顾佩华　编著

# 顾佩华工程教育文集

## 从设计导向的
## 工程教育到CDIO和新工科建设

（1999—2024年）

天津大学出版社
TIANJIN UNIVERSITY PRESS

**图书在版编目（CIP）数据**

顾佩华工程教育文集 ： 从设计导向的工程教育到CDIO和新工科建设 ： 1999—2024年 / 顾佩华编著. 天津 ： 天津大学出版社，2025. 9. -- ISBN 978-7-5618-7955-9

Ⅰ. G649.21-53

中国国家版本馆CIP数据核字第2025GT7738号

**GU PEIHUA GONGCHENG JIAOYU WENJI**

CONG SHEJI DAOXIANG DE GONGCHENG JIAOYU DAO

CDIO HE XINGONGKE JIANSHE (1999—2024 NIAN)

**出版发行** 天津大学出版社
**地　　址** 天津市卫津路92号天津大学内（邮编：300072）
**电　　话** 发行部：022-27403647
**网　　址** www.tjupress.com.cn
**印　　刷** 廊坊市海涛印刷有限公司
**经　　销** 全国各地新华书店
**开　　本** 787mm×1092mm　1/16
**印　　张** 23.75
**字　　数** 608千
**版　　次** 2025年9月第1版
**印　　次** 2025年9月第1次
**定　　价** 96.00元

---

# 前 言 Foreword

自1999年起我参与工程教育改革工作，截至2024年12月底，已历经25年。1999年7月，我担任卡尔加里大学（University of Calgary）机械与制造工程系主任后，与当时加拿大机械工程领域的三位资深教授和领导伊恩·耶洛利（Ian Yellowley）教授（不列颠哥伦比亚大学）、罗伦德·文特尔（Ronald Venter）教授（多伦多大学）和罗伊·皮克（Roy Pick）教授（滑铁卢大学），在加拿大自然科学与工程研究委员会（Natural Sciences and Engineering Research Council of Canada，NSERC）支持下，共同发起了加拿大工程教育改革，并创立了加拿大设计工程网络（Canadian Design Engineering Network，CDEN）。这场改革覆盖了加拿大所有设有工科专业的高校，旨在通过改革，大幅提升学生的工程设计和创新能力。

当时，我对工程教育改革认识尚浅，在Yellowley教授的指导和帮助下［Yellowley教授曾任教于麦克马斯特大学（McMaster University）机械工程系］，开始研究和实践Yellowley教授提出的设计导向的工程教育（design directed engineering education）。自1999年起，我系统地研读美国工程教育改革的文献资料，主动参加各类工程教育会议，并深入剖析多所高校的改革案例。同时我开始密切关注刚成立的欧林工学院（Olin College of Engineering）的工程教育探索与实践工作。

在卡尔加里大学工作期间，我参与了三次加拿大工程教育认证组织对机械工程系的专业认证考查。其中，第一次是作为教师身份参与，而后两次则是以系主任的身份参加（系主任是全系工作的负责人，包括负责接受认证考查的全过程）。作为系主任，我不仅要撰写认证自评报告，准备现场考查材料（包括每门课程的详细课程档案），回答上次认证现场考查所提的问题，展示专业教育的持续改进等，还要负责所有环节的准备工作。此外，作为系主任和注册工程师，我还参加了对其他大学的专业认证工作，因此对加拿大工程教育认证体系有了比较深入的了解与认识。

经过多年的学习、研究和在卡尔加里大学的亲身实践，我逐渐对加拿大及美国工程教育面临的主要问题和挑战有了更为清晰的认识，并积累了一些经验。

2005年，我同意借调到汕头大学担任副校长，希望把加拿大工程教育改革的经验用到汕头大学的工程教育工作中。在对CDEN改革有深入了解的基础上,我认真学习和研究了当时麻省理工学院和几所瑞典大学共同开展的CDIO工程教育。CDIO是麻省理工学院与三所瑞典大学在克努特与爱丽丝瓦伦堡基金会(Knut and Alice Wallenberg Foundation)的支持下开展的一项系统性工程教育改革。在这一改革过程中,形成了两个重要文件:一是CDIO能力大纲,明确了工程毕业生应具备的各项能力;二是实施CDIO工程教育改革的标准,这实质上也是CDIO改革的工作指引。2005年,我有幸与CDIO改革的领导者——麻省理工学院航空航天系爱德华·克劳利(Edward Crawley)院士会面,并在深入了解CDIO工程教育改革的进展后,决定在汕头大学开展CDIO工程教育改革实践探索。

2005年10月,汕头大学启动了"设计导向的EIP-CDIO工程教育改革",其中,E为职业道德(ethics),I为诚信(integrity),P为职业素质(professionalism)。由于我个人的学术背景和企业工作经验主要涉及机械工程(mechanical engineering)、制造工程(manufacturing engineering)以及机电一体化工程(mechatronics engineering)的教育与科研,因此我首先在机电工程系开展了这项教育改革。2006年,陆小华老师从新加坡理工学院加盟汕头大学土木工程系。他曾亲身参与新加坡理工学院的CDIO工程教育改革,积累了宝贵的系统性改革经验。他不仅领导了土木工程系的CDIO改革,还努力协助我在工学院全面推广这一模式。后来,包能胜老师及多位汕头大学的同事也积极投身其中,为推动CDIO工程教育改革提供了强有力的支持与协助。李嘉诚基金会为CDIO工程教育改革提供了500万元的专项经费,为深入推进CDIO改革提供了重要的资金支撑。

在汕头大学机电专业实施CDIO工程教育改革的实践过程中,依据CDIO能力大纲,在专业认证标准中的毕业要求与课程计划之间构建起了清晰的培养标准。具体而言,我们将毕业要求细化为能够用CDIO大纲进行描述的具体指标,并确保这些指标在课程目标和课程产出中得以实现。通过将所有课程目标和产出有机整合与迭代完善,我们不仅能够满足认证标准的毕业要求,还能够清晰地展示毕业要求是如何达成的。这一创新实践方法也得到了中国工程教育专业认证专家及相关委员会的肯定,机电专业获得了"6年无条件"的认证结论。

2008年4月,教育部高等教育司(简称高教司)发文成立CDIO工程教育研究与实践课题组。同年,在高教司理工处倡议和CDIO课题组的框架下,由18所院校组成的CDIO工程教育试点工作组正式成立,并按照机械、土木、电气和化工四大类别试点实施CDIO工程教育模式。到2010年,试点工作组已扩大至39个成员单位,很多非试点组高校也积极参与CDIO工程教育改革。为了更广泛地推动这一改革,我和汕头大学的同事们共同翻译了Crawley院士等专家出版的CDIO专著。为了满足更多高校加入CDIO试点组的需求,2016年1月成立了CDIO工程教育联盟的组织体系,首批加入联盟的成员高校达到104所,随后又有多所高校加入联盟。2024年我们进一步加强了CDIO工程教育联盟组织体系建设,期待为智能时代工程教育的变革与创新做出新的更大贡献。

2011年,我跟随李嘉诚基金会的领导访问了以色列理工学院(Technion Israel Institute of Technology)。鉴于以色列在科技创新和技术创业方面取得的卓越成就,李嘉诚基金会萌生了与以色列理工学院合作办学的构想,计划在汕头创办广东以色列理工学院。经过李嘉诚基金会的积极推动,2013年9月,在以色列特拉维夫,在广东省领导、李嘉诚先生和以色列方代表见证下，我代表汕头大学与以色列理工学院校长佩雷兹·拉维（Peretz Lavie）教授共同签署了合作办学备忘录。自2013年我们向教育部提交合作办学申请的初稿，至2016年12月教育部正式批准设立广东以色列理工学院（Guangdong Technion Israel Institute of Technology），汕头大学和以色列理工学院历经三年多的不懈努力，克服重重困难，最终达成了合作办学的目标。在此期间，Lavie校长主持了我在以色列理工学院所做的关于汕头大学CDIO工程教育改革的报告会并回答了大家提出的问题，以增强以色列理工学院的院系领导和骨干教授对合作办学的信心，报告会收获了积极的反响。

2018年9月，我加盟母校天津大学，投身新工科教育的改革与实践工作。在天津大学校领导和广大师生员工的支持下，我们于2018年底完成了新工科建设"天大方案"的初稿，并随即进入迭代完善进程。2019年4月，新工科建设"天大方案"在天津大学与美国佐治亚理工学院在深圳联合举办的中美新工科教育研讨会上正式发布，获得了广泛关注。2019年夏季，我参与了欧林工学院举办的夏季学院活动，与欧林工学院及来自各国的专家就"天大方案"展开深入探讨，并广泛征集各方的意见与建议。2020年1月，受麻省理工学院新工程教育转型（NEET）创始人Crawley院士的邀请，我参加了NEET战略研讨会，向NEET的领导和骨干介绍了"天大方案"。自2019年实施新工科建设"天大方案"以来，我们在实践中不断迭代优化。

自2022年11月ChatGPT上线以来，生成式人工智能（GenAI）技术和大语言模型（LLM）迅猛发展，广泛赋能各行各业，给未来发展带来了前所未有的不确定性和发展机遇。当前，人工智能技术正由狭义人工智能（artificial narrow intelligence）向通用人工智能（artificial general intelligence）演进，并不断为工程技术领域的实际应用注入强大动力。这一趋势无疑将重塑企业对工程技术人才的需求，促使工程教育与人才培养迎来新一轮的变革与创新。面向未来，工程教育应如何转型与发展？2023年6月，李培根院士发表文章指出，人类社会正处于历史的转折点，教育亟须率先变革，以积极的姿态应对未来的挑战。这开启了关于智能时代工程教育变革的深入探讨，成为值得我们深思并亟待解答的时代课题。

2024年4月，我收到美国《新闻周刊》（*Newsweek*）亚洲教育访谈的邀请，此后又陆续收到其他邀约，希望我分享对智能时代工程教育转型与发展的思考。2024年12月发布的"12 Days of OpenAI"活动以及谷歌"量子AI"团队推出的威洛（Willow）芯片，都预示着未来科技发展的不可预测性与无限可能性。虽然我还没有形成系统的思考与成熟的答案，但鉴于工程教育的长周期性和系统化特点，我认为工程教育需要不断探索能够克服高度不确定性的新模式和新体系，才能持续培养出适应AI时代产业发展需求的工程创新人才。

回顾过去25年来在工程教育工作中的经历，我对世界先进的工程教育模式有了较为深入的了解与认识。为更好地顺应智能时代发展趋势，我主动对过去在工程教育改革领域的探索与实践进行总结，将我与工程教育界同人及研究生们在2004—2024年期间撰写的有关工程教育的报告及论文汇编成册。对于过去的经验，需要以数智时代的思维进行全面反思，我也衷心希望同事们能够以批判性思维和专业视角，深入分析和剖析这些文章的内容，期待大家能够识别其中可能存在的认知偏差与潜在问题，并提出宝贵的改进建议，以便及时更正与完善相关内容。这将有助于我们共同思考智能时代下工程教育的转型与发展，推动其不断进步。

最后，我谨借此机会，向教育部高教司、教育部评估中心、中国工程教育专业认证协会、李嘉诚基金会，以及多所高校的领导、院士、专家和广大教师致以衷心的感谢。感谢大家在我参与 CDIO 工程教育改革、工程教育专业认证和新工科建设工作期间给予的大力支持与帮助。能够投身国家的工程教育事业，为其贡献力量，对一名工科教师而言，无疑是莫大的荣幸！

顾佩华<br>
天津大学新工科教育中心<br>
天津大学浙江国际创新设计与智造研究院<br>
2025 年 1 月 6 日

# 简 介 Introduction

顾佩华，天津大学浙江国际创新设计与智造研究院院长、新工科教育中心主任、机械学院教授。1997—2005年任加拿大卡尔加里大学（University of Calgary）工学院副院长和机械与制造工程系主任，2005—2010年从加拿大卡尔加里大学借调到汕头大学任副校长、执行校长，2011—2018年任汕头大学执行校长。

他是加拿大工程院院士（2004）、国际生产工程院会士（CIRP，2004）；教育部长江学者讲座教授（2004）；曾两度担任加拿大自然科学与工程研究委员会（NSERC）工业讲席教授（NSERC Industrial Chair）和工程设计讲席教授（NSERC Design Chair）；天津大学杰出校友、麦克马斯特大学杰出工程校友（Top 150）；2021年获光华龙腾奖·中国设计贡献奖金质奖章；曾获优秀大学校长奖、英国机械工程师协会颁发的约瑟夫·惠特沃思（Joseph Whitworth）优秀论文奖、CIRP设计年会最佳论文奖等多个奖项。

他长期从事智能制造研究，建立了可适应设计（adaptable design）方法，发明了多源多材料自由成型制造（multisource and multimaterial freeform fabrication）技术和多项智能制造技术；发表了300多篇文章，应邀在国内外学术大会做多次报告，连续被列入爱思唯尔（Elsevier）中国高被引学者和斯坦福大学发布的全球前2%科学家榜单。

他积极参与中国和加拿大工程教育改革。作为1999年建立加拿大设计工程网络的四名创始人之一，他带领卡尔加里大学制造工程专业获得2003年美国制造工程师学会的大学领先奖（University LEAD Award）。他领导国内开展CDIO工程教育改革，担任CDIO联盟理事长；参加卓越工程师教育培养计划和新工科建设工作；现任中国工程教育专业认证协会学术委员会主任，教育部高等学校机械类专业教学指导委员会副主任委员；获得国家教学成果特等奖（2022）、国家教学成果奖一等奖（2022）、国家教学成果奖二等奖（2014）。

顾佩华毕业于天津大学，获硕士学位；在麦克马斯特大学获博士学位。

# 目 录 Contents

# Design Directed Engineering Education

*Ian Yellowley, Peihua Gu*

**Abstract:**The authors examine the changes and opportunities in the educational environment as packaged courseware and virtual access to laboratories are assimilated into the engineering curriculum worldwide. The impact on universities and consequently on Canadian industry will be major unless there is a coordinated effort that can turn the challenge into an opportunity. The opportunity, the authors believe, is to use this new material to enable innovative approaches to education that use design to direct student learning. The major benefits would be a greater appreciation of technology and practice and significantly improved communication skills, both of which are regarded as essential by industrial employers. The authors believe that the engineering science background would be enhanced rather than weakened by the approach suggested.

## Introduction

The Canadian economy is becoming increasingly knowledge-based and activities are knowledge-intensive. This is true of most industrial nations; rapid technological advance is required to remain competitive. For Canada the situation is made more difficult by the fact that the country is in the process of moving away from a resource based economy. The response to the problem has to be improving education and enhancing skills. Canadian industry has clearly recognized the need for continuous professional development. The question for universities is what sort of engineering or technological education do we need to stay abreast in a world which is changing rapidly and where a knowledge of the basic engineering skills is extremely widespread? Engineering education in Canada must become more responsive and progressive, and it has to provide engineers who are well qualified in the traditional sense, but to compete on the international scene this is clearly not nearly enough.

Canadian universities, in common with all others, will soon see a rapidly increasing rate of change in the environment in which they try to educate the next generations. The internet and electronic media in general will drive this change. Programs, curricula and detailed course materials are widely available on the internet and of course, access to physical experiments and the development of ever better simulation tools coupled with internet enabled physical plant will allow extremely high class traditional tools to be available to all worldwide at very low cost. Various high profile initiatives are underway especially in the USA to make the best of courseware available on the internet free of charge. It is very clear that 5 years from now most, if not all, of the traditional materials and classic tutorial, laboratory or problem based approaches within traditional engineering programs will be widely and cheaply available. Each one of the engineering schools then needs to ask the question now: what real value we as educators can add to this material? Each university and each level of government needs to be asking what needs to be done, where the critical shortcomings are, and what will be the economic result to all of us. As a hint it is unlikely that building more real estate within the universities is a good idea when students need reduced access to traditional contacts through lecture, tutorial, or laboratory. The idea of simply adding more faculty is also an unlikely solution to the challenge.

The authors believe that radical change is required if students are to be innovative enough to help Canadian industry survive in the global economic environment they will find upon graduation. After graduation, there is not enough time, nor are there significant opportunities for these students to assimilate the technologies underlying the products they will be designing, using or competing against. Typically they will not have been exposed to many of the so-called soft but very important skills they need to be productive. Few large companies still have the training programs in the past. The typical new companies are smaller and leaner and they do not have the training resources, nor the luxury to allow several years of learning.

## 1 Engineering Program and Curriculum

Engineering competencies are regulated and controlled through engineering accreditation. According to the Canadian Engineering Accreditation Board (CAEB), engineering competencies in engineering programs are divided into five components which are: mathematics, basic sciences, engineering sciences, engineering design and complementary studies. A typical engineering program, such as mechanical engineering, has 1 to 2 years of common core engineering courses followed by 2 to 3 years of mechanical engineering courses, as well as complementary studies. The sequences of courses are controlled through prerequisites so as to ensure that students have a sufficient background to learn the course content. A typical engineering science course consists normally of lectures, laboratories and tutorials. Students are usually required to do assignments and projects to help them digest the learned materials. These evaluations may include assignments, laboratory reports, project reports, quizzes and exams. Most universities offer a design project course to expose students to real-world industrial or research projects.

Curriculum changes and controls have well-established processes and procedures to ensure that any proposed changes are discussed and evaluated thoroughly. The process is initiated by individual instructors or subject area committees, and proceeds through the departments and faculties. Incremental changes are normally carried out on a regular basis by individual instructors, since they have the most control over course content. Major changes must go through the formal process. If course instructors teach the same courses for a long time, course materials may not be changed, making the course content stable. On the other hand, course content must be current; a lack of up-to-date material may be undesirable.

Through the years of engineering education evolution and the exchanges among engineering schools through various forms, it is most likely that well-established disciplines in some engineering programs at Canadian universities are fundamentally similar (there are some enlightened schools that have taken a much more radical and sensible approach [1]). Delivery modes are also alike. The only major differences may be the quality of students, the competency of instructors and the learning environment, which includes support staff and materials, as well as laboratory facilities.

Design is generally regarded as the correct vehicle to integrate the various engineering and related courses. Many, if not most, schools have a real capstone design project, but relatively few have both ongoing open and simpler heavily constrained design exercises. Fig. 1 shows an example of an integrated engineering curriculum using design problems and specific design projects that would provide students with the opportunity to practice both technical and non-technical knowledge and skills in creating innovative products (new designs or engineering solutions). A few schools in North America do have such a continuous process, and have had for a while[1-2].

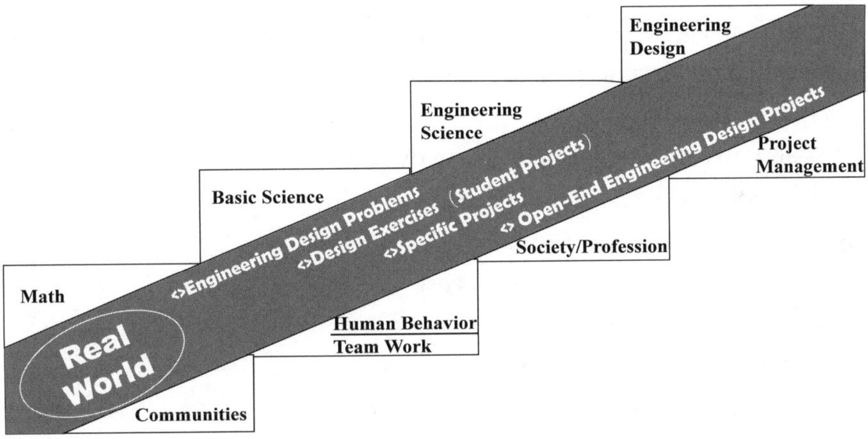


**Fig. 1 Integration of Engineering Curriculum Using Design Engineering**

## 2 The Industrial (User) Viewpoint

The viewpoint portrayed derives from an industrial workshop held with participants from several industrial sectors — engineering procurement and construction (EPC), oil and gas, engineering consulting, high-tech, manufacturing, and management consultants. The workshop took place in 2003 in Calgary Alberta. Participants were asked to provide input on the competencies that graduating engineering students should possess with respect to engineering design activities. Because of limited space, the following high-level competencies were identified as those that a new engineer-in-training (EIT) should have on the first day on the job.

*Scientific and Technical Knowledge*

- knowledge of mathematics, basic sciences, engineering sciences and engineering design and practices
- specific knowledge pertinent to an engineering discipline (i.e. mechanical or electrical engineering)
- technical risk management

*Process/Methodology*

- design process and methodologies
- design and analysis tools
- problem-solving skills
- data acquisition, analysis and interpretation
- application of scientific principles to identification and solution of practical engineering problems

*Creativity/Innovation*

- demonstration of knowledge and skill in design as a creative, iterative and open-ended process
- knowledge and application of idea generation and selection techniques
- understanding of the concept of problem and solution domains

*Team/Interpersonal/Personal*

- team skills, cross-functional teams, team dynamics, "service" work ethic, customer focus
- diversity, equity, personal ethics, integrity, humility

*Project and Engineering Management*

- time management, budgets, design to cost
- planning, estimating, scheduling
- management of facilities and processes
- management of human resources

*Communications*

- understanding of effective communication
- effective verbal, written and visual communication skills
- effective presentations

*Professional Practice*

- professional ethics, product liability, intellectual property, legal considerations
- role of the engineer in society
- technology and society
- sustainable design (lifecycle approach)

*General Feedback*

- The university can't hope to change students' behaviour but can create awareness in many key areas. Instructors can set expectations and provide feedback (e.g. 360° feedback, where students are evaluated by themselves, instructors and peers) as well as provide coping tools when warranted.

- The faculty needs to weave team-building skills, organizational skills, etc. into the program much earlier. It is not sufficient to provide students with "one big dose" through design projects in their fourth year.
- Students need to be aware that life-long learning is critical. Professional associations such as the Association of Engineers, Geologists and Geophysicists of Alberta (APEGGA) help to promote this view.
- Students need to be reminded that some of what they are learning now will not become relevant for a few years. For example, projects are conducted like a mini-company with students being responsible for all aspects of the project. Many of these aspects would not fall under the responsibility of an EIT.

*Work Experience*

- Students should be encouraged to take advantage of opportunities for internship/co-op placements. Historically, engineering students could often find summer work related to their engineering field but, in general, this is no longer the case. If internships or co-op placements aren't options, students should be encouraged to seek out volunteer opportunities through which they can learn and develop their skills.
- Students are often unaware of the opportunities available in various industries. Hopefully, an internship program can help identify the diversity of industries and related opportunities.
- Internship students and EITs seem to avoid "backwoods" assignments in favour of a downtown office tower. The participants stressed that the students/graduates who take advantage of these "backwoods" assignments tend to be better off in the long run.
- Students should be made aware of what a mentor is and how to find a mentor when they are in industry (either on internship or as an EIT).

*Industry Representation/Participation*

- At least some of the instructors within each engineering department should have significant industry experience so that they can relate the theory back to industry examples.
- Real-life projects involving people from industry will provide students with realistic feedback and increase their experience with practical business skills.

Following this workshop, an academic workshop was held with faculty members from all engineering disciplines in the Faculty of Engineering at the University of Calgary. The workshop identified the gaps between industrial needs and the competencies provided by the current engineering programs.

Table 1 is just a fraction of the competency matrix, but it demonstrates how the technical competencies are acquired through a 4-year engineering education. It is, by no means, complete. A more comprehensive and detailed design engineering competency matrix has been developed by the NSERC Design Chair Group[3]. The point of the exercise is to force the providers of the solution — the universities — with the requirements of the user — the engineering industry or society as a whole.

**Table 1 Competency Matrix (an excerpt)**

(I—Introduction, P—Primary Focus, S—Supporting)

| Technical | 1st | 2nd | 3rd | 4th |
|---|---|---|---|---|
| perform design and/or analyse functions of limited scope and complexity (e.g., create detailed design from preliminary design) | I | I | I | P |
| demonstrate substantial knowledge of technical subjects pertinent to their discipline | I | P | P | P/S |
| knowledge of mathematics fundamentals | I | P | S | S |
| knowledge of basic sciences | I | P | P | S |
| knowledge and skills in the area of engineering science and engineering design | I | I | P | P |
| solid grasp of engineering fundamentals | I | P | P | S |
| understanding technical requirements (purpose, good vs. bad) | I | I | P | P |
| build work products from specifications including prototypes for design proving | I | I | P | P |
| use design debug techniques and tools | I | I | P | P |
| demonstrate a basic understanding of simulation and modelling of products and systems | | I | I | P |
| understand component and material selection and use design layout/development tools | | I | I | P |
| document the design implementation in clear and concise terms | I | I | P | S |

## 3 Design Directed Engineering Education

The previous sections have indicated that traditional engineering programs are very uniform (and one has to admit that they are directed most clearly towards the needs of the student heading towards graduate studies or research rather than to a career in innovative engineering practice). Given industry needs now as briefly indicated above, and the fundamental changes one might expect to see in the infrastructures available to education worldwide, there are very considerable challenges and the need, it seems, for radical change. This is particularly the case for a large proportion of the students who see their career as being directed towards the design of new products, processes or systems (this may be approximately 30% of the typical student population in engineering with a large group headed to management or business and a smaller contingent headed to research).

The authors believe there is an opportunity to benefit greatly from the changes occurring by taking advantage of the enhanced accessibility to engineering science, not to teach engineering science in a traditional environment, but to use the presence of this material (within the design environment) to aid the exposure of students to the technology and practice of engineering through a design directed approach as opposed to traditional or problem based learning approaches. This is enabled by the changes in infrastructure and provides a route to a much richer education, as well as a redefined role for faculty and facilities. The authors believe that it is not enough to introduce engineering students to open format design problems, these problems should expose students to large bodies of specialized practice and technology that is found in all advanced technological fields. At the same time the student must learn to work as a member of a team and develop communication skills to interact with colleagues and characterize their work. Engineering science forms a framework for the efficient use and appraisal of this knowledge, but is not sufficient alone for the development of such technology or to make sensible decisions regarding utilization (without experience). The student exposed to engineering practice and technology over a wide range of sectors will also of necessity need to be introduced to engineering science in a rigorous manner, the reverse is not the case, because a large number of our students have little or no "engineering appreciation". The best analogy is perhaps to think of the technology and practice as the vocabulary of engineering, to think of the design process as composition and to think of engineering science as the grammar.

Fig. 2 shows the technology and practice clusters that can be profitably addressed in a very simple student design exercise concerned with the design of an electric powered bicycle. The exercise is such that 2nd year mechanical or electro-mechanical students will be easily capable of understanding all the basic science. The volume of technology though is large and requires explanation using additional engineering science. Several of the decisions (frame type, drive arrangement, etc.) need to be posed in a very general manner. The student should not be encouraged to perform detailed engineering analysis until the main conceptual options have been explored technically and economically to prune the solution space (this should be done by the students themselves). The students will profit from analogies and examples of practice from related fields, for example, in examining the frame design one might want to look at typical light weight structures from the aircraft, marine and building fields to stimulate thinking about innovative solutions. The drive system should be illustrated by examining light vehicles, golf carts and other related applications. To examine one solution may encourage duplication; to examine multiple very different solutions encourages analysis and innovation.

The use of design to encourage students to explore technology and practice and in turn to rigorously analyse possible solutions from technical, economic, and usage perspectives is extremely appealing. One might ask if this type of activity could be a substitute for the traditional engineering education. The authors believe that this is certainly the case in theory, but there are several background issues that need to be carefully addressed. The first is to confirm that the design exercises posed are exhaustive in their coverage of the basic engineering science. The second is to confirm that the student retains hands on access to basic laboratories or even better that component testing related to individual design exercises covers the materials that would normally be covered in laboratories.

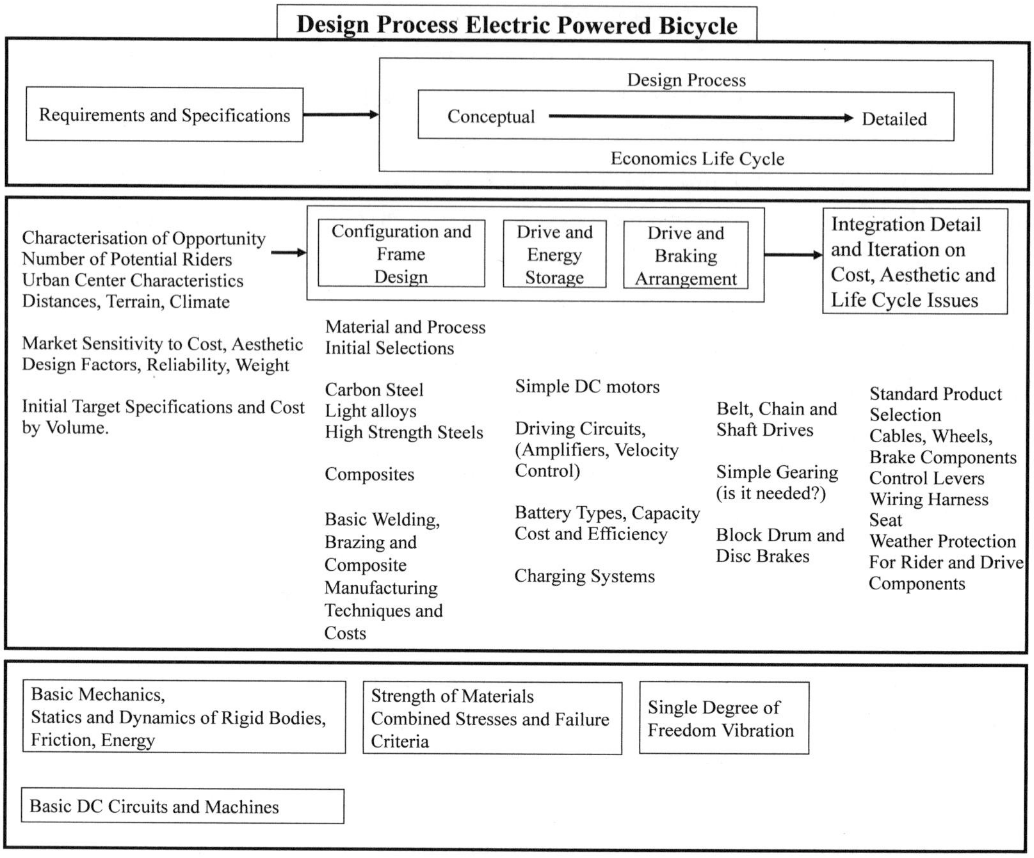


**Fig. 2 Technology and Practice within a Simple Design Exercise**

The idea of such a program is rather new and until now it has been very hard to persuade colleagues to take such steps. Clearly the changes being thrust upon us may change this. One of the authors, IY, has proposed an undergraduate product design program that would be accommodated within a design studio environment at UBC (the proposed facility would also be utilized for a joint industry/university masters level program in product and process design). It should be emphasized that after many years this is still not a reality, to this point there is not a critical mass within the faculty that would embrace such an initiative. The intention within this paper is to simply use this idea as a model of what might be common in the relatively near future. The typical student day in such programs would be divided as shown in Table 2. It is seen that the teaching function disappears in favor of first self-study, followed by rapid examination through tutorials and problem sets, and then rapid application in design exercises. The faculty requirements are a little higher than within a typical lecture program, and the background required of the faculty is expected to be very different from one might prescribe for lecture courses only. Without formal classes in the basic subjects, there will be a fair need for ongoing student support. TA's could be used to support groups of up to 6 students, say one hour per week per subject. Faculty would also have office hours and students would be allowed to make appointments (perhaps 5 hours per week total). The major reinforcement is intended to come from the problem sets and the design exercises. The design of the actual set of design problems to be used each year is the most challenging part of the curriculum design. A discussion follows.

The design exercises would be carried out in a studio environment, each student being provided with space and access to a design station which is also running a browser that has access to all basic engineering science materials as well as design catalog material, etc. One needs to design a set of challenging design problems for each year of the program, which are exhaustive in their coverage of the science in the parallel coursework. Likely, this needs a large number of faculty with varied experience to do it. A reasonable approach with small numbers of students (a maximum of 30), would be to have 6 different faculties design specific standard projects and have a single faculty with responsibility for overall course supervision. The typical standard project at the 2nd and 3rd year levels would last for four weeks with a single faculty supervising. In 2nd and 3rd years, at least one major design project per year would require the students to work in teams over the full year and to both build and test a prototype of their design. Final year would see the regular capstone design project in addition and a reduction of laboratory activity in favor of fabrication and test of design components.

**Table 2 Typical Daily 2nd and 3rd Year Schedule**

| 8:00-10:00 | 10:00-12:30 | 13:30-14:30 | 14:30-16:30 | 18:00-? |
|---|---|---|---|---|
| Complimentary Coursework (liberal studies, economics, law, etc.) | Personal study in design studio Engineering science Problem sets done here | Office hours and tutorials(-Mandatory) + Quizzes | Design studio 3/4 afternoons Laboratories 1 afternoon | |

## 4 Development of Design Teaching Materials

The types of program being suggested will benefit greatly from the presence of improved course materials in the traditional areas. This material is appearing at an ever increasing rate. There is still the need to develop modular teaching materials that cover the other areas of practice and technology, and put these areas, together with engineering science, into a design context. Some schools have started this but it is not an easy task and cannot really be designed, developed and maintained by any one school in the Canadian context. The approach then has been to try to form a network that would develop and share these resources for the benefit of all. The result of this was the formation of the CDEN/RCCI network whose aims at the time were communicated as follows.

"The CDEN/RCCI network is intended to facilitate the communication of best design practices between schools, promote the production and sharing of courseware, help inject more real design experiences into the university, and allow all schools to access the best available expertise in areas of detailed interest. The network will facilitate the joint development of multi-discipline design related courseware modules and put in place the mechanisms to ensure that the practice of design will be central to the education of the next generation of engineers" [4].

CDEN/RCCI had approximately a million dollars that was allocated equally among the formation of individual network nodes at each school, the development and improvement of specific modules and the development of specific high-level design competencies through research (the so-called design focus groups which are the last part of the overall CDEN/RCCI project process).

To try to maintain a modular structure CDEN/RCCI has developed the three-tier approach to design education materials shown in Fig. 3. Tier 1 is concerned with basic sciences, mathematics and engineering sciences. These scientific and mathematical principles are the foundations of engineering design. Tier 2 builds on Tier 1 and provides the technologies and engineering practices necessary for Tier 3. Tier 3 deals with open-ended design projects and case studies.

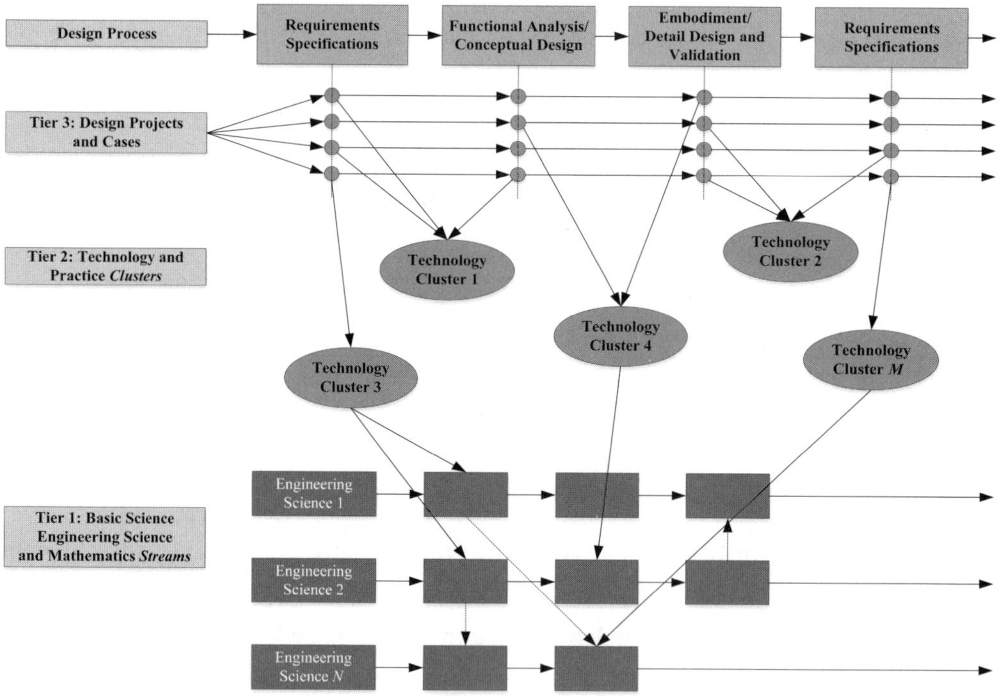


**Fig. 3 Three-Tier Structure of CDEN/RCCI Design Education Material**

For each tier, there are a number of specific modules and the others are common to all programs. Design educators across Canada have been invited to develop and contribute their design education materials under the three-tier system. The modules along with the tier structure, which will be made available on the CDEN/RCCI server, provide sufficient flexibility for design educators to assemble modules for their specific design education needs. It is expected that some of the modules will be available in early 2005.

## 5 Summary

The paper examines the main issues and challenges that engineering education will face in the near future. The authors propose the use of a design directed engineering approach to integrate new course material and formats in a manner that encourages the most positive overall education experience. This is a very preliminary attempt to stimulate a broad discussion on the future of engineering education. It is our hope that the ideas proposed go some distance towards the development of programs that use design as the major vehicle to integrate the tools of engineering science with technology practice and communication skills.

**References**

[1] PROULX D. The design experience at Université de Sherbrooke[C]// Proceedings of the 2001 Canadian Conference on Engineering Education. Victoria: Canadian Engineering Education Association (CEEA), 2001: 1-8.

[2] BRIGHT A, PHILLIPS J R. The Harvey Mudd Engineering Clinic: past, present, and future[J]. Journal of engineering education, 1999, 88(2): 189-194.

[3] Design Chair Group. Engineering design competency: final report[R]. Montreal: Canadian Design Engineering Network (CDEN), 2004.

[4] YELLOWLEY I. Engineering design: an essential component of university based research and education[C]// Proceedings of the 2001 CSME International Design Conference. Montreal: Canadian Society for Mechanical Engineering (CSME), 2001: 1-6.

# The Engineering Design Competency

*Jorge Angeles, Ron Britton, Liuchen Chang, François Charron, Peter Gregson, Peihua Gu, Peter Lawrence, Warren Stiver, David Strong, Paul Stuart, Brian Thompson*

**Abstract:**There is increasing global competition for better product and process functionality, higher quality, lower costs, and other considerations including energy and environmental challenges. This trend requires that Canadian industry be more innovative and responsive in order to stay competitive internationally. The Canadian capability in engineering design is at the core of our ability to achieve this goal. At both the undergraduate and graduate levels, we must improve the capability and capacity of engineering graduates so that they are capable of leading innovation, and converting research results into value-added products and services. This paper addresses the engineering design competency, identifies needs in engineering design training, and describes directions for the design content in engineering education programs.

## Introduction

In 1999, a new NSERC chair program was created in design engineering. The NSERC Design Chair Group has undertaken an initiative to develop a definition of the engineering design competency from which universities may draw inspiration in the design of new and innovative engineering education programs. In response to various factors including particularly a demand by the business and engineering communities for enhanced design competencies in graduating engineers, there is a trend in engineering accreditation towards "outcomes-based" assessments and the integrated engineering design curriculum. Under outcomes-based criteria, engineering programs must demonstrate that their graduates have an ability to apply knowledge of mathematics, sciences and engineering. This incorporates the evaluation of design competencies such as, for example, the ability to design and conduct experiments, and the ability to design a system, component, or process to meet desired needs.

Traditionally, quality in engineering education has been achieved by providing high-quality instruction, excellent lab facilities, and relevant tutorials and assignments. However, the engineering design competency cannot easily be developed in the traditional classroom setting. Various approaches are currently being adopted by universities in engineering design education including innovative strategies for engineering design content within individual degrees, employing interdisciplinary approaches, and project-based learning.

To further improve engineering design competency in graduates, a number of issues and challenges must be addressed which may touch the very foundation of university traditions. These include such factors as the current university reward systems, academic program development and approval processes, traditional engineering education models, engineering accreditation requirements and processes, and the academic culture in Canadian engineering schools. New thinking towards engineering education as well as research and innovation are essential in order to evolve Canadian engineering education to a new model that will produce engineering graduates who are design-ready and confident in their ability to innovate.

This paper is an abbreviated version of a white paper entitled "The Engineering Design Competency" prepared by the NSERC Chairs in Design Engineering.

## 1 Current Trends in Engineering Design Education

### 1.1 Accreditation

To ensure that engineering programs offered by education institutions meet educational standards acceptable for professional engineer registration, and that the quality and relevance of engineering education continuously improve, engineering associations of many countries in the world have established accreditation mechanisms to evaluate and accredit the undergraduate engineering programs of education institutions. Accreditation is usually a voluntary, nongovernmental process of peer review. In Canada, the Canadian Engineering Accreditation Board (CEAB), a standing committee of the Canadian Council of Professional Engineers (CCPE), has been responsible for the accreditation of Canadian engineering education programs since 1965.

In order to be accredited, an engineering program must meet or exceed the accreditation criteria established and published by CEAB. Accredited engineering programs must contain not only adequate mathematics, sciences and engineering content, but also adequate complementary studies that deal with central issues, methodologies and thought processes of the humanities and social sciences. The programs must also allow students to develop communication skills and an understanding of the environmental, cultural, economic and social impacts of engineering on society and the concept of sustainable development[1].

Engineering education has been progressing in response to the technological advances, political and economic realities, engineering job markets and public interests. As a quality assurance program, engineering accreditation is also evolving. The following trends have been observed in engineering accreditation in recent years.

*Outcomes Assessment*: Many engineering accreditation organizations outside Canada have shifted away from prescribing what engineering programs should be like, and are evolving toward examining the outcomes of engineering education. The old criteria set standards for faculty size, curricular requirements, and the quality of laboratories and other facilities. The new criteria focus increasingly on the educational objectives of engineering programs, and evaluation procedures that track whether objectives are met. For example, engineering graduates should have an ability to apply knowledge of mathematics, sciences and engineering, an ability to design and conduct experiments as well as to analyze and interpret data, an ability to design a system, component, or process to meet desired needs, and other similar outcomes[2].

*Engineering Design*: Under outcomes based criteria, engineering design has been emphasized as a key component by accreditation organizations. CEAB specifies a minimum of 225 academic units for engineering design, and expects the faculty teaching engineering science as well as engineering design to be registered professional engineers.

*Internationalization*: Globalization has been an important phenomenon in engineering professions, as marked by the cross-border mobility of practicing engineers and students across the borders of countries. International agreements on engineering education, accreditation and practice have thus been developed. One of the first agreements was signed in 1980 by the CEAB and the Engineering Accreditation Commission (EAC) of the United States, in which the two parties mutually recognize graduates of all engineering programs accredited by each party.

*New and Innovative Engineering Programs*: Rapid development in technology has led to the formation of numerous new engineering disciplines. Accreditation organizations have responded to these needs of the engineering community by accrediting new programs. Accredited examples that have been accredited during the past couple of decades include computer engineering, geomatic engineering, oil and gas engineering, software engineering and environmental engineering.

*Partnerships in Education*: Interactions and partnerships between engineering educational institutes and outside stakeholders such as engineering organizations and associations, and industry and businesses have been rapidly strengthened in recent years. Partnerships in engineering education have been ongoing in two areas: ① providing engineering students with real-world practical experience as an integral part of their academic program; ② inviting "outsiders" from engineering and business communities into the advisory and decision-making bodies controlling the engineering curriculum.

These activities, which triggered changes in curricula, led to the development of new ways of delivering engineering education, accelerated the emphasis on engineering design and project-based learning, and promoted the inclusion of "soft skills" such as communications and team work.

### 1.2 Strategic Issues in Engineering and Engineering Design Education

Tomorrow's engineers must cope with problems and challenges significantly different from their predecessors.

In the following points, some specific strategic decisions that must be addressed in the coming years and are related to engineering education are discussed.

*Program Structure by Discipline and Subject*

Canada's Innovation Strategy[3] points to the "need to encourage cross-training and a multi-disciplinary approach, in order to build capacity among MBAs and engineers for the commercialization of these new technologies". The new technologies referred to were environmental and green energy, but the statement could equally apply to any innovative technology.

"In the last half or more of the 20th century··· has found that the world of practical applications is increasingly cross disciplinary, and even more rapidly becoming interdisciplinary. The integration across fields in the world of practical applications is often delayed until the engineer has moved into a job rather than being part of his or her university education. Universities should move to meet their obligations to students and to society by moving toward true interdisciplinarity" [4].

The need for true interdisciplinary programs is driven by increased local and global competitiveness, both because industry is rewarded for being the first to market (first-mover advantage) and because markets are no longer defined geographically. To meet this need, product realization has become a more concurrent and less linear process in most companies, requiring a large variety of skills on the part of the design team. In addition, the rate of employment and innovation is now greatest in small to medium sized enterprises. These organizations require employees to have considerable familiarity with all aspects of the design.

Canadian universities and engineering faculties must continue to identify these market trends and create interdisciplinary programs and training opportunities which respond to our evolving needs.

*Engineering Curriculum Renewal with Technology Changes and Knowledge Growth*

The short- and long-term needs of engineering students and employers are often in conflict. If engineering education is to make students maximally employable in the short term, it would risk delivering training in the latest CAD software or the use of a particular instrument or process, rather than emphasizing a sound understanding of the principles on which these tools are based. However, to ignore the latest technology, the latest software or the latest code/regulatory changes leads to graduates who are out of step with the practice of engineering.

The rapid pace of knowledge growth in engineering presents a motivation for increased specialization within engineering curricula. Curriculum renewal continues to be faced with adding content to reflect new fields and new technologies, however, for every addition, some content must be removed.

*Continuity in Design Education*

Most Canadian engineering schools have a first year design course and a final year capstone design sequence including a design project. In the first year course, students tackle a relatively simple problem with considerable assistance from teaching assistants and faculty members. The capstone design sequence is based on open-ended projects offered by industry and/or faculty members. Each group of students typically undertakes a different project with the result that the ability to learn from one another is minimized. In this model, students can become frustrated as their design skills have not progressed sufficiently to handle the degree of open-endedness of an industry project.

Alternatively, a number of engineering schools offer a "continuum of design" throughout the curriculum. Harvey Mudd College[5] has been offering a sequence of design courses for approximately 40 years, and a number of Canadian engineering schools now offer a continuum of design courses (e.g., University of Guelph in all programs, University of Manitoba in Biosystems Engineering, University of Sherbrooke in several departments, and Electrical and Computer Engineering at Dalhousie University).

Providing a design continuum is critical, but requires significant cooperation between departments. The problems associated with ensuring extensive collaboration between faculty members with the requisite expertise are exacerbated by timetabling, resource allocation, space, and registration issues.

*Design Facilities*

Team-based design and design in general rely on a different mix of educational space than engineering science courses. Design studios, shop (machine or equivalent), storage space, advanced software, and large-format printers are just some of the unique needs. Design studios in particular are not commonly found in engineering schools in Canada, although some schools have developed them. In particular, the University of Western Ontario has developed studio-based design[6], Queen's University has the Integrated Learning Centre[7], and the Mechanical Engineering Departments at Sherbrooke University and the University of Calgary have created considerable design facilities and spaces for undergraduate students.

*Faculty Renewal*

In Germany, 10 to 15 years of industry experience was the rule until recently[8]. Some schools have implemented proactive programs to engage faculty and students with industry[9] so as to make faculty more familiar with the modern manufacturing environment and to keep faculty technically current.

Approximately one-third of the Canadian university engineering faculty in tenured or tenure-track positions are over the age of 50 and thus retiring within the next 15 years[10]. The significant faculty renewal that is now underway in Canada presents an opportunity for innovation and advancement in engineering education while at the same time presenting some risks.

Tenure, promotion and compensation policies play a critical role in shaping the activities and priorities of all faculty members, and are especially important for new faculty. An opportunity exists to reward interaction with industry, attract expertise from industry, and restructure some courses to better reflect the teamwork, communication and collaboration skills that are needed by industry and society[11-14].

For example, engineering design teaching is recognized as requiring considerably more time for course development, project selection and student consultation. Course loads for team-taught engineering design courses should be calculated appropriately to account the extra effort in course development and delivery.

The *Macleans Magazine* "Ranking Canadian Universities" (www.macleans.ca) has grown in influence and attention on many campuses. In faculty terms, measurement focuses on the percentage with PhD's and funding from the major granting councils. Additional important measures for engineering might include such things as industrial experience, P.Eng status, and collaboration/funding relationships with industry.

## 2 Back to Basics

Engineering design is iterative, creative, at times both analytic and synthetic, incorporating elements of problem-solving, and incorporating intuitive as well as heuristic methodologies. Design is decision-based and goal-directed; designers are presented with problems motivated by human need, related to products, processes, materials and systems of all kinds, and bring to bear rational tools and imagination in methodologies for developing optimal solutions[15].

The Canadian Engineering Accreditation Board has proposed the following definition of engineering design[1]. Engineering design integrates mathematics, basic sciences, engineering sciences and complementary studies in developing elements, systems and processes to meet specific needs. It is a creative, iterative and often open-ended process subject to constraints that may be governed by standards or legislation to varying degrees depending on the discipline. These degrees may relate to economic, health, safety, environmental, social or other pertinent factors.

In its guide on the professional practice of engineering in Canada[16], the Canadian Council of Professional Engineers defines the following characteristics of a profession.

A profession is a learned calling that requires advanced knowledge, understanding, and abilities gained from intensive and specialized education, training, and practical experience. Members of a profession limit their activities to their areas of knowledge and experience, doing so out of commitment to serve and protect the public. Professional practitioners also ensure that their competency is maintained throughout their careers.

In addition to theoretical and technical knowledge, effective professional practice requires reflective and practical knowledge and competencies for dealing with problems in the indeterminate zones of practice, that is, the areas that cannot be solved by technical or familiar solutions. These competencies are critically important to the education and development of professionals in the climate of rapid technological, cultural and economic change. A number of researchers in the field of professionalism and skills, such as Le Boterf[17], share this broadened vision of the profession.

## 3 The Engineering Design Competency

### 3.1 A Competent Design Engineer

A review of the literature offers many descriptions of professional engineering competencies in general. But what does it say about the design engineer? Is there a definitive list of skills, personality traits, behavior, and a body of knowledge that sets design engineers apart from other engineering practitioners?

North American educators typically approach design as a subset of skills for all engineers. But based on industrial demand[18], there are too few institutions that train engineers with explicit design competency.

Many engineering educators believe that students should understand how to generate design specifications and how to proceed from design specifications to a final artifact by establishing objectives and criteria, generating alternatives, synthesizing, analyzing, constructing, testing, and evaluating[19].

### 3.2 Established Skills for Design Engineers

This review examines the skills that set design engineers apart from other engineering practitioners.

*Technical Skills*

There is little apparent concern over the level of competency amongst design engineers in math, basic sciences and engineering sciences[20-22], although graduates have trouble applying those skills to proper technical design analysis[23].

*Experience and "Know-how"*

Above all other skill-level considerations, design engineers require some level of hands-on competency in the use of tools or processes relevant to their field[13,18,20-22,24]. These skills are lacking among North American engineering graduates, based on the frequency with which this issue appears in the literature.

Where design engineering skills have been identified as distinct from typical engineering science, there is a recurring principle of learning-by-doing[24]. Experiential competency is defined as an innate ability and as a "set of instincts about the likely consequences of certain choices which every professional faces every day"[22].

*Specific Design Activities*

Industry and academe cite a wide range of preferences in formal design methodologies. While each industry segment has its particular methods, design engineers should be able to implement the following:

• Methods and rules for the larger design process including Design for X[18,20,25-30], identification of constraints and needs such as QFD[20,31], quality control processes such as Six Sigma or TQM[18-20], and use of project management structures[18,20-21,32-35];

• Rules for design analysis and design improvement such as Failure Mode Effect Analysis, product testing, process integration, etc.[20-21,36-37];

• Methods for creativity such as brainstorming to TRIZ[18,20,38-40];

• Specific technical skills with special emphasis in design, for example solid modeling techniques[18], computer-aided process engineering (CAPE)[41], computer assisted design (CAD)[20,37,42-44], geometric dimensioning and tolerancing (GD&T)[18,20] and computational fluid dynamics (CFD)[45-46];

• Other design knowledge including safety methodologies[20,32,47-49], regulatory issues[20] and human factors[20,50].

*Attitudes Toward Design Engineering*

Professional attitude is widely cited as a key competency for engineers in general along with the ability to adapt to changes in circumstances[18,51]. Design engineering practice suffers from varying attitudinal pathologies. "Not-Invented-Here" attitudes[51], confusion of originality with creativity[52], notions of design as an individual activity[52], and unwillingness to leverage the knowledge of technicians or tradesmen[20] are recurring problems amongst new graduates of university engineering programs.

*Business Skills*

Recent literature suggests novice engineers require at least an introductory familiarity with business issues. These skills are identified as pertinent to all engineers, and not just design engineers. Important business issues for engineers (in general) include project management skills[20-21,53-54], customer awareness[55], knowledge of basic issues in business finance including cost of money, corporate ownership structures and liabilities[20-21,32,51], basic economic principles[54], risk analysis and budgeting[18], social skills applicable to a multicultural business environment[51,54], understanding of corporate culture and the global nature of business[18,23,51,56], and appreciation for intellectual property[51].

*Communications Skills*

Employers expect young engineers to be able to draft comprehensible, compelling reports[20], express themselves verbally[18,20,42], listen effectively, and be able to "sell" concepts, products and themselves to the technically savvy as well as to laypeople[42].

*Teamwork Skills*

Every comprehensive list of engineering competencies includes the ability to work effectively in teams. Typically, teamwork skills receive highest priority among the design engineering competency[18,20]. Yet, despite the importance of teamwork and other social skills, they are not assessed systematically in the process of educating design engineers[53,57].

Lauche[53] has surveyed several important communications and project management skills for the design process including negotiation with clients, problem solving, acceptance of responsibility, interpersonal skills, planning, exchanging information, coordinating activities, assessing capabilities of others, workload management, team building and collaboration.

## 4 Incorporating the Engineering Design Competency in the Curricula of All Engineering Disciplines

This section provides perspectives on design competency as they relate to the broad context of the practice of engineering. Table 1 provides a definition of the engineering design competency as applicable to all disciplines. It is not expected that a single graduate or an engineering program would be competent in all of the listed items. Only 2 of the engineering competencies in Table 1 are treated in this paper, however more details can be found in the complete Design Competency Document by the NSERC Chairs in Design Engineering[58].

**Table 1 Proposed Definition of the Design Engineering Competency**

| Type | Description | Engineering — All disciplines | |
|---|---|---|---|
| General knowledge | To understand a phenomenon, a situation, a problem, a process, etc. | Mathematics | Linear algebra, Calculus, Differential Equations, Probability, Statistics, Numerical Methods, Partial Differential Equations, etc. |
| | | Basic Sciences | Chemistry, Physics, Biology, Earth Science, etc. |
| | | Engineering Sciences | Mechanics, Materials, Fluid Mechanics, Circuits, Thermodynamics, Heat Transfer, Mass Transfer, System Control, etc. |
| Specific knowledge in a professional environment | To know the technologies, the rules, the standards, the culture, etc. | Technologies, standards, regulations, safety, liability, intellectual property, ethic, role in the society | |
| Knowledge of procedures | To know the procedures, the methods, the processes, etc. | Product development process, engineering design process, engineering design tools (market research, functional analysis, QFD, design for cost and cost estimation, etc.) | |
| Operational skills | To know how to use methods, procedures, technologies, etc. | To have executed and practiced the design process | |
| Experiential skills | To know how to use tacit knowledge | Design by similarity, design by experience, etc. | |
| Social/ Personal skills | To know how to listen, to co-operate, to work in a team, etc. | Teamwork, communication, leadership, negotiation, professionalism | |
| | Initiative, thorough, curious, etc. | Initiative, thorough, curious, practical, humble, responsible, adaptable, confident, awareness, respectable, entrepreneurialism | |
| | To manage life (personal and professional), to feel (intuition, perception, etc.) | Self-awareness, managing emotions, motivating oneself, empathy and handling relationships | |

续表

| Type | Description | Engineering — All disciplines |
|---|---|---|
| Cognitive skills | To solve problems, to design, to manage a project, to take decisions, etc. | To know your limitations, to create, to look at the big picture, to manage projects (including the system engineering perspective), to decide (decision-making), to learn how to learn, to manage information and knowledge, to define a problem, to define potential solutions, to learn from past experiences, to manage resources, to take and manage risk |

### 4.1 Specific Knowledge in a Professional Environment

In the words of the Canadian Council of Professional Engineers[59], Canadian engineers provide leadership to advance the quality of life through the creative, responsible and progressive application of engineering principles in the global context.

"Quality of life" is a broad term that recognizes the importance of economics, social and environmental domains that are all essential for realizing a high standard of living. These domains are the pillars of sustainable development[60]. CEAB accreditation guidelines reinforce that knowledge of the principles of sustainable development is essential for all engineers[1].

*Safety*: The practice of engineering is fundamentally about the protection of public safety. As designers, graduating engineers should have experience with one or more of the classical techniques for identifying and reducing safety risks. HAZOP, FMEA, and FTA are three common techniques.

*Ethics*: Morrison and Hughes[61] are leading reference on ethical aspects for Canadian Engineering practice.

*Codes, Laws and Regulations*: Codes, laws and regulations influence all engineering design. For example Workplace Hazardous Materials Information System (WHMIS), established in 1987, has become fully integrated into the Canadian workplace. All graduating engineers should be familiar with WHMIS and its impact on their designs[62].

*Standards*: Standards are critical to many aspects of our lives, although this is not obvious to most. When possible, design engineers should rely on standard components to design and build complex systems. They should know where to look to find standard specifications for a bolt or a pipe, and should customize only when necessary. Engineers should be aware of which standards are applicable to their work, and aware of testing and certification processes. The success and the growth of the ISO 9000 series in quality management and the ISO 14000 series in environmental management means student exposure to these standards is important within the engineering curriculum.

*Intellectual Property*: Many design engineers will create new intellectual property (IP) over the course of their career, and will use existing intellectual property in the development of solutions. Engineering graduates should be aware of the various forms of intellectual property (patents, trade-marks, copyright, and industrial designs). Most universities have an intellectual property office that can be an important resource in support of the curriculum.

*Technologies*: All graduating engineers should have some technical understanding of a broad range of technologies beyond the technologies of their engineering discipline. This breadth of awareness is necessary to support the development of creative solutions, understanding engineering systems and components, working in cross disciplinary teams and ultimately leading larger engineering projects.

### 4.2 Knowledge of Procedures

Knowledge of the design process and an awareness of the various design tools are the starting points for a design competent engineer.

*Design Process*

Knowledge of the design process should encompass the transition from an idea. This transition leads to the technical specifications of the product, process, or solution. Final implementation of the solution is the conclusive step in the design process. The design process is described in varying detail through numerous references including Dieter[38], Voland[63], Ullman[64], and Ertas[39].

Engineers should be well versed in the terminology associated with the design process. Conceptual design, feasibility study, preliminary design, final design, detailed design, concurrent design and embodiment design are all terms used to describe portions of the design process.

Additional knowledge includes the understanding of where R&D, testing, prototypes and pilot-scale activities fit into the process. Knowledge encompasses recognition that the process is usually iterative.

*Design tools*

Design tools are used to support the design process. They come in many forms depending on the stage of the process and on the nature of the design problem. The tools include people as sources for problem definition and data gathering. Libraries (as a title encompassing all information sources) are primary tools in the early information gathering stage. Knowledge of this tool must include awareness of the various types of sources (textbooks, journal literature, patents, gray literature, the web, standards, codes, regulations, and people) and the recognition that all sources are important.

Engineering drawings are essential tools for the process. Sketches, generated by pencil and paper, are the most frequent start to the process. Sophisticated Computer-Aided Drawing software has become integral to the process as a design matures. Knowledge means that the engineer is aware of the role of both ends of this spectrum.

Engineering calculations are key tools in the design process. Rough approximations will parallel the sketch drawing stage. Sophisticated Computer-Aided Engineering software, capturing the 3D and transient complexity of a system, is increasingly playing a role in preliminary and detailed design work. Again, knowledge means that the engineer is aware of the existence and capabilities of these tools.

*Performance Assessment against Criteria and Constraints*

Problem definition usually identifies appropriate constraints (the musts) and desired criteria (the wishes). The constraints must each be achieved. The criteria are dealt with in a collective balancing act. Quantifying each of the identified factors eases the subsequent decision making stage.

Cost is always a factor in engineering design and cost estimation has become an important field on its own. Cost estimation is necessary at various stages of the design process. Cost estimating relies on experience and thus depends on empirical relations. The chemical engineering field has well developed empirical relations to support cost estimating[41]. SAE provides a structured format for cost estimating for the student Formula SAE competition[65]. This format could be effectively used within engineering curriculum.

Environmental performance is another important factor. Since life cycle analysis is a growing capability, it should be an element of all engineers' knowledge base. The literature on engineering design and the practice of engineering design has introduced the use of the terms: "Design for Cost", "Design for Reliability", "Design for the Environment", and others[66-70]. Collectively, these are increasingly referred to as "Design for X" (see DFX terminology by Migliore[71]). The introduction of these concepts represents an effort to focus design attention on one particular criterion. They imply that attention paid to the design of "X" has been lacking. The aspect that so many "X's" have been used reflects the design challenge of simultaneously optimizing numerous criteria.

*Decision making*

Decisions are an integral part of the design process. Many formal decisions and many more informal ones are made throughout the process.

Formal decisions are often at the conclusion of conceptual, preliminary and final design stages as part of recommending the next step and seeking budgetary approval to proceed to the next stage. Procedures have been developed to formalize this decision-making process as part of fostering objectivity. Objectivity is important in all settings, yet it holds particular significance in the public sector. The decision-matrix method is one common formalized approach that is relatively simple to execute[64]. However, it is important for students and engineers to recognize that subjectivity quickly becomes a part of the decision matrix approach through selection of criteria weightings and scoring rules.

## 5 Conclusions

The essence of professional engineering is captured in the definition of design competency. This definition is complex and profound, yet also a living entity that evolves alongside professional practice.

Design competency can provide the necessary foundation for ongoing renewal of the undergraduate curriculum in engineering. When implementing design competency in current and future engineering programs, we must address a number of issues and challenges, which may even affect the very foundation of university traditions and operations.

New thinking about engineering education, the academic system, and research and innovation may be required. Only in this way can we effectively transform Canadian engineering education into a new model. This new model will produce engineering graduates who are innovative designers and lifelong learners with the necessary engineering competency.

**References**


[1] CEAB. Accreditation Criteria and Procedures 2002[S]. Ottawa: Canadian Engineering Accreditation Board, 2002.

[2] ABET. Criteria for Accrediting Engineering Programs: Effective for Evaluations During the 2002-2003 Accreditation Cycle[S]. Baltimore: Accreditation Board for Engineering and Technology, 2001.

[3] Government of Canada. National Summit on Innovation and Learning: Summary [EB/OL]. (2002-01-23) [2011-08-01]. http://www.innovationstrategy.gc.ca.

[4] COATES J F. Innovation in the future of engineering design[J]. Technological forecasting and social change, 2000, 64: 121-132.

[5] BRIGHT A, PHILLIPS J R. The Harvey Mudd Engineering Clinic: past, present, and future[J]. Journal of engineering education, 1999, 88(2): 189-194.

[6] THOMPSON B E. Studio pedagogy for engineering design[J]. International journal of engineering education, 2001, 18(1): 1-8.

[7] Integrated Learning Centre at Queen's University. ILCE homepage [EB/OL]. (2004-04-10) [2011-08-01]. http://appsci.queensu.ca/ilc/.

[8] ALTAN T. Mechanical engineering education and research in US and German universities[C]// Proceedings of the Workshop of the German Science Council. Cologne: German Science Council, 2003: 1-15.

[9] DENTON N L, HUTZEL W J. Venturing into engagement[C]// 2003 CIEC Conference. Tucson: CIEC, 2003: 12-15.

[10] CCPE. Canadian engineers for tomorrow: trends in engineering enrolment and degrees awarded [EB/OL]. (2003-01-15) [2011-08-01]. http://www.ccpe.ca.

[11] EEIC. Best practices summary report[R]. Arlington: Engineering Education Innovators Conference, 1997.

[12] DENTON H G. Multidisciplinary team-based project work: planning factors[J]. Design studies, 1997, 18(2): 155-170.

[13] BELL T E. Proven skills: the new yardstick for schools[J]. IEEE spectrum, 2000, 37(9): 1-8.

[14] GRINTER L E. Summary of the report on evaluation of engineering education[J]. Journal of engineering education, 1955, 46(1): 25-60.

[15] COVO D. Personal Communication[Z]. School of Architecture, McGill University, Mon-

treal, 2003.
[16] CCPE. Guideline on the professional engineering practice in Canada [R]. Canadian Council of Professional Engineers, 2001: 17.
[17] LE BOTERF G. Développer la compétence des professionnelles — construire les parcours de professionnalisation[M]. 4th ed. Paris: Éditions d'Organisation, 2002.
[18] FRISE P R, et al. Mechanical engineering skills needs in Canadian industry[C]// Annual Conference of the Canadian Society of Mechanical Engineers. Kingston: CSME, 2002: 1-12.
[19] SHEPPARD S D. Design as cornerstone and capstone[J]. Mechanical engineering, 1999, 121(11): 1-5.
[20] EGGERT R J. Response tables from industry members of ASME's design engineering division and the manufacturing engineering division: engineering design education: surveys of demand and supply[R]. Boise: Boise State University, 2002.
[21] CCPE. 2000 engineering work in canada, sectoral focus groups synthesis report [R]. Canadian Council of Professional Engineers, 2001: 11-12.
[22] FRISE P R. Identifying the design body of knowledge[C]// International Conference on Engineering Design. Stockholm: ICED, 2003: 1-10.
[23] DEMPSTER W M. Filling the gap: engineering design analysis within a mechanical engineering curriculum[C]// International Conference on Engineering Design. Glasgow: ICED, 2001: 1-10.
[24] HUBKA V, EDER W E. Design science[M]. Berlin: Springer-Verlag, 1992.
[25] BAJAJ A. Estimating for design costs [C]//AACE-International. Transactions of the Annual Meeting, 2002: EST081-EST086.
[26] OAKLEY M. Design management: a handbook of issues and methods[M]. Oxford: Blackwell Reference, 1990.
[27] BOOTHROYD G. Why DFM? [J]. Design engineering, 2001: 15-16.
[28] BOOTHROYD G. Product design for manufacture and assembly[M]. New York: Marcel Dekker, 1994.
[29] FU Y. Process design for the environment: a multi-objective framework under uncertainty[J]. Clean products and processes, 2000, 2: 92-107.
[30] GATTIKER T F. A hands-on application for teaching design for the environment (DFE) principles[J]. Quality management journal, 2003, 10(4): 32-39.
[31] RADCLIFFE D F, HARRISON P. Transforming design practice in a small manufacturing enterprise[C]// Sixth International Conference on Design Theory and Methodology. New York: ASME, 1994: 91-98.
[32] MCCOWAN J D, KNAPPER C K. An integrated and comprehensive approach to engineering curricula, part one: objectives and general approach[J]. International journal of engineering education, 2002, 18(6): 633-637.

[33] DEKKER D L. Difference between open-ended projects and design projects[C]// Proceedings Frontiers in Education Conference. Piscataway: IEEE, 1996, 3: 1257-1259.

[34] ASBORNJEN O A, HAMANN R J. Toward a unified systems engineering education[J]. IEEE transactions on systems, man, and cybernetics C: applications and reviews, 2000, 30(2): 175-182.

[35] EVBUOMWAN N. Survey of design philosophies, models, methods and systems[C]// Proceedings of The Institution of Mechanical Engineers, Part B: Journal of Engineering Manufacture. London: Imeche, 1996, 210(B4): 301-320.

[36] ZHANG G. Information-based engineering design and the ABET 2000[C]// Proceedings of the 1998 28th Annual Frontiers in Education Conference. Tempe: FIE, 1998: 1-6.

[37] LEWIN D R. Integrated process design instruction[J]. Computers and chemical engineering, 2002, 26(2): 295-306.

[38] DIETER G E. Engineering design[M]. 3rd ed. New York: McGraw-Hill, 2000.

[39] ERTAS A, JONES J C. The engineering design process[M]. 2nd ed. Hoboken: Wiley, 1996.

[40] TRIZ. Theory of Inventive Problem Solving Journal [EB/OL]. (2004-02-13) [2011-08-01]. http://www.triz-journal.com.

[41] PETERS M S, TIMMERHAUS K D, WEST R E. Plant design and economics for chemical engineers[M]. 5th ed. New York: McGraw-Hill, 2003.

[42] DAVIS D C. Competency-based engineering design projects[C]// 1996 ASEE Annual Conference. Washington, DC: ASEE, 1996.

[43] EVATT M A C. Industrial training — more than just work experience? [C]// International Conference on Engineering Design. Glasgow: ICED, 2001: 1-8.

[44] SORBY S A. Modernization of the mechanical engineering curriculum and guidelines for computer-aided engineering instruction[J]. Computer applications in engineering education, 2000, 7(4): 252-260.

[45] KUNDU A K, RAGHUNATHAN S. A proposition in design education with a potential in commercial venture in small aircraft manufacture[J]. Aircraft design, 2000, 3(4): 261-273.

[46] BIRTIGH A, LAUSCHKE G, SCHIERHOLZ W F, et al. CFD in chemical engineering from an industrial standpoint[J]. Chemie ingenieur technik, 2000, 72: 175-193.

[47] HALES C. Respect design or expect disaster! [C]// International Conference on Engineering Design. Stockholm: ICED, 2003: 1-8.

[48] GUZMAN B, VUDGDELIJA J. Operations & maintenance — when “wait and see” isn’t good enough: applying HAZOP at genelba — adapting hazards and operability techniques to power plant operation[J]. Modern power systems, 2003, 23(10): 33-37.

[49] KELLY G. Reducing risk and all that HAZ[J]. Safety and health practitioner, 2004, 22(3): 26-31.

[50] TOLF Y. Human-centred engineers — a model for holistic interdisciplinary communication and professional practice[J]. International journal of industrial ergonomics, 2003, 31(3):

195-202.
[51] WISLER D C. Engineering — what you don't necessarily learn in school[J]. Mechanical engineering, 2003, 125(8): 1-5.
[52] THOMAS C, AME E. Cultivating design competence: online support for beginning design studio[J]. Automation in construction, 2000, 9(1): 83-91.
[53] LAUCHE K. Non-technical skills training for designers[C]// International Conference on Engineering Design. Stockholm: Iced, 2003: 1-8.
[54] LAHIDJI B. Competencies in manufacturing engineering technology programs from employer's point of view[C]// Proceedings of the 33rd Annual NAIT Conference. Chicago: NAIT, 2000: 1-10.
[55] SANTIAGO C. The model engineer for GE[C]// Proceedings of the Conference on European Society for Engineering Education. Copenhagen: SEFI, 2001: 1-8.
[56] SEKIGUCHI S. Design skills and education of new employees[C]// International Conference on Engineering Design. Glasgow: ICED, 2001: 1-12.
[57] COWDROY R, WILLIAMS A. Assessing design activity: issues and actions[C]// Proceedings of the Seventh International Design Conference. Dubrovnik: IDC, 2002: 43-48.
[58] Nserc Design Engineering Group. Engineering design competency[R]. Ottawa: NSERC, 2004.
[59] CCPE. A vision for the engineering profession in Canada[R]. Ottawa: Canadian Council of Professional Engineers, 1997.
[60] World Commission on Environment and Development. Our common future[M]. Oxford: Oxford University Press, 1987.
[61] MORRISON C, HUGHES P. Professional engineering practice: ethical aspects[M]. 3rd ed. New York: McGraw-Hill, 2003.
[62] WHMIS. Workplace Hazardous Materials Information System [EB/OL]. (2004-03-12) [2011-08-01]. http://www.hc-sc.gc.ca/hecs-sesc/whmis/index.htm.
[63] VOLAND G. Engineering by design[M]. 2nd ed. Upper Saddle River: Pearson Prentice Hall, 2004.
[64] ULLMAN D G. The mechanical design process[M]. 2nd ed. New York: McGraw-Hill, 1997.
[65] BOWMAN B A, FARR J V. Embedding leadership in civil engineering education[J]. Journal of professional issues in engineering education and practice, 2000, 126(1): 16-20.
[66] DHILLON B S. Design reliability: fundamentals and applications[M]. Boca Raton: CRC Press, 1999.
[67] CORBETT J. Design for manufacture: strategies, principles and techniques[M]. Boston: Addison-Wesley, 1991.
[68] ROUSE W. Design for success: a human-centered approach to designing successful products and systems[M]. New York: Wiley, 1991.

[69] USEPA. US Environmental Protection Agency, Design for the Environment [EB/OL]. (2004-01-24) [2011-08-01]. http://www.epa.gov/dfe/index.htm.

[70] NRC. Canadian Codes Centre [EB/OL]. (2004-07-11) [2011-08-01]. http://irc.nrc-cnrc.gc.ca/codes/home_E.shtml.

[71] MIGLIORE H. Design for X[EB/OL]. (2004-01-22) [2011-08-01]. http://www.cecs.pdx.edu/~herm/capstone/mee9899/design/dfx/dfxterms.htm.

# The Development of Design Directed Engineering Curriculum based on the CDIO Framework

*Peihua Gu, Xiaohua Lu, Guangjin Xiong, Shengping Li, Minfen Shen*

**Abstract:** As economic reform in China has made significant progress in the last 25 years, there is an urgent need to reform higher education system to better serve increasing needs of society and industry. College of Engineering at Shantou University adopted CDIO education framework to re-design engineering programs. A design directed engineering education approach based on CDIO has been developed to re-design curricula and course contents. Since this is a college wide implementation of a new engineering education paradigm, detailed steps have been taken to ensure smooth transition from the current curricular to the new curricula. This paper discusses the implementation process and progress as well as potential challenges.

## Introduction

Over 2,000 universities in China graduate over 500,000 new engineers annually. Recent rapid economic expansion in China has created a number of new enterprises, and these companies have absorbed most of the recent engineering graduates. For the increasing number of multinational firms established in China, recruitment of qualified engineers has been considered critically important. According to research by the McKinsey Global Institute, these multinationals have been experiencing challenges in recruiting engineers and other professionals in China. The report identified a number of issues, one of which is that the Chinese educational system is "biased toward theory" where "Chinese engineering students received relatively little practical experience in projects or teamwork compared with engineering graduates in Europe and North America". In the last few years, major efforts have been made to reform engineering education both at the Ministry of Education and at universities.

Before the cultural revolution, the Chinese education system was designed more for the planned economy. Engineering programs were, therefore, narrowly focused with significant engineering science content and detailed specialized courses. Engineering students graduated from this kind of program readily worked at jobs on which the programs were based. Engineering graduates were provided with employment, based on their specialty and family location as well as other government considerations. With the planned economy and lifelong employment of almost all government corporation, such programs served the purpose of supplying engineering graduates to sustain the operations of crown corporations.

Since Chinese economic reform was launched in 1978, many private enterprises and crown corporations that have gone public require different kinds of engineers with broader based engineering training who can adapt to the changing needs of both companies and their customers. Graduating students are no longer provided with jobs, and they have to compete with others in the open job market. It is becoming increasingly clear that broad based engineering education with both strong theoretical and practical knowledge, as well as other skills, such as teamwork, leadership, communications, project management, knowledge of technology, appreciation of society, etc., is essential in engineering education reform. No private firms can offer lifelong employment, and individuals may have to change jobs a few times before retirement. Therefore, educational background, various software skills and interview skills have become critically important for those who are competing with many others for one job.

In the last few years, the importance of engineering education has been recognized by the leadership at various levels of educational systems. In north America, universities are autonomous, with protection by law for academic freedom and governance. For those professionally accredited engineering programs, professional bodies control the accreditation process to ensure that graduating engineers meet the minimum requirements for registration as a professional engineer after a few years of practice and passing the ethics exams.

In China, the Ministry of Education and provincial governments are formally in charge of the educational system, with authority ranging from degree granting status to quality control and textbook development. The quality control of engineering programs has been largely entrusted to the government, since formal engineering accreditation by an independent body has yet to be established. One of the major advantages of the current Chinese educational system is that radical reform of engineering programs can take place relatively more easily than in North America. Therefore, a relatively efficient approach has been adopted by Shantou University to develop new curricula for all engineering and computer science programs based on the CDIO education framework.

## 1 Engineering Education Reform at Shantou University

Shantou University was founded jointly by the Guangdong Province of China and the Li Ka-Shing Foundation in Hong Kong in 1981, when economic reform in China had just begun. The College of Engineering at Shantou University consists of four departments, offering five engineering programs: Civil Engineering, Computer Science and Engineering, Electronic Engineering, Electric Communication Engineering, and Manufacturing Engineering (formerly Design, Manufacturing and Automation Engineering in Chinese). Shantou University has been taking various initiatives in education reform, ranging from English enhancement to full credit systems. Therefore, both academic staff and students are more open to changes than many traditional universities in China.

One of the main objectives of engineering program reform is accreditation by ABET 2000 in the US and the Canadian Engineering Accreditation Board as soon as possible. To make all the engineering programs ready for accreditation within a five-year time frame, it is not practical to follow a well-established approach that normally requires a relatively long time to complete changes in the entire curriculum. The College of Engineering has decided to adopt the CDIO initiative and redevelop new curricula for all five programs based on the CDIO framework, because it provides a holistic and systematic educational model and the complete implementation of the CDIO education framework will provide the necessary assurance to meet US/Canada engineering accreditation needs. In addition, it is believed that design directed engineering education, based on CDIO, provides a rationale, methodology, resources and tools to develop the new engineering education paradigm in China, so as to produce a new generation of engineers capable of meeting the demands of both Chinese local enterprises and multinational corporations. While the curriculum redesign is still in progress, this article reports the process, experiences and difficulties in the development of the new engineering curricula, using the Manufacturing Engineering and Civil Engineering programs as examples.

## 2 Design Directed Engineering Program based on the CDIO Framework

In the Chinese educational system, with strong administrative influence, it is much easier to establish a consensus in developing new curricula based on the CDIO framework. To develop new engineering curricula for all engineering programs in a relatively short time, an approach with the following steps has been developed:

(1) Introduce CDIO to academic staff.

(2) Help academic staff become familiar with the CDIO education framework and the associated standards through training and workshops.

(3) Prepare students for program reform and changes.

(4) Analyze individual course content against the CDIO syllabus with Introduction, Teaching and Utilization.

(5) Select and train champions.

(6) Redesign curricula for all the engineering programs.

(7) Design new course content.

(8) Renovate laboratories and workspace, as well as upgrade experimental facilities.

(9) Select two courses from each program for pilot implementation.

(10) Revise the new programs and make changes based on feedback from experience of the pilot courses.

To prepare academic staff for adopting CDIO in creating new engineering curricula, the first step was to reach a consensus within the College Administrative Council. A series of meetings and discussions were carried out to discuss the development and implementation process. Then, a faculty council meeting with all academic staff was called to discuss this new initiative. Each department also called a series of meetings to reach a consensus on adoption of CDIO for developing new engineering curricula.

This initiative quickly spread among most engineering students. Some students were excited about this major change; others expressed concern for the potential impact on their studies. In parallel to the implementation process, we created the World Engineer Forum to discuss various topics that are important to engineering students and academic staff. The first forum was on engineering education. This three-hour session was used to explain to students the reasons for such changes and how this new initiative would impact on their studies and career development. Students became very supportive. For example, students currently in their junior and senior years will not have an opportunity to experience this change. Many students, therefore, demanded the implementation of as many courses as possible and as soon as possible so that they could learn in this new paradigm.

All engineering academic staff who were currently teaching engineering courses were provided with a copy of the CDIO syllabus in Chinese and were asked to provide analyses of their course content and the learned knowledge and skills. Each of the syllabus competency items was analyzed against the learned knowledge and skills of a course by the course instructor in terms of Introduction, Teaching and Utilization of a particular competency item. All of the course analyses were then collected to determine the differences between the current programs and the CDIO syllabus. This exercise accomplished two things: ① determination of what was being taught in the current programs; ② understanding of the CDIO syllabus and its meaning, as well as a more in-depth knowledge of CDIO. In fact, this was also a training and learning process and has proven to be worthwhile.

Champions were selected from each department to form a CDIO panel for developing the implementation plan, ranging from training workshops to course outline format issues. Several training workshops and faculty council meetings were organized to introduce CDIO and associated documents. As one individual had previously attended a CDIO workshop and two others were familiar with the contents, the workshop and initial implementation process seem to have gone well.

The new engineering curricula have been designed based on an engineering design directed approach. Engineering design, in a broad sense, is considered the essence of engineering. The proposed engineering design directed CDIO program will use engineering design as the theme to integrate all courses, as shown in Fig. 1.

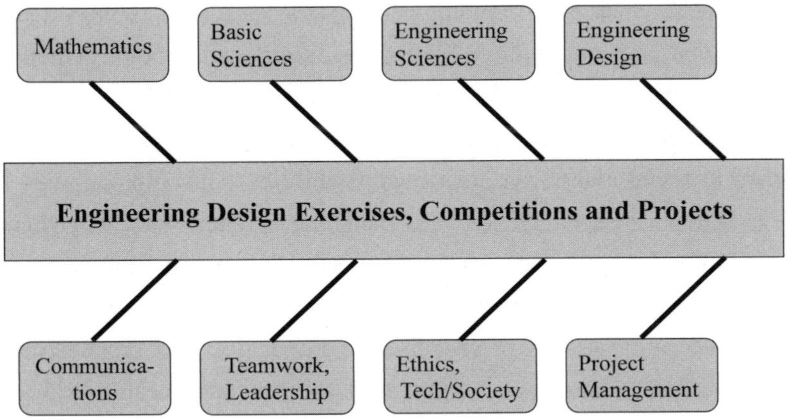


**Fig. 1 Design Directed CDIO Implementation**

Fig. 1 shows that the design directed engineering programs based on CDIO will integrate all engineering and non-engineering knowledge and skills. In addition to the previously existing final year design project, at least four design projects will be introduced in each of the five programs. These design projects will be distributed throughout the four-year programs to allow the students to gradually delve deeper in each stage. Table 1 shows the projects and their emphases for the Manufacturing Engineering program.

**Table 1 Planned Projects in the Curriculum of the Manufacturing Engineering Program**

| Project | Stage | Project specifications |
|---|---|---|
| Introduction to Engineering | Year 1 Semester 1 | 4 design mini-projects to stimulate the students' interest and creativity, to expose the students to the process of knowledge creation and development, to give the students a sense of responsibility in social and historical contexts |
| Engineering Design & Communication | Year 2 Semester 1 | To introduce the students to the design process, design process management, task decomposition and cooperation and team spirit |
| Mechatronic System Design & Prototyping Ⅰ | Year 2 Semester 2 | Market survey, product definition (functional analyses), feasibility analyses and conceptual design |
| Mechatronic System Design & Prototyping Ⅱ | Year 3 Semester 2 | Detailed design including specifications, forms, tolerances, materials, etc. |
| Mechatronic System Design & Prototyping Ⅲ | Year 3 Semester 2a (a mini 6-week semester after Semester 2) | Prototyping and validation including fabrication, inspection, assembly, testing, operating processes, etc. |
| Final Year Design Project | Year 4 Semesters 1 & 2 | Open-ended design projects coming from industry or faculty R&D programs, students will be required to complete the project from the planning and definition stage to the implementation stage |

As can be seen, design projects are staged in accordance with the students' development in learned knowledge and skills in their programs. The design directed curriculum puts the students in a design environment where they learn engineering science and technology and when they need to use them. In addition, they are required to work as design teams, exercise their communication, project management, leadership and other skills. Specifications for life cycle engineering requirements and environmental considerations give students the opportunity to relate their design activities and decisions to social and professional responsibilities. This approach is a major improvement from the traditional one, which provides the students with all the engineering science and technology materials but where most students have little or no "engineering appreciation". An analogy may depict the situation more clearly: imagine that "the technology and practice are the vocabulary of engineering, the design process as composition and engineering science as the grammar" [1]. Preparation of compositions puts the grammar and vocabulary in the right context and makes the learning much easier and fun. Of course, any composition assignment uses only limited vocabulary and grammar. Therefore rigorous training in these areas is necessary.

For the Civil Engineering program, the design processes are arranged in a more discrete fashion. This is due to the diversity of the different fields in civil engineering: material science, structural engineering, transportation engineering, geotechnic engineering, etc. Each project is designed with emphasis on a specific field. Table 2 shows the project plan.

**Table 2 Planned Projects in the Curriculum of the Civil Engineering Program**

| Project | Stage | Project specifications |
|---|---|---|
| Introduction to Engineering | Year 1 Semester 1 | 4 design mini-projects to stimulate the students' interest and creativity, to expose the students to the process of knowledge creation and development, to give the students a sense of responsibility in social and historical contexts |
| Sustainable Development Civil Engineering Ⅰ (Sustainable Development Civil Engineering Materials) | Year 2 Semester 1 | The students need to learn the fundamentals of construction materials; then work in groups to make mix designs of Portland cement concrete for specific purposes, to realize the mix, to test and validate the design, to present to the class, and to discuss and defend their ideas |
| Sustainable Development Civil Engineering Ⅱ (Human Habitat and Green Construction) | Year 2 Semester 2 | Team project work. Enhance communication abilities |
| Engineering System Design | Year 3 Semester 2 | A whole cohort of students (about 50 people) work together as a team to design a civil system, such as an arterial road system or a new city district |
| Structural and Geotechnic Engineering Design | Year 3 Semester 2 | Two structural teams and two geotechnic teams work together to design a given system |
| Final Year Design Project | Year 4 Semesters 1 & 2 | Work on a major construction development project, such as Shantou Metro system |

Teamwork and communication are always required throughout all projects. The personal, interpersonal and CDIO capabilities, as specified in the CDIO syllabus [2], are addressed where appropriate in the processes and assessments of the projects' implementation.

In order to introduce the new design projects, radical adjustments have been made to the existing curricula. Twenty to thirty percent of existing contact hours between academic staff and students have been cut. Some courses have been merged or may even be phased out.

Most of the details of the projects are still under design. This is partially because the stakeholders' survey is not yet complete. The survey results are needed to set up the educational benchmarks and to validate the educational objectives, as stipulated by CDIO Standards [3].

The development of course content is in progress. To further enhance faculty members' understanding of CDIO and the associated processes and standards as well as enthusiasm in the process, faculty members are involved in reformatting the course syllabi. A unified course syllabus template has been created for all courses. Two major changes have been introduced into the template. One is changing the former content oriented syllabus into an outcome oriented syllabus. For each item listed in the syllabus, the expected learning outcome is marked with the six levels of Bloom's taxonomy of cognitive domain [4]. The second change is the introduction of a table specifying the 14 CDIO syllabus second-level 2.1-4.6 objectives, similar to Figure 2 in reference [5]. The table is filled with the training/utilization expectations for each objective. This serves three purposes:

(1) All teaching staff have to make some efforts to understand the CDIO initiative and its syllabus.

(2) The filled table works as a kind of "promise" for what a specific course is to contribute to the program's CDIO initiative.

(3) The collection of all syllabi in a program's curriculum would easily enable an overall check of CDIO practices within the program's activities.

Laboratories and workshops are indispensable components that support the CDIO initiative. Apart from the existing 24 laboratories open to all project students, an integrated Student Innovation and Project Centre in the College of Engineering is being developed to provide students with the necessary infrastructure and facilities to work on their projects. The over 400 $m^2$ space will house facilities ranging from physical prototyping to civil, mechanical, electric and electronic, computational and communicational hardware and software. An estimated 11 million RMB (about $1.4 million US) engineering complex renovation and laboratory equipment upgrading project is also underway. These efforts will provide students and staff with a new facility to implement the new CDIO based engineering curricula.

The new curricula will be implemented for students enrolled in Fall 2006. There have already been some trial runs of design projects conducted within discrete courses. For example, in a Civil Engineering course, instead of assigning a given mix to the students and asking them to make the specimens and crush them, Construction Material lab practice has required the students to design their own mix to fit a specific purpose, like acid resisting, and to validate their designs. The students have come up with some unique designs of which the instructor was unaware. In this particular course, the students are also asked to read journal papers and make summaries relating to their material design project. Such practices have changed the mindset of the students, who now even actively request changes in other courses. These initial responses received endorsement from students. Hence, it is expected that more positive responses will come from students once the new courses are introduced in the fall of 2006.

Though the CDIO framework has been set up and is expected to be in operation soon, the real challenges will occur upon full implementation of the CDIO programs. Two major problems are anticipated:

(1) Lack of experience in running and managing the design directed education practice. The balance between rigorous training and hands-on experience can easily be lost. This problem can, of course, be solved through practice and exploration, provided that all faculty members believe in the initiative and commit themselves to it.

(2) There will be some unwillingness, inertia, doubt or resistance from faculty members. The initiative must finally be implemented in courses and projects; and, the motivation and responsibility of faculty are crucial. Therefore, there have to be some pioneers piloting the initiative and leading the implementation process. To this end, two courses per program have been selected to pilot the initiative at the course level. The results will be summarized by the end of June 2006.

## 3 Conclusion

The College of Engineering at Shantou University is the first university in China to develop new engineering programs based on the CDIO education framework. Since November 2005, in a period of less than 6 months, progress has been made on various fronts. New curricula for all engineering programs including Civil Engineering, Computer Science and Engineering, Electric Communication Engineering, Design, Manufacturing and Automation Engineering (equivalent to Manufacturing Engineering programs in North America), and Electronics Engineering have been developed. Detailed course content is being developed. Workspace improvements, including development of new design project spaces and upgrading of laboratory facilities, are underway. Two pilot courses from each of the engineering programs have been selected to implement the new curricula, and the implementation results are expected at end of June 2006. Between June and September 2006, minor changes will be made in the new curricula and course content, in order for the college to be ready to offer the new curricula in Fall 2006.

## Acknowledgment

The authors would like to acknowledge that many colleagues at Shantou University were involved in developing the new CDIO based engineering programs. The authors wish to thank the Li Ka-Shing Foundation in Hong Kong for providing financial support to this work.

**References**

[1] YELLOWLEY I, GU P H. Design directed engineering education[J]. Journal of engineering design and innovation, 2005, 1: 1-12.

[2] CDIO Adoption Centre. Appendix A: The CDIO Syllabus in Topical Form (v4.2.3) [EB/OL]. (2005-05-01) [2006-06-13]. http://www.cdio.org.

[3] CDIO. The CDIO Standards[S/OL]. (2005-08-01) [2006-06-13]. http://www.cdio.org.

[4] CDIO Adoption Centre. Appendix B: Bloom's Taxonomy of Educational Objectives [EB/OL]. (2005-09-13) [2006-06-13]. http://www.cdio.org.

[5] BANKEL J. Benchmarking engineering curricula with the CDIO syllabus[J]. International journal of engineering education, 2005, 21(1): 121-133.

# 从 CDIO 到 EIP-CDIO
## ——汕头大学工程教育与人才培养模式探索①

顾佩华　沈民奋　李升平　庄哲民　陆小华　熊光晶

**摘要:** 全球化已成为当今世界经济发展和竞争的一个主要特征,全球经济一体化发展对人才特别是专业工程技术人才以及其他专业性及技术服务行业人才,形成了一个通用的标准。在这样快速发展的全球竞争环境下,一个国家的工程教育无法完全孤立地发展,必须融入全球经济和社会循环。本文在回顾国际工程教育改革背景的基础上,从汕头大学工学院的工程教育与人才培养模式改革出发,提出了以工程设计为导向,以培养个人能力、团队能力和系统调控能力为主要目标的 EIP-CDIO 工程教育理念;根据本校实际,提出以实践性和探索性的设计项目为载体,以科学的课程安排(进度)促进能力培养的人才培养模式。本文对 EIP-CDIO 的培养模式、培养计划、课程设置、教学模式、教学质量评估监督体系等诸方面进行了详细探讨,并阐述了自己的改革经验与思考,期望能为中国的工程教育与人才培养模式探索一条新的改革思路,为培养符合现代企业要求的国际化工程技术人才做出贡献。

**关键词:** EIP-CDIO;全球经济一体化;工程教育;人才培养

## From CDIO to EIP-CDIO: A Probe into the Mode of Engineering Education and Talent Cultivation in Shantou University

*Gu Peihu, Shen Minfen, Li Shengping, Zhuang Zhemin, Lu Xiaohua, Xiong Guangjing*

**Abstract:** Economic globalization is one of the main characteristics in the development and competition of current world economy. The development of globalization has formed a general standard for talents, especially professional engineering and technical personnel, as well as experts in other specialized and technical service fields. Under such a circumstance, engineering education in each country is by no means isolated from the mainstream, in fact, it should be integrated into the cycle of global economic and social systems. On the basis of recalling the background of engineering education reform as well as the education reform in Shantou University, the paper puts forward such a conception of engineering education as EIP-CDIO, which focuses on taking engineering design as its direction, and taking cultivation of personal competence, team spirit, and system adaptability as its main target. Based on different situations in each university, it also suggests the mode of talent cultivation which takes the practical project of design as its carrier with the help of scientific curriculum arrangement. The paper has also illustrated the cultivation mode, curriculum design, teaching mode, the evaluation and supervision of teaching quality, as well as the author's own experiences. It is hoped that this will explore a

① 本文刊登于《高等工程教育研究》2008 年第 1 期 12~20 页。

new approach to reforming China's engineering education and talent development models, contributing to the cultivation of internationally competitive engineers who meet the requirements of modern enterprises.
**Keywords:** EIP-CDIO; global economic integration; engineering education; talent cultivation

## 引言

20 世纪下半叶以来，全球化逐步把世界纳入一个共同的基本价值和行为规则体系中。2001 年，我国加入世界贸易组织（WTO），经济与社会发展进一步加快，并开始融入全球一体化的浪潮。这一历史变革，也对高等工程教育产生了巨大影响。这种影响不仅表现在人才的培养质量、知识结构和教学的方法手段上，而且表现在工程教育必须适应日益扩大的国际经济交流和日益加剧的国际竞争的趋势上。实现人才和教育的国际化已成为不可回避的重要课题。

改革开放以来，特别是近几年来国内高等教育体系发生了不少积极变化，但从总体上看，我国的高等教育特别是工程教育与经济发展的需要还显得很不适应，培养的工程技术人才远不能满足现代企业的要求，这种状况将直接影响我国在国际上的竞争力。据麦肯锡咨询公司的研究报告统计，我国的工科毕业生只有不到 10%适合在跨国公司工作；因此，迫切需要进行深层次改革，以适应全球经济快速发展的需要。据瑞士洛桑国际管理发展学院（IMD）公布的国际竞争力排名，我国整体实力排名由 2005 年的第 31 位大幅上升到了 2006 年的第 19 位，但在同一排名榜上，我国培养的可获得资格的工程师数量却连年位居末座。笔者认为，在当前，以下几个方面的问题特别值得关注。

第一，我国目前还只能称为“生产大国”，要成为“生产强国”还面临着巨大的挑战。重中之重是培养一大批符合现代企业要求的人才，而要完成这一任务，我国现有的工程教育模式应当进一步改革。

第二，快速发展的中国目前正处于一个经济、社会转型阶段，在诚信、道德特别是职业道德等诸多方面都面临严峻挑战。合格的工程技术人才不仅要能解决实际工程问题，而且还必须具备相应的社会意识、人文精神、诚信和职业道德，以及对市场需求的敏锐反应。凡此种种，都对人才培养提出了更高的要求。

第三，随着高新科技的飞速发展和全球化经济竞争的不断加剧，各种相关因素的不确定性也日益增多，使得各国的产品在技术、标准，甚至在法律上产生了诸多矛盾。在创造性地解决这些问题方面，工程技术所起的作用至关重要，因此培养具备国际视野、继续学习能力以及敏锐洞察力的工程师就显得更加迫切。

最后，坚持中国特色与国际接轨应当受到同样的重视。如果仅限于跟踪和模仿外国模式，是无法实现超越与突破，也无法培养出符合未来中国发展与国际化要求的工程技术人才的。因此，必须根据中国实际情况开展全面的、深层次的工程教育改革，从而走出一条独具特色的工程教育新路。

## 1 国际工程教育大潮中的 CDIO

近 20 年来，发达国家都在系统和综合的视野下，从观念、目标、教育内容到教育方法对工程教育进行整体改革。环顾欧美各科技强国，不难发现，科技发展的加速化、综合化、产业化、国际化和一体化也对工程师并进而对各国的工程教育改革提出了新的更高的要求。

### 1.1 北美的工程教育改革

从 1986 年开始，美国国家科学基金会（NSF）逐年加大对工程教育和研究的资助；美国国家研究委员会（NRC）、美国国家工程院（NAE）和美国工程教育学会（ASEE）也纷纷展开调查和制订战略计划，积极推进工程教育改革；麻省理工学院（MIT）、斯坦福大学等名校的工程教育都进行了整体改革。20 世纪 90 年代，美国三大工程教育机构在三份文件——1994 年 ASEE 的《面对变化世界的工程教育》、1995 年 NSF 的《重建工程教育：重在变革》、1996 年美国工程与技术认证委员会（ABET）的《工程标准 2000》（Engineering Criteria 2000）——中提出了工程教育改革的全新思路与措施。《高等工程教育研究》曾载文对这三份重要文件中关于工程教育的标准进行详细评介。

其中，ASEE 1994 年的报告指出，工程教育的目的，除技术知识之外，还必须包括团队精神、交流能力、领导才能、系统视野等 12 条能力要求。

NSF 1995 年的报告则指出，工程教育要在学生、教师、学习经验、课程计划四个方面进行重建。NSF 还资助了一系列大学组（consortia of colleges）加入工程教育合作计划（National Science Foundation's Engineering Education Coalitions Program），每个大学组根据不同的战略思维重新设计课程计划和改善教学方法。美国总统竞争力计划（President's American Competitiveness Initiative）要求以创新（innovation）、探索（exploration）和卓越（ingenuity）来保证美国的领先地位，NSF 还发表《投资美国未来：2006—2011 年战略计划》予以回应。NSF 计划指出，科学的发现和发展极大地加速了科学和工程在所有领域的急速扩展，开拓了全新的探索领域，同时带来巨大的冲击。因应这一挑战的两大方面是支持转换研究、促进卓越的科学和工程教育，以激励创新、刺激经济、提高生活质量。在该计划支持下，探索性学习正成为各种正式和非正式学习的重要特点。

ABET 1996 年的文件已从传统的“规定工程专业应是什么样”，转变成“评估工程教育的结果”。迄今为止，ABET 已为全美包括 MIT、康奈尔等 350 所院校的 2000 个工程学位计划（program）提供了认证。NAE 也非常关注工程教育变革，不仅发表了一系列重要报告，而且相继实施了一系列举措。NAE 院长办公室的常设委员会 CEE 进行了一个名为“The Engineer of 2020”的项目，其 2004 年发表的第一阶段报告描绘了未来关于政府、雇主和工程师的愿景。

加拿大在 20 世纪 90 年代也进行了一系列工程教育改革，建立了国家创新战略；国家自然科学与工程研究基金（NSERC）设立了一系列工程设计讲座教授（NSERC chair professors）职位，旨在改变大学中重工程科学、轻工程设计的现象；加拿大建立了所有工学院都参加的加拿大设计工程网络（Canadian Design Engineering Network），旨在提升加拿大的工程设计教育水平。

### 1.2 欧洲的工程教育改革

1993 年，欧洲国家工程联合会（European Federation of National Engineering Associations，FEANI）启动了名为 EUR-ACE（Accreditation of European Engineering Programmes and Graduates）的计划，旨在成立统一的欧洲工程教育专业认证体系，参加成员为包括 FEANI 在内的 8 个欧洲教育认证组织，提出了著名的“FEANI 公式”，以指导欧洲大陆的工程教育改革。1999 年，欧洲 29 国政府签署了《博洛尼亚宣言》，制定并承诺执行博洛尼亚进程，以改革各国教育系统，促进各国学位、学制的统一和互认，加强欧洲大陆的竞争力。2005 年，欧洲高等教育区教育部长卑尔根会议制定了《欧洲高等教育质量保障标准与指南》（Standards and Guidelines for Quality Assurance in the European Higher Education Area）。同年，包括 FEANI 在内的 14 个欧洲教育认证组织成立了欧洲工程教育专业认证网络（European Network for Accreditation of Engineering Education，ENAEE）。欧洲工程教育的改革方向和侧重点与美国一样：在继续保持科学基础的前提下，着重强调加强工程实践训练，加强各种能力的培养；在内容上，强调综合与集成。

在此，本文要重点介绍 CDIO 模式。

CDIO 工程教育模式是近年来国际工程教育改革的最新成果。2000 年，麻省理工学院和瑞典皇家工学院等四所大学组成的跨国研究组织获得克努特与爱丽丝瓦伦堡基金会近 2000 万美元巨额资助，经过四年的探索研究，创立了 CDIO 工程教育理念，并成立了以 CDIO 命名的国际合作组织。CDIO 代表构思（conceive）、设计（design）、实现（implement）和运作（operate），它以产品研发到产品运行的生命周期为载体，让学生以主动的、实践的、课程之间有机联系的方式学习工程。CDIO 培养大纲将工程毕业生的能力分为工程基础知识、个人能力、人际团队能力和工程系统能力四个层面，大纲要求以综合的培养方式使学生在这四个层面达到预定目标。CDIO 的理念不仅继承和发展了欧美 20 多年来工程教育改革的理念，更重要的是系统地提出了具有可操作性的能力培养、全面实施以及检验测评的 12 条标准。瑞典国家高教署（Swedish National Agency for Higher Education）2005 年采用这 12 条标准对本国 100 个工程学位计划进行评估。结果表明，新标准比原标准适应面更宽，更利于提高质量，尤为重要的是新标准为工程教育的系统化发展提供了基础。迄今为止，已有几十所世界著名大学加入了 CDIO 组织，其机械系和航空航天系全面采用 CDIO 工程教育理念和教学大纲，取得了良好效果，按 CDIO 模式培养的学生深受社会与企业欢迎。

## 2 渗透 EIP 精神的 CDIO 理念

汕头大学工学院从 2005 年开始研究 CDIO 模式，并结合中国实际，提出了以设计为导向、将素质教育与 CDIO 四大能力相结合的 EIP-CDIO 培养方案。2006 年初，汕头大学工学院成为中国第一个 CDIO 国际合作组织成员；2007 年 11 月，CDIO 国际合作组织会议在汕头大学举行，显示了国际工程教育界对中国工程教育改革的关注。

2005 年底，汕头大学工学院引入 CDIO 理念，这是根据社会发展需求，结合国内和本校多年改革经验而做出的选择。我们认识到，在重视加强科学基础的前提下，当前我国工程教育更应强调个人能力、团队能力、系统调控能力，而达到这些目标的有效手段，就是参照 CDIO 理念进行改革。

鉴于我国现在的工程教育多以学科知识为核心，缺乏对历史、社会和环境的认知与责任教育，加上其他种种原因，诚信、道德特别是职业道德教育普遍缺失，个人利益至上，团队意识匮乏，使得许多工科毕业生的现有能力与现代企业的用人要求差距甚大。针对上述问题，汕头大学工学院在 CDIO 的基础上，提出了 EIP-CDIO 培养模式，即注重职业道德（ethics）、诚信（integrity）和职业素质（professionalism），并与 CDIO 有机结合。这一创新教育模式强调做人与做事结合，做人通过做事来体现，做事依靠做人来保证，在培养过程中注重人文精神的熏陶，使培养出的工程师具备良好的职业道德，诚实正直，富有责任感。EIP-CDIO 的培养框架如图 1 所示。

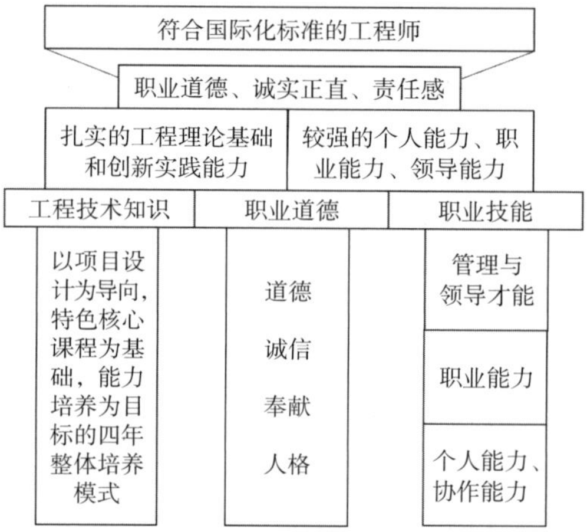


**图 1　EIP-CDIO 的培养框架**

EIP-CDIO 将“工程师职业道德”课程作为工学院全体学生的重要必修课，使学生了解作为一名合格工程师必须具备的素质与规范，并要求学生在未来的学习与实践环节中始终以工程师的道德标准与行为准则要求自己；在整个教学环节中，课程教学大纲对每一个项目和课程都有 EIP 方面的要求和具体考核规范；学院通过“世界工程师论坛”、成长沙龙、社会实践等多种活动，开展有关工程师职业道德和操守方面的教育与实践。

另外，基于 CDIO 理念提出的以设计为导向的 EIP-CDIO 工程教育模式，在专业培养上以实践性和探索性的项目设计为载体，以系统观念为指导，通过多种教学因素的集成来培养学生的个人能力、团队能力、系统调控能力。该培养计划和课程大纲已在 2006 级本科生中全面实施。

总之，汕头大学工学院 EIP-CDIO 模式的目标是：培养具有高度社会责任感、健全的人格、良好职业素质的国际化工程技术人才。

## 3 EIP-CDIO 的培养模式

EIP-CDIO 是一种以工程项目设计为导向、工程能力培养为目标的工程教育模式。工程项目设计是工程实践的精髓所在。功能、技术、经济以及环境、社会乃至历史的要求及其限制都要在项目设计的过程中得到反映，EIP-CDIO 培养模式就是通过项目设计将整个课程体系有机而系统地结合起来的。其特点是：所有需要学习和掌握的内容都围绕项目设计这个核心，形成一个有机的整体（图 2）。

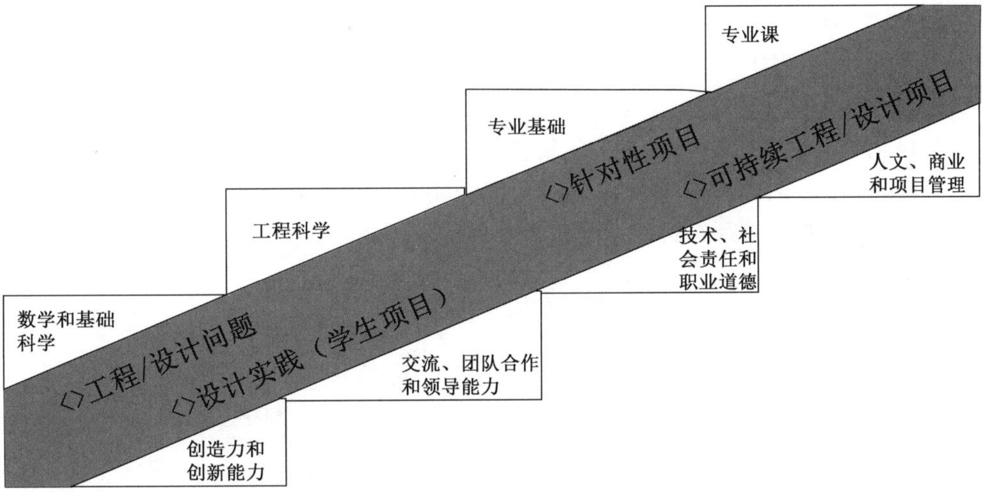


**图 2 以设计为导向的 EIP-CDIO 培养模式**

通过精心规划项目的 CDIO，引导学生对核心专业课程产生浓厚的学习兴趣，从而达到能力培养、综合发展的目的。EIP-CDIO 与以往培养计划的主要不同之处是：①通过导论性的基础课程，从起始阶段就将工程实践引导入门，让学生尽早领略工程技术之美；②在教学计划和教学实践中围绕项目设计将相关课程有机联系起来；③通过贯穿专业学习全过程的 CDIO 项目，让学生在学习专业知识的同时直接体验高级设计过程，使知识的学习和应用之间形成良性互动。

CDIO 项目按规模和范围划分为三级：1 级项目为包含本专业主要核心课程和能力要求的项目；2 级项目为包含一组相关核心课程、能力要求的项目；3 级项目是为单门课程而设的项目，旨在增强理解和培养相关能力，3 级项目的设立与否及采用何种形式由各门课程大纲根据需要确定。

1 级项目要求完整地、前后衔接地贯穿于整个本科教学阶段，使学生得到构思、设计、实现、运作的系统训练。每专业至少有两次 1 级项目训练。首次 1 级项目训练一般在一年级或二年级开始，学生在教师指导下通过解剖一个实例产品，了解其构成与设计，从而提前了解本专业核心内容与实际产品的关系，以工程师的角度去面对即将开始的专业课学习；同时，通过早期项目的构思与设计，激发学习兴趣，进行初步的创新思维与产品构思训练，并在一定程度上建立起与专业相关的整体概念。毕业实习+毕业设计为第二次1级项目训练。两次项目训练相互衔接。经过相关课程与项目的训练，要求学生利用所学知识，对一个产品项目完整地进行构思、设计、实现、运用，系统地完成一个工程实践，目的是让学生从解决工程问题的角度学习专业知识，进而形成对工程的兴趣，并初步掌握工程思维方法。

2级项目以相关核心课程群和相关能力要求为基础。作为1级项目的支撑，2级项目既是对相关课程群的综合，也是对整个教学体系的补充，主要培养学生综合应用相关知识的能力，尤其是创新思维能力与终身学习能力。训练一般以3~6个2级项目为载体，从而加强本专业核心课程的学习与应用。

3级项目是单门课程内的项目。在为学生提供强大基础知识背景和数学、科学方法训练的基础上，3级项目根据课程教学自身需要设立小规模实践项目，旨在加深和强化学生对课程内容的理解与应用。

基于CDIO框架的培养方案如图3所示。可以看出，整个培养计划以1级项目为主线，以2级项目为支撑，以3级项目与核心课程为基础，将核心课程教育与对专业的整体认识统一起来，并结合项目训练对学生自我更新知识的能力、人际和团体交流能力以及对大系统的掌握、运行和调控能力进行整体培养。

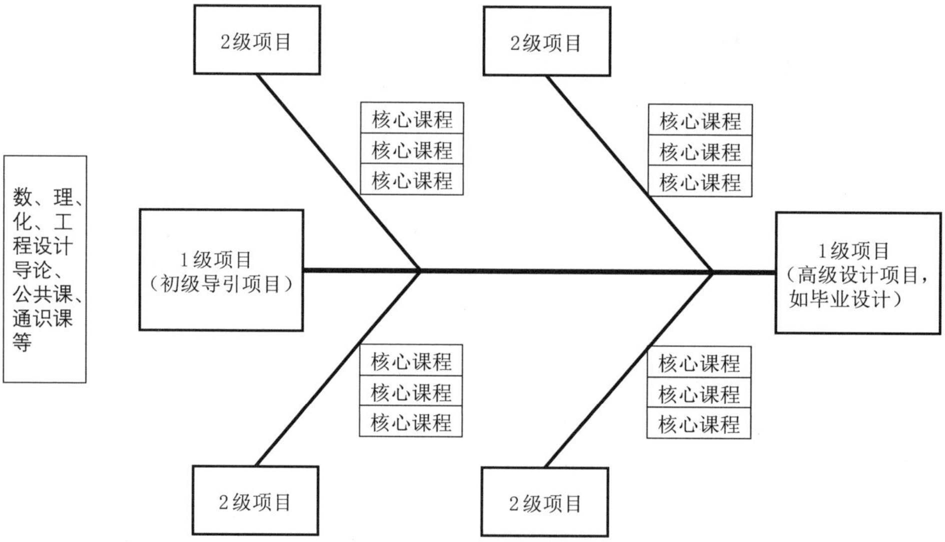


**图3 专业的CDIO培养鱼骨架图**

## 4 EIP-CDIO的课程体系

在整体确立EIP-CDIO培养模式的基础上，汕头大学工学院开展了以设计为导向的EIP-CDIO课程体系建设，修订了培养计划与课程大纲等一系列教学文件，并在全院5个专业全面实施。

## 4.1 EIP-CDIO 专业培养计划

按照 EIP-CDIO 培养计划，汕头大学工学院规划了公共基础课程和包括工程师职业道德在内的通识课程，并编制了相关文件。与原有的专业培养计划相比，各专业的 EIP-CDIO 培养计划除合理安排涵盖本专业基本科学知识、核心工程基础知识、高级工程基础知识、工程师职业道德和操守的课程外，更精心规划和设置了独具特色的构思、设计、实现、运行项目（CDIO 项目）。CDIO 所倡导的个人能力、团队能力、系统调控能力是需要反复训练和学习而逐步提高的，因此各门课程大纲对 CDIO 能力应有明确的接触、训练和应用要求并反映在课程考核中。各专业至少要有一门鼓励跨学科、鼓励创新、鼓励创业的基于产品设计、制造的选修课。所有实验课全部并入相关课程内，任课教师自然成为相关实验课教师之一，主导并统筹课程实验。重要的综合性设计实验也可以考虑单独设课。

在教学方法上，EIP-CDIO 培养计划要求教师预先明确所授课程在本专业知识结构中的地位和作用，以及学生学习本课程应该掌握的基本知识和能力，要特别强调相关知识和能力在实践中的有机联系；应从实际或已有知识中发现和提出问题，引导学生思考，应用所学知识探究规律和致力创新；教学中要安排丰富的设计性和综合性实验，尽量让学生自己动手和全身心投入；要引导学生主动学习，提供更多的动手实践机会；增强概念学习，强调发现问题、分析问题和解决问题能力的养成，建立和加强学习反馈机制。

学习效果评估增加项目报告、设计评估等形式，鼓励多学科融合，培养学生的创造性和创业精神，让学生通过自评、互评改变对学习和生活的态度并逐步掌握相应的工作技能。能力考核对号入座，专业知识采用口试或笔试方式，CDIO 相关能力则以记录、报告、自评、互评等形式进行，考核方式的多样化促进了学习方式的多样化，也有利于建立和完善评价系统。在学习构架上，建立教学计划、教学方法和考核方法之间互相支持、良性互动的机制，并提供良好的教学实践环境和设施。最后，通过建立各种规章制度，使管理者、教师和学生有章可循，接受合理的制度约束，包括院系领导、同行教师及教学督导员听课制度，教学质量学生联系小组工作制度等监督机制，以及各种教学奖励、年度考核、岗位聘任、学生综合测评等激励机制，确保教学方法的改进和教学效果的提高。

## 4.2 EIP-CDIO 专业课程设置

在分析国内外现行本科培养模式和社会需求的基础上，工学院各专业明确了培养国际化工程师的目标，以 EIP-CDIO 培养计划和培养三大能力的理念为指导，确定了以项目设计为导向的综合培养方式和 CDIO 课程设置方案。课程设置的主要特点体现在以下方面。

（1）通过“工程师职业道德”课程以及“世界工程师论坛”、成长沙龙、社会实践等多种活动与环节，开展 EIP 方面的学习与训练。

（2）通过导师制，加强教师对学生的学业辅导，并在职业道德、诚信和职业素质上予以指导。

（3）加强基础科学及人文科学课程的建设，特别注重数学分析能力的培养。

（4）以课程群的方式将全部专业核心课程有机结合起来，避免相关课程之间的重复，使教师能以相关知识有机联系的方式传授，学生能以多元因素合理联想的方式掌握专业知识，旨在有效培养学生掌握和运用科学知识的能力。

（5）加强实验与动手能力的培养，合理增加实验课时，将原计划外的实验纳入教学计划，使实验和其他实践环节能更好地与课堂教学结合。

（6）通过工程项目的团队设计，培养工程设计能力和协同工作能力，拓宽工程科学知识。以项目实施为主线，贯穿专业课教学的全过程，在这一过程中注重培养学生的创新意识、项目设计能力、团结协作精神和理论联系实际的作风。

（7）鼓励互动和探究式学习。

### 4.3 EIP-CDIO 课程大纲

经过反复研究和探讨，参照 CDIO 大纲并结合我国工程领域的实际情况，汕头大学工学院系统制定了 EIP-CDIO 课程大纲。大纲主要涵盖以下内容：一是工程师职业道德；二是基本理论知识；三是个人能力和职业技能；四是人际交流与合作能力；五是在企业和社会环境中构思、设计、执行和使用各种系统的能力。与过去相比，新大纲突出了工科学生的工程师职业道德意识、基本理论知识、个人综合能力的培养。作为课程教学过程的重要依据和指导性文件，课程大纲一方面指导学生选课，另一方面规范教师的教学及考核。大纲服务于专业课程计划（curriculum），在课程涵盖范围、学习目的及教学理念、方法和安排等方面接受课程计划的界定。它以纲要的形式规定每门课程的学科知识、技能范围、深度、体系结构以及教学进度。课程大纲由承担本门课程的教师或课程教学小组制定，由各系教学委员会审批。课程教学大纲模板则由院教学委员会制定，内容包括课程代码、名称、学分和总学时、目标、知识结构、教学方式、考核方式、对学生的要求、教科书及参考文献等。若课程中包含附属实验，需列明实验名称；课程描述部分应以不少于 150 字的篇幅进行简要介绍；课程目的应列举 3~6 条主要目的；对于知识，要列举本课程需要掌握的主要知识要点；对于技能部分，应列举学完本课程后应具有的主要技能或应用能力；授课安排通过列表形式，将每一学习单元的学时具体分配到各部分学习内容；考核部分要详细介绍本门课程的考核方法和要求；对学生的要求，如先修课要求等需明确说明；最终评分标准应通过列表给出总分和各部分的权重，以及成绩合格的特别要求；教科书及参考文献需提供书名、作者、出版社和出版时间等信息；此外，还需阐述与本课程相关能力的培养内容。

## 5 EIP-CDIO 的实施过程

### 5.1 以 EIP-CDIO 理念为指导，确立改革方向，明确未来任务

2005 年，加拿大工程院院士、中国教育部长江学者讲座教授顾佩华加盟汕头大学，引入 CDIO 教学改革理念，在工学院提出了培养符合国际工程教育共识的本科生这一全新的改革目标。为了加强组织领导工作，工学院成立了 CDIO 工程教育改革委员会，组织全院教师多次集体学习和研讨 CDIO 理念、培养大纲、教育框架和标准。对照大纲，找出差距，针对实际，明确目标，提出了七个方面的任务。

（1）改革课程体系、结构与内容。改变偏重工程科学知识、轻视工程实践训练，偏重专业知识传授、轻视综合素质与能力培养，偏重专业教育，轻视人文、经济、环保作用的传统培养模式，构建新的课程体系，特别是增加团队设计项目。

（2）更新教学观念，改革教学方法。主要是树立“以学生为中心”的新观念，引导学生“主动学习”，制订以设计为导向的培养计划。

（3）改革学科专业。不仅在本专业拓宽知识面，还将推进范围更广的“学科交叉”。

（4）改革评价教师的方法，提高教学水平。制定评估教师工作质量的新标准与分配制度；聘用有国外受教育背景的教师；注重青年骨干教师培养；聘请有实际工程经验的工程师来校教学和指导。

（5）改革学生考核方式。增加项目报告、设计评估等形式，让学生通过自评、互评等方式改变学习和生活态度，并逐步掌握必要的工作技能。

（6）改善教学实验条件。加大对教学实践环境和设施建设的投入，为学生提高实践能力提供更好的平台。

（7）提高工科学生入学水平。加强与本地区中学的合作，激发中学生投身工程职业的志趣。例如，设立“工学院开放日”，帮助中学师生和社会公众了解工程技术的魅力。

基于明确的改革任务，工学院开展了 EIP-CDIO 框架与内涵的全面研讨。2006 年 7 月，各专业均按 EIP-CDIO 理念、大纲、标准制订了以设计为导向的新培养计划，为每门课程制定了 EIP-CDIO 教学大纲；并在 2006 级 5 个专业全面执行 EIP-CDIO 培养计划。与 2005 年以前的教学计划相比，压缩 15%左右的授课学时用于研讨课，增加了 4~6 个团队设计项目，每个专业还安排了一个与外系交叉的团队设计项目。

### 5.2 进行 CDIO 课程实验，积累实验成果，逐步推广

为使改革稳妥进行，也为今后全面推广 CDIO 模式提供经验，从 2005 年秋季学期起，新生一入学，就进行 EIP-CDIO 理念培训，并通过“世界工程师论坛”、成长沙龙等不同形式，介绍 EIP-CDIO 的意义和内容，以配合教学改革。在 2006 级正式执行 EIP-CDIO 教学计划之前，在各专业 03、04 级选择 8 门试点课程进行初步探索，之后又在 04、05 级选择 16 门课程深化 EIP-CDIO 教学改革。

在教学方面实施探究式学习（inquiring-based learning）和主动实践学习（experimental learning），主要体现在对“构想”环节的需求分析，帮助学生明确所学内容在学科知识体系中的位置，找到建立和优化自身知识框架的方向和途径，使学生学习的方向性和主动性大大提高，课堂氛围也更轻松活跃。

实验课主要强调对实现（implement）环节的验证。在实验前，要求学生进行实验预习，重点训练工程推理能力，加强思维逻辑性；在实验过程中，促使学生认识到团队协作的意义，若实验受挫，则启发学生分析失败原因，以强化对相关知识的理解和运用。在实验总结中，强调对实验报告的规范性要求，不仅训练文字表述能力，而且培养系统思考和知识发现的能力。

为了评估试点课程的实施效果，通过问卷、座谈会等多种形式对学生进行调查。反馈结果表明，学生对 CDIO 教学改革是拥护的，对 CDIO 教学方式是认可的。工学院 CDIO 工程

教育改革领导小组、教学委员会和试点课程任课教师还就试点课程的授课方式、效果、学生的反映以及存在的主要问题等方面进行了研讨和总结。

### 5.3 加强硬、软件环境建设，为 EIP-CDIO 的全面实施创造条件

按照 CDIO 教学计划的要求，2006 年各系对教学实验室进行全面修缮，购置新的实验仪器设备，新建若干专业教学实验室，总投入经费达 800 万元。工学院于 2006 年 9 月建成 CDIO 创新实践中心，面积达 600 多平方米，拥有结构与金工实验室、计算机综合应用实验室和电子设计综合实验室三大功能区，并且配备了先进的设备，如高精度自动数控钻机、贴片焊接机、精密型 LCR 数字电桥、数字示波器及信号发生器、钻床、能力风暴机器人、多功能嵌入式开发套件等，具备了开展综合实践的条件。创新中心建成后，实行团队项目负责制，师生共同管理，培育了一批跨学科、跨年级的综合项目。

工学院还特别注重各种软环境的建设，包括人才引进、规章制度的建立与完善。两年来共引进 10 余名毕业于国内外知名高校的高学历、高水平人才。为使规章制度规范化、系统化，院系两级都建立了教学委员会，负责组织教师学习和研讨与 EIP-CDIO 相关的各种文件，审核各专业改革的指导思想、培养目标、培养计划、课程大纲、教学方法和考核方式。目前正在改革教师工作的评价体系与方法，鼓励“卓越教学”。同时鼓励广大教师积极参与国内外教学改革研究，如以 EIP-CDIO 为主题，工学院于 2006 年申请承担了教育部和广东省重点教改项目，这些项目都得到了同行专家的肯定。

### 5.4 积极参与 CDIO 国际组织活动

汕头大学工学院的部分改革经验与成果，已整理成若干篇论文发表在联合国教科文组织主办的《世界工程与技术教育学报》(*World Transaction on Engineering and Technology Education*)上。2006 年 1 月下旬，CDIO 委员会经过严格的审核后一致同意接受汕头大学成为中国高校中首个 CDIO 成员。2006 年 6 月 12—15 日，第二届 CDIO 研讨会暨合作组织会议在瑞典林雪平大学召开。汕头大学教师代表参加了会议，作了题为“Engineering Education Reform and Innovation based on CDIO”的专题报告，向大会介绍了汕头大学工学院的 CDIO 改革。鉴于上述工作与成绩，大会授权汕头大学组织做好以下工作：组织 2007 年 11 月的 CDIO 国际合作组织会议；筹备成立东亚区域中心并成为该中心的总部(现有北美、北欧、西欧和大洋洲四个区域中心)；编写 CDIO 手册(CDIO Implementation Manual)。国际 CDIO 同行的肯定，为我们走向国际化创造了一个良好的开端。

汕头大学的改革实践证明，成功的关键是通过培养方式和课程改革缩短与国内外核心工程技术发展的差距。例如，国外开展 CDIO 改革的学校几乎都调整了自己的课程，以达到 ABET 工程认证条件的要求。实际上，教学核心内容是相近的，只是各校改革都融入了自己的特色。这也证明，各校对工程技术培养目标的要求是清楚的，但如何使学生获得相应的职业技能与综合素质就不那么直观了。笔者认为，目前的改革与过去的区别体现在教师教学与学生学习的过程之中，体现在学习经验的获取方式上。在学生主动获取知识的能力方面，主要体现在能力、知识、态度、综合素质和学生的工程师职业技能训练方法上，同时也体现在

教师的自身理论、实践和教育水平的差别上，甚至体现在教师的职业态度与道德标准上。

在未来的工程教育改革中，以下问题值得关注与思考：一是由于知识迅速增加，国际化企业间竞争的加剧，公司很难有充分时间为毕业生提供在岗培训，现在的教育模式包括四年学制能否满足将来的发展要求？二是工程教育认证方法是否应更加深入和具体，从而能真正有效地考查学生的综合能力？三是如何建立工程教育质量和培养目标的保障系统？四是现在的大学，特别是研究型大学对优质教育是否给予了充分重视？五是如何正确处理好科研与教学的关系？学校及其领导层有何作为？六是提高教学质量不能只靠竞争，更要加强合作，那么怎样才能处理好良性竞争和诚信合作的关系？七是如何走出一条国际化与本土化有机结合的道路？

总之，我们将继续积极进行改革，密切观察实施进程，冷静分析成绩和不足，不断总结经验教训，期望能为中国的工程教育改革做些实事，提供新的改革思路，为培养符合现代企业要求的国际化工程技术人才做出自己的贡献。

## 致谢

本文所介绍的汕头大学工学院高等工程教育改革实践，得到了广东省教育厅和李嘉诚基金会的大力支持，也得到汕头大学工学院广大师生员工的积极配合，在此，我们致以衷心的感谢。此外，本文还得到以下项目的支持：①全国教育科学“十一五”规划 2006 年度教育部重点课题“符合国际工程教育共识的 CDIO 培养模式应用研究”；②2007 年广东省高等教育教学改革工程本科建设重点项目“EIP-CDIO 高等工程教育改革研究”；③2007 年广东省软科学研究计划项目重点研究。

## 参考文献

[1] BOEING. Boeing company offices attributes [EB/OL].（2005-10-09）[2008-01-28]. http://www.boeing.com/companyoffices/pwu/attributes/attributes.html.

[2] IMD. World competitiveness yearbook [EB/OL].（2005-04-10）[2008-01-28]. http://www.imd.ch/index.cfm?bhcp=1.

[3] 李培根. 育人为本 创新是魂 责任以行[J]. 中国高等教育，2006（Z1）：39-41.

[4] WULF W A. The urgency of engineering education reform[J]. The bridge, 1998, 28（1）：1-10.

[5] 钟秉林. 我国院校高等工程教育的改革与发展[J]. 中国机械工程，2000（Z1）：24-26，2.

[6] 刘微. 从国际比较看我国工程教育改革[N]. 中国教育报，2001-09-28（004）.

[7] 雷庆. 工程教育改革要有紧迫感[N]. 光明日报，2003-07-11.

[8] 时铭显. 面向 21 世纪的美国工程教育改革[J]. 中国大学教学，2002（10）：38-40.

[9] 杨叔子，余东升. 文化素质教育与通识教育之比较[J]. 高等教育研究，2007（6）：1-7.

[10] 翁史烈. 工程教育改革路在何方[N]. 解放日报，2004-11-05.

[11] 胡建华. 现代中国大学制度的原点：50 年代初期的大学改革[M]. 南京：南京师范大学出版社，2001.

[12] National Research Council. Engineering education and practice in the United States: foundations of our techno-economic future[R]. Washington, DC: National Academies Press, 1985.

[13] National Research Council. Engineering undergraduate education[R]. Washington, DC: National Academies Press, 1986.

[14] National Research Council. Engineering technology education[R]. Washington, DC: National Academies Press, 1986.

[15] National Research Council. Major issues in engineering education[R]. Washington, DC: National Academies Press, 1993.

[16] National Academy of Engineering. NAE homepage [EB/OL]. ( 2005-07-01 ) [2008-01-28]. http://www.nae.edu.

[17] National Academy of Engineering. Education for the manufacturing world of the future[R]. Washington, DC: National Academies Press, 1985.

[18] National Academy of Engineering. Focus on the future: a national action plan for career-long education for engineers[R]. Washington, DC: National Academies Press, 1988.

[19] American Society for Engineering Education. The green report: engineering education for a changing world[R]. Washington, DC: ASEE, 1994.

[20] National Science Foundation. Restructuring engineering education: a focus on change[R]. Arlington, VA: NSF, 1995.

[21] National Science Foundation. Investing in America's future: strategic plan 2006-2011[R]. Arlington, VA: NSF, 2006.

[22] Committee on Engineering Education. CEE homepage [EB/OL]. ( 2005-02-10 ) [2008-01-28]. http://www.nae.edu/engeducom.

[23] European Ministers of Education. The Bologna Declaration of 19 June 1999[EB/OL]. ( 1999-01-10 ) [2008-01-28]. http://www.ehea.info.

[24] FEANI. FEANI homepage [EB/OL]. ( 2005-12-01 ) [2008-01-28]. http://www.feani.org.

[25] MALMQVIST J, EDSTRÖM K, GUNNARSSON S, et al. The application of CDIO standards in the evaluation of Swedish Engineering Degree Programmes [J]. World transactions on engineering and technology education, 2006, 5( 2 ): 361-364.

[26] GU P H, LU X H, XIONG G J, et al. Development of design directed engineering curriculum based on CDIO framework[J]. World transactions on engineering and technology education, 2006, 5( 2 ): 1-10.

[27] YELLOWLEY I, GU P H. Design directed education[J]. Journal of engineering design and innovation, 2005, 1: 1-12.

# CDIO 在中国（上）①

顾佩华　包能胜　康全礼　陆小华　熊光晶　林　鹏　陈　严

**摘要：**CDIO 工程教育模式是近年来国际工程教育改革的新成果，在世界各地多所大学进行了实施并取得很好的成效。自 2005 年汕头大学率先实施 CDIO 工程教育改革以来，在教育部高教司理工处的指导和支持下，全国几十所试点高校和许多非试点院校实施 CDIO 改革，取得了很好的效果。汕头大学等试点高校重新思考工程教育改革的模式与路径，对人才培养的各个方面与相应的管理机制进行了重新构建，在明确专业培养目标、制定专业培养标准、构建一体化课程计划、实施探究式教与学方法、建立保障与持续改进体系等方面进行了实践和创新。CDIO 在中国的普及和实践，也为高质量实施卓越工程师教育培养计划打下了良好的基础，起到了积极的推进作用。本文对 6 年来 CDIO 在汕头大学及其他试点高校的实践和推广情况进行了回顾和总结，对中国工程教育面临的挑战和存在的问题给出了观察与思考，并对 CDIO 在中国做出展望。

**关键词：**工程教育改革；CDIO；专业培养；标准一体化课程；卓越工程师教育培养计划

## CDIO in China (Part Ⅰ)

*Gu Peihua, Bao Nengsheng, Kang Quanli, Lu Xiaohua, Xiong Guangjing, Lin Peng, Chen Yan*

**Abstract:** CDIO Initiative is the most recent development of an international collaborative endeavor for engineering education. It has significantly changed to and impacted on engineering education of many universities worldwide through adoption of the CDIO Initiative. Since 2005, Shantou University has been undertaking the CDIO based engineering education reform and has achieved significant results. The Department of Science and Engineering, the Bureau of Higher Education, the Ministry of Education have been providing strong leadership and significant support to the implementation of the CDIO Initiative in China. Over 40 universities in the China CDIO Pilot Group and Special Program of Ministry of Education, and many more other universities and colleges have been making good progress. Through adoption of the CDIO Initiative, Shantou University and many institutions have been undertaking a comprehensive review of all aspects of engineering education including definition of program objectives, detailed syllabus that codify the standards of the program objectives, development of the integrated curriculum, the implementation of active learning methods such as inquiry-based and project-based learning and establishment of quality assurance and continuous improvement system of programs. The adoption of the CDIO Initiative in engineering education in China has built a strong foundation for implementation of the Excellent Engineer Education and Training Plan. This paper summarizes the adoption process and experiences of the CDIO Initiative in engineering education at

① 本文刊登于《高等工程教育研究》2012 年第 3 期第 24~40 页。

universities and colleges in China. The challenges and the issues facing the Chinese engineering education have also been discussed.
**Keywords:** engineering education reform; CDIO; professional cultivation; standard-integrated curriculum; Excellent Engineer Education and Training Plan

## 引言

CDIO 工程教育模式自 2005 年引入中国以来，在短短几年内，就对中国工程教育产生了深远的影响。CDIO 代表构思（conceive）、设计（design）、实施（implement）和运行（operate），它以从产品研发到产品运行、维护和废弃的全生命周期为载体，建立一体化的相互支撑和有机联系的课程体系，让学生以主动的、实践的方式学习工程。CDIO 能力大纲和 12 条标准是实施 CDIO 工程教育模式两个最重要的指导性文件。与很多工程教育改革相比，CDIO 是一个国际性、广泛、较全面和系统的工程教育改革模式。2000 年至 2004 年的四年间，麻省理工学院（MIT）与瑞典的查尔摩斯工业大学、林雪平大学、瑞典皇家工学院在克努特与爱丽丝瓦伦堡基金会资助下，通过共同探索研究，创立了 CDIO 工程教育模式，成立了以 CDIO 命名的国际合作组织。自 2004 年正式成立以来，国际 CDIO 工程教育组织已发展到世界五大洲 81 所院校成员。2011 年，美国工程院院士爱德华·克劳利（Edward Crawley）教授也因创立 CDIO 工程教育模式而获得美国工程院最高教育奖项“戈登奖”。2005 年 10 月，汕头大学工学院开始实施 CDIO 工程教育改革，并从 2006 级本科生开始全面实施全新的以项目设计为导向的 EIP-CDIO 工程教育模式，在建立 CDIO 专业培养架构、构建 CDIO 专业培养标准体系、设计 CDIO 一体化课程体系、构建与实施基于项目学习的教学体系以及建立质量保障与评估改进体系等方面进行了有益的探索与实践。在教育部高教司理工处的指导下，国内众多其他高校也积极推进基于 CDIO 的教学改革，并取得了积极的进展。2010 年，汕头大学第一届以全新专业培养方案培养的学生毕业。2011 年 9 月开始，汕头大学进入了 CDIO 教学改革的新阶段。为了总结汕头大学以及其他试点高校近几年来推进 CDIO 工程教育改革的经验，以积极的态度推进本项工作向更深入发展，特撰写本文。

本文简单叙述背景后，在第一部分阐述 CDIO 改革的核心与特点，论述 CDIO 在工程教育改革方面的特色和地位，阐述选择 CDIO 作为改革模式的原因；在第二部分阐述 CDIO 在中国的传播与影响，着重总结 CDIO 在中国近年来的实施成效；在第三部分则重点阐述汕头大学以设计为导向的 EIP-CDIO 一体化教育改革，在目标体系、专业培养标准、课程体系、探究式教学方法等方面给出了全面的描述；随后在第四部分中阐述国内其他高校在 CDIO 工作中的特色，以及各高校不断创新的情况；第五部分总结几年来 CDIO 在中国传播与发展过程中的一些问题和不足，并在下一部分中引出作者对中国工程教育改革的观察与思考；最后，论文展望了 CDIO 今后在中国的发展前景。

本文简明扼要地回顾了 2005—2011 年 CDIO 在中国实施的情况，由于篇幅有限，不可能全面涵盖所有成功实施 CDIO 的院校的情况，不当之处在所难免，恳请读者指正。

# 1 CDIO 改革的核心与特点

## 1.1 CDIO 回答了工程教育的根本问题

任何试图改进工程教育的方法都必须考虑以下两个中心问题：第一，当工科学生毕业时，他们学到的全部知识和具有的能力、素质应该有哪些？掌握的水平如何？第二，如何更好地保证学生学到这些知识和能力？也就是任何教育者都必须面对的“做什么”（培养什么人）和“如何做”（如何培养人）的问题。CDIO 直接从这两个问题出发，制定了两个最重要的文件——CDIO 能力大纲和 CDIO 12条标准。

在“培养什么人”的问题上，CDIO 改革提出了三个总目标，要求学生能够：①更深入地掌握技术基础知识；②领导新产品、过程或系统的开发与运行；③理解研究与技术发展对社会的重要性与战略影响。这也就是说，CDIO 模式要培养具有更好的技术基础知识、能领导创新开发与运行并且具有社会与历史责任感的工程师。然而，如果仅仅提出这样的目标可能对实际操作没有什么建设性的意义。CDIO 的创新贡献是通过对工程师工作的分析（参见表 1），把工程师所需具备的知识、能力和素质分解整理为 CDIO 能力大纲（CDIO 专业培养标准），而这个能力大纲细化到可以直接观察学生的表现行为的程度，可以作为学生学习效果的测量依据。

**表 1 把构思—设计—实施—运行（CDIO）作为产品、过程和系统的生命周期模型**

| C（构思） | | D（设计） | | I（实施） | | O（运行） | |
|---|---|---|---|---|---|---|---|
| 使命 | 概念设计 | 初步设计 | 详细设计 | 元件制造 | 系统整合与测试 | 全生命支持 | 演化 |
| 商业战略 | 需求 | 需求定位 | 元件设计 | 硬件制造 | 系统整合 | 销售和铺货 | 系统改进 |
| 技术战略 | 功能 | 模型开发 | 需求确认 | 软件编程 | 系统测试 | 运行 | 产品家族 |
| 客户需求 | 概念 | 系统分析 | 失效和预案分析 | 资源 | 改进 | 物流 | 扩张 |
| 目标 | 技术 | 系统解构 | | 元件测试 | 取得认证 | 客户服务 | 报废 |
| 竞争 | 构建 | 界面要求 | | | 元件改进 | 投产 | 维护与维修 |
| 项目计划 | 平台计划 | | | | 交货 | 回收 | |
| 商业计划 | 市场定位 | | | | 升级 | | |

在“如何培养人”方面，CDIO 采用建构主义教育理论，并通过 CDIO 的 12 条标准指引工程教育改革的实施，这 12 条标准从基本理念（标准 1：背景环境）、培养目标（标准 2：学习效果）、课程体系（标准 3：一体化课程体系）、学习构建（标准 4：工程导论；标准 5：设计建造经验；标准 7：一体化学习经验；标准 8：主动学习）、工程实践环境（标准 6：工程实践场所）、教师能力（标准 9：教师工程能力；标准 10：教师教学能力）和考核与评估（标准 11：学生考核；标准 12：专业评估）等各个方面指导工程教育的实践，围绕培养目标，通过一体化实现工程教育的培养目标。

### 1.2　CDIO 提供了一体化的解决方案

工程教育所面临的挑战，并不仅仅是简单地加强基础、拓宽口径或增强实践能力的问题，而是全世界范围内工程教育的发展与科学、技术、工业和工程实践发展不协调所带来的问题。在我国，还面临着工程实践与教育市场国际化的问题。因此，工程教育的改革就需要整体考虑，探索一体化的解决方案，而 CDIO 提供了这样一个方案。

工程教育的内容应当完整地包含当代工程实践，包含工程人才所需要的知识、能力和素质。CDIO 能力大纲做到了这一点。该大纲与联合国教科文组织提出的教育四大支柱（学会求知、学会做人、学会合作、学会做事）、美国工程与技术认证委员会（ABET）《工程标准 2000》（Engineering Criteria 2000）的认证标准（3a~3k）、加拿大工程认证委员会（CEAB）工程教育认证标准（3.1.1~3.1.12）、英国工程职业能力与责任标准（UK-SPEC）、欧洲认证工程师（EUR-ACE）、欧洲博洛尼亚进程（Bologna Process）框架下的都柏林标准（Dublin Descriptors）以及瑞典工程教育标准（Swedish Ordinance）等各个国家和区域不同的工程教育认证标准都有较好的契合性，反映了这个时代工程实践和教育改革实践对工程教育培养目标的要求。

在实现培养目标方面，CDIO 的标准要求依照 CDIO 能力大纲整合课程体系（一体化课程计划），教学过程要给予学生知识、能力和素质培养的综合效应（一体化培养），通过教、学、考过程的顶层设计让学生取得一体化学习经验，并且需要建立以培养目标为基础的评估与改进制度（持续改进）。CDIO 工程教育改革在培养内容、课程体系、教学方法和评估改进等各个方面是一个整体，因此，CDIO 改革也需要至少在一个专业的层面上全面设计、逐层落实。

### 1.3　CDIO 融通了教育理论和工程实践

CDIO 提出以工程实践为工程教育的背景环境（context）。这与把工程实践作为工程教育的内容（content）有着本质的区别。把工程实践作为工程教育的内容意味着简单地增加实践、实习、操作训练，或“以典型产品组织教学”，或简单地在“做中学”。

把工程实践作为工程教育的背景环境具有两个方面的意义：其一，工程教育的目标是培养学生成为合格的工程实践者。因此，工程教育的目标要取自工程实践的要求，由此产生了 CDIO 的能力大纲；其二，工程教育的过程需要使学生能够把学到的内容应用于工程实践。因此，工程教育不仅要求学生对技术基础知识有更深刻的理解，更需要创造必要的环境和方法帮助学生理解工程实践并且学习在工程实践环境下工程人员的思维、能力和行为，CDIO 的标准从多个方面为这样的培养提供保障。

建构主义认知观认为应该使客观的知识结构通过个体与之交互而内化为认知结构。因此学习者的学习过程同时包含两方面的建构：一方面是对新信息的意义建构，同时又包含对原有经验的改造和重组。CDIO 改革通过其标准要求以 CDIO 能力大纲为培养标准，以从产品研发到产品运行、维护和废弃的全生命周期为背景环境，建立一体化的相互支撑和有机联系的课程体系，让学生以主动的方式学习和实践工程。

### 1.4 CDIO 提供了系统、全面、具体、可操作的实施指引

CDIO 能力大纲对工程教育的知识和能力目标进行了较完整的梳理,并且细化到能够在具体培养环节观察和评估的程度。比如,对于学生批判性思维能力的培养,大纲列举了 6 条学习效果目标:①分析问题;②选择逻辑论点和解决方法;③评价支持证据;④找出有矛盾的观点、理论和事实;⑤找出逻辑谬误;⑥验证假设与结论。这 6 条目标正是一个具有批判性思维习惯的人面对一个问题时所表现出的行为。因此,每个教师都有可能在自己的课程或学生的活动中找到合适的环节,要求学生按照这样的过程处理这门课程或活动中的问题。当学生在众多的课程和活动中经历同样的过程,他就不仅达到课程本身知识点的要求,而且同时养成了批判性思维的习惯(知识与能力的一体化培养)。

CDIO 的标准为实现 CDIO 教学目标提供了详尽、一体化的实施要求和指引。CDIO 还通过国际合作汇编了 CDIO 工程教育改革实施工具箱、启动指南和教学资源库。这些资源是国际合作的成果,是完全开放的。共享这些资源能够减少改革成本,增加改革成功的机会。

### 1.5 CDIO 改革为工程教育国际化提供了平台

CDIO 是国际工程教育合作的产物,CDIO 国际合作组织的成员来自全世界五大洲 20 多个国家,代表国际工程教育改革的一个方向。实施 CDIO 改革并参与国际 CDIO 工程教育改革经验交流,为我国工程教育国际化、加入国际工程教育认证体系以及我国工程毕业生进入国际人才市场参与国际竞争提供了重要的窗口和平台。

## 2 CDIO 在中国的传播与推广

### 2.1 CDIO 在中国的传播过程

自 2005 年汕头大学工学院进行 CDIO 工程教育改革以来,CDIO 工程教育模式在全国迅速传播。CDIO 之所以能在全国得到广泛响应,是因为它适合中国工程教育改革的时代需求,激发了我国高校工程教育改革的热情,在教育行政部门的指导和支持下,成为一种颇具影响力的创新型工程人才培养模式。

(1)国内高校联合启动。

2006 年汕头大学参加第二届国际 CDIO 会议并正式加入 CDIO 国际合作组织,此后几年,清华大学、北京交通大学、成都信息工程学院等学校先后加入 CDIO 合作组织。2007 年 11 月,CDIO 国际合作组织秋季会议在汕头大学召开,汕头大学借此机会组织了中国高等工程教育改革论坛,特邀中国工程院前常务副院长朱高峰院士、联合国教科文组织高等工程教育与产学合作教席查建中教授、浙江大学科教发展战略研究中心王沛民教授等我国工程教育改革的重要倡导者到论坛讲座,并借此传播 CDIO 工程教育改革理念。

2007 年,以 CDIO 工程教育改革为核心的"汕头大学工学院 EIP-CDIO 工程教育模式创新实验区"被批准为教育部首批人才培养模式创新实验区。2008 年 11 月,中国 CDIO 网站

开通，为 CDIO 在中国的传播提供了一个交流、合作及信息共享的平台，网站由汕头大学工学院维护。2009 年，教育部质量工程项目第二类特色专业建设项目设立了 CDIO 特色专业，全国 11 个专业获批建设，每个专业得到国家质量工程建设经费 80 万元的支持。

（2）成立课题组和试点工作组。

2008 年 4 月，教育部高教司发文成立 CDIO 工程教育研究与实践课题组，顾佩华教授任组长。2008 年 5 月，在汕头大学召开 CDIO 工程教育模式研讨会暨课题组第一次会议，全国超过 100 所学校的 200 多名代表参会，教育部高教司理工处领导和 CDIO 创始人，MIT 教授 Edward Crawley 出席会议。同年 9 月，课题组在北京交通大学召开了第二次会议，顾佩华教授、查建中教授陪同 Crawley 教授拜访了教育部章新胜副部长、工程院潘云鹤副院长。

2008 年 12 月，汕头大学组织 24 所院校交流 CDIO 教育模式的实施经验，在教育部高教司理工处倡议和课题组的框架下组成了由 18 所院校参加的 CDIO 工程教育试点工作组，分机械、土木、电气和化工四个大类试点实施 CDIO 工程教育模式。

在理工处的领导下，试点工作组每年召开 2 次会议，交流各自在改革实施过程中的经验和教训。会议对非试点工作组成员开放，并开办 CDIO 工程教育模式培训班，传播 CDIO 改革理念和方法。到 2010 年，试点工作组已扩大到 39 个成员，参加试点工作组会议的学校和代表也日益增多。2011 年 12 月在南京工程学院举办的试点工作组会议，参加代表超过了 300 人。因此，2012 年起试点工作组采用年会的形式组织会议。

各试点工作组成员学校（如成都信息工程学院和燕山大学）及浙江大学王沛民教授、联合国教科文组织产学合作教席查建中教授、《高等工程教育研究》常务副主编姜嘉乐教授等活跃在我国工程教育改革第一线的专家，在各自活跃的区域和场合对 CDIO 工程教育改革模式和经验进行了不遗余力的传播与辅导；汕头大学接待了 100 多所院校的访问与交流。

2011 年 5 月，北京交通大学组织了 CDIO 区域性国际会议，来自国内外的 400 多名代表参加会议，教育部高教司、中国工程院和国际 CDIO 工程教育合作组织领导到会致辞。

（3）出版相关论著。

汕头大学翻译出版了《重新认识工程教育——国际 CDIO 培养模式与方法》（高等教育出版社）、《CDIO 大纲与标准》（汕头大学出版社）和《CDIO 工作坊手册》（汕头大学出版社）作为 CDIO 教育模式传播与实践的参考资料。多所学校正在组织编写 CDIO 模式相关教材，方便任课教师使用。

（4）CDIO 对我国卓越工程师教育培养计划的影响。

2010 年 6 月，教育部联合中国工程院启动了卓越工程师教育培养计划（以下简称卓越工程师计划）。该计划是依据《国家中长期教育改革和发展规划纲要（2010—2020 年）》的安排，在国家层面上制定实施的高等教育重要改革计划，是一系列卓越教育培养计划中的首个计划。卓越工程师计划的目标是以该计划的实施为突破口，促进工程教育改革与创新，全面提高我国工程教育人才培养质量，建立具有世界先进水平、中国特色社会主义的现代高等工程教育体系，促进我国从工程教育大国走向工程教育强国。

此外，在实施卓越工程师计划之初，教育部高教司理工处安排汕头大学提供了申报卓越工程师计划的模板和本科培养方案的范例。汕头大学还在教育部高教司理工处的安排下分别向全国卓越工程师计划申报学校以及全国各省、市、自治区高教处处长和学位办主任汇报一体化教育方法的基本原理和实践。因此，CDIO 在中国应用的经验在很大程度上影响了卓越工程师计划的顶层设计，其方法是卓越工程师计划从顶层设计到实施过程的重要基础。卓越工程师计划培养方案的编制要求与 CDIO 一体化教育的要求基本符合，即在明确培养目标(国家通用标准—行业标准—学校标准)的基础上，所有培养环节围绕培养目标的实现进行一体化设计、实施与评估。

CDIO 的 12 条标准是实施 CDIO 改革的指引，这些标准在某种程度上也同样成为实现卓越工程师计划目标的指引。卓越工程师计划布置了五项主要任务，它们与 CDIO 要求的关系如表 2 所示。

**表 2 卓越工程师计划的主要任务与 CDIO 要求的对应关系**

| 卓越工程师计划的主要任务 | 对应的 CDIO 标准和大纲 |
|---|---|
| 创建高校与行业企业联合培养人才的新机制 | CDIO 标准第 1 条 |
| 创新工程教育的人才培养模式 | CDIO 标准第 2、3、5、7、8、11、12 条 |
| 改革完善工程教师职务聘任、考核制度 | CDIO 标准第 9、10 条 |
| 扩大工程教育的对外开放 | CDIO 本身就是国际合作的产物 |
| 制定卓越工程师计划人才培养标准 | CDIO 大纲 |

概括来说，CDIO 工程教育的方法为卓越工程师计划的设计与实施提供了借鉴。卓越工程师计划与 CDIO 在基本目标、任务、理念与方法以及内容上具有高度的相关性和兼容性。CDIO 工程教育改革的理念与方法为卓越工程师计划提供了重要的参考。

(5)CDIO 理论体系与工程实践的研究和总结。

国内教育界对 CDIO 理论体系与工程实践的研究和总结也迅速发展。在 CNKI(中国知网)中国期刊全文数据库中，以“题目”或“关键词”检索，发现与 CDIO 相关的文献有数百篇。作者单位有“985 工程”院校，有一般本科学校，还有高职高专；从论文作者单位的分布情况来看，其范围远远超出了全国 CDIO 工程教育模式试点高校和特色专业院校的范围。论文涉及 CDIO 的各个方面，从 CDIO 理念、理论到课程体系建设，从课堂教学到 CDIO 实践环境建设等等；从研究论文涉及的专业看，也不止全国 CDIO 工程教育模式试点工作组确定的 4 个工科大类专业，应用 CDIO 模式进行教学改革的专业已达到 20 多种，并且有许多人文社科类专业如英语、思想政治教育等。

## 2.2 CDIO 在中国高校推广的实施经验

(1)领导积极推动，营造改革氛围。

任何改革都必须有强大的推动力。比如，汕头大学的主要领导直接策划指导工学院的 EIP-CDIO 工程教育改革，多次向工学院教师和学生介绍推广 CDIO 工程教育模式，参加院内的 CDIO 研讨会和培训会；积极为工学院 EIP-CDIO 改革争取资源支持，清除改革过程中的障碍；积极推动工学院和麻省理工学院等国际知名院校交流改革经验。

为了营造工程教育改革的氛围，其他高校与汕头大学工学院一样，组织教师参加 CDIO

培训会，学习国外高校进行CDIO工程教育改革所总结的经验；对参加初期CDIO改革的学生进行调查并汇总他们对CDIO工程教育改革的评价和期待，向校友企业征求他们对参加CDIO工程教育改革的学生的评价并公开。同时举行CDIO研讨会，为教师提供思想交流和辩论的平台，回应一些教师对CDIO模式的质疑，探讨在实施中可能遇到的问题，进行“头脑风暴”，在集思广益的基础上统一认识。

在CDIO改革过程中，学院充分发挥改革积极参与者的榜样作用。学院先挑选具有较高学术能力和教学能力并有较高参与激情的教师率先进行试点，在他们使用实验设备和学院其他资源时给予最大方便，努力为这些教师从学校和其他方面争取资源，初期实施成功的榜样作用得以充分发挥。

（2）发挥教师主体作用，鼓励学生积极参与。

任何改革想要取得成功，都应该让所有组织成员积极参与其中。在CDIO工程教育改革中，学校教师的积极性被充分激发出来。试点高校的教师主动参与各种CDIO教学改革研讨会，参加CDIO国际会议，积极承担各级CDIO教改项目，CDIO能力大纲、课程计划、单门课程大纲、团队设计项目和学生考核方案都在教师集体参与的情况下制定并实施。

在CDIO教育改革中，学生居于关键的位置。在制定CDIO工程教育模式的教学大纲时，各高校调查并听取了在校学生、新老校友的建议和意见；在CDIO工程教育改革每一阶段实施完成后，都对学生进行调查以获取反馈，从而获得他们的评价和意见，改进下一阶段的改革；此外，还举办各种活动调动学生参与改革的积极性。

（3）建立持续推进改革的动力机制，将改革成果制度化。

在CDIO工程教育改革中，必须建立持续推进改革的动力机制。首先，汕头大学工学院要求做好工程教育改革文件、培训会和研讨会的会议记录、教师工作体会记录、学院制定的改革规划纲要、CDIO教学大纲、各专业的课程计划和各单门课程的课程大纲等所有文件和案卷的保存、整理和提炼工作，将主要文件整理并升格为制度规范。

其次，各高校都制定了新的教师考核考评机制。原有的简单以教学工作量（或授课学时数）计算岗位津贴的教师聘任标准和分配制度不利于推动教育改革工作，在CDIO工程教育改革的过程中，教师要投入大量时间和精力，授课时数可能因此减少。因此，这些教师的教学工作量和津贴可能会受到负面影响。为了消除“算工分”分配制度对教育改革的负面作用，汕头大学配合教学改革开展了教师的“年薪制”改革，将教师的教学态度和在教改工作中发挥的作用作为重要依据，确定一个聘期内的年薪待遇，从根本上鼓励教师进行教育教学改革和提高教学质量。

再次，建立ISO教学管理质量保证体系。基于ISO的系列标准，汕头大学工学院明确CDIO教学过程中的质量监控重点，设置合理的、可测量的长期及短期管理目标，并按照“计划—实施—检查—处理”的管理原则，定期对教学过程进行评估和改进，同时根据内部与外部的需要及评估反馈，对整个系统进行持续改进。目前汕头大学工学院已建立教学过程质量保障系统、文件系统、组织程序系统、业务流程系统、教学评估系统。

（4）协调好改革各方的关系，提供所需资源。

为持续改革提供必要的资源是至关重要的。若无法长期稳定地为改革计划提供资源，教育改革将难以实现预期目标。因此，各试点高校努力筹措资源，这些资源既包括资金、实验设备等硬件资源,也包括时间、组织权力、机会等软件资源,加大对 CDIO 改革的支持力度。

工程教育的目标是为企业界提供具有创新和管理能力的优秀工程师,企业是改革的直接受益者。只有高校与企业充分联手合作、优势互补,才能不断明确真正符合时代要求的人才培养标准,使社会资源在工程教育的过程中得到最有效的利用。为此,各高校采取了与企业建立实训基地、工程实践教育中心或联合办学等多种方式,为提高学生的工程实践能力提供良好的办学条件。

(5)积累实施经验,持续推进。

在 CDIO 工程教育改革中,汕头大学和其他试点高校不断遇到很多具体的困难,如改革的积极性问题、师资的问题、投入的问题、评价的问题等等。通过不断探索,积累了许多改革的经验,如表 3 所示。

**表 3　CDIO 在国内高校推广过程中的难题与解决经验**

| 遇到的问题与困难 | 汕头大学与其他试点高校的经验 |
| --- | --- |
| 如何入门与持续改进 | 组织学习 CDIO 的各个文件 |
| | 兄弟院校的相互学习与培训 |
| | 参加国内外工程教育改革研讨会 |
| | 定期进行全体教师研讨 |
| | 定期评估教学改革,发现问题,及时改进提高 |
| 教师的全员参与和教改热情 | 明确清晰的共同目标 |
| | 提升教师的职业道德与修养 |
| | 实行相应的奖励处罚措施 |
| 项目的指导与实践 | 清晰的操作流程 |
| | 完整的项目指导书 |
| | 教师自觉的行为 |
| 经费投入较少 | 设计和实施能有效提升学生能力与知识水平的小团队项目 |
| 教学改革、科研、服务等工作与聘任的关系 | 将教学改革工作纳入考核指标 |
| | 明确每位教师的教改任务职责 |
| | 设立专门的高层次教学岗位 |

## 3　汕头大学以设计为导向的 EIP-CDIO 一体化教育改革

### 3.1　汕头大学 CDIO 工程教育改革的再创新

汕头大学在学习 CDIO 基本框架的基础上,以推进先进本科教育为目标,积极推进工程教育改革,同时针对当前社会经济对工程师在工程创新能力以及职业道德(ethics,E)、诚信(integrity,I)和职业素质(professionalism,P)方面的特别要求,在 CDIO 的基础上融入 E、I、

P 等元素。

另外,中国正处于由传统的经济模式向知识经济转变的大潮中,创新与创造是其中的核心要素。从工程的角度来看,任何工程项目或产品都是基于需求进行设计的。创新与创造的灵魂在于设计,一个工程项目或产品的设计在很大程度上决定了其创新与创造的思维能力。因此,汕头大学在推进 CDIO 工程教育改革的过程中,以产品、过程和系统的 C-D-I-O 为背景,在一体化的课程体系中以设计项目为载体,通过各级设计使学生将学到的理论知识应用于实践,在完成设计项目的过程中实现工程能力和工程素质的提升,达到 CDIO 专业培养标准的要求。

以设计为核心,就是要通过一个以设计为导向的学习过程,帮助学生找到技术与工程实践的方向。这个设计导向的学习过程,跟传统或以问题为导向的教育方式不同。通过教育基本设施的改变构建的设计导向的学习过程,提供了一个更丰富的教育方式,也重新定义了教师资源和教学设施的规则。重新设计问题:这些问题只是告诉学生专业实践和技术中的大体目标和内容,具体必须通过 C-D-I-O 全过程来解答。与此同时,学生们必须学会在团队中工作,培养跟同事交流的沟通技巧,以及规划自己的工作,在不断强化的设计与实践过程中,逐步找到"对工程的感觉"。

通过以上学习与调研,再依据汕头大学自身的办学地位和特色,对 CDIO 进行了再创新。2005 年 10 月,汕头大学工学院开始实施 CDIO 工程教育改革,构建了以设计为导向的 EIP-CDIO 创新人才培养模式,自 2006 级本科生开始全面实施,并于 2010 年 7 月完成了第一轮全过程的改革。

### 3.2　汕头大学 CDIO 工程教育改革的总体思路

做任何事情,首先须明确思路,其次是注重细节和协调关系,最后就是全力实施。汕头大学 CDIO 工程教育改革的总体思路借鉴了现代质量管理的基本思想:P-D-C-A,即设立目标→实施目标→反馈→持续改进(参见图 1)。

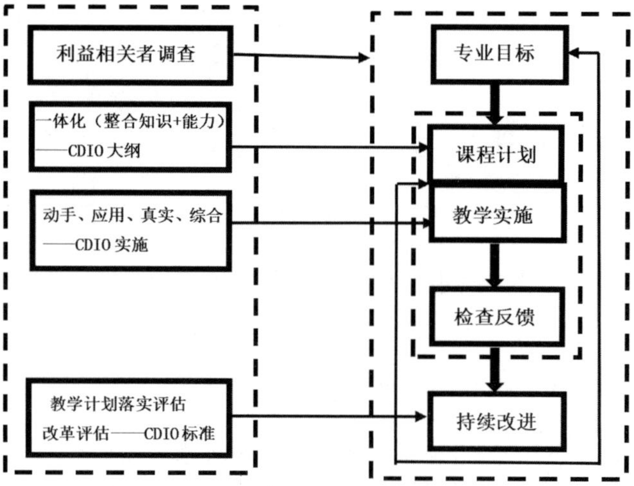


**图 1　汕头大学 CDIO 工程教育改革的基本思想**

依据改革的基本思想,按照 CDIO 的特色,汕头大学详细制定了如图 2 所示的一体化改革总体思路。以此为基础,学校全面推进以明确专业培养目标、制定专业培养标准(知识、能力与素质大纲)、构建一体化课程计划、实施教授与学习方法以及建立保障与持续反馈改进体系等工作为核心的一体化改革的全过程,并以一届四年从入学到毕业为周期,持续改进与提高。具体包括:①明确专业培养目标,即依据社会需求、学校定位、专业特色,明确适合本学校本专业的总体培养目标;②制定专业培养标准,即根据本专业培养目标,从社会、企业、校友和在校师生等各方面进行深入调研,制定出具体的、可操作的专业知识、能力和素质的学习产出效果目标,并形成一个目标集合;③构建一体化的课程计划,即依据专业培养标准的学习效果目标集合,整合课程,制定设计项目等实践环节,编写每门课程或设计项目的课程大纲和课堂教案,并明确各课程与设计对专业培养标准的贡献(教学目标达成矩阵),最终形成一体化的课程体系;④实施教授与学习方法,即实施主动学习和实践的教学方法,积极采用并探寻符合教学规律和人才成长规律的教与学的方法,比如基于项目的学习、基于问题的学习、探究式学习等,目的是实现专业培养标准所要求的培养目标;⑤建立保障与持续反馈改进体系,即建立管理、评估、反馈与持续改进体系,管理、检查、评估整个培养计划的实施过程、软硬件条件和最终的学习效果,并将工程师培养共同体各方的意见反馈到学校,促进学校对培养方案进行持续改进。

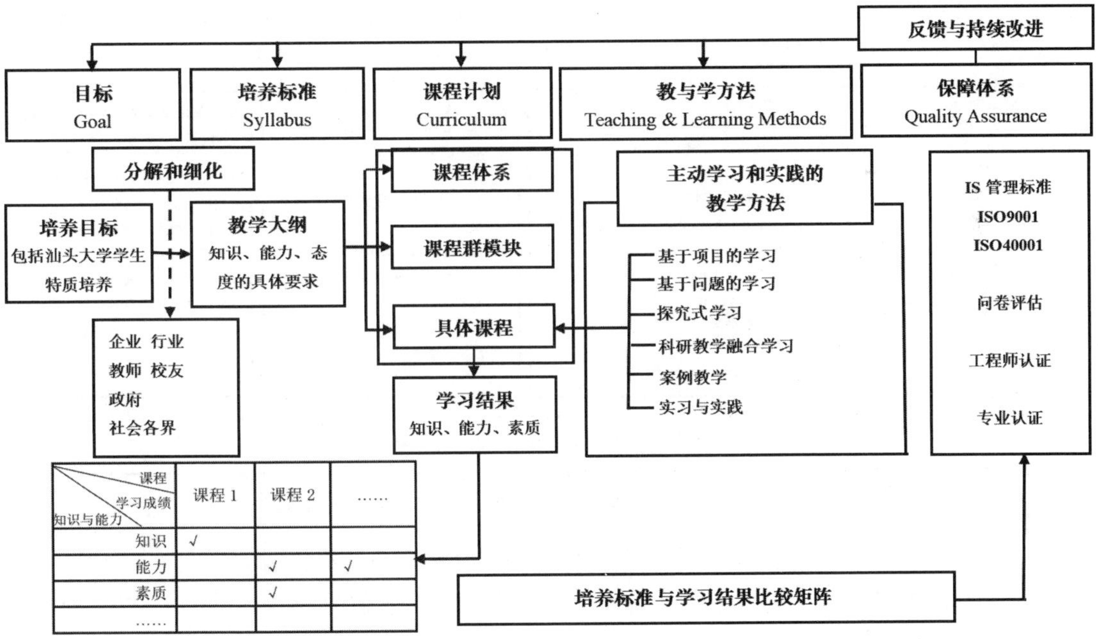


**图 2 汕头大学 CDIO 工程教育改革的总体思路**

### 3.3 汕头大学 CDIO 工程教育改革的核心工作

通过院系教师、学生、新老校友、企业和工程研究人员等利益相关者的研讨,以及全体教师、学生和企业界同人的共同设计与实践,汕头大学 CDIO 工程教育改革最重要的收获是完整地实施了一轮四年全过程的改革历程,并在此基础上不断地总结和深入,目前已进入一个新的实施阶段。依据改革的基本思想和总体思路，整个过程最核心的工作包括以下方面。

（1）以明确专业使命和培养目标为核心的顶层设计。

专业使命是依据专业的愿景、学校人才培养的要求以及本专业学科的定位，确定专业人才培养的大目标。

专业培养目标是依据未来专业的发展、现今专业的定位、社会的需求，以及未来专业从业人员的社会职责及角色，明确本专业的人才培养要求，涵盖毕业生应具备的知识、能力，以及要成为什么样的人才类型、达到的水平以及胜任的工作等方面。

图 3 给出了汕头大学机电专业的 CDIO 工程教育改革顶层设计框架，该框架的特色是以简洁明了的方式展示本专业的愿景、目标、战略以及实现以上目标所需要的知识、能力和素质等信息，使得所有的利益相关者能够快速了解本专业的培养使命和培养目标，并建立了后续所有工作的大框架，起到总体指导性作用。

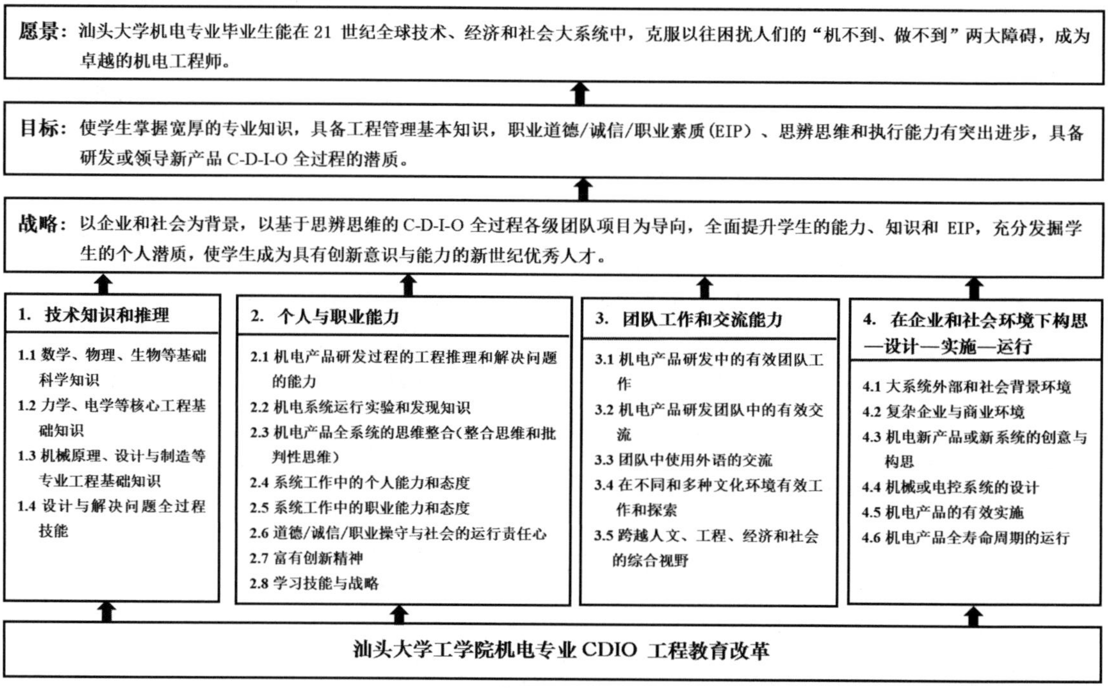


**图 3　汕头大学 CDIO 工程教育改革的顶层设计（机电专业案例）**

（2）以制定专业培养标准（知识能力素质大纲）为核心的详细设计。

为实现 EIP-CDIO 工程教育模式的专业培养目标，需细化分解顶层设计中对工科毕业生的学习产出要求。

在对工程教育各利益相关者进行深入调研的基础上，汕头大学工学院各专业制定出了详细、可操作，涵盖知识、能力、素质的学习产出目标集合，即 EIP-CDIO 专业培养标准。

以学校土木工程专业为例（见表 4），为了实现专业培养目标，制定的专业培养标准包括四个方面的内容：①技术知识和推理；②个人与职业能力（职业道德）；③人际交往能力，涉及团队工作和交流；④在企业和社会环境下构思—设计—实施—运行（CDIO）。这四个方面形成 EIP-CDIO 教学大纲的第一层内容。再将第一层内容进行细化和分解，例如“技术知识和推理”可细化为基础科学知识、核心工程基础知识、专业工程基础知识等,构成 EIP-CDIO 专业培养标准的第二层内容。照此类推,继续细化和分解,直至教师认为 EIP-CDIO 教学大纲中的知识、能力和素质能够在具体的课程和教学中实现并能够被测量和评估。这样,制定了土木工程专业集知识、能力和素质为一体的包含四层指标的 EIP-CDIO 大纲。

**表 4　汕头大学工学院土木工程专业知识、能力和素质大纲案例(部分)**

| | | |
|---|---|---|
| 1　掌握深厚的工程科学基础及土木工程专业技术知识<br>1.1　基础科学知识<br>1.1.1　数学<br>1.1.2　物理<br>……<br>1.2　核心工程基础知识<br>1.2.1　固体力学<br>1.2.1.1　理论力学<br>……<br>1.2.2　结构力学<br>……<br>1.3　土木工程基础知识<br>1.3.1　土木工程技术基础<br>1.3.1.1　工程制图<br>……<br>1.3.2　结构与岩土设计原理<br>…… | 2　具备整合思维能力,具备工程推理和解决问题的能力,具备合格的个人能力、职业能力和态度,展示职业道德和社会责任感<br>2.1　工程推理和解决问题的能力<br>2.1.1　发现土木系统问题和表述问题<br>2.1.2　构建土木工程结构模型<br>2.1.3　土木工程结构估计与定性分析<br>2.1.4　带有不确定性的土木工程分析<br>2.1.5　复杂土木工程解决方法和建议<br>2.2　具备对工程问题进行实验和调查、分析的能力<br>2.2.1　建立复杂土木系统的假设<br>2.2.2　查询各种印刷资料和电子文献<br>2.2.3　土木实验性探索<br>2.2.4　假设检验与答辩<br>2.3　具备整合思维能力<br>2.3.1　全方位思维<br>2.3.2　系统的显现和交互作用<br>2.3.3　确定主次与重点<br>2.3.4　解决问题时的妥协、判断和平衡 | 2.4　具备合格的个人能力<br>2.4.1　主动性与愿意承担风险<br>2.4.2　执着与变通<br>2.4.3　创造性思维<br>2.4.4　批判性思维<br>2.4.5　认知个人知识、能力和态度<br>2.4.6　求知欲和终身学习<br>2.4.7　时间和资源的管理<br>2.5　展示良好的职业道德<br>2.5.1　职业道德、正直、责任感并勇于负责<br>2.5.2　职业行为<br>2.5.3　主动规划个人职业<br>2.5.4　与土木工程领域发展保持同步<br>…… |
| 3　有效的交流及跨学科团队工作<br>3.1　团队工作能力<br>3.1.1　组建有效的团队<br>3.1.2　团队工作运行<br>3.1.3　团队成长和演变<br>3.1.4　领导能力<br>3.1.5　形成技术团队<br>3.2　交流<br>3.2.1　交流的策略<br>3.2.2　交流的结构<br>3.2.3　书面的交流<br>3.2.4　电子和多媒体交流<br>3.2.5　图表交流<br>3.2.6　口头表达和人际交流<br>3.3　使用外语交流<br>3.3.1　英语<br>3.3.2　区域内其他国家的语言<br>3.3.3　其他语言 | 4　在企业和社会背景下系统性地进行土木工程项目的构思、设计、实施和运行<br>4.1　认识社会和外部环境对土木工程的重要性<br>4.1.1　熟悉当代重要政治、社会、法律、环境课题和价值观<br>4.1.2　了解土木工程历史和文化背景<br>4.1.3　认识土木工程可持续性发展的重要性<br>……<br>4.2　认识各种企业文化成功过程的差异<br>4.2.1　重视不同的企业文化<br>4.2.2　企业战略、目标和规划<br>4.2.3　技术创业<br>4.2.4　成功地在一个组织中工作<br>4.3　构思复杂的土木工程系统<br>4.3.1　设立系统目标和要求<br>4.3.2　系统建模 | 4.4　设计复杂的土木工程系统<br>4.4.1　风险及不确定性评估<br>4.4.2　设计过程的解释与调整<br>4.4.3　知识在设计中的利用<br>4.4.4　同领域土木工程的设计<br>4.4.5　多学科设计<br>4.4.6　多目标设计(DFX)<br>4.5　实施复杂的土木工程系统<br>4.5.1　土木工程承包<br>4.5.2　系统土木工程施工<br>4.5.3　项目工程经济与管理<br>4.5.4　工程监理<br>4.5.5　工程检测和试验<br>4.5.6　工程成本核算与进度控制<br>4.6　运行和管理复杂的土木工程系统<br>4.6.1　大型土木工程构筑物及设施的运行、管理与维护<br>4.6.2　大气、水资源、垃圾处理等环境工程保护与运行<br>4.6.3　土木工程构筑物全寿命周期的检测、维修与加固 |

（3）以构建一体化课程体系为核心的具体设计。

为了达到 EIP-CDIO 专业培养标准中对工科毕业生学习产出的期待，必须设计和编制适当的一体化课程体系。由课程、项目、实习实践以及各类课外活动所构成的教学环节将专业特征目标所列出的知识、能力和素质以相互联系、相互支持的方式进行统筹与整合，一体化地实现专业培养目标。一体化课程体系要求全方位地考虑问题和解决问题，即要求课程体系依目标体系而设置，教学方法依目标要求而开发，学习方法配合教学目标和学生的个性与成长规律而采用，考核方式依据学习目标、学习方式、反馈要求而设计，以培养目标为依据进行评估反馈、持续改进。最后，要求明确课程体系中的每门课程或环节对专业培养标准的贡献，即绘制专业培养目标实现矩阵。

汕头大学工学院按照 CDIO 的培养模式，再结合自身学校和专业特色，提出了以三级团队设计项目为载体的一体化课程体系。以团队项目为骨架的设计，可以将学生的基础知识学习和综合能力训练、课程学习和探索兴趣结合起来，将知识学习和个人能力培养、团队合作精神以及大系统掌控能力等有机地结合起来。

以汕头大学工学院机械设计制造及其自动化专业为例，基于 EIP-CDIO 的能力-素质-知识教学大纲和对利益相关者的调研，按照 CDIO 模式一体化课程体系的设计流程，设计出以四个一级团队设计项目、四个二级团队设计项目、每门课程一个或几个三级团队设计项目为导向的一体化课程体系。同时采用了本文作者之一陆小华教授设计的以三级设计建造项目为基础的鱼骨型课程结构表达方案（如图 4 所示），清楚地显示了专业培养的基本方案和路径，连接了各学科课程与综合应用、实践能力培养。因为关系表达清晰、结构明确合理，鱼骨型课程结构表达方式在国内各试点高校获得了广泛认可。

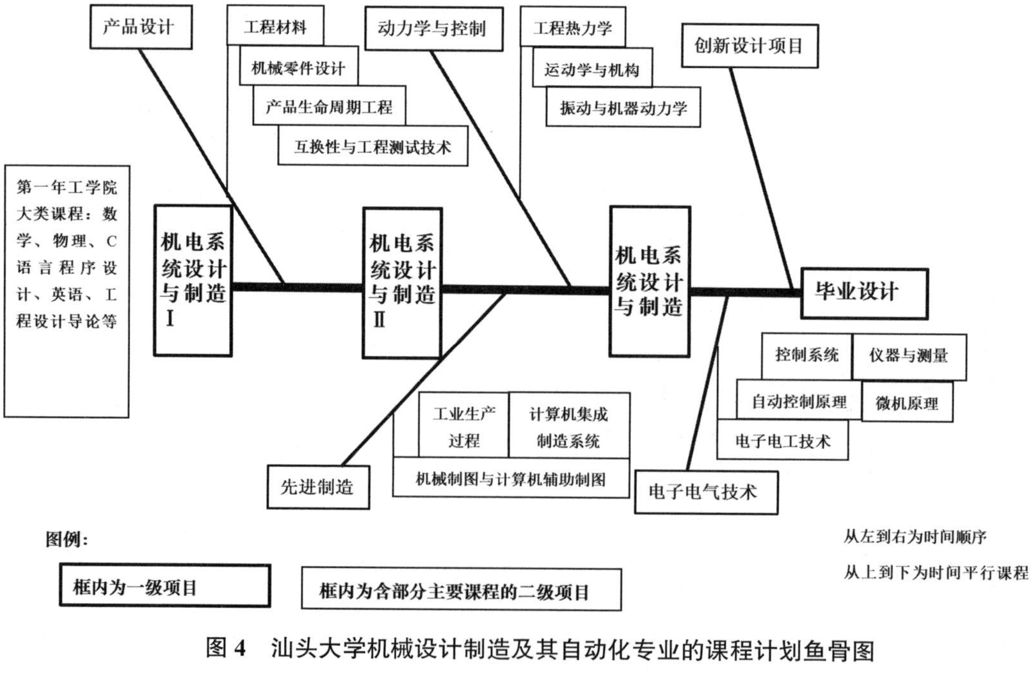


**图 4　汕头大学机械设计制造及其自动化专业的课程计划鱼骨图**

一级项目贯穿于整个本科教学阶段，包含本专业的主要核心课程和能力要求。在项目中，4~6 个学生组成一个团队，每个团队有一个具体的项目，从概念设计、系统设计、传动与机械结构设计、控制系统设计等，直到成功制造出来，经历一个完整的 C-D-I-O 过程。

在产品设计、先进制造、电子电气技术和动力学与控制（创新设计项目）四个二级项目中，每个项目都是基于课程群的综合性设计项目，能够有效地把相关联的课程知识点有机地结合起来，使学生认识到有机和关联的知识群而不是孤立的知识点。课程群建设与实践的结合可以避免内容重复，减少学时。

三级项目以单门课程为基础，在为学生提供强大基础知识背景和数学、科学方法训练的基础上，根据课程教学自身需要，设立小规模、低成本、短学时的实践项目，旨在加深和强化学生对课程内容的理解与应用。

在确立专业培养目标和课程计划之后，要求明确课程体系中的每门课程或环节对专业培养标准的贡献，即专业培养目标实现矩阵，如表 5 所示。专业培养目标实现矩阵将专业特征目标所规定的知识、能力和素质要求落实到具体的教学环节中。从专业培养目标实现矩阵中可以直观地看出课程计划与知识、能力和素质的密切关系，合理地回答为什么在本专业中需要设置这门课，以及这个培养环节和培养程度的期望。

汕头大学的专业培养目标实现矩阵以布鲁姆学习目标分类法（Bloom's Taxonomy）为基础，描述学生在学完本课程后应掌握的知识和具有的能力的程度，以 1（最低）、2、3、4、5、6（最高）来表示对此项知识、能力或素质要求达到的程度，无要求则留空。

（4）以建立课程档案为核心的课程文件详细设计。

建立专业课程体系之后，必须明确每一门课程的具体要求，而且这个要求只与课程有关。也就是说，这是课程的要求，与具体的授课教师无关，任何授课教师都必须严格执行。具体来说就是建立以课程档案为核心的课程文件详细设计。

因此，在每门课程的课程档案中，细化了每门课程/环节在专业培养计划中的贡献，并明确了课程的性质与目标、学时安排、教学方法、先修课程、后续有关专业课程和教学环节、课程综合记分方法、教科书与参考书以及重要的学习内容与时间节点等课程大纲内容。

更重要的是，在课程大纲中明确了本课程的学生需要掌握的知识点和程度、需要培养的能力及程度，以及实现掌握这些知识点和能力要求的教学环节，并且这些环节是可评估的。同时，由于三级项目是单门课程巩固知识点、培养能力和素质最主要的环节，因此专业的骨干课程都设计了体现核心知识和能力培养目标的小规模、低成本、短学时的三级项目，并要求给出详细的项目指导书。

三级项目指导书要求针对这门课程的知识、能力和素质培养目标，给出项目的总体目标、CDIO 学习目标、团队组织与管理事项、评估方法、所需要的软硬件资源、安全注意事项、具体的实施方法、制造与试验方法、评分标准以及特别重要的分析与思考、学生的讨论和思考问题等。其中，CDIO 学习目标、分析与思考、学生的讨论和思考问题是三级项目指导书的核心。

以机电专业的“工程热力学”课程为例，要求承担这门课的教师依据专业培养标准，撰写本课程详细的课程大纲和项目指导书并加以实施。表 6 和表 7 分别给出了“工程热力学”课程大纲中对知识、能力和素质的培养要求。

**表 5　汕头大学机械设计制造及其自动化专业培养目标实现矩阵**

| 课程名称 | 学分 | 课程性质 | 1. 技术知识和推理 | | | | 2. 个人与职业能力 | | | | | | 3. 团队工作和交流能力 | | | | | 4. 在企业和社会环境下构思—设计—实施—运行 | | | | | |
|---|---|---|---|---|---|---|---|---|---|---|---|---|---|---|---|---|---|---|---|---|---|---|---|
| | | | 1.1 数学、物理、生物等基础科学知识 | 1.2 力学、电学等核心工程基础知识 | 1.3 机械原理、设计与制造等专业工程基础知识 | …… | 2.1 机电产品研发过程的工程推理和解决问题的能力 | 2.2 机电系统运行实验和发现知识 | 2.3 机电产品全系统的思维整合 | 2.4 系统工作中的个人能力和态度 | 2.5 系统工作中的职业能力和态度 | …… | 3.1 机电产品研发中的有效团队工作 | 3.2 机电产品研发团队中的有效交流 | 3.3 团队中使用外语的交流 | 3.4 在不同和多种文化环境有效工作和探索 | 3.5 跨越人文、工程、经济和社会的综合视野 | 4.1 大系统外部和社会背景环境 | 4.2 复杂企业与商业环境 | 4.3 机电新产品或新系统的创意与构思 | 4.4 机械或电控系统的设计 | 4.5 机电产品的有效实施 | 4.6 机电产品寿命周期的运行 |
| 第一学年 | | | | | | | | | | | | | | | | | | | | | | | |
| 秋季学期 | | | | | | | | | | | | | | | | | | | | | | | |
| MAT1110 高等数学 I | 6 | 必修 | 3 | | | | | | | 2 | | | | | | | 2 | 2 | | | | | |
| ENC9105 工程设计导论 | 2 | 必修 | 2 | 2 | 1 | | 3 | 3 | 2 | 1 | 2 | | 3 | 3 | 3 | | | 1 | 2 | 2 | 2 | 1 | 1 |
| CST9910 程序设计 | 2 | 必修 | 3 | 4 | | | | | 2 | | | | | | | | | 1 | 1 | | | | |
| ENC9110 化学导论 | 1 | 必修 | 2 | | | | 2 | 3 | | | | | | | | | | 1 | 1 | | | | |
| ENC9120 生物学导论 | 1 | 必修 | 1 | | | | 1 | | | 2 | 1 | | 2 | 2 | 2 | 2 | 2 | | | | | | |
| COM011 计算机应用技能 | 2 | 必修 | 4 | | | | | | | 3 | 2 | | 2 | 2 | 1 | 2 | | | | | | | |
| 毛邓三 | 6 | 必修 | | | | | 2 | | | | 3 | | | | | | | | | | | | |
| 英语 | 4 | 必修 | 4 | | | | | | 2 | 3 | | | 2 | 2 | 4 | | | | | | | | |
| 体育 | 1 | 必修 | | | | | | | 2 | | 3 | | 2 | 2 | | | | | | | | | |
| 本学期必修学分小计 | 25 | 必修 | | | | | | | 2 | | | | | | | | | | | | | | |
| 春季学期 | | | | | | | | | | 2 | | | | | | | 2 | 2 | | | | | |
| MAT1210 高等数学 II | 6 | 必修 | 4 | | | | | | | 2 | | | | | | | 2 | 2 | | | | | |
| MAT1130 线性代数 | 2 | 必修 | 3 | | | | | | 2 | | | | | | | | | | | | | | |
| PHY030 普通物理学 | 4 | 必修 | 3 | 2 | | | 1 | 3 | 2 | | | | | | | | | | | | | | |
| PHY1000 普通物理实验 | 2 | 必修 | 3 | 2 | | | 1 | 2 | 2 | 2 | 3 | | 3 | 3 | 3 | | | 2 | 2 | 3 | 3 | 2 | 2 |
| MEC9500 机械制图与计算机辅助制图 | 4 | 必修 | | 4 | 3 | | 3 | 3 | 2 | | | | 2 | 2 | 4 | | | | | | | | |
| 英语 | 4 | 必修 | 4 | | | | | | 2 | 3 | 3 | | 2 | 2 | | | | | | | | | |
| 体育 | 1 | 必修 | | | | | 2 | | 2 | 3 | 3 | | | | | | | | | | | | |
| 形势与政策 | 2 | 必修 | | | | | | | | | | | | | | | | | | | | | |
| 公共课或者通识课自选 | | | | | | | | | | | | | | | | | | | | | | | |
| 本学期必修学分小计 | 25 | | | | | | | | | | | | | | | | | | | | | | |

**表 6 “工程热力学”课程大纲对知识点的培养要求(部分)**

| 知识点 | | | 程度 | 主要实现环节 |
|---|---|---|---|---|
| 一级 | 二级 | 三级 | | |
| 热力学 | 热力系统 | 热力过程 | 1 | 教学+三级项目(水力火箭) |
| | | 工质的状态参数 | 3 | 教学+三级项目(水力火箭) |
| | 热力循环 | 水及水蒸气物性 | 3 | 教学+三级项目(水力火箭) |
| | | 热力循环的分析方法 | 3 | 教学+三级项目(水力火箭) |
| | 传热学 | 导热 | 1 | 教学+研讨(暖气片的研讨等) |
| | | 对流 | 1 | 教学+研讨(暖气片的研讨等) |
| | | 辐射 | 1 | 教学+研讨(太阳能热水器的研讨等) |

**表 7 “工程热力学”课程大纲对能力和素质的培养要求(部分)**

| 能力和素质 | | | 程度 | 主要环节 |
|---|---|---|---|---|
| 一级 | 二级 | 三级 | | |
| 个人和职业技能和职业道德 | 2.1 工程推理和解决问题 | 2.1.1 发现问题和表述问题 | 4 | 三级项目(水力火箭) |
| | | | 3 | (实验一、二) |
| | | 2.1.5 解决方法和建议 | 3 | 三级项目(水力火箭) |
| | | | 2 | (实验二、三) |
| | 2.2 实验中探寻知识 | | 3 | (实验二、三) |
| | 2 3 系统思维 | | 2 | 教学、三级项目(水力火箭) |
| | 2.4 个人技能和态度 | 2.4.2 执着追求与变通 | 2 | 三级项目(水力火箭) |
| | | 2.4.4 批判性思维 | 3 | 教学、三级项目(水力火箭) |
| | | | 2 | (实验三) |
| | | 2.4.6 求知欲和终身学习能力 | 4 | 三级项目(水力火箭) |
| | | | 2 | 三级项目(水力火箭) |
| | 2.5 职业技能和道德 | | 2 | 三级项目(水力火箭) |

“工程热力学”课程的三级项目“水力火箭”指导书篇幅较大,在此仅给出“工程热力学”三级项目“水力火箭”指导书中“学生的讨论和思考问题”部分的设计内容:“①对于要求,你的解释是什么?你将如何解决对它们的误解?②你采用的创新是什么?灵感是什么?你如何知道什么时候进行创新,什么时候创建‘标准工作’?③你所做的研发工作有哪些?这些工作是否值得?你如何决定花在研发上的预算的多少?④你如何将你现有的热力学知识运用到分析设计的过程中?在实践的过程中你意识到你需要什么样的新知识?⑤你使用的设计灵感是什么?它是否像分析一样重要?更重要还是更不重要?⑥你是否理解设计好的文件资料的需要?为什么其这么重要?你是否按照图纸上的实际内容来建造实物?⑦你是怎样决定投资预算和时间资源的?你是否制订了一项计划?你是否按照这项计划实施?⑧你如何解释要制定的规定?你所做的设计是否足够承受这种潜在的改变?工程师在

参与要求和规章的变更中的责任是什么？⑨你是否了解高质量的实施的必要性？你是否意识到实践操作的重要性？⑩是否采用了建议的项目工程领导阶层结构？如果采用了，这种结构是否运作良好？如果没有采用，你采用什么方法来代替？你学到了什么？你是如何将这些知识概括应用到其他项目中的？”

从上述设计内容可以看出，学生实施“水力火箭”三级项目后，必须思考和回答更深层次的问题，进一步体现了CDIO中能力培养为先的原则。

（5）以服务课堂为核心的独具教师个人特色的课堂教案。

构建每门课程的课程档案之后，具体承担这门课程的教师形成以服务课堂为核心的独具教师个人特色的课堂教案，而非仅仅依赖以往的课程教学PPT或其他资料。

课堂教案一般以2个学时为单位，详细给出这门课程在这一上课时段的目标、上课内容、教学知识点、要培养的CDIO能力（选取四级指标），然后针对每一项主要授课内容和知识点，给出详细的讲授时间（分钟为计算单位）、辅助材料、授课方法与策略（提问、例题、小测验等）。表8给出了土木工程专业“工程力学Ⅰ”课程某一个单位学时部分的课堂教学教案，从中可以看出教师的个人特色。

**表8　土木工程专业“工程力学Ⅰ”课堂教学教案（部分）**

<table>
<tr><td colspan="2">姓名：王××</td><td colspan="4">时间：2011年9月14日</td><td colspan="2">学时：2小时</td></tr>
<tr><td colspan="2">课程：工程力学Ⅰ</td><td colspan="4">主题：约束与约束力、受力分析与受力图</td><td colspan="2">教室：E408</td></tr>
<tr><td colspan="8">内容：复习上节课的内容（讲解例题）；介绍工程常见约束与约束力；学习受力分析和画受力图</td></tr>
<tr><td colspan="8">目标：了解和掌握根据约束的性质确定约束力；分清施力体与受力体；应用二力平衡与三力平衡原理</td></tr>
<tr><td colspan="8">CDID相关能力在本课程中的培养</td></tr>
<tr><td></td><td></td><td>认知（1）</td><td>理解（2）</td><td>应用（3）</td><td>分析（4）</td><td>综合（5）</td><td>评判（6）</td></tr>
<tr><td>第1级：技术知识和推理</td><td>1.1 相关科学知识<br>■数学<br>■物理</td><td></td><td></td><td>√</td><td></td><td></td><td></td></tr>
<tr><td rowspan="8">第2级：个人和职业技能和职业道德</td><td>2.1 工程推理解决问题的能力</td><td></td><td></td><td></td><td></td><td></td><td></td></tr>
<tr><td>2.1.1 发现问题和表述问题<br>■制订解决问题的计划</td><td></td><td></td><td>√</td><td></td><td></td><td></td></tr>
<tr><td>2.1.2 建模<br>■应用假设简化复杂的系统和环境<br>■选择并应用概念性和定性模型</td><td></td><td></td><td>√</td><td></td><td></td><td></td></tr>
<tr><td>2.1.5 解决方法和建议<br>■综合问题的解决方案</td><td></td><td>√</td><td></td><td></td><td></td><td></td></tr>
<tr><td>2.4 个人能力和态度</td><td></td><td></td><td></td><td></td><td></td><td></td></tr>
<tr><td>2.4.3 创造性思维<br>■具有概念化和抽象化能力<br>■具有综合和通用化能力</td><td></td><td></td><td>√</td><td></td><td></td><td></td></tr>
<tr><td>2.4.4 批判性思维<br>■分析所陈述的问题</td><td></td><td></td><td>√</td><td></td><td></td><td></td></tr>
</table>

**续表**

<table>
<tr><td></td><td></td><td>认知<br>(1)</td><td>理解<br>(2)</td><td>应用<br>(3)</td><td>分析<br>(4)</td><td>综合<br>(5)</td><td>评判<br>(6)</td></tr>
<tr><td rowspan="2">第 3 级:人际技能:团队协作和交流</td><td>3.1 团队工作</td><td></td><td></td><td></td><td></td><td></td><td></td></tr>
<tr><td>3.1.2 团队运行<br>■确定目标和日程</td><td></td><td></td><td>√</td><td></td><td></td><td></td></tr>
<tr><td colspan="8">主题/内容:</td></tr>
<tr><td colspan="8">教学内容一:工程常见约束和约束力(35 分钟)<br>(1)辅助材料<br>■工程中常见约束的录像<br>(2)方法与策略<br>■基本概念介绍<br>约束力:约束对非自由体的作用力<br>主动力:约束力以外的力,如重力、风力、水压力等<br>约束力{大小——待定<br>方向——与该约束所能阻碍的位移方向相反<br>作用点——接触处<br>■以常见的工程为例,将抽象的约束实际工程化,便于学生理解<br>(3)效果<br>■以工程实例讲解抽象的约束,便于学生理解抽象的概念</td></tr>
<tr><td colspan="8">评估和总结(8 分钟)</td></tr>
<tr><td colspan="8">方法和策略<br>■总结课堂内容,强调重点和难点</td></tr>
<tr><td colspan="8">布置作业:<br>■作业 1-2</td></tr>
<tr><td colspan="8">课外练习题或需探究的内容<br>■课外练习题 1</td></tr>
<tr><td colspan="8">布置预习内容<br>■力系的等效与简化</td></tr>
</table>

课堂教学教案非常详尽,需要教师在多年工作积累和完善的基础上,以认真的态度完成并加以实践。它是每门课程具体承担教师的个人特色或魅力的教学方法的核心体现,不谋求千篇一律,鼓励各具特色的创新。

(6)以实施基于项目/问题等探究式主动学习为核心的教与学方法。

为充分发挥汕头大学 EIP-CDIO 一体化课程体系在课程群和三个层级项目上的优势,工学院实施了集成基于项目/问题的学习和探究式学习的一体化主动学习方法,以思维能力和创新能力为核心,将科学与技术知识和工程能力的学习方式由被动接受型转变为主动学习型。

基于项目的学习通过项目设计将课程体系有机、系统地整合起来。所有需要学习的知识、需要培养的能力和素质都围绕团队设计项目这个核心,形成一个整体。学生在项目进行的过程中学习探索,综合应用知识,锻炼团队精神,学习基本项目的组织和管理,培养 CDIO 能力。

以机械设计制造及其自动化专业为例，一级项目“机电系统设计与制造”分为以下四个阶段。第一阶段（“机电系统设计与制造Ⅰ”）从一年级第二学期开始，4~6 个学生组成一个项目团队，设小组长 1 名，由 1 名专职教师指导。要求每个项目团队选择一个具体项目或题目，比如“自动卫生快捷的取筷装置”，从市场分析与技术需求分析开始，完成项目的市场调研与技术分析报告。在第二阶段（“机电系统设计与制造Ⅱ”），在市场调研与技术分析报告的基础上，依据逐步学习的专业基础知识，通过与指导教师讨论、内部讨论、查资料等各种方式，提出多个总体设计方案，并比较优缺点，在控制总体成本的基础上，结合小组能力与现有条件，初步选择一个较为合适的总体设计方案。在第三阶段（“机电系统设计与制造Ⅲ”），在选定总体设计方案的基础上，通过进一步掌握的专业基础知识，进一步完善系统总体设计方案，并开始进行机械零部件设计和控制系统设计等过程。在第四阶段，通过前面机电系统设计与制造Ⅰ至Ⅲ的实践，经设计完善，开始加工、制造、安装以及综合调试。在这样一个完整的团队设计项目中，尽可能模拟行业企业的工程项目环境，让学生经历一个完整的 C-D-I-O 系统和过程；在这个过程中，学生可能会碰到诸如方案设计不合理、原材料与部件买不到、加工能力和经验不足等问题，在对一个个工程实践中出现的问题进行解决的过程中，学生必须主动探究相关知识，主动应用所学的专业知识，主动应用探究式学习和经验学习方法，这也有利于培养学生的人际交往能力、团队合作能力和职业能力等。

在单门课程的教学上，EIP-CDIO 模式首先要求改革课程教学大纲，将传统的只包含知识要求的教学大纲转变为集知识、能力和素质要求为一体的教学大纲；然后根据新教学大纲改革教学内容和教学活动，一般要求拓宽知识面（增加同其他课程的联系），减少课程讲授学时以增加研讨和团队设计项目学时；最后是改革对学生学习成绩的评定方式，减少笔试成绩的比例，增加团队设计项目成绩的比例。反思一方面可以启发学生积极进行批判性思考，对问题进行思考回答的过程就是深化课程学习目标的过程，另一方面也有助于学生进行深层次的学与问，加深对理论知识、学习过程等的认识。因此，在计算机专业的“Java 程序设计”课程中，针对课程特点，特别加强了“反思环节”，着重设计了如表 9 所示的项目报告会及其问题，积极引导学生思考，进而提高知识和思维、思辨能力的培养，实现本课程的培养目标。

**表 9 “Java 程序设计”课程实施的项目报告会及其反思环节**

| 项目报告会 | 问题 |
|---|---|
| 项目报告会Ⅰ | 问题 1：你对系统的需求是如何理解的？<br>问题 2：你所做的前期准备工作有哪些？这些工作是否值得？你如何决定花在前期准备上的预算的多少？<br>问题 3：关于系统的创新点，你设计的灵感是什么？你是如何认定你的系统是有新意的、能够吸引人的？ |
| 项目报告会Ⅱ | 问题 1：在哪些问题上你采用了面向对象的程序设计思想？你是否用到了软件设计模式？你的系统能否应对需求的变化？在设计过程中你发现面向对象技术的优势有哪些？<br>问题 2：你是怎样决定投资预算和时间管理的？你是否制订了一项计划？你是否按照这项计划进行？ |
| 项目报告会Ⅲ | 问题 1：你是否理解软件文档的需要？你是否按照文档中的规定来构建系统？如果你改变了文档中的某些规定来构建系统，那原因是什么？<br>问题 2：对于开发中的困难，你是否在设计之初设想到？如果设想到了，那你的解决方案是什么？如果没有设想到，那你下一步的解决办法是什么？你是否想过推翻整个系统重新来过？ |

续表

| 项目报告会 | 问题 |
|---|---|
| 项目报告会Ⅳ | 问题 1:面向对象的设计和面向过程的设计之间最本质的区别是什么?如果让你采用面向过程的方式开发这个系统,你觉得主要难点在哪里?可能性又是多少?<br>问题 2:分析系统成功或者失败的原因是什么?你认为在哪一个环节出了问题?你觉得一个成功的项目应该在哪些方面下足功夫?<br>问题 3:你学到了什么?你是如何将这些知识概括应用到其他项目中的? |

(7)以建立质量保障体系为核心的持续改进机制。

汕头大学工学院工程教育质量保证体系主要由对各利益相关者集团进行调查反馈、基于 ISO 的教学过程管理质量保证体系、专业认证和工程师认证四部分构成。

首先,对各利益相关者集团进行调查反馈,主要用来评估工学院各专业制定的 EIP-CDIO 教学大纲中对工科学生在毕业时的学习效果是否符合各利益相关者的要求,根据反馈意见及时调整工程人才培养方案。例如工学院土木工程专业的教师就对已经从事了近 10 年土木工程专业工作的工程人员进行了问卷调查,涵盖设计、施工、监理、管理、预算、造价等土木工程的各个领域,调查内容为大学里教师应该着重讲授的内容及注重哪些方面能力的培养。调查结果见表 10。从调查文件的结果可以看出,绝大多数的工程技术人员希望在基本概念、工程实际、分析能力、团队能力等方面加强培养的力度,而对很深的理论推导则希望能够弱化一些。因此,根据调查的结果,学院在土木工程专业的教学中注重加强培养学生分析解决问题和自学创新的能力,以及交流、沟通和团队协作等工程能力。

**表 10　工科中教师应该着重讲授的内容及注重培养的能力**

| 调查内容 | 基本概念、原理和方法 | 结合实际工程 | 很深的理论推导 | 结合相关规范 | 本学科前沿知识 |
|---|---|---|---|---|---|
| 同意的人数 | 76 | 71 | 8 | 66 | 73 |
| 百分比 | 97.4% | 91.0% | 10.3% | 84.6% | 93.7% |
| 调查内容 | 分析解决问题能力 | 结合设计软件 | 自学创新能力 | 交流沟通能力 | 团队协作能力 |
| 同意的人数 | 72 | 57 | 74 | 75 | 63 |
| 百分比 | 92.3% | 73.1% | 94.9% | 96.1% | 80.8% |

其次,采用基于 ISO 的教学过程管理质量保证体系,明确 EIP-CDIO 教学过程中的质量监控重点,设置合理的、可测量的长期及短期管理目标,并依据 PDCA(计划、实施、检查、处理)的管理原则,定期对教学过程展开评估和改进,同时根据内部与外部的需要及评估反馈,对整个系统进行持续改进。因此,学院制定了相应的教学质量保障体系。

再次,专业认证,指的是工学院各专业进行基于 CDIO 标准的专业评估工作。CDIO 标准着眼于工程教育的整个过程,因此学院按照 CDIO 的 12 条标准的要求采用审阅文件、与个人和专题小组面谈、问卷调查、教师工作体会备忘录、校外专家的专业审查和不同学习时期的分析等方法,分别评估各工程专业教育的专业目标和学习效果(标准 2)、课程计划(标准 3、4、5)、学习环境(标准 6)、教学(标准 7、8)、教师发展(标准 9、10)和学习考核(标准

11）等方面，以促进专业持续改进。

### 3.4 汕头大学 EIP-CDIO 工程教育改革的初步成效

经过 6 年多的探索和实践，EIP-CDIO 工程教育改革取得了初步成效。汕头大学工学院每年组织工业界专家对本科毕业生进行离校面试。根据毕业生面试的结果和用人单位的反馈，确认 CDIO 改革对学生的能力培养有显著效果。同时，学生的基本理论知识更加扎实，工程能力显著提高，EIP 素质得到加强，在国内外创新大赛连创佳绩（如在 2011 年的“第二届全国大学生工程训练综合能力竞赛”中获得一等奖）。

汕头大学工学院本科毕业生平均薪酬在 2009 年以前（还未有 CDIO 改革毕业生）基本低于广东省工科毕业生的平均工资。CDIO 改革后的首届毕业生（2010 届）的平均薪酬已高于广东省工科毕业生的平均工资。2011 年 9 月 1 日，汕头大学本科毕业生初次就业率达到 96.77%，居广东省第一批招生高校第一位。

汕头大学的 CDIO 改革也获得了教育行政部门、高教界和社会各界的普遍肯定：以 CDIO 改革为依托，学校获批为教育部人才培养模式创新实验区、联合国教科文组织教育模式示范基地、教育部卓越工程师教育培养计划第一批启动高校；机电专业和土木专业获批高等学校特色专业建设点，CDIO 教改项目获得广东省教学成果奖一等奖。同时出版多本 CDIO 专著、译著，发表 CDIO 教改论文几十篇，CDIO 教学改革也获得中国工程院、教育部、全国教育科学规划办公室、财政部、广东省教育厅、广东省财政厅立项资助研究。

汕头大学取得的成就得到国内外同行的肯定，引起了国内媒体的热切关注。《中国教育报》《光明日报》《科技日报》以及新华网、人民网等 60 余家报刊以及网络媒体多次报道汕头大学的 CDIO 教学改革成果。2008 年 9 月至今，共接待了国内外逾百所高校参观、考查或研讨 EIP-CDIO。汕头大学的 CDIO 工程教育改革也被中国科学院技术科学部“科学与工程教育创新”课题组列为典型创新案例向国内高校推介。

（未完待续）

### 参考文献


[1] CRAWLEY E F, MALMQVIST J, ÖSTLUND S, et al. 重新认识工程教育：国际 CDIO 培养模式与方法[M]. 顾佩华，沈民奋，陆小华，译. 北京：高等教育出版社，2009.

[2] 雷环，汤威颐，CRAWLEY E F. 培养创新型、多层次、专业化的工程科技人才：CDIO 工程教育改革的人才理念和培养模式[J]. 高等工程教育研究，2009（5）：29-35.

[3] 顾佩华，沈民奋，李升平，等. 从 CDIO 到 EIP-CDIO：汕头大学工程教育与人才培养模式探索[J]. 高等工程教育研究，2008（1）：12-20.

[4] YELLOWLEY I, GU P H. Design directed engineering education[J]. Journal of engineering design and innovation，2005，1（1）：1-7.

[5] 陆小华，熊光晶，陈珠琳. 设计导向的工程教育改革理念[J]. 高等工程教育研究，2007（6）：83-87.

[6] 邹晓东. 科学与工程教育创新[M]. 北京：科学出版社，2010.

[7] 中国工程院教育委员会. 探寻中国工程教育改革之路：“新形势下工程教育的改革与发

展”高层论坛纪要[J]. 高等工程教育研究，2007（6）：43-47.

[8] 熊玲，李忠. 新世纪我国高等工程人才需求调查报告[J]. 现代教育管理，2010（7）：3-6.

[9] 任荃. 工程教育能力缘何世界垫底？[N]. 文汇报，2007-09-25（005）.

[10] 陈金江，许晓东. 2007 年全国工程教育改革研讨会纪要[J]. 高等工程教育研究，2007（6）：48-49，77.

[11] 李晓强，孔寒冰，王沛民. 部署新世纪的工程教育行动：兼评美国“2020 工程师”《行动报告》[J]. 高等工程教育研究，2006（4）：14-18.

[12] 杨叔子. 谈谈我对“CDIO——工程文化教育”的认识 [J]. 中国大学教学，2008（9）：6-7，30.

[13] CRAWLEY E，MALMQVIST J，LRCAS W，et al. The CDIO syllabus v2.0—an updated statement of goals for engineering education[C]. Proceedings of the 7th International CDIO Conference. Technical University of Denmark，Copenhagen，June 20-23，2011.

[14] 陈新民. 应用型本科的课程改革：培养目标、课程体系与教学方法 [J]. 中国大学教学，2011（7）：27-30.

[15] 陈劲，胡建雄. 面向创新型国家的工程教育改革研究[M]. 北京：中国人民大学出版社，2006.

[16] 沈艳霞，潘庭龙，纪志成. CDIO-P 培养模式下运动控制系统课程改革探索 [J]. 江南大学学报（教育科学版），2009，29（3）：270-273.

[17] 王天宝，程卫东. 基于 CDIO 的创新型工程人才培养模式研究与实践：成都信息工程学院的工程教育改革实践[J]. 高等工程教育研究，2010（1）：25-31.

[18] 温涛. 基于 TOPCARES-CDIO 的一体化人才培养模式探索与实践[J]. 计算机教育，2010（11）：23-29.

[19] 熊和平，岳爱臣. CDIO 工程教育模式：误解的澄明与风险的规避[J]. 高等工程教育研究，2009（5）：48-51.

[20] 田国强. 关于改善学风、教风的建议[J]. 中国大学教学，2006（1）：4-8.

[21] 郝维谦，龙正中. 高等教育史[M]. 海南：海南出版社，2000.

[22] BLOOM B S，ENGELHART M D，FURST E J，et al. Taxonomy of educational objectives：handbook Ⅰ：cognitive domain[M]. New York：Longman，1956.

[23] ANDERSON L W，KRATHWOHL D R，AIRASIAN P W，et al. A taxonomy for learning，teaching，and assessing：a revision of Bloom’s taxonomy of educational objectives[M]. New York：Longman，2001：38-62.

# CDIO 在中国（下）①

顾佩华　包能胜　康全礼　陆小华　熊光晶　林　鹏　陈　严

**摘要：** CDIO 工程教育模式是近年来国际工程教育改革的新成果，在世界各地多所大学进行了实施并取得很好的成效。自 2005 年汕头大学率先实施 CDIO 工程教育改革以来，在教育部高教司理工处的指导和支持下，全国几十所试点高校和许多非试点院校实施 CDIO 改革，取得了很好的效果。汕头大学等试点高校重新思考工程教育改革的模式与路径，对人才培养的各个方面与相应的管理机制进行了重新构建，在明确专业培养目标、制定专业培养标准、构建一体化课程计划、实施探究式教与学方法、建立保障与持续改进体系等方面进行了实践和创新。CDIO 在中国的普及和实践，也为高质量实施卓越工程师教育培养计划打下了良好的基础，起到了积极的推进作用。本文对 6 年来 CDIO 在汕头大学及其他试点高校的实践和推广情况进行了回顾和总结，对中国工程教育面临的挑战和存在的问题给出了观察与思考，并对 CDIO 在中国做出展望。

**关键词：** 工程教育改革；CDIO；专业培养标准；一体化课程；卓越工程师教育培养计划

## CDIO in China（Part Ⅱ）

*Gu Peihua, Bao Nengsheng, Kang Quanli, Lu Xiaohua, Xiong Guangjing, Lin Peng, Chen Yan*

**Abstract:** CDIO Initiative is the most recent development of an international collaborative endeavor for engineering education. It has significantly changed to and impacted on engineering education of many universities worldwide through adoption of the CDIO Initiative. Since 2005, Shantou University has been undertaking the CDIO based engineering education reform and has achieved significant results. The Department of Science and Engineering, the Bureau of Higher Education, the Ministry of Education have been providing strong leadership and significant support to the implementation of the CDIO Initiative in China. Over 40 universities in the China CDIO Pilot Group and Special Program of Ministry of Education, and many more other universities and colleges have been making good progress. Through adoption of the CDIO Initiative, Shantou University and many institutions have been undertaking a comprehensive review of all aspects of engineering education including definition of program objectives, detailed syllabus that codify the standards of the program objectives, development of the integrated curriculum, the implementation of active learning methods such as inquiry-based and project-based learning and establishment of quality assurance and continuous improvement system of programs. The adoption of the CDIO Initiative in engineering education in China has built a strong foundation for implementation of the Excellent Engineer Education and Training Plan. This paper summarizes the adoption process and experiences of the CDIO Initiative in engineering education at

① 本文刊登于《高等工程教育研究》2012 年第 5 期第 34~45 页。

universities and colleges in China. The challenges and the issues facing the Chinese engineering education have also been discussed.

**Keywords:** engineering education reform; CDIO; professional cultivation; standard-integrated curriculum; Excellent Engineer Education and Training Plan

## 4 其他 CDIO 试点高校的工作特色与创新

2008 年 12 月以来,在教育部高教司理工处倡议和课题组的框架下组成了由 39 所院校参加的 CDIO 工程教育试点工作组,分机械、土木、电气和化工四大类试点实施 CDIO 工程教育模式。

几年来, CDIO 第一批、第二批试点和特色专业的几十所高校在推进 CDIO 工程教育改革方面取得了良好的进展和成效。在学习研讨 CDIO 的过程中,各校重新思考工程教育改革的模式与路径,在人才培养方案、课程体系、教学实施、实践环境、教师考评机制等方面进行了部分环节的重新构建,多方面探索 CDIO 的中国化、本土化和特色化。以下结合相关典型案例进行介绍。

### 4.1 自上而下,全面推进 CDIO 改革

CDIO 是一种新型的工程教育,回答了工程教育的重要问题。CDIO 创造了一个协调各个元素的综合方法,应对当代复杂的技术社会对工程教育的挑战。试点高校进行 CDIO 工程教育改革,第一步就是要转变教育思想和观念,全面推进 CDIO 改革。

比如,成都信息工程学院的校领导在改革之初就统一思想,宣传先行。学院工程教育改革领导小组设立专项宣传学习资金,制订系统的学习计划,通过组织召开各种类型的报告会、学习会、座谈会、研讨会,把专家、学者、干部、教师和学生等不同群体组织起来,开展丰富多彩的学习和讨论活动,深化对 CDIO 的学习和理解。在全校教职员工系统理解、全面认同的基础上,形成推进工程教育改革的良好氛围。

在此基础上,成都信息工程学院借鉴 CDIO 模式,形成了"以专业建设为主线的教育教学一体化改革"的方案,重新梳理专业的人才培养定位,制定人才培养的专业标准和培养方案,重新架构课程体系,特别是在人才培养的专业设置和课程教学方面突出自身的两大特点。

一是在理念上强调课程教学要"知识与能力"并重。在这样的要求下,一个专业应该首先确定面向社会和服务行业的专业知识与学生能力的培养标准,设置能达到培养标准的课程体系;再根据课程定位与课程特点,把知识与能力的培养按照课程进行分解,将能力培养通过能力指标量化到每门课程;最后将对学生的知识传授与能力训练落实到每门课程的课堂。要求本校教师课程教学改革的重点落在"如何改革教学方式以将能力培养落实到课堂"和"如何改革考核方法以全面评估学生所具备的知识和能力",积极推进和促进学校的 CDIO 工程教育改革。

二是学校推进各专业设置专门的工程实践教学环节,集中培养学生的 CDIO 能力。在保证专业知识体系的前提下,工程教育要求结合专业定位和课程教学开展工程实践项目,集

中培养学生的工程实践能力。积极引导企业参与，提供结合工程实际或工程应用的实践项目，或者让学生在企业环境中针对产品 C-D-I-O 的整个生命周期进行全面的能力训练。积极探索诸如如何在学校现有条件下开展学生的工程实践，如何设置工程实践项目才更利于学生 CDIO 等能力的全面培养，如何对工程实践中体现的学生能力进行评估等问题及解决方法。

成都信息工程学院同时将 CDIO 教育学和基本方法应用于非工科专业，如在管理专业的实施取得了很好的效果，也开创了 CDIO 教育改革的新领域，为四川省乃至全国的工程教育改革提供了成功经验。大连东软信息学院在充分考虑学校地位的基础上，提出了独特的 TOPCARES-CDIO 人才培养模式。两所高校成功加入 CDIO 国际合作组织，晋升为正式成员，与汕头大学、清华大学、北京交通大学等高校同属 CDIO 国际合作组织亚洲区域中心成员。

### 4.2 结合各专业实际，改革培养目标体系

CDIO 起源于欧美高校。在中国的传播过程中，难免出现简单模仿与移植的现象。但是试点高校在 CDIO 工程教育改革过程中，都尽量结合本校实际进行再认识、再构思、再设计，把 CDIO 的标准和能力大纲融入本校人才培养的全过程。

比如，大连东软信息学院高度重视 CDIO 的本土化和再创新。该校在 CDIO 工程教育改革过程中结合自身特色和 IT（信息技术）行业的人才需求标准，在充分考虑学生、教师、产业和社会等利益相关者需求的基础上，结合中国高等教育的实际和 IT 行业的人才需求标准，针对学院 IT 专业的设置情况，对 CDIO 能力培养大纲在继承基础上进行创新，调整并增加了部分能力指标，构建了具有东软特色的“八大能力”指标体系，形成独特的 TOPCARES-CDIO 人才培养模式（图 1）。

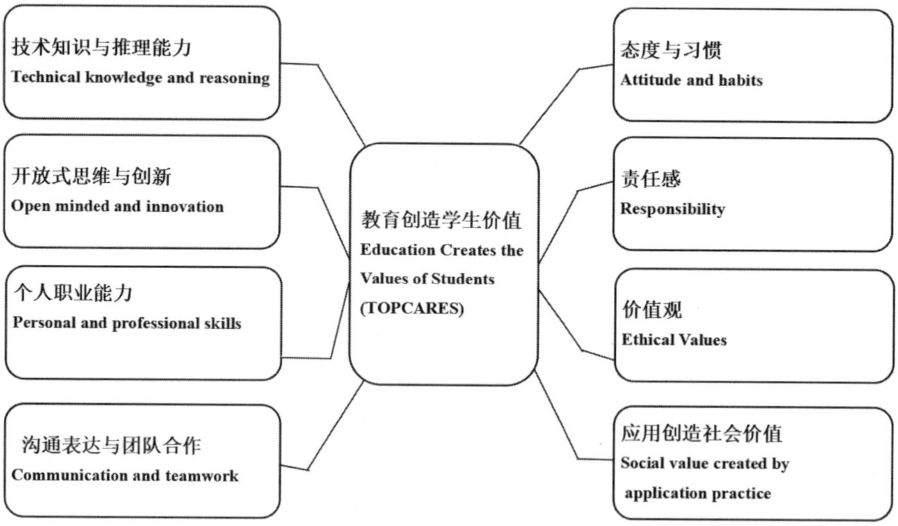


**图 1　TOPCARES-CDIO 模式中的 8 个一级指标**

“TOPCARES”中的每一个字母代表学生应当具备的一种能力。TOPCARES-CDIO 能力指标体系包含 8 个一级指标、32 个二级指标和 110 个三级指标，部分三级指标下面还根

据具体专业的不同要求细分出四级指标。一级指标、二级指标、三级指标和四级指标之间按照逻辑包含顺序和重要度加以组织。

成都信息工程学院的 CDIO 工程教育改革涉及全校各个学院和专业,也就是"全员、全程、全面"。该校依据 CDIO 理念、大纲和标准设计知识、能力、素质培养"三位一体"的培养方案。以该校电子信息学院为例,该学院采用"一个核心、一个导向、三个层次、一条主线"的改革路径(图 2)。其具体含义为:一个核心是指以角色为核心,以电子信息类学生未来可能从事的职业的基本需求为基础设定了三类角色(系统架构师、设计师、应用工程师);一个导向是指以工程师职业训练为导向;三个层次是指课程体系的结构和内容分解为应用系统、功能模块、基本单元三个层次;一条主线是以应用系统、功能模块、基本单元为主线贯穿课程体系的结构和内容的优化设计。

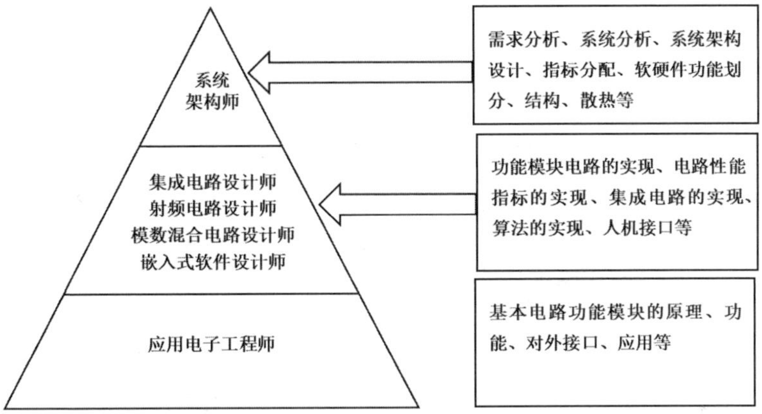


**图 2　成都信息工程学院电子信息学院的 CDIO 改革路径**

再如,上海应用技术学院结合本校的教育理念推行 CDIO,把本校的校训"明德、明学、明事"与 CDIO 联系起来。江南大学制药工程专业制定出一套突出生物制药特色、以制药工艺为工程特点、适合 CDIO 人才培养方案的教学计划和教学大纲。宁波工程学院建筑学专业以独特的"A+TCDIO"(艺科交融、创执并举)的教学理念,系统地进行工程教育改革,其理论课程体系全面体现了"艺科交融",实践课程体系全面体现"创执并举",将本专业的教改引向深入。

除上述高校外,浙江万里学院提出了基于 IEC-CDIO(Innovation & Enterprise Capability-CDIO)理念的计算机类专业课程的教学改革与实践。该理念的核心是以产品研发到产品运行的生命周期为载体,以验证性课程设计为知识"点",以模块级实践课程为方向"线",以行业、企业实际需求为应用"面",通过"点、线、面"一体化项目贯穿整个信息工程实践教学体系,在构思和设计阶段采用"研究性教学"培养学生的创新思维,在实施和运行阶段采用"合作性教学"培养学生的创业精神,从而全面提高学生的工程能力。

### 4.3　改进专业培养方案,构建一体化的课程体系

CDIO 工程教育模式建立了清晰、系统的能力大纲,培养目标明确,各高校易于构建一体化课程体系。因此,试点高校在课程体系和课程内容的改革等方面均取得了可喜的进步。

成都信息工程学院在厘清理念的基础上，设计了各专业的人才培养方案，重构了课程体系（图3）。该校的课程体系强调专业学习与素质教育、理论与实践、课内与课外、教书与育人、学习能力与创新思维培养的有机结合，让学生学会思考、学会学习、学会生活，注重知识和理解、技能和能力、判断和态度的提升；重新分配可用的时间和教学资源，压缩总课时，兼顾能力培养和学科知识，模块化设置课程，为学生拓展知识面和提高专业能力提供不同的选择。

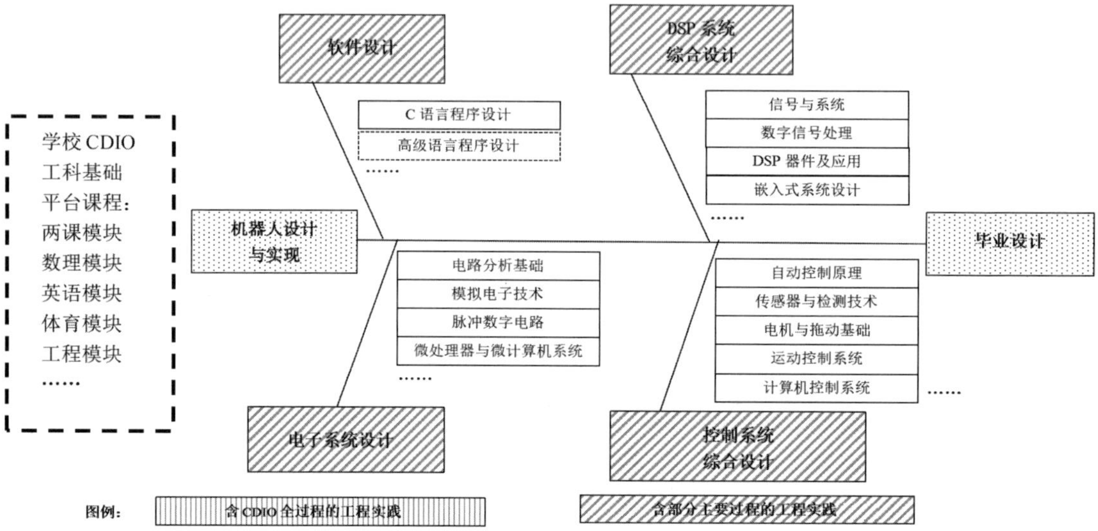


**图3　成都信息工程学院控制工程专业课程体系**

在重构课程体系的同时，成都信息工程学院还启动了CDIO教材的编写工作，已初步完成了电子基础系列教材的编写，包括《电路分析基础》《模拟电子技术基础》《数字电路与数字逻辑》《信号与系统》《单片机原理及应用》等。该系列教材采用基本原理结合典型工程应用实例的结构，引入新技术，精选内容，保证基础，突出工程应用。每章有贯穿始终的典型工程应用案例，有目标设定、目标测评、思考题、实践与提高、工程训练项目和习题等模块，并有小结和英文术语表。教材编写践行以理论为基础、以实践促提高、以能力为特色的理念。整套教材整体统一，各有特色。

燕山大学工程设计与分析专业以CDIO工程教育理念为指导，以现代冶金机械装备为主要对象，依托冶炼与轧钢专业特色优势，以培养具有机械类本科生专业基础知识、掌握现代化工程设计与分析技能的专门人才为目标，将传统机械设计理念与CAD（计算机辅助设计）/CAE（计算机辅助工程）技术等课程知识进行融合，构建了适合于冶金重型机械装备特点的项目式课程体系（图4），注重对学生工程应用和工程设计领域科研能力的培养，取得了很好的效果。

北京石油化工学院化学工程学院化学工程与工艺专业人才培养模式改革将大学四年的实践教学与理论教学通过系列"设计"结合起来，其课程计划的总体结构如图5所示。四个"设计"为基本设计、专业设计、工厂设计、产品与过程设计与研究；三个"实习"穿插在四个"设计"中间，初步实习主要培养学生参与社会的能力，职业实习主要增加学生对专业的印象并培养学生对未来职业的兴趣,专业实习主要加深学生对专业知识的理解和培养学生的专业实践技能。

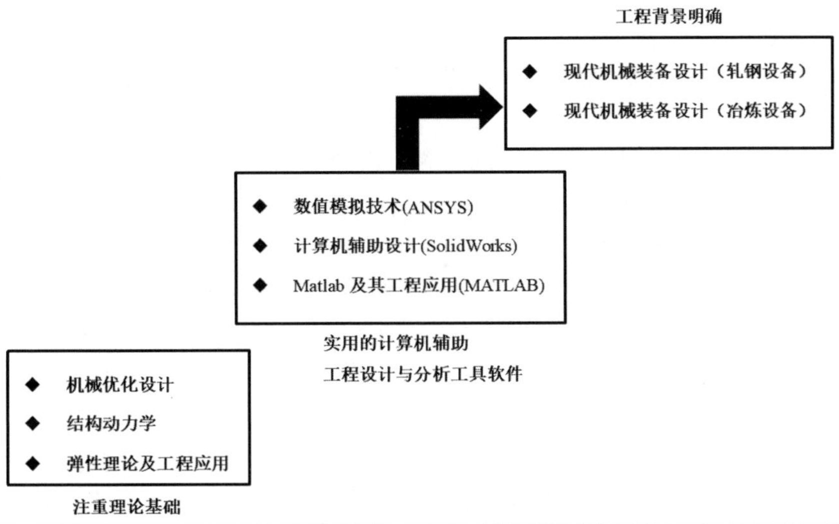


**图 4 燕山大学工程设计与分析专业课程设计路径**

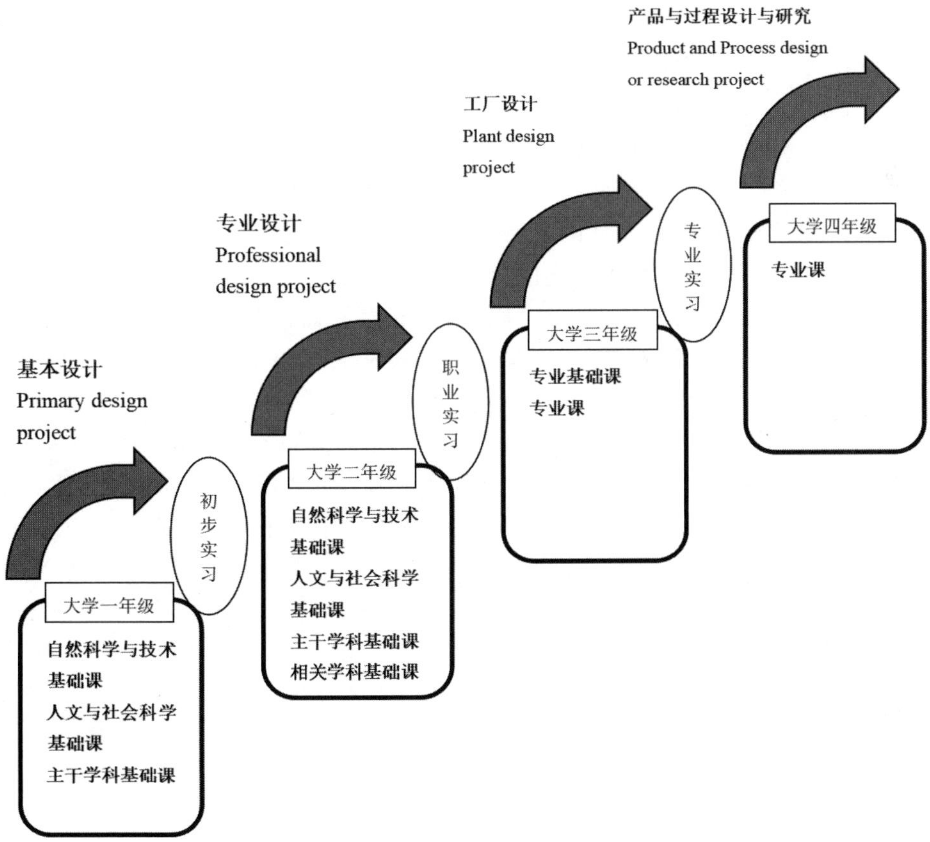


**图 5 北京石油化工学院化学工程学院化学工程与工艺专业的课程计划总体结构设计路径**

上海应用技术学院构建了基于CDIO的一体化专业培养方案(平台+模块)。“平台”提供工程技术基础课程,满足通识与知识系统性要求。“模块”满足个性化和分层要求,实现有限区别的能力培养目标,设置“基本型”“工程应用型”“工程设计和研究型”等模块和层次。增开了实践性课程,如“自动化工程设计”“全集成自动化技术”“西门子职业认证培训”“创意设计”“创新设计”“柔性制造系统设计”“技术创新与新产品研发管理”“工程管理”等课程。

江南大学通信与控制工程学院将CDIO教育理念应用到自动化专业培养方案的构建中,并在思想品德、科学精神、工程能力方面进行提升,提出了CDIO-P[P代表提升(promotion)]的人才培养模式,构建了以4级“项目”为核心的本科培养体系和多模式的研究生培养体系,创立了“理论学习、实践培训和工程应用”三结合的自动化创新人才培养方案,使学生具有扎实的基础理论、较强的项目开发设计能力、创新能力、团队精神和沟通能力[22]。

### 4.4 实施基于项目等的教学方法,探寻主动教与学

CDIO工程教育模式不仅要求教学目标的变革,相应的教学设计、教学方法也要进行改革。各试点学校都十分注重教学方式与方法的改革,在基于项目或问题的学习(project based learning/problem based learning)方面进行了有益探索与实践,强调以“工程的方法”培养学生。

燕山大学在实施基于项目等的教学方法、探寻主动教与学方面积累了诸多成功经验。以该校的机械工程学院设计与分析专业为例,该专业以CDIO工程教育理念为指导,共设置课程三级项目7项、三级实物项目1项、二级项目1项、一级项目1项;以课程项目为载体,构建“冶金机械装备结构与CAD/CAE技术、实验/实践”一体化项目课程体系(图6)。

该项目课程体系十分注重专业基础知识和工程应用能力的培养。

在做好项目课程体系顶层设计的基础上,又开始了各二级项目和三级项目的设计和实践。比如,学院成立跨专业的专业教学团队,整合了“机电一体化系统设计”“单片机”以及“机器人技术”3门课程及其项目,提出了以“智能车及灌篮机器人系统的设计与制作”为主载体的二级项目架构(图7),构建了集“课堂教学、讨论互动、动手实验、项目研究、课程设计”五位一体并且有机融合的课程教学体系,实现了多方位培养学生的综合能力和素质。

以2009年已完成的项目式教学为例,其共分两个阶段:第一阶段(三级项目实施阶段)为基于“机电一体化系统设计”和“单片机原理及应用”两门课程的三级研究项目,课程组选择的项目是智能小车的设计与制作,该项目需要综合运用以单片机控制技术为核心的机电一体化系统设计知识;第二阶段(二级项目实施阶段)为利用四周的专业课程设计周期,让学生将课程项目阶段完成的智能小车升级为简单的移动式抓取机器人和搬运机器人,并通过书面工作报告、汇报讲演和分组搬运物料竞赛等方式进行验收考核。学生自主完成从方案设计、工程设计、加工制作、集成调试直到比赛的全部过程。在项目的考核中引入了成本考核指标,并且创造性地引入了学生的自评分。

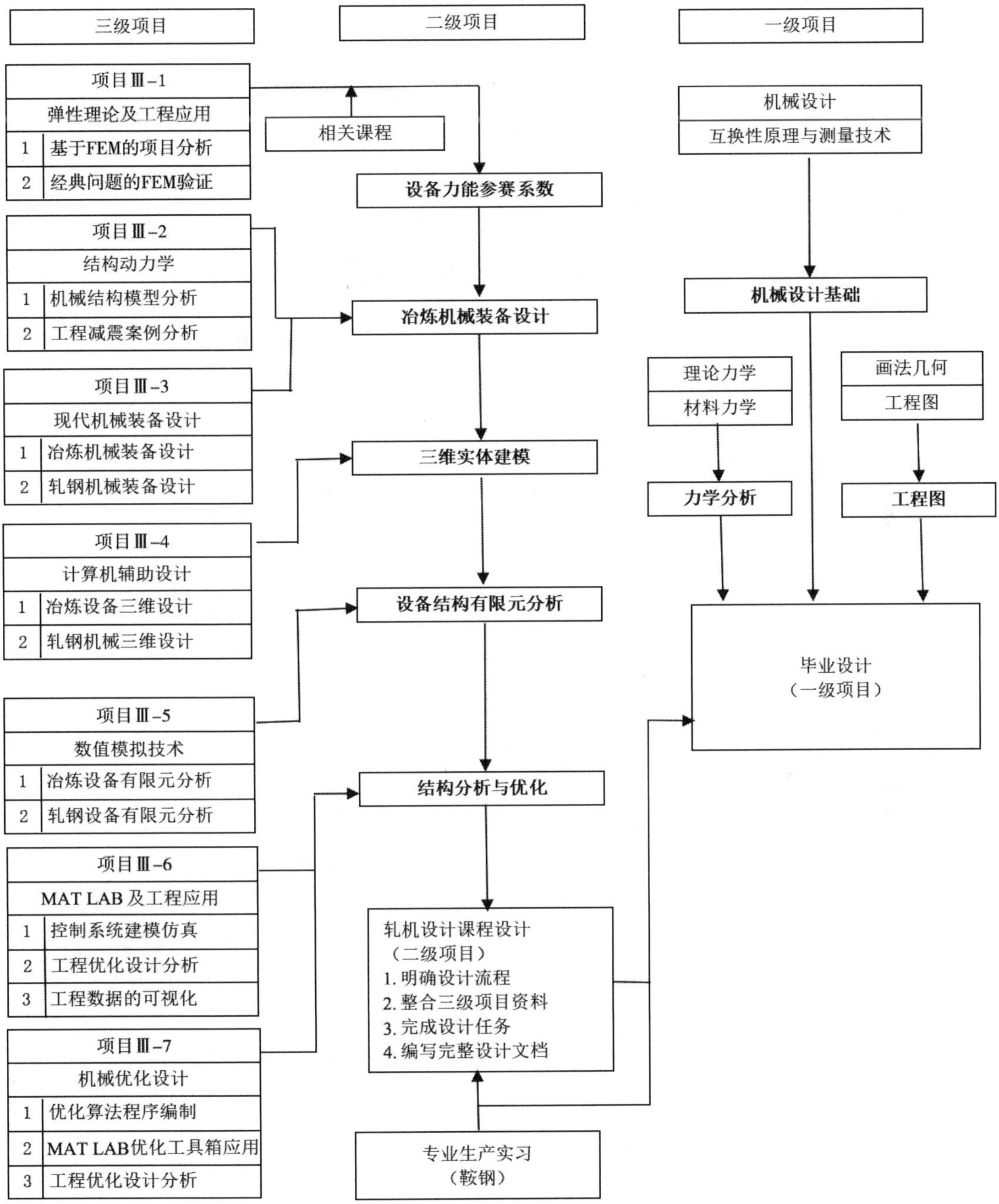


**图6 燕山大学工程设计与分析专业项目体系结构**

对于项目式教学改革的实践,学生们认为此种教学体验“是一场不同寻常的经历,全身心投入其中,用汗水浇灌出作品,并最终验收成功,是一道美丽的风景”;此种教学方式“使我们无论是课程知识,还是自身综合能力都有所提高,都学到了很多东西,充分发挥了自主创新能力,我们真正得到了成长”;这些收获“必将终身受用,使我们更有信心与能力面对更大的挑战”。

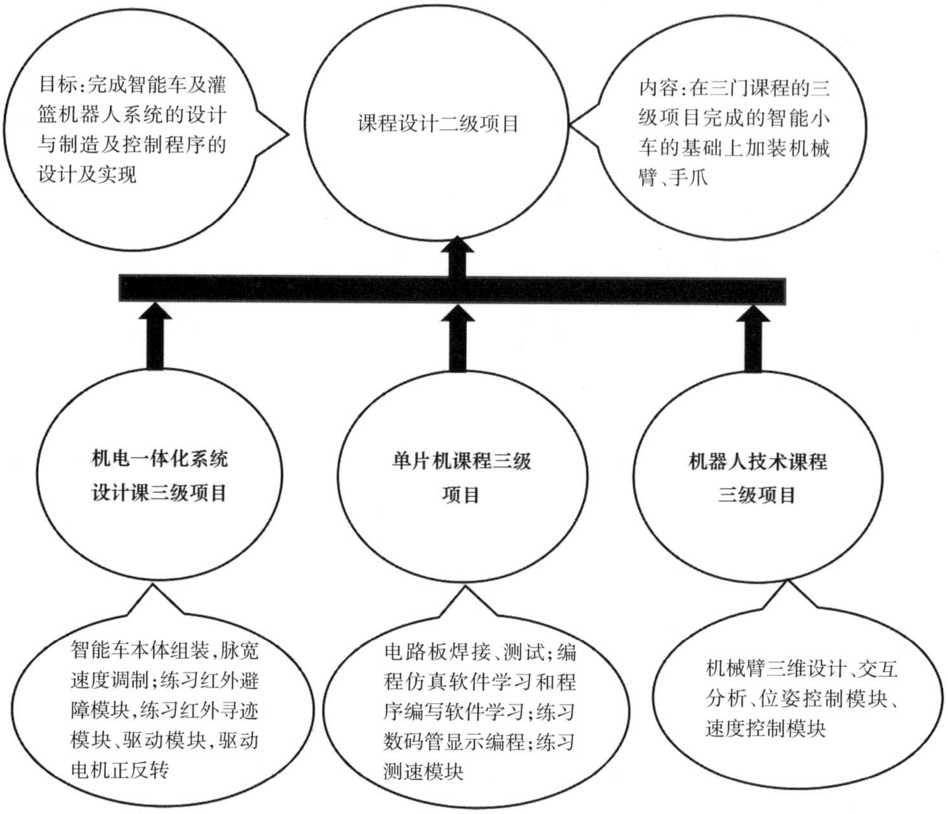


**图 7　智能车及灌篮机器人系统的设计与制作**

东北石油大学机械设计制造及其自动化专业在三级项目中，以 3~5 人为单位自发形成设计小组，完成下述内容。①项目调研：查阅资料，拟定项目范畴和设计内容。②项目申报：功能、原理、创新性、可行性论证。③项目开展：制订研究计划，分配设计任务，选择设计工具和仿真工具，开展项目设计。④项目汇报：提交项目日志、设计报告。在项目的全过程中，教师采取跟踪方式对学生进行辅导；每个阶段项目小组都要进行公开汇报，并且需要回答指导老师和其他项目小组提出的问题，及时改进，完善设计。小组项目部分占用一部分教学学时，教师和学生利用课余时间开展该项目内容。小组项目的实现流程如图 8 所示。

上海第二工业大学在“程序设计基础”课程教学中，由任课教师将学生分成 4 人一组的小组团队，并给学生配备课余上机机房；每次课内上机前，要求学生必须预先对所布置的实践作业进行认真、充分的尝试，遇到问题时先经过小组内讨论、研究，对解决不了的问题，带着思考在课内上机中聆听教师讲解，寻求解决办法。另外还开设了学习论坛网站，在网站上解惑答疑，推荐参考书，学生们可以相互交流，递交作业，下载资料；学习论坛网站受到了学生的欢迎，也大大提高了学生学习的积极性。

北京石油化工学院信息工程学院在“接口技术”课程中，应用问题教学法来革新。以问题为主线，贯穿课堂教学的整个过程；以问题来“抓住”学生，引领学生去思考；充分调动学生的学习积极性，吸引学生的注意力；活跃课堂气氛。在“多媒体技术与应用”课程中，采取了全新的网络互动教学模式组织教学，使现代教育技术的应用与学生学习过程的组织和管理融为一体。在“模拟电子技术”课程中，应用课题研究式教学法，强调以学生为中心，学生不是被动地接受知识，而是积极地建构知识；教师是学生主动构建知识的帮助者、促进者，而不是知识的传递者、灌输者。通过课题研究型学习，再结合其他教学方法，教师帮助学生，使学生各方面的能力得到发展和提高。

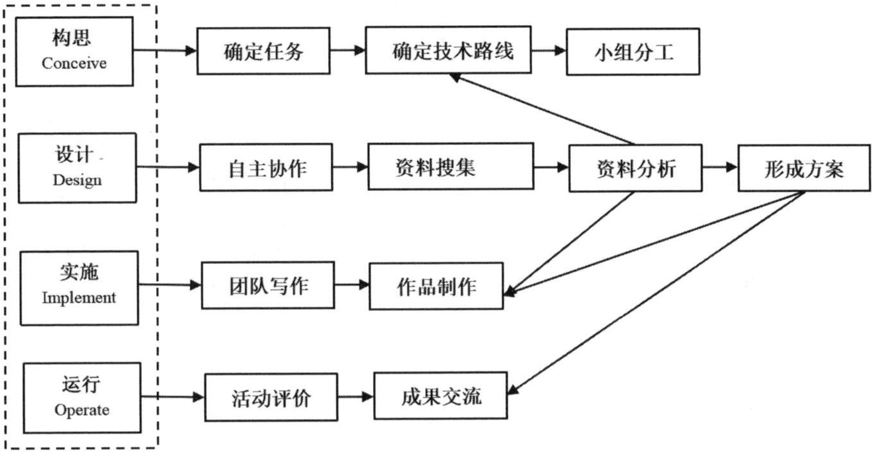


**图 8　东北石油大学机械设计制造及其自动化专业小组项目的实现流程**

上海应用技术学院在教学改革方面把教学典型性与工程相似性相结合，开展 CDIO 课程项目；压缩理论课时增加实践课时，摆脱实验台约束，增加实践性实验；通过小组合作实验、项目答辩、撰写小论文和报告，锻炼非课程能力等。

广州大学机械设计制造及其自动化专业构建“在实践中学习，在学习中实践”的主动学习、研究性学习等方法体系和教学模式。

### 4.5　改进教学管理流程，探讨学生能力的考核方法

为了适应 CDIO 中基于项目/问题等教学方法和教学流程的改变，各试点高校积极改进教学管理流程，探讨学生能力的考核方法，正逐步形成和完善自身特色的教学质量评估与保障体系。

成都信息工程学院依托自身优势，在教学过程监控与考核方面进行了诸多有益的探索，编制了创新团队及其项目的管理架构（图 9），并采取了计算机数据库管理的模式，极大地增强了基于项目式学习管理的便利性，并且制定了严格的实施计划节点（表 1）。

东北石油大学机械设计制造及其自动化专业针对传统的项目考核方式在能力考核方面存在的问题，如对学生协作能力、创新能力、组织表达能力、信息获取能力、社会活动能力以及沟通表达能力等方面考核的不足，设计了一种多元课程考核方法：学生综合成绩=笔试40%+讨论 20%+实验与实践 20%+平时成绩 20%。其中实验与实践成绩=个人成绩+团队成绩+答辩成绩。具体见表 2。

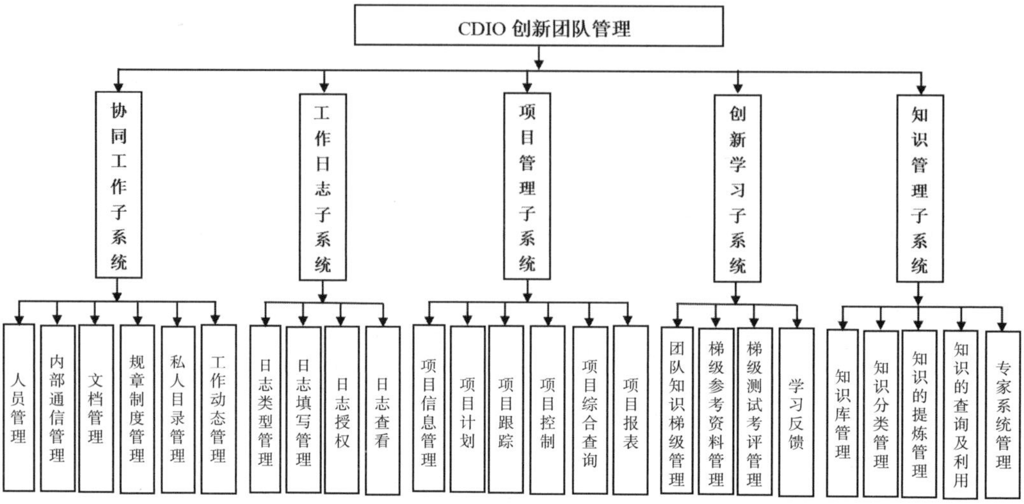


**图 9　成都信息工程学院创新团队及其项目的管理架构**

**表 1　成都信息工程学院设计的项目实施设计节点**

| 控制节点 | | 实施形式 | 执行时间 | | | 成果表现形式 |
|---|---|---|---|---|---|---|
| 阶段 | 实施内容 | | 学期 | 周 | 学时 | |
| 构思 | 机器人的入门说明 | 教师讲授 | 2 | 5 | 4 | 讲义/实物演示 |
| | 设计任务书编制 | 学生自主、教师指导 | | 6~8 | 12 | 提交设计任务书 |
| 设计 | 设计方案中期检查 | 小组答辩 | | 12 | — | 可行性分析报告、设计资料 |
| | 设计方案确定 | 分组答辩 | | 16 | — | 设计图纸 |
| 实施 | 方案实施要求说明 | 教师讲授 | 3 | 5 | 2 | 讲义 |
| | 方案实施计划检查 | 小组答辩 | | 7 | — | 提交实施计划 |
| | 方案实施中期检查 | 实物展示/小组答辩 | | 12 | — | 部件测试数据、部分实物（硬件或程序清单） |
| | 制作成果检查 | 实物展示/分组答辩 | | 16 | — | 实物（硬件或程序清单）、施工图纸/调试报告 |
| 运行 | 运行要求说明 | 教师讲授 | 4 | 5 | 1 | 讲义 |
| | 运行方案拟定 | 学生自主、教师指导 | | 6 | — | 提交运行方案书 |
| | 运行成果检查 | 实物演示/分组答辩 | | 12 | — | 实物（硬件或程序清单）、运行报告书 |
| | 资料整理、经验总结 | 学生自主、教师指导 | | — | — | 资料归档、优秀表彰 |

表 2　东北石油大学机械设计制造及其自动化专业项目设计能力评价表

| 类别 | 知识/能力 | 占比 |
| --- | --- | --- |
| 技术知识 | 本课程基本知识(1~10 分) | 30% |
| | 专业基础知识(1~10 分) | |
| | 专业学科知识(1~10 分) | |
| 工程能力 | 独立解决问题的能力(1~6 分) | 30% |
| | 应用知识、发现知识的能力(1~6 分) | |
| | 逻辑思维和系统思维(1~6 分) | |
| | 创造性思维和终身学习能力(1~6 分) | |
| | 职业态度、职业素质与社会责任感(包括质量、成本和环保意识等)(1~6 分) | |
| 团队能力 | 团队合作能力(包括领导、组织和执行力)(1~10 分) | 20% |
| | 表达交流能力(包括外语能力)(1~10 分) | |
| CDIO 能力 | 对企业文化的了解和社会多元文化的认识(1~10 分) | 20% |
| | 对开发产品全过程及相互关系的了解(1~10 分) | |

### 4.6　建设 CDIO 工程实践环境,加强实践能力培养

CDIO 标准 5 是设计建造经验,标准 6 是工程实践场所;CDIO 要求学生在教育过程中就接触到真正的工程实践,直接体验产品的全生命周期,在比较真实的环境中,培养学生系统全面的知识、能力和素质。

试点高校在构建 CDIO 实践场所与环境方面,或投入资金新建,或整合现有资源,以符合现代工程科技人才培养的要求。

东北石油大学机械设计制造及其自动化专业基于 CDIO 理念,筹建了创新设计与实践实验室,配置了必要的设备、配件和工具。例如,单片机实验系统,作为单片机原理及应用课程的实验手段和条件,用于训练学生的单片机初步应用能力,为机电一体化原理及应用课程奠定实践基础;自动控制雕刻机,作为数控加工技术课程与机电一体化原理及应用课程的实验手段和条件,用于培养学生的系统控制和数控加工方面的初步能力,为机电一体化创新设计奠定理论和实践基础;数控驱动卡与自动控制雕刻机配套使用,便于系统软件开发和升级;迷你型车床与迷你型铣床作为创新实验项目实施的必备工具,可以加工软金属和非金属材料制成的多种模型零件,既节省成本,也训练学生的实际操作能力,同时该设备作为机床主体,叠加单片机或 PLC(可编程逻辑控制器)等机电一体化控制系统,可以自主开发出小型数控机床,自身可以派生为创新项目;智能抽油机模拟实验装置作为石油钻采机械课程和机电一体化原理及应用课程的实验手段和条件,用于培养学生对主要采油设备的工作性能的理解和掌握,并有助于学生开拓思维,树立科技研发与创新的工程意识。

南京工程学院工程基础实验与训练中心在自动化(系统集成)专业全面实施 CDIO 工程教育模式改革研究与实践,遵循"学以致用"的办学理念,坚持校企合作的办学道路,在认真学习研究国外 CDIO 工程教育成功经验的同时,在人才培养方案、产学合作共建实验室、

理实一体化课程开发、综合项目实训、实施“做中学”等方面,全方位地进行了基于国际 CDIO 工程教育理念的人才培养模式的研究和探索。该学院借助校企共建实验实训中心平台,构建了技术知识、工程实践和综合素质三者结合的教学体系,在自动化(系统集成)专业进行教学改革实践,取得了良好的成效,学生的实践能力、综合能力、创新能力和就业层次得到明显提高。

## 5 CDIO 在中国发展中存在的问题

CDIO 模式在中国的影响日益扩大,实施 CDIO 改革的高校越来越多,成效也越来越显著。这些高校的 CDIO 改革可以分为如下几类:第一类,在深入思考工程教育改革的背景下,应用 CDIO 模式并有所创新;第二类,基本能够把握 CDIO 的主要特点,在学习其他高校 CDIO 改革的基础上,在本校进行 CDIO 改革;第三类,在人才培养的部分环节借鉴了 CDIO 方法,但整体上仍是传统的人才培养模式;第四类,标称 CDIO,但尚未实质进行 CDIO 改革。因此,CDIO 模式在中国的发展也存在一些理论上的误读和实践中的偏差,需要各方深入思考和探索。

### 5.1 在理解 CDIO 中存在的偏差

自中华人民共和国成立以来,中国工程教育逐渐引进了发达国家的人才培养模式。中华人民共和国成立初期,主要学习苏联模式以适应计划经济的人才需要;改革开放以来,学习美欧模式特别是美国的工程教育模式以适应市场经济的人才培养。但是在从计划经济下的专才培养模式向市场经济下的通才教育模式转变的过程中,还存在如何转变、转变的速度等问题。这是个渐变的过程,专才培养的特征还不可能一下子消除,还需要一段时间。这两种模式的支持者以及这两种模式的教育教学管理与研究人员同时存在,两种模式共存是现阶段工程教育的重要特点。其实这两种模式均在历史与现实的环境下受到前所未有的挑战,都在发生改变,变革的速度也是前所未有的。世界各国的各种工程教育改革火热进行,工程教育的认证标准也反映了这种变化。

CDIO 工程教育改革就是在这样的社会环境下产生和发展起来的。由于种种原因,我国工程教育界对 CDIO 有各种不同的态度:一种态度是,MIT 发起的一定是好的东西,以最快的速度引进,实施后可以告诉学生,学院和 MIT 的教育模式一样;另一种态度是,CDIO 是欧美的东西,与中国国情不符;还有的人认为,CDIO 强调工程实践,不适合“985 工程”大学和研究型大学的学生培养……

其实,以上这几种意见都有偏颇。汕头大学将 CDIO 引入我国的工程教育改革,是由于 CDIO 的两个重要文件:详细的 CDIO 能力大纲(专业培养标准)和 CDIO 的 12 条标准。CDIO 能力大纲是目前能在文献资料中找到的在工程教育目标上最为详细的知识、能力和素质的综合表述。CDIO 能力大纲的建立需要大量的时间和精力,它代表了工业界,包括研发单位、校友、工科教师和各种利益相关者的期待,经历了复杂的研究和反复改进的过程,它可适用于教学型和研究型大学的本科教育。此外,CDIO 的大纲满足美国工程与技术认证委员会和加拿大工程认证委员会工程认证的要求。CDIO 的 12 条标准凝聚了很多实施

CDIO 改革的学校和工程教育工作者、科研工作者的心血,积累了许多重要的实践经验,可以成为很好的教育改革指南。通过 CDIO 国际合作组织这个平台和 CDIO 会议,参加者可以分享教育改革的经验和成果。

汕头大学引入 CDIO 的目的很简单,就是在其他国家成功的工程教育改革的经验基础上,将该培养模式本土化,以适应中国国情和需要,以最快的速度学习国际水平的人才培养模式,并在此基础上再创新,探索建立自己的培养模式,培养出高水平的创新人才,使众多的企业具有国际竞争力,至于叫"CDIO"还是叫其他名字并不重要。

研究型大学工程人才的培养也应该有工程的能力和素质, CDIO 大纲也包括科研能力和设计创新能力的培养。这样来看,CDIO 能够适应各种教学和研究型大学。以美国参加 CDIO 协作组织的大学为例,麻省理工学院、斯坦福大学、密歇根大学、杜克大学等均是研究型大学。越来越多的国家的大学开展了 CDIO 的教育改革,在我国工业化、信息化、城镇化、市场化、国际化深入发展的背景下,进行教育教学改革,培养具有国际竞争力的工程科技人才是至关重要的。

### 5.2 在认识 CDIO 中出现的偏差

在 CDIO 的传播过程中,还存在将 CDIO 形式化、概念化、肤浅化的倾向。有些高校为改革而改革,重形式轻实质。

CDIO 引入我国以来,表现出强大的影响力,各类院校积极参与 CDIO 的研究与应用,队伍逐渐扩大。但是,也有些学校只是随波逐流或迎合改革热潮,或为了申请项目课题和得到教育行政部门的资源支持等而进行形式上的研究和改革,并未进行本质意义上的改革。这必然会导致资源的浪费以及改革质量的下降。关于这点,教育部高教司理工处的领导在 2008 年的中国 CDIO 工程教育模式研讨会上就强调指出,要针对工程教育目前存在的问题,进行改革探索,不要为了 CDIO 而 CDIO。

此外,我国 CDIO 改革中还有将 CDIO 改革模式单一化的倾向,一些高校模仿多于创新。CDIO 工程教育的理念、CDIO 能力大纲和 12 条标准,所有的工科院校和工科专业都可以借鉴和参考,但是不同类型和不同层次的高校,不宜照搬照抄,高校应更多地主动创造而不是互相模仿。不同层次和类型的高校,对未来工程师的培养要求不同,每个学校所处的社会环境与办学特色也不一样,那么所进行的 CDIO 改革也必然是不同的。

还有,在当前 CDIO 工程教育改革中,存在着一些照抄照搬、脱离本校历史与特色的现象,如个别学校的培养方案、课程体系、教学大纲,甚至实践项目,被一些学校简单模仿。当然,在改革初期,模仿是必要的。但是,随着改革的深化,每个学校、每个专业的创造性应该被高度激发出来。

### 5.3 在实践 CDIO 中出现的偏差

在我国 CDIO 改革实践中还存在着一些偏差,如误解、曲解 CDIO。例如,把 CDIO 工程教育简化为基于问题的教学,把 CDIO 工程教育等同于基于项目的教学,把 CDIO 工程教育曲解为典型产品组织教学,把 CDIO 工程教育简单地视为"做中学"[26]。这些偏差和误解影响了 CDIO 改革的正确、深入进行。

虽然基于问题的教学、基于项目的教学等教学方法都可用于 CDIO 教育改革中，但从本质上说，CDIO 不仅仅是这些教学方法的改变。CDIO 是一种符合国际共识的、全面的、系统的工程教育改革。它是一种工程教育的理念或者模式，贯穿于人才培养的各个阶段，涵盖教育改革完整的、全部的过程，它至少要在整个专业层面上规划、设计和实施，才能取得期待的改革效果。

## 6 对中国工程教育改革的观察与思考

近年来，中国工程教育的办学条件、财政投入、教学投入、实验设备、师资条件等方面有了较大的改善，许多经济发达地区的大学办学的硬件条件已经赶上国外同类院校。同时，从国家到省级的教育主管部门以及学校的领导，对工程教育的重视程度也不比发达国家低。但是，我们培养的人才同一些发达国家培养的人才在工程创新能力方面尚有差距，原因是什么？我们又该如何进一步努力？分析起来可能至少包括以下几个方面。

### 6.1 推进工程教育认证体系的建立与完善

以《华盛顿协议》组织成员为例，工程教育认证系统比较完善而且不断改进。该组织以职业协会为依托，根据建立的标准和严格的认证过程，以实事求是的态度，按照工业界对大学工程人才培养的要求对大学进行系统评价，从而对工程教育质量严格要求，促进其不断改进，对不符合要求（如办学条件差、水平低）的院校及时警告；对于认证通过的专业，一般也有改进建议和整改要求，以促使学系和专业不断进步。这样一来，学校就不得不注意吸收优质生源并重视办学的质量和水平。

我国近年来也尝试开展了工程教育认证，已经取得了又好又快的进步。但工程教育认证方法是否要更加深入和具体，真正考查学生的工程师能力？如何建立和实施工程教育质量和培养目标的保障体系？这一系列问题，仍需大家的思考。

### 6.2 工程教育内部质量保证体系与严格的教学管理制度

以美、加大学为例，其多年来形成了较严格和系统的教学过程管理体制，整合教学各个环节的管理，譬如课程改变（包括内容增加和去除课程），都有一个自下而上学术民主的充分论证过程，从专业、系、学院直至学校建立了一套系统的专业和课程增减与改变的严格管理过程和制度。各专业每年都会对课程进行调整和改进，逐渐形成稳定的培养方案和课程体系。

每一门课程的大纲确定后，任课教师必须严格执行课程大纲的要求，敢于淘汰学习很差的学生。当然，严格保证课程质量可能导致有些学生不及格，教师工作量和负担相应增加；也有可能导致有些学生不满意，可能影响教师课程评估结果等。但严格要求，恰恰是保证教育质量的基础。

国内的高校在工程教育内部质量保证体系与严格的教学管理制度建设方面与西方发达

国家的高校相比还有一些差距,通过工程认证、教学制度和质量管理系统的建立和完善,这些问题会逐渐得到解决。

### 6.3 校领导、教师与学生对待教学的态度

由于现有的评价制度,大学的校领导特别是研究型大学的校领导面对各种压力,特别是大学和学科排名的名次与科研成果和科研指标联系密切,因此校领导重视科研是可以理解的。教师是教学和科研的主体,且教师个人和教师整体是决定教育质量的主要因素。

大学教师的主要任务包括三个方面:教学、科研和服务。在这三者中,由于科研成果比教学成果显得更加“辉煌”,因此在中外大学特别是研究型大学中,存在不同程度的重科研、轻教学的现象。如何理解教学的研究和实践也是学术工作(scholarship),怎么解决这个问题,是中外大学的领导面临的共同难题。

教师是道德和良心的职业。教师可以不是顶尖的学者,但必须热爱教育、热爱教学、热爱学生。同是一门课或一节课,教师的不同态度决定了投入的时间与精力会相差巨大。特别是实施 CDIO 教育改革的项目,所用的时间和精力都会大幅度增加。许多教学改革导致授课学时减少,但教师投入的工作量可能反而会增加,如果还按授课学时计算岗位津贴,就会使教师岗位津贴减少。另外,如果要提高教学质量必定要用到更多的精力,而未必增加学时,因此以学时计算工作量或津贴是教学质量改进的障碍,领导必须予以充分考虑。教学的贡献虽然没有个人科研成果那么“辉煌”,但对培养学生和提高学校和国家工程人才的质量都非常重要。

工程教育改革需要学校领导与教师投入大量精力,需要扎扎实实地做好课程与教学实践,需要把学生的需求和教育质量放在学校的核心位置,而不仅仅是追求科研指标和名气。许多世界著名的优秀大学对本科教育和质量的重视,值得我国大学借鉴。因此,改革现有的教师职称评审制度,使教学优秀的教师(高水平的教学也是学问和重要的能力)一样可以晋升为教授等高级职务,改革工资津贴绩效分配制度,扭转学校特别是某些研究型大学重科研、轻教学的状况,可能是现阶段提高我国工程教育质量的关键步骤。

### 6.4 工业界与社会参与工程教育改革过程的积极性

以美国为例,工业界出于自身利益需要,通过职业协会和咨询机构的工作,积极参与高校的工程教育;有些企业对大学的工程人才培养提出意见和建议,为学生提供实习机会;工程师参与学生培养的各种活动,直接参加毕业设计/论文的指导,开设各种讲座;等等。CDIO 工程教育改革综合了工业界对人才的要求,并且强调教师工程实践能力对教育改革的重要性。

对我国现阶段大部分的高校来说,工业界与社会参与工程教育改革过程的积极性有待提高。他们渴望有更多适合企业文化的毕业生,也有热情参与学校或国家的工程教育改革进程,但现阶段相应的渠道或制度没有建立或者运行不畅。因此,这些方面亟待加强和完善。

## 7　CDIO 在中国的展望

自 2005 年汕头大学开展 CDIO 改革以来，中国已有许多所学校以各种方式用 CDIO 工程教育理念和方法对传统的工程教育进行改革。教育部高教司理工处的精心指导和有力的支持使 CDIO 在中国高等工程教育改革中得以有组织和有步骤地应用。从这几年国内高校的试点实践来看，CDIO 可以成为提高工程人才培养质量、实施"质量工程"的重要着力点，可以为专业结构调整、特色专业建设提供范例；CDIO 为改进人才培养模式提供了系统的方法，已经起到引领高等工程教育改革的作用，也会有力促进工程教育认证与大学内部质量保证体系的建立，还可以加速我国工程教育国际化的进程。教育部 2010 年启动的卓越工程师教育培养计划也为 CDIO 在中国工程教育中的应用提供了一个新机遇。CDIO 较好地回应了中国工程教育改革的挑战，CDIO 在中国的应用将更加广泛多样并富于变化。

从应用 CDIO 改革的高校类型来看，有研究型大学，也有教学型大学，还有高职高专。当然，研究型大学、教学型大学、高职高专几类学校在实施 CDIO 的改革中侧重点各不相同。研究型大学以培养学术型、研究型的工程科学人才、研究开发人员和设计工程师为主，毕业生也必须具备工程师所需要的能力和素质。教学型大学工程人才培养目标的定位可能要突出应用型，以服务地方经济建设为主，着力培养能在生产、工程第一线从事工程实施和管理的工程技术人才（生产工程师）。高职高专主要培养适应生产、建设、管理、服务第一线需要的高等技术应用型专门人才。中国高等职业教育研究会于 2010 年 6 月发布了《关于征集 CDIO 工程教育模式首批高等职业院校试点单位的通知》，试点的专业包括机械类、电气类（包括计算机）、土木类和化工类四个专业类别。

从应用 CDIO 的学科专业来看，我国一开始就突破了 CDIO 创立之初的机械工程、汽车、航空和电力工程专业。目前我国高校实施 CDIO 改革的专业，主要是试点工作组确定的机械类、电气类、土木类和化工类四大类，除此之外，大量自发实施 CDIO 改革的专业涉及几乎所有的工科专业，甚至应用于工程教育之外的专业。

从应用 CDIO 的教育层次来看，不管是中国还是外国，主要是在本科教育阶段。汕头大学工学院正在尝试在研究生教育中进行 CDIO 改革。欧洲一些高校也有兴趣将 CDIO 扩展到硕士生教育。旨在培养项目管理、交流能力和研究能力的博士计划也开始出现，特别是培养"工业博士"的计划。当然，这就带来了两个问题：硕士和博士的能力目标是什么？CDIO 大纲和标准中哪些可以适用于研究生教育，哪些需要改进和增减？

从 CDIO 改革本身来看，CDIO 将融汇更多高校的创造性经验，内涵将更加丰富。CDIO 是一个开放的系统，支持各国、各学校、各专业根据自己的实际情况进行自主改革。在未来的改革中，各院校应以开放的心态在国际工程教育改革的大背景下理解 CDIO，而不应被其桎梏，应该主动创新，探索多种培养方式。

汕头大学在实施 CDIO 的过程中，结合中国国情构建了以设计为导向的 EIP-CDIO，对 CDIO 教育模式进行了系统性的再创新，并在学校发展"先进本科教育"的理念指导下，融合了汕头大学人才培养目标体系的 18 个全校通用目标，今后还拟将汕头大学整合思维应用其中；汕头大学整合思维（STU-in-Thinking）是集成批判性思维、创造性思维和系统性思维模式的系统解决问题的方法。我们相信 CDIO 在中国的实施和再创新，一定会推动工科教育改革的深入，进一步提高工程教育的质量。

## 8 结论

汕头大学以及其他试点高校的实践经验告诉我们，要充分认识到成功实施 CDIO 工程教育改革是一个复杂的系统工程，要求校（院）领导的全力支持和周密思考与规划。在实施过程中要找准切入点，集聚一批热心教育改革、热爱教学的骨干，让学生积极参与其中。在全面实施前，要有计划地进行课程试点以取得经验。同时要改变教师薪酬分配制度，调动和保护热心教育改革、注重教学质量的教师的积极性。

我们相信，只要坚持细致认真做事，真诚努力不松懈，注重团队协作，经过几年探索与实践，就一定会看到我们培养的学生在知识、能力、素质等方面的明显提升。通过大家的共同努力，CDIO 工程教育培养模式在中国一定会结出硕果。

## 致谢

CDIO 在中国发展得到了当时教育部相关领导的大力支持，他们对 CDIO 在中国工程教育的实施、再创新和应用给予了强有力的领导。

成都信息工程学院周定文校长对中国 CDIO 试点工作组的工作给予了有力的领导与支持，《高等工程教育研究》的主编姜嘉乐自 2007 年以来为 CDIO 改革的工作做了大量工作，浙江大学的王沛民教授积极支持 CDIO 工作的实施，北京交通大学教授、联合国教科文组织教席查建中教授积极宣传和介绍 CDIO，为 CDIO 在中国实施做了很好的舆论工作。

CDIO 试点高校，如成都信息工程学院、燕山大学、北京石油化工学院、大连东软信息学院、南京工程学院、广州大学、东北石油大学、河北工程大学、黑龙江工程学院、上海第二工业大学、浙江万里学院等为本文的撰写提供了该校的 CDIO 试点总结报告。这些总结报告对完成本文的工作至关重要，再次深表谢意。

由于篇幅有限，不可能全面介绍所有成功实施 CDIO 的院校的情况，不当之处在所难免，请读者指正。

在汕头大学实施 CDIO 的过程中，李嘉诚基金会给予了强有力的支持和帮助，汕头大学工学院全体教师员工积极参与改革并做出了重要贡献，笔者在此一并表示衷心感谢。

### 参考文献

[1] CRAWLEY E F, MALMQVIST J, ÖSTLUND S, et al. 重新认识工程教育：国际 CDIO 培养模式与方法[M]. 顾佩华，沈民奋，陆小华，译. 北京：高等教育出版社，2009.

[2] 雷环，汤威颐， CRAWLEY E F. 培养创新型、多层次、专业化的工程科技人才：CDIO 工程教育改革的人才理念和培养模式[J]. 高等工程教育研究，2009（5）：29-35.

[3] 顾佩华，沈民奋，李升平，等. 从 CDIO 到 EIP-CDIO：汕头大学工程教育与人才培养模式探索[J]. 高等工程教育研究，2008（1）：12-20.

[4] YELLOWLEY I，GU P H. Design directed engineering education[J]. Journal of engineering design and innovation，2005，1(1)：1-7.
[5] 陆小华，熊光晶，陈珠琳. 设计导向的工程教育改革理念[J]. 高等工程教育研究，2007(6)：83-87.
[6] 邹晓东. 科学与工程教育创新[M]. 北京：科学出版社，2010.
[7] 中国工程院教育委员会. 探寻中国工程教育改革之路："新形势下工程教育的改革与发展"高层论坛纪要[J]. 高等工程教育研究，2007(6)：43-47.
[8] 熊玲，李忠. 新世纪我国高等工程人才需求调查报告[J]. 现代教育管理，2010(7)：3-6.
[9] 任荃. 工程教育能力缘何世界垫底？[N]. 文汇报，2007-09-25(005).
[10] 陈金江，许晓东. 2007 年全国工程教育改革研讨会纪要[J]. 高等工程教育研究，2007(6)：48-49，77.
[11] 李晓强，孔寒冰，王沛民. 部署新世纪的工程教育行动：兼评美国"2020 工程师"《行动报告》[J]. 高等工程教育研究，2006(4)：14-18.
[12] 杨叔子. 谈谈我对"CDIO——工程文化教育"的认识[J]. 中国大学教学，2008(9)：6-7，30.
[13] CRAWLEY E，MALMQVIST J，LRCAS W，et al. The CDIO syllabus v2.0—an updated statement of goals for engineering education[C]. Proceedings of the 7th International CDIO Conference. Technical University of Denmark，Copenhagen，June 20-23，2011.
[14] 陈新民. 应用型本科的课程改革：培养目标、课程体系与教学方法 [J]. 中国大学教学，2011(7)：27-30.
[15] 陈劲，胡建雄. 面向创新型国家的工程教育改革研究[M]. 北京：中国人民大学出版社，2006.
[16] 沈艳霞，潘庭龙，纪志成. CDIO-P 培养模式下运动控制系统课程改革探索 [J]. 江南大学学报(教育科学版)，2009，29(3)：270-273.
[17] 王天宝，程卫东. 基于 CDIO 的创新型工程人才培养模式研究与实践：成都信息工程学院的工程教育改革实践[J]. 高等工程教育研究，2010(1)：25-31.
[18] 温涛. 基于 TOPCARES-CDIO 的一体化人才培养模式探索与实践[J]. 计算机教育，2010(11)：23-29.
[19] 熊和平，岳爱臣. CDIO 工程教育模式：误解的澄明与风险的规避[J]. 高等工程教育研究，2009(5)：48-51.
[20] 田国强. 关于改善学风、教风的建议[J]. 中国大学教学，2006(1)：4-8.
[21] 郝维谦，龙正中. 高等教育史[M]. 海南：海南出版社，2000.
[22] BLOOM B S，ENGELHART M D，FURST E J，et al. Taxonomy of educational objectives：handbook Ⅰ：cognitive domain[M]. New York：Longman，1956.
[23] ANDERSON L W，KRATHWOHL D R，AIRASIAN P W，et al. A taxonomy for learning，teaching，and assessing：a revision of Bloom's taxonomy of educational objectives[M]. New York：Longman，2001：38-62.

# 基于“学习产出”( OBE )的工程教育模式
## ——汕头大学的实践与探索 ①

顾佩华 胡文龙 林 鹏 包能胜 陆小华 熊光晶 陈 严

**摘要:**受高等教育质量问责运动以及工程人才国际流动性增强等影响,欧美发达国家高等工程教育改革呈现出围绕预期学习产出( intended learning outcomes )组织开展教育教学的趋向。本文系统地阐述了 OBE 教育模式的概念、理论基础以及特点,介绍了汕头大学近年来 OBE 工程教育模式的实践与探索,就汕头大学 OBE 工程教育模式的实践架构、实施特点、实施重点、实施特色以及遇到的困难进行了详细阐述,以期为建设有弹性、高水平和可持续的 OBE 工程教育模式提供借鉴。

**关键词:**OBE;工程教育模式;预期学习产出;CDIO

## OBE Engineering Education Model
### —Practice and Exploration in Shantou University

*Gu Peihua, Hu Wenlong, Lin Peng, Bao Nengsheng, Lu Xiaohua, Xiong Guangjing, Chen Yan*

**Abstract:** In recent years, developed countries in Europe and America tend to shift their focus of higher education reform to a new model called "Outcome-Based Education (OBE)", due to the establishment of the higher education accountability system and the enhancement of international liquidity of engineering talents. This paper aims at providing a reference for the construction of a flexible, sustainable and high-quality OBE engineering education model. The first part elaborates on the conceptual framework, theoretical basis and distinguishing features of OBE model. The second part presents the research of Shantou University in exploring and practicing OBE model, by analyzing specific practice frameworks, distinguishing features, key implementation focuses and difficulties encountered during the process.

**Keywords:** OBE; engineering education model; intended learning outcomes; CDIO

## 1 OBE 概述

### 1. 概念

基于学习产出的教育模式( outcomes-based education, OBE )最早出现于美国和澳大利

① 本文刊登于《高等工程教育研究》2014 年第 1 期第 27~37 页。

亚的基础教育改革。从 20 世纪 80 年代到 90 年代早期，OBE 在美国教育界是一个十分流行的术语。美国学者斯派帝( Spady )撰写的《基于产出的教育模式:争议与答案》一书中对此模式进行了深入研究[1]。该书把 OBE 定义为“清晰地聚焦和组织教育系统,使之围绕确保学生获得在未来生活中获得实质性成功的经验”[1]。他认为 OBE 实现了教育范式的转换。因为,在 OBE 教育模式中,学生学到了什么和是否成功远比怎样学习和什么时候学习重要。西澳大利亚州教育部门把 OBE 定义为:“基于实现学生特定学习产出的教育过程。教育结构和课程被视为手段而非目的。如果它们无法为培养学生的特定能力做出贡献,它们就要被重建。学生产出驱动教育系统运行。”[2]特克( Tucker )认为,“outcomes-based education”与“outcomes focused education( OFE )”是同义词。无论是 OBE 还是 OFE,都是学习产出驱动整个课程活动和学生学习产出评价的结构与系统。

虽然定义繁多,但其共性较为明显。在 OBE 教育系统中,教育者必须对学生毕业时应达到的能力及其水平有清楚的构想,然后寻求设计适宜的教育结构来保证学生达到这些预期目标。学生产出而非教科书或教师经验成为驱动教育系统运作的动力,这显然同传统上内容驱动和重视投入的教育形成了鲜明对比。从这个意义上说，OBE 教育模式可被认为是一种教育范式的革新[3]。

**2. 框架**

OBE 是以预期学习产出为中心来组织、实施和评价教育的结构模式。阿查亚( Acharya )指出实施 OBE 教育模式主要有四个步骤:定义学习产出( defining )、实现学习产出( realizing )、评估学习产出( assessing )和使用学习产出( using )[4]。这涵盖了计划、实施、检查、行动各要素。

定义毕业生预期学习产出是首要的关键环节。学习产出定义要具有可操作性和具体性。参照欧美经验,布鲁姆的教育目标分类框架是被广泛使用的指南,它提供了描述学生知识、情感和技能掌握程度水平的词汇。为了实现预期学习产出,所有的教学计划和课程内容都遵循“回溯式设计”原则,实现完整的匹配矩阵。CDIO 工程教育改革的主要成果之一——CDIO 能力大纲就提供了关于工科毕业生学习产出的四层次分解方案,不同工科院校可根据办学定位和专业方向从中选择不同的组合与掌握程度。

评估学习产出是 OBE 教育模式中十分重要的环节,而这恰恰是国内高校做得较为薄弱的一环。按照美国高校学生学习评估实践的理论和经验,预期学习产出评估可划分为以下几个方面。按层次,学习产出评估可以分为课堂层面、专业层面和学校层面;按评估内容,可以分为直接评估和间接评估;按主体,可以分为教师、学生、校友、用人单位、管理者等。美国高校学生结果评估开展由来已久,已形成了较完善的体系。这一方面表现为开发了很多学校层面的、用于评估学生学习产出的工具,例如全国大学生学习投入调查( NSSE )和大学学习评价( CLA );另一方面是形成了各高校积极参与、评估中心定期进行学生评估的体系。最终结果是形成了全国性的学情数据库系统,这为动态地跟踪高等教育质量以及“学生学习增值”提供了有效证据和有力的信息反馈来源。相对而言,国内此领域的研究和实践十分薄弱。

**3. 理论基础**

OBE模式的产生和发展是基于一些教育理论或教育思想的。马伦（Malan）系统地总结了与OBE起源紧密相关的教育运动和教育思想[5]。一是泰勒运动。著名的泰勒原理（确定教育目标——选择教育经验——组织教育经验——评价教育经验）就是围绕“教育目标”这个核心展开课程设计的。二是布鲁姆的掌握学习理论。该理论认为：若能提供充裕的学习时间，绝大多数学习者都能达成学习目标。实际上，这构成了OBE教育模式得以成立的支撑假设之一。OBE在很多方面吸纳了掌握学习理论的特征：弹性的时间框架去实现教学目标；使用不同的资源去创设丰富的教育环境；使用形成性教学评价来反馈学习产出以改善教与学等。三是能力本位的职业教育（competency based education，CBE）。它产生于二战以后，以美国、加拿大为代表，主要应用于职业教育和技能培训中。其要旨是由学校聘请行业中一批专家组成专业委员会，按照岗位群的需要，层层分解以确定从事行业所应具备的能力。然后，再由学校组织相关教学人员，以这些能力为目标，设置课程、组织教学内容，最后考核是否达到这些能力要求。四是标准参照学习。标准参照测验并非为了选拔人才，而是通过测验来了解学生掌握知识和能力的水平，查漏补缺，让每个学生都能获得学业成就感。该理念受到了OBE教育模式的青睐。

## 2 OBE工程教育模式

### 2.1 产生背景

自美国工程与技术认证委员会（ABET）颁布和实施重视学生产出的《工程标准2000》后，20世纪末开始，欧美各国工程教育认证组织都先后改革认证标准，视学习产出为一项重要的质量准则，并由此延伸开来，在国家学位标准、高校教育目标、专业培养计划中都以学习产出为重要质量准则。

《华盛顿协议》成员大多数采取“成果导向”之认证标准，即将学生表现作为教学成果的评量依据，并以促进专业持续改进作为认证的最终目标。各成员认证规范追求其实质相当的内涵。例如，加拿大工程认证委员会（CEAB）认证哲学在传统上是基于输入的，集中于课程内容、班级规模、资源投入等内容。近来，其将建立基于学生产出的认证标准，规定参加认证的高校专业到2014年必须展示毕业生的12条能力。日本于2005年成为《华盛顿协议》正式成员。日本工程教育专业认证机构（JABEE）于2012年实施新的认证标准。新的认证标准是基于学生产出的，主要包括以下方面，即“plan”（清晰地描述学生产出）、“do”（实现学生能力）、“check”（持续地评估学生学习产出）和“act”（改善教学）。2004年9月启动的欧洲认证工程师计划（EUR-ACE）的认证标准也基于学习产出。

认证标准范式的变迁很快导入工程教育实践。例如，马来西亚工程认证委员会（EAC）鲜明地指出，工程教育改革与发展应体现OBE趋势；南非工程教育领域已于1998年开始推行OBE模式[6]。

有专家指出，世界各国的工程教育都在积极地采用“基于产出模式”（outcomes-based

education approaches),这并不足为怪。因为,工程活动本身就直接指向建造有形的结果,例如产品、系统或者基础建设。

### 2.2 特点

(1)重视定义工科毕业生品质(graduate attributes)。

在过去 20 年里,许多国家的职业工程师协会都建立了工程专业认证系统,并清晰地制定出工科毕业生的知识、能力和职业素养等要求。“毕业生品质”由一系列可以评定的学习产出组成,每项结果均表明毕业生可在相应水平上实践的潜在能力。例如,《华盛顿协议》《悉尼协议》《都柏林协议》分别对应规定了工程师(engineer)、技术工程师(technologist)和工程技术员(engineering technician)的 12 个品质。类似地, ABET 定义了毕业生的 11 条能力;CEAB 规定了 12 条能力;EUR-ACE 规定了 12 条能力。

(2)围绕预期学习产出(intended learning outcomes, ILOs)开展教学活动。

这一方面表现在课程计划的“反向设计”,即将规定的毕业生能力有机地导入课程计划,明确各门课程、每节课对实现 ILOs 的贡献,最终形成无缝的匹配矩阵。例如,表 1 显示了美国一所高校工学院课程与 ABET 对工科毕业生的 11 条能力要求的匹配情况,类似的课程计划思路在其他国家工程教育领域也较为普遍。

**表 1 美国某高校工程课程与 ABET《工程标准 2000》的匹配矩阵**

| 课程 | ABET《工程标准 2000》学习产出 | | | | | | | | | | |
|---|---|---|---|---|---|---|---|---|---|---|---|
| | a | b | c | d | e | f | g | h | i | j | k |
| 工程问题求解中的计算机应用 | | | X | | X | | | | | | |
| 工程仪器仪表 | X | | | X | X | X | X | | | X | X |
| 电路分析 I | | | X | | X | | | | | | X |
| 电路分析 II | | | X | | X | | | | | | X |
| 数字设计 | | | X | X | X | | X | | | X | X |
| 微处理器架构与编程 | | | X | X | X | | X | X | | X | X |
| 工程经济学 | | | | X | X | X | X | X | X | X | X |
| 线性控制系统 | | | X | | X | X | X | X | | X | X |
| 电子学 I | | | X | | X | | | | | | X |
| 电子学 II | | | X | | X | | | | | | X |
| 系统信息与噪声 | | | X | | X | | | | | X | X |
| 初级实验室 I | X | X | | | | | X | X | | | X |
| 电磁场理论 | X | X | X | | | | X | X | | X | |
| 电气与计算机工程项目 | X | X | X | X | X | X | X | X | X | X | X |

(3)十分重视学生学习产出评估工作。

学习产出评估工作是 OBE 教育模式必不可少的环节,也是牵扯教师精力最多、最复杂的环节。美国成立了全国学习产出评估机构(National Institute For Learning Outcomes Assessment),提供了交流各高校在学生评估方面的经验和进展的平台,并介绍了一些工科院校在评估学生学习产出方面的典型经验。从本质上讲,OBE 教育模式就是围绕“定义预期学习产出—实现预期学习产出—评估学习产出”这条主线而展开,学习产出评估构成了教育质量持续改进的闭环。图 1 是美国学者里查德(Richard)所提出的基于 OBE 模式的课程设计模型。可以看出,学生结果评估工作是该模型的三大要素之一。

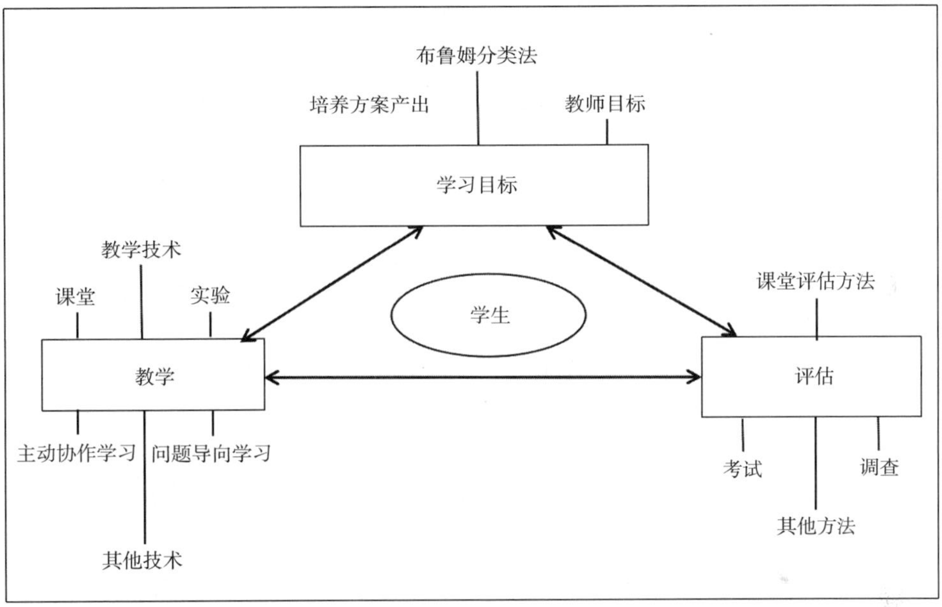


**图 1 基于 OBE 模式的教学设计**[7]

### 2.3 优点

(1)实现教育范式由“内容为本”向“学生为本”的根本转变。

在传统教学中,教学内容先于教学目标而存在并占据核心位置;而在 OBE 教育模式中,教学目标(学生预期学习产出)先于教学内容而存在,课程资源开发、学生管理和辅导等活动都要围绕预期目标而展开。因此,在 OBE 教育模式中,学生真正成为教学活动的中心。OBE 是一个循环的教育改革模式,它基于以学生为中心的哲学理念,这种理念聚焦于学生表现即产出(outcomes)的经验测评,相对于关注教学资源等产出的传统教学模式,OBE 没有提出对特定教学方式的要求,它只对学生最后的学习产出提出要求。表 2 和表 3[1]详细对比了基于内容和基于产出的学习系统和学生经验特征,描述了学生在 OBE 教育模式中的主动与中心地位,生动地体现了别敦荣教授提出的现代大学教学改革正在发生由“表演式哲学”到“实践哲学”转向的内涵。

**表 2　基于内容与基于产出的学习系统特征比较**

| 系统特征 | 基于内容 | 基于产出 |
| --- | --- | --- |
| 框架 | 预设课程评估和认证程序；结构是目的，不定义学习者产出 | 开放的课程、教学策略、评估和行为标准；教学结构支持目标实现，它是手段而非目的 |
| 时间 | 刚性的限制；教学日程表控制着学习和成功 | 使用可改变的资源——根据教育者和学习者的需求 |
| 绩效标准 | 比较与竞争的方法；预先设置好的正态分布曲线 | 学习者达到标准即可获得学分；没有通过比例或标准等的限制 |
| 学习评估 | 持续的测验和分数错误被永久记录；慢的学习者无法赶上学习节奏；永远没有提到学习者到底如何能成功 | 从宏观的视野来看待学习成就，错误是发展能力过程中不可少的；明确最终的成就是能做什么 |

**表 3　基于内容与基于产出的学习学生经验比较**

| 学生经验 | 基于内容 | 基于产出 |
| --- | --- | --- |
| 学生角色 | 被动的 | 主动的 |
| | 重点放在教师希望学生掌握的知识 | 重点在学习产出上学习者理解的和成为的 |
| 学习评价 | 间歇的总结性评价 | 持续的形成性评价 |
| 学习方式 | 死记硬背 | 批判性思考、推理和反思 |
| 学习计划 | 分解为单元的学科知识 | 与实际情景相联系的整合知识 |
| | 学习内容放置于严格的时间框架内，教学大纲具有刚性和不可协商性 | 灵活的时间框架——学习者根据自己的节奏学习，学习计划被视为引导教师创新的指南 |
| 学习动力 | 教师负责学习——激励源于教师的人格力量 | 学生负责自己的学习，动力来自反馈和积极的自我价值感 |
| 学习空间 | 停留于单一的机构直到完成学业 | 学习者可以在不同机构获得学分，直到达到规定的能力 |
| | 先前的知识和经验被忽略，每次都参加整个课程 | 先前的学习被承认；在预试之后，学习者学习产出被认证，可以省去重复环节 |

（2）有利于建立开放、透明、富有弹性和互认的教育结构。

学生。在 OBE 模式中，学生可以清晰地感受到来自教师的期望，通过持续形成评价获得成就体验。同时，只要能够实现预期学习产出，学生可以在不同教育机构中获得学习经验，可以参与不同类型的教育活动。而且，OBE 可以提高学生的可雇佣性，因为该模式下培养的毕业生可以向雇主自信地表述获得的能力。

教师。OBE 不限定教师采取什么样的教育方法和教育内容，只通过指定阶段性的学习期望来为教师指明方向。所以，OBE 教育模式为教师充分地展现教育艺术来实现既定目标提供了广阔空间，这会成为学校办学特色和个性的重要来源。

管理者。在 OBE 中，通过开展学习产出评估，管理者可以及时了解学生是否达到了阶段性教学目标，根据结果及时调整资源配置、师资培训和学生辅导等工作。同时，通过向家长、教育行政部门和社会公众等利益相关者展示学生发展情况，提供努力改善教学质量的证据，可以增进高等教育质量“透明性”，有利于实现高等教育问责。

高校。学生学习过程、学习产出或毕业生能力是比较容易交流的教育术语，“learning outcomes”是一张有效的“通行证”。因此，确立 OBE 教育模式，有利于不同类型高校之间、高校与工业界之间甚至不同国家和地区的高校之间展开有效沟通和交流，使得高校办学活动更加开放和包容。

高等教育国际化。学习产出是国际高等教育互认、学分转换的基础，是高等教育国际化和人才流动的基石。例如，学习产出对促进博洛尼亚进程（Bologna Process）起到了独特的促进作用。学习产出是“欧洲高等教育区”（EHEA）设想的核心，构成了“欧洲学分转换系统”（ECTS）的基础。

## 3 汕头大学 OBE 工程教育模式的实践与探索

汕头大学基于“学习产出”的工程教育模式，以 CDIO 工程教育改革实践为基础，深度借鉴、挖掘和利用 CDIO 工程教育所蕴含的思路与主旨，结合国际工程教育改革及工程教育认证发展趋势，进行了探索与再创新。

汕头大学 OBE 工程教育改革主要包括以下环节：①制定专业层面的预期学习产出；②通过一体化课程设计，建立课程与培养标准的匹配矩阵；③确定课程层面的预期学习产出，并设计相适应的教学策略；④做好专业层面与课程层面的实际学习产出评估。

### 3.1 制定专业层面的预期学习产出

基于对教师、学生、校友、用人单位等利益相关者的调查，结合本专业国内外发展趋势以及学校定位，来论证本专业的使命、愿景、目标以及实施这些目标所需要的知识、能力和素质。在借鉴 CDIO 能力大纲制定过程基本思路的基础上，确定专业层面的细化的可测评的预期学习产出，即 EIP-CDIO 能力大纲。图 2 为汕头大学机电专业的预期学习产出。

### 3.2 设计与专业培养标准相匹配的一体化课程体系

围绕专业预期学习产出，逆向设计各门课程，明确各门课程对实现预期学习产出的贡献及程度，实现一体化培养。

### 3.3 确定课程层面的预期学习产出及实现策略

专业层面的预期学习产出最终要落实到课程。确定课程层面的学习产出，特别是实现策略是核心环节。教师要根据学习产出类型，使用多样化的教学方法，基于学习科学理论创设丰富的教育环境，调动学生积极地参与教学过程，有效而非表面上实现预期学习产出，见表 4。

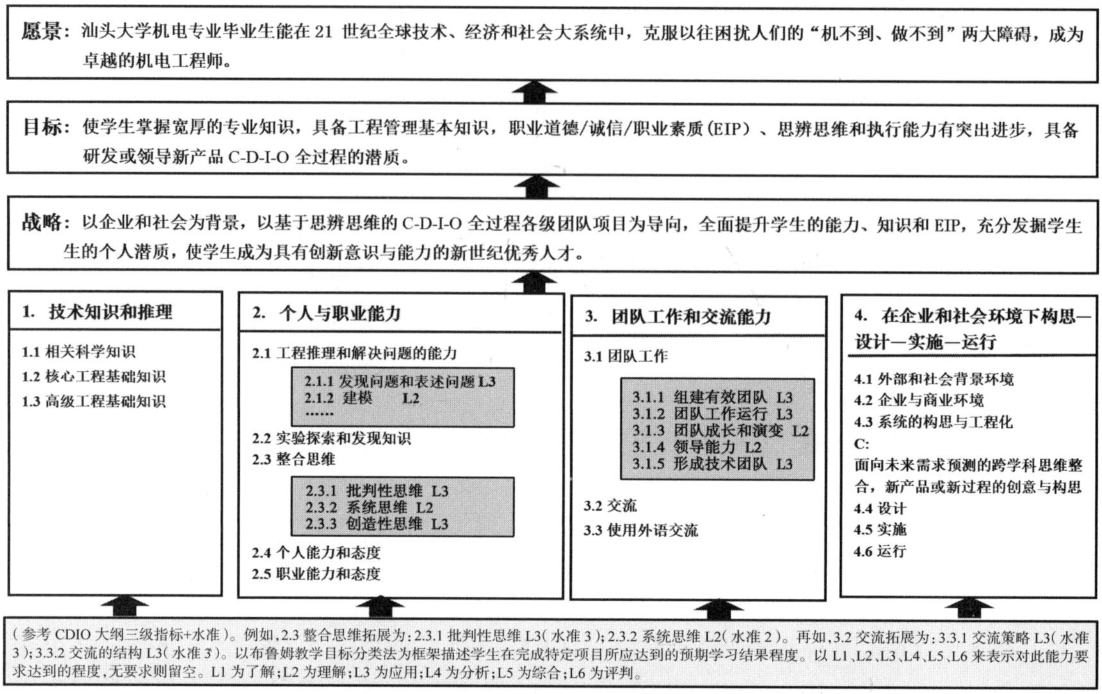


图 2　汕头大学机电专业的预期学习产出

表 4　工程热力学课程预期学习产出及教学策略(局部)

| 知识点 | | | 掌握程度 | 教学策略 |
|---|---|---|---|---|
| 一级 | 二级 | 三级 | | |
| 工程热力学 | 热力系数 | 热力学状态参数、理想气体状态方程、理想气体比热容、理想气体混合物 | 2 | 讲授 |
| | | 热力系统的储存能、热力学第一定律的实质、闭口系统的热力学第一定律表达式 | 3 | 讲授 |
| | | 热力学第二定律 | 3 | 讲授 |
| | | 水蒸气的产生过程、水蒸气的状态参数、湿空气的性质、湿空气的基本热力学过程 | 3 | 讲授 |
| … | … | … | … | … |

| 能力点 | | | | 掌握程度 | 教学策略 |
|---|---|---|---|---|---|
| 一级 | 二级 | 三级 | 四级 | | |
| 个人职业技能 | 工程推理和解决问题的能力 | 发现问题和表述问题(提出问题) | 评估水力火箭发射数据和问题表象 | 2 | 探究式项目 |
| | | | 分析假设和偏差源 | 3 | 探究式项目 |
| | | | 制定解决方案 | 2 | 探究式项目 |
| | | 估计与定理分析 | 估计量级、范围、趋势 | 2 | 探究式项目 |
| | | | 应用实验验证一致性和调整 | 3 | 探究式项目 |
| … | … | … | … | … | … |

### 3.4 做好实际学习产出评估

在课程层面,任课教师采用测验、问卷、项目、作业、报告等多样化评价方法,对学生实际学习产出进行形成性评估与总结性评估,参见图3。表5展示的是“工程热力学”课程评测的局部。在该门课中,任课教师为评测学生在水力火箭项目中的实际学习产出自编“水力火箭项目设计评分问卷”“水力火箭项目实验评分问卷”“水力火箭项目团队评分问卷”“水力火箭项目职业素养评分问卷”等,多侧面、多角度地考查学生是否达到教学目标。

上述环节构成了汕头大学OBE工程教育改革的整体图景。作为改革成果的物化,汕头大学在改革过程中形成了从宏观到微观、分层次的教学文档。在专业层面,有专业培养标准和课程匹配矩阵;在课程层面,有课程大纲、学生评测方案等;在项目层次,有项目指导书和实验指导书;在课堂层面,有详尽的教案。它们凝结着教师致力于教育改革的心血,成为汕头大学工程教育改革的扎实见证。

**表5 “工程热力学”课程实际学习产出的评测(局部)**

| 预期学习产出 | | | | | 实验学习产出 | | | |
|---|---|---|---|---|---|---|---|---|
| 预期学习产出 | | | | 教学策略 | 学习产出的形成性评估 | | 学习产出的总结性评价 | |
| 一级 | 二级 | 三级 | 水准 | | 水准 | 要求 | 水准 | 要求 |
| 个人职业技能 | 工程推理和解决问题的能力 | 发现问题和表述问题(提出问题) | 3 | 要求发现水力火箭飞行的不稳定性问题和水力火箭发射高度不同等问题 | 2 | 项目讨论的过程中提出了相关问题 | 3 | 在项目报告中提出水力火箭发射不稳定,以及气动阻尼的未知性等问题 |
| | | 估计与定性分析 | 3 | 要求对影响水力火箭发射稳定的因子进行定性分析 | 3 | 在项目讨论过程和实验设计方案中进行了相关分析 | 4 | 在项目报告中分析了水力火箭尾翼、瓶身形状等对发射稳定性的影响 |
| | 实验发现知识 | 解决方法和建设(结论与表达) | 3 | 要求能够设计出一些测量飞行高度和改变水力火箭外形的方法 | 3 | 项目讨论过程中和实验设计过程中提出设计方案 | 3 | 设计了利用恒速行驶的汽车测量弹簧拉力和通过理论与实验相结合等方法测量气动阻尼 |
| … | … | … | … | … | … | … | … | … |

## 4 汕头大学OBE工程教育改革的主要特征

### 4.1 实施框架:工程教育与工程教育认证双重变革

(1)从汕头大学工程教育结构来看,它是以预期毕业生能力(表现为EIP-CDIO能力大纲)驱动整个教育系统(课程计划、师资、教学方法、教学评价)的OBE模式。图4是汕头大学CDIO工程教育改革的总体思路。整个教育架构由培养什么样的人、怎么培养人、培养人的效果评价三部分组成,形成了环环相扣、以学习产出为导向的闭环系统。具体地讲,汕头

| 课程名称 | 学分 | 课程性质 | 1. 技术知识和推理 | | | | 2. 个人与职业能力 | | | | | | 3. 团队工作和交流能力 | | | | | 4. 在企业和社会环境下构思—设计—实施—运行 | | | | | |
|---|---|---|---|---|---|---|---|---|---|---|---|---|---|---|---|---|---|---|---|---|---|---|---|
| | | | 1.1 数学、物理、生物等基础科学知识 | 1.2 力学、电学等核心工程基础知识 | 1.3 机械原理、设计与制造等专业工程基础知识 | …… | 2.1 机电产品研发过程的工程推理和解决问题的能力 | 2.2 机电系统运行实验和发现知识 | 2.3 机电产品全系统的思维整合 | 2.4 系统工作中的个人能力和态度 | 2.5 系统工作中的职业能力和态度 | …… | 3.1 机电产品研发中的有效团队工作 | 3.2 机电产品研发团队中的有效交流 | 3.3 团队中使用外语的交流 | 3.4 在不同和多种文化环境有效工作和探索 | 3.5 跨越人文、工程、经济和社会的综合视野 | 4.1 大系统外部和社会背景环境 | 4.2 复杂企业与商业环境 | 4.3 机电新产品或新系统的创意与构思 | 4.4 机械或电控系统的设计 | 4.5 机电产品的有效实施 | 4.6 机电产品寿命周期的运行 |
| 第一学年 | | | | | | | | | | | | | | | | | | | | | | | |
| 秋季学期 | | | | | | | | | | | | | | | | | | | | | | | |
| MAT1110 高等数学 I | 6 | 必修 | 3 | | | | | | | 2 | | | | | | | 2 | 2 | | | | | |
| ENC9105 工程设计导论 | 2 | 必修 | 2 | 2 | 1 | | 3 | 3 | 2 | 1 | 2 | | 3 | 3 | 3 | | | 1 | 2 | 2 | 2 | 1 | 1 |
| CST9910 C语言程序设计 | 2 | 必修 | 3 | 4 | | | | | 2 | | | | | | | | | 1 | 1 | | | | |
| ENC9110 化学导论 | 1 | 必修 | 2 | | | | 2 | 3 | | | | | | | | | | 1 | 1 | | | | |
| ENC9120 生物学导论 | 1 | 必修 | 1 | | | | 1 | | | 2 | 1 | | 2 | 2 | 2 | 2 | 2 | | | | | | |
| COM011 计算机应用技能 | 2 | 必修 | 4 | | | | | | | 3 | 2 | | 2 | 2 | 1 | 2 | | | | | | | |
| 毛邓三 | 6 | 必修 | | | | | 2 | | | | 3 | | | | | | | | | | | | |
| 英语 | 4 | 必修 | 4 | | | | | | 2 | 3 | | | 2 | 2 | 4 | | | | | | | | |
| 体育 | 1 | 必修 | | | | | | | 2 | | 3 | | 2 | 2 | | | | | | | | | |
| 本学期必修学分小计 | 25 | 必修 | | | | | | | 2 | | | | | | | | | | | | | | |
| 春季学期 | | | | | | | | | | 2 | | | | | | | 2 | 2 | | | | | |
| MAT1210 高等数学 II | 6 | 必修 | 4 | | | | | | | 2 | | | | | | | 2 | 2 | | | | | |
| MAT1130 线性代数 | 2 | 必修 | 3 | | | | | | 2 | | | | | | | | | | | | | | |
| PHY030 普通物理学 | 4 | 必修 | 3 | 2 | | | 1 | 3 | 2 | | | | | | | | | | | | | | |
| PHY1000 普通物理实验 | 2 | 必修 | 3 | 2 | | | 1 | 2 | 2 | 2 | 3 | | 3 | 3 | 3 | | | 2 | 2 | 3 | 3 | 2 | 2 |
| MEC9500 机械制图与计算机辅助制图 | 4 | 必修 | | 4 | 3 | | 3 | 3 | 2 | | | | 2 | 2 | 4 | | | | | | | | |
| 英语 | 4 | 必修 | 4 | | | | | | 2 | 3 | 3 | | 2 | 2 | | | | | | | | | |
| 体育 | 1 | 必修 | | | | | 2 | | 2 | 3 | 3 | | | | | | | | | | | | |
| 形势与政策 | 2 | 必修 | | | | | | | | | | | | | | | | | | | | | |
| 公共课或者通识课自选 | | | | | | | | | | | | | | | | | | | | | | | |
| 本学期必修学分小计 | 25 | | | | | | | | | | | | | | | | | | | | | | |

图 3　汕头大学机械设计制造及自动化专业课程与预期学习产出匹配矩阵（局部）

大学在实施 OBE 的过程中，首先根据自身办学定位，在参考 CDIO 能力大纲的基础上，将相关利益群体对现代工程师所必备的知识、能力和素质等进行了系统分解，构成了毕业生可操作、可观察和可评测的预期学习产出（intended learning outcomes，ILOs），并依照著名教育学家布鲁姆的教育目标分类法来确定毕业生在各细化条目上的掌握水平。其次，紧密围绕预期教育目标，优化工程教育办学文化与环境、构建与预期培养目标相匹配的课程体系、实施主动性教学方法等一体化教育措施。最后，采取多样化教育评价手段评测学生学习效果，建立内部教学质量保障机制。

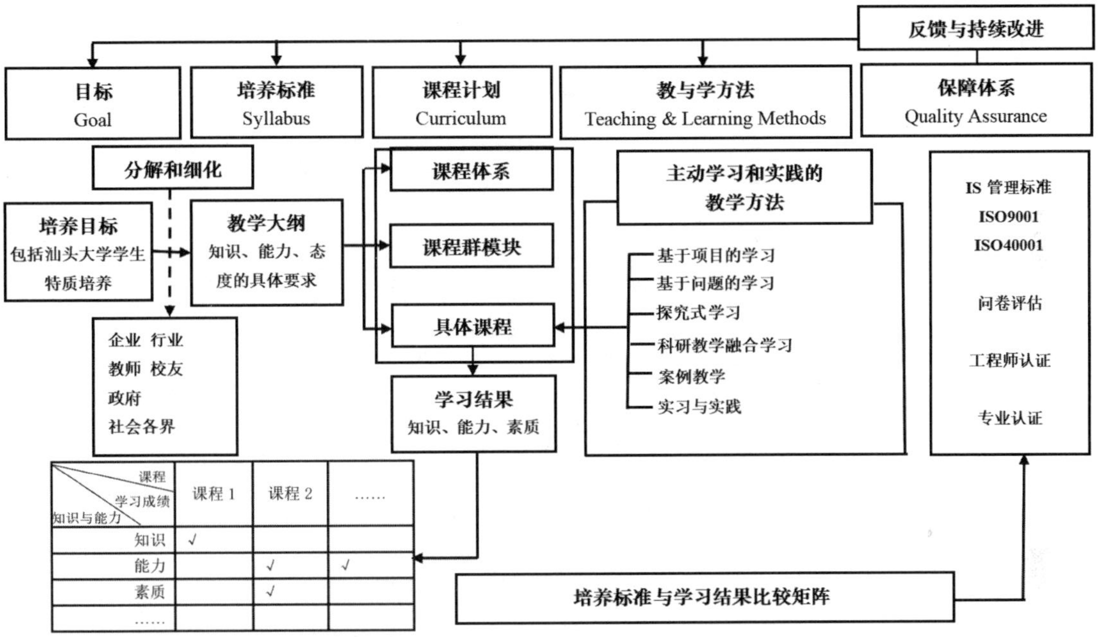


**图 4　汕头大学 CDIO 工程教育改革的总体思路**

（2）从汕头大学内部工程教育质量认证看，它是围绕预期学习产出寻找证据的过程。学习产出是内部教育质量认证的中心，学习投入和学习过程作为实现预期学习产出的手段或证据加以使用。这就形成了 OBE 工程教育认证模式。

汕头大学按照 CDIO 内在要求，在参考 CDIO 的 12 条标准的基础上，构建出工程教育内部质量保障机制。CDIO 的 12 条标准，全面地说明了满足 CDIO 要求的专业办学特点，可以作为教学改革和评估、实施 CDIO 基准和目标并制定持续提高的框架。这 12 条认证标准与欧美各国工程教育认证标准具有较好的匹配性，显示出 CDIO 工程教育模式较强的国际通用性。实际上，一些国家如芬兰和著名高校如悉尼理工大学就以 CDIO 的 12 条认证标准为本国或本校工程教育质量认证的标准。

图 5 是汕头大学工程教育内部认证标准的基本逻辑。标准Ⅱ学习效果构成了认证环节的核心，涉及课程建设的标准Ⅲ和Ⅳ，涉及教与学的标准Ⅴ、Ⅶ和Ⅷ，以及涉及教师发展的标准Ⅸ和Ⅹ，涉及工程教育环境的标准Ⅰ和Ⅵ构成了实现预期学习目标的保障因素，而标准Ⅺ则是学习效果评价。这些标准形成了“预期学习产出—教育投入与教育过程—评估学习产

出”闭环，呈现出典型的 OBE 风格。

### 4.2 实施特点：实现工程教育系统的三个根本转变

一是教育目标由知识客体转向学生主体。传统的工科专业课程设置模式是基于学科体系的，一般采用“三段式”固定顺序，即公共基础课、专业基础课和专业课，把系统理论知识作为工程教学的主要内容。汕头大学在 OBE 工程教育实践中，以培养学生的 C-D-I-O 能力为出发点，运用一体化原则设置课程，打破原有学科、课程之间的界限，平行设置专业课与基础课，交叉推进理论课与实践课，按照模块化工程设计项目驱动教学，实现教育目标由知识传授向能力培养的转变。

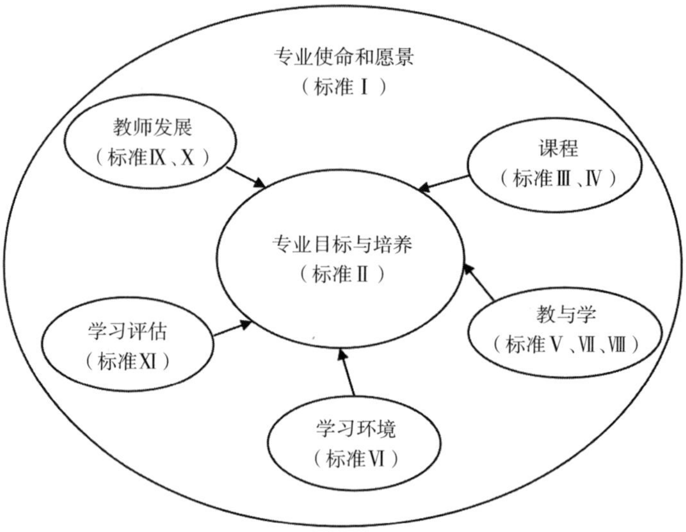


**图 5　汕头大学 CDIO 工程教育认证标准的基本逻辑**

二是教育导向由教育专家导向转向相关利益者代表导向。汕头大学在 OBE 工程教育实践中，建立了由产业界、校友、用人单位等相关利益者权威代表参与教育管理的机制与平台，其参与专业培养计划、培养目标、课程以及毕业生能力评估等决策与管理活动。当然，教育专家也是这些教育管理活动的主动参与者，以统筹协调各方要求，保证工程教育活动与产业发展紧密结合。

三是教育程式由传统的“教程”逐步向“学程”转化。汕头大学在 OBE 工程教育实践中，要求教师转变教育理念，成为学生达成预期学习产出的帮助者、促进者和组织者；建立弹性的教学管理系统，允许学生个性化的课程选修组合以及进度安排；在提高第一课堂教学质量的同时，努力丰富第二课堂和第三课堂，打造多样化的素质拓展平台，使学生积累工程实践经验，锤炼多方面的能力。

### 4.3 实施特色：将 OBE 理念融入探究式教学改革

OBE 教育模式的核心是培养学生能力，实现教育活动由“教师中心”向“学生中心”的转移。汕头大学工学院在 OBE 工程教育改革过程中，积极探索符合其要求的主动性教学方法。汕头大学于2010年申报教育部人文社会科学重点项目“工程科学教育中基于学习科学的探究式教育研究”。自立项以来，学校和学院领导高度重视，组建了包括教学副院长、各系主任、高教专家和一线教师在内的涵盖13门试点课程的39人研究团队，在工学院5个专业全面铺开试点，并以此作为深化工程教育改革、推进教学方式转变的抓手。

结合工程设计项目，汕头大学形成基于项目的探究式教学模式。该模式以工程科学概念和原理为基础，以面向实际工程技术问题或难题为驱动点，通过建立假说、实验设计、数据分析、验证结论等系列探究步骤来完成从项目构思、项目设计、项目制造到项目完成，即C-D-I-O代表的工业产品周期。按照由浅到深、由具体到抽象、由简单到复杂的原则，安排设计项目和课程之间的关系，形成多层次、渐进式的探究式教学模式。

在实施架构上，融入了OBE的基本环节，形成实施框架。首先，也是探究式教学改革最核心的工作，即精心设计能够贯穿本门课程主要核心知识点的探究项目。其次，预设探究式教学所要实现的预期学习产出。在此过程中借鉴CDIO能力大纲所提供的细化学习产出集，建立探究式教学模式各环节、各要素与CDIO能力大纲之间的匹配映射关系。再次，明确探究式教学各步骤的实施策略。CDIO能力大纲完整地涵盖了探究式教学模式的实施步骤，且CDIO能力大纲对识别问题、分析问题、实验假设、查询资料、得出结论等能力进行了细化。这就为教师设计实施策略提供了可资借鉴的参考资源。然后，充分利用CDIO能力大纲所提供的详尽的、可观测的目标体系，以此作为评估探究式教学实施效果的依据，使用多元化评价手段来考查学生知识掌握、能力培养以及态度养成的情况。最后，根据评估结果进一步完善教学。由此可见，实现教育闭环的过程也符合OBE教育模式的基本流程。

## 5 推进OBE工程教育模式的思考

### 5.1 有弹性的OBE

OBE模式虽然有许多优点，但如果操作不当，极有可能演变为行为主义操控下的僵化进程，使教育丧失基本的人文关怀。学者对该模式的批判集中于以下几点。

OBE模式基于行为主义心理学原理，强调学生对同一刺激做出同一反应，追求的是学生反应的同一性而不是多样性；以预先设置好的教学目标规定和影响教学过程，教学实际上成为按预定模式、预定路线和预定轨道对学生进行塑造的过程，这种标准化、程式化的教育，实质上是反创造性、反智慧的机械流程；可观测、可操作、外显化的行为目标是对教育肤浅的认识。即使学生在一定教学情境下达到相同的行为目标，其内心世界也是参差不齐的。任何教育都不能用一种规格来限制活生生的人；简单地把教育中“质”的问题进行“量”化处理，是反人性的。

汕头大学在实施OBE模式的过程中，汲取了一些学者对该模式的批评以及建议，进行了以下努力：将学生预期学习产出设为教学的最低标准，对学生发展程度不做上限规定，为师生发挥创造性预留弹性空间；在重视精确化“行为目标”的同时，还重视模糊的“表现性目标”，对学生的情意发展、审美意象以及高层次的能力不进行生硬的分解、量化和评价；将学习产出理解为阶段性的、周期性的，不为某节课、某单元设立细化的目标。使知识成为激发各种类型和不同水平理解的中介，而不是作为固定信息或标准答案让学生接受。力求平衡教育的预设性与生成性，达到“预设而不死板，生成而不游离”的境界。

### 5.2 高水平的 OBE

实施高水平和高质量的 OBE 工程教育模式，对教师教育理论素养提出了很高的要求。一是要求教师明确预期学习产出，并将其分解为可以操作的细化目标。二是要求教师善于利用各类教育资源、灵活选择各种教育策略来实现预期教育目标。三是要求教师掌握多样化的教学评价方法，动态地把握学生知识、能力和态度的发展水平。四是要求教师能够因材施教，为每一位学生制定个性化的发展方案。

为了构建与 OBE 教育模式相适应的高水平教师队伍，汕头大学做了以下努力：一是扎实做好工科教师专业发展与教学发展工作，成立“教师发展与评估中心”，服务于教师教学能力提高与发展；二是在工学院成立“CDIO 工程教育研究中心”，聘请高教所教师负责中心工作，全面介入、指导和帮助工学院教师从事教改工作；三是构建工学院教师学习共同体，经常开展教学改革研讨会，营造“研究学生，钻研教学”的文化氛围，并经常邀请国内外专家到校交流和指导。

### 5.3 可持续的 OBE

OBE 教育模式对教师的教学投入提出很高的要求。例如，教师需要投入大量精力，细致地进行教学目标分解、一体化课程设计和教学方法选择，动态评估学生发展水平，并根据学习产出评估反馈信息及时开展个性化学生辅导等工作。如果无法改变高校中普遍的“重科研，轻教学”的现状，无法调动教师参与教学改革的积极性，OBE 注定无法可持续开展。

为了持续、深入推动 OBE 工程教育模式，调动教师参与教学改革的热情，汕头大学做了以下努力：在文化上，实施“先进本科教育”的发展战略，营造重视教学的组织文化；在制度上，以“教学学术”理念为指导，变革教师业绩评价制度，改变教师评价与聘任中“重科研，轻教学”的现象；三是实施“年薪制”，消除“算工分”式分配制度对教师教学改革积极性的负面影响。通过实施综合教育改革，调动各方参与教育改革的积极性与创造性，从而保障了教学改革的持续性。

## 6 结语

我国是《华盛顿协议》第 21 个预备成员，且该协议各成员都实施了基于产出的工程教育模式。建立 OBE 工程教育模式，对提高我国高等工程教育的质量、加强工程教育与工业界的联系、建立与《华盛顿协议》规定具有“实质等效性”的工程教育体系具有重要推动意义。因为，工程教育国际化，核心是按国际标准培养工程科技人才[8]。

汕头大学的 OBE 工程教育模式实践，是一项时间跨度长、牵涉面广、改革纵深大的综合教育改革。它不是对原有教学薄弱环节的缝缝补补，也不是在教学、课程或产学研教育中移入 OBE 的某个要素。在实施之初，汕头大学便以 OBE 蕴含的理念为指导，在充分借鉴、整合 CDIO 改革经验的基础上，对培养目标、课程内容、教学方法和教学评价进行了变革。但是，随着改革不断深入，涌现出一系列制约教改推进的瓶颈。随后，汕头大学对制约教改开展的战略、文化、教师评聘、学生管理、科研管理等因素进行了全方位配套改革，初步构建起与 OBE 教改相适应的文化氛围与组织管理体制。

汕头大学的 OBE 工程教育改革实践表明，高校教学改革是组织持续创新的过程。教学改革必须与高校的战略、文化、组织和制度改革有机配合，通过复杂的非线性作用产生单独要素无法实现的整体协同效应，最终形成教学改革为战略、文化和制度等改革提出问题、提供思路和方向，战略、文化和制度改革围绕教学改革进行并为教学改革提供保障的良性互动格局。

在高校普遍存在着“重科研，轻教学”的语境中，实施 OBE 并非易事。但我们相信：只要认清国际工程教育改革与发展的趋势，坚持本科教学工作的中心地位，就一定能锐意进取、全面深化改革，形成科研与教学良性互动、教师发展与学生成长相得益彰的格局。

## 致谢

汕头大学基于学习产出的工程教育改革、CDIO 工程教育改革等受到各级教育行政部门、许多兄弟院校和知名学者的支持和鼓励。教育部高教司领导长期关注汕头大学工程教育改革的实施和推广，广东省教育厅分管高等教育的领导同志对汕头大学的工程教育改革也是一如既往地关心。《高等工程教育研究》常务副主编姜嘉乐先生亦多次到汕头大学考察和指导。他们的肯定与认可为汕头大学教育改革注入了不竭动力，成为汕头大学攻坚克难、深化教育改革的力量源泉。

汕头大学的工程教育改革，离不开李嘉诚基金会给予的强有力支持与帮助，离不开一线教师默默无闻地无私奉献。广大教师将大量精力与时间投入学生个性化辅导、教学文档撰写、构想预期学习产出、设计教学策略及评估等 OBE 改革中，承担着繁重的教改任务。没有他们对教育事业的崇高追求，没有他们对学生发展的高度责任心，OBE 教改就无法开展。笔者撰写的此文，仅是对他们一部分工作的简要整理。

谨向关心、支持和从事汕头大学工程教育改革的领导、专家和教师致以崇高敬意和衷心感谢！

## 参考文献

[1] SPADY W D. Outcome-based education：critical issues and answers[M]. Arlington，VA：American Association of School Administrators，1994.

[2] WILLIS S，KISSANE B. Outcome-based education：a review of the literature[M]. [S.L.]：Prepared for the Education Department of Western Australia，1995.

[3] DE JAGER H J，NIEUWENHUIS J F. Linkages between total quality management and the outcomes-based approach in an education environment[J]. Quality in higher education，2005，11（3）：251-260.

[4] ACHARYAC. Outcome-based education（OBE）：a new paradigm for learning[J]. CDT

Link, 2003, 7( 3 )7-9.
[5] MALAN B. The new paradigm of outcomes-based education in perspective[J]. Journal of family ecology and consumer sciences, 2000( 28 ): 22-28.
[6] COMBRINCK M. An international comparative perspective on outcomes-based assessment: implications for South Africa[J]. Perspectives in education: assessment of change in education, 2003( S1 ): 51-66.
[7] FELDER R M, BRENT R. Designing and teaching courses to satisfy the ABET engineering criteria[J]. Journal of engineering education, 2003, 92( 1 ): 7-25.
[8] 查建中. 论工程教育国际化 [J]. 高等工程教育研究, 2008( 5 ): 8-14.

# 从 CDIO 在中国到中国的 CDIO：发展路径、产生的影响及其原因研究①

顾佩华　胡文龙　陆小华　包能胜　林　鹏

**摘要：**CDIO 在中国的发展已逾十年，成为中国高等工程教育界重要的改革运动之一。CDIO 在中国的改革与发展表明，它能够提高人才培养质量，促进工程教育教学改革与研究，并推动其他中国高等工程教育重要改革项目。作为由汕头大学发起的一项工程教育改革，CDIO 之所以能够获得教育行政部门的大力支持和指导，并获得工程教育界的广泛认可，其根本原因是 CDIO 能够解决中国高等工程教育存在的系列问题，关键原因是 CDIO 能够提高人才培养模式改革的科学性、系统性和培养质量，重要原因是创建了 CDIO 改革共同体。此外，CDIO 改革主体表现出的教育改革实践的工匠精神也是促进其传播的重要因素。由于社会发展对人才培养提出了新要求以及 CDIO 本身具有特定的适用范围，CDIO 也要与时俱进。汕头大学改革团队在多年改革经验的基础上，提出了培养新工科人才、构架与《华盛顿协议》的立交桥等 CDIO 发展的建议，希望通过自我革新为中国高等教育发展贡献新思想和新智慧。

**关键词：**CDIO；高等工程教育；人才培养质量

## From CDIO in China to China's CDIO: Study on Development Path, Impacts and Its Causes

*Gu Peihua, Hu Wenlong, Lu Xiaohua, Bao Nengsheng, Lin Peng*

**Abstract:** With a developing history of over ten years in China, CDIO has become one of the most important reform movements in China's higher engineering education circle. Its reform and development in China shows that it can improve the quality of talent cultivation, promote the teaching reform and research in engineering education, and accelerate other important reform programs of higher engineering education in China. There are many reasons for CDIO, as an engineering education reform initiated by Shantou University, to have obtained strong support and guidance by education administrative departments and be widely accepted in engineering education circle: the fundamental reason is that CDIO can solve the serial problems existing in higher engineering education in China; the key reason is that CDIO can improve the scientificity, systematicity and quality of talent cultivation model reform; and the important reason is that it has created CDIO reform community. In addition, the spirit of the craftsman in educational reform practice showed by the main bodies of CDIO reform is also an important factor for it to spread. As there are new requirements for talent cultivation in social develop-

① 本文刊登于《高等工程教育研究》2017 年第 1 期第 24~43 页。

ment and CDIO itself has a specific application scope, it is also necessary for CDIO to keep up with the times. On the basis of years' reform experience, Shantou University's reform team puts forward the proposal of training new engineering talents and constructing an overpass according to Washington Accord to promote the development of CDIO, hoping to contribute new ideas and wisdom to the development of higher education in China through self-innovation.
**Keywords:**CDIO; higher engineering education; quality of talent cultivation

## 引言

改革开放以来,中国高校在人才培养模式改革和创新方面取得了很大成效,基本满足了我国阶段性工业化的人才需求。总体上看,在我国高等教育领域涌现出一批先进的办学模式,但代表性强和辐射性广的人才培养模式还不够多。原因很多,其中重要的一点是人才培养模式的系统性不够,多是根据教育实践者的经验凝练而成,甚至有的就是根据直觉,凭借以往多年办学经验而总结出的模式。这些模式确实有一定效果,但改革者却不能说清楚该模式作用的机制,可复制性不高,还没有将这些改革上升到科学化水平。

人才培养模式就是人才的培养目标、培养标准、培养过程和方式以及评价方法的合成系统,通过构成要素的优化组合可以构建出多种不同的培养模式。简言之,就是三个问题:"培养什么样的人""怎么培养人"和"培养人的效果如何"。培养理念和培养目标是人才培养模式的先导,它决定着办学者如何设计培养计划、选择教学方法和配置教育资源。传统教育模式最大的问题之一就是难以确切定义"培养什么样的人"。例如,什么是复合型人才,什么是人文素质,很少有人认真研究它们的内涵和特征。如果无法对培养目标进行可操作和可观察的设计,后继培养环节如课程、教学和评价等改革就会出现较大的随意性和主观性,人才培养模式改革的效果也很难进行比较可靠的建设性评定,就只能用一些成绩说明改革的成果,如由学生获奖和发表论文数量、教学成果奖等级和实验实习基础建设水平来印证改革成效。但是这些标志性成果只是人才培养改革成效的一些方面,改革者往往也很难厘清这些成效和教育模式改革之间到底有什么关系。

2005 年底,汕头大学开展了 CDIO 工程教育模式改革。十余年间,CDIO 在中国高等工程教育界逐渐萌芽、扎根、开花和结果,经历了不平凡的发展过程。CDIO 改革由汕头大学发起,教育部高教司理工处及时领导和支持,成都信息工程大学、燕山大学和南京工程学院等高校接力,工程教育研究者和实践者给予了高度关注与支持。经各方努力,CDIO 由最初的高校试点探索,演变为规模较大的工程教育改革运动。时至今日,CDIO 已成为推进高等工程教育改革、提升工程人才培养质量、推进工程专业认证的重要手段。值得关注的是,一些高校开始把 CDIO 改革的理念、思路、方法和经验推广到非工程专业。

2016 年 1 月 8—10 日,汕头大学牵头成立了 CDIO 工程教育联盟,在联盟成立会议上,讨论通过了《CDIO 工程教育联盟章程》,推选了 CDIO 工程教育联盟的理事单位、常务理事单位、轮值主席和秘书处。原 CDIO 工程教育模式试点高校工作组转型为包容性更广、组织结构和运行机制更加完善的民间学术交流平台。CDIO 工程教育联盟成立大会召开之际,已有 10 所"985 工程"高校、26 所"211 工程"高校和 69 所普通高校自愿加入联盟;现在,有更多的院校参与 CDIO 工程教育改革运动。联盟的成立及相应组织架构和运行机制的建立，标志着 CDIO 在中国的发展具备了更高的制度化和结构化水平。随着联盟平台日趋完善和联盟能力不断增强，CDIO 将会迎来新一轮发展高潮。2012 年，汕头大学在《高等工程教育研究》发表了《CDIO 在中国》（上、下）两篇文章，对 6 年来 CDIO 在汕头大学及其他试点高校的实践和推广情况进行了回顾和总结，对中国工程教育面临的挑战和存在的问题进行了观察与思考，并对 CDIO 在中国的发展做出展望[1-2]。

如今，高等教育处于更加全球化和创新的时代，面临着新的发展环境。新科技革命飞速发展，以前所未有的速度改变社会和我们的生活。供给侧改革、促进传统国有产业转型升级、信息技术革命和新型科技形态深刻地改变着时代面貌，制造强国战略的提出对工程人才培养提出了更高、更广、更新、更迫切的要求。大学应该也必须要适应时代的发展，应该走在时代的前面，迎接和创造新理念、新模式和新事物的挑战。在急剧变革的时代，高等教育领域没有一成不变的办学理念，也没有放之四海而皆准的教育模式。斯坦福 2025 计划的实施，有可能在各方面颠覆传统的大学教育。CDIO 也一样，需要与时俱进，不断进步与发展。如果墨守成规，CDIO 的影响力和生命力就会衰退和消失。只有结合时代特征和高等教育发展趋势，不断地进行理念与模式创新和发展，CDIO 才能适应中国高等工程教育变化的需求，才能为中国高等工程教育发展贡献智慧和力量。

本文希望通过总结 CDIO 在中国十年发展的过程，梳理 CDIO 理念和模式在中国高等工程教育界获得感知、接受、认同和肯定的历程，揭示 CDIO 在中国广泛传播和推广的原因与规律，并以此来探讨中国化 CDIO 的发展前景以及在国家新需求下的变革思路。在“大众创新、万众创业”的宏大叙事中，在高校如火如荼开展“双创”教育的环境中，本文期望通过 CDIO 模式的持续创新，使其能够更加紧密地把握高等教育脉搏，进而为高等教育工程模式创新提供一些理念和思路，为及时解决中国高等工程教育发展过程中出现的问题提供想法，继续引领高等工程教育人才培养模式改革的潮流与趋势。

## 1　CDIO 在中国发展的路径

### 1.1　基本历程

#### 1.1.1　CDIO 进入中国

CDIO 于 2005 年被引入中国。2005 年 10 月，加拿大工程教育改革组织——加拿大设计工程网络（CDEN）创始人和领导人之一、原加拿大卡尔加里大学机械与制造工程系主任、加拿大工程院院士顾佩华教授来到汕头大学工作，并担任工学院院长。耶洛利（Yellowley）教授和顾佩华教授早前曾探索构建了设计导向的工程教育模式（design directed engineering education）。实践表明：该模式能够有效整合自然科学、工程技术和交流能力[3]。顾教授带领汕头大学工学院教师团队，在充分调研国外工程教育改革和发展最新情况后，意识到能够解决北美和欧洲的工程教育改革和培养质量问题的 CDIO 模式，也应该能够解决中国工程教育面临的问题并提高工程教育质量[4]。

在前期工作的基础上，结合我国工程师职业化水平和职业伦理方面发展的需求，汕头大学提出并实施以设计为导向的 EIP-CDIO 培养模式改革。学院多次组织教师研讨 CDIO 理念、大纲、标准及框架，对照现状找差距，明确改革方向。在全面推行之前，先从 2003 级和 2004 级选择 8 门课程进行初步试点，积累经验后又在 2004 级和 2005 级中选择 16 门课程扩大改革试点。同时，通过问卷、访谈等形式评估改革效果。此后在 2006 级新生中实施新的专业培养计划，即全面开展 EIP-CDIO 工程教育改革。CDIO 在中国发展的序幕由此开启。

### 1.1.2 中国高校参与国际 CDIO 组织活动

2006 年，汕头大学加入国际 CDIO 合作组织，同年 6 月，汕头大学顾佩华教授应邀参加国际 CDIO 合作组织年会，介绍了汕头大学工程教育改革情况。同时，汕头大学获 CDIO 国际组织授权，筹备成立东亚区域中心并成为该中心的总部，编写 CDIO 实施手册。随后清华大学、成都信息工程大学、燕山大学等高校也加入国际 CDIO 合作组织。

中国高校也承担了加入国际 CDIO 合作组织所承诺的义务，承办了国际性的 CDIO 学术交流活动。2007 年 11 月，汕头大学在国内首先承办了国际 CDIO 研讨会。来自麻省理工学院、瑞典皇家理工学院、查尔姆斯理工大学、皇后大学、卡尔加里大学、蒙特利尔综合理工大学、利物浦大学、新加坡理工学院等 CDIO 国际组织成员大学的专家、学者在汕头大学进行为期 3 天的研讨工作[5]。2011 年 5 月，由北京交通大学主办的“2011 北京 CDIO 区域性国际会议”在京召开。2015 年 6 月，成都信息工程大学、汕头大学联合承办“CDIO 国际合作组织第十一届全球年会”，出席年会的代表主要有来自近 40 个国家的高水平工程类高等院校及科研院所的资深专家、教授 300 余人，这是 CDIO 国际合作组织全球年会第一次在中国举办。2016 年 3 月，燕山大学主办 CDIO 亚洲区会议暨亚洲工程教育会议。

汕头大学加入 CDIO 国际合作组织的消息引起了国内同行的关注。《高等工程教育研究》姜嘉乐副主编是最早关心 CDIO 改革的专家。早在 2007 年 6 月，他来到汕头大学工学院调研，专门就 EIP-CDIO 模式、学校为地方经济建设服务等问题与学院领导、教师进行了深入交流。姜副主编高度评价汕头大学率先开展的新模式改革，工学院以三层级设计项目为骨干的课程体系给他留下了深刻印象。随后，《高等工程教育研究》于 2007 年第 6 期刊登了陆小华教授等人撰写的《设计导向的工程教育改革理念》一文，汕头大学首次向全国同行介绍 CDIO 改革。此后，在 2008 年第 1 期又刊登了顾佩华教授等人撰写的《从 CDIO 到 EIP-CDIO——汕头大学工程教育与人才培养模式探索》一文。该文介绍了 CDIO 改革后汕头大学工学院的“鱼骨图”课程体系，引起工程教育界关注。至 2016 年 7 月 26 日，该文已被引 605 次，下载达 4252 次。

### 1.1.3 CDIO 在中国有组织地发展

鉴于汕头大学在工程教育改革方面的大胆尝试，在教育部高教司理工处支持下，汕头大学于 2007 年 11 月主办了“2007 年中国高等工程教育改革论坛”。在论坛上，各位专家学者充分肯定了汕头大学 CDIO 改革的思路与实践。会议认为，汕头大学大胆引进国际先进的 CDIO 工程教育模式，取得了初步的改革成效，必将为其他高校工程教育改革起到积极示范作用[6]。2008 年 4 月，教育部高等教育司发文成立 CDIO 工程教育模式研究与实践课题组。通知指出，课题组的任务是研究国际工程教育改革情况和 CDIO 工程教育模式的理念及做法；对我国工程教育改革情况进行调研并指导有关院校开展 CDIO 工程教育模式试点工作；组织开展 CDIO 工程教育模式的研讨与交流活动。在组织领导方面，汕头大学执行校长顾佩华教授担任课题组组长，秘书处办公室设在汕头大学。该课题组的成立，预示着 CDIO 工程教育模式获得了行政主管单位的认同，CDIO 具备了正式的交流和研讨平台，推动 CDIO 在中国的实践与发展。

2008 年 12 月，教育部高教司理工处和汕头大学联合主办了 CDIO 工程教育模式试点工作会议。会议确定了第一批 18 所 CDIO 试点高校名单，并成立了 CDIO 试点工作组，决定由汕头大学任试点工作组组长单位并作为秘书处常设地点，成都信息工程大学任副组长单位，燕山大学、成都信息工程大学、合肥工业大学、广州大学分别作为机械类、电气类、化工类和土木类的专业类小组召集单位。此次会议标志着 CDIO 工程教育模式在中国传播的体系性更强，它从研讨走向实践，由理念走向落实。2010 年 4 月，第二批 21 所 CDIO 试点高校产生，全国共计有 39 所高校在开展 CDIO 试点工作。此外，很多学校根据各自需要，开展基于 CDIO 的工程教育教学改革，实施 CDIO 的高校数量继续扩大。

自 2009 年起，试点工作组开展常态化活动，CDIO 发展、传播与研讨的平台日趋完善。在教育部理工处支持下，该工作组每年组织召开两次全国性的 CDIO 试点工作会议，对 CDIO 试点工作进行交流、研讨和总结；同时，试点工作组每年举办两次 CDIO 骨干教师培训班，为全国高校实施 CDIO 培养骨干人才。例如，2009 年 3 月和 10 月分别在北京和成都举办了 CDIO 工程教育模式骨干教师培训班，每次规模都在百人以上。为满足兄弟院校的参会需求，2012 年后，在教育部理工处支持下，CDIO 工程教育模式试点工作组为满足兄弟高校参会需求，将每年召开的 CDIO 试点工作组会议和 CDIO 骨干教师培训会合并为开放性论坛——“中国 CDIO 工程教育年会”。

### 1.1.4 CDIO 在中国自主协同地发展

2014 年，汕头大学作为秘书长单位，代表 CDIO 试点工作组加入全国高等学校工科教学改革协作组。全国高等学校工科教学改革协作组是在教育部高等教育司指导下联系全国高等学校教学管理人员、工程教育研究人员和教师的协作组织。为适应工程教育改革与发展新形势，经教育部高教司同意，协作组于 2014 年 7 月重组，吸纳哈尔滨工业大学、中南大学和汕头大学为新成员，旨在加强对卓越工程师教育培养计划、大学生创新创业计划、CDIO 工程教育改革等工作的统筹协调。

2016 年 1 月，汕头大学发起成立了 CDIO 工程教育联盟，并于 1 月 6—8 日在汕头主办了 CDIO 工程教育联盟成立会议。会议讨论通过了《CDIO 工程教育联盟章程》，规定了联盟的组织架构和运行机制，推选了 CDIO 工程教育联盟的理事单位、常务理事单位、轮值主席和秘书处。原有的教育部 CDIO 工程教育模式试点高校工作组转型为开放性更强的民间学术交流平台，CDIO 在中国的发展迈入新阶段。

## 1.2 发展特征

### 1.2.1 扩散上的自下而上自愿式推进

制度、政策或模式扩散与传播有两种路径:自上而下和自下而上。由上级政府及相关职能部门制定的政策或方针,一般直接通过各级政府或部门层层落实和执行,这是一种典型的"自上而下"式层级化制度扩散模式。这是教育行政主管部门经常采用的政策推广方法,具有效率高和权威性强的特点。20 世纪 80 年代以来我国制定和实施的重要教育改革和教育发展规划,其特点是重视"顶层设计",通过行政手段自上而下地推进。

与此相对应,CDIO 在中国的发展路径是"自下而上"的,在教育部的领导和支持下展开的,其中教育部高教司的领导和支持起到了关键作用。它是由汕头大学、成都信息工程学院、燕山大学和南京信息工程学院等高校发起的教育改革。这些高校认识到中国高等工程教育质量面临的系列问题之后,发挥首创精神和教学改革能动性,自愿地开展教育改革。当然, CDIO 在中国的发展离不开教育部的领导和支持,特别是成立 CDIO 试点高校工作组后, CDIO 迎来了发展的加速阶段。教育部理工处是通过试点工作组发挥 CDIO 在中国工程教育改革中的作用,并为 CDIO 发展提供改革项目、交流平台和发展咨询等公共服务的,这种影响是非主导或命令性的。

CDIO 的迅速发展,是地方基层改革者的积极性与行政主管部门的切实转变政府职能理念相结合的产物,开辟了一种自下而上的改革首创精神与自上而下的顶层设计相促进的教育创新与扩散模式。

### 1.2.2 历程上的局部到整体渐进式推进

从实际历程来看, CDIO 在一个学校成功实施后,从局部发展到整体,待发展相对成熟,教育行政部门将其改革实践纳入工程教育改革计划,并在高等工程教育领域加以倡导。综合各种因素,在中国的发展呈现出"吸纳-辐射"型特点,其逻辑链条为:汕头大学等高校的 CDIO 改革——引起兄弟院校和工程教育研究界关注——同行之间相互交流与模仿——获得教育行政部门认可,发文成立 CDIO 课题组——常态化的 CDIO 学术研讨会——CDIO 研究与改革成果展示——CDIO 权威性不断增强——吸纳更多的高校参与 CDIO 改革——加入全国重点工科高校教学改革协作组——成立 CDIO 工程教育联盟,转型为民间性学术组织。

制度理论认为,创新一种模式、成立一种新组织、传播一种新观念,都具有挑战性,需要克服"新进入缺陷",赢得相关利益群体的认可、赞同与支持,即获得关乎其生存与发展的所谓"合情理性"。这个"合情理性"是社会学和政治学的核心概念之一,用于分析特定社会现象或社会行动的发展与扩散机制。教育行政部门可以通过行政系统开展和推动改革,具备天然的高权威性;同时,在中国的国情下,如果某项改革由历史悠久的著名高校发起,鉴于其具备雄厚的声望、资源和影响力,其改革举措会比较容易成为被模仿和被学习的对象。而反观 CDIO 工程教育改革,其是由汕头大学一所地方高校发起,若干其他地方高校实施的、自下而上的工程教育改革。所以, CDIO 若要在高等工程教育界获得认可,获得较多的资源、情感和认知支持，必然要长期坚持，靠结果证明，因此需要付出巨大的努力。

2014 年，在教育部理工处的倡导下，汕头大学代表 CDIO 试点工作组，加入全国高等学校工科教学改革协作组，这使得由地方大学开展的 CDIO 工程教育改革与研究型大学主导的工程教育良好结合，促使 CDIO 在更多的平台上与各类型教学改革和人才培养模式开展交流。

## 2 CDIO 对中国高等工程教育的影响

### 2.1 改变了中国工程教育的思维模式

#### 2.1.1 学校层面

中国近几十年来的工业化进程对工程人才的需求迫切，因此各层级的学校都非常重视工程人才培养，从全国大学工科学生招生人数占全部大学生的比例就可以明显看出这一点。同时，各学校也在积极探索提高工程人才培养质量的有效途径。但是，在如何系统地解决"培养什么样的工程人才"以及"如何培养这样的人才"这两个根本问题上的讨论与实践仍然需要做大量工作。

对工程人才而言，这两个关键问题具体表现为：其一，工科学生毕业时，应具备哪些知识、能力和素质，且达到怎样的掌握水平？其二，如何能更好地保证学生学到这些知识和能力？这也就是任何教育者都必须面对的"做什么"和"如何做"的问题。CDIO 直接从这两个问题出发，制定了 CDIO 的两个最重要的文件——CDIO 能力大纲和 CDIO 12条标准。因此，CDIO 工程教育改革影响了很多学校的思维模式，学校开始重新思考，如何系统性地提高工程人才的培养质量，而不仅仅是想到什么就增加课程补什么，而是想清楚自己的学校要什么，如何去做，如何做得更好。

CDIO 模式不仅获得工程教育界的认可，而且很多高校都把工程专业 CDIO 改革的经验推广到全校其他非工科专业。例如，汕头大学把工学院 CDIO 改革经验推广到全校，构建了以 OBE 教学体系为骨架的"先进本科教育"。出现这种现象的原因并非偶然。一般认为，CDIO 工程教育模式有两个精华，即 CDIO 能力大纲和 CDIO 12条标准，它们为工程教育实践者提供了可操作的改革借鉴。但我们认为，蕴含在大纲和标准背后的是 CDIO 工程教育模式构建时体现的"科学性"和"系统性"取向，这可以启发教育改革者思考如何构建科学水平高的教育模式。

具体地讲，第一，在人才培养目标制定上，CDIO 通过实施复杂但有条理的量化调查方法，收集到不同利益相关群体对现代工程师所必备的知识、能力和素质及其掌握层级的观点。第二，为了使培养目标能够有效地导入教育活动中，CDIO 创建者根据布鲁姆教育目标分类理论和丰富的调查资料，构建起可测评的培养标准。这是至关重要的一步，也是传统上人才培养模式改革所缺失的环节。第三，在一体化课程计划设计上，充分体现了认知和能力螺旋式提高的规律，进行全程渗透式培养。第四，在培养结果评价上，综合使用定量与定性方法，衡量是否达到了预期学习结果。第五，总体上讲，CDIO 改革是专业层面上的培养目标导向的全方位的教育综合改革。

提高人才培养质量，要尽可能地对影响人才成长的整个环节进行设计、监测和改进。CDIO 模式（图 1）就是一套符合教育学和心理学规律的教育质量保障体系，它在培养目标、培养措施、培养方法和培养结果等任一环节都是经过反复思考和科学设计的，培养环节可以监控是否符合预期设计，整体改革的成效也是可以衡量并持续改善的。CDIO 模式所蕴含的针对教育改革的科学态度和科学方法，是它能够为人接受并能够推广到非工科专业的深层次原因。

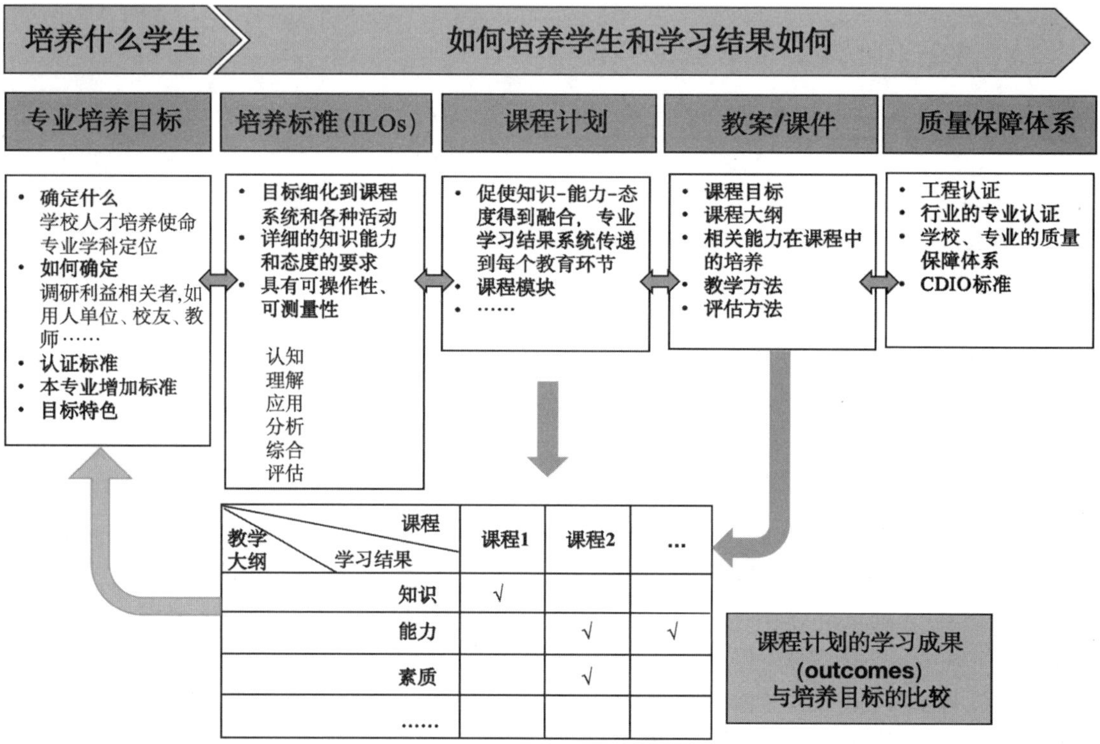


**图 1　CDIO 工作总体思路**

### 2.1.2　专业层面

工程教育改革过程中常常出现以下现象。在专业层面上认为，人才培养计划就是课程计划，专业培养目标不够具体，因此导致理解与实施不够系统，无论怎么实施总能自圆其说，并未系统地思考人才培养模式，因此很难在根本上系统地解决提高自身专业人才培养质量的问题。另外，在专业课程计划修订过程中，课程计划经常未认真细致地修订就延续使用，缺少系统地进行分析、论证和修改的严谨过程。在有些情况下，并不知道课程计划是如何产生的、是否合理、有哪些可改进的地方等等。再就是如果学校说要推进某个方面的改革，首先考虑的是增加这个方面的课程，其次是借鉴兄弟院校的课程计划，采用有新意的课程却没有思考这些课程是否适合自身专业的培养目标。因此，当前高等工程教育的主流还是学科中心，反映在培养方案上就是各自独立的学科课程和“缺啥补啥”的课程体系，而不是站在把学生培养成专业人员的角度进行培养方案的整合和优化。CDIO、OBE，尤其是工程专业认证的要求，正在扭转这一现象。

推进 CDIO 工作之后，大家逐渐明白人才培养不仅仅是课程计划，它包括在一系列人才需求的调研基础上，确定专业培养目标和毕业要求、专业培养标准、课程计划、课程教学大纲、课程教案等（图 2），评估与反馈的全过程。这一工作过程改变了很多专业领导者的思维，让他们在推进新一轮的改革工作、卓越工程师教育培养计划、工程专业认证等工作时，不自觉地融入了 CDIO 所推荐的思维模式，也就是今天工程专业认证所倡导的基于学习结果的教育（OBE）理念。

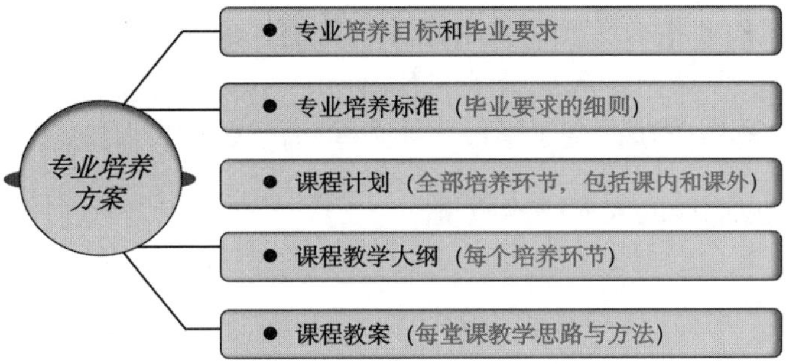


**图 2　汕头大学 CDIO 专业培养方案的构成**

### 2.1.3　教师层面

教师工作就是教学、科研、服务三大任务。以前的理解是，教学主要是上课，很少有教师思考自己所上课程在专业人才培养中的地位是什么、它为什么存在、它是如何产生的等问题，或者说，教师在这方面缺乏相应的意识。教师经常思考的是如何提高自身的授课能力和水平。

推进 CDIO 工作之后，部分骨干教师逐渐认识到，在专业人才培养体系中，课程的意义不仅在于知识传授，更重要的是要明确课程设置的缘由、课程的目标、与其他课程的关系、课程对专业毕业要求的贡献，以及如何通过多种方式达成课程目标。同时，教师也逐渐认识到，学校所要求的服务工作，其主体不仅仅是行政管理人员，教师也应该积极投身于教学改革工作。因此，教师在参与 CDIO 改革工作的过程中，逐渐理顺了思维逻辑，拓宽了教育视野，也更清晰地认识到自己在专业发展与人才培养中所处的位置和应承担的责任。

### 2.1.4　学生层面

对于广大学生，他们经常是被动的，学什么、为什么学、怎么学，这些问题一般都很少有明确的答案。相应地，学生很难主动规划自己的学习与成长。最典型的状态是，教师让选什么课就上什么课，对于为什么学和学了有什么用则思考较少。这不怪学生，传统的思维与做法，使得学生极少参与专业培养方案的建设。

推进 CDIO 工作之后，学校采取各种措施，包括课外宣讲、导论课、项目设计课、专业课等，尽力使更多的学生理解什么是 CDIO、CDIO 的内涵是什么、我们准备怎么做等一系列以前学生不关心的问题。通过这些举措，学生在思维方式上逐渐明白，在推进 CDIO 的工作中，自己不仅是主体，也是改革者和实践者，同样需要承担相应的责任。

### 2.1.5 用人单位层面

对于用人单位来说，一直以来，学校和专业做的工作较为狭窄，就是向用人单位推荐毕业生，期望他们多招聘自己的毕业生，这些单位往往是学校推荐毕业生的被动接受者，这些传统的思维与做法反映出学校和用人单位的思维模式都需要改变。

推进 CDIO 工作之后，特别是从专业层面系统性推进改革的工作后，用人单位的需求成了设计专业培养目标、专业培养标准的核心之一，用人单位的需求反馈成了专业培养方案修订的主要依据之一，有些培养方案还邀请用人单位深入地参加设计专业培养目标与专业培养标准、实施培养计划、调研培养成效等工作，使得用人单位也成为专业培养的主体之一。这些工作的开展与深入，逐步改变了学校与用人单位的关系和思维模式。

## 2.2 提高了试点高校的人才培养质量

### 2.2.1 汕头大学

汕头大学是 CDIO 试点工作组组长单位。以工学院学生毕业生平均年薪为例，在 2005 年 CDIO 改革以前，汕头大学工学院毕业生的就业率、平均工资低于广东省高校平均水平。自 2010 年起（2006 年第一届 CDIO 改革后的毕业生），就业率和平均工资就逐渐增加并高于省平均水平（见表 1、表 2）。例如，2011 年起，汕头大学就业率就高于省平均水平；2014 年，汕头大学工科毕业生初始平均薪酬比广东省工科毕业生平均水平高出 17.85%。汕头大学 2015 年毕业生的自主创业率为 1.3%，远高于广东省平均水平（0.38%）。学生在国内外科技竞赛中的获奖数量和级别显著提高，汕头大学发表了多篇高引用率的教学研究论文，建设了国家级人才培养模式创新实验区和多个国家级工程实践教育中心。

**表 1 汕头大学工学院各专业本科毕业生与广东省平均就业率比较**

| 专业 | 2009 年 | 2010 年 | 2011 年 | 2012 年 | 2013 年 | 2014 年 | 2015 年 |
|---|---|---|---|---|---|---|---|
| 通信 | 84.62% | 95.00% | 100.00% | 100.00% | 100.00% | 97.78% | 95.65% |
| 电子信息 | 91.01% | 92.00% | 100.00% | 97.40% | 97.33% | 98.67% | 98.48% |
| 机械设计、制造和自动化 | 94.44% | 100.00% | 98.61% | 100.00% | 95.60% | 99.00% | 96.77% |
| 土木 | 95.83% | 88.57% | 94.44% | 100.00% | 100.00% | 100.00% | 98.75% |
| 计算机 | 80.88% | 94.23% | 98.44% | 98.31% | 98.46% | 98.36% | 95.38% |
| 汕大工学院平均 | 88.99% | 94.76% | 98.60% | 98.99% | 98.28% | 98.76% | 97.02% |
| 广东平均 | 96.59% | 97.50% | 95.84% | 95.09% | 96.11% | 95.77% | 95.28% |

**表 2　汕头大学与广东省高校工科生初始平均薪酬比较**

| 年份 | 汕大工科毕业生初始平均薪酬/元 | 广东工科毕业生初始平均薪酬/元 | 差别 |
|---|---|---|---|
| 2009 年 | 2063 | 2108 | −2.13% |
| 2010 年 | 2553 | 2359 | 8.22% |
| 2011 年 | 2987 | 2732 | 9.33% |
| 2012 年 | 3590 | 3017 | 18.99% |
| 2013 年 | 3402 | 3094 | 9.95% |
| 2014 年 | 3916 | 3323 | 17.85% |

在汕头大学申报国家级教学成果专家鉴定会上，以清华大学原副校长余寿文教授为组长的专家委员会一致认为：汕头大学的教改工作经过长时间的实践检验，全面反映了“回归工程”的改革趋势，指导理念先进、方案设计科学、可操作性强，在创新人才培养模式、优化教育教学管理机制、提高人才培养质量、推广人才培养经验等方面成果显著，达到了国内领先水平。

### 2.2.2　燕山大学

燕山大学机械工程学院于 2007 年开始实施 CDIO 工程教育模式改革，参加了教育部 CDIO 模式教学改革试点课题组，并成为机械专业试点小组的牵头单位和 CDIO 中国区域中心成员。2008 年，在燕山大学修订的本科培养方案中，机械工程学院大部分课程都进行了“做中学”与“基于项目的教育和学习”有机结合的教学改革，目前，CDIO 模式教学改革已经辐射到燕山大学其他理工类专业教学[7]。各门课程出勤率、平均成绩以及课程设计、毕业设计质量均有明显提高。学生科技作品多次在校级、省级乃至国家级的学生科技作品竞赛上获奖。近几年学生一次就业率始终保持在 97%以上，就业形势一直在学校内保持领先水平，毕业生深受企业欢迎。

### 2.2.3　成都信息工程大学

成都信息工程大学倡导并实施 CDIO 工程教育理念和模式，在全校深入推进以专业建设为主线的教育教学一体化改革，成为全国 CDIO 工程教育模式试点工作组副组长单位和电气组召集单位、四川省教育体制改革试点院校。学校现有 4 个省级高校实验教学示范中心、2 个省级人才培养模式创新实验区、26 门国家级和省级精品课程。在近两届教学成果奖评选中，学校共获得国家级教学成果二等奖 2 项，省级教学成果一等奖 10 项、二等奖 7 项、三等奖 10 项；近五年来，学生在全国重大科技竞赛中获得全国性奖励 168 项，其中，全国大学生电子设计竞赛连续五届获奖总数位列全国高校前七位、一般高校第一。据麦可思人力资源信息管理咨询有限公司对高校毕业生的跟踪调研，成都信息工程大学学生的就业能力和就业质量连续多年位居全省高校前列[8]。

### 2.2.4　云南大学

云南大学软件学院是国家示范性软件学院。 云南大学软件学院创新性地提出 SE-

CDIO（SE 为 Software Engineering）工程教育模式，改变了 CDIO 试点专业主要集中在机械类、电气类、化工类和土木类的局面[9]。该软件学院从 2006 级本科生开始小规模实验性应用 CDIO 工程教育模式，于 2008 年完成第一轮全过程的实验性改革。同年，软件学院获准了国家教学质量工程项目“基于 CDIO 的国际化、工程化软件人才培养创新实验区”（简称实验区）。基于前面阶段 CDIO 实验应用的效果，正式提出 SE-CDIO 工程教育模式，并从 2008 级本科生开始，实施 SE-CDIO 模式的纵深发展与应用。到 2012 年，新一轮全过程改革与实践全部完成，SE-CDIO 工程教育模式得到了完善，无论是在课程体系、实践环境，还是在教学组织形式、教学运行和管理机制、国内及国际合作等诸多方面都取得了显著的成效，获得省级教学成果一等奖和国家级教学成果二等奖。SE-CDIO 模式被列入《云南大学“十二五”发展规划纲要》，用于开展拔尖学生培养模式改革，并在云南大学开始大规模推广应用。

### 2.3 促进了工程教育教学改革与研究

#### 2.3.1 CDIO 类高等教育教学改革成果不断涌现

2016 年 6 月，笔者登录各省、自治区、直辖市教育厅及教育部网站，查询近两届高等教育类教学成果公示结果，在成果名称中出现“CDIO”的省级教改成果共计 23 项，国家级教学改革成果 2 项，地域范围涉及 19 个省和直辖市。以 CDIO 思想或模式来统筹规划高校、专业及课程的教育改革，能够取得一定成效并获得省级及以上高等教育类教学成果奖，从一个侧面反映出 CDIO 对我国高等工程教育改革产生的积极影响。有些教学成果虽然名称中没有包含“CDIO”字样，其实其教学改革中贯穿 CDIO 模式的理念和做法，例如成都信息工程大学的教学改革成果“西部地方院校工程教育改革的实践与探索”，该成果获得 2014 年国家级高等教育类教学成果二等奖，它在内容和实践上充分体现了 CDIO 的改革思路。

#### 2.3.2 CDIO 类教研论文逐年增多

笔者于 2016 年 7 月 14 日以 CDIO 为主题词在中国知网（CNKI）数据库进行检索，检索到以 CDIO 为主题词的论文共 3323 篇（见图 3），内容涵盖“高等教育”和“职业教育”。自 2006 年以来，国内 CDIO 研究的总量大致逐年递增，并自 2009 年开始进入快速增长期，这种快速增长趋势直到 2012 年才开始逐渐放缓。2008 年是国内 CDIO 研究中国化发展过程中至关重要的一年，也正是从这一年开始，国内涉及 CDIO 的期刊论文数量稳步增多，以汕头大学为代表的主要研究机构开始由理论探讨走向实践探索。这一年，以 CDIO 工程教育改革为核心的“汕头大学工学院 EIP-CDIO 工程教育模式创新实验区”获批，汕头大学 EIP-CDIO 工程教育改革开始，多篇文献表明汕头大学的 CDIO 改革在这一年里取得了实质性进展。

需要指出的是，CDIO 模式并非工程教育领域的专利，其他学科也应用了 CDIO 模式开展改革。Crawley 等人在创立 CDIO 模式之初即已明确指出 CDIO 原理可以用于大多数高等教育专业，运用 CDIO 原理改革现有专业的优势包括：①为教育创设实践的环境；②学生在一系列给定的知识、能力和态度上达成的预期学习效果最终由利益相关者反馈决定；③课程计划与教学方法是一体化的，协同为达成学生的预期学习效果服务；④强调教学过程的持续改进，对学生的学习情况和整个专业的培养目标进行有效评估，并将评估结果及时反馈给师生[10]。

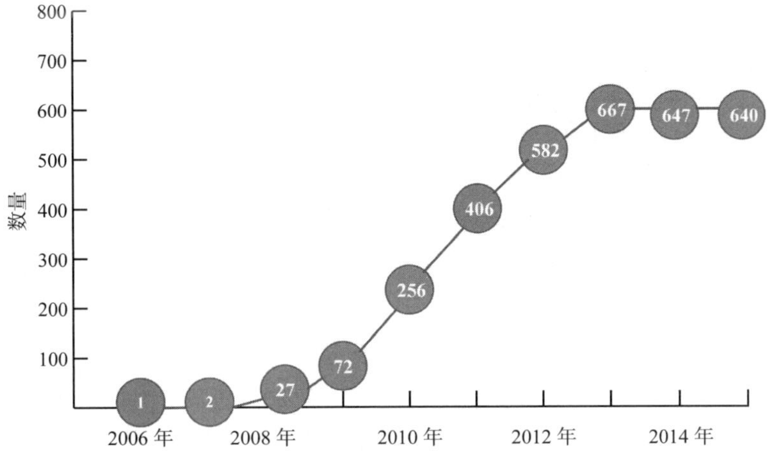


**图 3　分年度 CDIO 类论文数量**

近年来，随着研究的不断深入，国内 CDIO 模式的应用已从工程教育领域拓展到外国语言文学、宏观经济管理、美术、会计、医学等多个高等教育领域。其中，外国语言文学学科对 CDIO 模式的探究最为突出。截至目前，外国语言文学学科已发表关于 CDIO 模式探究成果的期刊论文 165 篇，占所有 CDIO 模式研究论文总量的 3%左右。

### 2.3.3　促进了工科教师的教学发展

2008 年 12 月，在教育部高教司理工处倡议和课题组框架下，成立了 CDIO 试点工作组。在理工处领导下，CDIO 试点工作组先后组织 8 次 CDIO 培训班。培训班的目的是让更多教育实践者掌握 CDIO 模式所蕴含的基本思路、解决工程教育问题的独特视角，展示 CDIO 工程教育模式的实用价值，探讨各高校改革经验的理论化，向一线教师骨干传授 CDIO 模式的实质、内涵及实施路径。这些培训工作有效地传播了 CDIO 模式，促进了骨干教师对 CDIO 模式特点的理解，使他们由衷地认可 CDIO 模式所蕴含的“一体化”思想、“工程文化”思想及 CDIO 能力大纲的可操作性。

以 2011 年全国 CDIO 工程教育改革会议暨教育部 CDIO 高级研修班为例，此次大会有以下特点。①参会人数空前，360 人的规模是历届 CDIO 会议之最，且在会议筹备后期，考虑到会场、住宿、餐饮等因素，会务组对人数进行了比较严格的控制，若无此措施，会议人数还会继续增加。②此次大会受到了越来越多“985 工程”“211 工程”高校的重视，如浙江大学、华中科技大学、北京邮电大学、国防科技大学、北京交通大学等，反映出 CDIO 工程教育改革在这些高校中的影响力越来越大。③报告数量和内容空前。此次大会的专题报告总计 34 个，报告人包括教育部领导和各高校校长、院长、系主任和一线教师，内容包括改革方案、培养模式、目标体系、课程与项目体系、课程与项目设计、教学方法与策略、过程管理与控制、结果考评与改进，涵盖了改革的宏观、中观、细观和微观层面。④报告人的主动性和积极性高。除少数特邀报告外，此次大会的大部分报告是征集而来的，而且筹备后期不断有试点高校要求做报告，报告人的主动性和积极性被充分调动，极大地促进了改革经验和成果的分享与交流。

### 2.4 推动了 OBE 改革及项目导向的课程模式

CDIO 实质上是一套实施“基于学习结果的工程教育模式”（OBE）的系统。它以可测评的 CDIO 能力大纲为导向，统筹配置教育内容、教育资源、师资队伍和教育评价。基于学习结果的教育模式，同传统上教育者熟悉的“重投入、重过程”的教育模式有较大不同。它强调教育者要切实树立“学生中心”的意识，对学生学习结果负责并建立完善的教育质量保障系统。我国于 2013 年成为《华盛顿协议》预备签约成员，2016 年成为正式成员。中国工程教育专业认证协会陆续开展了工程教育专业认证。构建与《华盛顿协议》实质等效的工程教育认证系统和质量标准，为了实现结果导向的毕业生标准要求，认证专业需要实施 OBE 工程人才培养模式改革。

由于 CDIO 与 OBE 的关联性，汕头大学后来提出了 CDIO-OBE 模式，即用 CDIO 大纲和标准实现 OBE 的培养要求，给出了满足以 OBE 为理念的工程专业认证要求的实施方法。这对促进工程教育改革者树立学习结果导向意识、实施专业认证以及后来的审核评估都具有积极影响。CDIO 另外一个重要影响是，在课程计划上，工程教育者普遍重视工程实践项目与理论教学的统筹安排，构建多层次设计项目导向的课程体系，这一做法也是 CDIO 模式本身的要求。这不仅克服了传统工程教育课程体系不科学的弊病，而且改变了工程教育课程计划先理论、后实践的结构。我们从各院校 CDIO 改革的实践中可以看到这些特点。

#### 2.4.1 汕头大学

汕头大学工学院构建了 CDIO-OBE 模式。自 2005 年实施 CDIO 改革以来，结合国际工程教育发展趋势，尝试以预期学习结果的“设计—定义—组织—实现—评价”为主脉络来构建新型工程教育模式。同时，在定义预期学习结果、设计课程计划、选择教学策略、评估学习结果和完善质量保障体系等方面又充分借鉴了 CDIO 能力大纲和 CDIO 的一体化教育理念。经不断探索，形成了以 OBE 为主线、充分借鉴 CDIO 精华的 CDIO-OBE 工程教育模式。汕头大学创建的 CDIO-OBE 工程教育模式，开辟了用 CDIO 去实现 OBE 的新思路和新途径，深化了对人才培养规律和教育规律的认识。多年实践表明，该模式能够提高人才培养质量，符合工程专业认证要求，且具有较强的通用性和普适性。

#### 2.4.2 成都信息工程大学

成都信息工程大学通信工程学院的 CDIO 改革，围绕“一个核心、一个导向、三个层次、一条主线”的改革路径[11]。①一个核心是指以角色为核心——以电子信息类学生未来可能从事的职业的基本需求为基础设定了三类角色（系统架构师、设计师、应用工程师）。②一个导向是指以工程师职业训练为导向。通过与专业充分结合的工程性（综合性）的一级项目、二级项目、三级项目的团队式训练（由一级项目所分解的子系统作为二级项目，以及由二级项目所涉及的单元性功能模块作为三级项目），将对工程学生的工程基础知识、个人能力、人际团队能力和工程系统能力的培养深度融入教育教学全过程。③三个层次是指课程体系的结构和内容分解为“应用系统、功能模块、基本单元”三个层次。④一条主线是以“应用系统、功能模块、基本单元”为主线贯穿于课程体系的结构和内容的优化设计中。

### 2.4.3 燕山大学

燕山大学机械工程学院的改革充分体现了 OBE 和 CDIO 的特点[12]。引入基于 OBE 教育理念的人才培养模式，要求各专业面向社会，立足行业，以满足社会需求为确立和完善人才培养目标的主要依据，要求“反向设计，正向施工”，注重对学生能力的培养与评估，强调培养学生运用专业知识解决实际工程问题的能力，注重对学生创新意识和实践能力的培养。同时，在 CDIO 教育理念的框架下构建了一体化项目式课程体系。该课程体系以学生为主体、教师为主导，并以工程能力培养为目标，而贯穿该体系的主线便是丰富多样的项目体系。它包含三个层次的项目，即三级项目（课程项目）、二级项目（专业综合项目）和一级项目。三级项目设置于专业基础和专业课程内，以本门课程基础知识的应用为主要内容，旨在加强学生对本门课程核心知识或技能的理解和运用；二级项目通常将多门专业核心课程内容相结合，并与三级项目相关联，旨在加强学生专业核心能力的培养；毕业设计一级项目主要是让学生参与教师为企业开发的新产品或关键技术改造的项目，培养学生综合运用专业知识和技术解决工程问题的能力，培养学生综合全面的能力与素质。

### 2.4.4 中国石油大学

中国石油大学理学院创建了 MPC-CDIO 教育教学模式[13]。以大学物理课程体系为例，根据人才培养目标和类型，该校在教材选用、教学内容、教学手段、课程项目等方面进行筛选和建设，教学内容体系注重理论与实践、物理与数学的结合，体现石油特色，注重学生“知识、能力、素质”一体化的协调发展。为了更有效地实现 CDIO 能力培养，学院按照专业人才培养需求，进行了 CDIO 能力分析，筛选出凸显数理能力和素养特征的核心能力条款，研发出相应的研究项目，并以这些研究项目作为纽带，对数理的核心课程及其内容等进行了优化与重组，形成了三级 MPC-CDIO 项目体系，最终实现学生数理的交叉融合和“知识、能力、素质”的协调发展，为专业基础课程群项目研究以及毕业设计项目研究奠定基础。

### 2.4.5 云南大学

云南大学软件学院实施了 SE-CDIO 改革[14]。软件学院基于 CDIO 教育理念，结合自身实际，按照课程的规模和范围，以 CDIO 能力培养大纲为目标，以项目的构思、设计、开发、运行为主线，构建了点、线、面相结合的三级课程体系，一级为单门课程或课程群（点），二级为专业实践和实训课程（线），三级为毕业设计和综合性改革（面），构建一体化的教育体系。

## 2.5 推动了中国高等工程教育重要改革项目

### 2.5.1 推动卓越工程师教育培养计划

2010 年 6 月，教育部启动和实施卓越工程师教育培养计划，该计划积极贯彻落实《国家中长期教育改革和发展规划纲要（2010—2020 年）》和《国家中长期人才发展规划纲要（2010—2020 年）》，是促进我国由工程教育大国转变为工程教育强国的重要措施。在教育部理工处的指导下，CDIO 试点组主动融入政府主导的工程教育重要改革项目，为推进项目开展和卓越工程师教育培养计划实施贡献智慧与力量，汕头大学等 CDIO 试点高校做出了不懈努力。

一是论证 CDIO 与卓越工程师教育培养计划的关联性。在《CDIO 在中国》（上）一文中，顾佩华教授等详细论证了卓越工程师教育培养计划五项重点任务与 CDIO 12 条标准之间的对应关系，阐述了卓越工程师教育培养计划与 CDIO 的基本目标、任务、理念与方法以及内容，指出二者具有高度的相关性和兼容性[15]。2011 年 12 月，在全国 CDIO 工程教育改革会议暨教育部 CDIO 高级研修班上，时任成都信息工程学院校长的周定文教授作了题为“深化 CDIO 改革，推进卓越工程师教育培养计划”的主题报告。他在报告中指出，卓越工程师教育培养计划是我国工程教育改革的目标，而 CDIO 是实现这个目标的手段之一，并阐述了两者之间的相通之处。

二是为卓越工程师教育培养计划申报单位开展培训。为帮助第二批申报卓越工程师教育培养计划的高校理解该计划的基本精神和申报要求，教育部高教司于 2010 年 12 月在北京分两批组织召开了卓越工程师教育培养计划申报工作研讨会。时任汕头大学教务处处长的陆小华教授应邀为研讨会作了题为“一体化教学的基本思想与课程设计”的两场专题报告，阐明卓越工程师教育培养计划学校标准和学校方案的制定原则，阐述卓越工程师教育培养计划在教育理念与方法上对 CDIO 工程教育改革的借鉴。2013 年 6 月，教育部高教司、研究生司在天津召开教育部省级区域卓越工程师教育培养计划工作交流会。陆小华处长介绍了一体化培养模式与课程体系设计。北京石油化工学院介绍本校制定和实施国家卓越工程师教育培养计划方案的经验。一体化培养模式与课程设计是卓越工程师教育培养计划学校方案编制所采用的方法基础，是从 CDIO 工程教育试点工作中提炼而来的。一体化培养模式在卓越工程师教育培养计划中采用是教育部所领导的 CDIO 工程教育试点工作组的重要成绩，也是 CDIO 对我国工程教育改革所作的贡献。

三是 CDIO 试点高校为实施卓越工程师教育培养计划提供典型案例。2010 年 6 月，教育部高教司从卓越工程师教育培养计划第一批 61 所高校中挑选了六个典型案例，CDIO 试点高校就有两个，分别是北京石油化工大学（化学工程与工艺专业）和汕头大学（机械设计制造及其自动化专业）。同时，教育部编写了包含 12 所高校的《“卓越工程师教育培养计划”部分高校方案汇编》，其中有 4 所高校借鉴和使用了汕头大学首创的“三级项目”和（或）“鱼骨图”课程构架。实际上，众多一线教师在实施卓越工程师教育培养计划时，也借鉴了 CDIO 的基本理念与方法。例如，吕九芳等在家具设计与工程专业中应用了 CDIO 模式[8]；郭长虹等在构建工程图学卓越工程师教育培养计划教学体系时应用了 CDIO 模式[9]；周海等在实施机械设计课程教学时也借鉴了 CDIO 理念和方法[10]。类似的案例还有很多。

姜嘉乐副主编在汕头大学的一次调研中曾说，汕头大学等高校的 CDIO 改革促进了 CDIO 中国化，深刻地影响了国内众多高校的工程教育改革，并成为影响教育部卓越工程师教育培养计划实施最深刻、最全面和最具有普适意义的案例。

### 2.5.2 推动工程专业认证

2013 年 7 月，中国成为《华盛顿协议》预备签约成员。我国工程教育采用与《华盛顿协议》实质等效的培养标准，达到《华盛顿协议》规定，实现与各签约成员工程教育质量的实质等效。因此，需要构建学习结果导向的工程教育体系，形成持续改进的质量保障体系。CDIO 工程教育模式，特别是细化的 CDIO 能力大纲，不仅可以与工程认证标准中的毕业要求完全对应，而且比其要求更加细化且可以操作，所以可以将 12 条毕业要求分解成具体的可观察和评价的能力、知识和态度。汕头大学等 CDIO 试点高校提供了如何把《华盛顿协议》对毕业生能力的要求落实到教育各环节中的案例，并通过培训、报告和论文等形式把它传播到工程教育界，有助于推进工程专业认证的开展。

一是受邀在中国工程教育专业认证协会培训会上交流经验。2014 年 4 月，中国工程教育专业认证协会组织第一期工程教育专业认证培训会，汕头大学执行校长顾佩华教授应邀为学员做了题为"面向工程认证的 CDIO-OBE 工程教育模式"的报告。顾佩华教授在报告中介绍了国内外基于学习结果的工程教育发展历程、特点以及汕头大学对 CDIO-OBE 工程教育模式的探索。2014 年 9 月，教育部高等教育教学评估中心举办了工程教育认证交流研讨会。作为通过专业认证的代表单位之一，汕头大学工学院委派林鹏教授详细分享了在土木专业中运用 CDIO-OBE 工程教育模式组织和开展工程教育认证的经验。

二是承办中国工程教育专业认证协会培训会。鉴于汕头大学较早地探索和实践了用 CDIO 实现工程专业认证，教育部高等教育教学评估中心委托汕头大学承办 2014 年 12 月第三期工程教育专业认证培训会。全国 105 所高校的 600 余名教师代表参加了研讨会。教育部高等教育教学评估中心吴岩主任、周爱军副主任，中国工程教育专业认证协会副理事长余寿文教授以及教育部理工处领导参加了培训会。汕头大学执行校长顾佩华介绍了工程教育专业认证与 OBE 教育模式，教务处处长陆小华介绍了汕头大学 OBE 教育模式的设计与执行，工学院副院长林鹏汇报了土木专业认证工作以及 OBE 教学体系的构建与实施，土木工程系喻莹副教授、王英姿副教授分别介绍了基于 OBE 的课程、项目设计的构建与实施。在大会交流环节，参会代表针对中国工程教育专业认证的具体要求、汕头大学如何进行工程教育专业认证、如何推进 OBE 工作等问题进行提问。此外，汕头大学全面地向与会人员展示了专业认证工作流程、教学文档资料整理和自评报告撰写等认证活动。此次会议使参会人员了解了工程教育认证的体系和标准，初步认清了工程教育专业认证发展趋势，开阔了工程教育专业办学思路，为很多高校拟启动的工程教育专业认证前期准备工作提供了启示。

三是系统总结运用 CDIO-OBE 模式组织和实现工程专业认证的经验。顾佩华、胡文龙在《基于"学习产出"（OBE）的工程教育模式——汕头大学的实践与探索》一文中全面详细地介绍了用 CDIO 实现工程认证的做法[11]。该文总结了汕头大学运用 CDIO 实现 OBE 的新思路和新途径，有助于深化对人才培养规律和教育规律的认识。多年实践表明，该模式能够提高人才培养质量，符合工程专业认证要求，且具有较强的通用性和普适性。

四是 CDIO 试点高校成为《华盛顿协议》考查学校。2013 年，我国加入《华盛顿协议》，成为预备成员，2016 年初接受转正考查。燕山大学是国内首批加入 CDIO 教育改革的高等院校之一，并作为机械类组的牵头单位于 2008 年春季学期开始实施基于 CDIO 模式的教育教学改革。鉴于燕山大学工程教育改革方面的成果，中国工程教育专业认证协会秘书处建议燕山大学作为《华盛顿协议》组织考查的观摩单位之一。在多年 CDIO 改革基础上，按照工程专业认证要求，燕山大学材料成型及控制工程和电子信息工程两个专业基于学习产出

（OBE）的理念对专业人才培养目标、毕业要求的合理性、课程教学等各教学环节的设计与实施、达成度评价等各个环节进行了全面梳理，达到了认证标准并通过了专家考核。燕山大学的专业认证组织工作得到了《华盛顿协议》组织秘书处的高度评价，教育部高等教育教学评估中心致函对燕山大学组织认证的工作表示肯定。

## 3 CDIO在中国发展的原因分析

作为一种工程教育模式，CDIO首先要面对的是它能否有效地解决中国工程教育中存在的问题（培养什么样的工程人才和如何培养这两个根本问题），体现出此模式相对于传统模式的优越性。托尔伯特（Tolbert）等认为，“合理化”要完成两大关键任务[12]：一是明确组织失灵的原因并进行抽象分类，为解决不同类型的组织失灵进行局部创新；二是论证创新的正当性，即证明在实践中新理念比旧理念更具优越性。这样，局部创新才能在较大的范围内扩散推广。新制度模式要经过从理论到社会实践再到制度规则这样的过程转变才能真正成型。也就是说，针对中国高等工程教育界存在的问题，CDIO要证明自身较之其他人才培养模式的优越性和适用性，否则就很难令人信服和自觉地接受。

### 3.1 从CDIO自身视角

#### 3.1.1 内因：CDIO自身的系统性为解决高等工程教育难题提供了方法

CDIO能够兴起和发展，是因为与传统工程教学模式相比较，CDIO的系统性使得它有条件有效地解决中国高等工程教育的系列问题，而且通过众多高校的不断实践，逐渐给出和丰富了它具体的实施方法，这是其存在的根本性原因。CDIO的系统性最重要的体现就是CDIO人才培养模式是由培养目标、培养标准、课程体系、教学方法和教学评价等要素构成，系统地回答了“培养什么样的人”以及“如何培养这样的人”这两个根本问题。

近年来，我国工程教育界探索并形成了多样化的人才培养模式。但是，高等工程教育领域尚未涌现出标志性的改革成果，人才培养质量无法满足建设创新型国家和走新型工业化道路的需求。具体地讲，工程教育面临以下问题。

（1）改革成果缺乏对教育因素的顶层设计。由于缺乏人才培养模式改革的顶层设计，当前的工程教育改革多是局部性和修补式的，缺少系统性和可持续性。

（2）工程教育难以突破理论教学与实践环节的隔阂。由于持“工程是科学的应用”这一观念，工科课程计划长期无法突破基础课、专业基础课、专业课的“三段式”划分和安排。基础课，甚至相当部分的专业基础课，是按科学教育的逻辑组织实施的，主要考虑的是学科体系的完整性，而不是按工程需要加以组织；实践课则主要安排在高年级，这使得实践教学难以发挥激发工科生专业兴趣、活化知识联结的功能。重理论、轻实践，理论与实践的分割在工程教育中普遍存在。

（3）工程教育急需对《华盛顿协议》等国际认证标准进行前瞻性审视。当前，工程教育界的国际化程度日益提高。在工程科技人才国际流动性增强以及中国成为《华盛顿协议》成员的背景下，要实现中国工程教育质量和人才培养标准的国际化、高水平，关键在于在全面满足《华盛顿协议》对工程教育人才培养标准要求的基础上，依据人才需求打造各学校的特色，按照"结果导向"的工程教育理念与模式推进专业教育改革。

（4）工程教育界需要标志性改革成果。改革开放以后，高等教育教学领域虽然涌现出一批成果，但总体来看还没有出现辐射广泛、影响持久且深远、为业界广泛认可的成果。

CDIO 产生的背景就是美欧工程教育存在"理论与实践"脱节的问题，导致教育质量和培养结果无法满足工业界的需求。CDIO 为解决上述问题提供了解决思路，因此提高了工程教育质量。CDIO 人才培养模式由培养目标、培养标准、课程体系、教学方法和教学评价等要素构成。实施 CDIO，至少要求在专业的层面，人才培养模式各要素协同演化、同步变革。

以汕头大学为例，为改变理论课与实践课截然分开、先理论后实践的课程设计方式，汕头大学等 CDIO 试点高校构建了以三层级设计项目为导向的课程体系，三层级项目贯穿工科生四年的学习历程。在低年级开设的"工程导论"课程中通常会包含一些基本的三级项目，通过这些项目让学生获得基本的设计-实现经验，引导学生形成解决工程问题的思路，活化基本的学科知识，增进学生对工程的兴趣；高年级则侧重于设置二级或三级项目，提供实际机会让学生对工程系统进行分析、设计、建造、测试以及可能的运行，使学生获得高级的设计-实现经验，项目主要来源于与工业界的合作项目或是实际的工程问题。其典型的展示方式就是汕头大学陆小华教授首创的鱼骨型课程表达方案。由于它清楚地显示了专业培养的基本方案和路径，连接各学科课程与综合应用、实践能力培养，被国内各高校广泛使用。

另一方面，汕头大学较早地认识到，在工程科技人才全球流动性增强的情况下，中国工程教育办学理念、标准和质量要达到与《华盛顿协议》标准实质等效的要求。从 2005 年实施 CDIO-OBE 改革以来，汕头大学就重视构建与《华盛顿协议》实质等效的培养标准，对 CDIO 能力大纲进行梳理和研究，实施新的培养质量标准体系。事实证明了汕头大学的预判。2013 年 6 月，中国成为《华盛顿协议》预备成员。第二年，即 2014 年 5 月，经住房城乡建设部高等教育土木工程专业评估委员会审议和表决，汕头大学土木工程专业顺利通过专业认证（评估），认证专家高度认可汕头大学土木工程专业细致、扎实和深入的教育改革。鉴于汕头大学较早地探索和实践了用 CDIO-OBE 工程教育模式来组织和实施工程专业认证，教育部高等教育教学评估中心委托汕头大学承办了 2014 年 12 月第三期工程教育专业认证培训会。

### 3.1.2 外因：中国教育体制改革提供了 CDIO 成长的土壤

《国家中长期教育改革和发展规划纲要（2010—2020 年）》在教育体制改革总体部署中，第一次提出了人才培养体制改革和人才培养模式创新的任务。人才培养模式，是在一定教育思想和教育理论的指导下，由教育制度、人才培养目标、培养方案、过程诸要素构成的相对稳定的教育教学过程与运行机制的总称。《国家中长期教育改革和发展规划纲要（2010—2020 年）》把人才培养观念、模式、制度作为一个整体，把创新人才培养模式作为人才培养体制改革的核心环节，突出了全球化时代国家对高校创新人才培养模式的紧迫感。

中国高等教育实现大众化后，各高校为了提高本科教育质量和培养创新型人才，根据学校定位和专业特点，探索出多样化的人才培养模式，如复合型、应用型、领军型、创新型等。

针对科技理性膨胀和人文精神式微，许多高校实施人文素质教育和通识教育等育人模式，在培养知识和技能的同时注重培养大学生广博的视野和社会责任感。与此同时，如何通过特色化办学实现高校内涵式和跨越式发展，提高高等教育质量，提高大学的声誉和品牌，进而吸引优质生源，是每一位高校领导和管理者所思考的问题。十年间，CDIO 在中国的发展由点到面、由浅入深，成为影响中国高等工程教育发展的重要事件之一，在一定程度上引领着工程教育改革的潮流，影响了一线教师教学改革的理念与实践。

在“十三五”期间的教育改革浪潮中，各高校若要抢占先机，就需要开动脑筋，发挥主观能动性，把自己置于“制度创业者”的角色。通过敏锐地抓住高等教育教学改革中出现的矛盾，积极动员和调动各方改革资源，实现学科建设、人才培养和办学模式等方面的“制度创业”，进而为高等教育发展提供新理念、新思想或新模式。

CDIO 在中国萌芽、传播、发展以及制度化的过程，也是以汕头大学、燕山大学和成都信息工程大学等试点高校为代表的“制度创业者”抓住高等教育大众化后面临的系列矛盾，协调 CDIO 试点高校动员各方资源，冲破“重科研，轻教学”的束缚，变革高等工程教育模式、理念与方法，把 CDIO 规则、理念和行为模式推广到高等工程教育界的过程。

### 3.2 从 CDIO 实施者视角

#### 3.2.1 内因：CDIO 改革主体表现出的教育改革实践的工匠精神

（1）CDIO 改革者的教育改革实践的工匠精神，表现在坚持不懈。

汕头大学是李嘉诚基金会资助的公立学校。李嘉诚先生在办学之初，就希望汕头大学能够把学生培养好。李嘉诚基金会在学校确立了“先进本科教育”战略，学校在资源配置、师资建设和管理机制等方面出台了一系列向教学倾斜的政策，组建了有创新思维、有执行力、能坚持的领导团队，认真落实本科教学工作的中心地位，并在复杂的办学环境里保持了战略定力。汕头大学的 CDIO 改革从 2005 年开始，截至目前已过了十多年，未曾有中断，反而根据高等教育发展形势不断地促进 CDIO 实现本土化。例如，汕头大学构建了 CDIO-OBE 模式，并以此模式来组织专业认证并获得了初步成果。在近 10 年的中国高校发展进程中，一所高校能够坚持不懈地长时间实行并完善 CDIO 模式改革，体现了对大学培养人才这一永恒使命的忠诚。

燕山大学是国内首批加入 CDIO 教育改革的高等院校之一，并作为机械类组的牵头单位于 2008 年春季学期开始实施基于 CDIO 模式的教育教学改革。该校机械工程学院在所有专业课和几乎全部教学环节中实施了教学改革，改革涉及学院的所有教师和所有本科生。燕山大学严格遵循 CDIO 大纲及标准，重新建立了以项目为主线的课程教学体系，制定了以设计为导向、以工程能力培养为目标的培养方案；构建了三级项目为主导的分级教学模式，将课堂讲解、实验教学、研究讨论、项目实施、汇报竞赛等多种教学形式和教学内容有机地结合在一起，形成了对学生理论知识、实践运用、综合提炼、总结表述等全方位综合能力的训练；建立了注重过程和综合能力的全程监控的课程考核机制，既保证了学生全程参与教学活动，又调动了学生的积极性，有效提高了人才培养质量。

（2）CDIO 改革者的教育改革实践的工匠精神，表现在精益求精。

在汕头大学 CDIO-OBE 模式改革中，每位课程负责人或任课教师都需要明确所授课程对细化培养标准的贡献，都要撰写详细的、可查性强的教案，都要时刻分析学情，评估并改善学习结果和教学质量。为保留学生学习状态的“证据”，教师要详细地记录这些细微的课堂教学活动，并编撰成厚厚的课程档案。课程档案的内容包括教学大纲、教案、PPT、作业、评估以及反思报告等。它凝结着任课教师的心血，体现着精益求精和精雕细琢的工匠精神。无怪乎，凡是实地考察或参观过汕头大学 CDIO 改革，或者看过汕头大学工学院任课教师课程档案的人员，都会被这种细致入微、精雕细刻的教学行为震撼。在这一过程中，一线教师在 CDIO 教学改革中，已经摆脱了经验和直觉的束缚，开始自觉地运用教育目标分类理论、学生发展理论以及建构主义理论等思想来指导自身的教学行为。

此外，CDIO 试点高校工作组堪称中国高等工程教育界的劳模。例如，汕头大学先后接待过百余次兄弟高校来访，工作组曾举办过 8 次全国性的 CDIO 骨干教师培训班以及若干次年会，向与会教师和代表分享 CDIO 实施经验，还为推进卓越工程师教育培养计划和工程认证献计献策。教育实践的工匠精神与劳模精神交相辉映，促进了 CDIO 在中国的传播与发展。

### 3.2.2 外因：CDIO 改革共同体表现出的担当与责任

社会领域的改革需要各方利益相关者围绕改革初衷，开展理论设计、目标制定、方案选择、资源获取与分享、效果评估等行动。没有构建教育改革“共同体”或“强关系网络”，是以往教育改革无法深入和持久的原因之一。这表现在以下方面。

一是管理者与改革者相分离。长期以来，中国高等教育改革与发展战略、路径和规则由政府制定，通过行政系统层层落实。各方行动者（高校、教育研究者和企业界等）被动地参与和跟进政府主导的教育实践。在这种情况下，教育领域是一个资源和有效推动力匮乏、行动者间有效互动少、参与度低的“弱场域”。

二是研究者与实践者相脱节。许多教育研究机构保持着理论研究风格，对中国高等教育重要历程或事件的敏感性尚需提高。因此，许多教育研究成果是脱离现实教育现象或教育问题的思辨式概念游戏，对教育改革家或教育实践者的启发价值较小。

三是工程教育界与产业界关系疏远。由于体制和机制等因素的制约，双方在培养计划和培养管理等方面的深度合作，找不到适合的抓手与载体，双方还没有达到“优势互补、资源共享、互利双赢”的局面。

CDIO 是由地方高校发起的教育改革。若想将其推广至高等教育界，需通过多种途径来推动合作、调动资源、建立新联盟。其最终目的在于唤起集体性行动，共同构建一个多方认可的新系统，从而实现自身存在的合法性。如前所述，汕头大学在 CDIO 改革之初，就注意构建工程教育改革共同体，多次邀请著名的高等教育研究学者、政府主管部门领导、企业界和媒体到校考察，为 CDIO 改革献言献策；通过系统化和理论化展示 CDIO 改革成果，获得政府主管部门认可，教育部 CDIO 工程教育模式实践课题组的成立，极大地提升了 CDIO 的社会影响力，增进了高校对 CDIO 的信任。在教育部 CDIO 工程教育模式实践课题组框架下，多次义务组织全国性 CDIO 培训活动，最大范围地动员一线教师参与 CDIO 改革。经不懈努力，在工程教育界形成了 CDIO 合力，构筑了 CDIO 改革共同体（见图 4）。具体体现在以下方面。

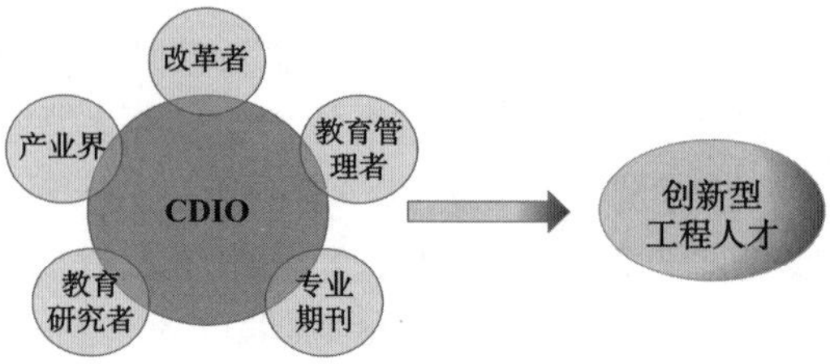


**图 4　CDIO 改革共同体**

一是教育行政部门与教育改革主体良性互动。通过及时地邀请主管部门领导实地考察 CDIO 改革,向上级部门汇报 CDIO 改革的进展、经验、成效和困难,增进主管部门对 CDIO 的理解;在此基础上,教育主管部门为 CDIO 发展提供政策支持(如发文成立课题与实践组)、信息支持(CDIO 如何融入国内外工程教育改革趋势中)和情感支持(主管领导每次都莅临 CDIO 工作会和研讨会)等。政府主管部门的支持对提高 CDIO 的公信力和权威性,推进 CDIO 沿着正确方向迅速发展起到了至关重要的作用。

二是高等教育研究者与改革者相互促进。以汕头大学为例,为更好地凝练 CDIO 改革经验,解决 CDIO 改革出现的问题,汕头大学主动邀请国内著名高等教育研究者到校考查或参加 CDIO 类学术会议,让专家为 CDIO 发展出点子、拿主意。例如,曾邀请厦门大学教育研究院潘懋元教授、别敦荣教授到校考察。在 2012 年中国 CDIO 年会上,邀请别教授做了主题报告——“一个教育学者眼中的 CDIO 教学改革”。在报告中,别教授深刻地分析了 CDIO 工程教育改革中存在的障碍:学科文化障碍、教学能力障碍、制度习惯障碍和领导能力障碍。他提出了推进 CDIO 工程教育改革的四点策略:加强工程教育改革研究,提高工程教育改革的领导力,改善教师和学生的教学行为,将 CDIO 工程教育纳入卓越工程师教育培养计划。

汕头大学还多次邀请我国著名工程教育研究专家、浙江大学王沛民教授到汕头大学考察,参加 CDIO 学术研讨会。在 2013 年中国 CDIO 工程教育年会上,王沛民教授追溯了工程教育的历史沿革与传统,提炼了工程教育一次革命和二次革命的特征,指出工程教育正在经历着第二次“转换范式”的革命,认为 CDIO 是 MIT 应用“工程问题求解范式”开发的一个全新的教育概念,内涵是以概念设计为先导、以技术设计为核心、以先进制造为重点、以应用服务为契机,旨在培养出有专业技能、有社会意识、有企业家敏锐性的工程师。需要重点强调的是,《高等工程教育研究》常务副主编姜嘉乐,自汕头大学开始 CDIO 改革之初,就敏锐地意识到 CDIO 发展的前景。一是姜副主编促进了 CDIO 模式理论化。他多次到汕头大学开展调研,研讨 CDIO 改革的经验与问题,指导 CDIO 工程教育改革进程,凝练 CDIO 模式特点,为 CDIO 发展出谋划策。二是姜副主编促进了 CDIO 在中国的传播与推广。《高等工程教育研究》早在 2008 年就刊发了由汕头大学顾佩华教授等作者撰写的《从 CDIO 到 EIP-CDIO:汕头大学工程教育与人才培养模式探索》一文,该文在业界产生了较大影响。此外,姜副主编亲赴汕头大学,与一线教改骨干教师共同商讨《CDIO 在中国》(上、下)的构思与撰写(该文分两次发表在《高等工程教育研究》2012 年第 3 期和第 5 期)。同时,姜副主编在各种学术论坛或报告中介绍 CDIO 模式的研究成果。三是姜副主编利用他在高等工程教育领域的影响和人脉，推动 CDIO 改革者与管理者和研究者的双向互动与交流。

通过邀请工程教育研究专家、著名学术期刊代表、教育行政部门人员、企业界人士和媒体记者等到校参观和考查 CDIO 改革的进展、做法与成果，增进了上述各方人士对汕头大学工程教育改革的理解、支持与认可，把中国高等教育领域长期以来相对分离的各方力量（管理者、研究者、改革者和企业等）汇集起来，形成了改革共同体，共谋 CDIO 发展大计。CDIO 在中国的发展，也为我们提供以下启示：任何教育改革，只有调动教育管理者、教育研究者、教育改革者以及企业等主体的参与积极性，才能保障改革方向的正确性、改革路径的可操作性、改革动力的持续性以及改革资源的充裕性。

## 4 CDIO 面临的挑战

著名历史学家阿诺德·汤因比曾指出，文明如同人类个体一样，也有着新生、成长、成熟、衰老、朽亡的生命周期。文明的生命力，表现在它应对内外挑战的能力。在新生、成长、成熟的阶段，文明能以合适的方式和力度应对挑战，最终解决问题，成长壮大。而在衰老、朽亡的阶段，文明则无力应对挑战或者用力过猛，导致问题越拖越严重，最终导致文明衰落[13]。汤因比的话，不仅可以解读文明和文化的兴衰，同样适用于解释社会现象和教育思想或模式的发展周期。

CDIO 在中国发展的环境发生了巨大变化。如前所述，CDIO 在中国兴起的根本原因，并不是由于它来自 MIT 等著名高校，而是它本身具备的系统性、科学性和可操作性等特点，可以为解决了中国高等工程教育的棘手问题提供新思路，具备传统工程教育模式所不具备的优势，能够显著提高高等工程教育质量。CDIO 获得的地位和影响力并非“天然的”，是由于其解决中国高等工程教育特定时期的问题，完成了特定的时代使命。这些特点和优势只在特定历史阶段有效，不存在一成不变的经验或模式。随着时代主题、社会矛盾和教育问题的变化，一种模式即使过去创造过无数辉煌，如果不与时俱进，丧失自我更新的能力，就会衰落。美国 20 世纪三次教育运动（进步主义、要素主义和平民主义）指导思想的转变，充分说明只有能够应对时代挑战的教育思想和模式才可能独领风骚，否则就会被历史淘汰。

### 4.1 宏观层面

#### 4.1.1 科技快速发展与经济结构转型带来新型工程人才需求的迫切性

进入新世纪以来，我国经济社会发展步入新常态。经济增长正从高速增长转向中高速增长，经济发展方式正从规模速度型粗放增长转向质量效率型集约增长，经济结构正从增量扩能为主转向调整存量、做优增量并存的深度调整，经济发展动力正从传统增长点转向新的增长点。与此同时，我国经济面临国外更低劳动力成本国家的竞争，以及发达国家“再工业化”的双重挑战。为了迎接这一挑战，党中央、国务院依据“创新、协调、绿色、开放、共享”的发展理念，提出了供给侧结构性改革等发展战略，确定了以“创新驱动”为核心的各产业转型升级行动计划。

制造强国战略的提出，对高等教育人才培养质量，特别是工科人才，以及工科与医科、金融、商科、设计、传媒等其他学科的多学科融合人才培养质量提出了更高的要求。我国于2013年成为《华盛顿协议》预备签约成员，2016年成为正式成员。中国工程教育专业认证协会陆续开展了各类工程专业认证，并正加速实施，如何适应这一新形势，需要CDIO做出变革。

### 4.1.2 最新的人才培养理念与方法带来的CDIO再思考

新世纪以来，社会的变革不断给各国的高等教育带来压力，促使高校探索更加符合时代发展的新模式。国内外的一流高校都在探索这一问题："世界日益增长的社会政治、经济、生态的相互联系已经向我们发起了严峻的挑战，我们必须以更宽广的视角来看待教育公民的意义，重新审视这些变化如何影响我们的本科教育，我们究竟想让学生在本科教育中收获什么，以及如何才能更好地为学生扮演地方、国家乃至世界公民的角色做准备？"

而与此同时，随着近年来科学技术尤其是计算机网络技术的发展，在线网络课堂悄无声息地改变着传统教育模式，慕课（MOOC）以及翻转课堂等的出现更是冲击着传统的课堂教学，一些更深层次的问题摆在了各个高等院校的面前：当今大学应如何应对信息化社会的挑战？如果网络课堂可以承担传播知识的职责，那么未来的大学校园会以何种方式存在？学生在大学校园里的生活与学习方式会有哪些改变？

在迎接这些挑战时，斯坦福大学提出的"斯坦福2025计划"以颠覆性的概念给人以震撼。"斯坦福2025"计划以"开环大学"（open loop university）、"绕轴翻转"（axis flip）、"自适应教育"（paced education）、"目的性学习"（purpose learning）四个方面为核心，围绕学制改革、教学重点转移、课程体系重构、学习方式变革等方面提出了大胆的改革构想，旨在突破当前本科教育四年学制的束缚，构建开放式大学，强调学生的主体地位并实施个性、自主教育，重视培养学生的可迁移技能以及整合多学科资源解决全球性问题的意识与能力。国外这些最新的人才培养理念与方法，使CDIO面临着迫切需要重新思考的局面。

## 4.2 微观层面

### 4.2.1 新型工程人才需求需要重新开始顶层设计

鉴于前文所述国家快速发展与转型带来新型工程人才需求的迫切性，在制定人才培养方案时，需要重新思考并设计专业培养目标与标准。比如制造强国战略对各类型工科人才的具体要求是什么，新形势下工科与医科、金融、商科、设计、传媒等其他学科的多学科融合人才培养的具体要求是什么，不同类型的学校如何设计更符合学校发展实际的专业培养标准等一系列新问题。CDIO工程教育模式提供的CDIO能力大纲和CDIO 12条标准还不能回答这些问题，需要在学校和专业的层面重新开始顶层设计。

### 4.2.2 人才培养目标需要更进一步落实

落实难是人才培养的重要挑战，它涉及人才培养主体的方方面面，需要时间且难以评估。CDIO 能力大纲给出了多层级、细化的能力培养目标，这些培养目标如何在各个培养环节中得到贯彻，是一个很值得讨论的问题。比如，落实的环节有哪些？MOCC 对人才培养落实有何贡献？博雅教育在其中发挥怎样的作用？课堂教学又该如何进行改革？许多教改难以落实，原因在于，虽然提出了美好的目标和愿景，但在具体的教学管理落实过程中，往往只是简单地将目标转化为内容和比例。例如，对实践能力的要求仅体现在实践环节占比由20%提高到 25%，卓越工程师教育培养计划提出的一年企业实习要求，也缺乏深入思考和具体实施方案。再比如，学校要求教师"认真做好教学"，改革教学方法、考试方法等，这些过去只作为单项要求提出来，往往顾此失彼，并且目标指向不明，没有评估指标，没有观测点，最终也就没有评估。

### 4.2.3　工程人才培养成效的评估需要更创新的方法

学生经过四年大学培养之后，目前各高校提供的只是单科课程的成绩单。但是，从人才培养的目标角度来看，应用知识的技能与综合能力这两方面才是最核心的。可惜的是，到目前为止都实施得很不理想。这要从两方面考虑：一是从专业的层面来看，毕业生进校的能力如何？每个学期的能力变化如何？最终离校的能力又如何？这些都是用人单位关心和考虑的。二是从培养环节层面来看，学习一门课程前学生应用知识的技能以及综合能力达到何种程度？学习这门课程后又提升到何种程度？种种挑战需要 CDIO 给出更创新的方法，需要回答如何评估学生、评估什么、怎么评估、谁有能力来评估等一系列问题。更合理的结果应该是，每个学生在离开母校之前，能够拿到自己在学校四年的能力成长图，知道自己想做什么、能做什么，能够更好地定位自己的职业生涯。

## 5　CDIO 在中国的新发展

CDIO 工程教育模式必须认真回应经济社会发展新态势对工程人才培养的新需求，在动态地回应挑战、积极参与高等教育改革重要事件的过程中，促进 CDIO 在中国的发展。CDIO 之所以能够持续在中国发展，得益于汕头大学、成都信息工程大学和燕山大学等 CDIO 试点高校主动应对制度与竞争环境压力。最为典型的案例就是，面对高等工程教育的重要改革项目——卓越工程师教育培养计划和专业认证，CDIO 试点工作组通过积极地参与，创建 CDIO-OBE 模式，为参与计划和专业认证的高校提供可供思考的资源和可借鉴案例，使 CDIO 度过了可能被边缘化的危机，发展得更加深入人心。因此，在快速变化的社会环境中，高等教育制度创业、模式创业和特色化办学之路，即使获得初步的成果，创业者也不能一劳永逸，更不能试图改变环境或采用"鸵鸟策略"对现实变化无动于衷，要时刻准备着对新模式的再创新和再发展。

### 5.1　总体思路

作为中国 CDIO 模式的倡导者和践行者，汕头大学 CDIO 改革团队对形势有清醒的认识。CDIO 改革团队多次召开工程教育改革研讨会，围绕下一步 CDIO 的改革思路与方案展开深入研讨与头脑风暴。一系列的研讨会回顾了 CDIO 取得的经验和问题，展望了社会科技发展态势和高等教育发展趋势，顾佩华教授提出了汕头大学面向未来的新教育改革构想。

该创新计划的总体思路如下：围绕建设“国际化特色的高水平大学”办学目标，借鉴“斯坦福 2025”计划，明确汕头大学创新型工程人才培养目标，注重培养学生运用知识技能与综合能力解决复杂工程问题的能力，同时融合品格和公民意识建设，开展以博雅教育与 OBE 专业教育联合、先进课程内容、学生个性化培养为核心的先进本科教育，构建人才培养全生态系统，改革传统的人才培养理念，建立工科人才培养的全新模式，达成汕头大学“五个一”教育质量工程的承诺。

## 5.2 具体想法

### 5.2.1 建立融合多视角下的新工科人才培养模式

2016 年 5 月 11 日的国务院常务会议新闻通稿首次提出“品质革命”，加之 2016 年政府工作报告中首提“工匠精神”，一场与大众生活息息相关的“品质革命”即将开启。据统计，目前我国生产的消费品中，有 100 多种产品产量居全球首位。其中，家电、制鞋、棉纺、化纤、服装等产能占全球的 50%以上，轻工、纺织出口占全球的 30%以上，是名副其实的消费品制造、消费和出口大国，但难称制造强国，消费品有效供给不足日益凸显，品种结构、产品品质、品牌培育等方面与发达国家存在明显差距。

汕头大学 CDIO 改革团队认为，CDIO 要面向创新型国家建设需求，不断学习和借鉴国际上最先进的人才培养理念与方法，重视人的能力培养，特别是创新、创业、创造能力，主动学习的能力与习惯，将想法转化为工程实践的能力，以及解决复杂工程问题的能力，为培养高层次新型工程人才发挥作用。以未来工程人才需求为导向，从用人单位、学生、学校、国家等多视角出发，丰富、发展 CDIO 能力大纲和 CIDO 12条标准，更好地迎接新科技革命的挑战，基于汕头大学创新人才培养生态系统（见图 5），建立融合多视角下的新工科人才培养模式，并开展新工科人才培养实践。

### 5.2.2 搭建 CDIO 与工程专业认证的互通桥梁

针对今后几年各高校的现实需求，根据我国《工程教育认证标准》，以 CDIO 的能力大纲为基础，将认证标准中的 12 条毕业要求分解为具体的能力、知识点及实践要求，然后建立一套完整的从毕业要求到结果导向的课程计划、课程设置及教学活动的实施系统和方法，使所有希望专业达到认证的 12 条毕业要求，又不知道如何实施的学校，能够根据这一套系统的方法、路线图和实践案例，制定出 12 条毕业要求达成度的结果导向的培养计划和课程体系。结合对传统的招生、选专业、制定四年培养计划、注重成绩和考试等方面的全面改革，希望中国工程教育能够引领世界工程教育特别是新工科领域的培养理念、模式和实践。

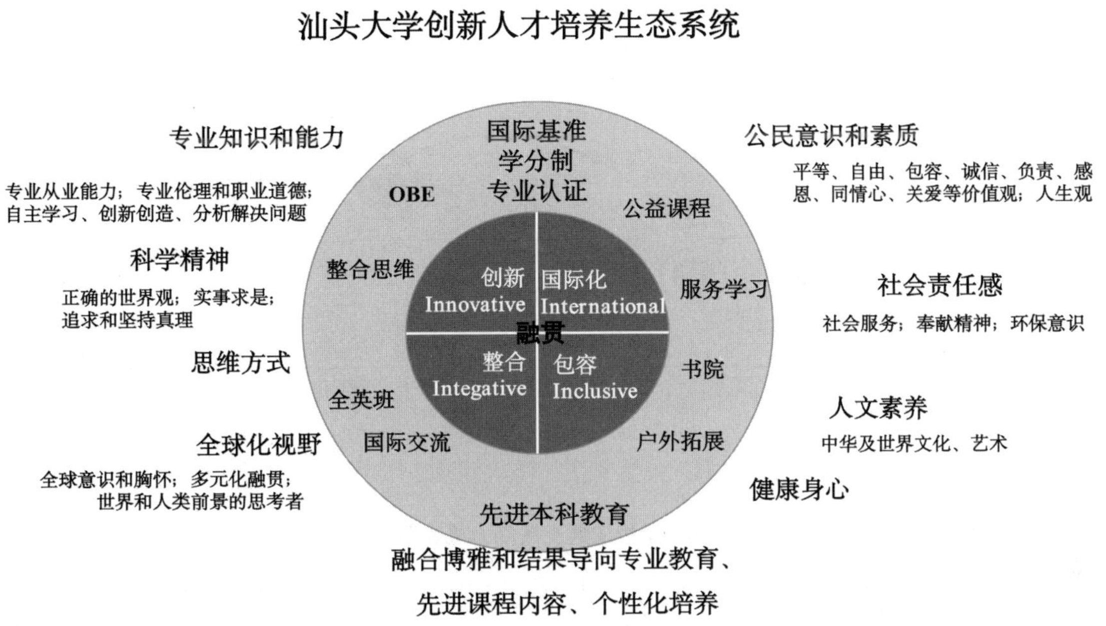


图 5 汕头大学创新人才培养生态系统

### 5.2.3 落实专业培养目标达成的各环节

针对 CDIO 实施过程中暴露的专业培养目标落实不理想的问题，进一步梳理、整合和更新以三层次设计项目为骨架的课程体系，使项目更贴近产业界的需求，体现科技发展的最新前沿，梳理课程核心知识点和概念，借助 MOOC、精品课等资源提升课程深度与难度，用更具探究性的项目设计激发学生潜能、挑战其智能极限；此外，根据 CDIO 模式重视创意和设计的特点以及中国高端工程人才缺失的现状，在研究工业设计、创意认知及心理学特征的基础上，进一步提高 CDIO 能力大纲的针对性和独特性。汕头大学已开展了一些探索，例如，在国内高校中第一个开设“整合思维”课程，培养学生的批判性思维和创造创新思维；开设“道德推理”核心课程，培养学生的伦理智能和批判性思考。这种注重思维与伦理培养的课程设置思路，也是很多著名高校多年来人才培养的有效做法。

### 5.2.4 创新工程人才培养成效评估的方法

为实现所提出的工程人才培养目标——每个学生在离开母校前，能拿到自己四年的能力成长图和能力表，明确自身兴趣与能力，从而更好地为职业生涯定位。汕头大学将进一步创新工程人才培养成效评估的方法，组建融合用人单位、学生、学校、国家等教育主体单位的评估团队，利用产业界人才评估模型与方法，分别开展学生知识应用技能评估和综合能力素质评估工作，并给出毕业生核心能力的成长路线（见图 6），以及对学生今后发展的综合建议。

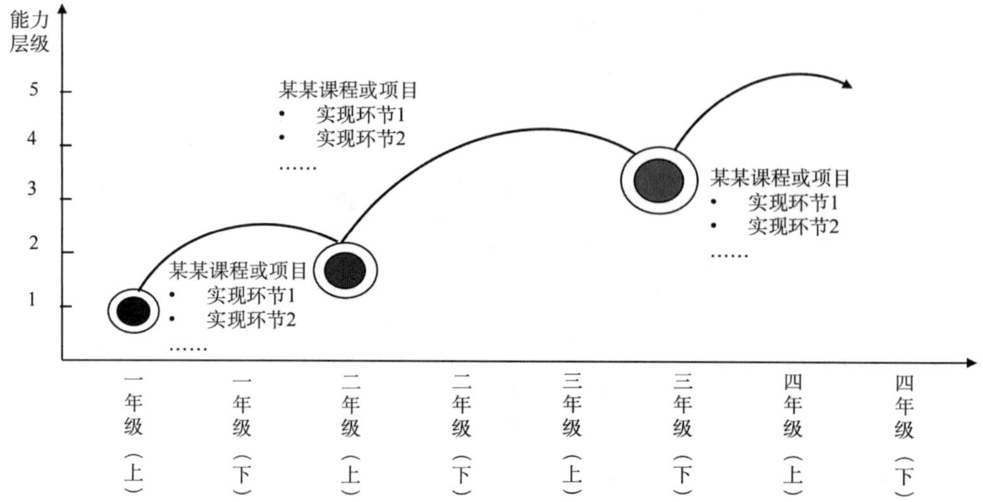


**图 6 学生沟通交流能力成长路线**

今天,基于 CDIO 的工程教育改革正站在新的历史起点上。作者撰写此文,并非为总结 CDIO 的辉煌,因为任何成绩只属于过去。相反,作者怀着强烈的危机感,清醒地认识到,任何社会运动都具有"兴起—发展—转型—衰落"的生命周期,风靡一时的"实用主义"教育思想在美国社会曾经历类似的历程, CDIO 也概莫能外。如果 CDIO 工程教育改革不能自我革新,无法应对高等教育变革的挑战,就可能会被教育界遗忘。作者怀着对中国高等教育强烈的责任感和自我批判精神,希望能够根据未来发展的需要,对 CDIO 改造升级,更好地满足未来中国社会发展对工程人才的需求,通过不断地转型和再造,使其实现凤凰涅槃,再续辉煌。

## 参考文献


[1] 顾佩华,包能胜,康全礼,等. CDIO 在中国(上)[J]. 高等工程教育研究,2012(3):24-40.

[2] 顾佩华,包能胜,康全礼,等. CDIO 在中国(下)[J]. 高等工程教育研究,2012(5):34-45.

[3] YELLOWLEY I, GU P H. Design directed engineering education[J]. Proceedings of the Canadian Engineering Education Association(CEEA), 2005:1-7.

[4] CRAWLEY E F, MALMQVIST J, ÖSTLUND S, et al. 重新认识工程教育:国际 CDIO 培养模式与方法[M]. 顾佩华,沈民奋,陆小华,译, 北京:高等教育出版社, 2009.

[5] 王天宝,程卫东. 基于 CDIO 的创新型工程人才培养模式研究与实践:成都信息工程学院的工程教育改革实践[J]. 高等工程教育研究,2010(1):25-31.

[6] 钟寿仙,张瑛,郭绍辉. MPC-CDIO 教育教学模式的探索与实践[J]. 高等工程教育研究,2015(2):169-175.

[7] 李彤,张璇,王旭,等. SE-CDIO 工程教育模式的探索与实践[J]. 高等工程教育研究,2014(1):52-57.

[8] 吕九芳,关惠元,葛林毅."卓越工程师教育培养计划"下基于 CDIO 模式的家具设计与工程专业教学改革初探[J]. 中国林业教育,2012,30(5):25-28.

[9] 郭长虹，马筱聪，李大龙，等. 构建基于“卓越工程师教育培养计划”和 CDIO 的工程图学教学体系[J]. 图学学报，2014，35(1)：121-126.

[10] 周海，黄传锦，郁倩，等. 基于卓越计划与 CDIO 模式的机械设计课程教学改革与实践[J]. 现代制造技术与装备，2014，(3)：98-99.

[11] 顾佩华，胡文龙，林鹏，等. 基于“学习产出”(OBE)的工程教育模式：汕头大学的实践与探索[J]. 高等工程教育研究，2014(1)：27-37.

[12] TOLBERT P S，ZUCKER L G. The institutionalization of institutional theory[M]. London：SAGE，1996.

[13] 汤因比. 历史研究[M]. 刘北成，郭小凌，译. 上海：上海人民出版社，2014.

[14] 刘怡，张炜. 一流大学卓越工程师核心素养构成及发展状况调查：基于学生视角的探索性研究[J]. 高等工程教育研究，2023(6)：59-65.

[15] 胡德鑫，徐文君，常乔丽，等. 国际注册工程师资质认证制度的建构逻辑与改革趋向：基于美、英、日、澳四国的范例[J]. 高等工程教育研究，2023(2)：87-95.

# 新工科与新范式：概念、框架和实施路径①

顾佩华

**摘要**：自2016年新工科建设理念提出后，从"复旦共识""天大行动"到"北京指南"，教育部发布新工科项目，相继成立了工科优势高校组、综合性高校组、地方高校组，积极推进新工科建设工作。在总结过去多年工程教育改革探索与实践的基础上，参考新工科建设的研究和工程教育范式转变的探索，本文试图回答什么是新工科、为什么叫新工科等基本问题，探讨新工科教育以及新工科教育范式；根据以往工程教育改革实践经验，以汕头大学为例，提出新工科建设的技术路径、组织实施方法，并讨论了需要关注的问题。

**关键词**：新工科；新范式；技术路径；组织实施

## The Concept, Framework and Implementation Approaches of Emerging Engineering Education (3E) and the New Paradigm

*Gu Peihua*

**Abstract:**Since the concept of emerging engineering education(3E) was put forward in 2016, the Ministry of Education has started several projects ranging from "Fudan University Consensus", "Tianjin University Movement" and "Beijing Guidance". And also, many groups have been established to promote the construction of 3E, such as groups consisting of engineering universities, comprehensive universities and local universities. Based on the experiences of the reform and practice of engineering education in the previous years and the study of 3E and the reform of engineering education model, the paper tries to explain what 3E is, why 3E got its name, discuss the 3E and its education paradigm, and puts forward technological paths and implementing approaches of the construction of 3E based on the previous experiences and deals with other issues.

**Keywords:** emerging engineering education (3E); new paradigm; technological path; organization and implementation

## 1 新工科提出的背景和重要性

互联网、物联网、大数据、人工智能、新材料、新能源等新科技与新商业模式的涌现，正快速重塑现代工业格局、推动经济社会发展变革，并深刻影响劳动力市场。国家实施的创新驱动发展、共建"一带一路"倡议、"互联网+"等重大战略，为中国的创新发展提供了新机遇，注入了新动力。科学发现向技术或产品的转化周期持续缩短，知识更新与新知识产生的速度

① 本文刊登于《高等工程教育研究》2017年第6期第1~13页。

日益加快,这些变化对现代工程技术人才的知识储备、专业能力和技能、职业素养及视野格局都提出了更高要求。为了支撑快速发展的新经济,培养新型工程创新人才,高等工程教育必须进行全面、深刻的改革和创新。新工科教育理念和教育改革就是在这样的背景下提出的,因此需要新思维、新体制机制、全面创新工程教育,培养创新人才,支撑和引领新经济。

2016年新工科概念提出后,教育部高教司经过反复研讨、调研和论证,于2017年正式推出新工科计划,并先后形成了"复旦共识""天大行动""北京指南"等指导性文件[1-3]。按照教育部的部署,工科优势高校组、综合性高校组和地方高校组都积极响应和启动新工科建设战略,新工科教育改革发展迅速,多篇新工科教育改革文章发表,为实施新工科教育创造了良好开端。

吴爱华等[4]根据新经济发展对工程技术人才的知识、能力和职业素质的新要求,分析了国际工程教育发展的情况,在总结前期新工科教育改革和探索成功经验的基础上,提出了工程教育的新理念、构建新型工科和传统工科相结合的新结构、探索工程教育人才培育的新模式、建立具有国际竞争力的新质量标准、建立中国特色的工程教育新体系,对新工科建设进行了系统概括并提出整体发展思路。

钟登华[5]在《新工科建设的内涵与行动》一文中阐述了什么是新工科、为什么要建设新工科和如何建设新工科这三个基本问题,从而揭示了新工科建设的内涵,给出如何面向国家需求、聚焦工程教育的挑战、实施新工科建设的战略。李培根[6]讨论新工科的"新"的内涵,提出工程人才的培养应该注重新素养、空间感、关联力、想象力、宏思维和批评性思维等方面的能力。从专业、课程和知识体系方面讨论新结构,提出新工科的教学和学习等方面需要新方法。赵继等[7]从经济与科技发展以及大学自身创新发展的需要出发,讨论了新工科和工程教育创新,以及建设和发展新工科的必要性,提出了新工科的通宽性、前瞻性、交叉性、开放性、实践性,并阐述了工程教育创新需要解决的问题。林健[8]提出新工科的广义概念和新工科的边界范畴,提出要重视理科、管理、法律等学科的影响,不但要关注当前的需要,更要面向未来,培养德才兼备的工程人才。陆国栋[9]从经济社会发展的现实对新工科建设的需要的视角,讨论了建设和发展新工科的主要瓶颈,进而提出了新工科建设的基本路径、思考与探索。

徐雷等[10]从理科特别是应用理科的角度讨论了综合性大学建设新工科和新工程教育的内涵,认为应包括知识、能力、价值观等方面的培养,打破本科和研究生培养界限,实行多元化培养,改革教师评价机制,推进产业和学校协同创新。陈慧等[11]分析了综合性大学在新工科人才培养方面的优势,讨论了中山大学的新工科专业建设和立足珠三角的战略布局,以及以新工科建设助推21世纪海上丝绸之路的战略;在分析面临的问题后,提出推动综合性大学新工科建设的思路。

夏建国等[12]分析了在新工科建设的背景下,地方高校如何进行工程教育改革和创新,总结了地方高校工程教育改革的实践探索经验,提出了地方高校工程教育改革的发展路径并提供了参考实例。施晓秋等[13]从新工业对工程人才的新需求出发,依托产教和科教融合、创新和创业融合,提出了地方高校建设新工科的人才培养体系和原型系统。叶民等[14]认为新业态是实施新工科建设的基础,新工科建设是面对新业态的挑战,阐述了工程教育的理念、课程体系和教育体制、设计工程范式和教育体制创新等,对未来的新工科建设提出了建议。

王巨宏等[15]从工业界的角度分析新工科建设，特别讨论了建设政产学研融合的工程教育新生态，着重剖析该新生态在新经济下工程教育面临的挑战；以腾讯为例介绍新经济下校企协同育人的探索，在新经济下构建工程教育新生态体系，在体制机制创新、生态体系建设、引导社会力量支持工程教育等方面展开研究，并提出了新生态建设路径。

在总结过去多年工程教育改革探索与实践的基础上，参考新工科建设方面的研究，本文试图回答什么是新工科、为什么叫新工科等基本问题，探讨新工科教育以及工程教育的新范式；根据以往工程教育改革的实践经验与教训，提出汕头大学新工科建设的初步技术路径、组织实施策略与方法，并讨论了几个需要关注的问题。

## 2 新工科基本概念

新工科中的“新”是“emergent”或者“emerging”，新工科指的是“emergent or emerging engineering”。为了解析新工科的内涵，有必要对工程、科学、应用科学、技术的定义、内容和本质区别进行梳理和界定。经过分析和比较，发现工程和应用科学的边界尚需更清晰地界定。新工科可以理解为科学、应用科学、工程科学和工程实践的创新进步，以及多学科交叉融合所形成的新兴工程学科、领域及新范式和新工科教育等综合概念。新工科涉及现代工科领域的新定义、新认识、新工程范式、新工科教育、新工程研究与创新、新工程实践等多方面。

为何称为新工科？“emerging engineering”或者“emergent engineering”可译为“新工科”或者“新工程”。在教育语境下，“新工科”这一表述更为贴切。其对应概念并非“旧工科”，而是“现有工科”或“传统工科”，后者已经形成了共同的认识。

新工科的学科或领域可以理解为刚出现、正在形成或将要形成的新兴工程学科、领域或方向，可以是一级、二级或交叉学科，也可以是学科方向。新兴学科或领域的特点是新颖，代表工程和科技的新发展，与快速发展的产业和新经济联系紧密。由于“新”(emerging)，就有某些不确定性或模糊性。在工程教育领域，从跟随和并行向引领的过渡过程，需要逐渐适应引领的过程中面对的某些不清晰、不确定性甚至暂时不完全正确的认识和理解，这是引领者必须面对的现实。如果什么都完全清楚和确定了，那就不新了，也就无须引领了。

新工科的学科或领域伴随着所服务的产业和经济发展，经历形成、发展、成熟等阶段后，成为常规学科或领域。而后续新的工科领域又继续涌现，经历同样的过程。应以发展的思维，理解从新到传统学科的发展过程，推动新工科建设与发展。

以工程教育新理念、新模式、新方法、新内容、新质量等作为学校新工科建设和教育改革的基本内容，构建新工科专业或改造现有专业，培养新经济和满足学校所服务的产业需要的新型工程技术人才。新工科人才培养应该使学生掌握更先进的知识，包括自然科学、数学、工程科学、人文社科等方面的知识；具备综合能力，包括应用所学知识解决实际工程问题、工程设计、创新创造创业能力、团队沟通交流和领导能力、终身学习能力以及专业所涉及的核心技能和职业态度等。

## 3 新工科教育范式

### 3.1 新工科教育范式的基本框架

新工科教育范式或者称为工程教育新范式是新工科建设和改革的核心任务之一。为了定义新工科教育范式,首先分析范式(paradigm)的定义。范式可以理解为例子、模式、框架等。涉及范式讨论和研究,常常会提到科学范式的形成和发展。牛顿物理学时代,物理学界曾经普遍认为根据牛顿力学原理,很多力学研究被认为是可预见的;这种物理学范式的理解,被后来出现的爱因斯坦相对论而改变,现代科学发展还在不断挑战已有的科学范式。由于人类有了认识世界的新设备、新仪器、新工具,人类对科学的探索将不断深入,新的科学范式还会出现。托马斯·库恩(Thomas Kuhn)在《科学革命的结构》(*The Structure of Scientific Revolution*)一书中定义了科学范式,用于指导科学研究和回答科学问题。在这个科学范式框架下,根据需要研究和回答的问题,确定实验观察和分析的内容。按照科学的方法设计具有代表性且可重复的实验,获取实验数据,确定解释实验结果的方法,从而回答科学的问题。当这样的科学范式研究问题的框架用于人文和社会科学领域,定义需要扩展。Kuhn 也认识到严格的科学范式定义并不完全适合非自然科学领域。对范式在不同领域的定义有了新的理解,如可以理解为基础思考的框架,在这个框架下,利益相关者具有相似的认识和理解。李茂国等[16]对工程教育范式进行了详细讨论,自 20 世纪 90 年代提出工程教育“回归工程”的范式,至今已经有 20 余年的探索和实践;通过研究中美两国的工程教育的发展和范式转变,从工业革命和科技革命的视角,以及根据三种新工业模型,提出工程教育从回归工程向“融合创新”范式转变。

根据科学范式定义的逻辑和思考框架,可以定义工程和工程教育的范式。在尝试定义工程教育范式时,应该考虑工程教育专家及工程教育利益相关者所共同遵守和接受的理念、原则、标准、教育教学方法、内容、评价体系等,而这些就构成了工程教育的范式基础框架。

为了定义工程教育的新范式,需要认识范式的形成过程。根据 Kuhn 的科学范式和范式转变的论述,可以理解为某科学领域进步证明,现有范式不能解释和指导该领域的科学工作,范式开始转变并形成更加合理的范式。因此工程教育范式转变可以理解为,在传统的工程教育范式下,工程教育培养的人才服务于工业和经济社会发展。当科技和社会进步改变了产业和工业发展,导致已有工程教育范式不能满足产业对工程技术人才的需求,工程教育界就会开展教育教学改革,转变工程教育范式。目前的工程教育范式转变,源于多年前就开始的各种工程教育改革尝试。新工科教育改革的讨论和实践,使中国工程教育界形成共识,建立新的工程教育范式。新工程教育范式形成一段时间后,随着科技和社会的进步,又会出现新发展、新知识、新认识和对工程教育的新理解,将会开始更新一轮的工程教育范式的转变,因此工程教育范式的转变、形成、稳定和再转变是一个动态和发展的过程。在这个过程中,适应当前发展的工程教育范式的内容被保留和传承,不适应的部分在这个过程中就会消失。因此,工程教育范式转变是传承和渐变,很少是颠覆性的推翻重来。

确定新工科教育范式的基本框架,需综合考量学校层面工程教育的范围、内容和内涵。

参考吴爱华等[4]提出的新工科的核心内容即新理念、新结构、新模式、新质量、新体系，引用李茂国等[16]提出的“融合创新”范式作为新工科教育范式。“融合创新”体现了现代工程教育的协同创新、理工和多学科融合、产学融合、校企融合、在线-新媒体-移动学习与校园内培养的融合、教研学融合等多方面创新的相互融合和促进，使只限于学校内部、学院内部甚至系和专业内部的教育改革与创新，成为开放式、全方位、所有利益相关方参与和协同互动、可持续、全面的融合创新。笔者对新工科教育范式框架基本内容的初步认识如图 1 所示，涉及新工科教育的理念、培养模式、教学方法、教学内容、质量标准等方面。虽然现在还无法证明这些方面是不是能构成工程教育新范式的基本元素，但它们都是直接关系到建设新工科专业和改造现有专业（包括跨学科专业）等教育教学改革的基本内容。将创新工程教育的理念、质量标准、模式、培养体系、教育教学方法以及动态更新的教学内容，与理工和多学科融合、产学融合、校企融合、教研学融合等相结合，构建新工科教育范式的基本框架。随着新工科教育研究与实践的深入，新工科教育范式的框架和涉及的内容会更加清晰、合理和全面。下面对融合创新范式涉及的主要元素进行简单描述。

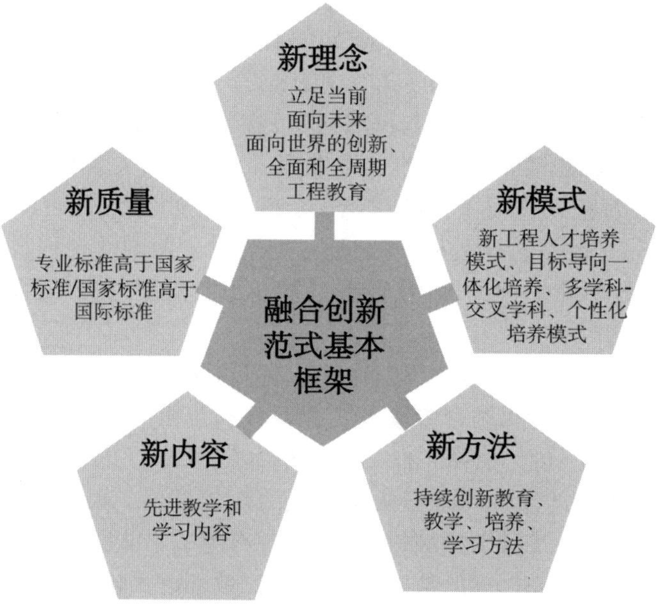


**图 1　融合创新范式基本框架**

（1）新理念[4]。工程教育要贯彻落实“创新、协调、绿色、开放、共享”的新发展理念，全面革新工程教育观。立德树人，培养具有综合人文素养和卓越工程能力的现代工程技术人才。一是树立创新工程教育理念，深化工科教育改革，注重学生的工程和科技创新能力的培养、多学科和跨界领导力的培养；二是树立全面综合的工程教育理念，改变工科专业过窄过细的弊端，加强跨学科、多学科知识和能力、人文和管理能力、运用所学知识解决真实世界复杂工程问题的综合能力培养；三是要树立全周期工程教育理念，培养学生树立对产品、系统和过程全生命周期的系统工程观；四是要以更加开放和广阔的视野，立足当前需求、面向未来、面向国际，以学生为中心，建设贴近业界、聚焦需求、结果导向、持续改进的工程教育。

（2）新模式[4]。建立工程教育新模式需做到：一是总结中国工程教育改革经验，借鉴适配国情的国际成功模式，打造兼具中国特色与世界水平的人才培养新模式；二是综合国际工程专业认证要求的知识、能力和职业素质，根据科技、产业和社会发展，分析未来工程技术人才应具备的知识、能力和技能、职业素质等；三是根据产业和现代工程师职业的需求，确定人才培养目标和毕业要求，制定系统完备的人才培养计划和课程体系，将创新创造创业能力贯穿到整个人才培养过程中，营造创新型工程师培养的生态系统，不断发展适应和引领工程发展的工程教育，培养从研发、设计、建造到运行的多元化、创新型的现代工程技术人才。

（3）新方法。在新理念指导下，基于工程教育新模式的需求，创新工程教育、教学培养方法和手段。根据培养计划，制定详细课程、教学内容和学习结果。根据课程内容和学习结果的要求，整合教学资源，包括互联网开放教学资源，如慕课（MOOC）、其他网络和数字化教学资源；及时吸收新的教学和人才培养经验和手段，创新教育、教学和学习方法。鼓励教师采用体验式学习（experiential learning）、基于项目的学习（project-based learning）、基于问题的学习（problem-based learning）、探究式学习（inquiry-based learning）、各种主动学习方法，运用案例教学、翻转课堂等教学方法。随着科技和社会进步，教师与学生在学习习惯、学习方法和工具使用等方面会有差别，教师应与时俱进，熟练使用先进的教学和学习工具、先进的教学方法。将先进的方法、工具和学习内容集成起来，完善人才培养体系。应该广义理解新方法，它既包括传统意义的教学和学习方法，也包括现代的教育方法。教育、教学和学习的方法将随着脑科学、认知科学和学习科学研究的不断深入而发展，更加科学的新方法将会不断出现，工程教育应及时探索和应用这些科研成果，提高教育、教学和学习质量和效果。

（4）新内容。有了新理念、新模式、新方法，还必须有先进的教学和学习内容。快速发展的科学与技术，促进知识更新和新知识产生，因此要求教学和学习内容特别是涉及快速发展的工程科技领域的专业内容应及时更新，体现当前科技发展的新成果和新知识。以笔者为例，当年在大学时代学习的机械制造工程的专业内容与今天制造业广泛使用的数字化设计和制造技术、加工和成型技术、3D 打印和智能控制等技术所需要的知识和能力要求完全不同。当代工业使用的互联网技术、大数据、人工智能、云计算、新材料、3D 打印、虚拟现实、信息物理系统等，要求工程教育的知识体系、能力水平、技能和工具使用、职业素质不断更新。教师可通过科研、学术交流、职业发展、学术休假等方式和机会，及时不断地提高学术水平、各种能力和更新知识。教师应掌握最先进的知识和能力，以保证教学内容与现代企业和社会发展要求的知识和能力相匹配。

有了新理念和新模式，如果课程内容不及时更新，学生学到的知识将趋于陈旧，难以养成契合现代工业需求的工程能力、技能和学习习惯，就无法满足当前和将来企业的需求，这样的教育也无法满足现代企业对工程技术人才的要求。所以，不断更新教师教学和学生学习的内容至关重要。

为了在制度上保障学生学习的内容体现当今时代的先进水平，学校和专业必须建立定期修订课程计划的长效机制，定期更新课程内容，将本领域的最新发展、最新科研成果（尚未写入教科书）及时介绍给学生，使他们学到的知识是当时最先进的。学生走上工作岗位后，就会发现他们的知识、能力和技能有用武之地。此外，教育和教学行政管理部门要建立一个体制机制，定期审查和改革教学内容，及时更新教学内容和教学手段。

（5）新质量。建设工程教育强国，工程教育必须具有国际竞争力，代表国际最先进的水平和最高的质量标准。因此需建立国家工程教育的质量标准和质量保障体系，推动建立行业人才培养和要求的标准，包括专业培养标准。根据这些标准和要求，学校制定工科专业的培养标准，从而形成国家、行业、学校的质量标准和保障体系。工程认证标准是国家和行业标准中的重要组成部分，根据国家发展的需要，工程认证标准既要满足国际等效的要求如"华盛顿协议"的相关规定，也要体现国家对工程科技人才更高的要求。为了确保工程教育教学的高水平和高质量，学校的专业质量标准应该超过国家的教学质量和认证标准，而国家的教学质量和认证标准应该超过国际认证标准的要求。

需要说明的是，新理念、新模式、新方法、新内容、新质量中的"新"的含义包括"新"和"创新"（英文是三个词，即 emerging、new 和 innovative），从这些方面构造融合创新的工程教育新范式的基本框架，希望能够体现新工科教育在专业层面包括多学科和跨专业培养和改革需要考虑的基本内容。对这五个"新"的理解应该是相对的，比如"结果导向"概念并不新，但是作为工程教育实践，由于很多学校包括发达国家的工程教育没有实施或实现，从实践的角度看仍然是比较新的。因此上述五个方面的"新"，可以理解为特定维度的革新，或是新工科改革所提倡要求的，并非绝对意义上的全新概念。此外，随着科学技术和工程的发展与进步、教育进步和社会发展，将会有更新的理念、模式、方法、内容和质量标准出现，以动态和发展看待这些"新"的含义，有助于从聚焦概念转向聚焦实质性新工科教育和新范式的内涵和内容。

为了进一步说明这一点，下面举一个例子。当前讨论的人工智能和 3D 打印等新技术（emerging technologies）其实多年前已经出现了，3D 打印是 20 世纪 80 年代出现的，人工智能技术出现得更早。笔者博士研究期间的第一篇文章是用人工智能的专家系统规划三坐标测量机的检验过程"Expert System for Inspection Planning"，1987 年发表在 *Annals of CIRP*。但是今天讨论的这些技术已与早年不同，这些技术不断成熟，正在和将会改变产业和经济社会，所以仍然称为新技术。

### 3.2 基于融合创新范式框架建立新工科专业和改造现有专业

新工科教育改革包括两大方面：①建设新工科专业或专业方向；②根据新工科教育范式的框架改造现有专业。后者即依据新理念、新模式、新方法、新内容与新质量标准，对工科专业教育进行改造。无论是办新工科专业还是改造现有专业，目标都是培养好学生。在办好本专业的基础上，推进跨学科融合、校企产学研合作及教研学协同创新，做好人才培养工作。根据每个学生的具体情况，尽可能提供个性化的培养。比如机械工程专业的学生中，有的喜欢智能机器人，有的对新能源应用感兴趣。机械工程专业可设立多个专业方向，满足学生个人学习和事业选择方面的需求。如果现有专业和专业方向无法满足某些优秀学生的学习志向，应鼓励学校为这样的学生提供既符合其个性化发展的专业培养计划，又满足专业质量标准的新工科专业教育。在这方面，"斯坦福 2025 计划"[17]值得认真学习和参考。

吴爱华等[4]对设立新工科专业或者改造现有专业提供了指导，面向未来的技术和产业的重点领域，如空天、海洋、信息技术和安全（大数据、人工智能、网络安全）、生命科学、核工业技术、智能制造等领域，进行新工科建设和对现有专业进行教育改革。新的科技进步使传统产业发生了深刻变化,对工程技术人才的需求也发生了很多变化。比如现代制造业需要的人才,应该掌握数字制造、创新设计、增材制造、工业机器人、人工智能等方面的先进技术。对于地方大学,应根据地方产业需求,改造现有的专业,使学生有良好的就业前景,支撑地方工业和经济发展,这是新工科建设的重要内容。

无论是工科优势高校、综合性高校还是地方高校,新工科教育注重学生创新创造创业能力的培养,而这些能力的培养不能只依靠一门课程,而是贯穿于整个培养计划,可以预见新工科教育培养的毕业生,其技术创业率会大幅度提高,有些院校的创业率一定能够跻身亚洲乃至世界最高水平。

## 4 汕头大学工程教育范式转变和新工科建设路径的思考

### 4.1 OBE-CDIO 工程教育范式转变案例

20 世纪 80 年代开始,世界上很多国家和地区的工业界都意识到,当时工科毕业生解决工程实际问题的能力不足。当时的工程教育以工程科学知识学习为主,对学生工程实践经历、产品设计能力、团队精神、沟通能力、创新能力,特别是对解决复杂工程问题能力的培养不够;因此学校开展各种工程教育改革,如秉持"回归工程"的教育理念,着重加强学生的工程设计能力培养,采用基于问题和基于项目的学习模式,强化工程师社会责任感与可持续发展意识的培养等。这些改革可以理解为对当时工程教育范式的转变的尝试。中国作为工程教育大国,基于国情和国家需求,多年来主动开展各种工程教育改革,如微电子学院、软件学院、工程教育认证、卓越工程师教育培养计划、CDIO、实践教学、创新创业等,这些工程教育改革和实践是工程教育范式转变的典型实例。

2004 年成立的 CDIO 协作组织是由麻省理工学院和几所瑞典大学通过几年教育改革实践,在总结教育改革经验和成果的基础上成立的。基于 CDIO 工程教育框架,多个学校实施教育改革,形成工程教育范式转变的成功案例。

2005 年汕头大学在总结国内外工程教育改革经验的基础上,开展了基于 CDIO 的工程教育改革。CDIO 工程教育实质上是培养未来工程师的创新教育框架,它主要包括工程教育愿景和核心理念、CDIO 大纲和一套实施 CDIO 教育改革的标准。CDIO 的 380 多条能力大纲(或者称为预期学习产出,即 intended learning outcomes),是除专业知识外,对学生能力和职业素质较全面的要求,它包含了毕业生从事工程师工作的综合能力要求。CDIO 的 12 条标准是实施 CDIO 工程教育综合改革实践和评估的准则,这 12 项标准能够确定 CDIO 改革的特征,作为教育改革与评估的原则,设立国际通行的基准与目标,构建促进教学持续提升的框架。

CDIO 工程教育框架、CDIO 大纲和 CDIO 标准构成专业层面的系统改革,它为学生提供了一个真实世界产品、过程和系统全周期培养环境。CDIO 实质上回答了两个问题:①在现代产业环境下,工程师需要哪些知识、能力、态度(职业素养);②学校如何培养学生的这些知识、能力和职业素养。这就是 CDIO 框架的整体思路。

汕头大学在应用 CDIO 实现结果导向工程教育改革(OBE-CDIO)的过程中,建立了实施路线、模板、工具、三级项目和设计导向等，这是汕头大学对工程教育改革的贡献。实施路线首先依据企业需求、认证标准和专业定位，明确专业综合培养目标（包括培养目标、毕业要求和专业特色）；接着将综合培养目标细化为系统培养标准；再依据培养标准制订一体化课程培养计划；随后从计划出发，确定具体课程、教学和学习方法；最后按照国家、学校和专业质量要求，构建教学质量保障系统，开展教学质量评估工作。作为毕业生竞争力的一个指标，学校跟踪改革前后学生毕业后的就业变化，自 2006 年实施 OBE-CDIO 改革后，每届工学院毕业生的就业率和起始薪酬都比广东工科毕业生平均薪酬高。特别是毕业时的工资，在实施教育改革前工学院毕业生的工资低于广东省工科毕业生的平均值，2010 年后（2006 年实施 CDIO 培育模式和课程计划），每年工学院毕业生的工资高出广东省工科毕业生平均工资 8%~20%。

### 4.2　汕头大学工程教育范式转变总结

汕头大学的工程教育范式转变尝试具有以下特征。

（1）以学生为中心，可适应培养。

从毕业生的就业率和就业质量上看，毕业生能够满足企业的用人要求。教学方法比较先进，体现企业、产业和教育主管部门的要求。适应学生的个性化学习要求（双学位、主辅修、跨专业选课等）。特别注意培养学生自主学习、适应新环境和新挑战的能力。

（2）融合通识和专业培养。

学校建立了 18 个通才培养目标和一组专业目标（专业自定）。通才目标通过学校层面的必修和选修课程体系、书院培养、服务学习（公益学分），配合体育、科技竞赛等方面的课外活动来实现。五个工科专业采用结果导向的一体化课程体系，保证专业知识和工程能力在四年中完成培养。

（3）教学和质量保障体系。

除了满足工程教育认证和教育部教学质量要求外，学校借鉴欧洲管理发展基金会工商管理认证标准和英国大学教学质量保障系统，建立了一套校内教学质量管理和质量保障体系。

汕头大学 OBE-CDIO 工程教育改革在新理念、新模式和新质量方面比较接近新工科教育范式的要求；在新方法方面尚有差距，特别是翻转课堂、现代化教学手段等方面要进一步提高；在学习内容更新方面特别是在高科技相关领域方面差距较大。结论和毕业生反馈的结果比较吻合，在新工科建设过程中，要下大功夫改进（表 1）。

**表 1　新工科教育范式的基本框架和 CDIO 教育改革特点对比**

| 融合创新范式框架 | STUOBE-CDIO | 注解 |
|---|---|---|
| 新理念 | 学生为中心、结果导向、持续改进等 | 基本符合，需要扩充 |
| 新模式 | CDIO 能力大纲、一体化培养体系等 | 需要加强创业能力培养 |
| 新质量 | 工程认证质量标准和特色培养 | 需要扩充与完善 |
| 新方法 | 基于项目、三级项目、设计导向、教学案例 | 一定差距 |
| 新内容 | 思维教育和移动编程等 | 较大差距 |

### 4.3 汕头大学新工科建设技术路径

在总结2005—2017年教育改革经验教训的基础上,深入学习"复旦共识""天大行动""北京指南"等新工科文件,以及教育部高教司领导讲话与相关学术成果,以融合创新工科教育范式基本框架为指导和参照,汕头大学进行了新工科建设路径初步思考,如图2所示。

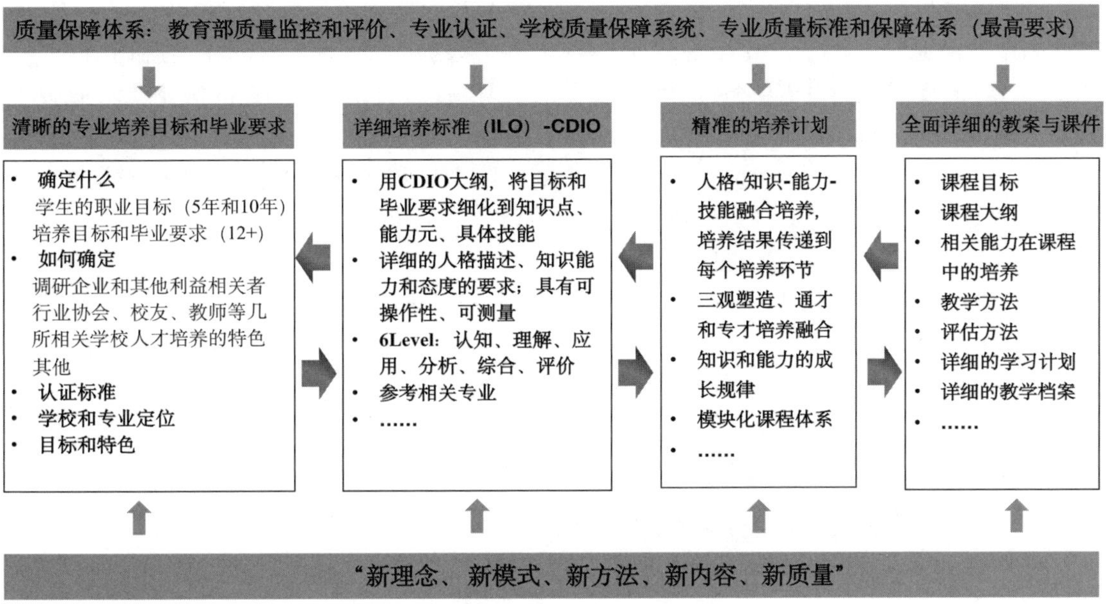


**图2 汕头大学新工科建设的技术路径**

#### 1. 根据"天大行动",问产业需求办专业

多数工科毕业生期望从事与专业相关的工作,而对于有志于技术创业的学生,洞悉企业和市场需求尤为关键。调研企业、行业对专业人才的具体要求,涵盖专业知识、岗位技能、创新和创业能力及工程技术人员的综合素质等,以此作为专业、设置改造(包括跨学科和多学科专业)和制订培养计划的重要参考依据。根据美国高等教育协会2013年对企业的调查[18]发现,95%接受调查的企业优先聘用能够为企业创新做贡献的毕业生。因此系统调查本专业所服务的产业界需求,对指导专业建设、毕业生的就业、服务和支撑产业发展都有重要意义。

在专业的设置方面要采用开放的态度,尽量给学生提供多学科和跨学科专业学习、双学位和主辅修等机会,从"斯坦福2025计划"[17]和香港科技大学个性化专业设置的发展趋势判断,将来会有愈来愈多的学生带着很强的个人兴趣或者事业使命到大学学习,如果现有专业不能很好地满足学生个人的学习意愿,在满足专业培养标准和学校要求的同时,应尽可能为学生提供个性化的专业学习。

以新理念为指导,充分了解产业当前和将来的人才需求,针对学生的学习要求和职业发展目标,结合学校的定位、相关学科的水平和专业特色及培养能力,确定所办专业、专业方向和规模。

**2. 以新理念和新模式为指导，调研利益相关方和比较目标基准，确定专业综合培养目标体系**

基于新工科建设需求与人才培养导向，专业综合培养目标体系的建立至少要包括三个方面的内容（图 3）。

（1）培养目标定位在毕业 5 年后毕业生从事本专业相关工作应该能够担当的责任，比如在一个产品制造公司工作 5 年后，应该达到产品开发技术部门负责人的能力和水平。

（2）毕业要求是学生毕业时达到的水平，比如工程教育认证的 12 条毕业要求或者 12 条要求加上其他方面的要求。

（3）专业特色应体现本专业独特的地方，如团队管理和沟通能力，或者工程设计和创新能力等。不同学校和专业的要求不同，在专业特色方面应该有所体现。

具体工作和过程至少应该包括以下内容。

（1）教师团队学习和研讨工程教育认证通用和补充标准，提炼专业培养目标和 12 条毕业要求等核心内容。

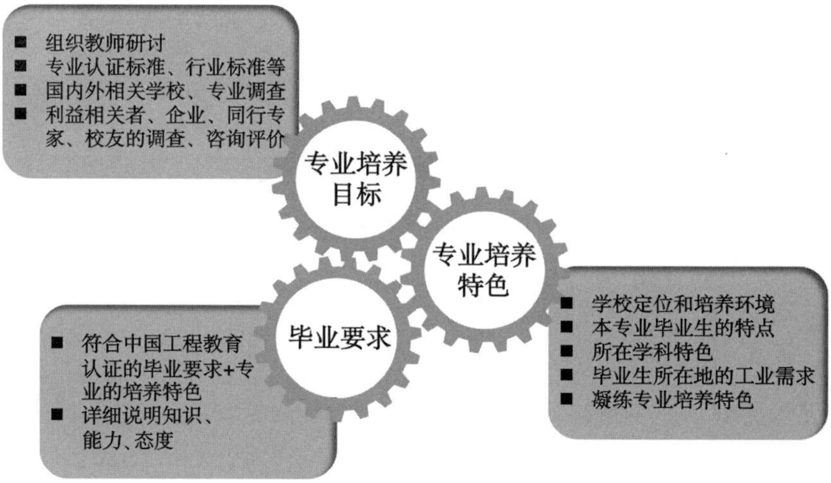


**图 3　专业综合培养目标**

（不同学校或同一学校不同专业的专业综合培养目标可能不同，除了在培养目标和专业特色方面可以体现外，在毕业要求方面也应该有所体现。虽然都要满足工程认证的毕业要求，不同类型和水平的学校，具体要求和水平应该有所不同）

（2）调研主要用人单位（问卷调查和访谈）、调研校友（根据需要可以调查 3 年、5 年和 10 年内毕业生）等利益相关方。

（3）选择国内相关学校专业和国外对标学校专业，分析比较关键指标体系和数据。

（4）建立初步专业培养目标、毕业要求、专业特色。

（5）广泛征求意见，包括征求国内外专家、校友和企业的意见，经相关委员会审核通过，根据学校质量保障体系规定，最后确定专业综合培养目标体系。

**3. 根据新模式的要求和专业综合培养目标体系，分解细化为专业培养标准（intended learning outcome，ILOs），把握精准度**

培养标准或ILOs包括知识、能力和技能、工程师职业素质，并且按照布鲁姆分类法确定知识掌握的水平（1~6级）。比如《华盛顿协议》或我国《工程教育认证标准》中毕业要求的第一条为学生能够运用数学、自然科学、工程基础和专业知识解决复杂工程问题。为培养学生的这项能力，需要将这条要求分解成知识点和能力级，这个细化和分解过程就是在建立详细的培养标准（intended learning outcomes）。专业知识可以参照专业要求，如电子专业可以参照中国电子专业教学指导委员会规范和标准，或者参考IEEE的电子专业知识要求，分解到课程体系，可以在课程和教学环节中直接培养。对于专业知识以外的能力和职业素质要求，例如创新、创造和创业能力要求等，380多条新版CDIO大纲应该可以覆盖。对于专业知识掌握程度的要求，可以参考使用布鲁姆认知分类法（remembering、understanding、applying、analyzing、evaluating、creating，即认知、理解、应用、分析、综合、评价）。能力和技能分类需按照职业的要求分级，知识、技能和能力均要求学生在毕业时掌握，因此，需要精心设计四年的知识、能力和技能以及职业素质要求的成长轨迹，并规划好课程培养计划，保证学生毕业时的知识、能力和技能、职业素质达到预期要求。因此，精准的培养计划和考核培养结果非常重要。

学生培养的一个重要部分是人格和三观的塑造，这是人才培养的重要核心。这不可能用一门课程完成，应该作为工程师职业素质部分或工程人才培养的特别要求，贯穿整个培养计划，包括课外活动。

**4. 建立课程体系和培养计划**

课程体系和培养计划是一个整体，依据专业知识与能力培养的连续性和相关性，对课程进行分组，形成课程群。以机械设计制造及自动化专业为例，涵盖产品设计与制造、流体-传热-热力学、控制与自动化等课程群。根据培养标准和布鲁姆分类法及能力的分级，每个课程群需明确核心知识、能力和技能要求，并制定相应的保障与评估机制，确保达成要求并展示成果。对课程群中的每门课程，确定课程目标、学习内容和结果，根据学习内容和掌握程度，确定学习结果的评价方法。

为了更好实现核心知识、能力和技能以及职业素质的培养，对于一个专业（包括跨学科和多学科专业），希望通过一个或多个实际工程项目的实施和培养，全面展示学生的整体专业能力和水平、综合工程设计和创新能力，以及工程实践能力。每个课程群都要有一个项目，可以是综合课程设计项目，通过完成课程群的项目，培养学生课程群要求的核心知识、能力和技能及职业素质。对于每门课，特别是核心课程，鼓励设置一个课程层面的项目作为载体，通过这个项目培养学生与这门课相关的核心知识、能力和技能以及职业素质，如图4所示。

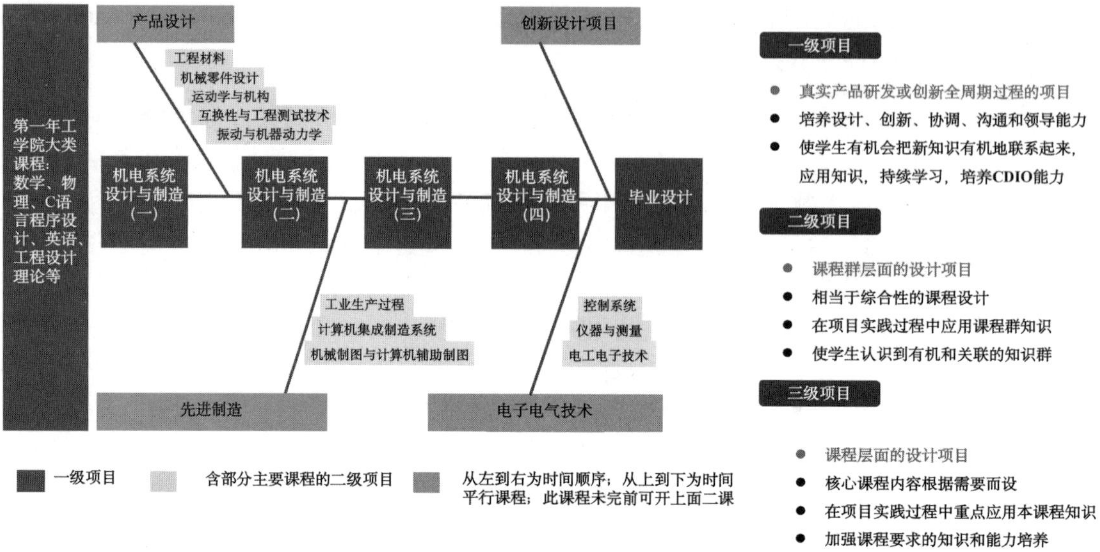


**图 4　课程体系的组织和三级项目鱼骨图**

除了课堂学习外，学校的其他教育和培养环节（如课外科技创新竞赛、工程扶贫项目、体育和户外拓展项目、朋辈互助学习等），均需对照专业标准培养，形成全面立体化的人才培养体系，实现立德树人的整体培养目标。

**5. 以新方法和新内容为指导，确定课程目标、课程内容、课程档案和课件**

所有知识的学习以及能力和技能的培养，均需通过课程和具体教学活动来完成。每门课程涵盖课程内容、ILO（知识、能力、技能等）、每节课的计划和课件、实验，以及针对 ILO 的测验和考试等内容。将每门课程的 ILO 组合在一起，就是整个专业的培养结果。

根据技术发展改造教学内容，根据学生的志趣来改变培养方法。新工科教育范式包括新方法和新内容，这两项与课堂教学直接相关。先进的教学和培养方法会激发学生的学习兴趣，促进学生主动学习和自主学习，因此选择的教学方法和辅助工具对课程学习效果有直接影响。为提升学生主动学习的能力、动力与学习效率，鼓励采用翻转课堂开展教学，基于问题、基于项目、探究式、体验式等主动学习方法，助力学生养成主动学习的习惯。为学生提供各种学习工具、参考课件与资料，有助于学生自主学习和时间管理能力的培养，提高学习的兴趣和能力。

课程教学和学习内容的先进性至关重要，特别是专业课程内容更要及时更新，至少体现当前的科技进步和发展。这就要求教师不但要将自己和行业内的前沿科研成果及时介绍给学生，也需要系统更新教学内容，更新自己的知识和提高学术和教学水平。对于快速发展的行业，企业可能掌握当时的先进技术和知识，从企业聘用经验丰富和专业水平高的实践型教师，邀请企业界的工程师或技术人员给学生开讲座，也可以弥补课程内容更新周期带来的知识滞后问题。总之，教学内容的先进性，应该反映当前和将来的发展。

为了确保教学内容和教学质量的连续性和持续改进，每一门课程都要有完整的教学档案。汕头大学工学院的教学档案包括：教学大纲；课堂教案和课堂 PPT；作业题目、小测验题目、考试题目、概念口试题目、实验报告及评分标准与说明；学生的学习成果，包括作业、小测验答题、考试答题、实验档案、项目设计档案等，一般存档两份最好、两份中等、两份较差的样件；访谈题目、访谈结果分析（视不同课程而定）；调查题目、调查结果分析（视不同课程而定）；课程学习目标的评估及分析；教师反思报告；等等。这些档案不仅能够作为工程专业认证的重要支撑材料和证据，而且在改变课程授课教师的情况下，不会因换人而影响教学质量。

**6. 根据新质量标准，建立工科专业的教学质量保障体系**

工程教育教学质量保障体系主要涵盖以下三个方面内容。

（1）国家教育主管部门的教学质量评估和保障制度。

（2）工程教育专业认证。

（3）学校教学质量保障体系，其中包括专业教学质量保障制度。

作为一个原则，建议学校内工程专业的质量标准高于学校层面的教学质量要求和国家工程教育认证的标准，学校的要求超过国家教育质量的标准，国家的教育质量要求包括专业认证标准应该超过国际工程教育专业认证标准。用这样的理念指导建设专业教育教学质量标准和保障体系，可保证每个教学环节、每门课程、整体培养质量持续改进和提高。

为确立并实现高标准专业质量要求，应秉持对标国际前沿的态度，深入研究国际工程教育在新知识、新能力、新政策和新标准等方面的发展动态，在此基础上制定符合国情并且更高的质量要求。专业质量保障需融入日常的教学活动和管理，全面规范教学和培养环节，持续完善质量监控系统，促使教师和教学行政服务人员自觉落实质量保障措施，建立详细的教学过程数据档案，以现代化的数据分析和过程控制手段持续改进教学质量，保证专业的教育教学质量标准高于工程教育专业认证标准的要求。

根据新建和改造现有专业的实际情况，将以上六步实施路径再细分为更详细和便于操作的路线。虽然在实施路径中没有将协同创新、理工和多学科交叉融合、产学合作、校企合作、教研学融合等单独列出，但是这些方面的内容应该在设计详细路线中体现。如前所述，新理念和新模式主要指导和应用于一至四部分，新方法和新内容主要指导第五部分，虽然新质量的实施重点是第六部分，实际上新质量体现于整个过程中。在设计专业的详细实施路线时，以融合创新工程教育范式的基本框架为指导和对照分析每一步，有助于新工科改革在教育实践中得到落实。

## 4.4 新工科建设的组织实施建议

基于汕头大学 OBE-CDIO 工程教育改革的实践经验，当技术路线确定后，高效的组织实施成为工程教育改革成功的关键所在。与科研工作的性质不同，教师教学的兴趣需要培养和鼓励。教育改革要求教师主动提升教学标准，在教学与人才培养过程中投入更多精力，以实现更高的考核目标，这是一个比较有挑战的命题。因此新工科教育改革的组织者要清醒认识到这个挑战，及时出台相关政策，鼓励教师自愿投入新工科教学改革，这是保证顺利实施的关键因素之一。

**1. 学校的承诺和支持是新工科建设的保障**

学校领导需明确承诺支持新工科建设，统筹整合校内外资源，全力构建新工科教育改革生态体系。新工科专业需要跨学科、跨专业、跨学院、产学研合作、校企合作等，为学生提供一个全面、丰富和现代化、多元化的培养生态环境。学校需协调校内各个相关学院深度参与新工科建设，提供充足的资金支持。同时，制定政策时，在教师考核与激励等方面充分考虑新工科建设的特殊性。与普通教学任务相比，新工科建设需要投入更多时间和精力，并克服各种挑战。应成立学校层面包括学院领导参加的领导小组，协调学校相关部门，出台相关政策和配套资源，推动新工科专业建设和用新工科教育范式改造现有专业的工作。

**2. 建立工业指导委员会**

基于新工科专业建设与现有专业的改造需要，组建工业指导委员会（Industrial Advisory Council/Committee，IAC），为新工科建设提供专业协助与指导。工业界的直接参与不但加强了学校和工业界的联系，工业专家的知识和经验也是新工科教育教学改革重要的资源。

在 IAC 的指导和帮助下，根据学校毕业生的去向和所在地区的工业发展情况，较详细地调研产业当前和将来的科技、产品和服务发展的需求，包括对人才的知识、能力和专业素质的要求等，获取这些数据，对推动建设工作非常重要。

此外应该充分发挥校友和校友负责的企业和部门的作用，给新工科教育改革提供更多外部联系和支持，包括办学和人力资源、校企和产学合作的支持。

**3. 建立新工科教育指导委员会**

根据需要组建新工科教育指导委员会（Emerging Engineering Education Advisory Committee，简称新工科教指委），统筹指导新工科教育改革工作。根据学校情况和需要，委员会专家成员以校外专家为主，涵盖工科领域高水平院校或同类院校的专业学者、工业界资深人士、科技领域专家以及国外专家，具体构成可依据学校实际需求灵活调整。委员会可以协助学校开展新工科建设，包括听汇报、提建议、审核建设方案、参与教育质量和水平评估等工作。委员会也能起到与外界沟通与交流的作用。

**4. 学院、系和专业组织实施计划**

无论是建设新工科专业、专业方向，还是改造现有专业，新工科教育改革均属于对专业的全面系统改革，需要院长的支持和系主任直接领导，院长和系主任都是第一责任人。专业培养涉及四个方面：本系负责的专业的相关课程、通识课程、基础课程（数学、物理、化学、生物等）和课外活动（包括科技创新活动）。本专业课程的改革由课程群组织教研小组负责。对于专业外的课程和培养，需要学校领导小组和教学主管部门协调和帮助。

**5. 建立新工科专业建设（改造）工作组**

该工作组由系主任担任组长，成员涵盖专业负责人、教研小组负责人和教学骨干，主要负责新工科建设具体工作的推进，参照新工科建设技术路线，设计实施方案、制订行动计划、调配所需要的资源、协调校内外工作等等。整个专业教育改革的关键是整体化和系统的思维,制订较全面的计划,调动全专业所有教师参与。与新工科建设技术路线不同的是,新工科的实施过程不能简单认为就是按照技术路线时间顺序的线性过程,而是立体交叉的复杂过程。比如在制订新工科建设计划的过程中,组织几名骨干教师,选择他们负责的课程作为试点课,尝试新教学方法和更新教学和学习内容,从而取得经验,为后续的整体改革过程奠定基础,在选择和进行试点课程时,其他新工科改革还要同步进行。

**6. 教师发展、教学评估、质量保证组织**

在新工科建设过程中,教师的专业发展与能力提升十分重要。教师发展包括提升教学能力,掌握新型教学方法,更新专业知识体系,参与企业调研和实践以增强工程实践能力,进而优化教学内容、提升教学质量。学校的教师发展中心、教学质量评估单位应该积极地为教师提供必要的支持和帮助。在试点过程中,教学评估方面及时进行课程改革工作,为试点课程提供教学质量保障,确保教师能够成功地完成试点课程,总结课程改革的成功经验,用于后续的改革实践。

根据汕头大学工程教育改革的经验,为了有效实施上述技术路线,以下两个方面的工作非常关键。

其一,学校各级领导的决心和承诺。新工科教育改革是全方位的系统工程,不仅有教学方面的改革,如跨学科教学与人才培养改革,还有教师的聘任、考核、资源分配等方面的改革,涉及每位参与的教职工,触及的利益也是多方面的,有成功的案例作为参考,但是没有捷径可走。本科教学与科研工作存在本质差异,办好本科教育需要调动大多数教师和员工的积极性,尤其是多数任课教师的深度参与。学校主要领导的决心和承诺是改革成功的关键因素之一;学院院长和系主任(包括跨学科和多学科专业相关学院院长和系主任)的全力推动是新工科教育改革成功的关键因素之二,本科教学改革涉及专业所有课程的每一位教师,院系领导的日常推动是必要条件;骨干教师和多数教师的积极参与是成功的关键因素之三,骨干教师虽然没有行政职务,但他们的带头作用非常重要。院系领导鼓励学术和学科带头人和教学骨干积极参与新工科教学改革,成功完成试点课程,为全面推动新工科建设提供成功的基础。此外,在这个过程中要发挥校友和学生的促进作用,让学生意识到新工科改革的直接目的就是培养好他们,他们需要有主人翁的意识和责任感。

其二,在实施新工科改革的技术路线的过程中把握精准度。工程师在日常工程工作中清楚地知道,精准和精确是工程的生命线。对工程教育而言,精准度也是关键。从确定专业综合培养目标、分解和确定培养标准、课程计划和培养体系、每门课程教学方法和课程内容,到教学质量保证系统和评估等每一步的准确程度决定了最终的培养质量和水平。将新理念、新模式、新方法、新内容、新质量扎扎实实和尽量精准地落实到位,才能培养出新一代创新型工程技术人才。

汕头大学在过去的 OBE-CDIO 改革基础上,按照新工科教育的融合创新范式的基本框架,以新理念为指导,尝试工程人才培养新模式,建立专业教育教学质量的新标准,探索和使用先进的教学方法、手段和工具,激发学生主动学习的兴趣,提高学生自主学习的能力,保证学习效率和效果,及时更新和建设课程教学的新内容,采用创新的方法为学生提供本专业和跨学科的新知识,使学生掌握专业和学科领域的前沿;拓宽和营造更好的办学环境,更加主动地开展理工、人文和多学科交叉融合、产学和校企合作与协同创新、教研学融合等，开放办学，加强国际合作和交流，进一步凝练汕头大学工程教育特色，实施国际化、精细化、个性化、多元化的现代新工科教育。

## 5 新工科和新范式的讨论

(1)从广义上来说，理解新工科应该从整个新工程学的角度来思考，其内涵极其丰富，泛指整个工程学科和体系、新工程范式，以及对现代工程、学科、科研、工程教育等的全新理解。目前聚焦的新工科教育，是面向经济社会发展、面向未来、面向世界的全新工科教育体系和范式。无论建设新兴工科专业，还是改造现有专业，都要考虑根据新工科教育的内涵，参考近年来工程教育改革的成功经验，坚持立德树人，培养现代中国特色的工程科技人才。

(2)以新工科教育整体理念为基础，组织系统研究新工科，创新性实施新工科教育改革。工科优势高校、综合性大学和地方大学在实施新工科教育改革时，需要采用不同的方法和实施手段；当培养理念和目标确定后，要具体落实到课程计划、知识学习、能力和素质的培养；结合机械工程、计算机技术、土木工程等专业知识要求，CDIO 的 380 条能力大纲和 12 条标准，在新工科教育改革实施过程中能够发挥重要作用。

(3)新工科教育是一场全面、系统的教育改革，涵盖整个工科专业领域，强调跨学科和多学科融合，涉及专业定位、培养目标、毕业要求、专业特色、培养标准、结果导向的课程计划、每门课程和教学活动的学习结果、考核与评价等。这些改革都体现在教师和学生之间的各种教育活动如课堂、实验室、项目的实施、科教和产学的融合实践中，聚焦人才培养质量和水平的命题上，最终还是要把学生培养好。所以新工程建设不仅是理念和概念，更应该以科学的态度认真推进和实施课程和课堂教育改革的各项工作。

(4)研究型大学，尤其是“双一流”建设大学，在实施新工科建设中有多种选择，从新办工科专业、新专业方向、本硕博连读、多学科和跨专业培养、双学位和主辅修，到科技创新创业等等；研究型大学应该营造一个融合教育、科技创新和创业、多元化、现代化的新型大学生态环境。尽量为本科生提供参与高水平科研和科技创新的机会，鼓励本科生和研究生通过科研和技术研发取得知识产权，积极开展技术创业。

(5)对于地方高校，不能盲目办新专业，更要避免用“新瓶子装旧酒”。新工科教育提倡用融合创新工程教育范式改造现有专业，比如在机械设计制造及自动化专业实施新工科教育改革，结合地方制造业发展对数字化和智能技术的需求，从培养理念、培养模式、课程内容、教学和学习方法、培养质量标准等方面全部改革和提高，培养出现代制造业需要的工程技术人才。

(6)对于希望提高现有工科专业人才培养水平和质量的高校，可以用融合创新工程教育范式对现有专业进行改造和提升，提高学生的知识水平、专业技能、工程设计与解决复杂工程问题的能力、创新创业能力、团队合作和沟通交流能力、领导多学科团队和跨界整合资源能力等。虽然专业名称没有改变，但是专业培养的理念、模式、教学方法、学习内容和水平、质量标准都得到根本改变和提高。

(7)在新工科教育改革过程中要避免出现领导热情高、普通教师冷淡、学生不关心的状态。新工科教育的实施需要学校领导和师生员工的共同努力,建立健全配套政策、制度以及学校文化,确保改革成功。

## 6 结语

从工程和工程教育的发展历史看,当前的新工科建设是中国对现代工程教育发展的新贡献,也是从工程教育大国走向工程教育强国的新起点。自新工科建设提出以来,充分发挥体制优势,快速推进相关工作,新工科发展已呈现良好态势。接下来要扎实推进新工科教育改革,提高人才培养质量和水平,特别是创新创业创造型人才的培养,达到并超越世界先进水平。以动态发展的眼光看待新工科建设,在实践过程中,不断提高认识、及时调整发展和实施战略,真正做到引领世界工程教育的新发展。

工程教育新范式的形成和成熟需要时间,在探索工程教育新范式的转变和形成过程中,会面对各种不确定性、模糊性所带来的阶段性困难和挑战。在教育部高教司的领导下,优势工科高校、综合性高校和地方高校工作组积极协调和推进新工科建设任务,通过交流和总结,共同学习和相互借鉴,及时解决改革过程中出现的问题,推动新工科建设的实施和进步,建立适应经济发展的新工程教育范式。如前所述,新工程教育范式形成后,随着科技和社会的进步,又会出现新发展、新知识、新认识和对工程教育的新理解,将引起更新一轮的工程教育范式的转变,因此工程教育范式的转变、形成、稳定和再转变是一个动态和发展的过程。在这个过程中,适应当前发展的工程教育范式内容被保留和传承,不适应的部分会消失。因此,工程教育范式转变基本是传承和渐变的。

笔者清楚地认识到,受学识、经历、经验和视野的限制,笔者对新工科教育和新范式的理解、认识等可能不深入、不全面甚至不正确。随着新工科研究和实施的深入,可以预见,一个更加全面、合理和清晰的新工科教育范式会逐渐形成。

### 参考文献

[1] 中华人民共和国教育部.“新工科”建设复旦共识 [EB/OL].(2017-02-18)[2017-07-01]. http://www.moe.edu.cn/s78/A08/moe-745/201702/t20170223-297122.html.

[2] 中华人民共和国教育部.“新工科”建设行动路线(“天大行动”)[EB/OL].(2017-04-08)[2017-07-01]. http://www.moe.edu.cn/s78/A08/moe-745/201704/t20170412-302427.html.

[3] 中华人民共和国教育部. 新工科建设形成“北京指南”[EB/OL].(2017-06-10)[2017-07-01]. http://moe.gov.cn/jyb-xwfb/gzdt-gzdt/moe-1485/201706/t20170610-306699.html.

[4] 吴爱华,侯永峰,杨秋波,等. 加快发展和建设新工科主动适应和引领新经济[J]. 高等工程教育研究,2017(1):1-9.

[5] 钟登华. 新工科建设的内涵与行动[J]. 高等工程教育研究,2017(3):1-6.

[6] 李培根. 工科何以而新[J]. 高等工程教育研究,2017(4):1-4,15.

[7] 赵继,谢寅波. 新工科建设与工程教育创新[J]. 高等工程教育研究,2017(5):13-17,41.

[8] 林健. 新工科建设:强势打造“卓越计划”升级版[J]. 高等工程教育研究,2017(3):7-14.

[9] 陆国栋,李拓宇. 新工科建设与发展的路径思考[J]. 高等工程教育研究,2017(3):20-26.

[10] 徐雷,胡波,冯辉,等. 关于综合性高校开展新型工程教育的思考[J]. 高等工程教育研究,2017(2):6-12.

[11] 陈慧,陈敏. 关于综合性大学培养新工科人才的思考与探索[J]. 高等工程教育研究,2017(2):19-23,47.

[12] 夏建国,赵军. 新工科建设背景下地方高校工程教育改革发展刍议[J]. 高等工程教育研究,2017(3):15-19,65.

[13] 施晓秋,赵燕,李校堃. 融合、开放、自适应的地方院校新工科体系建设思考[J]. 高等工程教育研究,2017(4):10-15.

[14] 叶民,钱辉. 新业态之新与新工科之新[J]. 高等工程教育研究,2017(4):5-9.

[15] 王巨宏,刘婷婷,马东娜,等. 构建新经济下政产学研融合工程教育新生态[J]. 高等工程教育研究,2017(3):27-30.

[16] 李茂国,朱正伟. 工程教育范式:从回归工程走向融合创新[J]. 中国高教研究,2017(6):30-36.

[17] Stanford University. STANFORD 2025[EB/OL].(2016-08-17)[2017-07-01]. http://www.stanford2025.com.

[18] American Association of Colleges and Universities. It Takes More Than a Major:Employer Priorities for College Learning and Student Success[EB/OL].(2013-04-10)[2017-07-01]. https://www.aacu.org/research/it-takes-more-than-a-major-employer-priorities-for-college-learning-and-student-success.

# 新工科与新范式：实践探索和思考 ①

顾佩华

**摘要：**在分析科技革命和创新经济对工科毕业生需求特点的基础上，天津大学提出了新工科的天大方案（CCII-EEE）。该方案以培养未来卓越工程师、企业家、工程科学家和领军者为核心理念，提出了一种以立德树人统领人才培养全过程，融合新文理教育、多学科和跨学科工程教育的个性化专业教育的新工科教育模式。天大方案定义了面向未来的工程科技人才的综合能力特征，突破单一学科课程支撑专业教育的传统教育模式，构建了面向未来科技和产业发展主题的开放式多学科培养平台，包括5种项目为节点的融合贯通课程体系及建设路线，以及相应的教学质量标准和保障体系。正在试点实施中的天大方案，鼓励以创新为主题的多种工程教育改革，探索工程教育新范式。结合后疫情时代新需要，本文还讨论了新工科再深化、再拓展、再突破等方面的工作，愿能与工程教育同行共同探讨和学习。

**关键词：**新工科；CCII-EEE；多学科培养平台；新范式

## Practical Exploration and New Paradigm Transformation of Emerging Engineering Education

*Gu Peihua*

**Abstract:** Based on an analysis of the characteristics of the demand for engineering graduates amid the technological revolution and innovative economy, Tianjin University developed a plan namely Coherent-Collaborative-Interdisciplinary-Innovative Plan of EEE Transformation—CCII-EEE Plan. The implementation of the CCII-EEE Plan integrates new liberal education, multi- and inter-disciplinary engineering education and individualized major studies for educating future engineering innovators, entrepreneurs, engineering scientists and leaders. The CCII-EEE Plan defines the comprehensive ability characteristics of future engineering and technological talents, breaks through the traditional education model where professional education is supported solely by single-discipline courses, and constructs an open multidisciplinary cultivation platform oriented towards the themes of future technological and industrial development. This platform includes an integrated curriculum system with 5 types of projects as nodes, a construction roadmap, as well as corresponding teaching quality standards and guarantee systems. Currently under pilot implementation, the CCII-EEE Plan encourages various engineering education reforms centered on innovation and explores new paradigms of engineering education. In combination with the new needs of the post-COVID-19 era, this paper also discusses efforts to further deepen, expand, and make breakthroughs in emerging engineering education,

① 本文刊登于《高等工程教育研究》2020年第4期第1~19页。

hoping to engage in joint discussions and learning with peers in engineering education.

**Keywords:** emerging engineering education; CCII-EEE; multi-and inter-disciplinary education platform; new paradigm

## 引言

从工业发展的历史来看，尽管不同国家和地区存在差异，但每次工业革命均彰显了特定时期工业发展的主题和内涵，工业发展需要工程技术的人力资源支撑，因此，推动了工程教育的不断变革与发展[1-4]。如图 1 所示，纵观工业革命与教育发展之间的关系，每一次革命都定义了一个时代的教育。第一次工业革命时期的蒸汽机发明，开始改变传统的手工作业方式，对机械化专业技能人才的需求，推动高等教育迈入 1.0 时代，为工业发展提供了人力资源的支持。第二次工业革命时期的电气化实现了制造业的批量化生产，新制造技术促进了包括铁路、石油、钢铁等在内的工业和经济发展。那个时期建立了各种类型的高等院校，包括麻省理工学院（MIT）等理工科高校和学院。值得一提的是哈佛前校长查尔斯·埃洛伊特（Charles Eloit）教授对当时美国高等教育课程体系不能服务工业化建设不满，于 1896 年发表《新教育》（The New Education）一文，希望改革美国高等教育[5]。第三次工业革命以电子通信、计算机、Web 互联、信息技术等为特征，推动了自动化技术、设备和系统的发展。同时，高等工程教育全球化和国际化得到很大发展，建立了国际工程教育认证实质等效体系，并支持学生和注册工程师的移动性（mobility）以及学习与工作地点的选择。第四次新工业革命的开始阶段经历了人工智能、物联网、传感技术、云计算、大数据存储与计算、区块链、新材料、生物科技、新能源等新科技的涌现，推动创新技术和产业的快速发展，对应第四次工业革命的教育 4.0 将经历变革性的发展。

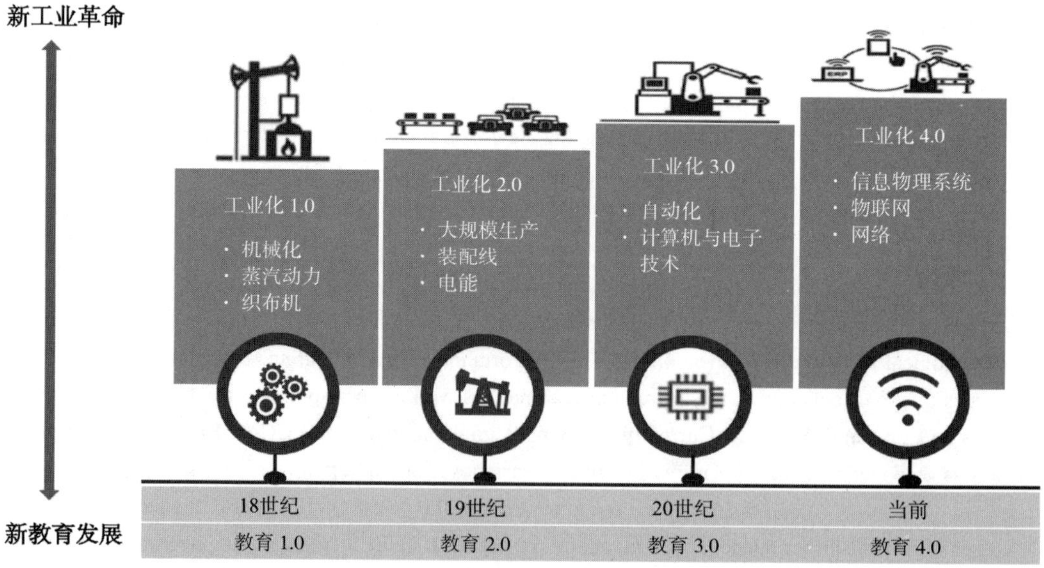


**图 1　工业革命与教育发展**

实践表明，传统工程教育在模式、课程体系、课程内容、教学方法等方面，已难以适应新产业和新经济的发展需求，教育部提出新工科建设，旨在培养符合当前与未来科技发展及产业革命需求的卓越工程创新人才，实现面向未来、面向世界、面向需求，聚焦学生培养持续创新的工程教育。新科技革命的特点是新技术的快速和加速发展，物质科学、先进信息科技和生物科技的直接交叉融合，产生了很多颠覆性新技术，这些新技术催生一大批新产业，同时也颠覆了一些传统企业，形成全新的人力资源需求。展望未来，工程教育发展需要新的试点、新的思考，特别是对工程教育产生重大影响的技术发展，在科技快速变化的时代，需要关注工程与技术伦理、智能时代人与工具的边界等重要问题[6]。

新工科建设是我国主动适应和引领新经济发展，为应对 21 世纪工程教育挑战贡献中国智慧与方案的关键举措。全国高校和相关行业积极响应国家新工科建设号召，纷纷组织各类研讨会，推动新工科建设迅速发展为全国性的工程教育改革行动。高等工程教育和产业界在培养面向未来、面向世界、面向产业的新型工程科技人才，支撑创新时代新经济发展等方面积极合作，推动新工科教育发展[7-10]。天津大学于 2019 年 4 月发布了新工科“天大方案”（CCII-EEE）[11-12]，其基本框架和主要内容如图 2 所示，随后电子科技大学发布了“成电方案”[13]、华南理工大学发布了“新工科 F 计划”[14]等。

本文内容组织如下：全面介绍新工科天大方案设计与实施的各个方面；讨论新工科教育模式和范式；试图探讨后疫情时代的新工科再深化、再拓展、再突破和再出发；最后得出结论。

## 1　新工科天大方案设计与设施

### 1.1　新工科教育变革与创新的需求

自从教育部提出新工科建设，历经 3 年多的研讨和实践，高等工程教育界达成了基本共识：新工科教育不是简单地按照传统模式增设新专业，在开展新工科建设之前，学校也办新专业；也不是在传统工程教育模式和课程体系上简单增加新内容，各学校在修订专业课程计划时也会增加新内容；当然更不是将传统的课程体系冠以新的名词。新工科教育应该是面向新工业革命与未来科技和工业发展的工程教育系统性变革与全面创新；探索工程教育的新理念，根据新理念建立工程教育的新模式，基于新工程教育模式，构建新的人才培养和新课程体系，为了实现新培养体系，需要建设新课程内容，根据新课程学习要求，利用数字教育教学资源，探索更有效的新的教与学方法，为了持续提高教育教学和人才培养质量，建立工程教育的新质量标准；以新理念、新模式、新培养体系、新课程内容、新的教与学方法、新质量标准和新要求建设新工科专业，系统性改造和创新现有工科专业；促进新兴工程教育领域与教育实践的发展，探索工程教育的新模式和新范式，培养未来科技和工业发展需要的工科毕业生，支撑国家创新经济发展。

为培养契合未来工业和社会需求的工科人才，未来工科毕业生在满足工程教育认证标准和要求的同时，还需要具备哪些新工业革命时代的知识、技能、态度、能力和素质？基于对创新经济、新科技革命和新产业发展需求的观察、调研、分析和研究，提出了以下新工业革命

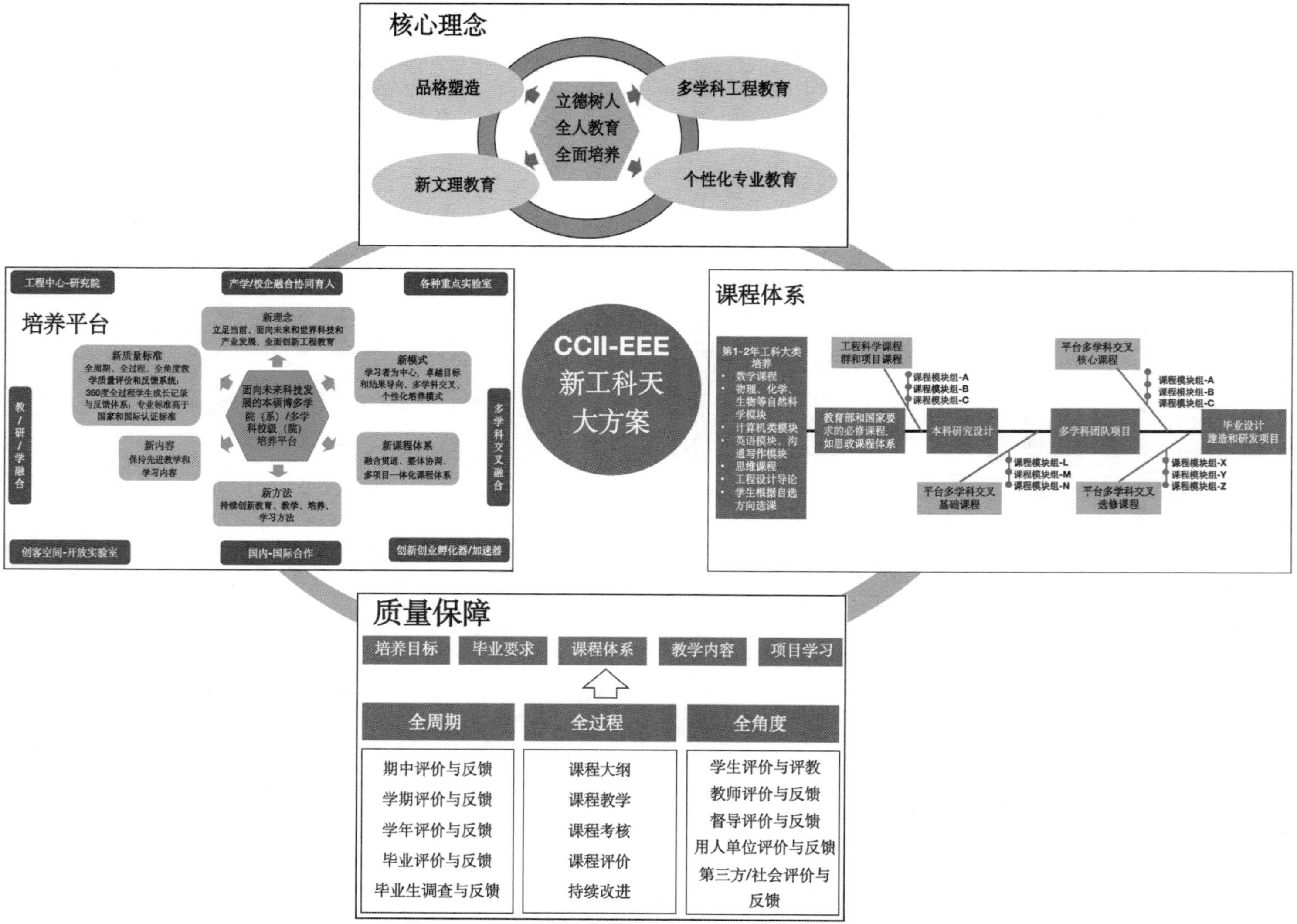


图 2　新工科天大方案的基本框架和主要内容

时代和创新经济发展需要的基本工程素质：

（1）适应未来职业变化与发展的能力（adaptability）；

（2）较高的伦理道德标准和职业责任的自觉意识；

（3）正确的工作动机和职业行为准则，以及克服挑战的持久毅力；

（4）养成自主和自觉学习的习惯，具备学习动力、学习毅力和学习能力，坚持持续学习和终身学习，保持工程专业素养和职业发展能力；

（5）较强的自然科学、数学和工程科学基础，多学科、跨学科的工程和技术知识，设计、建造、创造和创新、技术和产品研发、解决复杂的工程问题的能力；

（6）思维、团队合作、沟通、创业、管理、执行和领导等能力与素质。

将上述要求结合工程教育专业认证标准中的培养目标、毕业要求及天津大学专业特色，构成天津大学专业综合教育目标（CEG）。

### 1.2 天大方案培养模式

天津大学在分析和总结欧林学院、哈维穆德学院、OBE-CDIO、麻省理工学院-新工程教育转型等工程教育改革成功经验和最佳实践的基础上，创新提出了新工科天大方案。天大方案的核心理念是以立德树人统领学生培养全过程，融合新文理教育、多学科交叉工程教育和个性化专业教育，为学生提供全人教育和全面培养，培养未来卓越工程师、企业家、工程科学家和领军者。天大方案实施的重点包括：

（1）以学生发展为中心；

（2）建立开放、协同、多学科人才培养平台，以面向未来科技发展为主题，支撑多学科和跨学科的工程教育，实现教—研—学融合、校企融合和国内国际教育合作；

（3）建立书院，提供通识教育和有组织的课外活动；

（4）设立导师组指导学生的个性化学习；

（5）根据CEG，以5种项目为连接点，制订融合贯通的一体化课程计划和模块化课程体系；

（6）建立新的教学质量标准和保障体系，持续改进教育质量；

（7）评估毕业生培养结果，改进新工科天大方案，形成新工科天大模式。

新工科天大方案主要包括核心理念、培养平台、课程体系、质量保障，如图2所示。下面详细介绍这四部分内容。

#### 1.2.1 天大方案培养模式的核心理念

如前所述，新工科天津大学方案的核心理念是以立德树人统领人才培养全过程，通过融合新文理教育、多学科交叉工程教育和个性化专业教育，塑造学生的人格和核心价值观，培养学生卓越的专业素质和能力，实现全人教育和全面培养，如图3所示。

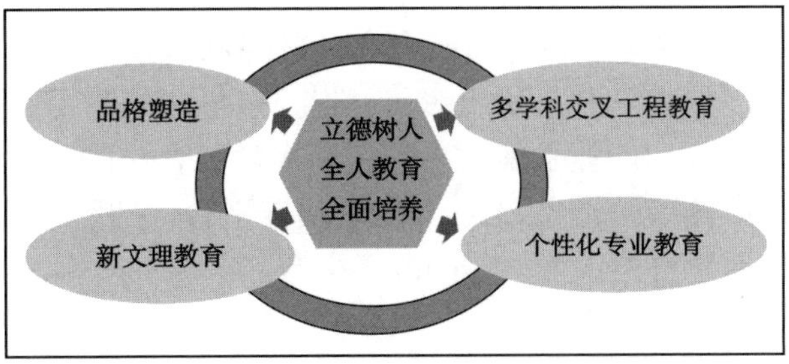


**图3 新工科天大方案CCII-EEE模式核心理念**

品格塑造：大学教育旨在培养具有社会责任感、良好道德品质、正确价值观和有知识、有能力、高素质的公民。天津大学坚持立德树人，培养品学兼优的创新人才。学校各级领导和教职员工都需要参与设计和建立培养体系，实现"三全育人""五育并举"，通过课程、项目、课外活动和社会服务等方式，培养学生的家国情怀、伦理道德和核心价值观，塑造高尚人格，实现全人教育与全面培养。

新文理教育：中华民族五千多年的灿烂文化，为人类文明和进步做出了卓越的历史贡献。以中国传统与现代人文、社科与艺术精髓丰富和改造传统文理教育，培养学生的人格、价值观、思维想象力、创造力、科学精神、科学态度、分析和判断、伦理推断、沟通、写作、团队合作、创业、管理、领导和终身学习能力，以适应未来职业变化与发展。

多学科交叉工程教育：工程项目通常是多学科团队合作完成的。为学生提供多学科和跨学科工程教育是培养综合工程能力的基本要求，打破传统的学科界限束缚和限制，培养学生宽厚的自然科学、数学和工程科学基础，严谨的工程态度，多学科和跨学科的工程知识，分析和决策能力，设计和建造能力，解决复杂工程问题的能力和工程创新能力等。

个性化专业教育：传统的本科教育，对同一专业学生的培养体系基本相同，学生可自选的课程很少，跨学院、跨学科选修课程更加困难。"斯坦福 2025 计划"提出根据学生的职业发展目标，构造个性化的培养体系。借鉴"斯坦福 2025 计划"的特点，以卓越目标和学生职业发展为导向，从体制机制上解决跨学院和跨学科选修问题，为学生提供最新的专业知识、能力、职业素质培养，鼓励学生修读双学位、主辅修，实现个性化的专业培养。

### 1.2.2 建设多学科-跨学科-全开放培养平台

当前本科专业教育主要以院系或学科为培养基础，为培养多学科和跨学科工程科技创新人才，亟待打破传统单一学科办学格局。各国大学的院系设置有所不同，我国是按照教育部的学科和专业分类进行建设，比如机械系（学科）支撑机械工程、机械电子工程、机械设计制造及其自动化等专业的教育教学，而北美的机械系通常支撑机械工程专业，虽然都是机械系，但是教师队伍和课程体系差别非常大。比如笔者非常熟悉的一个只有 35 名教师的机械和制造工程系，具有多个一级学科领域。又如 MIT 的机械系约有 80 名教师，其学术背景涵盖了我国的十多个一级学科，所以在课程体系、培养环境、科研和实验室等方面为学生提供了更多的选择。在当前强调建设一流学科的要求下，突破学科思维，在传统的大学组织结构中有效地实施多学科交叉融合，是实现科技和教育创新的一个重要途径，值得甚至是必须认真对待。

在现有大学由单一学院和学科组织专业课程的教学框架下，天大方案通过建立多学科、跨学科和多学院教育平台，突破体制机制以及组织结构的限制，探索建设面向未来科技发展主题的教学和科研组织，为学生提供多学科和跨学科工程教育。图 4 显示的是一种面向未来科技和产业发展的多学院和多学科合作的跨学科人才培养组织形式，也可以是未来技术学院的一种构建方式。其中，培养平台包括跨学院的多学科人才培养的校级平台，以及跨系和跨学科的人才培养的院级平台。

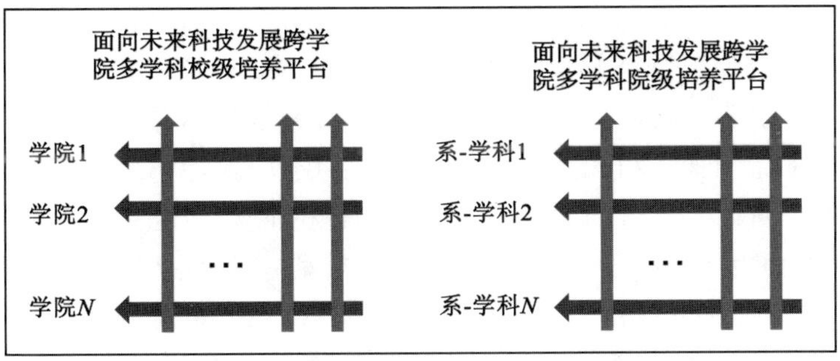


**图 4　校院两级多学科培养平台与院系和学科的关系**

国内外很多高校虽然都实现了跨学院、跨系、跨专业选课，以满足学生发展和个人兴趣需求，但这不是真正意义上的多学科交叉融合工程教育。多学科或跨学科的工程教育是根据培养目标和要求，通过设计和实施多学科交叉融合的课程体系，达到毕业生的培养目标和毕业要求，是整个专业系统性、规范性与可持续的，也是真正意义上的多学科交叉融合工程教育。众所周知，学科与知识体系相关，而专业与职业相关。如机械设计制造及其自动化专业培养制造工程师，但该专业传统聚焦的冷加工业和机床制造业已发生颠覆性变革，其多年形成的专业课程体系需要紧跟产业变化做出系统性修订和课程内容更新。

新工科天大方案规划建设聚焦未来科技/产业发展的主题式培养平台，如未来智能机器和系统培养平台、未来智能医疗与健康教育平台等。聚焦平台科技和产业主题，整合不同专业课程体系的共同要求，如智能机器与系统的自然科学和数学，智能产品和技术研发、思维，多学科团队工作、沟通、项目管理等共同要求，通过平台必修课实现共同的培养要求。不同专业聚焦的重点有所不同，如智能制造工程专业与测控技术与仪器专业在未来智能机器与系统方面的专业知识和能力的要求不同，这些不同专业的要求通过专业必修课实现。因此，不同专业课程体系通过聚焦同一科技主题，进行系统性整合，形成多学科交叉融合的课程体系，实现真正的多学科工程教育。

组建跨学院教师团队，负责设计平台的多学科和跨学科专业课程体系及其实施方案。在设计培养计划的过程中，根据新工科教育的理念、模式、课程体系、教学方法、课程内容、质量标准的要求，充分考虑适应性和可操作性，以未来的科技培养今天的学生，使他们现在就具备创造未来新技术和新产品的能力。

图 5 给出了一个典型的 CCII-EEE 培养平台。建设面向未来科技发展的开放型、多学院、跨学科的本硕博贯通的校-院两级培养平台。其中，校级平台由多学院/单位联合建设，院级平台由学院下设的系/学科联合组建。

"四融-四合-六新"的平台优势与特色：产学-校企融合、多学科交叉和跨学科融合、国内-国际培养融合、教-研-学融合，即四融；学校重点实验室、工程中心、创客空间和创新创业孵化器/加速器与教学和人才培养的深度合作，即四合；新工科人才培养理念、模式、课程体系、教学方法、教与学内容和质量标准的全面和持续创新，即六新。

面向未来建设以科技和产业发展为主题的本硕博培养平台，如未来智能机器与系统平台（可以建设为未来技术学院，如未来智能机器与系统技术学院）。面向世界选择对标的世界一流工程教育最佳实践，推动各种形式的国际合作，培养学生的国际交流、跨文化沟通和团队合作与领导能力。面向产业推动产学合作,企业深度参与培养计划和课程体系制定、校企共建培养/平台,为学生提供企业导师和各种产品/技术研发项目等。建设跨学科、跨学院、跨学校合作,真正实现多学科和跨学科人才培养。教研学融合推动科研支持教学,国家/省部重点实验室、研究院、工程中心等科研平台向学生开放,教师将最新科技前沿成果融入教学,指导学生科研和创新项目,提高学生科研创新能力,体现研究型大学培养特色。为学生提供创新创业教育和指导,建设孵化器和加速器,推动建立创业基金,支持学生技术创业。多学科培养平台也为研究生教育提供一个新机制和新环境,拓宽从单一学科支撑研究生培养到多学科交叉融合的研究生培养机制,不同学院的研究生在平台上合作研究,实现研究生的多学科交叉融合培养,对科研创新具有重要意义。

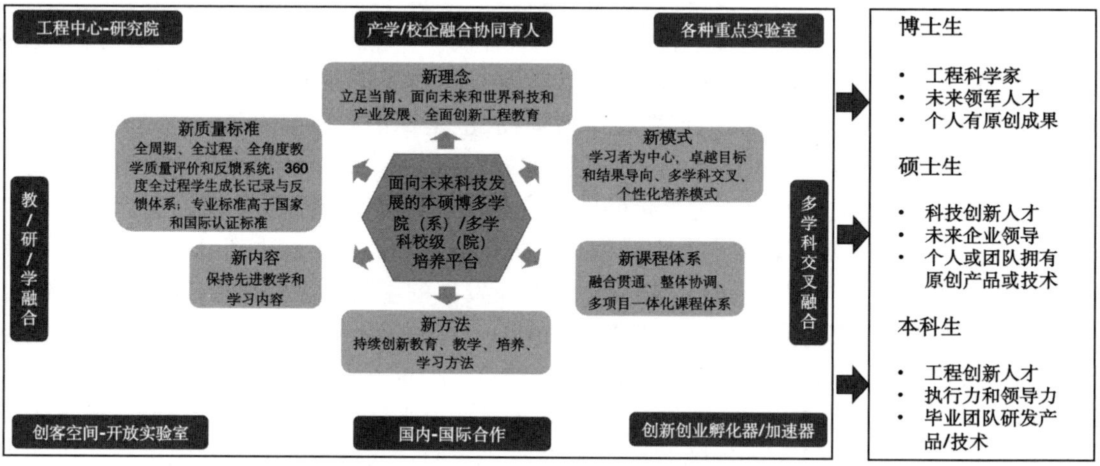


**图 5　面向未来科技和产业发展的多学科交叉融合培养平台**

### 1.2.3　建设融合贯通一体化课程体系路线图

本文作者在参考文献[15]中对课程体系建设路径做过较详细的描述,这部分虽然讲的是天大方案的课程体系,但结果导向的设计过程和路径基本相同。新工科培养方案和课程体系突出"通""融"和"新",按照学校的专业 CEG 设计课程体系,课程体系建设路线如图 6 所示,主要包括以下主要步骤:

(1)确定专业 CEG;

(2)分解 CEG 为详细的培养标准(或称为预期学习结果/学习产出, intended learning outcomes,简称 ILOs);

(3)设计结果导向的课程体系,实现 ILOs;

(4)根据结果导向课程体系和课程的 ILOs,确定详细课程内容;

(5)比较课程体系计划达到的总培养标准与第二步的 ILOs,根据比较结果,进行迭代。

确定综合教育目标是制定人才培养方案的第一步,如图 7(a)所示,一般建议完成下列工作:

(1)调查毕业五年内、五至十年及十年以上的校友代表(对象的选择、覆盖面和问卷设计要符合调查研究的规范和要求);

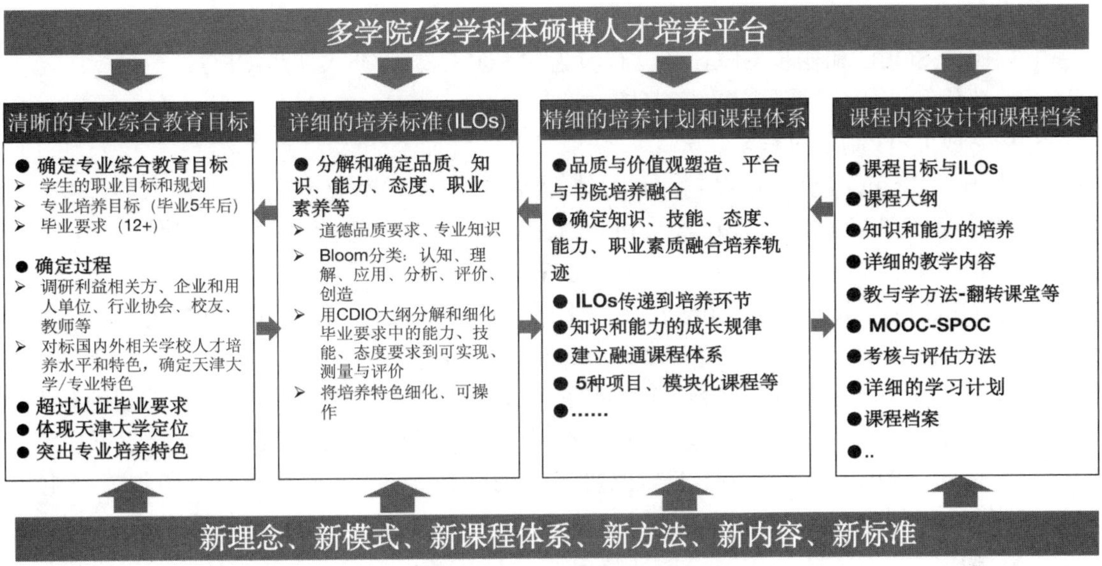


**图 6　融合贯通一体化课程体系建设路线**

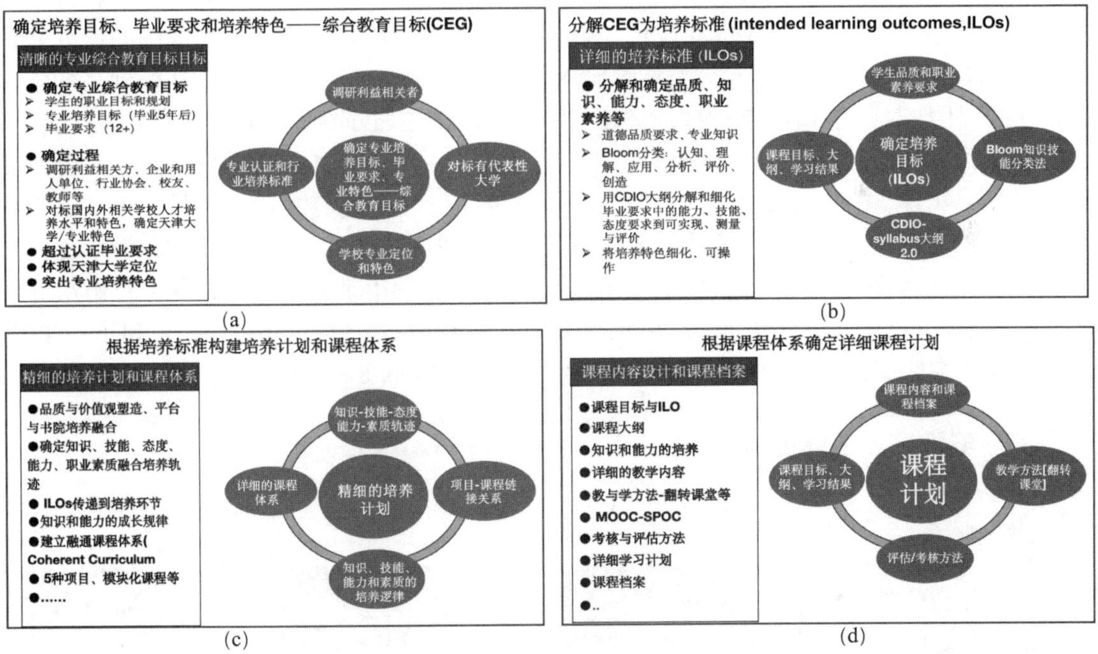


**图 7　课程体系建设路线主要步骤的详细说明**

（2）调查毕业生的用人单位，用人单位聘任的毕业生来自多个学校，能够提供毕业生表现的客观资料和比较优势分析；

（3）对标国内相关大学/专业培养水平和特色；

（4）对标国际相关大学/专业培养水平和特色；

（5）研讨工程教育专业认证标准中的培养目标、毕业要求和专业相关补充标准；

（6）提出初步综合教育目标（CEG）；

（7）比较 SQEC 和初步 CEG，将没有包含的 SQEC 条款补入初步 CEG；

（8）评价和迭代，邀请外部专家审核；

（9）完成 CEG 制定过程。

如上所示，CEG 包括专业培养目标、毕业要求、学校和专业特色等内容，大学和专业的培养特色表现为其毕业生的特殊素质和能力，是本校该专业毕业生有别于其他大学同类专业毕业生的主要体现。

鉴于 CEG 内容较为宏观，无法直接用于课程体系的设计，需要将其分解为具体的培养标准（学习结果或学习产出，intended learning outcomes，简称 ILOs），过程如图 7（b）所示。然后根据培养标准，设计培养计划、课程体系、具体课程内容和教学活动。科学基础和专业技术知识的设定，可以参照教指委或专业行业协会制定的标准，例如电子行业可以考虑 IEEE 的"Body of Knowledge"；技术知识要求、技能、态度、职业素质等工程和非工程能力，可以参考 CDIO 大纲 2.0 给出的 380 多项关于个人能力、团队合作和沟通等技能，以及企业、社会和环境背景下的构思、设计、实施和运行能力等[15]。在确定培养标准后，可以应用 Bloom 分类法进一步对知识掌握水平和技能要求进行分级。

如图 7（c）和（d）所示，设计融合贯通课程体系和课程内容，将培养标准（ILOs）分配到课程等教学环节，然后进行评价和迭代，这是一个从抽象到具体、从宏观到详细的反复迭代的设计过程。需要根据 Bloom 分类所界定的知识和技能的水平，明确学生从低到高的学习成长路径，比如对某个知识点或技能要求达到 Level 6（Evaluation），需要设计出从 Level 1（Knowledge）到 Level 6（Evaluation）的成长路径，将 Level 1 至 Level 6 的进步过程分布到不同课程中实现，保证 Level 6 的达成。此外，应关注自然科学、数学、工程科学等基础知识的系统性和专业科技知识的先进性，定期更新专业课内容。以不同类型项目为学生提供产品和技术研发、创新和创造产品和技术的经历和经验，使学生掌握运用结构化方法解决非结构化工程实际问题（use structured methods to solve unstructured engineering problems）的技能和能力。设计过程完成融合贯通的一体化课程体系，如图 8 所示。

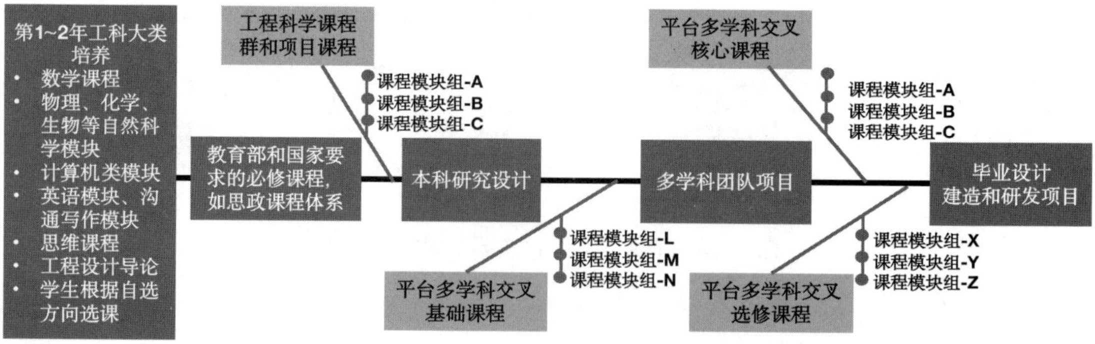


**图 8　以 5 种项目为节点的融合贯通课程体系的鱼骨图**

融合贯通课程体系中定义了 5 种项目，课程项目由教师根据课程内容需要，以项目为载体，使学生掌握和应用课程核心知识。在一年级引入基于项目的学习，通过体验式学习的

Kolb 循环，让学生体验和掌握主动学习模式。课程群项目旨在培养学生应用课程群涉及的领域核心知识解决实际工程问题的能力。多学科团队项目是符合培养平台主题的多学科工程技术项目，解决较复杂的工程问题或者开展一项技术研发。本科研究项目是指本科生参加重点实验室等研究机构的科研项目、指导教师的科研项目、竞赛或企业提供的研发项目等。毕业设计研发项目要求学生团队（多学科、大团队）开发新产品或新技术。课程内项目和课程群项目主要培养学生掌握和应用知识。科研项目、多学科团队项目和毕业项目培养学生的科技创新能力。

在项目的组织方面，参与平台建设的多个学院整合了丰富的实验室优势资源，比如参与建设未来智能机器与系统培养平台的学院就包含有两个国家重点实验室、多个省部级重点实验室、研究院和研究中心等，这些科研平台对学生项目提供了大力支持。学生项目特别是三年级的科研项目、多学科学生团队项目和四年级的毕业项目可以与重点实验室和研究院科研项目相结合，本科生与教师和研究生团队一起组成大团队，完成科技创新和产品研发任务。项目的组织可以参考佐治亚理工学院的纵向集成项目[16]和新南威尔士大学工学院的 ChallENG 项目[17]。

#### 1.2.4 建立教学质量新标准及评价体系

建立教学质量保障体系，首先要建立教学质量标准。如图 9（a）所示，专业在制定质量标准时需要考虑国家的教育教学质量要求、工程教育专业认证标准、行业的人才资质评价标准以及学校的人才培养质量要求。如前所述，一流大学和专业的人才培养质量标准应高于国家和国际工程专业认证标准。其次是教学质量的持续改进，如图 9（b）所示。天大方案构建了全周期、全过程、全角度的评价反馈体系：全周期是指对学生在学期中、学期末、学年、毕业和毕业后的评价与反馈；全过程是指对课程大纲、课程的教学过程、课程考核、课程评价方法及课程的持续改进；全角度指多方教育教学的利益相关者的评价与反馈，包括学生、教师、督导、用人单位、社会和第三方等。

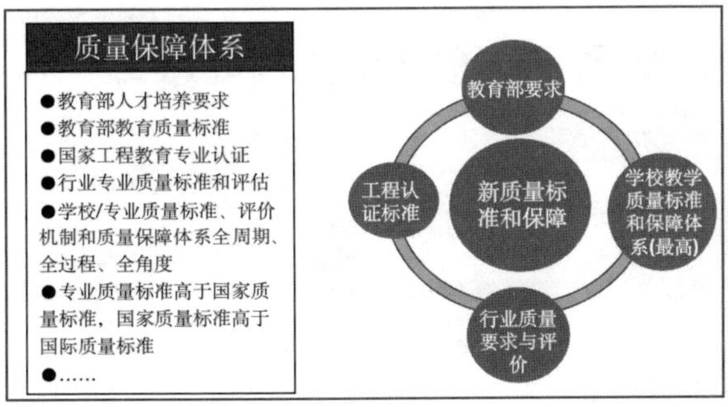


(a)

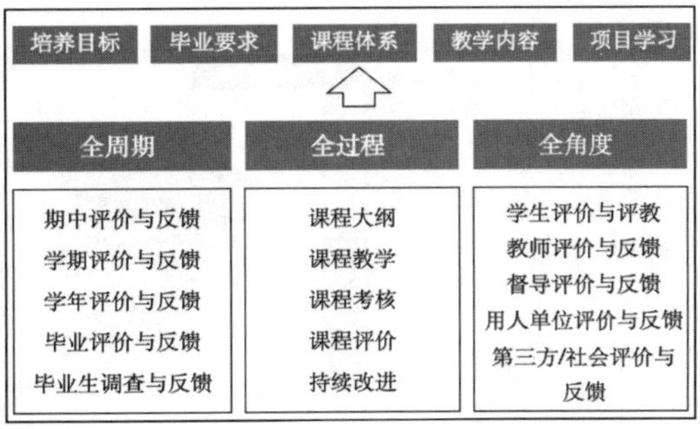


(b)

**图 9 教学质量标准及评价体系**

### 1.3 天大方案的试点实施

天大方案的实施过程是一个工程教育系统性变革的实践过程，涉及机构组织、教学组织、人事、财务等机制、体制方方面面的改革，在国内现有大学组织结构下，实施这样的系统性教育改革计划，大学书记和校长的坚强领导和支持至关重要。只有在学校一把手领导和支持下，经过从上到下和从下到上的多轮广泛协商，才能制定出可行的实施计划和具体工作方案。天津大学以建立“未来智能机器与系统”平台开展试点实施，及时评估和修订行动方案，为全校范围内的推行打好基础。作为试点探索，除了范围和规模外，试点工作一般要能够涉及全面实施的所有方面的重要工作，探索实施路径、潜在问题和挑战。试点实施主要包括以下内容：①建立多学科教育平台；②组建多学科教师团队；③设计课程体系和课程内容；④试点平台招生；⑤实施试点课程计划；⑥评估试点工作的阶段性进展，找出存在的问题并及时改进。

### 1.3.1　建立多学科教育平台

针对未来重要科技发展方向，结合学校教学和科研规划，如结合“双一流”建设规划，设计校院两级多学科和跨学科人才培养开发式平台。在当前高校组织结构下，建设校级平台具有一定的挑战性。试点平台的核心任务在于，探索在现有大学体制下，如何建立多学科和跨学科工程教育，构建新型教育科研机构，丰富和补充传统大学院系建制，创新人才培养机制。

如图 10 所示，未来智能机器与系统（future intelligent machines and systems，FIMS）是天津大学的首个试点校级培养平台，FIMS 平台以机械工程学院、电气自动化与信息工程学院、精密仪器与光电子工程学院、微电子学院、智能与计算学部、管理与经济学部的宣怀学院等为组建主体，联合其他单位和部门，为平台提供涵盖文理教育、项目、科研、创新创业等方面的支持。两个国家级重点实验室（精密测试技术及仪器国家重点实验室、内燃机国家重点实验室）、两个省部级重点实验室（机构理论与装备设计教育部重点实验室、天津市装备设计与制造重点实验室）、智能技术研究院和工程实践中心以及宣怀学院（创新创业）等对学生项目、课程、创新创业需求开放。

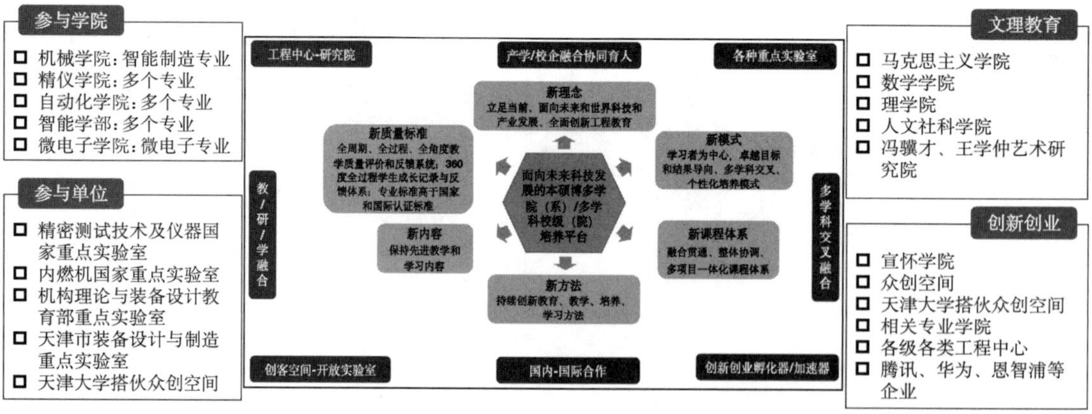


**图 10　未来智能机器与系统培养平台**

FIMS 平台的高效管理和稳定运行，是落实天大方案的培养模式和实现多学科工程教育的核心环节。FIMS 平台目前的管理体系包括平台管理委员会、求是学部以及教学委员会。成立于2009年的求是学部，是学校教育改革工作的综合试点部门，拥有基本完备的人员构成和运行体系，负责FIMS的日常运行。平台管理委员会负责制定政策和重要决策，平台管理委员会主任由校级领导担任，委员由参与平台建设的学院院长和主管教学的副院长及求是学部领导组成。教学委员会由参与平台建设的学院的副院长和骨干教师组成，负责教学和课程及相关学术事务。

### 1.3.2 组建多学科教师团队

多学科教师团队由参与学院的教师组成，各学院推荐热心本科教学和积极参加本科教育改革的教师进入培养平台。从准备平台课程到第一学期结束前的几个月，FIMS平台共召开了50多次建设研讨和教学研究会议，研讨平台教学计划和课程内容。特别值得一提的是，来自几个学院的教师们在学校教师考核标准没有修改的情况下，工作仍然非常努力，在几个月的试点工作过程中，没有一位教师问过工作量如何计算，这体现了教师对本科教育的重视以及自觉投入教学工作的热情。所有参与平台建设的学院的教学副院长也积极参与课程建设。校院（部）领导和教师团队的积极投入是试点运行顺利的根本保证。

### 1.3.3 设计课程体系和课程内容

课程体系设计分为以下两步。

（1）根据图6、图7、图8描述的课程体系建设路线，修订已有专业的课程体系，设计新建专业的课程体系。

（2）将修订后的现有专业课程体系和设计的新专业课程体系围绕“未来智能机器与系统”的主题进行整合，建立平台融合贯通课程体系。平台的课程体系包括平台必修课、专业必修课和平台选修课。在FIMS平台内，围绕主题设计平台必修课，整合各专业基础课和技术必修课，保留各专业必修核心课。一个专业的必修课，可以成为其他专业的选修课程，再与各专业已有选修课整合为平台选修课。学生根据个人职业发展和学习兴趣，选择平台选修课、主辅修或双学位课程，实现多学科个性化专业培养。

平台试点必修课程的内容在后面会具体介绍。

### 1.3.4 试点平台招生

FIMS平台首批招生采用二次选拔方式，通过笔试和面试从一年级新生中选拔具备良好学习动力并愿意参加试点项目的学生进入平台培养，第一批140名学生是从1000多名申请者中选拔出来的。FIMS平台的课程比常规专业的课程难度高、课程负担重，主动学习方法和项目制学习很具挑战性，这些挑战激发了学生的学习动力和自觉性。

### 1.3.5 实施试点课程计划

第一学期FIMS平台必修课程注重基础性和课程项目，由教师团队根据平台主题设计，FIMS平台学生在修读全校必修课程外，还需修读以下平台必修课程：①工程数学分析A（代替高等数学）；②设计与建造；③智能电子创客设计与应用；④思维与创新。

工程数学分析[18]是一门分三个学期开设的课程，工程数学分析A是第一学期课程，后续两个学期分别开设工程数学分析 B 和工程数学分析 C。本课程不仅为学生传授数学分析的内容，培养数学思维，而且引导学生将所学知识应用于 FIMS 相关领域的工程实践，特别是跨学科项目和研究中。根据课程大纲的要求，经过课程教师调查和评价，第一学期的工程数学分析 A 课程达到了预期目标，该课程的学生在学习动机和学习意愿上表现出很强的主动性。表 1 是非平台学生修读的高等数学与新开设的工程数学分析 A 课程内容的简单比较。

**表 1　高等数学与工程数学分析 A 课程内容比较[18]**

| 比较项 | 高等数学 | 工程数学分析 A |
|---|---|---|
| 学习目的 | 掌握专业学习需要的数学知识 | 掌握专业学习与研究需要的数据基础知识 |
| 数学能力 | 掌握基本的微积分公式及应用 | 掌握微积分主要知识的产生和发展过程 |
| 聚焦 | 主要集中在解题 | 培养学生发现和提出问题的能力 |
| 训练 | 主要训练解题技巧和细节 | 培养学生解决问题的思维方法 |
| 逻辑推理 | 简单逻辑训练 | 严谨的逻辑推理能力训练 |

设计与建造[18]课程的主要目标是通过学习产品设计与开发过程，实施基于项目的学习，培养学生运用现代设计技术与方法解决产品和系统设计方面问题的能力。授课内容包括产品设计流程、产品设计表达与软件工具使用、制造与控制技术、项目管理技术和工程伦理等。学生通过完成智能派送机器人小车项目，获得项目实践经验和团队工作经历，对产品和技术开发有了更深刻理解，培养了团队合作、沟通交流和项目管理的基本能力。表 2 显示了主要课程内容及其组织形式。通过课程内容学习和项目实践，掌握基础制造过程等产品设计和建造技能。学生团队制作的智能派送机器人小车能够沿着规定的路径运行，在规定的车站放下物体。图 11 显示了与课程内容对应的项目流程进度。在课程进行的每个阶段，要求学生提交报告或者展示项目进展，教师评价学生的阶段性工作，并提供反馈意见。这门课对教师团队成员而言是全新的教学体验，在课程准备期间，教师团队多次开会讨论、规划和准备课程，在课程进行中每周召开教师团队会议，共同备课、试讲和说课。课程项目评估包括阶段性报告、PPT 汇报、最后项目展览和竞赛。

**表 2　设计与建造课程内容和组织[18]**

| 讲课（14 学时） | 研讨（14 学时） | 实验（28 学时） |
|---|---|---|
| 第一章　工程设计概论 | | |
| | 任务分工/工程师的职责 | |
| 第二章　产品规划 | | 三维软件使用上机（4） |
| | 客户需求分析，目标树 | 手绘实践（2） |
| 第三章　概念设计 | | 三维软件使用上机（4） |
| | 概念设计，方案选择 | |

续表

| 讲课(14 学时) | 研讨(14 学时) | 实验(28 学时) |
|---|---|---|
| 第四章　产品设计表达 | | 产品设计上机(4) |
| | 产品详细设计 | VR 软件使用(2) |
| 第五章　机电控制 | | 产品设计上机(4) |
| | 产品控制部分设计 | 产品制作(2) |
| 第六章　产品制作 | | |
| | 零部件制作与装配 | 产品制作(2) |
| 第七章　经济分析 | | 产品制作(2) |
| | 产品总结 | 产品制作(2) |

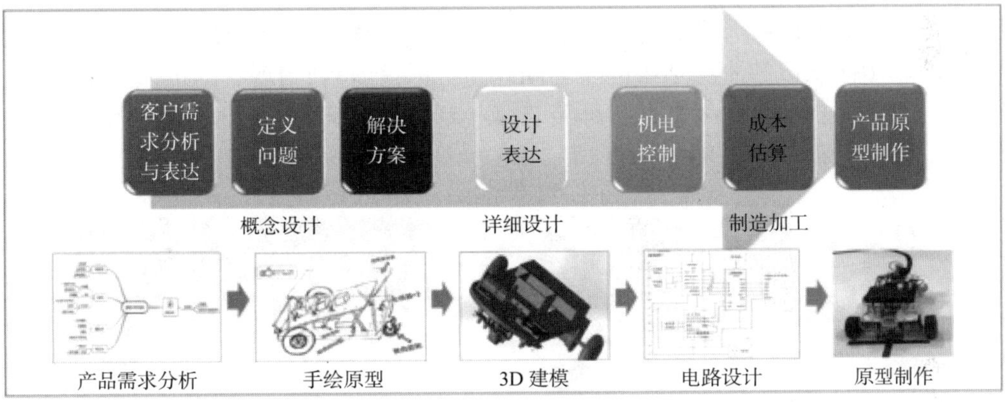


**图 11　设计与建造课程主要内容与学生团队项目进度[18]**

智能电子创客设计与应用[18]课程改革传统按学科组织教学内容的方式,打破机械、电子、软件和硬件的课程界限,将分散在传统课程体系 1~4 年级的课程内容,包括电路基础、编程、工程图学、自动控制原理、模拟和数字电路、电机学、微机原理、单片机应用和过程和运动控制等,按照功能重新整合为“ Capture”“Control”“Compute”“Communication”四个模块,每个模块都包含相关机械、电子和软硬件知识。表 3 展示了课程主要授课内容。

教师团队由来自电气自动化与信息工程学院、微电子学院、智能与计算学部、机械工程学院和精密仪器与光电子工程学院的 7 名教师组成。课程负责人在自动化和信息领域具有多年教学经验,虽然可以自己承担课程教学,但为了给学生提供更好的多学科教育体验,邀请了各个领域的专家组成多学科教学团队,在课程涉及的各个领域提供专家教学和指导,如传感器方面的教学由来自精仪学院的著名传感器教学专家承担。教学实践表明,多学科的课程由多学科教师团队负责,才能达到理想的教学效果。

表 3　智能电子创客设计与应用课程内容[18]

| 课程 | 内容 | 课程 | 内容 |
| --- | --- | --- | --- |
| 1 | 基于 Arduino 的创客电子案例 | 6 | 适用于 Arduino 的各类新型传感器 |
| 2 | Arduino 基本语法与数字 IO 设计 | 7 | 适用于 Arduino 的驱动器和执行器 |
| 3 | Arduino 基本语法与模拟 IO 设计 | 8 | 面向 Arduino 的手机控制 App 开发 |
| 4 | 工程文档撰写和电路板设计软件 | 9 | 适用于 Arduino 的通信设计 |
| 5 | 3D 打印 | — | — |

在学生课堂学习之外，引导学生通过自学、朋辈学习，践行主动学习和自主学习的理念和方法。除了培养学生多学科知识和能力外，课程重点培养学生的创造力。具体措施是通过课程内容和项目激发创意灵感、构思创意方案、进行同行评审、鼓励拓展创意，进而实施创意并亲身体验创意的实现过程。教师团队向学生介绍各种“黑技术”，如用于绿色种植的“土壤传感器”、用于确定降雨量的“雨量传感器”以及“PM2.5 传感器”，激发学生的想象力和创造力。学生团队以解决生活中的实际问题为目标，综合利用现有的机械电子装置，完成创意项目。如图 12 所示，43 个项目涉及日常生活衣食住行的各个方面，学生通过项目构想、设计和实现，获得学以致用的体验。

图 12　从 43 个项目选出 4 个案例[18]

思维与创新[18]是一门兼具重要性和挑战性的新课程，其核心目的在于培养学生的思维能力。由于我国高中应试教育的性质和学生面临的高强度学习压力，很难为学生提供充分的思维能力培养和训练。而传统工科课程以学习学科有关知识为主，对学生思维能力的培养重视程度不够。思维与创新课程的主要内容包括批判性思维、创造性思维、系统性思维、逻辑学与推理、设计思维、融合设计与创新等，培养学生的各种思维及分析、创新创造和决策能力。课程的组织方式是授课、研讨会和辅导课。从课程内容可以看出，很难找到一位教师掌握所有这些思维的知识、技能和能力，因此，需要组建满足课程要求的教师团队。一位法学院教师负责批判性思维，一位建筑和设计学院教师负责创造性思维，一位系统工程方面的教师负责系统性思维，一位科技哲学方面的教师负责逻辑学和推理，一名具有设计思维教学经验的管理学教师负责设计思维部分，一名熟悉思维领域的机械工程教师负责融合思维与创新方面。培养学生的思维能力不能单靠一门课程，这门课程的作用是引导学生认识和运用思维知识和技能，在今后的学习和工作中，有意识地培养和锻炼思维方面的能力，一些学生将会成为优秀的思考者。

学生对这门新课程的反应非常积极，同时提出了一些建设性的改进意见。由于这是学生第一次接触思维方面的知识和技能训练，通过课程学习，他们认识到有效思考的重要性。

该门课程目前的主要挑战是没有合适的教材。图 13 是学生的一些反馈。

| 答案文本 |
| --- |
| 能激发同学们思考、有亲和力 |
| 批判性思维学到了，短短几节课，还是懂得了一些批判性思维，感觉很有用的，对自己思维培养有帮助 |
| 引导同学们积极参与辩论，课堂参与度高 |
| 准备到位，积极参与 |
| 老师和蔼可亲，授课很好 |
| 和蔼可亲，讲的也很好 |
| 老师很热情，和学生互动很多，有自己的想法 |
| 思想活跃，清晰明了 |

从反馈意见来看，多数学生对课程高度肯定，认为对思维提升有很大帮助。

- 还记得之前了解到思创课堂老师多来自文科学院，对于一名日常钻研于工程设计的学生来说，与其说是一门传统的课程还不如说是一次心灵的交流，思维模式的创新。其实，我们的世界还很大，我还很想去看看，去看看那更远的远方，给心灵一次洗礼，灵魂一次升华。
- 在未来的生活中，去做出更多的选择，将会是我们的宿命，更是我们的必然，无论是成功还是失败，这条路，都必将由自己一步一个脚印地走过，任何人或物，也无法替代，面对选择，面对人生，我希望自己在走过她的时候，内心是充满了预测完趋势之后的自信和“不怕意外跌倒，一路向前”的焕发着光芒的坚持与毅力品质。
- 着重眼界的开拓与思维的创新，更应该从日常做起，是一种日常类似于报刊的定时更新与熏陶，而不仅是单纯的长时间的课程。

**图 13　思维与创新课程学生反馈案例说明[18]**

### 1.3.6　试点课程的反思与改进意见

根据以往的经验，按照北美的学术体制，未来智能机器与系统平台建立、招生、学生培养各方面需要 1~2 年的时间才能完成教学和学术程序的准备工作。我国虽然学术体制不同，但平台的教师队伍建设、课程、招生等方面的准备工作也面临很多挑战。为应对这些挑战，学校采取了边试点、边改进的方式开展工作。求是学部凭借 10 年在教育教学改革试点工作、招生和新课程建设等方面积累的经验，为平台试点的具体工作开展和有效管理提供了强有力的支撑。在主要校领导和主管校领导的支持和领导下，在参与学院及求是学部领导的积极协助下，在各位老师的共同努力下，试点工作得以顺利推进。平台相关各方不断思考、总结与改进，优化试点工作。在思维与创新课程的总结过程中，提出了存在的问题和改进的建议（图 14）。

| | |
| --- | --- |
| 课程学时 | ◆ 问题：学时较少，内容难以全面展开，小班研讨受限<br>◆ 建议：增加学时或分设课程 |
| 授课团队 | ◆ 问题：师资来源较广，协调存在一定困难<br>◆ 建议：分专题组建较为稳定的团队，特别要考虑新老校区问题 |
| 内容建设 | ◆ 问题：各部分内容之间的衔接不够紧密，尚未形成有效合力<br>◆ 建议：加强课程定期研讨，完善授课内容与形式 |
| 学生意识 | ◆ 问题：部分学生对课程的目标和意义认识还不到位<br>◆ 建议：强化全校通识教育，多方塑造人文氛围 |
| 激励机制 | ◆ 问题：授课教师投入的工作量难以在绩效考核中被充分认可<br>◆ 建议：尽快出台相关文件，从制度层面予以保障 |

**图 14　对思维与创新课程的改进意见[18]**

## 1.4 天大方案培养模式与试点实施分析

### 1.4.1 培养模式的理念创新和实践可行性

对学生人格和价值观的塑造贯穿四年学习全过程，在制定人才培养计划和课程体系时，对学生道德品质、价值观、人文素养、科学精神、职业素质等方面的培养，部分是通过课程和项目等教学活动来实现的，其他方面的培养则是通过思想工作、书院学习、讲座、课外活动、义工活动、文化艺术活动等形式来实现的。负责学生工作的学工组织将为学生在品格、理想、道德、价值观、人文素养、职业技能等方面的培养提供重要支撑。2019 年 12 月，天津大学提出“三全育人”“五育并举”人才培养综合改革方案，旨在通过新工科教育实现立德树人的目标，塑造学生的人格和价值观。

世界上一些优秀大学，如哈佛大学和耶鲁大学的办学经验证明了文理教育的优势。随着科技发展和社会进步，传统文理学院和综合性大学的文理教育面临着培养目标、教育模式和培养内容与时俱进的挑战。“天大方案”提出的新文理教育以中国传统和现代人文、社科与艺术等方面的精髓改造和丰富传统文理教育，致力于塑造学生的人格与价值观，培养学生的思维、想象力、创造力、科学精神、分析和判断、伦理推断、沟通、写作、团队合作、创业、管理、领导和终身学习等方面的能力，以适应未来职业变化与发展。第一学期的思维与创新课程致力于培养学生的批判性、创造性、系统性思维以及设计思维等思维能力，使学生掌握科学与逻辑推理等方面的知识与能力。设计与建造和智能电子创客设计与建造课程培养学生在想象力、创造力、团队、沟通、写作、创新等方面的能力。工程数学分析 A 和大学化学课程培养学生的思维能力、分析问题能力和科学态度等。思想道德修养与法律基础、形式与政策等全校通识教育课程培养有中国特色的人文社科素养。

多学科工程教育是在跨学院和跨学科培养平台上实现的。平台培养的学生可以选择在 5 个学院的 10 多个专业中学习并毕业。第一学期的课程包括全校必修课和 4 门平台必修课。工程数学分析 A 和思维与创新可以推广为全校课程。设计与建造和智能电子创客设计与应用体现了多学科培养平台的优势。设计与建造课程已成为电气自动化与信息工程学院、微电子学院、智能与计算学部、精仪与光电子学院多个专业的必修课。智能电子创客设计与应用已成为机械工程学院、精仪与光电子学院、智能与计算学部学生的必修课。如果没有多学科和跨学科培养平台，就不会建设这样的多学科课程，一个学院的学生也很难在第一学期实现跨学院修课。后续还设计有多门这样的课程，以实现多学科工程教育。

平台上一个专业必修课可以成为其他专业的选修课，再与各专业选修课整合起来，成为平台学生的选修课。通过选修课的合理组合，形成多个课程模块，由学生选择，实现个性化培养。天大方案的培养模式鼓励学生攻读主辅修、双学位以及研究生。在面向未来科技主题平台上的多学科和跨学科主辅修和双学位的课程基础上，增加了创新创业、管理与领导力和工程科学等三类课程模块，实现平台专业+创新创业、管理与领导力以及工程科学主辅修或双学位，最终实现卓越工程师、企业家和工程科学家及未来领军者的培养，如图 15 所示，三类个性化培养都可以成为未来的领军者。

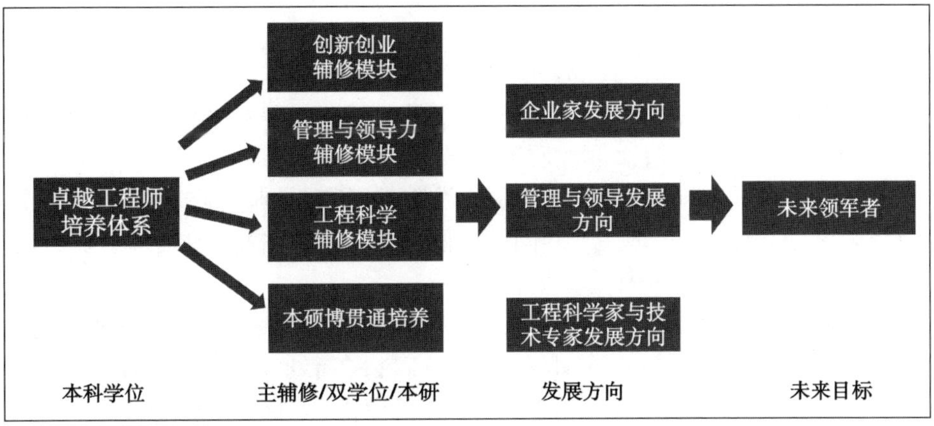


图 15　培养未来卓越工程师、企业家、工程科学家和领军者的关系

#### 1.4.2　新工科教育是一把手工程

国内外大学本科教育的成功经验证明，一流本科教育的建设离不开学校和学院一把手的高度重视，主要领导不仅需肩负办好教育的责任，还应具备调配资源的能力。大学主要领导要高度重视本科教育和人才培养，全力推动新工科建设，主管校领导、教务部门、学工系统和科研系统要协助校领导推动学生培养工作。各学院（部）院长（部主任）和系主任是实施新工科教育工作的责任主体，因为学生培养和课程教学都在院系，一流本科教育最终体现在教师和学生之间高效且优质的教与学互动工作中。只要学校、院、系领导把学生培养放在中心地位，新工科建设方案一定能落实好。

### 1.5　新工科天大方案的国际比较

#### 1.5.1　天大方案与 MIT-NEET

（1）天大方案是系统性的整体改革，在现有体制机制下，具有实施的可行性。NEET 在不改变现有专业要求的基础上增加跨学科的新课程和新内容。天大方案是学位项目，NEET 是证书项目。

（2）天大方案和 NEET 都强调多学科培养。NEET 要求学生修读一个现有工科学位，同时完成跨学科项目和课程学习。跨学科方向包括先进材料机械、自主机械、数字城市、活体机械和可再生能源机械。天大方案以未来科技为主题建立跨学科多学科培养平台，如“未来智能机器与系统”校级培养平台和“未来建成环境与建筑”院级培养平台。天大方案要求根据专业综合教育目标，系统修订和建立相应的课程体系并在平台上进行整合，实现多学科交叉和跨学科的学位课程培养。

（3）天大方案和 NEET 都强调基于项目的学习，NEET 要求在跨学科新机器方向完成几个项目，天大方案提出包括 5 种项目的课程体系，强调毕业生有原创技术/产品。

（4）天大方案和 NEET 都有思维教育的要求。

### 1.5.2 天大方案与欧林学院培养模式

(1)天大方案和欧林学院模式都是整体性和系统性改革。Olin 是新建学校,可以按照学校定位和建设目标进行系统建设;天大方案需要在现有的院系结构和培养体系基础上开展系统改革。两者都具有挑战性,但性质不同。

(2)两者都强调多学科培养。欧林学院不设院系,所有教师都在一个学院工作,由于学校规模小,教师之间合作密切,是一个共同的团队;天大方案则需要建设跨学院的教师团队,在组织、文化和人事制度等方面都有很大挑战。

(3)在课程体系方面,天大方案强调课程体系的融合贯通和一体化;欧林学院没有这方面的明确要求,而且学生可以在巴布森学院修读商科,在韦尔斯利学院修读人文社科课程,学生培养的课程体系(课程组建设)和课程学习的指导很具创新特色。

(4)关于项目制学习,欧林学院毕业生大学期间每人平均完成 25 个项目,学生每学期完成各种项目并参加展览,展示各类设计和建造项目成果;天大方案提出 5 种项目,没有具体项目数量要求。

欧林学院和 MIT 培养的毕业生证明了其工程教育模式的先进性和成功经验。天大方案设计是在分析和总结世界先进工程教育经验和最佳实践基础上的再创新,天大方案具有一定的先进性,并有持续改进和持续创新的要求。必须清楚地认识到,这只是一个方案,只有方案全面实施后,以学生培养的水平和教育质量才能真正证明此方案的先进性。

## 1.6 新工科天大方案的创新点与特色

21 世纪以来,全球工程教育变革浪潮中积累的成功经验和最佳实践,为天大方案奠定了坚实基础。其中,多年来持续开展的基于项目的学习模式,超过 10 年的 OBE-CDIO 工程教育改革与创新,融合博雅通识教育与结果导向的先进本科教育,借鉴欧林学院和哈维穆德学院的工程博雅教育,以及 MIT-NEET 和"斯坦福 2025 计划"等先进经验,有助于天大方案在此基础上再创新,面向国家未来经济发展需要、面向未来科技发展、面向企业需求、面向国际竞争与机遇,建设可复制和可参考借鉴的新工科教育模式和体系。新工科天津大学方案具有以下特点。

(1)大学机构和人才培养体制机制创新。方案创造性地提出多学科人才培养平台,在传统大学体制中,实现系统性和规范性的多学科交叉和跨学科工程教育。传统大学工科教育是以院系(或者学科)为单位的专业教育体制,现在建立面向未来科技和产业发展的多学院和跨学科人才培养平台,不是要改变现有院系建制,而是对现有大学体系的丰富和补充。多学科培养平台不仅支撑交叉学科和跨学科的本科教育,而且为研究生培养提供了一个新方向。每一位工作在跨学院多学科人才培养平台的教师都隶属一个学院和系,教师的科研团队不仅不变,而且可以向多学科和交叉学科的科研方向发展和整合,科研成果仍然归所属学科,教师的教学任务在培养平台完成。这样就形成传统院系和多学院、多学科平台建制相结合的模式,实现面向未来的创新工程教育和科技创新的体系。

(2)整体性和可操作性。方案紧扣创新经济和新工业革命的产业特征,精准提炼出个人适应能力、正确工作动机、职业行为准则、克服挑战的持续毅力、学习动力和能力等应对未来职业变化的基本素质要求，结合大学立德树人的培养目标、工程专业认证的毕业要求和大学自身的特色和优势，构建起新工科人才综合培养目标，提出了新文理教育、多学科工程教育和个性化专业教育的新工科培养体系。通过人才培养平台、专业学院与书院育人机制，实现对学生的全人教育和全面培养。

新工科建设方案是一个较完整的多学科和跨学科培养体系，方案构建了从整体到局部紧密关联的完整培养体系，各部分都有明确的内部实施体系（例如平台建设、融合贯通的课程体系、5 种项目与组织、质量保障体系、平台-书院-导师融合体系等），从建立培养目标、毕业要求、专业特色到形成培养标准、构建课程体系、开发课程内容等具体环节的路线，建设聚焦以未来科技和产业发展为主题的多学科培养平台，将多学院和多专业课程体系集成为平台必修课、专业必修课和平台选修课，配合创新创业、企业家和领导力等模块，支持学生个性化发展需要。方案具有可操作、可落实的特点，培养模式核心组成模块之间可做到柔性连接，便于局部实施和持续改进（具有适应性和可拓展性特点），由院长、系主任或专业负责人领导的团队可以实施局部或整体方案。

（3）适应性和可拓展性。此方案适用于研究型大学，也适用于只有本科教育的普通高校。方案可以整体实施，也可以部分或局部实施。如果学校没有重点实验室或工程中心，就不必在培养方案中要求。没有博士和硕士授予权，就只建设本科生培养方案。根据实际情况，建设培养平台。如果局部实施，可以只建设课程体系，只建设符合学校/学院实际的培养平台，只建立质量保障体系，只深化校企合作办学，只加强各种项目的学习，只建设书院-导师制，只加强创新创业培养等。适应性也体现在可以对方案整体或某些部分进行适应性调整和修改，例如若科技和工业发展的人才需求发生变化，人才培养目标或毕业要求等就需要相应修改，课程体系也相应做出新的调整或重建。可以预见，后疫情时代的产业调整、新基建、新产业和产业链建设等会对工科人才提出一些新要求。针对新的变化，要根据课程体系建设路线，建设新的课程体系或者修改已有课程体系，满足新的培养目标和毕业要求。

方案设计基于持续改进和持续创新理念，今天的新一定会成为未来的旧。方案的可适应性使方案在局部和整体层面均具备优化和拓展空间，保证方案与时俱进。随着外部需求变化，可及时修订毕业要求与培养目标，更新专业课程，包括取消、增加课程，增加、减少、修改项目类型，更新教育理念、培养模式、教与学方法、教与学内容、质量标准等。

（4）本科生项目要求与研究生项目比较。研究型大学教师重视研究生培养，项目研究的成果对教师科研兴趣、个人和学校发展都很重要。尽管研究生教育和本科教育存在本质区别，从教师指导学生项目的角度思考，如果本科生的多学科、大团队项目成果与研究生个人项目成果相当，我们期望教师将更有兴趣和动力投入对本科项目的指导。

新工科的培养方案强调扎实的数理基础，要求学生完成多个项目，包括一个三年级的多学科团队项目和本科研究项目，四年级的毕业项目，而且必须是原创的产品或技术。学生团队具有多学科、大规模（15~20 人团队）的特点。学生可以将三年级和四年级的项目集成起来，致力于原创科技和/或产品的研发。由于本科生团队规模较大，在教师的指导下，团队成员投入的时间和精力有望催生出创新技术。如图 16 所示，技术研发为三年级研究项目与四年级毕业项目联合，要求毕业生团队产出技术和专利（或论文）。产品研发为三年级多学科项目与毕业项目联合，学生团队完成三年级多学科项目和四年级毕业项目，毕业要求产出产品样机或技术专利。

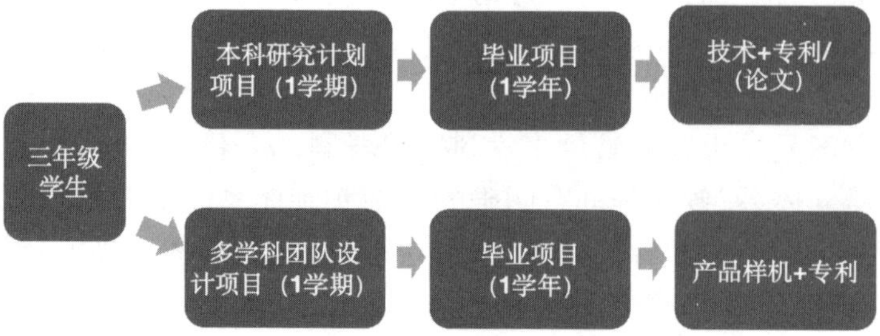


**图 16　学生 3~4 年级团队项目组织和要求**

传统本科教学与科研工作联系不紧密。新工科培养鼓励教师团队教学，发挥教师团队的学术专业知识和经验优势。教师通过指导学生完成多个原创项目，将人才培养融入科研工作之中，实现教师教学与科研的相互支持。如图 17 所示，CCII-EEE 模式便是这一理念的重要实践。该模式明确要求毕业生团队产出原创成果，在这样的机制下，学生能够在科研实践中提升专业能力与创新素养，教师也能通过指导学生项目进一步深化科研成果、拓展学术领域，从而实现学生培养和教师发展在成果要求方面的共赢。

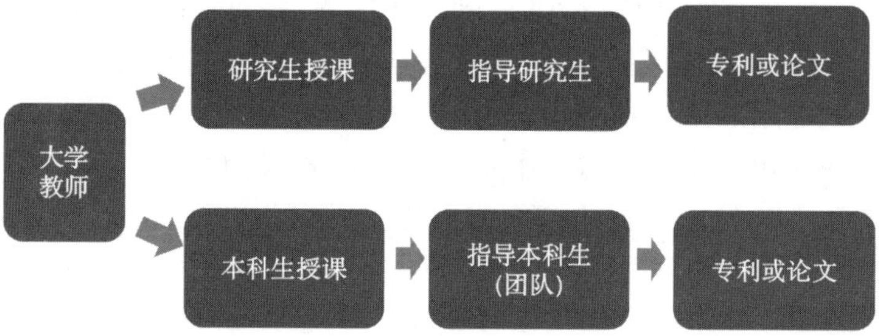


**图 17　教师的本科生和研究生项目指导工作比较**

## 2　新工科教育范式——“X-创新”

新工业革命时代呼唤工程教育范式的新转变。近 30 年来，我国持续推进一系列工程教育改革，显著提升了工程教育质量，培养了大量产业和社会需要的工科毕业生。这些教育改革也推动了工程教育模式和范式的转变。为了适应快速发展的新科技革命和产业变革的紧迫需求，现在和未来一段时间的教育改革力度更大、速度更快、系统性更强，进而促进工程教育范式的加速转变。

工程教育的发展历程，经历了从技术范式、科学范式到工程范式的演进。对从工程实践、工程科学、回归工程到目前讨论的新范式转变的思考，是一个系统性工程教育的思考框架。范式转变和形成需要实践和时间，是一个连续和渐变的过程，在形成和稳定一定时间后才能更好地总结。一次工业革命的开始和结束时间很难精确界定，而精确界定开始和结束时间未必重要，但是工业革命的主题和内涵却是十分重要的。同样，对于工程教育范式转变过程、内容及内涵比起始和结束时间更加重要。

工程教育范式的转变,体现在理念、模式、课程、方法、内容、标准等各方面的系统性和根本性变革。从当前工程教育范式向新工科教育范式转变,通常是一系列的变革、探索和调整。从基于知识传承和经验借鉴等方式而形成的传统工程专业课程体系,向面向未来、以学生全面发展为导向,融合贯通、持续改进的课程体系转变。从以知识传授为主的传统教学模式,向以立德树人为本的系统化的全人和全面教育模式转变。从以单一学科办专业的传统模式,向多院系合作、多学科、跨学科教育的模式转变。从依靠一个学校的资源和能力的传统办学模式向主动运用网络教学资源、产业资源、兄弟院校资源和国际资源的开放型办学模式转变。从培养能够胜任当前企业需要的工科毕业生,向培养既服务当前又面向未来的新工科毕业生转变。如图 18 所示,天大方案的 CCII-EEE 模式具有上述转变的特征,是较全面和系统性的工程教育变革和创新,构建以未来科技发展与创新为导向,开放和融合的工程教育。因此, CCII-EEE 模式属于开放融合创新范式,这种范式具有较广泛的工程教育模式代表性,可以支撑多种工程教育改革与创新,为工程教育的发展提供了新的思路和方法。

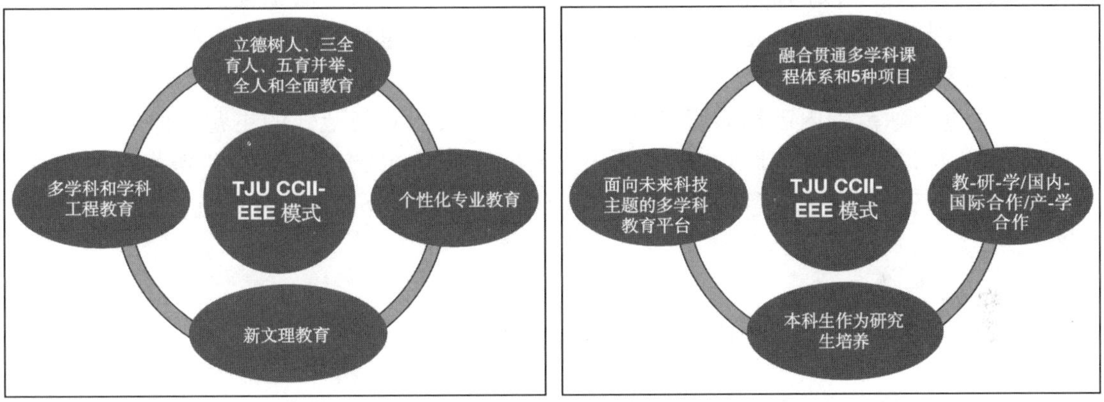


**图 18 天大方案的 CCII-EEE 新工科教育范式的说明**

天大方案代表或属于的教育范式仍然是在教育界、工业界和社会民众理解的框架下的工程教育变革与创新,而快速发展的科技革命,必将带来更加深刻、更加根本性的产业革命,对工程教育理念和模式必将产生颠覆性的影响。探索未来工程教育模式与范式需要突破传统的思维定式,需要更加自觉地去理解工业创新体系或国家创新体系的内涵,需要多方面的创新人才,不同的工作性质需要不同类型的创新人才,研究型人才适应研究性质的工作,但不一定能成为运行性工作的卓越专家。同样,一位优秀的实施方面的专家,可能成为不了高水平研究人才。未来的世界、科技、产业和人类发展需要突破传统教育的思维定式,斯坦福大学的“斯坦福 2025 计划”是对未来办学非常有意义的尝试,展示了一流研究型大学如何深刻探索未来本科教育。除了斯坦福大学的积极探索,在面向产业需求和学生职业发展方面,澳大利亚的查尔斯特大学等多所学校也在做有意义的尝试[19]。未来教育需要更加颠覆性的思考,更加具有根本性甚至激进的变革与创新,才能形成多元化的发展。因此,我们需要思考一些更加基础的问题,比如:为什么大学要四年制?为什么要设置 2 个、3 个或 4 个学期?MOOC、基于 VR 和 AR 技术的在线试验等对未来的学习产生什么影响?不同定位的学校或专业应该怎样办学？如何办好学生、产业和社会需要的专业、学院和大学？现在是一个面向新工业革命、新科技革命、新产业革命的大变革时代，为这样的时代培养未来的工程科技创新人才，需要突破传统工程教育思维束缚。可以预见，21 世纪将会有更多、更大规模、更系统甚至更彻底的工程教育模式的创新，形成一个多元化的人才培养大系统，建设能够支撑和引领新工业、新科技、新经济发展的新工程教育。

基于这样的思考，当今处于新工业革命和科技大变革的前期，现在就确定某一种工程教育新范式的主题可能不利于今后工程教育模式和范式大胆探索和颠覆性创新，可以预见"创新"应成为这个时代工程教育新范式的一个重要内容。因此，为了激发更多的工程教育新模式和新范式探索，结合上述思考和以下两个主要原因，本文尝试提出"X-创新"范式（X-Innovation Paradigm）作为当前工程教育新模式和新范式的代表，它不但能够代表天大培养模式，也能够代表多元化工程教育的创新模式与范式。

（1）在新工业和科技革命快速发展和变化的时期，特别是后疫情时代，未来 20~30 年将涌现出多种颠覆性创新的工程教育模式探索，以满足 21 世纪各国、各地区创新经济发展和后疫情时代新产业发展的需求。"X-创新"中的"X"可以代表任何工程教育创新模式和范式，甚至"X-创新"本身在一定时间内也可以代表新范式，是代表一个多元化工程教育模式和范式创新发展的现实。

（2）通过全球范围内工程教育转变与创新的探索，当对新范式的主题和内涵达成广泛共识后，"X"可以被具体的新范式的主题内涵所取代，形成创新工程教育的新范式。如通过系列范式的探索，工程教育界达成广泛共识，以"开放融合创新"为新范式，"X"="开放融合"。

## 3 新工科再深化、再拓展与再突破的思考

自 2017 年新工科建设启动以来，政府部门、产业界、高校等多方积极响应并协同合作，取得了令人鼓舞的进展。2019 年 12 月 28 日，教育部在天津大学召开深化新工科建设座谈会暨卓越大学联盟高校新工科教育研讨会，对新工科建设的现状、进展、问题进行了梳理，对新工科的未来发展提出了再深化、再拓展、再突破、再出发的要求。

新工科的再深化与再拓展旨在从深度和广度两个方面推进新工科教育向纵深与更广阔的层面发展。比如将先进新工科教育理念深化到教学实践中，制定出可操作和可复制的实施方案，将方案付诸实践后，持续改进。在实践中，从注重宏观培养目标和毕业要求的理念，深化到培养过程的各环节，提高培养目标与培养结果的吻合度和一致性，切实提高了学生培养质量。在教学过程中，从以教师课堂教学为中心，依靠教材、作业和考试的传统模式，向以学生学习和发展为中心转变，聚焦学生主动学习，实施基于项目的学习、基于问题的学习和探究式学习等主动学习方法，鼓励学生拓展教材以外的学习内容，从重点关注知识和考试的传统教学方式，向培养学生能力、知识、技能、态度的综合要求深化。在教育教学过程中，始终坚持实事求是的态度是深化新工科教育，提高质量与水平的关键所在。

有些新工科项目实践还停留在教改项目的亮点总结。新工科的再拓展要求，从亮点总结拓展到整体实施，从局部亮点到专业层面的整体亮点拓展，从一个试点班到整个院系多专

业拓展,从少部分学生的先进学习经历向全院系学生的学习经历拓展,只有绝大多数学生的培养质量和水平得到切实提高,才能真正体现新工科教育模式和培养体系的先进性。新工科的再拓展也包括从相对窄的学科支撑专业教育,拓宽专业领域,以便更好地支撑学生今后的职业发展;从单一学科支撑专业人才培养,拓展到由多学科支撑专业人才培养;从本科生教育向研究生教育的拓展。

如果新工科再深化与再拓展是量的要求,那么再突破与再出发就是质的改变。再突破首先是观念和认识的突破,是对思维模式或习惯定式的突破。只有实现了突破,才会建立新方向和新目标,才能再出发。建设工程教育强国、科技和工业强国,必须搞好教育,必须搞好本科教育,必须搞好本科工程教育。大量工科本科毕业生进入企业,支撑企业、产业和工业发展;同样大量本科毕业生读研,成为科技骨干力量。因此,无论是进入企业还是继续读研,本科毕业生是建设科技和工业强国的重要力量。搞好本科工程教育不仅要在观念上实现对本科教育重视程度的突破,还要对新时代工程教育变革和创新在认识上有所突破。

国际科技和产业竞争的根本是人才的竞争,哪个国家有了人才优势,就在建设科技和工业强国方面具有竞争优势。技术的创新靠企业,而企业的竞争力,除了体制机制的因素外,还是靠人才,特别是工程科技创新人才。大学和学院的首要任务是培养学生,多数大学是教学科研型和教学型大学,少数是研究型大学。如麻省理工学院、斯坦福大学这样的一流研究型大学也是把人才培养放在学校工作的重要位置,一流的本科毕业生继续读研,对大学的科研事业无疑是巨大的支撑。中华民族具有重视教育的传统,每个家庭只要有条件,无论是幼儿园、小学、中学和大学等,家长都会积极努力争取为孩子提供最好的教育。所有高等院校领导和教师也都知道教育和人才培养的重要性,我国每年培养出世界最多的高校毕业生,如果我们能够培养出世界最多最好的学生,我们一定是世界教育强国。新工科教育正是建设工程教育强国的举措,也是建设科技及工业强国的举措。对本科教育和本科工程教育重要性的理解从理念层面转为具体的行动,体现在校领导的重视中,体现在教师考核和教职工的追求中,这必将成为一所大学的价值观,这是一个重要的突破。

当我们深刻认识到传统课程体系和内容,与快速发展的新技术和产生的新知识不适应时,多年传承的工科教育课程内容和教学方法已不能满足产业对工科毕业生的新知识和新技能需求,传统的工程教育模式已不能适应新产业和新经济发展的需求,工程教育需要根本性变革和全面创新,就会突破对“新工科”等名词的关注,聚焦新工科教育内涵和内容的探索。只要实现上述突破,就会给新工科教育发展建立新方向和新目标,再出发就是在新的方向上和新的目标要求下的新发展。

各种分析表明,新冠疫情对未来工业和经济社会产生了重大影响。世界各国都对产业链和供应链进行了分析、修复和完善,建设了战略性企业和产业等。疫情后,我国的新基建、新产业、新科技、新经济的建设与发展,必将对工程教育和人才培养提出新的要求,这也是新工科再深化、再拓展需要思考的方向,也是新工科再突破的切入点和再出发的新起点。

以数字和智能科技创新发展和应用为代表的新基建十大战略发展方向,包括智能数字基础设施,数字化和科技创新基础设施,发展现代资源、能源与交通物流基础设施,先进材料与智能绿色制造基础设施,现代农业和生物产业基础设施,现代教育、文旅、体育与卫生健康等基础设施,新型生态环境基础设施,空天海洋新型基础设施,国家总体安全基础设施和治理现代化基础设施等[20]。这些新基建所需人才的知识结构、专业领域、数量和水平及专通人才要求等，将是新工科新起点的发展方向。高等教育系统响应国家需求，及时调整培养体系，支撑新基建各领域以及新产业新经济的人才需求，是新工科教育的新使命。

## 4 结语

新科技和产业革命推动创新经济发展，引发人才需求的变革，进而推动新工科建设发展的再深化、再拓展、再突破和再出发，实现从卓越工程师教育培养计划 1.0 向卓越工程师教育培养计划 2.0 的跨越。作为世界上最大的工程教育国家，我国通过新工科的持续深入发展，为 21 世纪世界工程教育变革和创新贡献中国智慧、提供中国方案、做出中国贡献。

新工科天津大学方案以立德树人统领人才培养全过程，通过融合新文理教育、多学科和跨学科工程教育和个性化专业教育，实现对学生的全人与全面教育，培养从科学发现、技术发明到工业应用全范围的未来卓越工程师、企业家、工程科学家和领军者。天大方案的人才培养模式提出了以面向未来科技和产业发展为主题的多学科、开放式培养平台，以 5 种项目为节点的融合贯通、一体化课程体系，以及对应的建设路线，试点实施效果良好，说明该方案和新模式具有可行性。

为探索新工业革命时代的工程教育新范式，天津大学提出的工程教育方案，可以作为开放融合创新范式的代表。鉴于当前处于新工业革命早期，随着时间推移以及科技创新和教育的发展，势必会涌现更多的工程教育创新模式。为激发和鼓励更多新模式和新范式的探索，最大限度增加多元化新范式发展，本文提出了“X-创新”教育范式，代表以创新为主题的工程教育范式，当未来工程教育界就新范式达成广泛共识后，可以赋予“X”一个具体的范式名称。

新冠疫情后，世界各国评估和反思产业链和供应链在战“疫”过程中发挥的作用，重新审视工程科技人才培养和工程教育的贡献与挑战。后疫情时代，我国的新基建、新产业、新科技、新经济发展需要大量工程科技创新人才，势必对工程教育和人才培养提出新的要求，为新工科再深化、再拓展指明新方向，这也是新工科再突破和再出发的新起点。

本文作者受专业背景和经历等局限，难免对新工科教育的理解有不全面或不正确的地方，愿就天大方案的培养模式与范式，对新工科再深化、再拓展、再突破、再出发的认识，与工程教育同行共同探讨和学习。

### 参考文献


[1] National Academy of Engineering of United States. Understanding the educational and career pathways of engineers（2018）[M] .Washington，DC：The National Academies Press，2018.

[2] 孔寒冰，叶民，王沛民. 多元化工程教育历史传统[J] . 高等工程教育研究，2013（5）：1-12.

[3] SCHWAB K. The fourth industrial revolution[ M] .[S.l.]：World Economic Forum，2016.

[4] HATCH M R. The maker revolution：building a future on creativity and innovation in an ex-

ponential world[ M] .Hoboken：Wiley，2017.
[5] ELIOT C W. The new education[J]. Atlantic monthly，1869，3( 136 )：229-247.
[6] 李培根. 未来工程教育几个重要视点[J]. 高等工程教育研究，2019( 2 )：1-6.
[7] 吴岩. 勇立潮头，赋能未来：以新工科建设领跑高等教育变革[J]. 高等工程教育研究，2020( 1 )：1-5.
[8] 吴爱华，侯永峰，杨秋波，等. 加快发展和建设新工科主动适应和引领新经济[J] . 高等工程教育研究，2017( 1 )：1-8.
[9] 钟登华. 新工科建设的内涵与行动[J]. 高等工程教育研究，2017( 3 )：1-6.
[10] 吴爱华，杨秋波，郝杰. 以"新工科"建设引领高等教育创新 变革[J]. 高等工程教育研究，2019( 1 )：1-8.
[11] 天津大学新工科建设方案发布[EB/OL].( 2019-04-26 )[2020-04-30]. https://baijiahao.baidu.com/s? id=1632010249910491506&wfr=spider&for=pc.
[12] 李家俊. 以新工科教育引领高等教育"质量革命"[J]. 高等工程教育研究，2020( 2 )：6-11.
[13] 曾勇，黄艳，向贵君，等. 从新生项目课开始：新工科建设"成电方案"的设计与实践[J]. 高等工程教育研究，2020( 1 )：14-19.
[14] 高松. 实施"新工科 F 计划"，培养工科领军人才[J]. 高等工程教育研究，2019( 4 )：19-25.
[15] 顾佩华. 新工科与新范式：概念、框架和实施路径[J]. 高等工程教育研究，2017( 6 )：1-13.
[16] GEORGIA TECH. Vertically Integrated Projects[EB/OL].( 2020-01-01 )[2020-04-30]. https://www.vip.gatech.edu/.
[17] University of New South Wales. The ChallENG Projects[EB/OL].( 2019-06-10 )[2020-04-30]. https://www.challeng.unsw.edu.au/about.
[18] 史国良，张冠伟，陈曦，等. 天津大学智能机器与系统平台课程总结交流研讨[Z].2020.
[19] GRAHAM R. The global state of the art in engineering education[R]. Massachusetts：Massachusetts Institute of Technology ( MIT )，2018.
[20] 潘教峰，万劲波. 新基建十大战略方向[EB/OL].( 2020-04-26 )[2020-04-30]. http://www.xinhuanet.com/2020-04/30/c1125929139.htm.

# 工程教育专业认证标准的国际比较研究 ①

王 庚 朱 露 胡德鑫 闫广芬 顾佩华

**摘要:**新一代科技革命和产业变革快速发展,对工程教育人才培养质量提出更高要求。持续提升教育质量已成为世界各国工程教育改革与发展的重要目标。专业认证作为工程教育质量保障的重要机制和手段,其地位与作用也愈加重要。本文聚焦13个《华盛顿协议》成员,从毕业要求、认证通用标准以及区域与国别三个维度对其展开分析。结果显示,大部分国外认证组织在毕业要求设计中都遵循《华盛顿协议》的核心要求,但也根据本国国情与需要进行本土化改革与整合。在通用标准体系设计中最为趋同的是设施和学校支持标准项,差异最大的是课程体系标准项。从区域与国别维度来看,各组织可分为奠定基础型、本土加工型与模仿借鉴型三种类型。国外工程教育认证标准改革的基本态势,即明确本国特色,着眼赋能创新;坚持实质等效与本国实际并存;建构独立自主的内部驱动发展逻辑。中国特色专业认证标准改革的未来方向是强化立德树人要求、认证标准弹性化、认证标准特色化、本硕标准贯通制、工程师衔接制度化等。

**关键词:**工程教育;专业认证;《华盛顿协议》;新工业革命

## International Comparative Research on the Accreditation Standards of Engineering Education

*Wang Geng, Zhu Lu, Hu Dexin, Yan Guang fen, Gu Peihua*

**Abstract:**The rapid development of new technologies and industrial transformation demands a new generation of engineering talents which in turn, requires a higher quality of engineering education. Continuous improvement of the quality of education has become an important goal of the reform and innovation of engineering education in all countries in the world. To ensure the quality of engineering education, engineering accreditation has become a critical means for the engineering education community. This article selects 13 signatories from the list of the Washington Accord for comprehensive analysis from three dimensions: graduate attributes, general criteria, and regional perspective. The research results show that the most signatories follow the core requirements of the Washington Accord in the design of their graduate attributes, but they also take the national and regional needs into consideration. In the design of general criteria, the most similar items are the facilities and institutional support, and the biggest difference is in the curriculum. From the regional perspective, the signatories can be divided into three types: foundation type, localization type, and imitation type. Furthermore, it points out the basic trend of international engineering education accreditation reform: reflect the national characteristics and focus on empowering innovation;insist on the coexistence of substantive

① 本文刊登于《高等工程教育研究》2022年第2期第35~44页。

equivalence and domestic reality; construct an independent internal development logic. Finally, it discusses the future direction of the reform of accreditation standards with Chinese characteristics to strengthen the requirements of cultivation of talents, the adaptability and elasticity of accreditation standards, the special features of accreditation standards, the integrated standards for undergraduate and master engineering education, and the connection with professional engineers registration.

**Keywords:** engineering education; accreditation; Washington Accord; new industrial revolution

## 1 问题提出

进入21世纪以后，随着全球科技革新骈兴错出，以数字化、网络化、智能化为主要特征的新一轮科技革命加速发展。为应对新工业革命带来的机遇与挑战，世界多个国家相继出台相关战略，抓住新一轮工业革命提供的发展机遇，推动工业和经济发展[1]，例如澳大利亚的“技能生态系统战略”（2012年）[2]、德国的“工业4.0战略”（2013年）[3]、英国的“工业战略”（2019年）[4]。为有效应对新一轮工业革命的机遇和挑战，形成创新驱动发展的工业振兴新格局，我国在2015年正式提出制造强国战略的第一个十年行动纲领。面向未来科技发展、面向产业需求、面向世界竞争与挑战，为培养未来的卓越工程师、企业家和工程领域领军人才，2017年教育部提出新工科建设计划，通过“复旦共识”“天大行动”和“北京指南”三部曲深入推进新工科建设实施，探索中国工程教育发展的新模式与新路径[5]。面对新工业革命带来的挑战，我国工程教育必须进行深刻变革和全面创新，以适应新经济、新科技、新产业对工程教育的人才培养目标、模式、内容、方法和质量标准等提出的新要求[6]。

新工科建设的一个重要目的在于提高工程教育人才培养质量，为推动“质量革命”，建设“质量中国”贡献力量。专业认证制度作为工程教育质量保障的重要机制和核心手段，在教育教学理念、培养模式、培养目标确定、课程体系建设、教与学方法研究、教师团队建设以及质量持续改进等方面发挥着重要的引领和指导作用[7]。在我国正式成为《华盛顿协议》签署成员以及全面推进新工科建设的背景下，以13个签署成员为研究对象，从《华盛顿协议》认证标准的毕业要求与通用标准（中国通用标准包含毕业要求，这种拆分是为了对比分析各认证组织的毕业要求）这两个维度对标这些成员的认证体系和成功经验，并从区域与国别维度分析其运行机制与基本逻辑，以期为未来建构起具有中国特色、世界实质等效的新工程教育质量标准与认证体系提供参考与借鉴。

## 2 研究设计

### 2.1 研究对象

本文以《华盛顿协议》13个签署成员——美国、英国、爱尔兰、加拿大、澳大利亚、新西兰、秘鲁、中国、日本、韩国、新加坡、马来西亚和南非的工程教育专业认证标准为研究对象。13个签署成员分布在六大洲，其专业认证标准各具特色，对我们制定面向未来科技与产业发展的专业认证标准改革具有借鉴意义。在《华盛顿协议》签署成员范围内，工程教育领域专业认证体系都基于产出导向的标准,描述了工程专业毕业生应具备的能力素质要求。每个专业必须证明其毕业生满足这些要求。毕业要求形成了一系列可单独评估的结果,这些结果是毕业生获得工程与实践能力的组成部分,它们适用于所有工程专业。

### 2.2 比较分析框架

由于13个研究对象之间既存在相似性,又有相异之处,这就需要构建一个比较分析框架。本文以认证标准中的“毕业要求”“除毕业要求的其他认证通用标准”以及“区域与国别”三个维度为基底建立比较分析框架。由此可见,在产出导向的认证标准中毕业要求的重要性。认证通用标准是对专业本科办学质量的综合性评价,在本部分着重分析除毕业要求之外的其他核心要素。区域与国别强调各组织根据本国国情和发展实际开展的专业认证标准化改革,体现的是国际化与本土化的深度融合。本文将对标13个《华盛顿协议》签署成员的毕业要求(graduate attributes)以及工程教育专业通用标准(general criteria)进行相关内容的分析,并基于这两个维度的关键性因素,在区域与国别维度进行分类与归置的比较研究。

## 3 工程教育专业认证标准的国际比较

### 3.1 毕业要求维度的比较

本文选取的13个签署成员的专业认证标准中的毕业要求在很大程度上都遵循《华盛顿协议》的认证标准中的核心要素,但部分成员并未与之保持完全一致,而是根据自身实际情况需要,进行本土化处理或整合(表1)[8]。美国毕业要求(在美国专业认证标准中称为“学生产出”)标准项涵盖《华盛顿协议》工程知识和问题分析,即能够应用工程原理、科学、数学识别、规划和解决复杂工程问题[9]。澳大利亚的认证标准设计与美国类似,其设置的“知识和技术基础”标准项也涵盖了这两项标准的内容[10]。

针对毕业要求中的设计/开发解决方案、调查研究以及使用现代工具,澳大利亚设置的工程应用能力涵盖了这三项指标,而爱尔兰和日本并未单独列出使用现代工具这一项,英国制定的工程专业本科毕业要求中关于设计/开发解决方案、研究以及使用现代工具这三个方面设置了更细化的指标[11]。

美国的第二项毕业要求强调伦理和职业责任,以及工程对全球、经济、环境和社会的影响,涵盖了《华盛顿协议》中工程与社会、环境和可持续发展以及伦理规范这三项。爱尔兰和日本的毕业要求也呈现出与美国类似的现象。澳大利亚的第三项一级指标“专业与个人素养”涵盖了《华盛顿协议》后七项毕业要求。此外,美国、韩国和南非都未单独设置项目管理这一标准。综上可见,各国认证标准在毕业要求总体上保持基本一致的前提下,结合本国实际对相关要求进行组合或修订,与实质等效原则并不冲突。

综合分析来看,按照13个签署成员遵循《华盛顿协议》毕业标准的程度,将这些成员分类并归置为完全遵循、略有差异和个性化较强三类。

(1)完全遵循类。在13个签署成员中,专业认证标准的毕业要求大多都遵循《华盛顿

**表 1　毕业要求层面各项标准维度分析**

| 毕业要求 | 签署成员 | | | | | | | | | | | | |
|---|---|---|---|---|---|---|---|---|---|---|---|---|---|
| | 美国 | 加拿大 | 英国 | 爱尔兰 | 澳大利亚 | 新西兰 | 韩国 | 日本 | 中国 | 南非 | 马来西亚 | 新加坡 | 秘鲁 |
| 工程知识 | 1. 应用工程、科学和数学原理，识别、阐述和解决复杂工程问题的能力 | 证明毕业生具备适用于本专业的大学数学、自然科学、工程基础和专业工程知识 | 工程由科学、数学以及其他相关学科所支撑，由相关的专业工程学会定义 | (a)掌握并能理解数学、工程科学和技术中的工程知识 | 1. 知识与技能基础（包含1.1~1.6） | 1.3.1 工程知识基础 WA1 | 应用数学、基础科学、工程、信息技术知识解决实际工程问题 | (c)(d)掌握对数学及自然科学等相关知识的应用能力 | 3.1 工程知识，对学生提出“学以致用”的要求 | Exit Level Outcome 2：应用数学、自然科学等知识解决工程问题 | (i)工程知识 | a)工程知识 | (a)工程相关知识 |
| 问题分析 | | 具备使用合适的知识和技能识别、归纳、分析和解决复杂工程问题，得到确凿结论的能力 | 应用工程知识和工具解决工程问题 | (b)识别、规划、分析和解决工程问题的能力 | 2. 工程应用能力（包含2.1~24） | 1.3.2 工程问题复杂性分析 WA2 | 能够理解实际工程技术问题并运用相关数据来分析 | (a)具有从全球性视角出发，多元的思考能力和素养 | 3.2 问题分析，学生应学会基于科学原理思考问题，并掌握问题分析的方法 | Exit Level Outcome 1：有创造性地识别、规划和解决问题的能力 | (ii)问题分析 | b)问题分析 | (e)问题分析 |
| 设计/开发解决方案 | 6. 开发和操作合适的实验，分析和解释数据，运用工程判断得出结论 | 就复杂、开放的工程问题设计解决方案，包括设计系统、部件和程序以满足特定需求 | 创造和发展一种在经济上可行的产品、过程或系统，以满足特定的需求 | (c)设计系统、组件或过程以满足特定需求的能力 | | 1.3.3 待解决工程问题的广度和唯一性 WA3 | 设计系统、单元(部件)或工艺流程来解决现实工程问题 | (e)根据社会需求，具有灵活运用各种科学、技术和信息化手段进行设计的能力 | 3.3 设计/开发解决方案，学生应了解“面向工程设计和产品开发全周期、全流程设计/开发解决方案”的基本方法和技术 | Exit Level Outcome 3：能够有创造力地设计系统、组件或过程 | (iii)设计/开发解决方案 | c)设计/开发解决方案 | (c)设计并开发解决方案 |
| 研究 | | 包含于上述标准中 | 包含于前两条标准中 | (d)设计和进行试验，并在指导下进行研究或高级技术活动的能力 | | 1.3.4 调查和实验的广度和深度 WA4 | 能够设计实验，并运用相关数据解决现实工程技术问题 | 包含于(c)、(d)、(e)中 | 3.4 研究，按照“调研、设计、实施、归纳”的思路开展研究 | Exit Level Outcome 4：能够设计并执行探究以及实验 | (iv)调研 | d)调研 | (b)研究 |
| 使用现代工具 | 包含于第1、2、6条中 | 在一系列工程活动中，从简单到复杂地创造、选择、应用、调整和拓展相关技术、资源和现代工程工具，并了解相关的制约因素 | 工程技能的实际应用，需结合理论和经验，使用其他相关的知识和技能 | 包含于(a)、(b)中 | | 1.3.5 对工具适当性的理解程度 WA5 | 选择应用最新的技术以及工具，解决现实工程技术问题 | 包含于(c)、(d)、(e)中 | 3.5 使用现代工具，对学生提出“开发、选择和使用”的要求 | Exit Level Outcome 5：能够运用适当的工程方法、技术、工具，包括信息技术工具 | (v)使用现代工具 | e)使用现代工具 | (k)现代工具的使用 |

续表

| 毕业要求 | 签署成员 | | | | | | | | | | | | |
|---|---|---|---|---|---|---|---|---|---|---|---|---|---|
| | 美国 | 加拿大 | 英国 | 爱尔兰 | 澳大利亚 | 新西兰 | 韩国 | 日本 | 中国 | 南非 | 马来西亚 | 新加坡 | 秘鲁 |
| 工程与社会 | 2. 考虑公共卫生、安全和福利以及全球、文化、社会、环境和经济因素，应用工程设计得到满足特定需求的解决方案的能力 | 了解职业工程师在社会中的角色和责任，特别是保护公众和公共利益的角色 | 毕业生需有能力管理工程活动，并意识到各种法律和道德约束 | （e）了解工程实践中对高道德标准的需要，包括工程对人和环境的责任 | 3. 专业与个人素养（3.1~3.4） | 1.3.6 背景知识的水平以及责任意识 WA6 | 理解工程解决方案所产生的一系列影响 | （b）理解工程活动的影响 | 3.6 工程与社会，理解工程项目的实施不仅要考虑技术可行性，还必须考虑其市场相容性，即是否符合社会、健康、安全、法律以及文化等方面的外部制约因素的要求 | Exit Level Outcome 7：工程问题解决方案对社会、工业、环境的影响有批判性的意识，以及责任 | （vi）工程与社会 | f）工程与社会 | （j）工程活动与社会 |
| 环境和可持续发展 | | 分析工程活动的社会和环境因素的能力 | | | | 1.3.7 可持续性与重要性 WA7 | | | 3.7 环境可持续发展，要求学生必须建立环境和可持续发展的意识 | | （vii）环境与持续性 | g）环境与持续性 | （h）环境与可持续性 |
| 伦理规范 | | 履行职业道德，具有承担责任和维护公平的能力 | | | | 1.3.8 伦理原则 WA8 | 遵守工程实践中的职业道德，履行社会责任 | | 3.8 职业规范，对工科沉重的人文社会科学素养、工程职业道德规范和社会责任提出了要求 | Exit Level Outcome 10：对伦理原则和职业道德有批判性意识，并能够承担相应责任 | （viii）伦理 | h）伦理 | （f）伦理 |
| 个人和团队 | 5. 能够有效在团队中发挥作用，在团队成员的领导下，营造协作和包容的环境，建立目标，计划任务，并达成目标 | 在多学科环境中，以个人或团队领导的角色进行有效工作 | 毕业生必须以学习产出的技能为基础，发展各种情况下都有价值且可传递的技能 | 包含于（f）中 | | 1.3.9 在团队中的作用 WA9 | 为解决现实工程技术问题，能够作为团队成员贡献力量 | （i）具有在团队中工作的能力 | 3.9 个人和团队，要求学生能够在多学科背景下的团队中，承担不同的角色 | Exit Level Outcome 8：能够在团队中承担不同角色 | （ix）个人和团队协作 | i）个人和团队协作 | （d）个人和团队协作 |

续表

| 毕业要求 | 签署成员 | | | | | | | | | | | | |
|---|---|---|---|---|---|---|---|---|---|---|---|---|---|
| | 美国 | 加拿大 | 英国 | 爱尔兰 | 澳大利亚 | 新西兰 | 韩国 | 日本 | 中国 | 南非 | 马来西亚 | 新加坡 | 秘鲁 |
| 沟通 | 3. 有能力与社会公众进行有效沟通 | 与职业人员和社会大众沟通复杂工程概念的能力 | 包含于上一条标准中 | (g)与工程界和整个社会在专业工程活动上有效沟通的能力 | 3. 专业与个人素养(3.1~3.4) | 1.3.10 沟通能力 WA10 | 能够有效沟通 | (f)具有沟通技巧及逻辑表达和演讲与辩论的能力 | 3.10 沟通. 对学生就专业问题进行有效沟通交流,及其国际视野和跨文化交流的能力提出了要求 | Exit Level Outcome 6：能够在口头和书面上与同行及公众有效交流 | (x)沟通 | j)沟通 | (g)沟通 |
| 项目管理 | 包含于第1、2、6条中 | 在工程实践中,适当地结合包括项目,风险和变更管理在内的经济和商业实践,并了解其局限性 | 包含于上一条标准中 | (f)在团队和多学科背景下高效工作的能力和终身学习的能力 | | 1.3.11 管理能力 WA11 | | (h)在特定的限制条件下,具有系统推进工作和完成任务的能力 | 3.11 项目管理,按照工程项目或产品的设计和实施的全周期、全流程进行的过程管理. 包括多任务协调、时间进度控制、相关资源调度,人力资源配备等 | | (xi)项目管理 | k)项目管理 | (l)项目管理 |
| 终身学习 | 7. 根据需要使用适当的学习策略来获取和应用新知识 | 识别和表达在变化社会中自身的学习需求,与时俱进,致力于知识的进步 | 包含于上一标准中 | | | 1.3.12 深入继续学习的准备 WA12 | 在工程技术变革的背景下能够终身学习 | (g)积累不断学习的能力并培养终身学习的素养 | 3.12 终身学习,学生必须建立终身学习的思维和行动能力 | Exit Level Outcome 9：具有独立学习的能力 | (xii)终身学习 | l)终身学习 | (i)终身学习 |

协议》认证标准，但其中完全与《华盛顿协议》保持一致的只有新西兰、中国、秘鲁、加拿大、马来西亚和新加坡这 6 个成员。

（2）略有差异类。此类包括美国、爱尔兰、南非、日本和韩国。其中，作为《华盛顿协议》的发起成员，美国和爱尔兰在遵循《华盛顿协议》的基础上，不断改进和修订本国的认证标准；韩国、日本和南非在坚持与《华盛顿协议》实质等效的基础上，结合本国的认证需求，对一些标准进行了调整。韩国、日本和南非的认证标准在一定程度上进行了类似美国和爱尔兰的操作。韩国的毕业要求（韩国称为“专业毕业要求”）由 10 条标准构成，对《华盛顿协议》的部分标准进行了整合，将“工程与社会”“环境和可持续发展”这两项要求合并为一条，即“社会影响，能够理解工程解决方案对健康、安全、经济、环境和可持续发展所带来的影响”。日本的毕业要求（日本称为“学习产出”）由 9 条标准构成，将《华盛顿协议》毕业要求中的“工程与社会”“环境和可持续发展”“伦理”三项能力要求整合为一条，即“能够理解专业活动对社会、自然的影响，同时能够理解专业人员应对社会做的贡献与承担的责任”[12]。在南非的专业认证标准中，毕业要求（南非称为“出口水平产出”）将《华盛顿协议》中的“工程与社会”与“环境和可持续发展”整合为一项，即“工程活动的影响”[13]。

（3）个性化较强。此类包括澳大利亚和英国。这 2 个成员虽然没有完全按照《华盛顿协议》的 12 条标准模式来制定认证标准，然而其制定的毕业要求基本涵盖了《华盛顿协议》12 条毕业要求规定的关键要素。澳大利亚以知识与技能基础、工程应用能力以及专业和个人素养这几大关键能力为对标方向，制定了更加详细且自成体系的标准要求。英国为使高等工程专业的本科生能成为未来的工程师，制定了 18 个毕业要求，比《华盛顿协议》12 条毕业要求更为细化。

总的来看，13 个成员所设置的毕业要求与《华盛顿协议》相差较大的几项是工程与社会、环境和可持续发展、伦理规范、使用现代工具、项目管理。例如，美国的毕业要求由 7 条能力要求构成，与《华盛顿协议》相比，其差别主要表现在以下三个方面：其一，上文提到美国第一项毕业要求将“工程知识”和“问题分析”合并；其二，将“工程与社会”“环境和可持续发展”“伦理规范”合为一项；其三，第 1、2、6 条中体现了《华盛顿协议》中“使用现代工具”以及“项目管理”的相关要求。爱尔兰对《华盛顿协议》12 条毕业要求中的部分内容进行整合，主要表现在将“使用现代工具”融合进其设置的“问题分析”“设计”“研究”这三项标准中，同时，将《华盛顿协议》中的“工程与社会”“环境和可持续发展”“伦理规范”整合为“专业与伦理责任”，将“个人和团队”“终身学习”整合为“团队与终身学习”，从而精简了认证标准。此外，每项标准中都包含对该项学习成果的详细说明，指出学习成果达成的指标点，增强了认证过程的可操作性，为专业解读认证标准提供了明确指导[14]。

### 3.2 认证通用标准维度的比较

除毕业要求外，各国专业认证的通用标准中还包括学生、专业培养目标、持续改进、课程体系、师资队伍、设施、学校支持等方面（图 1）。在设施和学校支持这两项中，本文所选的 13 个《华盛顿协议》签署成员的认证标准的内容趋于一致，即均规定了设备、现代工具等相关教学设施与学习资源的开放性，并建立了相应的维护与更新机制。同时，制定了相关的安全规范与准则，对学生使用设施设备提供指导。此外，从经费、人员等方面为专业教学、专业发展提供服务与支持,完善教学管理与服务规范。

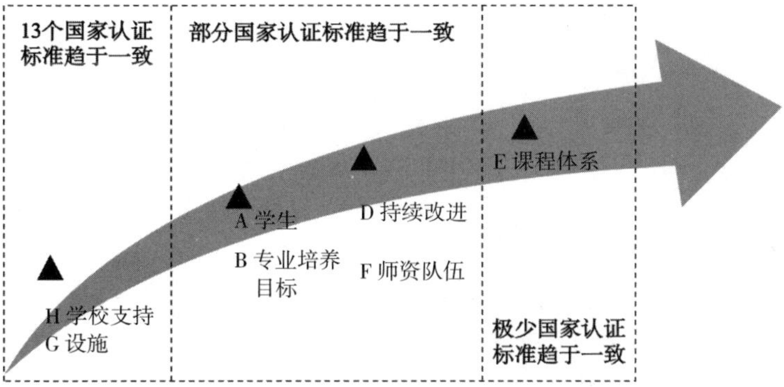


**图 1　通用标准层面的各项标准维度分析**

在学生、专业培养目标、持续改进、师资队伍这四项中,只有部分成员在这几项认证标准中具有一致性,有一些成员把这些项的关键性因素整合到其他标准中。例如,韩国、中国、秘鲁、美国把“学生”作为独立的认证标准,而爱尔兰在“专业管理”、新西兰在“质量保障与管理体系”、日本在“教育方法”中提及与学生相关的认证要求。

从专业培养目标标准项来看,新西兰、加拿大、日本没有提出与此项相关的认证要求,爱尔兰仅在“目标、资源和可行性”这一标准中指出制定专业培养目标应考虑不同利益群体的需求,发动学校各部门及教师的力量。美国、韩国、中国、秘鲁把培养目标作为一项独立的认证标准。一些成员并没有专门列出“持续改进”这一项标准,而是在所设置的学生评价或者质量保障等项中体现。例如,爱尔兰设置了“学生表现评价”,新西兰设置了“达到预期要求评价”。

在师资队伍方面,美国、爱尔兰、新西兰、中国、秘鲁主要从教师的数量与质量两个方面提出了认证要求。在数量上,要求师资队伍能够胜任不同课型的教学,满足师生互动、学生指导等教学需要;在质量上,要求教师具备合格的从业资质,资质审核包含教师的教育背景、实践经历、教学技能、综合素养、专业权威等方面。其中,美国、爱尔兰、新西兰由于建立了完备的注册工程师制度,在资质审核时,还将教师的工程师资质纳入考查范畴,而中国除对教师的从业资质做出规定,还要求教师有足够的时间和精力投入本科教学、学生指导,积极参与专业的持续改进工作。日本、韩国有关师资队伍的认证标准有所不同,日本要求专业为课程教学的顺利实施提供师资与支持体系,韩国对师资数量与结构提出要求,同时强调教师应积极促进专业的持续发展。

在 13 个签署成员中,课程标准体系展现出的差异性最大,这一点也比较容易理解。虽然课程体系不同,毕业要求还是要达到实质等效。美国、加拿大、韩国、中国、日本、马来西亚规定了专业需包含的主要课程类型,以及每种课程所应达到的最低学时。其中,加拿大提供各类课程学时换算方法,可供国内所有高校工程类专业直接应用。爱尔兰有关课程的规定更多是对毕业要求的细分和深度解读,阐释如何帮助学生达到预期的毕业要求。新西兰从专业设计的角度提出课程体系应关注的重点领域,突出强调项目设计、学生研究、工业实践经历三个要素在课程体系中的重要性。日本有关课程体系的规定要求:专业是否有课程相关政策，课程设计是否有利于实现学习成果，课程实施是否遵循教学大纲，课程教学是否鼓励学生的自主学习等。澳大利亚从专业和课程设计、专业结构和实施框架、专业实践、专业课程四个方面对课程的关键性要素进行要求。南非对课程体系本身并未设置标准，但对教与学的质量进行了规定。

### 3.3 区域与国别维度的比较

#### 1. 各区域所选国家毕业要求的特点

本文选取了分布在六大洲的 13 个《华盛顿协议》签署成员作为研究对象，在区域维度上也进行了比较分析。总体来讲，这 13 个签署成员区域内的一致性并不明显，同在一个大洲的几个签署成员会存在差异性较大的情况（表 2）。

表 2 毕业要求层面的区域维度分析

| 区域 | 所选国家的特点 |
|---|---|
| 欧洲 | 英国的工程教育专业认证标准并没有完全遵循《华盛顿协议》标准，爱尔兰则在《华盛顿协议》标准基础上进行少部分整合 |
| 北美洲 | 美国在《华盛顿协议》标准基础上进行一定条目的整合和修改，而加拿大与《华盛顿协议》标准基本保持一致 |
| 南美洲 | 秘鲁的工程教育认证标准完全遵循《华盛顿协议》标准 |
| 大洋洲 | 澳大利亚的工程教育专业认证标准基本上自成体系，而新西兰则完全遵循《华盛顿协议》标准 |
| 亚洲 | 中国、新加坡和马来西亚完全遵循《华盛顿协议》标准，而日本和韩国在《华盛顿协议》标准基础上进行了小范围整合 |
| 非洲 | 南非在《华盛顿协议》标准基础上进行了补充和加工 |

（1）在欧洲，选取英国和爱尔兰作为研究对象，尽管两国在制定毕业要求标准时存在一定的差异，但均体现了《华盛顿协议》12 条标准的关键性因素。爱尔兰制定的毕业要求较为详细，对每个要求都进行了细节性说明，指出学习成果达成的指标点。然而，英国的毕业要求对标技术工程师的标准，需要本科生在获得荣誉学位时达到此要求，这些毕业要求虽未像爱尔兰那样列出指标点，但相比《华盛顿协议》的毕业要求，提出了更多的要求，设计/开发解决方案、研究以及使用现代工具这三项标准更详细，并非常注重项目管理这一标准。

（2）在北美洲，加拿大的毕业要求与《华盛顿协议》保持一致，美国的毕业要求则列出 7 项，与《华盛顿协议》相比做出了一定调整。

（3）在大洋洲，新西兰的毕业要求与《华盛顿协议》保持一致，而澳大利亚的毕业要求则自成体系，并未沿袭《华盛顿协议》的框架模式，但也体现协议标准中所有必备的关键性因素。

（4）在亚洲，中国、新加坡和马来西亚都完全遵循《华盛顿协议》的毕业要求，这三个国家认证标准的一致性也较为突出，韩国和日本制定的毕业要求与《华盛顿协议》略有差别，特别是日本调整的标准较多。

（5）在南美洲，与亚洲的一些国家一样，秘鲁的毕业要求也与《华盛顿协议》保持一致。

（6）在非洲，南非的毕业要求在《华盛顿协议》标准的基础上进行了补充和加工。

**2. 各区域所选国家通用标准的特点**

从通用标准层面来看，本文所选取的13个签署成员，或自成体系，或受到《华盛顿协议》发起成员的影响（表3）。

（1）在欧洲，英国通用标准的制定基于本国的工程教育发展历史积淀，基本上自成体系。在爱尔兰，通用标准最具特色的便是其课程体系的标准。与美国和加拿大等国不同的是，爱尔兰并没有对专业应包含的课程类型、最低学分提出相应要求，而是对“专业领域”这一标准进行分解和阐释，旨在说明这项标准是什么，它对工科毕业生有什么重要性，并简要说明为达到预期的毕业要求，学生应被置于什么样的学习或教学环境之中，教师可采取哪些教学措施，专业可提供哪些教学支持等。

**表3　通用标准层面的区域维度分析**

| 区域 | 所选国家的特点 |
|---|---|
| 欧洲 | 英国的工程教育专业认证标准基本上自成体系，爱尔兰通用标准最具特色的是其课程体系的标准 |
| 北美洲 | 美国为世界工程教育认证提供了参考范本，加拿大在美国的认证标准的基础上进行了细化 |
| 南美洲 | 秘鲁的工程教育认证标准基本参考了美国的认证标准　， |
| 大洋洲 | 澳大利亚的工程教育专业认证标准基本上自成体系，而新西兰则与其他国家类似 |
| 亚洲 | 中国、韩国、新加坡和马来西亚基本趋于一致，日本则自成体系，个性化突出 |
| 非洲 | 南非在参考了美国认证标准的基础上进行了补充和加工 |

（2）在北美洲，美国工程与技术认证委员会（ABET）制定的八项通用标准体现了美国工程教育专业认证的新思考。加拿大在课程体系方面进行了细化，对专业教育的几大方面提出学时要求，以及计算方法。

（3）在大洋洲，从澳大利亚和新西兰的通用标准中可以看出，这两个国家并未受到其他国家的影响，且彼此也未互相影响，基本上自成体系。澳大利亚对标三大能力，包含三大一级指标；新西兰在美国的认证标准的基础上制定了五项一级指标。

（4）在亚洲，中国、韩国、新加坡和马来西亚都参考美国ABET的通用标准，所以这几个国家的通用标准制定基本趋于一致。然而，日本的通用标准自成体系，包含四项一级指标。在亚洲范围内，日本的认证标准个性化最为突出。

（5）南美洲、非洲的一些国家与美国的通用标准差别不是很大。

**3. 基于国别维度的分析**

通过对《华盛顿协议》13个签署成员的工程教育认证标准进行分析，基于国别维度，本文所选国家大致可以分为奠定基础型（美国、英国、加拿大、爱尔兰、澳大利亚、新西兰）、本土加工型（日本、韩国、南非）、模仿借鉴型（马来西亚、新加坡、中国、秘鲁）三类。

（1）奠定基础型。在美国、英国、加拿大、爱尔兰、澳大利亚、新西兰6个发起成员中，由于美国最早实施产出导向的认证，对其他国家认证标准的制定影响深远。ABET也是世界上最早的全国性工程教育专业认证的统一组织和管理机构。ABET 的主要职责体现在三个方面:一是对国内外的专业认证机构进行审查和授权,以保证其具有开展认证工作的专业水平;二是通过下属的工程认证委员会、应用科学认证委员会等四个专业性机构制定本学科领域的认证标准、程序以及操作性实践框架;三是为各院校和社会公众提供信息咨询、战略规划和技术支持服务。

(2)本土加工型。日本对《华盛顿协议》中的 12 条毕业要求进行了整合与分解,同时增加新的毕业要求。例如,将"工程与社会""环境和可持续""伦理规范"三项能力要求整合为一条,即"能够理解专业活动对社会、自然的影响,同时能够理解专业人员应对社会做的贡献与承担的责任",且将"问题分析""研究""使用现代工具"三条要求融合进前四项认证标准之中,将"工程知识"分解为"能够运用全球战略性知识进行多元思考""掌握对数学、自然科学、信息技术等相关知识的应用能力""具备专业领域知识及其应用能力"三项内容,从全球视野、多元思考能力等方面提出新的要求。韩国工程教育认证委员会(Accreditation Board for Engineering Education of Korea, ABEEK)十分注重韩国工程教育质量,并因其严谨的认证审查机制,获得韩国各高校的认同以及产业界的支持。在通用标准中,强调各专业必须重视"教育质量持续改善",定期评估工程教育质量并能持续改进。与韩国类似的是,南非的通用标准也对"持续改进"进行强调,特别是从专业设计、教师、资源等维度出发制定若干细化标准。此外,南非对课程体系这一项并没有设置标准,而是针对教与学的各环节(教学内容、学习目标、教学手段、教学评估方式等)的质量保证制定了一系列标准。

(3)模仿借鉴型。该类型认证组织加入《华盛顿协议》时间较晚,并且国内并未形成较为完善的工程教育专业认证标准以及与之衔接的注册工程师制度。加入《华盛顿协议》标志着这几个国家走向了工程教育国际化之路,并通过多边认可工程教育资格,促进工程学位互认和工程师的国际流动。

## 4 工程教育专业认证标准国际比较的讨论

### 4.1 毕业要求维度:实质等效与本国实际并存

从毕业要求维度来看,本文选取的 13 个签署成员的专业认证标准中的毕业要求在很大程度上都遵循《华盛顿协议》的认证标准中的关键性因素,但部分国家并未与之保持完全一致,而是根据本国的实际情况有所变通,将一些标准进行本土化的处理或整合。可见,在毕业要求总体上保持基本一致的前提下,结合本国实际提出特色性要求,或者对相关要求进行组合,与实质等效原则不冲突。马来西亚、新加坡、中国等国家的毕业要求与《华盛顿协议》高度一致。美国、爱尔兰、韩国等国家的毕业要求则与《华盛顿协议》相比进行了一些标准的整合或精简。澳大利亚和英国虽没有按照《华盛顿协议》的 12 条标准的模式进行认证标准的制定,但其标准体系都囊括了《华盛顿协议》中所要求的关键性因素。在《华盛顿协议》的 12 条毕业要求中,工程与社会、环境和可持续发展、伦理规范、使用现代工具和项目管理是被整合或调整最多的标准。目前,我国认证体系的设计理念,尤其是毕业要求,与《华盛顿协议》保持了较高的一致性,但尚未结合本国实际提出具有特色的要求。习近平总书记多次指出，坚持党对教育事业的全面领导，坚持把立德树人作为根本任务。面向未来发展，中华优秀传统文化、社会主义核心价值观和立德树人等要求应在毕业要求中进一步体现，以建立面向未来的中国特色、国际实质等效的新认证标准和体系。

### 4.2 认证通用标准维度：明确本国特色，着眼赋能创新

本文所选取的13个签署成员在通用标准中的课程体系呈现出最鲜明的本国特色以及个性化特征；在学生、专业培养目标、持续改进、师资队伍4项中，一些国家（如日本、马来西亚、韩国、秘鲁等）与美国认证标准有较多相似，但是根据各自需求进行了本国标准化处理；13个国家只有通用标准中的设施和学校支持这两项标准呈现较强的一致性。我国的认证通用标准借鉴美国ABET认证标准，采用“结果导向”的基本原则，即将学生的素质和潜能表现作为衡量教学成果的依据，并以促进其持续改进作为认证的最终标准。从认证标准设计来看，我国在标准弹性化、特色化和标准结构层次以及标准衔接方面面临诸多挑战，必须对认证标准设计进行二次赋能创新。首先，认证标准设计并没有充分考虑到不同层次高校需求的差异性，并没有针对不同高校的办学实力设计具有层次的认证标准。因为认证难度太大或太小都会影响高校参与认证的积极性。其次，我国工程类14个专业类委员会的专业补充标准保持高度一致，在相当程度上也忽略了各专业类本身的特色和实际。再次，我国的工程教育专业认证层次仅限于本科层次，但从中国的实际发展情况来看，我国硕士层次的工科学生数量十分庞大，而且呈现出急剧增长的态势，需要专业认证制度来保证其培养质量。最后，随着新一轮科技革命提质增效，跨国型工程科技人才流动日益加剧，我国尚未建立起相对完整的专业认证制度和工程师注册制度的衔接机制，其资质的认可度也无法得到有效保障。

### 4.3 区域与国别维度：建构独立自主的内部驱动发展逻辑

从区域与国别维度来看，本文所选13个签署成员在区域内的一致性并不明显，即便同在一个大洲，各成员之间也存在较大差异，其中一部分成员受美国等《华盛顿协议》发起成员影响较大。从20世纪90年代初期我国着手在建筑领域开展专业认证试点、2005年全国工程师制度协调改革小组组建、2015年中国工程教育专业认证协会正式成立，到2016年我国成为《华盛顿协议》正式成员，我国专业认证制度已经逐步走向成熟，逐渐建立起一套相对完善的认证机构组织、认证标准以及认证程序等。但是，我国的专业认证制度与体系建设在参考《华盛顿协议》成员诸如美国认证体系的基础上，需要进行本土化处理，以适应国内工程教育专业认证要求[15]。目前，我国工程教育相当程度上缺乏独立自主的内部驱动发展逻辑，而作为全球工程教育发展典范之一的德国在实际改革过程中在相当程度上保持着本国的文化特色与历史传统，并没有完全严格按照《华盛顿协议》的认证标准来开展创新设计，在面临本土化与国际化的冲突时，甚至选择退出《华盛顿协议》[16]。因此，在落实立德树人根本要求的基础上，未来我国工程教育专业认证毕业要求与一般要求的修订要适应未来新兴科技和产业创新发展对工程专业人员的需求，以数字和智能科技创新发展和应用为代表的新基建等大战略发展方向表明了国家所需的人才结构、专业领域、数量和水平等[17]。在

修订我国的工程教育专业认证标准的过程中要注重在设计和开发解决方案时的灵活性、创造性、创新性以及思维能力培养；在团队工作中强调多样性和包容性；在制定解决方案时要考虑不同的环境、社会、文化、经济因素以及全球责任；在保留工程专业能力培养的同时，加强数字化学习，提高终身学习方面的能力培养[18]。

## 5 工程教育专业认证的中国标准建构

在新工业革命的时代背景下，我国认证标准建构尚处于不断探索与实践之中，需面向未来产业发展需求、国际工程教育新发展趋势以及 GAPC21 认证标准的新要求，对我国工程教育专业认证标准进行创新性重构，以便更有效地服务于我国未来工程教育发展的战略需求，形成中国特色的工程教育专业认证体系。具体来看，在满足 GAPC21 的要求的基础上，未来工程教育专业认证的中国标准的建构方向应聚焦并强化立德树人和全面培养的要求、认证标准的弹性化和适应性、特色化、本硕标准贯通以及工程师衔接制度等方面。

一是强化立德树人的要求，即在认证标准中强调坚持立德树人，引导学生树立社会主义核心价值观[19]。在“培养目标”中，应体现社会主义事业建设者和接班人的培养总目标。这些总目标需要体现在认证标准和学校人才培养计划中，关键是如何落实和如何评价。在西方如加拿大的培养体系中，人文社科的培养是通过补充学习实现的。我国需要制定能够实现培养目标的教育体系，将理念切实付诸实施。在毕业要求中有关工程伦理和职业责任的指标中，应强调培养有较高的职业道德标准、社会责任感和敬业奉献精神，对党和国家及人民忠诚的人。此外，还应该考虑世界面临的共同挑战，如环境保护和“双碳”目标、资源和能源、社会和网络安全、老龄化社会等全球共同关注的问题。在“课程体系”和“师资队伍”标准中，应将教师的职业伦理规范、对教育教学工作和育人的投入、课程思政和师德师风作为教师队伍建设和课程体系建设的首要任务进行强调。

二是认证标准的弹性化和适应性，即在认证标准建构中要特别关注不同类型、层次、需求、办学定位的院校的认证要求。对中国众多高校而言，其办学定位和目标与自身综合实力之间往往存在差距。对于部分“双一流”研究型大学来说，师资队伍、办学资金投入、学生水平、设施和设备等方面，比较容易满足工程教育认证标准。而对部分地方院校来说，在这些方面可能需要努力才能达到工程认证标准[20]。因此，在未来标准建构中，需注重增强标准的弹性和挑战度，既要符合不同高校的办学实际，又要提升我国工程教育的国际竞争力。

三是认证标准的特色化，即推进认证标准的专业类特色化建设。各专委会应充分考虑不同专业类的本质差异及其实际情况，制定专业类补充标准，同时为保证标准目标的实现，还要对毕业生的能力要求与课程体系进行设计。此外，针对各专业类的特色，认证标准还要对配套的指标体系及操作程序进行建构。

四是构建本硕标准贯通制，即完善本科与硕士贯通性的专业认证标准。目前，我国工程教育专业认证层次主要聚焦于本科层次，尚未形成具体可行的本硕标准贯通制度设计与实施程序。英国、爱尔兰等已经建立起相对完善的本硕贯通制认证标准体系，这些经验与做法值得我国深入研究与借鉴。从一些签署成员的认证标准中可以看出，本科与硕士的专业认证标准和毕业要求的各个维度虽然相同，但两者对学生的能力素养以及知识结构要求的层次却不同，硕士的认证标准和毕业要求实际上是本科认证标准和毕业要求在各个维度的延伸，这在很大程度上考虑到知识的连贯性和层次性，以及本硕两个层次的认证标准的逻辑性。

五是推动工程师衔接制度化，实现工程教育专业认证与注册工程师制度的有效衔接。目前，我国大部分专业未建立起行之有效的专业认证与注册工程师衔接机制。反观美国、加拿大等国，都已经建立了较成熟的工程师注册制度，有效地对接工程教育专业认证标准与注册工程师标准。面向未来，我国应积极推进两者衔接改革，政府、高校和工业界等利益相关主体应共同协作，制定符合各方利益诉求的工程师技术资格与工程教育专业对接体系。

## 6 结语

当前科技革命和产业变革快速发展，需要大量工程科技创新人才，对工程教育人才培养质量提出了更高要求。工程教育专业认证是工程教育质量保障的重要机制和质量提升的手段。本文对 13 个《华盛顿协议》签署成员的认证体系进行比较研究，根据工程教育专业认证的通用标准以及标准中的毕业要求进行分析，将认证标准维度和区域维度的关键性因素进行比较研究。这些国家专业认证标准中的毕业要求大多遵循《华盛顿协议》的关键要素，但部分国家并未与之保持完全一致，而是根据本国的实际情况和需求，进行本土化的处理或整合。在毕业要求总体上保持基本一致的前提下，各国结合本国实际情况，提出符合本国或地区工程教育专业认证特色的要求，这与实质等效原则并不冲突。在区域维度上，这 13 个签署成员所在区域内的一致性并不明显，同在一个大洲的几个签署成员存在差异性较大的情况，这些分析研究为未来《华盛顿协议》认证标准修订和制度建设与发展提供了有参考价值的信息。作为世界上最大的工程教育国家，我国通过持续深入发展新工科，将为 21 世纪世界工程教育变革与创新贡献中国智慧、提供中国方案、做出中国贡献。建立中国特色、国际实质等效的认证标准，并由此进一步推动和强化高等教育落实立德树人根本要求。在未来的工程教育专业认证发展中，如何根据我国的实际情况以及对工程专业人员的需求，在专业认证标准上提出特色性要求、创新能力要求，以及对相关要求进行组合和修订，需要进一步深入研究和持续实践。

### 参考文献

[1] 林健，胡德鑫. 国际工程教育改革经验的比较与借鉴：基于美、英、德、法四国的范例[J]. 高等工程教育研究，2018(2)：96-110.

[2] National Centre for Vocational Education Research(NCVER). Australia’s shifting skills ecosystem：contemporary challenges in education. training and immigration[EB/OL]. (2018-02-09)[2021-08-31]. https://www.voced.edu.au/content/ngv%3A76052.

[3] Federal Ministry for Economic Affairs and Energy. Industrie 4.0 [EB/OL]. (2021-08-31) [2021-08-31]. https://www.bmwi.de/Redaktion/EN/Dossier/industrie-40.html.

[4] The National Archives. The UK’s Industrial Strategy [EB/OL]. (2020-03-04)[2021-08-31]. https://www.gov.uk/government/ topical-events/the-uks-industrial-strategy.

[5] 顾佩华. 新工科与新范式：概念、框架和实施路径[J]. 高等工程教育研究，2017(6)：1-13.
[6] 顾佩华. 新工科与新范式：实践探索与思考[J]. 高等工程教育研究，2020(4)：1-19.
[7] DE PAOR C. The contribution of professional accreditation to quality assurance in higher education[J]. Quality in higher education，2016，22(3)：228-241.
[8] International Engineering Alliance. Washington Accord[EB/OL].(2019-06-25)[2021-08-31]. https://www.ieagreements.org/accords/washington/.
[9] ABET accreditation. Setting The Standard Worldwide[EB /OL].(2021-08-31)[2021-08-31]. https://www.abet.org/accreditation/.
[10] Engineers Australia. Accreditation of Engineering Education Programs[EB/OL].(2021-08-31)[2021-08-31]. https://www.engineersaustralia.org.au/About-Us/Accreditation.
[11] Engineering Council. The Engineering Council[EB/OL].(2020-08-31)[2021-08-31]. https://www.engc.org.uk/.
[12] Japan Accreditation Board for Engineering Education. About JABEE[EB/OL].(2020-10-21)[2021-08-31]. https://jabee.orgen/.
[13] Engineering Council of South Africa. Overview[EB/OL].(2021-08-31)[2021-08-31]. https://nationalgovernment.co.za/units/view/424/engineering-council-of-south-africa-ecsa.
[14] Engineers Ireland. Accrediting Bodies[EB/OL].(2020-03-04)[2021-08-31]. https://accreditation.org/accrediting-bodies/ireland.
[15] 胡德鑫. 新工业革命背景下工程教育专业认证制度国际改革的比较与借鉴[J]. 高校教育管理，2019，13(5)：72-81.
[16] 胡德鑫. 德国专业认证制度改革的行动方略与演绎逻辑[J]. 高教探索，2020(11)：58-65.
[17] 潘教峰，万劲波. 新基建十大战略方向[EB/OI].(2020-04-26)[2021-08-31]http://www.xinhuanet.com/2020-04/30/c1125929139.htm.
[18] 刘鑫桥. 新常态下新工科建设形势趋同的制度逻辑[J]. 黑龙江高教研究，2019(4)：1-4.
[19] 李志义，赵卫兵. 我国工程教育认证的最新进展[J]. 高等工程教育研究，2021(5)：39-43.
[20] 胡德鑫. 赋能未来：工程教育专业认证制度改革的国际比较与标准重构[J]. 天津大学学报(社会科学版)，2020，22(3)：223-229.

# 工程教育专业认证标准的国际案例研究①

朱　露　王　庚　胡德鑫　闫广芬　顾佩华

**摘要：**工程教育专业认证标准受科技发展、产业变革、工程师职业要求变化、国家和地区教育政策等多种因素影响。以分别位于欧洲、北美洲、大洋洲和亚洲的《华盛顿协议》的四个成员——爱尔兰、美国、澳大利亚、日本的工程教育专业认证通用标准为研究样本，基于标准的内涵逻辑与实施程序，剖析各成员组织认证标准的共性与差异，从层次结构调整、内容更新、实施程序优化三个维度，探讨对我国未来专业认证标准改革与创新的参考价值。

**关键词：**工程教育专业认证；标准；内涵逻辑；实施程序

## An International Case Study on Accreditation Criteria for Engineering Programs

*Zhu Lu, Wang Geng, Hu Dexin, Yan Guangfen, Gu Peihua*

**Abstract:** The accreditation criteria for engineering education programs are influenced by various factors such as the development of science and technology, industrial transformations, the change of requirements of professional engineers, national and regional education policies and so on. Taking the general criteria for accrediting engineering education programs in four members of the Washington Accord in Europe, North America, Oceania and Asia — Ireland, the United States, Australia and Japan as research samples, based on the connotation logic and implementation procedures of the criteria, this paper analyzes the similarities and differences of the accreditation criteria of each member organization from the three aspects of hierarchical structures, content updating and implementation procedures to explore the reference value for the reform and innovation of accreditation criteria for engineering education programs in China in the future.

**Keywords:** accreditation for engineering education programs; criteria; connotation logic; implementation procedures

## 引言

为构建中国特色、国际实质等效的工程教育认证新标准和新体系，从内涵逻辑与实施程序入手，对欧洲的爱尔兰、北美洲的美国、大洋洲的澳大利亚和亚洲的日本的工程教育专业认证通用标准进行案例深度解析，以期为未来我国认证标准改革和创新提供参考。

① 本文刊登于《高等工程教育研究》2022 年第 3 期第 32~45、73 页。

## 1　研究设计

### 1.1　案例设计

《华盛顿协议》的21个成员遍布全球，本研究分别从欧洲、北美洲、大洋洲、亚洲各选取一例（爱尔兰、美国、澳大利亚、日本）作为研究样例，对其工程教育专业认证通用标准进行案例分析。样本选取还考虑到成员认证制度的发展历史与发展特色。爱尔兰、美国、澳大利亚作为《华盛顿协议》的原始成员，认证制度的建立时间较早，认证标准体系较完善，具有一定的探究价值。日本作为专业认证领域具有后发优势的国家，认证标准的层级划分与内容构成独具特色，能给同为亚洲国家的我国推进认证标准改革带来一定启发。

### 1.2　分析框架

案例分析主要从两个方面着手：标准的内涵逻辑、标准的实施程序。在研究标准的内涵逻辑时，一是从层次结构出发，重点分析通用标准项及各通用标准项内涵观测点的逻辑结构关系；二是从内容设计出发，重点分析通用标准的内涵概念与功能定位，并将毕业要求项作为独立的分析单元。在研究标准的实施程序时，依据现场（线上）考查、自评报告等具体资料，对认证组织如何开展认证、学校如何为接受认证做准备两个维度进行分析。通过上述研究，探讨四个国家工程教育专业认证通用标准在内涵逻辑、实施程序中的共性与差异，总结对我国未来认证标准改革的经验与启示。

## 2　案例分析

### 2.1　爱尔兰

爱尔兰工程师协会（Engineers Ireland，EI）是爱尔兰工程教育专业认证的主体机构，它兼具工程教育认证与工程师资格认证两项重要职能，不仅负责制定、修订与实施爱尔兰工程教育和工程职业的认证标准，还致力于在二者之间创建关联。爱尔兰工程师的职业头衔有三类：特许工程师、助理工程师、工程技术员。针对各类型的职业头衔，EI提出不同教育要求，制定相应的工程教育专业认证标准，同时，为鼓励仅有学士学位的特许工程师通过进一步深造获得硕士学位，还增设与特许工程师进修相关的教育认证标准。爱尔兰的工程教育专业认证标准与欧洲资历框架相适应，适用于高等教育证书、普通学士学位、荣誉学士学位、综合硕士学位等不同学历等级。

#### 2.1.1　标准的内涵逻辑

爱尔兰工程教育专业认证标准的通用标准项数量较少，其标准设计注重各项指标之间的关联性，并增加部分具有本国特色的认证标准项。如图1所示，认证标准由3项通用标准、20 项通用标准观测点构成。通用标准包含毕业要求、专业领域和专业管理三大内容。其中，毕业要求基于《华盛顿协议》的 12 条毕业要求，制定 8 项与学生学习产出相关的规定；专业领域对毕业要求进行进一步解读，从七个方面详细说明专业如何使工科毕业生达到预期的毕业要求；专业管理的内容较为丰富，涉及与学生、资源、目标、质量保障等相关的要求。

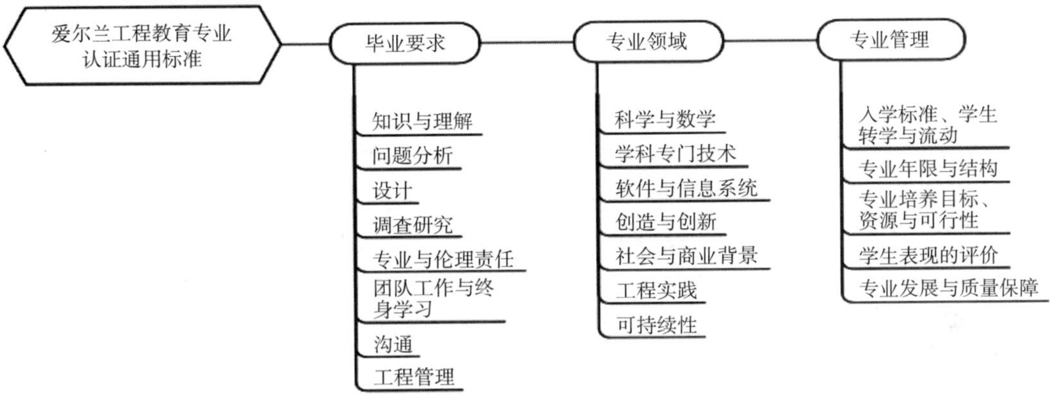


**图 1　爱尔兰工程教育专业认证标准的基本框架**

具体内容如下[1]。

毕业要求由知识与理解、问题分析、设计、调查研究、专业与伦理责任、团队工作与终身学习、沟通、工程管理 8 项能力标准构成，与《华盛顿协议》的 12 条毕业要求相比，并未保持完全一致，而是根据本国的实际情况有所变通，在坚持实质等效原则的基础上对部分内容进行优化组合（表 1）。此外，每项标准中包含对该项毕业要求的详细说明，指出毕业要求达成的指标点，增强了认证的可操作性，为专业解读认证标准提供了明确指导。

**表 1　《华盛顿协议》12 条毕业要求与爱尔兰毕业要求标准项的对应关系**

| 《华盛顿协议》12 条毕业要求 | 爱尔兰毕业要求标准项 |
| --- | --- |
| 工程知识 | 1. 知识与理解 |
| 问题分析 | 2. 问题分析 |
| 设计/开发解决方案 | 3. 设计 |
| 调查研究 | 4. 调查研究 |
| 现代工具的使用 | 包含于第 1、2、3、4 条标准中 |
| 工程师与社会 | 5. 专业与伦理责任 |
| 环境与可持续发展 | |
| 伦理 | |
| 个人和团队工作 | 6. 团队工作与终身学习 |
| 沟通 | 7. 沟通 |
| 项目管理和财务 | 8. 工程管理 |
| 终身学习 | 包含于第 6 条标准中 |

专业领域涵盖科学与数学、学科专门技术、软件与信息系统、创造与创新、社会与商业背景、工程实践、可持续性 7 项内容。与其他国家的课程认证标准有所不同，课程主要对专业应包含的课程类型、最低学分提出要求，而专业领域则侧重于从教学角度阐释如何实现毕业要求，基于每项标准回答“这项标准是什么，它对工科毕业生有什么重要性”“各项标准应帮助学生实现何种学习目标，学生在认知、技能或态度等方面应取得怎样的成果”“为达到预期的学习成果，学生应被置于怎样的学习或教学环境中，教师可采取哪些教学措施，专业可提供哪些教学支持”等问题。专业管理涉及学生、培养目标、师资、设施、学校支持、持续改进等多个方面。就学生而言，爱尔兰要求专业制定最低入学条件，拥有与学分互换、学生流动相关的政策要求，专业年限和结构应符合国际（欧洲学分累积与转换体系）、国内（国家资历框架）相关的制度规定，同时注重评价学生表现，定期监测毕业要求的达成情况。就培养目标而言，专业培养目标应符合学校、教师、行业、学生等不同利益相关者的诉求，制定过程要有不同利益群体的共同参与。就师资而言，一方面，教师数量必须保证教学有效开展，另一方面，结合注册工程师制度，从学历、实践经验、教学能力、专业影响力等方面对教师的从业资质做出规定。就设施与学校支持而言，要求学校配备满足专业教学需要与学生学习需求的资源，例如，实验室、图书馆、设备、团队工作室等，同时拥有充足的支持性人员，能够为师生使用设施、设备提供指导及安全训练，为专业开展实验、项目教学等活动提供支持。就持续改进而言，主要包括“专业发展与质量保障”和“学生表现的评价”这两条标准，涵盖四个方面：其一，拥有涉及毕业要求制定过程与实现过程的正式书面文件；其二，对于通过认证的专业，学校应至少每五年提交一次基于上次认证建议的专业改进报告；其三，学校应对专业进行定期审查，并基于审查结果促进专业的持续改进；其四，注重评价学生表现，以实现对毕业要求达成情况的动态监测。

### 2.1.2 标准的实施程序

#### 1. 认证组织层面

在实施认证的过程中，认证组织将开展以下方面的工作（表 2）：审核认证材料、进行现场（线上）考查、撰写认证报告、得出认证结论。

**表 2 爱尔兰工程教育专业认证的实施流程（认证组织层面）**

| 审核认证材料 | 现场（线上）考查 | 撰写认证报告 | 得出认证结论 |
| --- | --- | --- | --- |
| ·自评报告<br>·线上证明材料 | ·专业小组/认证小组的非公开会议<br>·与高校管理人员及专业负责人的会议<br>·与学生、毕业生及用人单位的沟通<br>·专业小组/认证小组内部的进一步协商<br>·与专业负责人/特定人员的深度交流，介绍初步考查结果 | ·学校及专业基本信息，对先前认证建议的回应<br>·专业特点与优势<br>·毕业要求达成度<br>·其他认证标准的达成情况<br>·调查结果及建设 | ·完全符合认证标准：认证结论适用于五届毕业生<br>·专业不能满足一个、多个或部分毕业要求：认证结论最多适用于三届毕业生<br>·专业不满足大多数毕业要求：无法通过认证 |

材料审核注重考查自评报告中所提及的内容是否有线上材料作为支撑，是否符合认证标准的各项要求。审查过程中，评审员将对自评报告中有疑问或需现场考查的地方进行标注，以便在现场（线上）考查环节能更好地向专业团队、学生、毕业生及用人单位提问。现场

（线上）考查由专业小组或认证小组成员组织开展，对于每一个参与认证的专业，认证管理员都会派出一个专业小组，专业小组由一名主席和两名评估员构成，若有多个专业接受认证，则通过合并专业小组以形成认证小组的方式实施评估[2]。现场（线上）考查时长为一天，在此期间，考查小组将通过参观学校设施设备，与高校管理人员、专业负责人、学生、毕业生、用人单位等沟通交流，了解专业发展概况。

认证报告由评估人员共同完成。认证组织不仅制定标准化的认证报告模板，给出各部分内容的字数建议，而且明确评估员在报告撰写过程中的职能分工。同时，相关政策文件从各认证环节的注意事项、现场（线上）考查可能问及的问题等方面加强评估员培训，为其深度理解认证标准、有效撰写认证报告予以指导。认证结论采用三级评定制，结论有效期最长为五年。

**2. 学校层面**

在参与认证的过程中，学校需准备好以下材料：自评报告、线上证明材料。认证组织并未提供统一的自评报告模板，但规定了专业自评应包含的 13 个方面的内容（表 3），涉及专业基本信息、认证标准达成度评价、相关支撑材料三个方面。专业基本信息与国家资历框架相适应，包含专业名称、工程师培养类型以及寻求获得的认证状态等内容（表 4），若之前接受过认证，还需阐述基于上一次认证建议的专业改进措施。认证标准达成度评价涵盖通用标准中的三大指标，细分为组织结构与人员配备，培养目标与资源条件，入学标准、学分互换、学生流动的相关政策要求，专业年限、结构与课程分布，学生表现的评价，专业管理与发展，质量保障程序，对毕业要求的理解、毕业要求的实现过程等 8 个自评要素[3]。进行认证标准达标举证时需把握不同要素之间的关联性，结合院校实际对专业发展概况做出整体性评价。例如，在阐述专业毕业要求及其实现过程时，需说明不同课程模块与毕业要求之间的映射关系，构建包含课程类型、学分数量、不同课程对实现各项毕业要求的贡献度等信息的矩阵（表 5）。相关支撑材料是为了增强自评报告的真实性与说服力，涉及毕业设计的项目列表、学生考试成绩的统计数据、毕业生及用人单位的调查报告等内容。

**表 3　爱尔兰工程教育专业认证学校**

<table>
<tr><th colspan="2">自评报告</th><th>线上证明材料</th></tr>
<tr><td rowspan="2">专业基本信息</td><td>专业名称、工程师培养类型、寻求获得的认证状态</td><td rowspan="10">1. 线上证明材料索引<br>2. 含有每一课程模块支撑材料的文件夹<br>3. 设施设备的说明<br>4. 教职工概况<br>5. 外部审查员的专业审查报告<br>6. 专业管理与质量评价材料</td></tr>
<tr><td>对先前认证建设的回应</td></tr>
<tr><td rowspan="8">认证标准达成度评价</td><td>组织结构与人员配备</td></tr>
<tr><td>培养目标与资源条件</td></tr>
<tr><td>入学标准、学分互换、学生流动的相关政策要求</td></tr>
<tr><td>专业年限、结构与课程分布</td></tr>
<tr><td>学生表现的评价</td></tr>
<tr><td>专业管理与发展</td></tr>
<tr><td>质量保障程序</td></tr>
<tr><td>对毕业要求的理解、毕业要求实现过程（主要说明不同课程模块与各项毕业要求之间的映射关系）</td></tr>
</table>

续表

| 自评报告 | | 线上证明材料 |
|---|---|---|
| 相关支撑材料 | 毕业设计的项目列表 | |
| | 学生考试成绩的统计数据 | |
| | 毕业生及用人单位的调查报告 | |

**表 4　爱尔兰自评报告中专业基本信息的填写示例[3]**

| 专业名称 | 缩写 | 国家资历框架中的等级标准 | 工程师培养类型 | 寻求获得的认证状态 |
|---|---|---|---|---|
| 电气工程高级证书 | HC | 6 | 工程技术员 | 再认证 |
| 土木工程学士学位 | BEng | 7 | 助理工程师 | 首次认证 |
| 机械工程(荣誉)学士学位 | BE | 8 | 特许工程师进修 | 再认证 |
| 电子工程硕士学位 | ME | 9 | 特许工程师 | 首次认证 |

**表 5　爱尔兰自评报告中毕业要求及实现过程的填写示例[3]**

| 课程模块 | 学分 | 毕业要求 | | | | | | | |
|---|---|---|---|---|---|---|---|---|---|
| | | PO1 | PO2 | PO3 | PO4 | PO5 | PO6 | PO7 | PO8 |
| 模块 1 课程代码与名称 | 5 | 4 | 3 | 1 | 1 | 1 | 2 | 3 | 4 |
| 模块 2 课程代码与名称 | 10 | 2 | 4 | 2 | 3 | 2 | 4 | 1 | 3 |
| 模块 3 课程代码与名称 | 5 | 1 | 3 | 4 | 1 | 2 | 3 | 4 | 4 |
| 模块 4 课程代码与名称 | 5 | 4 | 4 | 1 | 4 | 2 | 2 | 1 | 2 |
| 模块 5 课程代码与名称 | 5 | 4 | 4 | 3 | 2 | 2 | 2 | 3 | 1 |
| … | … | … | … | … | … | … | … | … | … |

除了自评报告，学校还需在线提供其他证明材料(具体内容见表 3)，线上证明材料与自评报告中的支撑材料有所区别，但具有一定互补性，用以辅助说明认证标准的达成情况。

## 2.2　美国

美国工程与技术认证委员会(ABET)是经美国高等教育认证理事会(CHEA)认可的非政府、非营利性专业认证组织，负责对应用与自然科学、计算机、工程、工程技术等学科相关专业实施认证，认证范围涵盖副学士、学士、硕士三个学历层次，认证标准由通用标准和专业补充标准组成，本文仅对 ABET 下属的工程认证委员会(EAC)认证标准的通用部分进行探讨。

### 2.2.1　标准的内涵逻辑

美国工程教育专业认证标准由 8 个通用标准项构成，即学生、培养目标、毕业要求、持续改进、课程、师资、设施、学校支持。通用标准分类较细，除了毕业要求，其他标准多以段落的形式加以阐释，指标的层级划分较为简洁。

具体内容如下[4]。

“学生”这一标准要求评价学生表现，监测学生进步，予以学生课程及职业生涯指导，制定并执行与招生、学生流动、学分转换相关的政策，同时有相关文件或措施保证毕业生达成所有的毕业要求。

“培养目标”规定专业应制定符合学校定位、利益相关者需求的培养目标，并对培养目标进行定期审查，审查过程有不同利益群体的参与，从而保证培养目标对不同需求的适应性。

“毕业要求”由 7 条能力要求构成，整合了《华盛顿协议》12 条毕业要求中的主要内容（表 6）。此外，与《工程标准 2000》( Engineering Criteria 2000 )中的 11 条毕业要求相比，标准数量有所减少，内容却更加丰富[5]，能力评价注重整体性和系统性，同时，增加多样性、包容性等考查要素，较为关注社会对工程项目的全面影响以及工程师的全球责任，对工程人才质量提出更高要求。

**表 6 《华盛顿协议》12 条毕业要求与美国毕业要求标准项的对应关系**

| 《华盛顿协议》12 条毕业要求 | 美国毕业要求标准项 |
|---|---|
| 工程知识 | 1. 通过应用工程、科学和数学原理，识别、阐述和解决复杂工程问题的能力 |
| 问题分析 | |
| 设计/开发解决方案 | 2. 考虑公共卫生、安全和福利，以及全球、文化、社会、环境和经济因素，应用工程设计得到满足特定要求的解决方案的能力 |
| 调查研究 | 6. 开发和操作合适的实验，分析和解释数据，运用工程判断得出结论 |
| 现代工具的使用 | 包含于第 1、2、6 条标准中 |
| 工程师与社会 | 4. 能够在工程环境中认识到伦理和专业责任，并做出明智的判断，必须考虑工程解决方案对全球、经济、环境和社会环境等因素的影响 |
| 环境与可持续发展 | |
| 伦理 | |
| 个人和团队工作 | 5. 能够有效地在团队中发挥作用，在团队成员的领导下，营造协作包容的环境，共同建立目标、计划任务，并实现目标 |
| 沟通 | 3. 有能力与社会公众进行有效沟通 |
| 项目管理和财务 | 包含于第 1、2、6 条标准中 |
| 终身学习 | 7. 根据需要使用适当的学习策略来获取和应用知识 |

“持续改进”涉及三点要求：一是对毕业要求达成情况予以评价；二是将评价结果用于专业的持续改进；三是通过其他可获得的信息来促进专业的持续发展。

“课程”规定了专业应开设的主要课程类型，包括基础科学类课程、工程专业类课程、通识教育类课程、复杂工程设计体验类课程。同时指出各类课程所应达到的最低学分，标准规定了课程应涵盖的主要领域，但没有对专业应开设的具体课程做出限制。

“师资”一方面要求教师数量充足，不同类型课程都有相应的师资团队，且教师数量能保证师生互动，学生咨询，大学服务活动，专业发展，与行业及专业从业者、用人单位互动等活动的顺利开展；另一方面，要求教师具备合格的从业资质和足够的专业权威，例如，教师拥有注册工程师资质。

“设施”要求学校配备充足的教室、办公室、实验室、图书馆、设备等资源，这些资源具有开放性与可获得性，并建立起相应的维护与更新机制，在资源使用上予以学生恰当指导，同时，图书馆服务、计算机与信息基础设施要能为师生的专业活动提供有效支持。

“学校支持”指学校提供的支持与领导足以保证专业质量提升与可持续发展；学校服务、经费、人员要能满足专业教学需要；专业资源要足以吸引优秀教师，稳定教师团队，促进教师发展；学校要为专业获得、维护、运行基础设施和设备提供支持，帮助专业营造有利于学生达成毕业要求的学习环境。

### 2.2.2　标准的实施程序

#### 1. 认证组织层面

美国工程教育专业认证大致按以下流程实施：学校呈递认证申请，同时提交用于专业考查的自评报告或中期报告；认证组织组建现场考查小组，并与学校商榷具体考查时间；认证组织根据认证标准及相关政策要求，对申请认证的专业实施综合考查或中期考查；学校核实认证结论报告草案，期间可提供反馈意见以及支撑最终声明的依据；专业委员会基于认证结论草案、学校反馈意见及其他相关信息，拟定最终宣布内容，从而做出认证决议。认证结论主要包括：下一次综合考查、中期报告、中期访问、原因陈述报告、原因陈述访问、延长报告、延长访问、延长出示原因、不予认证[6]。认证结论的类型取决于三个条件：专业是否存在未达成项和弱项等问题，是否需要提交进度报告以说明专业改进措施，是否需要对专业改进措施的实施情况进行现场考查。结论有效期最长为六年，其余通常为两年或四年。

专业审查是专业认证中的重要环节，包括中期考查和综合考查。中期考查旨在考查上次审查中的未达成项和弱项是否得以解决，可细分为：不需要现场考查的中期考查，只需要审查中期报告或原因陈述报告；需要现场考查的中期考查，需进行现场访问或原因陈述访问。综合考查旨在通过自评报告审阅与现场考查以全面评估专业对认证标准、政策和程序的达成情况，考查内容涉及以下方面[6]：支撑学校教学与学习环境的设施设备；包含课程大纲、教材、作业、试卷等在内的课程相关材料；专业培养目标符合利益相关者需求的证据；对专业培养目标进行定期审查的制度设计；评价毕业要求达成度的证明材料；促进专业发展所采取的改进措施；有利于实现学校使命、专业培养目标、毕业要求的学生支持服务；确保专业学习完成及学位授予的程序。综合考查有两项重要任务：审阅自评报告，实施现场（线上）考查。自评报告审阅旨在判断专业对认证标准的达成度，发现报告中未能提及的考查要点，以便在现场（线上）考查中加以核实。现场（线上）考查由专门的考查小组执行，考查小组由一名主席和若干名评估员（每个专业委派一名）构成，小组最小规模为 3 人，其中可包含观察员，观察员一般是 ABET 会员组织新培训的评估员（我们称认证专家）、各州执照和注册委员会的成员或者 ABET 国际认证合作伙伴的代表，主席通常是对应专业委员会的现任成员，评估员则从牵头成员组织批准的名单中选出[2]。在现场（线上）考查的过程中，考查小组将访谈教师、学生、行政人员等专业利益相关者，参观学校设施设备、审查毕业论文和项目设计等反映学生学业成绩的材料。

**2. 学校层面**

在接受认证的过程中，学校需要撰写自评报告、提供相关支撑材料，同时准备用于现场（线上）考查的材料。

自评报告由三大内容组成：专业基本信息、认证标准达成度评价、相关支撑材料[7]。认证标准达成度评价是自评报告的主体部分，其内容可划分为两类：评价数据与专业数据。评价数据又可细分为直接评价数据与间接评价数据。直接评价数据由不同任课教师通过评价课程目标的达成度而获得，间接评价数据则来自对学生、教职员工、用人单位等利益相关者的调查。属于评价数据的标准项有专业培养目标、毕业要求、课程、持续改进；属于专业数据的标准项有学生、教师、设施、学校支持[8]。根据 ABET 的自评报告模板可知，里面包含了对每条认证标准的要素分解，要求学校逐条说明各项指标的达成情况（图 2）。例如：在阐释课程这一标准的达成情况时，学校需通过表格展示专业开设课程的基本信息（课程名称、课程性质、课程类别、学期与学年注册人数、学分、学时等），说明课程如何促进实现专业培养目标与毕业要求，专业如何满足通用标准或专业补充标准中对主要课程类别在课时数与学习深度方面的要求，课程的通识教育部分与专业教育部分如何协同促进实现专业培养目标，工程设计体验类课程如何帮助学生实现知识应用、技能提升、素质发展等。同时，学校还需呈现符合通用标准或专业标准中课程相关要求的课程大纲。

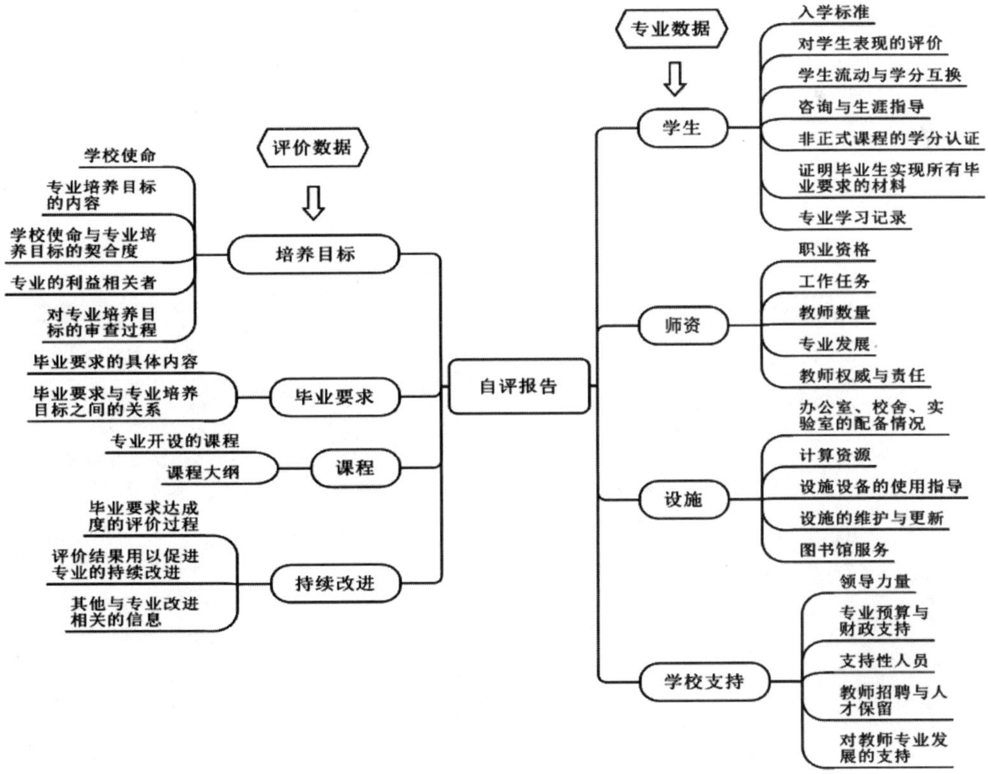


**图 2　美国工程教育专业认证自评报告的考查内容**

（资料来源：根据参考文献[7]整理而成）

自评报告的支撑材料与现场(线上)考查的材料有所不同,相关政策文件对其进行了区分。支撑材料一般以附录形式呈现于自评报告中,主要包括课程大纲、教师简历、设备的举例说明、学校基本信息等内容。支撑材料不必在现场(线上)考查中重复提供。用于现场(线上)考查的材料主要有[6]:解决自评报告中问题的材料;专业在提交自评报告后所采取行动的材料;证明符合认证标准和政策的材料(自评报告中提交的除外);毕业论文、顶石项目(capstone project)设计等反映学生学业成绩的材料。

### 2.3 澳大利亚

澳大利亚工程师协会(Engineers Australia, EA)是促进工程技术进步和会员专业发展的全国性组织,致力于专业认证、工程师移民技能评价、专业发展、工程师注册等工作。作为澳大利亚和海外值得信赖的高等工程教育认证机构,EA 基于注册工程师、工程技师、工程助理的初级能力标准制定了适用于三个职业等级的工程教育专业认证标准。认证标准对接澳大利亚资历框架(Australian Qualifications Framework, AQF)中学历等级、学习年限等相关规定,同时因 EA 加入工程教育国际互认协议(《华盛顿协议》《悉尼协议》《都柏林协议》)而具有国际实质等效性。

#### 2.3.1 标准的内涵逻辑

澳大利亚工程教育专业认证标准由 3 个通用标准项、15 个通用标准观测点构成,指标的层级划分较为清晰,各项指标有着明确的考查目的,并确立了指标达成的操作要点(详见表 7~表 9)。通用标准包含学术专业、专业的实施环境、质量体系三大内容,三者之间的关系可用一个教育项目的功能模型加以解释,在这一模型中,学术专业与专业的实施环境是促使教育功能得以发挥的使能器,而质量体系是控制系统,三者相互作用,协同帮助学生达成毕业要求[9]。

**表 7 “学术专业”标准的内容构成及操作要点[10]**

| 通用标准项 | 通用标准观测点 | 操作要点 |
|---|---|---|
| 学术专业 | 人才培养规格 | 要求根据澳大利亚工程师协会的初级能力标准,制定清晰明确的毕业要求,同时基于工程实践、工业发展等多方面需求定期审查、评价毕业要求 |
| | 专业与课程设计方法 | 要求阐述实现毕业要求的宏观路径。例如,如何对毕业要求进行制定、审查与达成度评价,是否在不同学习单元强调了自主学习、反思性练习、批判性复习、自评与同伴评价,是否有系统的课程审查机制等 |
| | 专业结构与实施框架 | 要求说明教育理念及培养方案的实施程序。例如,专业提供了有效的工程教育的双学位培养模式,有合作学习、远程学习、出国留学等多样化的学习形式 |
| | 对专业实践的参与 | 要求阐释专业实践能力的培养过程。例如,在学术单元中融入了综合性的工程实践学习活动,拥有记录、跟踪、评价学生工程实践能力的体系等 |
| | 专业课程(毕业要求、学习内容、教学方法、教学评价) | 要求说明毕业要求如何在具体的学习单元中得以实现。例如,每个学习单元的学习内容、预期达成的毕业要求、学习任务及评价方法是什么,不同学习单元如何协同促进毕业要求的整体实现等 |

表 8 “专业的实施环境”标准的内容构成及操作要点[10]

| 通用标准项 | 通用标准观测点 | 操作要点 |
| --- | --- | --- |
| 专业的实施环境 | 组织结构以及对工程教育的责任 | 要求说明专业各部门的职责权限及相关制度的运行机制。例如,拥有长效的责任机制与战略管理措施保证专业发展与资源的有效供给,领导和管理工程专业的组织实体职责明确等 |
| | 学术与支持性人员情况 | 要求阐述专业的员工概况以及不同人员如何促进教育教学与专业发展。例如,教师数量充足、结构合理、能力多元化,工程实践经验丰富,拥有注册工程师头衔或工程学会会员身份,有恰当比例的技术与行政人员等 |
| | 学术领导力与教育文化 | 要求说明专业如何组建了有效的领导团队,如何营造了良好的教与学的氛围。例如,对教学团队实施了有效领导,推动了教育教学改革与发展,形成了充满活力的、包容多元的合作型学习社会等 |
| | 资金、设施与物质资源 | 要求阐述学校如何为专业教学、学生发展、专业改革等提供了全方位的资源保障。例如,拥有能支撑专业学习与实践的实验与项目基础设施,确立了恰当的资金分配原则 |
| | 学生的战略管理 | 要求说明与学生相关的政策规定与发展规划。例如,拥有监测招生趋势、毕业率、留级率等的制度,制定了专业准入标准等 |

表 9 “质量体系”标准的内容构成及操作要点[10]

| 通用标准项 | 通用标准观测点 | 操作要点 |
| --- | --- | --- |
| 质量体系 | 外部利益相关者的参与 | 要求说明如何及时吸纳外界人员的反馈以促进专业可持续发展。例如,组建了包含工业界、社区及专业机构代表的正式顾问团体,能够对毕业要求的制定、修订、达成度评价提供建议 |
| | 学生的参与 | 要求阐述获取学生反馈的方法与措施。例如,拥有师生咨询论坛、专题小组或其他意见反馈机制,能恰当使用调查工具和其他手段获得系统性反馈 |
| | 专业的持续发展 | 要求阐述如何让持续改进成为专业教育改革的常规性活动。例如,有开设专业、修订专业的正式书面程序,全体教职工积极参与专业的持续改进过程等 |
| | 教育期望的传达 | 要求说明在正式教学前,帮助学生全面了解了预期的学习成果。例如,向学生反馈了学习单元与毕业要求之间的关联,传达了各教学单元的学习目标、学习活动及评价方法等 |
| | 标准检查 | 要求阐述专业标准与其他标准之间的适切性。例如,采取了相关措施比较毕业要求、学生评价标准与雇主之间的差距 |

具体内容如下[10]。

“学术专业”旨在对专业人才培养现状做出评价,尤其是通过“人才培养规格”“专业与课程设计方法”“专业结构与实施框架”“对专业实践的参与”“专业课程(毕业要求、学习内容、教学方法、教学评价)”五项指标说明专业如何帮助学生达到预期的能力标准。

“专业的实施环境”包含“组织结构以及对工程教育的责任”“学术与支持性人员情况”“学术领导力与教育文化”“资金、设施与物质资源”“学生的战略管理”五个通用标准观测点,分别从职能分工、人员构成、领导力量、文化建设、资源条件、政策规划等方面对专业运行系统做出规定。

“质量体系”是为了对专业的可持续发展能力做出评价,由“外部利益相关者的参与”“学生的参与”“专业的持续改进”“教育期望的传达”“标准检查”五个通用标准项观测点构成。一方面，专业需在正式教学前让受教育者全面把握、深度理解毕业要求的内涵与实现路径；另一方面需结合不同利益相关者的意见对专业进行定期审查与持续改进，注意毕业要求、学生评价标准等对接雇主期望、国家/行业标准。

澳大利亚工程教育专业认证有关毕业要求的规定源于澳大利亚工程师协会的初级能力标准，初级能力标准适用于注册工程师、工程技师、工程助理三个职业等级。以注册工程师为例，其能力标准包含三个群组：①知识与技能基础，反映工程实践的技术性要求；②专业与个人素养，强调工程实践的人文性特征；③工程应用能力，注重工程问题解决方案的技术性要素与人类需求之间的关联[11]。根据《华盛顿协议》12 条毕业要求与澳大利亚初级能力标准的对应关系（表 10）可知，澳大利亚在保留《华盛顿协议》毕业要求核心内容的基础上，一方面对《华盛顿协议》的部分能力要求进行要素整合与关联，将 12 条毕业要求归为知识与技能基础、工程应用能力、专业与个人素养三大类；另一方面，结合工业与社会发展需求，增加新的能力标准，例如，要求学生具备创新创造能力、能够有效利用与管理信息等。

**表 10 《华盛顿协议》12 条毕业要求与澳大利亚初级能力标准的对应关系**

<table>
<tr><th>《华盛顿协议》12 条毕业要求</th><th>澳大利亚初级能力标准</th></tr>
<tr><td>工程知识</td><td>1. 知识与技能基础<br>1.1 对自然科学、物理科学以及工程学科基础知识在理论层面有全面理解<br>1.2 对工程学科的数学、数值分析、统计学、计算机和信息科学有概念性理解<br>1.3 对工程学科内的专业知识体系有深入了解<br>1.4 对工程学科内的知识发展和研究方向有洞察力<br>1.5 了解工程设计实践以及影响工程学科的背景因素<br>1.6 理解特定学科中可持续工程实践的范围、原则、规范、责任和界限</td></tr>
<tr><td>问题分析</td><td rowspan="5">2. 工程应用能力<br>2.1 能够应用既定的工程方法解决复杂工程问题<br>2.2 能够熟练运用工程技术、工具和资源<br>2.3 能够实施系统性的工程集成与设计流程<br>2.4 能够在工程项目实施和管理中应用系统化方法</td></tr>
<tr><td>设计/开发解决方案</td></tr>
<tr><td>调查研究</td></tr>
<tr><td>现代工具的使用</td></tr>
<tr><td>项目管理和财务</td></tr>
<tr><td>工程师与社会</td><td rowspan="6">3. 专业与个人素养<br>3.1 拥有道德操守和职业责任<br>3.2 能够在专业和非专业领域进行有效的口头和书面交流<br>3.5 能够有序进行自我管理，遵守专业行为规范<br>3.6 能够有效维护团队成员关系，发挥团队领导能力</td></tr>
<tr><td>环境与可持续发展</td></tr>
<tr><td>伦理</td></tr>
<tr><td>个人和团队工作</td></tr>
<tr><td>沟通</td></tr>
<tr><td>终身学习</td></tr>
<tr><td>—</td><td>3.3 拥有创造性、创新性和积极主动的行为举止</td></tr>
<tr><td>—</td><td>3.4 能够对信息进行专业化使用和管理</td></tr>
</table>

### 2.3.2 标准的实施程序

#### 1. 认证组织层面

认证相关事宜主要由澳大利亚工程师协会任命的评估小组执行。评估小组的人员构成具有多样性,包括主席、2~10 名核心小组成员(包括主席)、澳大利亚工程师协会会员。其中,有不参加考查的顾问、来自澳大利亚及海外认证机构的小组观察员。不同成员分工明确、各司其职,协同参与材料审核、校园考查等工作[2]。校园考查以认证标准为依据,以实地检验专业对标准的达成情况,历时 2~3 天,考查工作授权评估小组实施,考查日程将依据院校、学院、专业的特点而专门制定,但大多数会按照一个相对固定的流程进行,即会见专业所在学院的高层管理人员、专业负责人、教师、学生、行业咨询机构成员、用人单位、毕业生代表等专业利益相关者,参观学校的设施设备,查看自评报告中未包括的记录资料,例如,学生作业、教学材料、质量保障程序等。校园考查通常以现场考查的方式进行。

考查结束后,评估小组将依据材料审阅结果及校园考查情况拟定认证报告初稿,并提交至认证委员会接受审核,如果审核通过,则将初稿送到学校征询校方反馈,参考校方意见后对其进行定稿,最后将修改后的报告送至认证委员会进行认证结论审议。认证结论包括[12]:无条件授予或继续授予为期五年的全面认证;授予或继续授予为期五年的全面认证,需在规定期限(通常为一年)内向委员会提交中期改进报告;授予或继续授予五年以内的全面认证,在认证期满时提交后续申请,并接受考查,从而保持认证状态;对于新专业或有重大修改的专业采取临时认证,当专业有一定数量学生完成培养方案后再对其进行进一步审查;在一定期限内延缓认证,在此期间,要求教育机构解决委员会提出的实质性问题,委员会将根据问题解决情况决定是否继续认证;拒绝或撤销认证。

#### 2. 学校层面

在接受认证的过程中,学校所需准备的材料主要包括:自评报告及其证明材料、学校与学院相关信息资料、用于校园考查的材料。

自评报告是以认证标准为评价指标,对专业发展概况做出的简洁而连贯的自我分析。学校在撰写自评报告时,需准确阐述每条认证标准的达成情况,并提供相关支撑材料,例如学生的毕业率与留级率、毕业生反馈与就业数据、教师的简历信息等,报告应尽可能地简明扼要,在说明“专业的实施环境”与“质量体系”这两项标准的达成情况时,要立足学院大环境,而不能局限于某一个专业[12]。自评报告由导言、认证标准达成举证、附件三部分构成。第二部分简单列出学校自评时所需阐释的指标点,没有附加的指导性说明[13],为专业解读认证标准预留了空间,学校在陈述认证标准达成度时具有一定的灵活性和自主性。

除了自评报告及其支撑材料,学校还需提供学校、学院相关的信息资料,即校历,包含有专业公开声明的手册、日历增刊或其他官方出版物,专业宣传资料中所提及的主要项目以及网站对这些项目的参考情况。

同时,学校需准备用于现场考查的材料,以便评估小组依据认证标准对专业概况做出客观全面的评价,具体材料类别及考查目的见表 11。

表 11　澳大利亚工程教育专业认证校园考查的材料类别及其考查目的[12]

| 材料类别 | 考查目的 |
| --- | --- |
| 专业教学团队会议、专业设计与评审会议、外部咨询委员会或其他行业咨询机构会议、专业年度审查报告等记录 | 了解教育教学设计、专业审查、持续改进的程序 |
| 师生咨询委员会及其他有关学生反馈机制的材料、学生反馈意见的调查记录 | 了解专业在持续改进过程中对学生反馈意见的听取情况 |
| 学习评价、学业成绩的相关材料，如考试材料、学生作业、实验与实践成果等 | 了解专业对学生能力的培养情况 |
| 小组作业或设计项目的主要内容、实施过程及评价标准 | 了解学生在小组作业、大型设计项目中的表现情况 |
| 部分毕业年级学生的论文与设计项目 | 了解顶石活动（capstone activities）对毕业生能力评价的有效性 |
| 实践报告或相关证明材料 | 了解专业实践情况 |
| 学生的反思性实践成果 | 了解学生是否具备自我批判能力，能否反思学习经历和未来工程师职业生涯的价值 |

## 2.4　日本

日本工程教育认证委员会（Japan Accreditation Board for Engineering Education，JABEE）是一个非政府性的第三方认证机构，以公众对专业人员期望的知识和能力以及社会需求为基准，对高等教育机构的工程、农业、科学等相关专业进行认证。JABEE 的认证标准具有国际等效性，经认证专业毕业的学生可以免去注册专业工程师的第一阶段考试。工程教育专业认证标准由通用标准和专业补充标准构成，其中，专业补充标准覆盖学士、硕士两个学历层次，本文仅对通用标准部分进行探讨。

### 2.4.1　标准的内涵逻辑

日本工程教育专业认证标准由 4 个通用标准项、11 个通用标准观测点构成（图 3）。认证标准层次清晰，归整了部分具有关联性的指标。

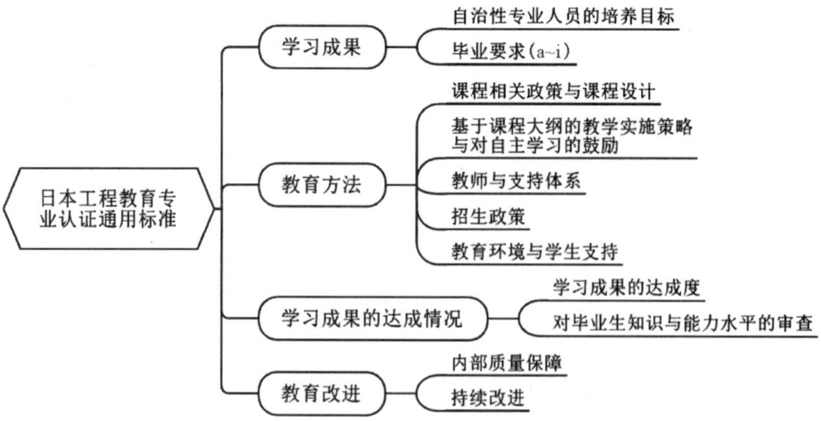


图 3　日本工程教育专业认证通用标准的基本框架

具体内容如下[14]。

"学习成果"包含两点要求：一是制定并公开专业培养目标，目标制定应充分考虑教育传统、资源、毕业生就业领域、社会发展需求、学生个体发展要求等影响因素；二是根据 9 条毕业要求，设定毕业生在知识、能力、素养等方面应达到的标准。将 9 条毕业要求与《华盛顿协议》的 12 条毕业要求对比后发现（表 12），日本对 12 条毕业要求进行了整合与分解，同时补充新的能力要素，例如从全球视野、多元思考能力等方面提出新的要求。

**表 12 《华盛顿协议》12 条毕业要求与日本毕业要求标准项的对应关系**

| 《华盛顿协议》12 条毕业要求 | 日本毕业要求标准项 |
|---|---|
| 工程知识 | （a）能够运用全球战略性知识进行多元思考<br>（c）掌握对数学、自然科学、信息技术等相关知识的应用能力<br>（d）具备专业领域知识及其应用能力 |
| 问题分析 | 包含于（a）、（c）、（d）、（e）四项标准中 |
| 设计/开发解决方案 | （e）根据社会需求，具有灵活运用各种科学、技术和信息化手段进行设计的能力 |
| 调查研究 | 包含于（a）、（c）、（d）、（e）四项标准中 |
| 现代工具的使用 | 包含于（a）、（c）、（d）、（e）四项标准中 |
| 工程师与社会 | （b）理解职业活动对社会和自然的影响以及工程技术人员应承担的社会责任 |
| 环境与可持续发展 | |
| 伦理 | |
| 个人和团队工作 | （i）具有在团队中工作的能力 |
| 沟通 | （f）具有沟通技巧及逻辑表达、演讲和辩论的能力 |
| 项目管理和财务 | （h）在特定条件下，具有管理和完成任务的能力 |
| 终身学习 | （g）具有自主学习和终身学习的能力 |

"教育方法"涵盖的内容较为丰富，涉及课程、教师、学生、教育环境等方面。就课程而言，要求专业制定各项毕业要求的评价标准与方法，确定每门课程与毕业要求之间的关系，并向师生公开教学大纲，专业教学应以教学大纲为基础，鼓励学生开展自主学习。就教师而言，要求专业为课程实施提供合格的师资，例如教师具备注册工程师执业资格，积极参与学科前沿性研究，坚持持续职业发展等。同时，要求建立起相应的支持体系，支持体系包括基于课程协调的教学实施保障机制、基于教师教学活动评价的质量改进机制。就学生而言，要求专业制定招生相关政策，并严格按照招生政策招录学生。就教育环境而言，一方面要求学校配备完善的设施、资源和组织结构体系，并对其进行定期维护、操作与更新，另一方面要求为学生学习提供支持。

"学习成果的达成情况"可概括为：基于教学大纲中的评价方法和评价标准对毕业要求达成度进行定期评价；拥有相关政策以认定学生在其他学校或学院获得的学分，审查并证明毕业生实现了培养目标，满足所有毕业要求。

"教育改进"规定学校应有完善的内部质量保障制度，向师生公开内部质量保障相关活动，定期审查内部质量保障机制，在此过程中，征询学生、社会等不同利益群体的需求。同时，专业应构建起持续改进机制，将审查或评价结果用以促进专业持续发展。

### 2.4.2 标准的实施程序

#### 1. 认证组织层面

日本工程教育专业认证工作由评估小组实施，小组成员学科背景多元，包含主审查员、副审查员以及审查研修员，同时建立新任审查员的岗前培训制度，注重主审查员领导力培训，形成相对固定的审查研修员后备力量[15]。其评估工作可分为两类：现场考查与书面审查。现场考查适用于首次评估、延长认证期的评估、专业结构发生变化的评估、陈述理由的评估以及部分中期评估，书面审查则主要针对一部分中期评估[16]。

现场考查包含考查前、考查中、考查后三个阶段的工作。考查前，评估小组成员将基于自评报告及支撑材料对专业概况做出初步评估，确定自评报告中缺失或需进一步核实的内容，列出现场考查需要学校提供的材料。自评报告审查结果告知学校后，学校需在规定时间内做出回应、补充相关支撑材料，评估小组则根据学校反馈及小组成员意见，拟定现场考查计划，完成考查前的专业审查报告，确定考查重点。考查中，评估小组内部、评估小组同专业利益相关方需召开多次会议，评估小组将与学生、专业负责人、教师等群体进行面谈，审查反映认证标准达标情况的证明文件，参观专业相关的设施和设备，并根据现场考查情况完善专业审查报告。考查结束后，评估小组将依据专业审查报告及学校的补充说明，撰写一期评估报告，并向学校征询一期评估报告的反馈意见，学校可提交书面异议及改进报告，评估小组则根据学校提交的回应材料修改和完善一期评估报告，形成二期评估报告。

书面审查只需对专业提交的自评报告做出评价，适用于需要中期评估的专业，与现场考查的实施流程相比，省略了实地考查的环节。

最终认证结论将根据认证标准达成度的评定结果做出，主要采用“S”“W”“D”三级评判制：S 为 satisfy，意为符合认证标准，结论有效期为六年；W 为 weakness，意为基本符合认证标准，但须通过持续改进以增强标准达成度，结论有效期为三年，期满需接受中期检查；D 为 deficiency，意为不符合认证标准，未通过认证[16]。

#### 2. 学校层面

材料准备是学校接受认证过程中必不可少的环节，与其他国家类似，日本工程专业认证所需准备的材料主要包括自评报告及其支撑材料、用于现场考查的材料。

自评报告由三部分构成：概要、自评结果与附录。概要部分要求阐述专业基本信息、专业发展概况、近期的专业改进措施、对自评结果的总结。自评结果部分以一般疑问句的方式提出专业所需回答的问题，要求专业列表展示认证标准各项指标的达成情况，表格的内容包括自评结论、对专业如何满足认证标准各项指标的陈述、自上次认证以来的改进或变化、证明材料名称及所在位置。其中，自评结论可用“XX”“X”“R”加以标注，“XX”表示专业满足了认证标准的所有要求，并进行了额外的改进工作，“X”表示专业满足了认证标准的所有要求，“R”表示尽管专业满足了认证标准的所有要求，但仍有改进空间[17]。附录部分要求附上需要大量时间审查的证明材料的代表性样本，所需提交的材料有：上一次评审结果的复印件、毕业要求与 9 条学习成果标准(a)~(i)之间的对应关系、毕业要求各项指标的评价标准与评价方法、课程设计与课程实施的相关政策、基于毕业要求的课程体系设计、自评报告附录部分的材料清单、用于现场考查的材料清单、专业相关的数据信息(如招生数量、毕业生数量、全职与兼职教师数量、专业课程的学分数量等)[17]。

现场考查需要专业提供的材料有两类:学业成绩的记录材料、反映毕业生学习成果达成度的相关材料。前者包括近两年的考试试卷、成绩分析记录表、报告、毕业论文等文件,后者特指反映毕业生知识和能力水平的证明文件,达成 70%~80%学习成果标准被认定为合格毕业生的衡量指标[17]。

## 3　四国工程教育专业认证标准的共性与差异分析

### 3.1　认证标准内涵逻辑的共性与差异分析

(1)通用标准的内容实质对等,层级划分特色鲜明。

从整体上看,四个国家工程教育专业认证的通用标准都有与学生、毕业要求、课程、持续改进、设施、支持条件等相关的要求。但不同国家认证标准的层次结构具有差异性,美国的通用标准分类较细,没有独立设置通用标准观测点,各通用标准项的具体要求多以段落形式加以陈述,爱尔兰、澳大利亚、日本认证标准的层级划分清晰,通用标准项数量较少,下设通用标准观测点,通用标准观测点多以"标题+解释性语句"的形式呈现,把握各项认证标准之间的关联,同时增加部分具有本国特色的认证标准。例如:爱尔兰设置"专业领域"这一标准,从七个方面为专业达成预期成果指明方向;澳大利亚在通用标准观测点中强调"对专业实践的参与",将工程实践作为专业与课程设计的一个重要考查因素;日本把"学习成果的达成情况"设为独立的认证标准,进一步凸显定期审查学习成果、评价学习成果达成度对专业持续改进的重要性。

(2)四国毕业要求在与《华盛顿协议》保持基本一致的前提下均有所变通。

从毕业要求这一维度看,四个国家在坚持实质等效原则的基础上,均对《华盛顿协议》的 12 条毕业要求进行了一定调整,主要表现为整合、分解、增设、提高四类措施。整合即对关联性较强的能力要求进行归类或融合。归类频率较高的毕业要求有三条,即工程师与社会、环境与可持续发展、伦理。融合是指将现代工具的使用、项目管理和财务等毕业要求暗含于其他能力要求中。分解即对已有毕业要求的细化或分列,例如,日本将"工程知识"拆分为"能够运用全球战略性知识进行多元思考""掌握对数学、自然科学、信息技术等相关知识的应用能力""具备专业领域知识及其应用能力"三项能力要求。增设即新增除 12 条毕业要求以外的其他成果标准,例如,澳大利亚在"专业与个人素养"中要求毕业生具备创新创造能力、信息运用与管理能力,日本在学习成果中强调全球性视角、多元思考能力与素养的重要性。提高即对现有毕业要求的更新或升级,升级的典型代表是美国在修订毕业要求时关注现代工程问题的复杂性和综合性,将"工程知识"与"问题分析"合并为一条能力要求,对能力的考查更加注重整体性和系统性。

(3)四国有关课程的规定侧重点不同,均强调以毕业要求为指引,支撑毕业要求的达成。

从课程这一维度看，四个国家均强调课程体系设计以毕业要求为指引，课程教学应支撑毕业要求达成。美国规定了专业需包含的主要课程类型以及每种课程类型所应达到的最低学时。爱尔兰有关课程的规定更多是对如何帮助毕业生达成毕业要求的深度解读。澳大利亚要求说明专业与课程设计方法、毕业要求在具体学习单元内的实现路径以及专业实践能力的培养过程。日本注重考查专业是否有课程相关政策，课程设计是否有利于实现学习成果，课程实施是否遵循教学大纲，课程教学是否鼓励学生的自主学习等。

（4）爱尔兰、澳大利亚的认证标准对接国家资历框架中学历等级、学习年限等相关的规定。

爱尔兰、澳大利亚工程教育专业认证通用标准与国家资历框架相适应，在保障工程教育整体质量、推进各类工程人才培养协调贯通、实现教育资历互认等方面发挥着重要作用。爱尔兰、澳大利亚基于国家资历框架中学历等级、学习年限等相关规定，针对不同工程人才培养类型，制定入学门槛、专业结构与年限等认证标准，推进各级各类工程教育的相互衔接与一体化发展。同时，爱尔兰还在认证标准的学时计算中采纳欧洲学分转换与累积制度，以促进工程人才的国际流动与欧洲范围内学历的相互承认。

（5）四国在师资审查中凸显对教师专业与工程师职业资格的重视。

从教师这一维度看，四个国家主要从教师的数量、质量、结构、专业发展、支持体系、管理制度等方面提出认证要求。在质量上，要求教师具备合格的从业资质，资质审核包含教师的教育背景、实践经历、教学技能、综合素养、专业权威等。由于工程教育的特殊性，各国尤为重视从业人员的专业身份与职业资格，例如，要求教师成为工程相关专业学会或行业协会会员，鼓励教师兼任企业技术顾问、积极参与校企协同育人等。在建立完备注册工程师制度的基础上，各国还将教师的工程师资质纳入资质考查的范畴，实现了工程教育专业认证与工程师职业资格制度的有效衔接。

（6）四国秉持持续改进理念，质量管理贯穿于人才培养全过程。

从持续改进这一维度看，各国主张通过内外部质量保障促进专业的可持续发展，相关认证要求贯穿于人才培养的全过程、多方面，可概括为以下几点：有相关文件说明培养目标、毕业要求的制定与实现过程；对教学过程实施质量管理，通过多元评价手段监测学生表现；有效评价、定期审查毕业要求及培养目标的达成度与合理性，评价或审查过程有不同利益相关者参与，吸纳多元利益群体的诉求；评价结果能用于完善课程体系，改进各教学环节，促进专业的持续发展；能基于上次的认证报告改进专业中存在的问题。

### 3.2 认证标准实施程序的共性与差异分析

整体而言，四个国家均建立了较为完善的认证标准运行机制，将标准的达成度评价贯穿于认证全过程，各国的认证程序主要包括：认证申请，提交自评报告及相关支撑材料，材料审阅，现场（线上）考查，撰写认证报告，意见征询，得出结论。

（1）现场（线上）考查的内容与流程具有相似性。

现场（线上）考查内容涉及专业成果达成度、专业人才培养过程、专业实施环境、专业质量保障四个方面。为了从多元视角了解专业实际情况，考查时会与教师、学生、专业负责人、高层管理人员等不同利益相关者进行沟通交流，参观设施设备，审查各类文件材料。访问结束后，评估小组将根据考查结果撰写认证报告草案，总结专业对认证标准的达成情况，不同国家在标准达成度的表述上略有差异。最后，报告草案需返至学校征询反馈意见，评估小组根据反馈意见修订报告，形成最终认证报告，然后提交给认证组织审批。

（2）四国确立了认证小组组建原则，强调成员构成多样化与专家培训制度化。

能否通过现场（线上）考查对专业概况做出有效评价，很大程度上取决于认证小组的考查能力，因此各国在认证相关文件中明确了认证小组的组建原则。例如：美国、澳大利亚注重小组成员构成的多样性，要求形成认证机构内部成员与其他机构成员、考查人员与顾问人员并存的异质考查小组；爱尔兰主张对多个接受认证的专业实施联合认证，即通过合并专业小组以构建认证小组的方式进行评估；日本强调小组成员学科背景的多元化，针对不同成员建立起独具特色的培训制度与管理办法。

（3）美国、澳大利亚认证结论类型多样，爱尔兰、日本分类较为简洁，四国认证结论具有周期性。

认证结论基于认证标准达成度的评估结果做出，为了贯彻持续改进的认证理念、帮助学校形成周期性审查的专业发展文化，其结论具有动态性和实效性。各国认证结论的类型多样，“认证通过”的有效期通常为五或六年，在“通过”与“不通过”之间还增设了补件再审、有条件通过等情况，结论有效期从两年至四年不等。其中，爱尔兰、日本的认证结论分类较为简洁，主要采用三级评定制，将认证标准的达标情况划分为符合、大部分符合、不符合三类，针对各类型设定不同的认证有效期。美国、澳大利亚根据认证过程中发现问题的大小及可能遇到的特殊情况，对认证结论进行细分，尽量规避认证决议的笼统性和不公平性。

（4）四国自评报告的内容构成具有相似性，但自评指导独具特色。

四个国家自评报告的内容构成具有相似性，主要包括专业背景信息、认证标准达成举证、附录三项内容。虽然各国均指出自评要以认证标准为依据，但在指导评估认证标准达成度上却存在差异。爱尔兰基于认证标准的核心要求及专业的概况信息，规定自评报告应包含 13 项内容，对原有认证标准进行详尽解构与要素重组，明晰了自评要点；美国在自评报告模板中逐条对认证标准进行要素分解，要求专业对细化后的标准的达成情况做出判断，为专业解读认证标准提供了明确指导；日本基于认证标准的各项指标提出不同问题，这些问题多采用一般疑问句的句式，可用简单的表述加以回答，从而规范了自评程序，降低了自评难度；澳大利亚仅在自评报告模板中列出认证标准，没有过多的指导性说明，为专业解读认证标准预留了空间。四个国家均强调自评报告撰写应注重实证性和系统性，具体而言，自评是基于事实的评价，需以一定数量的证明材料作为支撑，要为审查员提供最大信息量以供其执行评估，同时，自评时应注意把握认证标准各项指标之间的内在逻辑关系，以专业成果为导向，以人才培养过程、专业实施环境为支撑，以专业质量管理为保障。

（5）美国、澳大利亚、日本明确了各认证环节材料审查的重点。

美国、澳大利亚、日本详细说明学校所需提供的材料类别，且对自评报告中的支撑材料与用于现场考查的材料加以区分。纵观两类材料，同一份材料，有的国家要求在自评报告或线上平台呈现，有的国家则要求在现场考查中提供，两种材料可概括为以下几个类别：反映毕业要求制定与修订过程、毕业要求达成度的证明材料；与专业管理与质量保障相关的政策文件；反映课程体系设计、课程实施过程、课程与毕业要求之间关系的证明材料；上一次的专业评审结果；设施设备的举例说明；专业相关数据信息（如招生与毕业生数量、教职工人员构成）等。

## 4 经验与启示

我国于2016年正式加入《华盛顿协议》，在保障工程教育质量以及促进工程教育国际互认上取得了重要进展。由于工程教育专业认证起步较晚，工程教育体量大和大学层次多，加之社会发展对工程技术人才需求的变化，我国工程教育专业认证体系尚处于不断完善阶段。因此，要根据工程教育和科技发展趋势，对作为专业认证核心的认证标准进行定期审查与持续改进。通过分析爱尔兰、美国、澳大利亚、日本的工程教育专业认证通用标准及相关政策文件，从标准的层级结构、内容构成、实施程序三个维度，总结得到的对未来认证标准变革的启示如下。

（1）优化认证标准的层级划分，把握各项标准之间的内在关联。

我国工程教育专业认证的通用标准包含学生、培养目标、毕业要求、持续改进、课程体系、师资队伍、支撑条件七大内容，涉及专业产出、专业人才培养过程、专业实施环境、专业管理与质量保障四个方面，通用标准分类较细，下设的通用标准观测点多以简短的句式加以阐述。建议探究工程教育质量保障中的核心要素，分析现有通用标准之间的关联性与相互作用原理，通过优化认证标准的层次结构，厘清各项指标的内涵逻辑与运作机制。同时，进一步明确每项标准达成的操作要点，为专业解读认证标准以及实施自我评价提供有效指导。

（2）立足本国国情，通过整合、分解、增设、提高等方式适时修订毕业要求。

我国通用标准中的毕业要求主要沿用了《华盛顿协议》的12条毕业要求，受科学技术创新、可持续发展理念日益深化等因素的影响，社会对未来工程技术人才的需求应时而变，为了建立中国特色、国际实质等效的认证标准，需适时修订毕业要求。建议借鉴爱尔兰、美国、澳大利亚、日本四国的实践，通过整合、分解、增设、提高等方式对毕业要求加以调整：其一，对关联性较强的毕业要求进行归类、融合与升级；其二，对现有毕业要求中笼统模糊、内容缺失、不合时宜的部分进行细化、补充及更新；其三，顺应社会发展、技术更新、产业升级等的变化趋势，增加除现有毕业要求以外的其他能力要求，如创新创业能力。同时，为进一步强化“立德树人”的根本要求，应考虑如何将中华优秀传统文化与社会主义核心价值观中的和谐、诚信等要素融入认证标准中。

（3）重视师资队伍建设，强化认证标准对教师专业权威与工程师资质的审查。

通用标准从教师的数量、结构、职业能力、职责等方面对师资队伍做出了规定，但部分参与认证的专业并未对教师的工程经验、工程背景设立相应门槛与判断依据，不能说明这些经验、背景在教学活动中的作用，以至于无法明确师资队伍是否达到了认证标准要求。建议通用标准进一步强化对教师专业水平、工程经验等职业能力的审查，确立各项指标达成的操作要点，例如，要求教师具备相关专业领域的工程师执业资格，拥有一定年限的企业工作经历，积极参与专业学会或行业协会活动等。因此，需加快建成我国工程师执业资格制度，通过建立完备的注册工程师制度，将工程师资质纳入工科专业课教师资格审查的范畴。

（4）增设与人才培养过程相关的认证要求，将对课程的考查与教学相结合。

我国通用标准中从属于专业人才培养过程的仅有课程体系，对培养方案实施路径、学习形式等的考查较为薄弱，因此，建议制定有关如何实现毕业要求的认证标准，在宏观层面强调多样化的人才培养模式，在微观层面鼓励丰富的课程学习形式。同时，将课程考查与教学结合起来，增加针对课程教学组织形式、教学方法等的具体认证要求。例如，可借鉴澳大利亚的做法，在认证标准中制定相关规定，明确毕业要求实现路径、教育理念及培养方案实施程序等内容，从毕业要求、教学内容、教学方法、教学评价等维度对专业课程提出认证要求。

（5）加快建设国家资历框架，推动实现工程教育专业认证标准与资历框架标准体系对接。

国家资历框架是以学习结果为导向，按照统一标准对国家范围内的各种资历进行合理编排而形成的有关知识、能力、技能水平的资格阶梯，发挥着融通教育体系、促进资格转换与鉴定、指导制定具体资格标准等功能，对完善工程教育专业认证标准具有一定的启发意义。我国于2016年首次以政策性文件提出制定国家资历框架，目前还处于探索发展阶段，顶层设计尚未完成。建议加快建设国家资历框架，促进工程教育专业认证标准与资历框架中资格等级标准、资格类型标准、资格类型规范的部分规定相适应。

（6）建立常态化的认证专家遴选与培训机制。

我国工程教育专业认证的现场考查和材料审核工作通常由本专业领域专家和相关行业技术专家承担。建议完善认证专家遴选条件，优化遴选程序，拓宽遴选渠道，注重专家库人员构成的多样性与异质性。现场考查专家组除了认证专家和秘书，还可适当增加顾问人员和观察员，顾问人员不必直接参与考查。同时，加强对认证专家的管理与培训，通过理论培训、现场考查见习、定期轮训、周期性评价等办法，提高认证专家的评估与考查能力。

（7）采取线上与线下相结合的考查方式。

为提高工作效率，增强认证方式的灵活性与适用性，建议优化认证程序，采取线上与线下相结合的考查方式，学校及专家组应根据实际情况，有针对性地进行选择。线上考查通过现代信息化手段展开，可由部分人员执行或在部分环节中实施，线下考查主要指专家入校的现场考查。这一混合考查方式应明确各环节的考查重点，强化材料审核工作，严格把控学校各类材料的真实性，紧扣毕业要求的制定、落实与评价，关注专业是否对产出目标的达成情况做出了有效评价。

（8）丰富认证结论的类型，增强认证弹性。

我国工程教育专业认证结论有三种：通过、不通过及有条件通过。“有条件通过”适用于存在问题或需关注事项的专业，专业应在第三年提交改进情况报告。为贯彻持续改进的认证理念，同时为鼓励更多专业参与认证，建议丰富认证结论的类型，增强认证的弹性与适用性。一方面，根据专业存在问题的大小，设定不同有效期的认证结论，此处可借鉴美国或日本的做法，将问题细分为不足（weakness）、缺陷（deficiency）两类；另一方面，针对专业存在的特殊情况，例如新兴专业、有重大调整的专业，可采取临时认证或在一定期限内延缓认证的方式。

（9）完善自评报告模板，加强专业自评指导。

我国现有自评报告指导书以认证标准的各项指标为基本单元，对学校需要说明的情况及所需提供的材料做出明确规定。虽然为学校解读认证标准提供了详尽指导,但也可能导致专业出现套用模板、堆积制度文件的现象。建议在自评指导中突出毕业要求的主线要求及产出评价机制的底线要求,为学校解读和实现认证标准预留一定空间,减轻学校撰写自评报告的压力及专家审阅负担,对于部分较难把握的认证标准,可进行适当解构,提取出考查要点或通过设置简单问题以供专业回答。同时,需引导专业注重自评的系统性、实证性与特色化,使其把握各项标准之间的内部关联,对专业实际开展的工作进行客观描述,突出专业发展的个性特征。

(10)明确自评报告审阅与现场考查的重点,增强二者之间的互补性。

自评报告审阅应高度关注专业是否建立了面向产出的教育体系,包括审查人才培养方案、教学大纲等材料,以初步判断认证标准达成度;现场考查应注重核实自评报告关键内容的准确性,考查自评报告中未能反映的问题,从而进一步评价认证标准达标情况。此外,建议相关文件对自评报告中的附件材料及现场考查所需审阅的材料加以区分,避免材料的重复提供,现场考查除了审阅反映学生能力达标情况的学习材料外,还可适当查阅部分教学材料及产出目标(培养目标、毕业要求、课程目标)的评价记录等。

## 5 结语

在新一轮科技革命与产业革命的历史交汇期,我国深入推进新工科建设,将工程教育的质量标准建设列为重要攻关目标。为构建新标准、引领新质量,需积极探索国际工程教育质量标准的变革趋势,加快构建中国特色、国际实质等效的工程教育专业认证标准。本文以《华盛顿协议》四个成员为研究对象,从内涵逻辑与实施程序两个维度,对各国工程教育专业认证的通用标准进行了案例分析,总结了经验和启示,希望为我国认证标准变革提供有价值的参考。为了充分证实研究结论的有效性与适用性,还有待后续学者选择《华盛顿协议》的其他成员以及认证标准的其他维度(如认证标准变革的深层原因与利益博弈)进行进一步研究。

### 参考文献


[1] Engineers Ireland. Accreditation Criteria[EB/OL].(2021-01-03)[2021-05-30]. https://www.engineersireland.ie/listings/resource/519.

[2] 吴岩. 国际高等教育质量保障新视野[M]. 北京:教育科学出版社,2014.

[3] Engineers Ireland. Procedure for Accreditation of Engineering Education Programm-es[EB/OL].(2021-04-05)[2021-06-02]. https://www.engineersireland.ie/listings/resource/587.

[4] ABET. Criteria for Accrediting Engineering Programs[EB/OL].(2020-10-31)[2021-06-03]. https://www.abet.org/wp-content/uploads/2021/02/E001-21-22-EAC-Criteria.pdf.

[5] ABET. Rationale for Revising Criteria 3 and 5[EB/OL].(2015-10-30)[2021-06-05]. https://www.abet.org/ration-ale-for-revising-criteria-3-and-5/.

[6] ABET. Accreditation Policy and Procedure Manual[EB/OL].(2020-10-31)[2021-06-05]. https://www.abet.org/wp-content/uploads/2021/01/A001-21-22-Accreditation-Policy-and-

Procedure-Manual.pdf.
[7] ABET. ABET Self-Study Questionnaire：Template for a Self-Study Report for Engineering Accreditation Commission（2021-2022 Review Cycle）[EB/OL].（2020-10-31）[2021-06-06]. https://www.abet.org/accreditati-on/accreditation-criteria/self-study-templates/.
[8] RASHID M.A systematic approach of data preparation for ABET accreditation[J]. International journal of engineering education，2021，37（1）：1-13.
[9] Engineers Australia. Accreditation Criteria User Guide-Higher Education[EB/OL].（2019-08-26）[2021-06-10]. https://www.engineersaustralia.org.au/sites/default/files/2019-09/AMS-MAN-10_Accreditation_Criteria_User_Guide-Higher_Education_v2.0.pdf.
[10] Engineers Australia. Accreditation Standard-Higher Education[EB/OL].（2017-12-15）[2021-06-10]. https://www.engineersaustral-ia.org.au/sites/default/files/2019-08/AMS-STD-10_Accreditation_Standard-Higher_Education_v1.0.pdf.
[11] Engineers Australia. Stage 1 Competency Standard for Professional Engineer[EB/OL].（2019-11）[2021-06-12]. https://www.engineersaustralia.org.au/sites/default/files/2019-11/Stage1_Competency_Standards.pdf.
[12] Engineers Australia. Procedures Manual-Higher Education[EB/OL].（2018-07-16）[2021-06-13]. https://www.engineersaustralia.org.au/sites/default/files/2018-07/AMS-MAN-11_Procedures_Manual-Higher_Education_v1.0.pdf.
[13] Engineers Australia. Accreditation Submission（Self-study Report）[EB/OL].（2019-11-03）[2021-06-13]. https://www.engineersaustralia.org.au/About-Us/Accreditation/AMS-2019.
[14] JABEE. JABEE Common Criteria for Accreditation of Professional Education Programs Applicable in the year 2019 and later[EB/OL].（2019-01-15）[2021-06-17]. https://jabee.org/doc/Common_Criteria2019.pdf.
[15] JABEE. 審査団の構成基準[EB/OL].（2020-12-23）[2021-06-17]. https://jabee.org/doc/2021team.pdf.
[16] JABEE. 認定？審査の手順と方法[EB/OL].（2020-12-23）[2021-06-19]. https://jabee.org/accreditation/basis/examination/doc.
[17] JABEE.2020 年度認定？審査用資料[EB/OL].（2020-10-01）[2021-06-19]. https://jabee.org/doc/2020shiryo.pdf.

# 国际工程教育专业认证体系的发展与改革
## ——基于《华盛顿协议》与欧洲工程教育专业认证体系的对比分析 ①

朱 露 胡德鑫 何 桢 顾佩华

**摘要:**国际工程教育专业认证形成以美国等为代表的《华盛顿协议》(WA)体系和以德、法等为代表的欧洲工程教育专业认证(EUR-ACE)体系两大阵营。本研究基于多维比较研究的视角,从历史沿革、组织结构、认证标准、认证程序、运行机制五个维度对EUR-ACE体系和WA体系进行对比分析;以双体系典型参与国——俄罗斯为样例,对其发展现状、运行机制与典型特征进行深度解析。研究结果显示:①WA体系和EUR-ACE体系坚持持续改进的基本工作逻辑,遵循组织体系日臻完善、认证范围不断扩大、国际化价值取向日益突显的演化规律;②建构决策层、管理层、服务层和执行层四级联动的组织架构,形成集合作、监管、协调为一体的组织运行机制;③EUR-ACE体系采取标签授权制,而WA体系实行成员组织授权制,二者均赋予相关认证机构认证高度自主权;④WA体系与多边协议相关联,强调各参与组织认证标准的等效性和可比性,而EUR-ACE体系各组织的认证标准更具全面性、灵活性;⑤作为两大认证体系的交叉成员组织,俄罗斯融合吸收二者的精髓,很大程度上实现认证制度的特色化构建。借鉴两大体系成熟的经验,指出未来我国工程教育专业认证体系建设与革新方向。

**关键词:**工程教育专业认证;《华盛顿协议》;欧洲工程教育专业认证体系

# Development and Reform Trend of International Engineering Education Accreditation Systems
## —Comparative Analysis based on Washington Accord and European Engineering Education Accreditation Systems

*Zhu Lu, Hu Dexin, He Zhen, Gu Peihua*

**Abstract:** There are currently two international engineering education accreditation systems: the Washington Accord (WA) system represented by the United States and the European Engineering Education Accreditation (EUR-ACE) system represented by Germany and France. Based on the perspective of multidimensional comparative research, this paper performs a comparative analysis of EUR-ACE system and WA system from five dimensions: historical evolution, organizational structure, accreditation criteria, accreditation procedures and operation mechanism. Taking Russia as an example, an in-depth analysis on its development status, operation mechanism and typical characteristics

① 本文刊登于《高等工程教育研究》2022年第4期第P38~51页。

was documented. The results are as follows. ①The WA system and the EUR-ACE system adhere to the basic working principles of continuous improvement, and follow the evolution process of improving the organizational system, expanding the scope of accreditation and highlighting the international value orientation. ②We should build a four-level linkage organizational structure of decision-making level, management level, service level and execution level, and form an organizational operational mechanism with integrated cooperation, supervision and coordination. ③The EUR-ACE system adopts the label authorization system, while the WA system implements the member organization authorization system, both of which give the relevant accreditation bodies a high degree of autonomy in accreditation. ④The WA system is related to multilateral agreements, emphasizing the equivalence and comparability of accreditation criteria of participating organizations. The accreditation criteria of various organizations of the EUR-ACE system are more comprehensive and flexible. ⑤As a cross member organization of the two certification systems, Russia integrates and absorbs the essence of the two systems and realizes the characteristic construction of the accreditation system to a great extent. Based on the mature experience of the two systems, this paper also discusses future perspectives of the development and innovation of China's engineering education accreditation.

**Keywords**: engineering education accreditation; Washington Accord; European Engineering Education Accreditation System

## 引言

目前，工程领域有两大国际认证体系在全球占主导地位，一是由国际工程联盟（International Engineering Alliance，IEA）管理的《华盛顿协议》（Washington Accord，WA）体系，二是由欧洲工程教育专业认证网络（European Network for Accreditation of Engineering Education，ENAEE）建立的欧洲工程教育专业认证（European Accredited Engineering Programs，EUR-ACE）体系。前者致力于四年制本科工程教育的国际互认工作，后者专注于欧洲乃至全球的学士和硕士层次工程教育专业认证。IEA 与 ENAEE 虽然各自保持独立的认证体系，但也在多方面进行交流合作。2015 年，两大体系联合发布《工程教育专业认证的最佳实践：一个范例》（*Best Practice in Accreditation of Engineering Programs*：*An Exemplar*）文件，从政策、程序、标准三个维度阐释了对工程教育专业认证最佳实践的理解[1]，为世界各国工程教育专业认证体系的建立与完善带来启发。我国成为《华盛顿协议》的正式成员已接近六年，虽然本科工程教育得到国际认可，但工程教育专业认证在实现“形似”到“神似”的转变过程中仍面临难题[2]，例如如何强化立德树人要求、如何增强认证弹性、如何建立本硕有效衔接的工程教育专业认证标准等。因此，亟须进一步汲取国际经验，立足本国国情，着力构建中国特色、国际实质等效的工程教育专业认证体系。以 WA 与 EUR-ACE 体系为研究对象，本文着重从历史沿革、组织结构、认证标准、认证程序和运行机制五个方面对二者进行比较，同时选取双体系典型参与国——俄罗斯进行案例分析，在此基础上探讨两大认证体系的基本特征与形塑逻辑，指出未来我国工程教育专业认证体系的革新方向。

## 1 WA 和 EUR-ACE 体系的多维对比分析

### 1.1 历史沿革的比较

从兴起原因看，EUR-ACE 体系和 WA 体系都旨在实现工程专业的多边互认，增强工程师的国际竞争力，促进工程技术人才的跨界交流与合作。EUR-ACE 体系是在博洛尼亚进程以及欧洲工程师国际流动需求的双重驱动下产生的。一方面，为克服欧洲学位体系的多样性给学位与专业资格认可带来的困难，1999 年，欧盟成员国在意大利博洛尼亚签署《博洛尼亚宣言》，提出建立一个易于解读且具有可比性的学位转换体系，确定到 2010 年建成欧洲高等教育区的发展目标。自此，博洛尼亚进程正式启动，资历框架、学位体系、学分系统、质量保障标准的相互协调推动着欧洲高等教育区域内工程专业的跨国互认。另一方面，受工程国际化、经济全球化、新学位和新教育机构日益增加等趋势的影响，欧洲迫切需要一个全洲认可的工程教育专业认证体系，以适应全球就业市场对工程师国际流动的需求[3]。相比之下，WA 体系的签订源于 6 个原始成员（澳大利亚、加拿大、爱尔兰、新西兰、英国、美国）主张通过签署本科工程教育互认协议，承认签约成员之间认证标准、认证程序、认证相关政策的实质等效性[4]，使得工科毕业生更容易在其他国家获得专业注册，从而增加就业机会，并为注册工程师在全球范围内的流动提供便利。

从发展历程（图 1）看，WA 体系经过 30 余年的发展，成员数量遍布全球，工程相关协议不断丰富，国际影响力日渐提升；相比之下，欧洲工程教育专业认证体系的发起时间略晚于 WA 体系，经过明晰组织职能，规范 EUR-ACE 标签授权程序，实施 EUR-ACE 推广计划等一系列发展，走出了一条既具欧洲特色又与国际接轨的专业认证之路（图 2）。

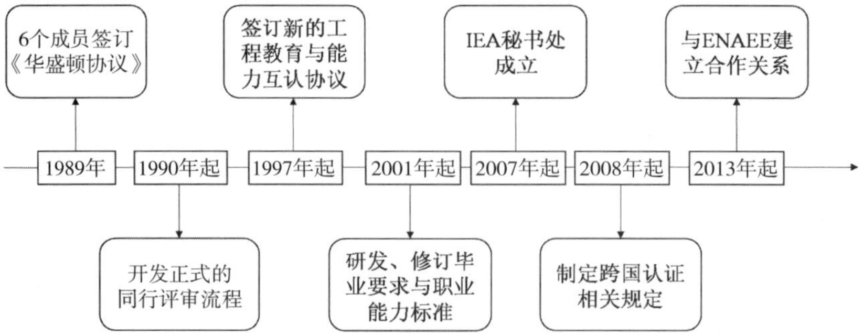


**图 1 WA 体系发展历程**

两大认证体系在历史进程中表现出三个共性特征。其一，组织体系不断趋于完善。1997—2019 年，WA 体系成员针对注册工程师、技师和技术员分别签署工程教育与工程师资格互认协议；ENAEE 的前身是欧洲工程职业与教育常设观察站（European Standing Observatory for the Engineering Profession and Education，ESOEPE），2006 年，ESOEPE 正式更名为 ENAEE，成为注册性的国际非营利组织，同时设立 EUR-ACE 标签委员会负责监管 EUR-ACE 标签的授权工作[5]。其二，注重认证标准及其指导性文件的定期修订。IEA 从 2001 年开始研发、修订毕业要求与职业能力标准（Graduate Attributes and Professional Competencies，GAPC），目前已正式颁布四版GAPC（2005版、2009版、2013版、2021版）[6]。2013版GAPC成为广大签约组织制定毕业要求与职业能力标准的重要依据，至今仍被使用。2019年，世界工程组织联合会与IEA、联合国教科文组织、国际工程教育中心等机构签订合作协议，启动第三版GAPC的修订工作，2021年正式颁布第四版GAPC，在毕业要求中对可持续发展、智力灵活性、创新性等做出规定[6]。ENAEE于2004年制定针对第一学位阶段和第二学位阶段的认证标准[5]，此后定期审查和修订认证标准，修改力度较大的是2015年发布的EUR-ACE标准框架与指导性方针（EUR-ACE Framework Standards and Guidelines，EAFSG），与原始版本（EUR-ACE Framework Standards，EAFS）相比，修订版更加简洁明晰，充分吸纳利益相关者的反馈意见[7]。其三，注重国际组织之间的交流与合作。作为国际上占主导地位的工程教育专业认证组织，ENAEE与IEA始终保持着密切联系，并于2015年联合发布有关工程教育专业认证最佳实践的报告。此外，EUR-ACE体系与WA体系之间存在交叉性组织，典型代表即爱尔兰工程师协会（Engineers Ireland）、英国工程委员会（Engineering Council UK）和俄罗斯工程教育协会（Association for Engineering Education of Russia）。

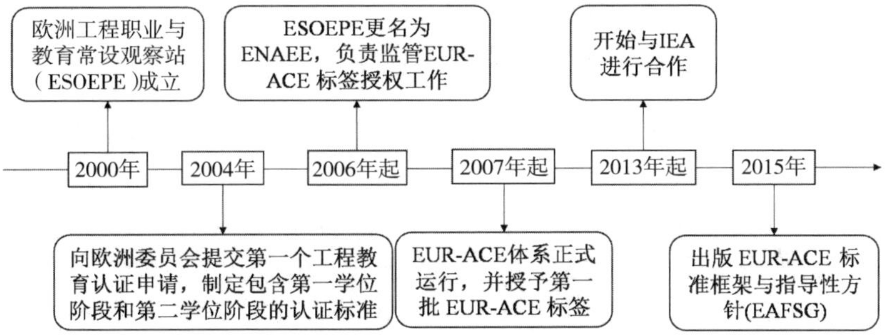


**图2 EUR-ACE体系发展历程**

从未来趋势看，随着工程教育办学模式的多元化发展，EUR-ACE体系和WA体系除了对成员组织本国范围内的认证提出要求外，还不断补充、完善跨国认证的相关规定，发挥了国际认证体系在境外工程教育中的质量保障作用。例如，EUR-ACE体系明确成员组织在本国以及欧洲高等教育区以外开展认证的细则，提出双学位及联合学位的专业认证办法[8]；2014年以前，WA体系规定境外工程教育的认证工作只需由教育提供方的认证组织进行，2014年后，要求实施双重认证，即境外工程教育的认证工作需由教育提供方与教育接受方的认证组织合作进行[9]。此外，为扩充成员数量、增强国际影响力，WA体系与EUR-ACE体系持续顺应国际工程技术人才需求的变化趋势，积极探索工程教育专业认证的最优路径，有效开展国际对话与合作，注重审视自身认证体系的局限性，主动借鉴对方认证实践的成功经验，努力实现资源利用最优化、整体功能最大化。

### 1.2 组织结构的比较

ENAEE作为EUR-ACE体系的直接管理者，建立起上下联动、层次清晰的组织架构（图3）。全体大会是ENAEE的最高决策团体，由各成员组织的一名代表构成，具有政策审批、选举或罢免会员、修订宪章等权力;行政委员会在组织运行中发挥着承上启下的作用,负责处理各委员会的建议,管理 ENAEE 的日常活动,并为全体大会处理政策、会员身份、财务等相关事宜建言献策;行政委员会下设 EUR-ACE 标签委员会、相关委员会和工作组,且注重二者之间的协调性,前者由具有 EUR-ACE 标签授予权的专业认证组织的代表构成,旨在协助行政委员会处理欧洲高等教育区域内 EUR-ACE 标签的授权工作,后者主要根据实际工作需要选择性设立,同时,行政委员会还可成立常设秘书处,以更好地为机构的日常管理提供支持[10]。ENAEE 的成员构成具有多样性,凡是对工程教育及工程师职业发展感兴趣的组织或机构都可申请入会,会员资格有两类[11]:正式会员和准会员。正式会员多为具有合法权限的工程教育专业认证组织;准会员除了专业认证组织,还包括代表教育培训机构或工程专业学生的协会和以维护工程师利益为目的的法律实体。全体大会由 ENAEE 的正式会员组成,行政委员会的成员则由全体大会选举产生,申请 EUR-ACE 标签授权可以不具备 ENAEE 的会员身份[11]。

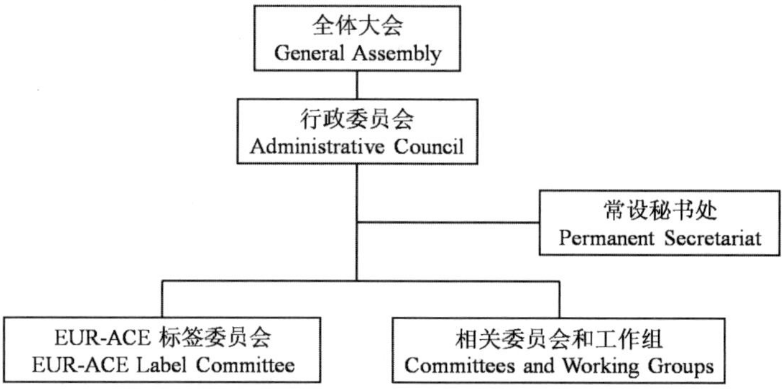


**图 3 ENAEE 组织结构**

WA 体系是 IEA 管辖的工程教育互认协议之一。作为一个由多边协议构成的全球非营利性组织, IEA 从国际视角为各国在制定工程教育要求和工程师能力要求方面建立基准和提供参考(图 4)。多边协议包括七个国际协议,涉及工程人才成长的两个阶段(工程教育阶段与工程实践阶段),面向工程人才培养的三种人才类型(注册工程师、技师和技术员)。协议的成员资格有两类:正式成员和预备成员。不同协议的成员组织之间具有交叉性,例如,若一个专业机构兼具工程教育专业认证资格和工程师职业注册资格,则可同时申请加入工程教育互认协议与工程师能力互认协议。管理组是 IEA 的决策机构,由多边协议的代表成员组成,负责开发、修订工程教育标准和工程师职业能力标准,制定适用于多边协议的管理制度和政策文件,监管秘书处和相关工作组的日常活动等;秘书处是 IEA 的日常事务机构,旨在为管理组、各大协议、相关工作组提供支持与服务;管理组还可设立特定工作组,代表 IEA 调查问题或拟定建议,该工作组以协商一致的方式运作[12]。

EUR-ACE 体系和 WA 体系组织结构的异同可从治理主体与客体两个方面进行比较。就治理主体而言, ENAEE 和 IEA 合理划分职能部门,明确各部门的职责权限,形成决策层、管理层、服务层、执行层四级联动的治理主体群。IEA 的决策管理工作由管理组统一负责,而 ENAEE 分设两个部门,全体大会是决策机构,行政委员会是管理机构。ENAEE 和 IEA

服务层的主体均为秘书处,但执行层的主体略有不同,前者是 EUR-ACE 标签委员会、相关委员会和工作组,后者是七大协议和相关工作组。就治理客体而言, ENAEE 和 IEA 的成员资格可分为准会员和正式会员两类,会员来源具有多样性。ENAEE 会员包括质量保障机构、工程师协会、学生联合会、专业认证组织等异质团体[13],为多元利益相关者参与协同治理、形成治理合力带来契机,此外, ENAEE 的会员身份不是获得 EUR-ACE 标签授予资格的必要条件,这便有利于吸引更多认证组织申请 EUR-ACE 标签授权。IEA 多边协议的广泛关联性决定其成员构成的多样性,既有专门性的工程教育专业认证机构或职业资格注册机构,又有集工程教育专业认证与工程师职业资格注册为一体的专业组织。

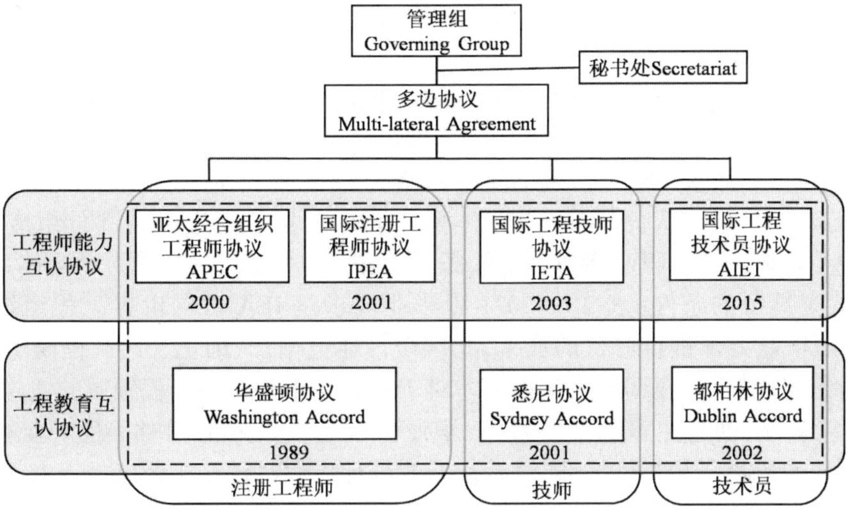


**图 4　IEA 组织结构**

### 1.3　认证标准的比较

#### 1. 适用范围

EUR-ACE 体系与 WA 体系的适用范围有所不同。受欧洲高等教育多元发展以及博洛尼亚精神的影响, EUR-ACE 体系构建了本硕贯通的工程教育专业认证标准,该标准与欧洲高等教育区的资历框架相适应,基于资历框架中对应等级的学习成果标准,制定了工程专业学士和硕士应满足的能力要求,同时,根据欧洲学分转换与积累体系规定了不同学位层次应达到的最低学分数,且不设学习年限上的限制[7]。由于 WA 体系原始成员遵循以美国为代表的工程教育模式(学习四年后获得学士学位,再额外学习一至两年后获得硕士学位),工程人才的培养年限具有一定共性,基于此,签订适用于四年制本科工程教育的互认协议,面向的工程师培养类型是注册工程师。与之相配套的还有面向三年制技师培养项目的《悉尼协议》和面向两年制技术员培养项目的《都柏林协议》,三者共同构成 IEA 工程教育互认协议,IEA 针对三项协议,基于毕业生能力要求和学习年限,在注册工程师、技师、技术员培养之间设置严格的界限[14]。与 WA 体系相比, EUR-ACE 体系覆盖的学位层次更广,包容国家教育体系之间存在的差异,在学习产出、学习时间和实现路径之间建立起更加灵活的联结。

### 2. 内容构成

EUR-ACE 体系的认证标准可概括为工程教育专业认证标准和工程教育专业认证机构的指导性标准两部分（图 5）[7]。工程教育专业认证标准包括学生学习量标准、毕业要求标准、专业管理标准三个子项。学生学习量标准规定工程专业学士、硕士（包括综合硕士）学位应修得的最低学分总数。毕业要求标准在学位层次上区分为学士和硕士两个等级，在能力要求上涵盖知识与理解、工程分析、工程设计、调查、工程实践、判断、沟通与团队合作、终身学习八个方面，尽管两个等级标准的内容框架基本一致，但从学士到硕士，具体要求的深度和广度有所提高，体现了工程专业毕业生能力水平的进阶。专业管理标准注重全方位、多维度地考查专业人才培养情况，从培养目标，教与学的过程，资源，学生入学、流动、发展、毕业，内部质量保障等方面提出认证要求。工程教育专业认证机构的指导性标准旨在为认证机构的有效运作提供全面指导，其标准可细分为认证评估的指导性标准和质量保障的指导性标准，前者对认证方法和策略、认证相关文件出版、认证实施流程、认证决定过程、认证结论公开做出规定，后者关注认证机构的质量保障水平，从管理体系建设、认证机构性质、相关资源供给三个方面制定认证标准。WA 体系认证标准相关规定由两部分组成：一是源于 2021 版 IEA《毕业要求与职业能力》的 11 条毕业要求（表 1），二是成为 WA 体系临时成员或正式成员应具备的条件（表 2）。2021 版毕业要求是 IEA 协同世界工程组织联合会对 2013 版 12 条毕业要求进行修订的成果，此次修订通过增加、细化、分列、提高等方式，纳入联合国可持续发展目标，强调未来工程人才对于新兴技术及新兴工程领域的适应力，同时考虑创新性、包容性、创造性等能力要素[6]。毕业要求通过系列指标对工程专业毕业生的知识、能力、素质水平进行概括性描述，没有从专业设计、专业目标、实现路径等方面做出规定，高校可根据实际情况灵活选择人才培养模式、教育教学方法。毕业要求标准项规定工程专业毕业生应达到的能力水平，并对其中所提及的复杂工程问题、知识体系和工程活动范畴加以说明[6]，为认证机构及学校制定学习产出标准提供参考。此外，专业质量不仅取决于既定的培养目标和毕业要求，还受到课程体系设计、相关资源保障、教育教学过程、学生评价方法等因素的影响。因此，《IEA 协议规则和程序》从上述各方面提出认证机构制定认证标准应达成的指标，这些指标包含在认证机构加入 WA 体系须具备的基本条件之中，即认证机构成为临时成员或正式成员应满足的要求（表 2）。成为临时成员的相关要求对认证机构特点、认证体系运作、认证标准内容做出规定，成为正式成员除了满足成为临时成员的所有要求之外，还需在健全认证体系、规范认证程序、优化管理机制、建立毕业要求实质等效性等方面有所突破[15]。

EUR-ACE 体系和 WA 体系的认证标准均涉及毕业要求、专业管理、认证机构指导三大内容。

（1）毕业要求。出于增强毕业要求兼容性与可接受性的目的，EUR-ACE 体系的类目划分较为简洁，整体描述较为宽泛，毕业要求由六大指标构成，各指标下设具体观测点，而 WA 体系的毕业要求分类较细，对工程问题、工程活动、工程知识和素养等关键词做出解释，并以单独成项的方式突出强调个别能力素质的重要性。虽然二者类目划分不同，但在内容构成上存在一定对应关系。与 WA 体系相比，EUR-ACE 体系单项毕业要求的概括性更强，内容覆盖面更广。例如，虽然 EUR-ACE 体系未将工程师与世界、伦理、项目管理和财务列为单独的毕业要求项，但在工程分析、工程设计、工程实践和判断中渗透有相关内容。

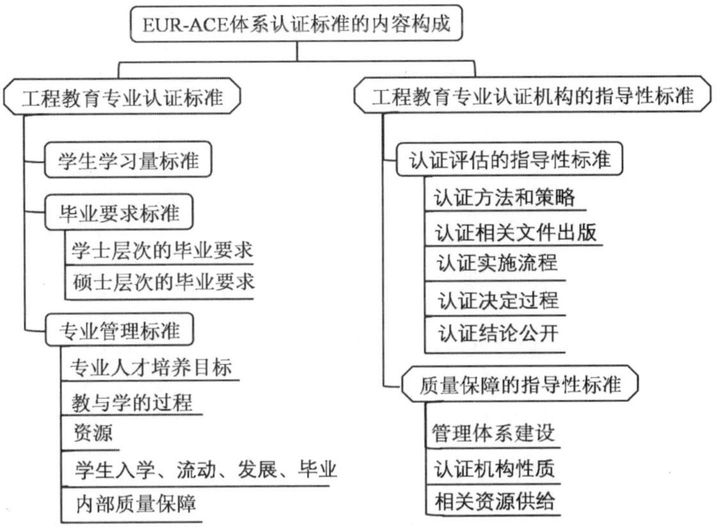


**图 5　EUR-ACE 体系认证标准的内容构成**

（资料来源：根据 https://www.enaee.eu/wp-conte/uploads/2021/05/eafsg_brochure_2017_online.pdf 整理而成）

**表 1　WA 体系的 11 条毕业要求**

| 要求 | 具体内容 |
|---|---|
| 工程知识 | WA1：运用数学、自然科学、计算机和工程基础知识以及 WK1~WK4 中规定的工程专业知识，开发复杂工程问题的解决方案 |
| 问题分析 | WA2：利用数学、自然科学和工程科学的第一原理，结合对可持续发展的整体考虑，识别、表达、研究和分析复杂工程问题，以得出有根的结论（WK1~WK4） |
| 设计/开发解决方法 | WA3：为复杂工程问题设计创造性的解决方案，并设计系统、部件或流程，以满足特定需求，同时适当考虑公共健康和安全、全寿命周期成本、净零碳，以及资源、文化、社会和环境因素（WK5） |
| 调查研究 | WA4：运用研究方法对复杂工程问题进行调研，包括基于研究的知识、设计实验、分析和解释数据，以及通过信息综合得出有效结论（WK8） |
| 工具的使用 | WA5：为解决复杂工程问题、开发、选择和应用恰当的技术、资源、现代工程工具和信息技术工具，包括预测和建模，并认识其局限性 |
| 工程师与世界 | WA6：在解决复杂工程问题时，分析和评估问题解决方案对可持续发展产生的影响，涵盖社会、经济、可持续性、健康与安全、法律以及环境（WK1、WK5、WK7） |
| 伦理 | WA7：运用道德准则，遵守职业伦理以及工程实践责任和规范，遵守相关国家法律和国际法律，并理解多元化和包容性的必要性（WK7、WK9） |
| 个人和团队协作 | WA8：在多元化和包容性的团队中，以及在多学科、面对面、远程和分布式的环境中，作为个人、成员或领导者有效地发挥作用（WK9） |
| 沟通 | WA9：与工程界和整个社会就复杂工程活动进行有效的、包容性的沟通，例如，能够理解和撰写有效的报告和设计文档，有效地进行演示，并考虑到文化、语言和学习差异 |
| 项目管理和财务 | WA10：理解和掌握工程管理原理和经济决策方法，将其用于自己的工作，并作为团队成员和领导者，在多学科环境中管理项目 |

续表

| 要求 | 具体内容 |
|---|---|
| 终身学习 | WA11：认识到需要并具备以下能力：①自主学习和终身学习；②适应新技术；③在最广泛的技术变革背景下进行批判性思考（WK8） |

资料来源：根据 https://www.ieagreements.org/assets/Uploads/Documents/IEA-Graduate-Attributes-and-Professional-Competencies-2021.1-Sept-2021.pdf 整理而成。

**表2　加入WA体系须满足的基本标准**

| 成为临时成员须满足的标准 | 成为正式成员或保持认证身份须满足的标准（除了符合成为临时成员的所有标准外，还须符合下列标准） |
|---|---|
| 1. 认证机构的特点：<br>（1）非政府性；<br>（2）享有注册地所属国的合法管辖权；<br>（3）是所属辖区内无可争议、最具权威性的认证机构；<br>（4）是一个法定或专业认可的权威机构，经认证专业的毕业生将满足获得在所属辖区内执业资格（如许可、注册）的学术要求；<br>（5）对具有高等教育学位授予资格的院校的专业进行认证；<br>（6）拥有制定、批准、评估和执行认证标准及认证程序的相关政策；<br>（7）独立于在其管辖范围内提供专业教育的教育机构；<br>（8）在做认证决定时享有不受利益相关者干涉的自主权 | 1. 认证机构的认证体系和认证程序应满足下列要求：<br>（1）认证机构对认证的专业性、伦理性和客观性提出了较高要求；<br>（2）参与专业评估的所有人员擅长认证体系运作，是享有较高地位的教育工作者或专业从业人员；<br>（3）能够公平地实施认证标准和认证程序，并且注重二者之间的相关性；<br>（4）为支撑认证决定，认证报告详细地记录认证建议并证明其合理性，且对建议与要求加以明确区分；<br>（5）决策机构具备困难决策能力，从长远来看可能对工程团体有益 |
| 2. 认证机构有一套可操作的认证体系，其程序和做法须符合下列要求：<br>（1）正式记录、公布认证标准和程序，并按照既定政策实施；<br>（2）该体系认证单个专业或由不同专业协调组成的专业群；<br>（3）专业评估员是学术和行业领域的同行评审员；<br>（4）拥有培训专业评估员的机制和文件；<br>（5）专业评估要求进行自我评估和现场考查；<br>（6）为保持认证身份，需定期进行重新评估；<br>（7）个别专业评估需秘密进行；<br>（8）在认证的所有阶段都有利益冲突协调机制；<br>（9）须公布已经认证的专业名单；<br>（10）拥有相关上诉程序 | 2. 毕业要求与《华盛顿协议》的12条毕业要求实质对等，并反映在下列标准之中：<br>（1）机构成文规定的毕业要求标准；<br>（2）在专业教育教学实践中所制定的标准 |
| 3. 认证机构的认证标准须符合下列要求：<br>（1）符合专业人才培养目标的毕业要求；<br>（2）拥有为工程实践提供广泛基础的课程体系；<br>（3）具备合适的专业教学环境；<br>（4）具备充足的专业领导力量；<br>（5）拥有工程实践背景的师资队伍；<br>（6）制定适当的入学和升学标准；<br>（7）具备充足的人力、物力、财力资源 | 3. 下列信息反映了认证机构及其认证体系具有可持续性，且得到了充分管理，如：<br>（1）能证明高校在所属辖区内寻求过认证的数据；<br>（2）能证明专业在所属辖区内寻求过认证的数据；<br>（3）专业经历完整认证周期且已被重新评估的具体情况；<br>（4）在现场考查和决策会议期间进行深入考虑，这有利于根据一系列有关专业质量的证据做出恰当认证决定；<br>（5）定期审查认证政策、准则及程序的机制；<br>（6）专业评估人员接受培训的深度足够；<br>（7）专业认证由在工程教育、工程实践和教育质量保证领域的专家实施；<br>（8）政策制定与认证决定的分离；<br>（9）保持认证决定持续性和一致性的机制；<br>（10）该机构参与国际工程联盟其他教育协议的历史（如果有的话），并证明该机构总体上始终符合已公布的认证政策和程序 |

资料来源：根据 https://www.ieagreements.org/assets/Uploads/Documents/Policy/Accord-Rules-and-Procedures-July-2018-version-2019.1.pdf 整理而成。

（2）专业管理。EUR-ACE 体系的相关描述更为详尽，对各项指标的具体内容做出明确解释，而 WA 体系仅在关于协议临时成员需符合的标准中提及相关内容，未进行过多阐释，二者在内容构成上既有交叉性，又彰显了自身特色，交叉部分的内容包括专业培养目标，相关资源保障，学生入学、升学等规定。此外，EUR-ACE 体系特别关注教与学的过程和专业质量保障，WA 体系突出强调专业领导力建设以及教学环境营造，虽然二者都提到课程建设，但 WA 体系以“教什么”“学什么”为着眼点，要求专业构建为工程实践提供广泛基础的课程体系，EUR-ACE 体系以“怎么教”“怎么学”为突破口，重点关注课程设计如何通过教与学的过程帮助学生达成毕业要求。

（3）认证机构指导。EUR-ACE 体系从两个方面、七个维度对认证实施、认证管理提供指导，而 WA 体系的指导性标准分布于成为协议临时成员和正式成员应满足的要求之中，相关规定的条目分类更细，内容描述更具体，针对不同等级的成员，从认证机构特点、认证体系运作、认证实施程序等方面予以指导。

### 1.4 认证程序的比较

EUR-ACE 体系和 WA 体系均强调工程专业毕业生质量的国际互认，但秉持的理念和遵循的原则却有所不同。EUR-ACE 体系的互认源于认证机构之间建立的共享的认证标准框架和指导性方针，之所以能实现共享，是因为博洛尼亚进程推动了欧洲高等教育一体化，相互承认的学分系统、资历框架、质量保障体系为欧洲建立工程教育的通用质量标签提供了便利。ENAEE 并不直接对工程相关专业施以认证，而是基于 EAFSG 评估认证机构的政策和程序，决定其是否获得 EUR-ACE 标签授予权，从本质上看，采取的是自下而上的申请授权制。EAFSG 是一个具有兼容性和广泛适用性的通用参考框架，而非对各国认证标准和认证程序的取代，而是为各国特色化工程教育专业认证体系的构建预留了空间。WA 体系在成员之间建立起工程教育专业认证项目的实质等效性，即由任意成员认证机构认证过的专业的毕业生可在其他国家得到认可，这种互认建立在各国认证机构的认证标准、认证程序、认证相关政策具有可比性的基础之上。在遵循 WA 体系相关规定的前提下，认证机构可灵活制定、独立实施具有可比性的认证体系。

EUR-ACE 标签的授权程序与 WA 体系的入会程序具有相似性。EUR-ACE 标签的授权程序如下[16]：认证机构向秘书处提交正式申请，并通过自评审查用以说明认证机构对 EAFSG 的达成情况；审查团主席根据材料的完整性与有效性，决定认证机构是否获得候选认证机构身份；标签委员会组建 ENAEE 审查团（ENAEE Review Team，ERT）；实施现场考查，对于单一学位的授权申请，ERT 将分别在两所高校的至少一个专业中进行，对于本硕两级学位或综合学位的授权申请，ERT 将至少在两所高校不同学位层次的专业中进行；审查团撰写认证报告，征询认证机构反馈，并向标签委员会提供建议；行政委员会做出最终认证决定（认证结论包括：条件性授权，有效期为 2 年；正式授权，有效期为 5 年；拒绝授权）。认证机构在成为 WA 体系正式成员前，通常会经历至少两年的预备成员身份期，申请成为预备成员须具备以下条件[15]：有一套符合 WA 体系相关标准及规定的认证体系；有两个正式缔约方的支持；获得签约成员三分之二的投票。预备期满后认证机构欲申请转正，须经历以下环节：认证机构提供自评报告、认证数据等申请材料；评估员进行现场考查，证实毕业要求、认证程序、认证标准的实质等效性；评估员撰写认证报告，并寻求利益相关者的意见；缔约方投票得出认证结论，认证机构获得全票通过即可被授予正式成员资格，有效期为六年。从整体上看，EUR-ACE 标签的授权程序与 WA 体系的入会程序均包括申请、材料审核、现场考查、认证报告撰写、意见征询、做出认证决定等环节，略有不同的是，成为 WA 体系签约方前会经历较长时间的预备考查期，申请转正须获得正式缔约成员的全票通过，而 EUR-ACE 标签的申请授权者在成为候选认证机构后的较短时间内即可获得正式标签授予权，最终授权决定由行政委员会做出。

### 1.5 运行机制的比较

WA 体系注重组织运行的三个维度，即民主性、系统性和科学性，构建以协商决策民主化、监督指导一体化、权责分配合理化为显著特征的组织运行机制。协商决策民主化是指组织内部不是一个人说了算，而是通过实行民主集中制以促进各签约组织集体决策、协同管理、共谋发展。WA 体系的所有成员每年定期召开一次大会，就审议接纳新成员、修订协议条款、终止或继续会员身份等事宜进行探讨，对于重大问题的决议，每个正式成员均享有一票表决权，预备成员享有参与讨论权，决议通过需获得三分之二以上正式成员的同意[15]。大会期间，为促进成员组织之间的良性互动，可随时举办研讨会。闭会期间，各成员组织为协商处理一些紧急情况，可专门召开特殊会议。监督指导一体化是指 WA 体系厘清了监督与指导之间的逻辑关系，通过构建整体的制度环境发挥了持续改进机制的作用和功能，包含两个方面：其一，协议章程规定，签约方的身份有效期最长为六年，期满后须对成员组织的认证体系是否具有实质等效性进行资格审查，形成了周期性审查制度；其二，WA 体系建立起完善的入会指导体系，通过委派指导员的方式为参与认证评估、谋求预备成员身份转正等提供支持。监督机制与指导机制相辅相成，推动整体功能发挥及持续质量改进。权责分配合理化是指 WA 体系明文规定了正式成员和预备成员享有的权利和应尽的义务，权责之间界限清晰，适用范围明确，实现了权责统一。例如：正式成员享有重大事项的投票表决权，而预备成员仅享有大会旁听权；预备成员须履行财政义务、参会义务以及为认证专业的毕业生提供福利的义务，正式成员的义务包括实施现场考查、提供审查评估员、指导申请机构或预备成员等[15]。

EUR-ACE 体系在建立层次清晰的组织结构的基础上，形成科学合理的组织运行机制。一是多元利益相关者介入机制。EUR-ACE 体系由 ENAEE 负责管理，但 ENAEE 的成员身份并不是获得 EUR-ACE 标签授予权的先决条件，EUR-ACE 标签的授权对象有两类，即工程教育专业认证机构和负责工程及其他学科学校审查与专业认证的质量保障机构[16]。相比之下，ENAEE 成员组织的来源更广，除专门的认证机构和质量保障机构以外，还包括与高校、雇主、学生相关的团体，这为多元利益相关者参与管理 EUR-ACE 体系、增进授权组织与工程教育相关领域的互动搭建起桥梁。二是系统科学的质量监控与评价机制。ENAEE 通过出台工程教育专业认证标准框架与指导性方针、EUR-ACE 标签授权程序等系列文件，建立起一套规范化的集评价、指导、发展为一体的授权审查机制，不仅为认证组织构建或完善认证体系、有效申请 EUR-ACE 标签授权提供明确指导，而且形成全面灵活的工程教育质量评价框架。三是融通互动的沟通交流机制。一方面，ENAEE 清晰的组织架构有利于不同层次的责任主体保持多方联动。全体大会、行政委员会、EUR-ACE 标签委员会、相关委员会和工作组、秘书处共同构建起以决策、管理、执行、服务为目标节点的互动链。另一方面，ENAEE 的各组织层定期召开会议，通过建立常态化的会议制度，在组织章程中明确会议准则和条例，促进了成员之间以及不同部门之间的协商对话。

EUR-ACE 体系和 WA 体系运行机制的异同可从合作机制、监管机制、协调机制三个维度进行比较。就合作机制而言，二者皆强调成员机构之间的互惠共赢、责任共担、资源共享，通过健全会议制度和完善组织结构，畅通信息获取途径，搭建沟通交流平台，保证了决策民主性、协作长效性以及管理科学性。就监管机制而言，EUR-ACE 体系以规范化、具有广泛适用性的授权审查制度为显著特征，而 WA 体系突显周期性审查与常态化指导相结合的管理特色。二者均设置不同会员身份的有效期，WA 体系在这方面积累了丰富经验，通过协议章程对周期性审查制度予以详细说明。就协调机制而言，EUR-ACE 体系注重标签授权工作与社会各界的广泛联系，通过吸纳具有多元背景的 ENAEE 成员和明确不同主体的权利与职责，为利益相关者参与管理 EUR-ACE 体系提供了保障。WA 体系也在章程中规定不同身份成员的权利和义务，避免了参与方因社会属性、入会诉求不同而带来的利益冲突。

## 2 双体系典型参与组织的认证制度解析——以俄罗斯为样例

俄罗斯作为 EUR-ACE 体系与 WA 体系的共同成员，其工程教育专业认证制度兼具国际认证体系的基本特征，在对接国际标准时，实现了放眼国际与扎根本土、原则坚守与灵活变通相结合。探究其认证制度建设经验，不仅有利于把握 EUR-ACE 体系与 WA 体系的核心要义、实践要求，而且能为我国认证制度的本土化构建提供借鉴与参考。

### 2.1 俄罗斯工程教育专业认证体系的基本介绍

《俄罗斯联邦宪法》规定，俄罗斯采取两种方式的认证：国家认证和专业认证。国家认证由联邦政府执行，旨在对高校办学水平进行全面考查；专业认证由第三方机构实施，旨在对专业发展概况进行有效评估，以保障毕业生质量满足专业标准和劳动力市场要求[17]。在俄罗斯，通过国家认证是参与专业认证的前提，同时，专业认证结果也将为国家认证提供重要评估信息。俄罗斯工程教育专业认证工作由俄罗斯工程教育协会（Association for Engineering Education of Russia，AEER）负责，具体认证事项由认证中心承担。2006 年，AEER 成为 ENAEE 正式成员，并获得 EUR-ACE 标签授予资格。2012 年，AEER 加入 WA 体系，在国际层面赋予俄罗斯工程教育实质等效价值。AEER 的活动范围较广，不仅积极探索工程教育专业认证的优化策略，而且致力于工程师职业资格注册工作，不断建立和扩大与国外高等教育协会、基金会、教育机构之间的联系与合作。

2002 年，AEER 制定首套工程教育专业认证标准，这一时期的标准以要素性输入为导向，一级指标包含专业培养目标、专业教学内容、学生、师资队伍、专业资格、设施与资源、信息基础设施、财政政策与管理、毕业生九项内容，覆盖学士、硕士、专家三个学位层次[18]。随后，受国际工程教育专业认证体系的影响，AEER 对原有认证标准进行审查和修订，2013 年，出台最新版工程教育专业认证标准，此套标准与 EUR-ACE 认证标准及指导框架相适应，满足了 WA 体系在毕业要求等方面的规定，在适用范围上涵盖中等职业教育和高等工程教育两个层次，可细分为适用于中职相关专业的认证标准、适用于学士的认证标准、适用于专家的认证标准、适用于硕士的认证标准四个类别[19]。满足中职相关专业的认证标准可进一步申请成为工程技术员，满足学士、专家相关专业的认证标准可进一步申请成为注册工程师。此外，认证标准坚持成果导向原则，注重审查学生对不同性质工程问题的解决能力。例如：中职工程专业毕业生对狭义工程问题的解决能力、工程专业学士和专家对复杂工程问题的解决能力、工程专业硕士对创新工程问题的解决能力。在内容构成上，不同类型的认证标准均包含专业培养目标与学习成果、专业教学内容、教育教学过程、师资队伍、专业资格、专业资源、毕业生七大板块，各类认证标准在板块的具体内容上存在差异[19]。

AEER 严格规定认证工作的实施程序，其认证程序与 EUR-ACE 体系和 WA 体系其他成员类似，主要包括认证申请、专业自评、自评报告审查、现场访问、认证报告撰写、认证结论审议等环节。为加强认证指导，AEER 编写详尽的认证专家指导手册，确立评估小组的组建原则（至少由四名专家构成，包括主席、专业评估员和工业界代表），从专业化水平、利益冲突的解决办法、保密性等方面制定了认证专家的基本行为准则，并对不同认证环节的操作技巧和注意事项予以说明[20]。同时，为帮助学校有效进行专业自评，AEER 还提供了自评报告模板，对认证标准进行详尽解构，明确标准达成的指标点，一定程度上降低了专业自评的模糊性与不确定性。

AEER 在认证体系建设中，对 EUR-ACE 体系和 WA 体系相关规定进行深度解读，在保持国际认证体系基本框架的前提下进行灵活变通。以认证标准中的专业资格为例，专业资格是对工科毕业生能力水平的预设，EUR-ACE 体系和 WA 体系均提供了毕业要求的参考性框架，AEER 在保留框架基本要素的前提下，一方面适时增补新的能力要求，另一方面对框架中的能力要求进行优化组合。例如：EUR-ACE 体系没有涉及不同工程问题的解决能力，没有明确提及工程伦理的相关要求，而 AEER 在认证标准中突出强调这两大内容；WA 体系没有对毕业要求进行类别划分，而 AEER 将能力标准分为专业能力和一般能力两大类，并将部分能力要求（如现代工具的使用）融入其他能力要求中。

### 2.2 俄罗斯工程教育专业认证体系的特征解析

自 1992 年成立以来，AEER 广泛汲取国际认证体系的价值精髓，积极探索工程教育专业认证的优化路径，在促进认证体系的规范化与专业化发展，建立贯通衔接、层次递进的认证标准体系，推动认证制度的本土特色化建设等方面取得了显著成效。

#### 1. 注重认证体系的规范化与专业化发展

就国家层面而言，俄罗斯在认证体系建设中，以相关法律条文为基础，保证了工程教育专业认证制度的规范性与合法性。2002 年，AEER 与俄罗斯教育科学部签署合作开发工程教育专业认证体系的协议，AEER 获批负责俄罗斯工程与技术相关专业的认证工作。2005 年，该协议被俄罗斯联邦高等教育和科学监管局的一份文件所取代，俄罗斯教育部决定，在对高等院校进行国家认证时，将 AEER 认证结果作为有利因素加以考虑[21]。2008 年，修订后的《俄罗斯联邦教育法》规定，参加专业认证的高等教育机构必须以通过国家认证为前提。就组织层面而言，AEER 注重提高认证机构的专业化水平，通过建立常态化的专家遴选机制、编制详尽的评估员指导手册、开发统一的自评报告模板及认证报告模板等措施，为认证工作人员和参与认证的院校提供指导。

**2. 构建起贯通衔接与层次递进的认证标准体系**

AEER 在构建认证标准体系时，坚持了同中求异的原则。“同”表现为：各类标准的一级指标构成具有一致性，毕业要求标准项都以工程问题的解决能力为核心，标准设计都遵循成果导向原则。“异”则体现在认证标准的适用范围及各级指标的具体要求上。关于适用范围，认证标准覆盖不同学位层次，面向不同工程师类型，AEER 在工程教育专业认证与工程师资格认证之间建立起衔接机制，即申请注册为某一类型的工程师，必须获得对应层次经认证专业的毕业资格。关于具体要求，不同认证标准有着程度和水平上的差异，例如，虽然各类标准都注重评价学生的工程问题解决能力，但通过“复杂”“狭义”“创新”等词对工程问题的性质加以区分，要求不同学历层次的学生具备不同水平的工程问题解决能力。

**3. 对接国际标准的同时强调认证制度的本土特色化建设**

加入 WA 体系与 EUR-ACE 体系是俄罗斯推进工程教育国际化的重要举措，构建起与国际工程教育相容的认证体系，实现了以国际通行的标准和惯例培养多层次、多类型工程技术人才的目标。与此同时，俄罗斯在认证制度建设过程中，避免盲目进行制度移植与做法效仿，注意把握 EUR-ACE 体系和 WA 体系的本质要求，通过融合国际化与本土化以激发创造力的方式，构建起立足本土需求、对接国际一流的认证制度框架。一方面，深悉 WA 体系“实质等效”的内涵，结合本国教育实际以及国际工程界对工程人才要求的最新变化，在满足 WA 体系相关规定的基础上，于认证体系融入特色化元素；另一方面，考虑到 EUR-ACE 体系具有兼容性和广泛适用性的特点，在保持 EUR-ACE 体系基本框架的前提下对其进行改良和创新。

## 3 WA 和 EUR-ACE 两大体系的基本特征与形塑逻辑

### 3.1 坚持持续改进的行动逻辑

EUR-ACE 体系和 WA 体系坚持持续改进的行动逻辑，遵循组织体系日臻完善、认证范围不断扩大、国际化价值取向日益突显的演化规律。在历史进程中，两大体系的发展呈现出一些共性特征。就理念层面而言，二者始终坚持“持续改进”的行动逻辑。“持续改进”体现在以下三个方面：入会审查机制中包含周期性审查、持续性跟踪监测等相关要求；ENAEE 和 IEA 定期审查和修订认证标准、入会条件、协议章程等文件；要求认证机构引导参与认证的学校定期审查、适时修订专业培养目标、毕业要求、课程目标，使其将“持续改进”作为成果导向教育的重要方法论。就实践层面而言，EUR-ACE 体系和 WA 体系的组织体系日臻完善，统筹兼顾多元利益诉求，为进一步推进工程教育的国际化进程，二者不断扩大认证范围，跨国认证、全球性工程教育专业认证框架等一系列认证推广计划逐渐获得关注。

### 3.2 形成决策层、管理层、服务层和执行层四级联动的组织架构

两大认证体系形成决策层、管理层、服务层、执行层四级联动的组织架构，建立起集合作、监管、协调为一体的组织运行机制。EUR-ACE 体系和 WA 体系注重认证体系的组织建设，为实现组织结构合理化与功能最大化，不断优化组织的层级结构，在职能部门划分、职责权限划定上进行了有益探索。同时，二者统筹考虑高等教育机构、工程专业学生及毕业生、雇主、专业性工程组织、认证机构等利益相关者的诉求，通过建立集协作、监管、协调为一体的组织运行机制，营造多元协同的治理环境，为认证标准变革、认证决议等重要事项的实施奠定了良好组织基础。

### 3.3 赋予认证机构认证高度自主权

EUR-ACE 体系采取标签授权制，而 WA 体系实行成员组织授权制，二者均赋予认证机构认证高度自主权。EUR-ACE 体系强调权力重心下移与去中心化[22]，认证机构可参考 EUR-ACE 体系的认证标准框架与指导性方针，自主制定、实施认证标准和认证程序，从而获得在其认证证书上添加 EUR-ACE 标签的权利。WA 体系强调权力重心上移与中心化，成员身份是获得国际认证的前提，认证机构在坚持实质等效原则的基础上，可独立实施具有本国特色的认证体系。虽然两大认证体系的运作模式有所不同，但均主张在保持框架统一性的同时，尊重各国的认证自主权，认证机构享有变通执行相关规定的权力。

### 3.4 标准设计理念各具特色：统一性与多样性

WA 体系与多边协议相关联，强调成员组织认证标准的可比性与等效性。实质等效是 WA 体系秉承的核心理念，也是组织之间实现国际互认的重要前提。实质等效并不要求签约组织采用完全相同的认证标准，但要求其认证标准具有可比性。WA 体系提供了毕业要求标准项的参考框架，成员组织无需与其保持完全一致，但要求认证实施效果实质对等，即任意成员组织认证的工程专业毕业生在能力发展上应达到整体一致。纵观 WA 体系 21 个签约组织的认证标准，均涉及学生、毕业要求、师资队伍、课程体系、资源条件、持续改进等方面，其内容构成具有一致性，但标准的划分依据略有不同，大致分为四类：按职业划分（如澳大利亚、爱尔兰、新西兰）；按专业划分（如美国、新加坡、秘鲁）；按学位层次划分（如日本、土耳其）；按学校类型划分（如印度）。

与 WA 体系相比，EUR-ACE 体系的认证标准更具全面性和灵活性。WA 体系主要针对传统四年制本科工程教育，单一学位层次的认证使其遭受质疑，不断面临来自 EUR-ACE 本硕贯通认证体系的挑战[23]。EUR-ACE 体系根据欧洲资历框架，对不同学位层次加以区分，形成本硕贯通的学习产出标准框架。同时，要求认证机构在专业评估时考虑培养目标、教与学的过程、资源等要素，制定专业管理标准，并建立工程教育专业认证机构的指导性方针。认证标准的覆盖面广、内容丰富。它跨越两个学位层次，适用于所有工程学科，与博洛尼亚进程保持一致，尊重国家间教育和认证实践的差异，没有对学习年限、教学方式等做出限定，这使得高等教育机构享有发展新兴专业和特色化专业的自主权，构建起工程教育质量保障的泛欧洲框架。

### 3.5 具有较高的耦合性和交叉性

EUR-ACE 体系和 WA 体系的互认互通有利于成员认证制度的发展。目前,两大体系的成员构成存在交叉,交叉成员组织在把握国际认证体系共性规律的基础上,融合吸收二者的发展特色,变通性地参考和借鉴国际工程教育的认证框架,正确处理国际化与本土化之间的关系,注重认证制度的创新性建设。俄罗斯便是典型案例。俄罗斯的工程教育专业认证制度对接注册工程师制度,根据工程师的职业类型制定多层次的认证标准,注重认证制度的规范化与专业化发展,在满足国际工程教育专业认证基本框架的同时,对框架体系进行适度调整,构建起特色化的认证制度。

## 4 未来我国工程教育专业认证制度体系改革的初步思考

### 4.1 增强认证组织的专业性和功能性

中国工程教育专业认证协会(China Engineering Education Accreditation Association, CEEAA)形成了包含决策层(会员大会)、管理层(监事会和理事会)、执行层(各专业类认证委员会、学术委员会和认证结论审议委员会)的组织架构,具有纵向设计层级化的特征。同时划分不同职能部门,例如,秘书处包括学术部、综合部、培训咨询部、信息部等部门,由此明确各部门的工作范畴,具有横向设计部门化的特征。

CEEAA 由教育部授权,其秘书处和教育部高等教育教学评估中心合署办公推进工作,CEEAA 理事会及秘书处的领导按照学术组织任命。这种工作模式既保证了政府的核心地位,为认证协会提供所需资源,又为 CEEAA 进行自主决策和自我管理预留了空间。但各部门职能的清晰度和专业性还有待进一步提升,亟须建立持续改进的组织管理体制与运行机制。一方面,明确不同层级的管理特色,实现决策层的合作管理、管理层的自治管理、执行层的市场运作管理;另一方面,在完善自上而下传导机制的基础上,健全自下而上的反馈机制和长效互动机制,充分发挥专业类认证分委员会的作用,并进一步发挥学校、行业协会、专业学会等多元利益群体在协会管理和认证工作中的作用,畅通意见反馈渠道,搭建信息沟通平台,拓宽资源共享路径。

### 4.2 设计基于分层分类的弹性化认证标准体系

专业认证不是为了追求学校工科专业发展的统一化、模板化,在认证标准设计和变革过程中除了关注“系统性”“一致性”“明确性”之外,还应关注“类型性”“层次性”和“差异性”,换言之,就是要增强认证标准的科学性和必要的弹性,为学校自主发展与创新预留一定空间。目前,我国工程教育专业认证主要面向工科本科专业,尚未建立起专科、研究生层面的认证标准体系。同时,认证标准未考虑学校类型上的差异,所有学校采用一套通用标准及专业补充标准——这也是多数《华盛顿协议》成员的实际情况,由于部分学校还没有完全理解认证标准要求的本质,容易导致专业发展趋同。因此,建议通过分层分类的方式增强认证标准弹性,力求实现认证标准的创新设计。目前我国开设工科教育的院校主要有 5 类:研究型、研究教学型、教学研究型、本科教学型和专科教学型[24]。在层次上可划分为专科、本科和研究生;在人才培养类型上可划分为研究型(设计型)和应用型。基于此,工程教育专业认证标准可首先从层次上建立起专科、本科、研究生的三级衔接机制;再根据本科、研究生人才培养类型的不同,从研究型、应用型两大类对认证标准做进一步细化,引导学校在人才培养上办出特色和水平,同时设计出一套适用于新兴专业、交叉学科专业的认证要求与实施办法。

### 4.3 推进工程教育专业认证制度与注册工程师制度的有机衔接

加入 WA 体系使我国工科毕业生满足成为注册工程师的教育要求,为确保毕业生拥有国际认可的专业技术资质,还需健全注册工程师制度,推动工程师资格的国际互认。2005年,由原人事部等 18 个成员单位组成的全国工程师制度改革协调小组开始全面推进注册工程师制度改革,但发展较为缓慢,除个别领域和特种行业外,我国工程师制度基本与职称待遇挂钩,社会组织作用不突出,评价标准与全球行业标准有待进一步融合[25]。因此,为建立与工程教育衔接、国际等效且持续发展的注册工程师资格体系,需在认证标准、管理制度、运行模式、动力机制等方面展开探索。具体而言,包含以下方面:一是要建立注册工程师制度,完善工程师能力评价标准,实现工程师能力评价标准与工程教育专业认证标准相衔接;二是要进一步加强认证组织建设,创新认证制度、体系和管理模式;三是要发挥专业团体与社会组织在工程教育治理中的作用;四是剖析新工业革命背景下注册工程师国际互认面临的机遇和挑战,借鉴《华盛顿协议》成员的成功经验,筹备和计划未来加入国际注册工程师资格互认协议。

### 4.4 建构国际深度交流与合作的常态化机制

工程教育的国际互认是经济全球化、高等教育国际化共同作用的产物,外部环境的动态多变对工程教育的识变、应变与求变能力提出更高要求,认证机构应进一步加强国际交流与合作,紧随工程教育发展前沿,建立我国工程教育专业认证体系的定期自我审查与修订机制,准确预测、积极回应工业与社会发展对工程技术人才需求的变化。我国加入 WA 体系后,虽然认证标准和认证程序满足了国际要求,但还应该积极探索国际认证体系的未来发展新需求,与其他成员认证组织保持密切联系,了解国际工程教育专业认证的发展新动向。因此,建议加强工程教育专业认证协会各功能委员会建设,如强化学术委员会的功能与作用,吸收更多工业界成员,从多视角剖析、诊断认证标准中存在的问题,为标准完善提供修订意见。同时,加强与国家其他部门的合作,从多维度预测、分析工程人才需求的变化趋势,通过一定的统计分析手段判断标准修订措施的合理性与科学性。

### 4.5 坚持统一性和特殊性相结合的认证原则

WA 体系的毕业要求标准与成员准入标准为各签约成员制定认证方案提供了参考,WA 体系虽然强调内容实质等效,但未要求各国认证标准、认证程序完全一致,成员组织在坚持实质等效原则的基础上,可采用符合国家或地区实际情况的标准和程序。因此,我们应该更全面地解读 WA 体系的相关规定，把握实质等效原则的深层内涵，在对接国际标准与彰显本国特色之间保持合理平衡。此外，由于我国工程教育规模庞大、涉及的专业门类繁多、工程技术人才的类型多样，认证标准设计应力求全面、清晰且兼容，明确各项指标达成的操作要点，合理设置定性指标与定量指标的占比，避免指标设定繁杂、解读不一、可操作性差。在衡量和评价专业对各项标准的达成情况时，不能片面强调指标数量达成，应考虑不同学校及专业的发展特色与运作模式，自评报告审核和现场考查注重相关领域专家和企业的参与。

### 4.6 逐步扩大认证规模和认证范围

近几年来，我国工程教育专业认证的规模不断扩大，通过认证的本科专业点数量逐年增加，截至 2019 年底，共有 241 所高校的 1869 个专业通过认证[2]。然而，通过率较高的专业主要集中在机械、材料等传统工科领域，根据《普通高等学校本科专业目录（2020 年版）》对工学的专业分类可知，目前我国工程教育专业认证仍有多个工科专业类和工科专业尚未涉及。加之我国通过专业认证的高校数量在地域分布上具有明显差异，中部和东部地区通过率明显高于西部地区。因此，需要加大工科专业结构的优化调整力度，扩大认证的专业覆盖面，采取政策倾斜和激励指导措施，吸引更多专业参与认证。同时，为服务国家“一带一路”倡议，应积极探索共建“一带一路”国家工程教育质量的实质等效性，通过对相关国家的工程教育实施认证，促进双边及多边学历学位互认。而规模和范围的扩大需要以一定的质量保证为基础，还需加强和加快认证专家队伍建设，扩大专家遴选范围、提高专家遴选标准、注重专家能力培养。

### 4.7 补充国际实质等效和中国特色要求

作为《华盛顿协议》成员，中国工程教育专业认证标准需要遵守实质等效原则，同时尊重本土的特殊性。中国高等教育包括工程教育坚持“立德树人”的基本原则，在人才培养过程中，通过加强思政、工程伦理、工程师社会责任等教育，培养学生的职业道德和职业责任意识。目前，我国工程教育专业认证标准在“毕业要求”标准项中对工科学生的人文社科素养、社会责任感以及工程职业规范提出要求[26]，但在“课程体系”“师资队伍”等标准项中，尚未涵盖工程师职业素养培养和工程伦理教育相关规定。因此，要进一步明确“立德树人”为人才培养目标，在认证标准中细化工程师职业责任培养和工程伦理教育相关要求，引导专业培养职业道德高尚的卓越工程师。具体而言：一是要求专业设置工程伦理、工程师职业素养和社会责任等方面的培养内容，在培养过程中，通过工程和社会实例说明工程伦理和工程师职业责任的重要性；二是要求专业加强师资队伍建设，聘任具有工程职业伦理经验的兼职教师，开展师资培训，组建由不同学科背景教师构成的联合教学团队[27]。未来，在建设我国注册工程师体系的过程中，应注重工程教育专业认证的伦理和职业素养要求与注册工程师标准相结合，达到制度性保障。

## 5 结语

在深入探究国际工程教育专业认证最佳实践的基础上，有选择地对接水平较高的认证体系，既有利于借鉴国际成功经验推动工程教育专业认证改革，又能实时掌握工程教育的最新动态，提高工程人才培养的国际适应性。目前，EUR-ACE 体系和 WA 体系逐渐打破区块分割现象，呈现互融互通、共建共享的发展态势，这一动态塑造着未来工程教育专业认证的国际图景。因此，我们要深悉国际工程教育专业认证体系的发展动向，科学、理性地认识两大认证体系的发起背景、运作环境、价值取向等制约因素，融合吸收二者的价值精髓，推进认证制度的本土创新。在此过程中，要正确处理国际化与本土化、多元化与包容性之间的关系，避免盲目进行制度移植，应结合本国的政治体制和工程教育现状，构建适切的内生制度环境，融入特色化的中国元素，例如，充分把握"一带一路"的发展机遇，通过组建合作共同体，促进相关国家工程教育的双边或多边互认，使工程教育专业认证始终服务于国家战略需求。

**参考文献**


[1] IEA. Best Practice in Accreditation of Engineering Programs：An Exemplar [EB/OL].（2015-04-13）[2021-09-19]. https://www.ieagreements.org/assets/Uploads/Documents/Policy/Best-Prct-Full-Doc.pdf.

[2] 李志义，赵卫兵. 我国工程教育专业认证的最新进展[J]. 高等工程教育研究，2021（5）：39-43.

[3] AUGUSTI G. Accreditation of engineering programs：European perspectives and challenges in a global context[J]. European journal of engineering education，2007，32（3）：273-283.

[4] IEA. 25 Years of the Washington Accord：1989-2014 Celebrating International Engineering ducation Standards and Recognition [EB/OL].（2014-06-01） [2021-09-20]. https://www.ieagreements.org/assets/Uploads/Documents/History/25YearsWashingtonAccord-A5booklet-FINAL.pdf.

[5] ALAM F，KOOTSOOKOS A. Engineering education：accreditation & graduate global mobility[M]. London：CRC Press，2021：53.

[6] IEA. Graduate Attributes & Professional Competencies [EB/OL].（2021-06-21）[2021-09-22].https://www.ieagree-ments.org/assets/Uploads/Documents/IEA-Graduate-Attributes-and-Professional-Competencies-2021.1-Sept-2021.pdf.

[7] ENAEE. EUR-ACE® Framework Standards and Guidelines（EAFSG）[EB/OL].（2015-03-31）[2021-09-22]. https://www.enaee.eu/wp-content/uploads/2021/05/eafsg_bro-chure_2017_online.pdf.

[8] ENAEE. Standards and Procedures on Transnational Accreditation For ENAEE Authorized Agencies [EB/OL].（2020-09-18）[2021-09-23]. https://www.enaee.eu/wp-content/uploads/2020/10/Transnational-Accreditation-approved-GA_-18-September-2020-1.pdf.

[9] KOOTSOOKOS A，ALAM F，CHOWDHURY H，et al. Offshore Engineering Education：Assuring Quality Through Dual Accreditation[J]. Energy Procedia，2017（110）：537-542.

[10] ENAEE. Internal Rules [EB/OL].（2020-06-28）[2021-09-23].https://www.enaee.eu/wp-content/uploads/2021/09/New-Internal-Rules_GA-28-Jun-2021.pdf.

[11] ENAEE. Statutes [EB/OL].（2021-06-28）[2021-09-24]. https://www.enaee.eu/wp-content/uploads/2021/09/English-version-New-Statutes_-GA-28-June-2021.pdf.

[12] IEA. Governance Structure and Procedures [EB/OL].（2021-06-21）[2021-09-24]. https://www.ieagreements.org/assets/Uploads/Documents/Policy/IEA-Governance-Structure-and-Procedures.pdf.

[13] ENAEE. ENAEE Member Organizations [EB/OL]. [2021-09-25]. https://www.enaee.eu/members/.

[14] 胡德鑫. 赋能未来：工程教育专业认证制度改革的国际比较与标准重构[J]. 天津大学学报（社会科学版），2020，22（3）：223-229.

[15] IEA. IEA Accords Rules and Procedures [EB/OL].（2018-06-01）[2021-09-29]. https://www.ieagreements.org/as-sets/Uploads/Documents/Policy/Accord-Rules-and-Proce-dures-July-2018-version-2019.1.pdf.

[16] ENAEE. EURACE Label Authorisation Process [EB/OL].（2017-03-14）[2021-09-27]. https://www.enaee.eu/eur-ace-system/awarding-eur-ace-label/#authorization-pe-riod.

[17] POKHOLKOVY P，CHUCHALINA I，MOROZOVAE A，et al. The accreditation of engineering programmes in Russia[J]. European journal of engineering education，2004，29（1）：163-169.

[18] CHUCHALINA I. Developing the Unified Accreditation System for Engineering and Technology Programmes in Russia[C]. Orleans：43rd Annual SEFI Conference，2015.

[19] AEER. Accreditation Criteria [EB/OL].（2013-09-19）[2021-09-27]. http://aeer.ru/en/acc_criteria_eng.htm.

[20] AEER. Normative Documents [EB/OL]. [2021-09-27]. http://aeer.ru/en/norm-document.htm.

[21] POKHOLKOVY P，GERASIMOVS I. Professional Accreditation of Engineering Programmes and EUR-ACE Labels in Russia[C]. Kazan：Proceedings of International Conference on Interactive Collaborative Learning，2013.

[22] AUGUSTI G. Accreditation of engineering programs at European level[J]. International journal of electrical engineering education，2007，44（2）：101-108.

[23] AUGUSTI G. EUR-ACE：the European accreditation system of engineering education and its global context [M]. Engineering Education Quality Assurance，2009：47.

[24] 林健. 卓越工程师培养[M]. 北京：清华大学出版社，2013.

[25] 黄梅. 国外工程师制度模式与我国工程师制度改革[J]. 中国人事科学，2018（6）：66-74.

[26] CEEAA. 工程教育专业认证通用标准解读及使用指南[EB/OL].（2020-02-08）[2022-03-01]. https://www.cee-aa.org.cn/gcjyzyrzxh/rzcxjbz/gjwj/gzzn/index.html.

[27] 林健，衣芳青. 面向未来的工程伦理教育[J]. 高等工程教育研究，2021（5）：1-11.

# 国际注册工程师资质认证制度的建构逻辑与改革趋向
## ——基于美、英、日、澳四国的范例 ①

胡德鑫　徐文君　常乔丽　顾佩华

**摘要:**经济全球化与新工业革命演进交织下,注册工程师制度对国家和地区工业科技迭代发展、产业结构转型升级、卓越工程师人才培养等发挥着重要支撑作用。对美、英、日、澳四国注册工程师资质认证制度建构逻辑与改革趋向的研究表明:认证主体与组织上,形成功能多样且分工明确的多元主体协同机制;认证程序与标准上,分层考试和申请考核并行,注重非技术能力培养;认证对象发展路径上,进行多样化职业生涯分类设计,注重发展继续教育;认证融通与国际互认上,打造专业认证与工程师资质认证紧密衔接的国际互认机制。

**关键词:**注册工程师;资质认证;专业认证;卓越工程师;非技术能力

# Construction Logic and Reform Trend of Global Registered Engineer Qualification Certification System
## —Examples of USA, Britain, Japan and Australia

*Hu Dexin, Xu Wenjun, Chang Qiaoli, Gu Peihua*

**Abstract:** Under the intertwining of economic globalization and the new industrial revolution, the registered professional engineer system plays an important role in supporting the iterative development of industrial science and technology, the transformation and upgrading of industrial structure, and the training of outstanding engineers in these countries and regions. Based on examples in the USA, Britain, Japan and Australia, this paper analyzes the construction logic and reform trend of the registered professional engineer systems from four dimensions: in terms of certification subjects and organizations, a multi-agent coordination mechanism with diverse functions and clear division of labor is established; for the certification procedures and standards, the layered examination and application assessment are in parallel, and the cultivation of non-technical capability is emphasized; on the development path of the certification object, diversified career classification design is carried out with focus on continuing education; with respect to certification integration and international connection, creating an international mutual recognition mechanism that closely connects professional certification and engineer qualification certification.

① 本文刊登于《高等工程教育研究》2023 年第 2 期第 87~95 页。

**Keywords**: registered engineer; qualification certification; accreditation; outstanding engineer: non-technical capability

## 1 问题提出

18 世纪中叶英国工业革命以来,全球先后历经蒸汽时代、电气时代、信息时代三次工业革命。21 世纪,以人工智能和互联网技术广泛应用为标志的新一轮工业革命悄然而至,世界正经历百年未有之大变局,面对新工业革命浪潮的冲击,各国通过制定面向未来的高技术发展战略或政策积极应对,以维持国际竞争地位。如英国《产业战略:建立适应未来的英国》(2017 年)、德国《国家工业战略 2030》(2019 年)、日本《科学技术创新综合战略 2020》(2020 年)和美国《无尽前沿法案》(2021 年)等。工程科技成为改变全球综合国力格局的重要因素,工程科技的重大突破会催发社会生产水平与组织结构深刻变革,工程科技迭代发展需要大批卓越工程师提供支撑。习近平总书记明确指出,要培养大批卓越工程师,努力建设一支爱党报国、敬业奉献、具有突出技术创新能力、善于解决复杂工程问题的工程师队伍。为有效提升工程人才培养质量和服务国家重大战略需求,我国先后启动两轮卓越工程师教育培养计划,基于新工科建设计划撬动高等教育整体性变革,正在形塑中国特色、世界水平的卓越工程师教育培养体系。数据显示,当前中国工程师超过 7000 万人,成为名副其实的工程大国。但瑞士洛桑管理学院《世界竞争力报告》显示,中国合格工程师的数量和总体质量连续多年在参与排名的 55 个国家中居相对末位。美国《财富》数据表明,中国满足全球化能力要求的工程师数量仅占总数的 1/10 左右[1]。这两项数据提醒我们,工程师群体的综合能力和国际竞争力还有较大提升空间。

经济全球化背景下,技术贸易、资本转移活动日趋活跃,工程师规模性跨国流动成为必然趋向。相当部分国家通过加入《华盛顿协议》(Washington Accord)、《国际职业工程师协议》(International Professional Engineers Agreement)等国际协议,实现工程教育专业认证和注册工程师资质认证的有效衔接与国际融通。我国于 2016 年 6 月加入《华盛顿协议》,成为第 18 个正式成员,实现了工程教育学历层面的国际可比与实质等效,通过组建中国工程教育专业认证协会来开展全国性专业认证的组织与实施工作。但目前尚未建立全国统一的注册工程师资质认证制度,缺乏专业认证与注册工程师资质认证间的有效衔接,同时,由于未加入相关国际协议,我国工程师职业资质并未被其他国家认可,涉外项目中承担大量工程任务却得不到相应权益保护的情况时有发生。

因此,无论是从国家层面培养大批卓越工程师以有效支撑国家重大战略,还是从国际层面保障我国工程师跨国(境)工作的合法权益、提升国际话语权,推进建立完善的中国注册工程师资质认证制度并加入国际相关协议,都极具重要性和必要性。美国、英国、日本、澳大利亚等国经过长期探索和实践,建立了较完备和相对成熟的注册工程师资质认证制度,在规范工程从业人员准入门槛、促进工程师职业发展、保障工程师群体国际流动等方面发挥着重要作用。本文旨在从认证主体与组织、认证程序与标准、认证对象发展路径和认证融通与国际互认四个维度,解析美国、英国、日本、澳大利亚四国注册工程师资质认证制度的建构逻辑与改革趋向,为我国工程师资质认证制度的未来建构提供借鉴与参考。

## 2　注册工程师资质认证制度建构与改革

### 2.1　认证主体与组织:功能多样且分工明确的多元主体协同机制

新制度主义认为,制度变迁的基本模式分为强制性与诱致性。前者强调制度变迁的驱动主体主要来自政府力量,自上而下推进,以政策规划、行政指令、资金分配为基本手段,带有激进性及存量革命性的特点;后者强调驱动主体主要来自基层,自下而上推进,侧重先试点后推广和从外围向核心突破相结合,改革通常是渐进性的,带有边际革命和增量调整的特点[2]。美国、英国、日本、澳大利亚四国在注册工程师资质认证制度的组织建构方面,均形成非官方民间专业机构,并拥有完善的组织架构与功能分工,驱动逻辑大致分为日本代表的强制性和美国、英国、澳大利亚代表的诱致性两种类型。四国均建立了专业认证和注册工程师资质认证紧密联系机制,组织建构模式主要分为综合型组织和独立型组织两种,前者以英国、澳大利亚为代表,后者以美国、日本为代表(表 1)。为更清晰地比较两种类型,需要结合四国组织建构的历史演变进行分析。

**表 1　注册工程师资质认证机构与组织架构**

<table>
<tr><th>国别</th><th>工程教育专业认证机构</th><th>注册工程师资质认证机构</th><th>组织架构</th></tr>
<tr><td rowspan="5">英国</td><td colspan="2" rowspan="5">英国工程理事会(EUCK)</td><td>认证标准委员会</td></tr>
<tr><td>质量监督委员会</td></tr>
<tr><td>智囊团与法规委员会</td></tr>
<tr><td>国际顾问委员会</td></tr>
<tr><td>财务审计与薪酬委员会</td></tr>
<tr><td rowspan="3">澳大利亚</td><td colspan="2" rowspan="3">澳大利亚工程师学会(EA)</td><td>以地域为基础的组织</td></tr>
<tr><td>以学科为基础的组织</td></tr>
<tr><td>以科技社团为基础的组织</td></tr>
<tr><td rowspan="5">美国</td><td rowspan="5">美国工程与技术认证委员会(ABET)</td><td rowspan="5">美国工程与测量考试委员会(NCEES)</td><td>考试类委员会:专业工程师考试委员会、专业测量师考试委员会、考试审计委员会、考试政策与程序委员会</td></tr>
<tr><td>法律法规类委员会:法律实施委员会、程序规范与立法委员会</td></tr>
<tr><td>理事会咨询委员会</td></tr>
<tr><td>工程教育委员会</td></tr>
<tr><td>常规类委员会:执照局成员事务委员会、提名委员会、时务委员会、授奖委员会</td></tr>
<tr><td rowspan="4">日本</td><td rowspan="4">日本技术者教育认证机构(JABEE)</td><td rowspan="4">日本专业工程师协会(IPEJ)</td><td>管理运营组织</td></tr>
<tr><td>地域组织</td></tr>
<tr><td>部会组织</td></tr>
<tr><td>委员会组织</td></tr>
</table>

从历史变革看，日本注册工程师资质认证制度演进轨迹更多体现强制性制度变迁的特点。1951 年日本在政府支持下成立日本技术士会开始进行专业认证路径探索，其主要职能较为单一，主要从事工程科技咨询工作。1957 年的《日本技术士法》赋予日本技术士会管理注册工程师资质认证的法律地位，认证工作专业化和完备性极大提升。2001 年，随着日本技术士会在全球工程科技界影响力的提升，其更名为日本专业工程师协会，向国际工程师资质互认方向发展。文部科学省作为统筹日本教育、科技、文化和体育等事务的中央政府行政机关，在认证制度建构中发挥着重要驱动与引导作用，其下设工程科技相关的学术政策局、研究振兴局和研究开发局，分别发挥起草并制定科技基本政策、沟通协商相关机构的科技业务、全面振兴科学技术的作用[3]。此外，文部科学省与日本专业工程师协会、各类专业学会开展深度合作，共同促进组织职能日益完善，保障日本注册工程师资质认证制度稳定发展。日本专业工程师协会下设四大组织统筹运营日常工作，分别是作为协会核心的管理运营组织、负责各地区事务的地域组织、管辖不同工程师部门的部会组织以及主管调查事项的委员会组织[4]。四大组织相互协调、合作，在政府主导下共同为日本工程师资质认证工作服务，具体包括协调技术士考试、协助工程人才培养改革、推动本国工程师国际流动和与国外相关组织的工程师交流合作等。总的来看，日本注册工程师资质认证制度建构更多地受政府为主导的外部环境刺激，强调以权力为核心、自上而下的强制性建构逻辑。

英国、美国和澳大利亚三国注册工程师资质认证制度建构的演进更多体现诱致性制度变迁的特点。

英国工程师群体在早期工业革命影响下自发形成了许多同行业定期聚会，逐渐演化为“工程师社团”即各种学会组织的前身。随着学会数量和规模急剧扩大，建立权威性组织协调各学会关系和建构行业标准的呼声越来越强烈，英国皇家委员会对各行业组织进行调研后决定成立权威机构，建立相关的工程师认证制度。1981 年，皇家宪章特许的注册工程师资质认证的顶层机构——工程委员会（The Engineering Council）应运而生，成为工程界不断专业化、规范化和标准化的重要推动力。1996 年，工程委员会与英国执政党签署谅解备忘录，其合法地位得到政府机构正式认可。2002 年，经过组织调整，英国工程理事会（Engineering Council UK）从工程委员会中独立出来成为注册工程师资质认证的核心部门[5]。它由理事会和五个常务委员会组成，理事会为最高管理机构，理事会成员从工程学会和工程各界代表中选举而来：常务委员会包括认证标准委员会、质量监督委员会、智囊团与法规委员会、国际顾问委员会和财务审计与薪酬委员会，分别负责制定与审核学会的认证标准、认证过程中的授权和监督、搜集信息意见为做出合理决策提供建议、借鉴国际经验和在国际事务上代表英国国家利益、核算学会支出等。各委员会成员由理事会成员、专业学会和工程界代表等共同组成，充分吸纳政府学会和企业的意见和诉求，通过多方合作的方式保证注册工程师资质认证工作平稳推进。

20 世纪初，随着美国工程行业的发展，工程师群体规模迅速增长，衍生的质量危机凸显。公众要求消除工程师资质隐患的强烈呼声，逐渐催生美国工程师资质认证制度的立法和执照局设立，而后逐渐形成一套较完善的注册工程师资质认证体系。1920 年，美国成立负责全国注册工程师资质认证工作的美国工程与测量考试委员会（National Council of Examiners for Engineering and Surveying）。美国工程与测量考试委员会由 12 个常务委员会组成，包括4个负责考试事项的考试类委员会、2个管理政策法律法规制定的法律法规类委员会、1个提供咨询的理事会咨询委员会、1个负责与高等工程教育增强合作的工程教育委员会和4个承担促进各机构合作和内部协调任务的常规类委员会。委员会成员由工程师、州执照局官员、行业代表和教育界人士组成，代表企业、政府、行业和高校等多方利益，把促进工程师专业发展及工程行业内信息的交流作为最终使命，政府不直接介入工程师资质认证，而主要负责审查和监督考试内容，提出注册工程师资质认证法律法规和政策制定方面的建议，充当“守门员”角色[6]。

随着20世纪初工业经济规模快速扩张，澳大利亚逐渐出现大批以研讨专业知识、交流工程信息、专注工程实践和项目开发为目标的科技团体。1919年，澳大利亚工程师学会(Engineers Australia)成立[7]。该组织主要由以地域为基础的组织、以学科为基础的组织和以科技社团为基础的组织三部分组成，各组织下设分部和委员会。三类组织分别在区域、学科领域和社团的专业工程师沟通与信息交流、提供继续教育活动等方面发挥作用。与美国类似，澳大利亚政府对资质认证工作同样仅侧重监督，不直接介入。

英国、美国和澳大利亚认证组织的职能大致相同，主要包括确立工程师资质认证标准和程序、组织与实施资质认证考试/审核工作、在国际事务上代表本国工程师权益三大职能。

### 2.2 认证程序与标准：分层考试和申请考核并行，注重非技术能力培养

#### 1. 注册工程师资质认证程序

注册工程师资质认证程序主要分为分层考试和申请考核两种。前者以美国、日本为代表，强调考试形式在认证过程中的作用，通过分层考试量化毕业生的各项能力，以此检验其是否达到相应注册工程师资质标准；后者以英国、澳大利亚为代表，强调考核形式在判定注册工程师资质认证中的作用。

美国是基于分层考试制开展注册工程师资质认证的典型。工程师资质认证由美国工程与测量考试委员会统一组织，需通过工程基础考试(The Fundamentals of Engineering)和工程实践与原理考试(The Principles and Practice of Engineering)。工程基础考试为闭卷考试，主要考查经美国工程与技术认证委员会(Accreditation Board for Engineering and Technology)认证的工程本科教育四年的全部课程内容，考试时长为8小时，涵盖8个学科领域，分上午工程基础部分和下午专业基础部分，工程基础部分所有考生的考试内容一致，专业基础部分根据不同学科领域进行针对性考查。工程基础考试可全面、客观量化学生的学习产出成果是否达到实习工程师资质要求。工程实践与原理考试在8个学科领域的基础上细分为23门考试，考试时长为8小时，包括上午专业广度考试和下午专业深度考试，试题覆盖实际应用中专业工程师所需的全部专业知识与技能。工程基础考试侧重基础，工程实践与原理考试侧重实践，二者作为工程师类型分层的桥梁和纽带，有效衔接工程师资质认证全过程，使毕业生从实习工程师逐步成长为专业工程师。日本与美国类似，申请人成为专业工程师也需经历两类分层考试。第一类为闭卷笔试，内容同样为工程学科基础知识，包括以科学技术基础知识为主的基础科目、以工程师应遵循的义务和要求为主的适应科目和以必要相关专业知识为主的专业科目三大部分。第二类为笔试加面试，笔试包括必考科目和选考科目，

侧重专业性和实践性，面试考查专业知识、应用能力、问题解决能力等。（表 2）

**表 2　美国和日本的分层考试制**

<table>
<tr><th>国别</th><th>第一次考试名称</th><th>考试时长</th><th>考试组成部分</th><th>共同点</th><th>第二次考试名称</th><th>考试时长</th><th colspan="2">考试组成部分</th><th>共同点</th></tr>
<tr><td rowspan="2">美国</td><td rowspan="2">工程基础考试</td><td rowspan="2">8 小时</td><td>工程基础部分</td><td rowspan="6">考查内容为所学本科工程教育课程，侧重基础知识广度</td><td rowspan="2">工程实践与原理考试</td><td rowspan="2">8 小时</td><td colspan="2">专业广度考试</td><td rowspan="6">考查内容为某一学科领域，强调专业知识深度和实践能力水平</td></tr>
<tr><td>工程专业部分</td><td colspan="2">专业深度考试</td></tr>
<tr><td rowspan="4">日本</td><td rowspan="4">第一类考试</td><td rowspan="4">4 小时</td><td>基础科目</td><td rowspan="4">第二类考试</td><td rowspan="2">3.5 小时</td><td rowspan="2">笔试</td><td>必考科目</td></tr>
<tr><td rowspan="2">适应科目</td><td>选考科目</td></tr>
<tr><td rowspan="2">20~40 分钟</td><td rowspan="2">面试</td><td>应用能力</td></tr>
<tr><td>专业科目</td><td>工程伦理</td></tr>
</table>

澳大利亚和英国是基于申请考核制开展注册工程师资质认证的典型。澳大利亚注册工程师资质认证程序在设计上相当程度地借鉴了英国经验，其认证程序包括四个阶段，以申请审核为主，不采用考试形式。其资质认证程序包括以下内容：第一阶段，申请人缴纳申请费、递交材料，工作人员检查申请人提交的申请材料；第二阶段，由认证专家评估申请人提交的文件和相关支撑材料；第三阶段，由认证面试官进行综合面试，重点评价申请人的理论知识掌握情况和实践能力水平；第四阶段，面试官和认证专家共同对整个过程进行评估并通知申请人其认证结果。若没有通过认证，申请人可联系相应专业学会获得反馈和个人能力提升建议。申请材料在申请审核过程中起至关重要的作用。申请材料包括：申请表、学历证明及其他资格证书；在校学习成绩单；个人简历及经历证明；三份不超过 2000 字的关于专业学习和工作经历的自我陈述；英语语言能力相关证明和个人身份证明。其中自我陈述是最重要的资料，是向评审官证明申请人掌握进入工程职业所需知识基础和能力素质的凭证。相较于美国和日本的国家性分层考试制，澳大利亚和英国的申请考核制具有以下特点：一是更注重信用和承诺，它们的工程师认证制度以个人诚信为基础，以推荐人为保障；二是针对性和灵活性强，澳大利亚和英国由各专业学会和委员会负责认证，可根据专业领域的不同特点酌情进行不同类别的认证标准处理，如英国的化学工程师学会充分考虑化工行业的特性，面对统一认证标准时侧重安全和环境部分能力素质标准的考查。

### 2. 注册工程师资质认证标准设计与能力要求

能力标准对工程人才培养和工程师未来职业发展具有重要指导和导向作用。《华盛顿协议》对工科毕业生明确要求的基本能力包括工程知识、问题分析、设计/开发解决方案、调查研究、现代工具的使用 5 项技术性能力，工程师与社会、环境与可持续发展、伦理、个人和团队工作、沟通、项目管理和财务、终身学习 7 项非技术能力，要求工程师人才培养重视技术能力与非技术能力协同发展。分析四国注册工程师资质认证标准相关文件发现，随着新工业革命对工程师复杂工程问题解决能力要求的提升，认证标准不断完善和修正，相比于传统工程技术能力，当前更强调非技术能力要求，如工程伦理、协同合作、终身学习等。因为工程活动是集体性社会活动，随着新一代信息技术革命和产业革命不断深入，未来工程活动的不可预见性增加，工程师需要的不仅是技术知识与通用能力，更需要具备应对各种复杂工程难题的非技术能力[8]。2020 年的《英国专业工程师能力素质标准》( The UK Standard for Professional Engineering Competence and Commitment )包括知识与理解，设计、开发和解决工程难题，责任、管理和领导，沟通和人际交往能力，个人和职业承诺五个部分。前两部分强调技术能力，要求理解并应用工程知识，创造性地分析并解决工程难题；后三部分强调非技术能力，其中沟通和人际交流能力包括用英语沟通的技术和与同事、客户、供应商及公众有效沟通两个部分，个人和职业承诺要求工程师表现出对适当职业行为准则的承诺，确认对社会、职业和环境的义务( 表 3 )[9]。澳大利亚基础资质标准《阶段一：能力标准》包括知识基础、工程能力和专业素质三部分，知识基础、工程能力部分与《英国专业工程师能力素质标准》相似，强调理解和应用自然、物理、数学、统计学等工程通用知识和专门知识，强调对复杂工程问题的处理，如系统合成与设计、项目管理等，注重技术能力的培养。专业素质包括道德行为和职业责任，创意、创新和积极主动的行为，有序管理自我和职业行为，有序协调团队成员，有效领导团队等，注重非技术能力的培养[10]。工程人才特许资质标准《阶段二：能力标准》大大提高了特许工程师非技术能力的要求，包括个人和职业承诺、社会义务、职场价值以及技术能力四大部分中，前三部分均蕴含非技术能力要求。日本《技术士伦理纲领》对工程师伦理道德的要求形成纲领性文件，包括以公众利益优先、保守商业秘密、确保环境可持续发展的可能性、遵守法律法规、致力于钻研科学技术和促进公共事业的发展与人才培养等内容。随着社会发展和科技变革不断对纲领进行完善，使其适应社会情境并引领日本工程师的职业道德塑造。这几个国家对于不同类型的工程师，设计的能力素质要求也各不相同。英国《英国专业工程师能力素质标准》对工程技师、主任工程师和特许工程师三类工程师群体设计了各具特色但紧密衔接的分类能力评价标准。如设计、开发和解决工程难题对工程技师能力素质的要求为参与产品、设备、工艺、系统或服务的设计、开发、制造、建造、调试、退役、操作或维护；主任工程师的能力素质要求为应用适当的理论和实践方法设计、开发、制造、建造、委托、操作、维护、退役和回收工程过程、系统、服务和产品；特许工程师的能力素质要求为运用恰当的理论和实际方法，创造性地分析和解决工程问题。虽然都是工程实践能力的标准和要求，但具体标准随工程师职业类型进阶而不断提高，工程师的能力要求从参与工程活动过程到将知识和原理应用于实践，再到创造性地分析和解决问题，逐步提升。

**表 3 《英国专业工程师能力素质标准》具体要求**

| 能力要求 | 工程技师 | 主任工程师 | 特许工程师 |
|---|---|---|---|
| 知识与理解 | 理解和运用工程知识，应用技术和实践技能 | 结合一般和专门工程知识应用现有和新兴技术 | 结合普通和专业工程知识优化先进和复杂系统 |
| 设计、开发和解决工程难题 | 参与产品、设备、工艺、系统或服务的设计、开发、制造、建造、调试、退役、操作或维护 | 应用适当的理论和实践方法设计、开发、制造、建造、委托、操作、维护、退役和回收工程过程、系统、服务和产品 | 运用适当的理论和实际方法创造性地分析和解决工程问题 |
| 责任、管理和领导 | 接受并履行个人责任 | 提供技术和商业管理 | 提供技术和商业领导 |

续表

| 能力要求 | 工程技师 | 主任工程师 | 特许工程师 |
|---|---|---|---|
| 沟通和人际交往能力 | 运用有效的沟通和人际关系技巧 | 表现有效的沟通和人际关系技巧 | 展示有效的沟通和人际关系技巧 |
| 个人和职业承诺 | 表现出对适当的职业行为准则的个人承诺,确认对社会、职业和环境的义务 | 表现出对专业标准的个人承诺,承认对社会、专业和环境的义务 | 证明对专业标准的个人承诺,承认对社会、专业和环境的义务 |

### 2.3 认证对象发展路径:多样化的职业生涯分类设计,注重继续教育

(1)多样化的职业生涯分类设计基于本国工程教育特色和工业经济发展实际,设计各具特色的工程师职业发展路径,这些路径主要包括链式进阶型和分类平行型两类。链式进阶型工程师专业发展路径以日本和美国为代表,该模式不进行工程师职业类型划分,只设置从实习工程师到正式工程师的单向性发展路径。分类平行型工程师专业发展路径以澳大利亚和英国为代表,该模式根据工程教育不同学历和工程师群体不同功能划分平行路径,申请人可根据自身学历水平选择相应路径,最终注册成为不同类型的工程师。

作为链式进阶型专业发展路径的典型,美国以工程和技术认证委员会认证的工程教育学历为起点,申请人通过美国工程与测量考试委员会组织的工程基础考试,就可成为实习工程师;在此基础上,若具有 4 年以上工作经验,就可参加工程与测量考试委员会组织的工程实践与原理考试,通过后,可取得专业工程师的资质[11]。同样,日本受美国工程师制度影响,根据国情开辟两条既平行又汇合交叉的专业发展路径:第一条为以获得通过专业认证的工程教育本科学历为起点,通过日本技术者教育认证机构(Japan Accreditation Board for Engineering Education)认证专业毕业的学生可以免试,自动成为实习工程师:第二条为其他学历(获得非通过专业认证的本科专业学历)教育背景认证对象的专业发展路径,由于起点不同,毕业生需首先通过第一类考试才可成为实习工程师。申请人可基于三种情况进行经验积累进而参加第二类考试,分别为作为实习工程师积累 4 年及以上工作经验、具有主管领导监督下 4 年及以上工作经验或具有超过 7 年工作经验。通过第二类考试后登记注册即可获得专业工程师的资质[12]。

作为分类平行型专业发展路径的典型,英国根据中等、学士、硕士学历的不同,设计不同专业发展路径。通过积累职业发展和工作经验及专业评审面试达到各自路径的目标——工程技师、主任工程师和特许工程师,三者分别侧重承担工业实践中的技术工人、工业管理者和技术研发者等不同角色。澳大利亚工程师专业发展路径以获得经过专业认证的工程教育学历为起点,包括 3 种职业发展路径:4 年工程本科教育学位对应负责专业领域的职业工程师、3 年工程技术本科教育学位对应负责技术领域的工程技师、2 年工程高级文凭对应负责实践领域的助理工程师。3 类工程师相互平行、各自独立,分别通过继续教育、专业评审和面试等环节晋升至特许职业工程师、特许工程技师和特许助理工程师(图 1)。全面化、综合化的成长路径将纵向阶梯式晋升与横向工程师职业类型相结合,成为澳大利亚工程师专业发展路径的重要支撑和保障。

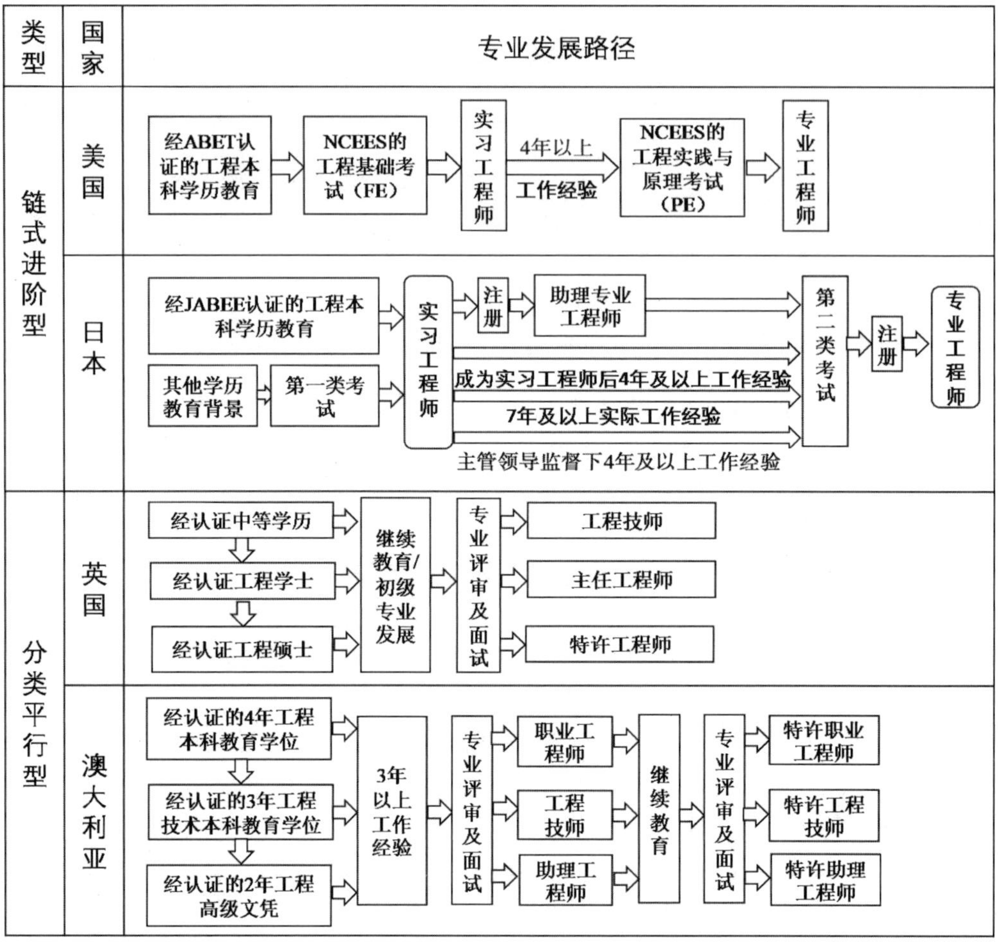


**图 1　英、美、日、澳工程师专业发展路径**

（2）开展继续教育，注重持续专业发展。人工智能、大数据、区块链等新技术变革正驱动工业生产模式快速迭代，要求工程师群体不断自我学习，不断提升应对社会变革的能力。作为专业工程师获得执照后自我提升的重要途径，继续教育成为工程师职业生涯发展路径不可或缺的一环，是对专业技术人员进行知识更新、补充、拓展和能力提升的高层次追加教育[13]。意识到继续教育的重要性，各国积极制定相关政策或要求以保证工程师的长期职业发展。美国的工程师资质并非终身制，每 5 年进行重新审核与更新，继续教育被视为评判专业工程师是否有资格更新执照的重要凭证。美国工程与测量考试委员会通过《继续专业能力准则》（Continuing Professional Competency Guidelines）建立全国统一的继续教育能力标准，该标准通过学时转换机制量化继续教育情况，量化内容主要包括大学课程、短期培训、高质量研讨会、专利成果、工业实践等。英国取得特许工程师资质需具备的条件之一为在职专业发展训练，即在职继续教育。英国工程理事会根据《英国专业工程师能力素质标准》的宗旨和原则制定专业发展准则，要求专业工程师自觉管理自身专业发展：专业学会对持续专业发展具有一定的支持和监督作用，专业学会对专业发展活动进行认证，组织和实施相关课程，对个人专业发展活动进行备案和评估。澳大利亚同样重视继续教育的作用。一方面，继续教育与工程师资质认证绑定，申请者提供申请前 5 年继续教育活动的记录才能进入特许工程师资质认证阶段。另一方面，继续教育也是特许工程师必须履行的义务，如果后续无法满足继续教育的要求，特许头衔将被撤销。澳大利亚工程师学会的继续教育政策要求专业工程师 3 年内须参与至少 150 小时的继续教育活动，具体包括不少于 50 小时的相关职业实践活动、不少于 10 小时的风险管理实践活动和不少于 15 小时的商业和管理技能实践活动，剩余学时需涵盖与工程职业生涯相关的一系列活动[14]。日本的继续教育与持续专业发展等同，持续专业发展被视为获得国际专业工程师相关证明的必备条件，对日本国内工程师与国际专业工程师资质互认起到至关重要的作用。日本专业工程师协会于 2017 年发布《技术士 CPD 指南》第三版，制定了专业工程师继续教育评估标准，以提高其专业素养与道德伦理水平[15]。日本专业工程师协会为有志于进修的工程师搭建资源丰富的学习平台，如通过持续专业发展讲座、参观会和研讨会等加强工程师之间的信息交流和资源共享。

### 2.4 认证体系国际融通：专业认证与注册工程师资质认证紧密衔接的国际互认机制

英、美、日、澳四国普遍建立了工程教育专业认证与注册工程师资质认证的融通机制。工程学历教育是工程师资质认证的起点，要取得专业工程师资质，须先取得相应经认证的教育背景，或证明自身具备同等学力。英、美、日、澳四国通过认证组织、认证标准、认证学历要求等内部和外部形式建构工程教育专业认证和注册工程师资质认证的融通机制，实现二者无缝对接。从认证组织看，美国和日本分别建立了相应认证职能的组织机构，美国设立美国工程与技术认证委员会进行工程教育专业认证，设立美国工程与测量考试委员会开展工程师资质认证工作；日本与美国类似，设立日本技术者教育认证机构组织工程教育专业认证的开展，设立日本专业工程师协会负责工程师资质认证。英国和澳大利亚虽由唯一机构（英国工程师理事会、澳大利亚工程师学会）统筹管理认证工作，但其内部分工明确，职责清晰，既负责工程教育专业认证的资源组织，又授权相应学会和委员会进行工程师资质认证。澳大利亚工程师学会的学科委员会主管工程教育专业认证，考查工程教育中的课程设置、师资、学时等内容，认证委员会负责开展澳大利亚工程师资质认证的相关工作。从认证标准看，工程学历教育标准与对工程师知识和能力基础的要求之间具有较高的逻辑连贯性，同时在形式上存在异质性。如英国工程教育专业认证和工程师资质认证都以“素质能力”为标准和基础，工程教育专业认证的指导性文件《高等学位教育认证》是《英国专业工程师能力素质标准》的子文件，以毕业生通过能力所展现出的学习效果作为认证标准。美国工程教育专业认证标准包括知识和思维能力、实践技能、一般通用能力等通用标准和各领域的专业标准，与美国工程与测量考试委员会组织的工程基础考试和工程实践与原理考试的考试内容的设计理念一致。从认证学历要求看，工程教育专业认证是工程师资质认证的起点，取得已认证专业的学位是获得职业资格的基本门槛[16]。英国工程技师对学历要求较低，获得经认证专业毕业的中等学历教育的个人可以申请；主任工程师的直接教育路径为获得认证专业的工程学士学位；特许工程师的直接教育路径为获得认证专业的工程硕士学位。美国专业工程师的申请要求申请人具有认证专业的 4 年及 4 年以上学位。澳大利亚工程师认证制度中，具有认证的教育背景是取得工程师资质的前提。职业工程师申请学历的要求是获得4年认证专业的工程学士学位，工程技师的要求是获得3年认证专业的工程学士学位，助理工程师的要求是获得2年认证专业的高级工程文凭。

随着工程师跨国流动日益频繁，执业资质能否被其他国家认可，成为工程教育和工程师职业资质管理领域的重要议题。由于各国工程教育专业认证标准不同、工程师专业发展路径多元，各国国内专业认证和注册工程师资质认证制度难以满足工程师参与国际合作工程项目的资质要求，建立专业认证与注册工程师资质认证高度协同的国际互认机制就非常必要。国际工程联盟（International Engineering Alliance）作为最大的全球性非营利工程组织之一，极大促进着各国专业认证与注册工程师资质认证的相互融通与国际互认。国际工程联盟由《华盛顿协议》《悉尼协议》《都柏林协议》三大工程教育专业认证互认协议，以及《国际职业工程师协议》《亚太工程师协议》《国际工程技术员协议》《国际工程技师协议》四大注册工程师资质认证互认协议组成。三大专业认证协议与四大工程师资质认证协议相互对应，形成协同体系。《华盛顿协议》是对工程专业教育四年本科教育学位水平的互认，与《国际职业工程师协议》和《亚太工程师协议》两个针对专业工程师资格的互认协议在毕业生学历水平上对应，《亚太工程师协议》在亚太经合组织经济体内互认，《国际职业工程师协议》在世界范围内更广泛地适用；《悉尼协议》认证的工程教育学位水平与《国际工程技术员协议》相对应，为三年制副工程技术学位；《都柏林协议》专业认证的学位水平则与《国际工程技师协议》相对应，为两年副学士学位[17]。英、美、日、澳四国均已加入面向4年本科工程学位水平的《国际职业工程师协议》，并根据本国工程教育发展实际加入其他不同的国际互认协议（表4），有助于简化工程师在其管辖地区申请从业的程序，实现工程师能力评价标准的相对统一。具体来看，该协议创建了工程师专业工程能力的国际标准框架，授权成员组织成为国际专业工程师注册的有效组成部分，承认各国建立的工程师知识掌握与实践运用能力标准的实质等效性[18]。《国际职业工程师协议》不仅促进各国人才流动壁垒的消除和工程师群体的国际合作，各国还可根据其创建的工程师能力资质框架不断完善本国的注册工程师制度，从而有效提升本国工程师的质量。

**表4　澳、美、英、日加入的国际互认协议**

<table>
<tr><th>序号</th><th>国家</th><th>专业认证互认协议</th><th>工程师互认协议</th></tr>
<tr><td>1</td><td>澳大利亚</td><td rowspan="3">《华盛顿协议》<br>《悉尼协议》<br>《都柏林协议》</td><td>《国际职业工程师协议》<br>《亚太工程师协议》<br>《国际工程技术员协议》<br>《国际工程技师协议》</td></tr>
<tr><td>2</td><td>英国</td><td>《国际职业工程师协议》<br>《国际工程技师协议》</td></tr>
<tr><td>3</td><td>美国</td><td rowspan="2">《国际职业工程师协议》<br>《亚太工程师协议》</td></tr>
<tr><td>4</td><td>日本</td><td>《华盛顿协议》</td></tr>
</table>

## 3 中国工程师资质认证制度的建构路径

### 3.1 构建政府主导、市场本位与高校协同多主体参与的认证治理共同体

我国虽在部分工程领域建立了准入类和水平评价类注册制度，但两类制度特色鲜明且相对独立，既不能覆盖所有工程领域，也未建立全国统一的工程师制度，管理体系上与国际通行做法尚未接轨。因此，注册工程师资质认证制度未来建构要多方协作，形塑“政府宏观主导、市场驱动、高校深度协同”的生态格局。从四国经验看，不论是强调权力主导的自上而下的强制性建构模式，还是强调知识主导的自下而上的诱致性建构逻辑，都离不开政府、职业协会、企业、高校、公众等多元主体的协商共建。从我国现状看，当前存在工程师资质认证治理主体单一、全国统一资质认证机构尚未建立、多元利益主体参与度不足等问题，亟须建构多主体深度协同参与的注册工程师资质认证治理体系。第一，加强顶层设计。通过政策规划、法律制定等方式，系统谋划注册工程师资质认证制度的建立、发展与完善路径。第二，依托2021年成立的中国工程师联合体，逐步构建全国统一的注册工程师资质认证机构，科学设计机构运行结构、能力评价标准制定、资质认证程序、专家队伍组建等事项，赋予相应法律地位。第三，厘清监管部门、职业协会、企业、高校及公众等多元主体的职能边界与角色定位，尤其要提升职业协会、企业等主体在注册工程师资质认证制度设计与实施过程中的话语权与参与度。

### 3.2 推进工程师制度分类与分层设计

过于简单的工程师群体分类既不适应日益复杂的知识生产模式转型需求，也无法契合诸多新兴工程领域快速技术革新迭代的趋势，科学合理的工程师类型划分与职业生涯发展路径设计，既有利于工科专业动态调整人才培养方案与目标，也有利于工程师群体按自身未来职业发展需求的资质标准不断提升技术能力和非技术能力，从而实现人才供给与行业需求的高度匹配。四国工程师发展路径的实践经验可为我国工程师制度分类与分层设计提供参考。首先，纵向看，强化专业认证作为工程师资质认证的起点，针对三年制硕士、四年制本科等不同学历层次的毕业生规划发展路径，满足我国多类型工程师群体的需求。其次，从横向看，结合中国工业发展实际和国情特点，以及国际产业科技革命发展趋势，确立相应的工程师职业类别。例如，借鉴英国或澳大利亚经验，按研发、设计、生产和服务四类功能对工程师群体进行划分。研发工程师主要从事复杂产品或大型工程项目的研究、开发和咨询；设计工程师主要从事产品、工程项目或生产过程的设计与开发；生产工程师主要从事工程项目的建造；服务工程师主要从事工程项目建成后的运行、维护与管理[19]。再次，根据不同类型、层次工程师群体的特色与实际，建立分层考试制与申请考核制相结合的资质认证程序，实现实习工程师向专业工程师的阶梯式晋升。最后，注重继续教育，建立赋能工程师群体知识更新与能力提升的长效机制，促进工程师未来的持续专业发展与职业生涯发展。

### 3.3 建构专业认证与注册工程师资质认证的衔接机制

资料显示，大部分《华盛顿协议》参与组织已建立起专业认证与注册工程师资质认证的有效衔接机制，从而在制度层面构建完善的工程教育质量保障机制。从组织架构来看，主要分为两种类型：一是兼具专业认证和注册工程师资质认证职能的综合性认证管理机构，以英国、澳大利亚为代表；二是针对专业认证、注册工程师资质认证分别成立独立认证管理机构，建立两种机构紧密合作的机制，以美国、日本为代表。我国仅有工程教育专业认证机构——中国工程教育专业认证协会，尚未设立全国性统一的注册工程师资质认证机构，尚未构建工程师能力评价标准体系，缺乏专业认证与注册工程师资质认证之间的有效衔接机制。首先，应着手建立工程师注册机构和构建工程师能力评价体系，制定兼顾各方利益的工程师技术资格与工程教育学科专业分类对接机制，为推进两者的有效衔接奠定基础。其次，整合专业认证与工程师注册相关机构的组织结构与功能定位，构建系统性的制度运行框架，有效提高衔接机制建设的科学设计与执行效率。再次，加快国家层面资质框架建设，为专业认证和工程师注册搭建桥梁，使工程教育专业认证标准与国家资质框架的学历标准、准入标准等相衔接，注册工程师资质与国家资质框架中的资格等级标准、资格类型标准相契合[20]。最后，在逐步建构注册工程师资质认证制度的同时，积极推动加入以《国际职业工程师协议》为代表的国际互认协议，为我国工程师群体走向全球提供具有国际互认质量标准的通行证。总之，通过建立专业认证与注册工程师资质认证的紧密衔接机制，加入相关国际协议，能够有效赋能我国培养大批具备复杂工程问题解决能力的卓越工程师，有效支撑中国特色、国际一流的工程教育强国建设目标。

## 参考文献


[1] 倪军. 好的工程教育是教学生解决问题[N]. 中国教育报，2012-02-06（002）.

[2] 胡德鑫. 我国世界一流大学建设的制度逻辑与路径选择[J]. 复旦教育论坛，2019，17（3）：74-80.

[3] Ministry of Education，Culture，Sports，Science and Technology. 组織図の紹介[EB/OL].（2022-01-01）[2022-05-16]. https://www.mext.go.jp/b_menu/soshiki2/04.htm.

[4] The Institution of Professional Engineers，Japan. 組織｜公益社団法人[EB/OL].（2022-01-01）[2022-05-16]. https://www.engineer.or.jp/c_topics/000/000042.html.

[5] Engineering Council UK. History [EB/OL].（2022-01-01）[2022-05-16]. https://www.engc.org.uk/about-us/our-purpose-and-or-ganisational-structure/history/.

[6] National Council of Examiners for Engineering and Surveying. Bylaws 2020[EB/OL].（2020-01-01）[2022-05-16]. https://ncees.org/wp-content/uploads/Bylaws-2020.pdf.

[7] Engineers Australia. Engineers Australia History [EB/OL].（2022-01-01）[2022-05-22]. https://www.engineersaustralia.org.au/About-Us/Overview/History.

[8] 张彦通，韩晓燕. 美、德两国工程教育专业认证制度的特色与借鉴[J]. 中国高等教育，2006（2）：60-62.

[9] Engineering Council UK. The UK Standard for Professional Engineering Competence and

Commitment( UK-SPEC )[EB/ OL].( 2022-01-01 ) [2022-05-16]. https://www.engc.org.uk/media/3877/uk-spec-v12-web.pdf.

[10] Engineers Australia. Stage 1 Competency Standard for Professional Engineer [EB/OL].( 2017-03-01 ) [2022-05-22]. https://www.engineersaustralia.org.au/sites/default/files/resource-files/2017-03/Stage%201%20Competency%20Standards.pdf.

[11] 王瑞朋，王孙禺，李锋亮. 论美国工程教育专业认证制度与工程师注册制度的衔接[J]. 清华大学教育研究，2015，36( 1 )：34-40.

[12] The Institution of Professional Engineers，Japan. 技術士入の道[EB/OL].( 2021-05-07 ) [2022-05-22]. https://jabee.org/doc/giju tusi 210507.pdf.

[13] 廖娟，李小忠. 美国工程师培养模式研究[J]. 中国高教研究，2011( 2 )：52-55.

[14] Engineers Australia. Continuing Professional Development [EB/OL].( 2022-01-01 )[2022-05-01]. https://www.engineersaustralia.org.au/membership/cpd-requirements.

[15] The Institution of Professional Engineers Japan. 技術士 CPD( 継続研鑽 )ガイドライン第 3 版[EB/OL].( 2017-04-01 ) [2022-05-28]. https://www.engineer.or.jp/cmtee/kensyuu/170401CPDguideline3.pdf.

[16] 郑娟，王孙禺. 英国工程教育专业认证与工程师职业资格衔接机制研究[J]. 中国大学教学，2017( 2 )：88-96.

[17] 王玲，秦戎，张鸣天，等.《国际职业工程师协议》研究及我国工程师资格国际互认发展前景分析[J]. 高等工程教育研究，2020( 4 )：34-40.

[18] International Engineering Alliance. IPEA Agreement [EB/OL].( 2022-01-01 ) [2022-05-28]. https://www.ieagreements.org/agreements/ipea/.

[19] 林健. 工程师的分类与工程人才培养[J]. 清华大学教育研究，2010，31( 1 )：51-60.

[20] 朱露，王庚，胡德鑫，等. 工程教育专业认证标准的国际案例研究[J]. 高等工程教育研究，2022( 3 )：32-45，73.

# 工科本科生解决复杂工程问题能力评价模型①

朱　露　唐浩兴　胡德鑫　顾佩华

**摘要**：培养解决复杂工程问题能力是工程教育的重要目标之一，但对如何评价该能力，高校和工程教育专业认证组织尚未建立成熟的标准，相关理论研究与实践探索有待深入。通过德尔菲法构建工科本科生解决复杂工程问题的能力评价指标体系，其包含5个一级指标和33个二级指标；运用层次分析法给指标赋权；基于该指标体系对120名工科应届毕业生进行模糊综合评价。研究结果显示：解决复杂工程问题能力是包含多项能力的高层次认知操作序列，由发现问题、表征问题、设计方案、实施方案、评价与改良五种能力构成；设计方案和实施方案是关键评价指标，探索精神、多学科和交叉学科知识应用、系统思维、方案比较与优化意识、持续改进理念、职业道德修养和实验技能是相对重要的评价点；样本高校学生解决复杂工程问题能力总体处于中等水平，工程设计能力良好，发现问题与实施方案能力偏弱，与技术能力相比，非技术能力亟待提高。
**关键词**：工科本科生；复杂工程问题；解决复杂工程问题能力；评价指标

## Models for Evaluating Undergraduate Engineering Students' Ability to Solve Complex Engineering Problems

*Zhu Lu, Tang Haoxing, Hu Dexin, Gu Peihua*

**Abstract:** Cultivating students' ability to solve complex engineering problems is one of the most important goals for engineering education. However, as to how to evaluate this ability, higher education institutions and engineering education accreditation organizations have not yet established mature evaluation criteria and associate methods as well as tools. More theoretical research and practical explorations are needed for developing effective and efficient evaluation approaches. Therefore, this paper applies Delphi method to construct an evaluation index system to assess students' ability for solving complex engineering problems, the evaluation index system consists of 5 primary indicators and 33 secondary indicators; the hierarchical analysis is used to assign weights to each indicator; the fuzzy comprehensive evaluation is carried out to obtain the evaluation results. A case study of 120 engineering graduates based on the evaluation index system was conducted, the results of the study showed that the ability to solve complex engineering problems is a high-level cognitive-operational sequence with five types of abilities: problem identification, problem characterization, solution design, solution implementation, and evaluation and improvement. The design and implementation of solu-

① 本文刊登于《高等工程教育研究》2023年第4期第86~99页。

tions are key evaluation indicators, and the spirit of exploration, the application of multidisciplinary and cross-disciplinary knowledge, systematic thinking, the awareness of solution comparison and optimization, the concept of continuous improvement, professional ethics and experimental skills are relatively important evaluative criteria. Students' ability to solve complex engineering problems in the case study university is generally at a medium level. Their engineering design ability is good, but the ability to find problems and implement solutions is relatively weak. In comparison with students' technical ability, their non-technical ability needs to be improved.

**Keywords**: engineering undergraduates; complex engineering problems; the ability to solve complex engineering problems; evaluation index

## 1 研究背景

根据世界经济论坛未来就业报告，雇主最看重的多项能力中，解决复杂问题能力稳居前列[1-2]。现代工程朝综合集成方向发展，复杂程度不断提高，工程实践从狭窄技术领域拓展至生活、生命和生态领域[3]，工程问题演变为以科学、技术为基础，融合经济、社会、环境、人文、健康、安全等非技术元素于一体的复杂系统，解决复杂工程问题能力成为工程师必备的能力。2013 年起，《华盛顿协议》毕业要求与工程师能力标准中明确了复杂工程问题的内涵和基本特征，要求成员组织认证的工程专业按国际实质等效原则培养学生解决复杂工程问题的能力；2021 年对复杂工程问题的定义做出调整，突出复杂工程问题的非技术性、创造性、跨学科性和系统性，结合修订的毕业要求对学生解决复杂工程问题能力提出更高要求[4]。我国 2015 版《工程教育专业认证标准》开始特别强调学生解决复杂工程问题的能力，尤其是 2016 年加入《华盛顿协议》后，该能力已成为专业认证考评、专业培养的重点和难点。评价学生解决复杂工程问题的能力，需运用多种方法相互佐证、综合评判，常用评价方法有项目设计与开发、专题研讨、综合分析报告、复杂部件作品设计等[5]。然而，为增强能力的可测量性与评价的客观性，实施评价还要以一定的能力指标为参照，量规表（rubrics）是制定能力评价标准的重要形式。目前，已有学者研制出工程设计能力评价量规[6-8]，但对如何评价学生解决复杂工程问题的能力，专业认证组织和高校尚未开发出成熟的通用性评价量规。此外，从既有研究看，国内学者多从国内外专业认证组织视角对复杂工程问题和解决复杂工程问题的能力进行概念界定[9-12]，较少从教育者、受教育者和工程实践者视角探究解决复杂工程问题能力的构成及如何有效评价。本研究在前期成果和政策文本的基础上，结合对工程教育专家、工科教师、学生和行业企业界代表的问卷调查与访谈，深入探究工科本科生解决复杂工程问题能力的概念框架与测量维度，研制评价指标体系，以为认证协会和高校评价学生解决复杂工程问题的能力提供工具支持。

## 2 概念界定

### 2.1 复杂问题与复杂工程问题

问题指特定情境的未知实体（体现目标状态与原始状态之间的差距）[13]。从认知心理学角度看，问题可分为结构良好的问题和结构不良的问题，结构良好问题的原始状态、目标状态及转化状态的方法均明确界定，结构不良的问题上述三者至少有一项未明确界定[14]。复杂问题是结构不良问题，复杂问题通常产生于特定环境或情境，问题描述不清楚、界定不清晰，解决问题所需的信息未包含于问题状态中，问题解决方案具有多样性和不可预测性，需运用多学科知识进行探索[15]。

关于复杂工程问题的内涵，国际工程组织及部分国家认证协会做出了解释。《华盛顿协议》在细化工程知识与态度框架的基础上，明确了复杂工程问题的七大特征，WP1 为任何复杂工程问题须具备的基本特征，同时，复杂工程问题还应具备选择性特征 WP2~WP7 中的一项或多项[4]。此外，亦有研究从教学实践者角度探讨复杂工程问题的内涵和特征，强调复杂工程问题源于真实情境，是多个结构良好问题的集合，可生成多种问题解决方案，会随外部环境变化产生难以预期的子问题等[16-17]。本文将复杂工程问题界定为包含技术要素与非技术要素、融合多学科知识、由诸多子问题组成的工程问题或新兴问题。复杂工程问题没有明确的解决方案，难以运用既定工程标准和实践规范解决，解决复杂工程问题需采用系统方法，协同多元利益群体，具备抽象思维和创新创造能力。

### 2.2 解决问题的过程与解决复杂工程问题的过程

解决问题是指通过系列认知策略消除障碍，将问题的原始状态转化为目标状态的过程[14]。行为主义心理学家最早对解决问题的过程进行阶段划分，代表性成果即杜威五阶段论[18]。诸多阶段论模型在此基础上建立，如华莱士将解决问题的过程分为知识准备、沉思酝酿、灵感突现、方法验证四个阶段[19]。在认知理论家们看来，这些观点过于简单，只是对解决问题过程的描述性解释[20-21]。认知心理学诞生之后，心理学家和教育学家开始把解决问题的过程视为高阶认知活动，尝试使用认知领域的术语（如问题表征、图式激活）对解决问题的各阶段进行深度探究。纽威尔和西蒙指出，解决问题就是对问题的内涵表征和信息搜索[22]。吉克认为，解决问题包含建构与表征、寻求解决方法、尝试应用、评价四个环节[23]。布兰斯坦福和斯坦提出解决问题的 IDEAL 模型，涉及识别问题、定义和表征问题、探索可能的问题解决策略、执行问题解决方案、回顾和评价活动效果五个阶段[24]。

目前，学界有关解决问题过程的研究较少区分简单问题和复杂问题[25]，对解决复杂问题的过程进行阶段划分时，多将解决问题的一般理论模型融入具体学科的复杂问题[26]。本文选用解决问题的 IDEAL 模型，结合工程活动的特殊性（如工程实践强调设计与创新，注重对社会的广泛影响），将解决复杂工程问题的过程分为发现问题、表征问题、设计方案、实施方案、反思与评价五个阶段。

### 2.3 解决问题的能力与解决复杂工程问题的能力

已有研究多将解决问题的能力视为高层次认知操作序列。根据国际学业测评项目（Program for International Student Assessment，PISA）的定义，解决问题的能力是个体在问题解决方案尚不明确的情况下，通过认知加工以理解和解决问题的能力，包含个体参与问题情境的意愿，这种意愿将促使个体成为具有建设意识和反思精神的公民[27]。弗布克从培训视角将解决问题的能力细分为识别、分析、沟通、行动、运用方法技巧和学习等能力[28]。费舍尔和诺伊伯特提出 KSAO 模型，即知识（knowledge）、技能（skill）、能力（ability）和其他特质（other characteristics），强调一般能力和特殊能力对解决问题的双重影响[29]。多纳认为，解决问题包含获取信息、明确与平衡目标、制订计划与做出决策、自我管理四项操作智能[30]。概言之，解决问题的能力是兼具操作性和创造性的高级思维方式与智力活动[28]，包含知识基础、认知能力、元认知调节能力、情绪、动机等多种能力要素[25]。

鉴于解决问题能力的要素构成具有多元化和系统性的特征，本文以既有成果为基础，将解决复杂工程问题能力界定为包含多种子能力的高层次认知操作序列，同时结合工程技术人才培养的特殊性，突显解决复杂工程问题与解决其他学科复杂问题所需能力素质的不同。具体而言，解决复杂工程问题能力是在真实或模拟真实的工程情境下，个体感知问题、分析问题、探索解决问题的策略、落实解决问题的方案、评价方案实施效果并不断修正和改进方案的能力，在此过程中，实践主体综合运用工程知识和多学科原理，充分利用工程工具、技术和资源，注重团队交流与合作，严格遵守工程师职业规范、专业技术标准和行业政策法规，积极承担社会责任、维护国家利益、促进全球发展。

## 3 研究方法

采用混合研究方法，从五方面对资料、数据进行质性和量化分析。一是通过政策文件、学术论文、访谈文本获取解决复杂工程问题所需能力的相关规定和描述，借助 NVivo 12 软件对三个来源的质性资料进行编码和类属划分，初步拟定工科本科生解决复杂工程问题的能力指标项；二是采用德尔菲法，以匿名方式征询专家对初拟指标的意见和建议，经多轮调查、汇总和反馈，得到较一致的标准建设方案，据此构建工科本科生解决复杂工程问题的能力评价指标体系；三是基于层次分析法构造判断矩阵，邀请专家通过两两比较方式对各指标的重要性做出判断，根据专家判断结果计算指标权重；四是参照量规表设计方法，确定二级指标的评价等级，提供有关各等级行为表现的具体描述；五是以设计好的指标体系为评价工具，对 L 高校（地方高校）四个工科本科专业共计 120 名毕业生解决复杂工程问题的能力进行模糊综合评价。

## 4 研究过程

### 4.1 评价指标初拟

初步构建评价指标体系分三步进行。第一，查找相关文献，了解已有研究对解决问题过程的阶段划分，结合工程实践的特殊性，探究解决复杂工程问题的主要阶段，确定工科本科生解决复杂工程问题的能力测评维度。研究发现，解决问题一般包括识别、界定、假设、验证、反思等心理过程。因此，基于现代认知心理学解决问题的 IDEAL 模型，同时考虑工程活动重设计、重社会影响的特点，最终确定解决复杂工程问题所包含的五个阶段为发现问题、表征问题、设计方案、实施方案、反思与评价，将其作为工科本科生解决复杂工程问题的能力测评维度,从这五个维度细化评价指标。第二,收集质性文本资料。资料来源有三类。一是从官方网站获得的关于工科本科生毕业要求、解决复杂工程问题所需能力的政策文件,为实现工科生能力指标与工程师职业要求相衔接,将工程师职业能力标准纳入分析范畴,最终获得包含国际工程联盟的毕业生素质和工程师能力标准、欧洲工程教育专业认证体系的本科层次专业成果标准、欧洲国家工程协会联合会的工程师专业胜任力要求、CDIO能力大纲、中国卓越工程师教育培养计划本科层次通用标准、十国(英国、美国、爱尔兰、新西兰、澳大利亚、加拿大、新加坡、日本、德国和俄罗斯)工程教育专业认证协会的毕业要求标准等在内的15份政策文本。二是通过谷歌学术、中国知网等数据库查找有关解决问题能力、解决工程问题能力、工科本科生毕业要求、工程师职业要求、未来人才能力素质期望等学术论文,筛选出有效文献48篇。三是选取6名工科应届毕业生(来自智能制造工程、冶金工程、电气工程及其自动化、光电信息科学与工程、机器人工程、化学工程与工艺6个专业)、6名工科教师(教授2名,副教授2名,讲师2名,专业包含机械、材料、电气、化工、电子信息和自动化)、5名企业代表(正高级工程师2名,高级工程师2名,工程师1名),从学科知识、技术能力、非技术能力和综合素质四方面进行访谈,了解不同利益群体对工科本科生解决复杂工程问题应具备的能力的看法。第三,以NVivo 12软件为分析工具,从发现问题、表征问题、设计方案、实施方案、反思与评价五个维度,对质性文本资料进行编码和类属划分,最终形成5个一级指标和27个二级指标构成的评价指标体系(表1)。

**表1　解决复杂工程问题的能力评价指标体系(草案)**

| 评价维度 | 指标层 |
|---|---|
| a 发现问题 | a1 好奇心、探索欲和批判精神<br>a2 关注学科前沿和社会发展需要<br>a3 提出专业领域亟待探究的问题<br>a4 分析工程问题产生的原因并确定研究目标 |
| b 表征问题 | b1 正确选用分析工具和分析技术<br>b2 灵活运用多学科知识<br>b3 熟悉工程师职业规范和相关法律法规<br>b4 有效获取并利用文献和其他信息资源<br>b5 工程伦理意识和社会责任感 |
| c 设计方案 | c1 运用工程的系统化原则进行方案设计<br>c2 确定利益相关者的需求并考虑采用新技术<br>c3 提出不同设计方案<br>c4 确保设计方案符合工程准则和实践规范<br>c5 预设方案成果<br>c6 制订详细的方案实施计划<br>c7 利用相关资源、工具和技术进行实验设计<br>c8 设计满足特定需求的系统、部件或工艺流程 |
| d 实施方案 | d1 运用恰当的工具、技术和资源开展实验<br>d2 做好项目实施前的准备工作<br>d3 在项目实施过程中进行团队协作<br>d4 在多元化、包容性环境中进行有效沟通<br>d5 严格遵守工程师职业规范和相关法律法规 |

续表

| 评价维度 | 指标层 |
|---|---|
| e 反思与评价 | e1 反思问题解决过程<br>e2 判断问题解决方案的目标达成度<br>e3 多维度评价工程创造物的价值<br>e4 虚心接受批评和建议<br>e5 及时修正方案 |

### 4.2 评价指标筛选

评价指标筛选主要采用德尔菲法。德尔菲法又称专家咨询法，由调查者制定函询表征求专家意见，专家根据调查者反馈材料背对背匿名交流，经过数轮反馈后，专家意见渐趋一致，最终获得具有统计意义的专家集体判断结果[31]。本研究运用德尔菲法进行了两轮专家调查，在整合专家评议结果的基础上，研制出工科本科生解决复杂工程问题的能力评价指标体系。

#### 1. 专家选择

本研究共邀请 17 名专家参与咨询，包括 7 名工科相关专业教师、4 名工程教育研究领域专家、6 名企业专家（背景信息见表 2）。专家组人员涵盖教学实践者、教育研究者和工程实践者，能从多元视角探索工科本科生解决复杂工程问题的能力测评维度，有利于评价指标的系统建构。

表 2　专家组成员基本信息

| 专家类别 | 背景信息 | | 人数 |
|---|---|---|---|
| 工科教师（7 人） | 职称 | 教授 | 4 |
| | | 副教授 | 2 |
| | | 讲师 | 1 |
| | 工作单位 | 工科优势高校 | 3 |
| | | 综合性高校 | 2 |
| | | 一般地方院校 | 2 |
| | 研究领域 | 传统工科专业 | 4 |
| | | 新工科专业 | 3 |
| 工程教育研究领域专家（4 人） | 核心期刊论文发表数 | 1~5 篇 | 1 |
| | | 6~10 篇 | 2 |
| | | 10 篇以上 | 1 |
| | 省部级以上项目主持数 | 1~2 个 | 2 |
| | | 3~4 个 | 1 |
| | | 4 个以上 | 1 |
| | 从事工程教育研究年限 | 5~7 年 | 2 |
| | | 8~10 年 | 1 |
| | | 10 年以上 | 1 |

续表

| 专家类别 | 背景信息 | | 人数 |
|---|---|---|---|
| 企业专家（6人） | 职称 | 工程师（中级） | 2 |
| | | 高级工程师（副高级） | 2 |
| | | 正高级工程师（正高级） | 2 |
| | 工作年限 | 5~7年 | 1 |
| | | 8~10年 | 3 |
| | | 10年以上 | 2 |

**2. 专家函询过程**

以初拟评价指标为调查内容，通过编制调查问卷，要求专家采用经典李克特五级量表[32]判断各项指标的重要程度（1表示非常不重要，2表示比较不重要，3表示一般，4表示比较重要，5表示非常重要），设置“修改意见”栏和“新增”栏，以便专家指出需增加、删除或修改的指标项。同时，要求专家说明对研究内容的熟悉程度，给出判断指标重要程度的依据。专家咨询共进行了两轮，收回调查数据后，统计各项指标的均值、中位数、满分率和变异系数，计算两轮咨询结果的肯德尔协调系数，根据专家意见集中程度和专家评价结果一致性程度，对指标进行增删和修改。

**3. 专家积极性**

专家积极性用问卷有效回收率表示，回收率大于70%，表示专家积极程度较高[33]。第一轮专家咨询发放17份问卷，获得有效问卷15份；第二轮专家咨询发放16份问卷，获得有效问卷15份。两轮问卷回收率分别为88.24%和93.75%，说明专家参与调查的积极性较高。

**4. 专家权威性**

专家权威性常由两个因素决定：一是专家判断指标重要程度的依据（用判断依据系数$C_a$表示），包括理论分析、实践经验、参考国内外文献资料和凭直觉选择，量化方式见表3；二是专家对研究问题的熟悉程度（用熟悉程度系数$C_s$表示），包括很熟悉、熟悉、较熟悉、一般、较不熟悉和很不熟悉，分别计分0.9、0.7、0.5、0.3、0.1、0[34]。专家权威性（用$C_r$表示）为$C_a$和$C_s$的算术平均值，$C_r$的取值为0~1，$C_r \geqslant 0.7$视为可接受[35]。计算可知（表4），两轮专家的$C_r$值均分布于0.7~1之间，平均值分别为0.843和0.860，说明专家具有较高的权威性，调查结果较为可靠。

**表3 专家判断依据及其影响程度量化表[35]**

| 判断依据 | 对专家判断的影响程度 | | |
|---|---|---|---|
| | 大 | 中 | 小 |
| 理论分析 | 0.3 | 0.2 | 0.1 |
| 实践经验 | 0.5 | 0.4 | 0.3 |

续表

| 判断依据 | 对专家判断的影响程度 | | |
|---|---|---|---|
| | 大 | 中 | 小 |
| 参考国内外文献资料 | 0.1 | 0.1 | 0.1 |
| 凭直觉选择 | 0.1 | 0.1 | 0.1 |

**表 4　专家权威程度**

| 专家编号 | 第一轮 | | | 第二轮 | | |
|---|---|---|---|---|---|---|
| | $C_a$ | $C_s$ | $C_r$ | $C_a$ | $C_s$ | $C_r$ |
| 1 | 0.9 | 0.9 | 0.9 | 1 | 0.9 | 0.95 |
| 2 | 0.9 | 0.7 | 0.8 | 0.9 | 0.7 | 0.8 |
| 3 | 0.9 | 0.7 | 0.8 | 0.9 | 0.7 | 0.8 |
| 4 | 1 | 0.9 | 0.95 | 1 | 0.9 | 0.95 |
| 5 | 1 | 0.9 | 0.95 | 1 | 0.9 | 0.95 |
| 6 | 1 | 0.9 | 0.95 | 1 | 0.9 | 0.95 |
| 7 | 1 | 0.7 | 0.85 | 1 | 0.7 | 0.85 |
| 8 | 1 | 0.7 | 0.85 | 1 | 0.7 | 0.85 |
| 9 | 0.9 | 0.7 | 0.8 | 1 | 0.7 | 0.85 |
| 10 | 0.9 | 0.7 | 0.8 | 1 | 0.7 | 0.85 |
| 11 | 0.9 | 0.7 | 0.8 | 0.9 | 0.7 | 0.8 |
| 12 | 0.9 | 0.7 | 0.8 | 0.9 | 0.7 | 0.8 |
| 13 | 0.9 | 0.7 | 0.8 | 1 | 0.7 | 0.85 |
| 14 | 0.9 | 0.7 | 0.8 | 0.9 | 0.7 | 0.8 |
| 15 | 0.9 | 0.7 | 0.8 | 1 | 0.7 | 0.85 |
| 均值 | 0.933 | 0.753 | 0.843 | 0.966 | 0.753 | 0.86 |

### 5. 第一轮专家咨询结果

指标筛选以专家意见集中程度和专家评价结果一致性程度为依据。专家意见集中程度通过各项指标得分的均值、中位数和满分率反映。均值和中位数大于 3.5，满分率大于 20%，视为可接受[36]。专家评价结果一致性程度用肯德尔协调系数（$W$）和指标变异系数（$C_v$）表示。肯德尔协调系数介于 0~1 之间，越接近 1，专家评价结果的一致性越好[37]。$C_v$ 用以反映专家意见的离散程度，取值越小，专家意见协调程度越高[38]。综合以上指标，本研究将均值和中位数大于 3.5、满分率大于 20%、肯德尔协调系数大于 0.6、变异系数小于 0.25、显著性小于 0.05 作为筛选指标和终止专家咨询的标准。

第一轮专家咨询中，一级指标的肯德尔协调系数为 0.623，显著性（$P$ 值）小于 0.05，卡方值为 37.377，5 项指标的变异系数均小于 0.25，各指标的平均值和中位数在 4 及以上，满分率大于 20%。可知，专家对 5 个一级指标的认可度较高，专家意见之间的协调性较好，一级指标的构成要素可取，5 项指标均予保留。

对于 27 个二级指标，$W$ 值为 0.393，专家协调程度一般，$C_v$ 有 3 项（$C_5$、$E_1$、$E_4$）大于 0.25，且有一项指标（$E_4$）的平均值小于 3.5。基于数据结果和专家意见，对二级指标体系进行修正：删除 3 个变异系数大于 0.25 的指标（$C_5$、$E_1$、$E_4$）；结合专家反馈（表 5），新增 9 个指标（a3、b5、c4、c6、d2、d4、d8、e1、e5），同时对内容残缺或表述不当的指标予以修改，最终形成包含 33 个二级指标的新问卷，随后进行第二轮专家咨询。一级指标与二级指标的相关统计数据见表 6 和表 7。

**表 5　第一轮专家咨询意见**

<table>
<tr><th>内容残缺项</th><th>修改建议</th><th>表述不当项</th><th>修改建议</th><th>建议新增项</th></tr>
<tr><td>B2 灵活运用多学科知识</td><td>补充交叉学科知识</td><td>A3 提出专业领域亟待探究的问题</td><td>“提出”改为“预测或识别”</td><td rowspan="3">a3 了解用户（或市场）需求<br>b5 综合集成、非线性的工程思维<br>c4 识别、评估风险并确定防范措施<br>c6 制定工程验收标准<br>d2 判断、评定与减少误差<br>d4 运用系统方法进行项目实施和管理<br>d8 家国情怀、全球视野和社会责任感<br>e1 查找设计方案和问题解决过程中的不足之处<br>e5 坚持持续质量改进的工程管理理念</td></tr>
<tr><td>C3 提出不同设计方案</td><td>除提出不同设计方案，还要通过比较与优化，选择最优方案，建议补充“证明最优方案的合理性”</td><td>C2 确定利益相关者的需求并考虑采用新技术</td><td>“确定”改为“平衡”</td></tr>
<tr><td>E5 及时修正方案</td><td>如果方案存在问题，则需修正；如果暂时未发现问题，也要坚持持续改进理念，不断改进和完善方案，建议将“修正”改为“修正或改进”</td><td>D3 在项目实施过程中进行团队协作</td><td>对团队合作进行进一步说明，如以成员或领导者等不同身份进行团队合作</td></tr>
</table>

**表 6　第一轮专家咨询一级指标统计结果**

| 指标编号 | 中位数 | 满分率 | 平均值 | 标准差 | 变异系数 |
|---|---|---|---|---|---|
| A | 5 | 80.00% | 4.80 | 0.414 | 0.086 |
| B | 4 | 33.33% | 4.13 | 0.743 | 0.180 |
| C | 5 | 86.67% | 4.87 | 0.352 | 0.072 |
| D | 4 | 40.00% | 4.20 | 0.775 | 0.185 |
| E | 4 | 33.33% | 4.13 | 0.743 | 0.180 |

**表 7　第一轮专家咨询二级指标统计结果**

| 指标编号 | 中位数 | 满分率 | 平均值 | 标准差 | 变异系数 |
|---|---|---|---|---|---|
| A1 | 4 | 46.67% | 4.47 | 0.516 | 0.115 |
| A2 | 5 | 53.33% | 4.40 | 0.737 | 0.168 |
| A3 | 5 | 60.00% | 4.60 | 0.507 | 0.110 |
| A4 | 4 | 40.00% | 4.33 | 0.617 | 0.142 |

续表

| 指标编号 | 中位数 | 满分率 | 平均值 | 标准差 | 变异系数 |
|---|---|---|---|---|---|
| B1 | 4 | 33.33% | 4.13 | 0.743 | 0.180 |
| B2 | 5 | 53.33% | 4.47 | 0.640 | 0.143 |
| B3 | 5 | 60.00% | 4.53 | 0.640 | 0.141 |
| B4 | 5 | 66.67% | 4.67 | 0.488 | 0.104 |
| B5 | 5 | 60.00% | 4.40 | 0.828 | 0.188 |
| C1 | 4 | 40.00% | 4.20 | 0.775 | 0.185 |
| C2 | 4 | 33.33% | 4.00 | 0.845 | 0.211 |
| C3 | 4 | 33.33% | 3.93 | 0.884 | 0.225 |
| C4 | 5 | 66.67% | 4.60 | 0.632 | 0.137 |
| C5 | 4 | 26.67% | 3.73 | 0.961 | 0.258 |
| C6 | 4 | 40.00% | 4.20 | 0.775 | 0.185 |
| C7 | 5 | 80.00% | 4.80 | 0.414 | 0.086 |
| C8 | 5 | 60.00% | 4.53 | 0.640 | 0.141 |
| D1 | 4 | 40.00% | 4.20 | 0.775 | 0.185 |
| D2 | 4 | 46.67% | 4.40 | 0.632 | 0.144 |
| D3 | 5 | 60.00% | 4.33 | 0.900 | 0.208 |
| D4 | 4 | 46.67% | 4.27 | 0.799 | 0.187 |
| D5 | 5 | 66.67% | 4.67 | 0.488 | 0.104 |
| E1 | 4 | 40.00% | 3.93 | 1.100 | 0.280 |
| E2 | 4 | 33.33% | 3.87 | 0.915 | 0.236 |
| E3 | 4 | 46.67% | 4.07 | 0.961 | 0.236 |
| E4 | 3 | 20.00% | 3.47 | 0.990 | 0.285 |
| E5 | 4 | 46.67% | 4.33 | 0.724 | 0.167 |

**6. 第二轮专家咨询结果**

调查结果显示，第二轮专家咨询的肯德尔协调系数为 0.614，显著性（$P$ 值）小于 0.05，卡方值为 294.734，各项指标变异系数均小于 0.25，平均值和中位数在 4 及以上，满分率大于 20%。可见，专家对修正后的二级指标体系认可度较高，彼此之间协调性较好，33 项指标全部保留。同时，有专家指出，专业技术标准和行业产业政策是工程人才必须掌握的非技术性知识，解决复杂工程问题的诸多环节，不仅要严格遵守工程师职业规范和相关法律法规，还要及时了解最新行业标准和产业政策，建议涉及工程师职业规范的指标项中增补相关内容，并在解决问题的不同环节予以强调。另有专家认为，解决复杂工程问题是一个循环往复、持续改进的过程，评价方案实施效果固然重要，但更重要的是根据评价结果修正或改进方案，建议将一级指标“反思与评价”修改为“评价与改良”。吸纳专家意见后，再次对评价指标做出修改，最终构建工科本科生解决复杂工程问题的能力评价指标体系，一级指标和二级指标具体内容和相关统计数据见表 8。

**表 8　第二轮专家咨询指标统计结果**

| 一级指标 | 二级指标 | 中位数 | 满分率 | 平均值 | 标准差 | 变异系数 |
|---|---|---|---|---|---|---|
| a 发现问题 | a1 好奇心、探索欲和批判精神 | 5 | 80.00% | 4.80 | 0.414 | 0.086 |
| | a2 关注学科前沿和社会发展需要 | 4 | 26.67% | 4.07 | 0.704 | 0.173 |
| | a3 了解用户（或市场）需求 | 4 | 33.33% | 4.20 | 0.676 | 0.161 |
| | a4 识别或预测专业领域亟待探究的问题 | 5 | 66.67% | 4.67 | 0.488 | 0.104 |
| | a5 分析工程问题产生的原因并确定研究目标 | 4 | 26.67% | 4.00 | 0.756 | 0.189 |
| b 表征问题 | b1 正确选用分析工具和分析技术 | 4 | 33.33% | 4.13 | 0.743 | 0.180 |
| | b2 灵活运用多学科和交叉学科知识 | 4 | 26.67% | 3.93 | 0.799 | 0.203 |
| | b3 熟悉工程师职业规范、专业技术标准和行业政策法规 | 5 | 73.33% | 4.73 | 0.458 | 0.097 |
| | b4 有效获取并利用文献和其他信息资源 | 5 | 80.00% | 4.80 | 0.414 | 0.086 |
| | b5 综合集成、非线性的工程思维 | 5 | 86.67% | 4.87 | 0.352 | 0.072 |
| | b6 工程伦理意识和社会责任感 | 5 | 80.00% | 4.73 | 0.594 | 0.126 |
| c 设计方案 | c1 运用工程中的系统化原则进行方案设计 | 4 | 33.33% | 4.07 | 0.799 | 0.196 |
| | c2 平衡利益相关者的需求并考虑采用新技术 | 4 | 40.00% | 4.13 | 0.834 | 0.202 |
| | c3 提出不同设计方案并证明最优方案的合理性 | 5 | 66.67% | 4.67 | 0.488 | 0.104 |
| | c4 识别、评估风险并确定防范措施 | 4 | 26.67% | 3.93 | 0.799 | 0.203 |
| | c5 确保设计方案符合工程准则、实践规范和行业政策法规 | 5 | 80.00% | 4.80 | 0.414 | 0.086 |
| | c6 制定工程验收标准 | 4 | 26.67% | 3.93 | 0.799 | 0.203 |
| | c7 制订详细的方案实施计划 | 5 | 86.67% | 4.87 | 0.352 | 0.072 |
| | c8 利用相关资源、工具和技术进行实验设计 | 5 | 80.00% | 4.73 | 0.594 | 0.126 |
| | c9 设计满足特定需求的系统、部件或工艺流程 | 4 | 33.33% | 4.00 | 0.845 | 0.211 |
| d 实施方案 | d1 运用恰当的工具、技术和资源开展实验 | 4 | 26.67% | 3.93 | 0.799 | 0.203 |
| | d2 判断、评定与减少误差 | 5 | 73.33% | 4.67 | 0.617 | 0.132 |
| | d3 做好项目实施前的准备工作 | 4 | 33.33% | 4.07 | 0.799 | 0.196 |
| | d4 运用系统方法进行项目实施和管理 | 5 | 93.33% | 4.93 | 0.258 | 0.052 |
| | d5 作为成员或领导者进行团队协作 | 5 | 86.67% | 4.87 | 0.352 | 0.072 |
| | d6 在多元化、包容性环境中进行有效沟通 | 5 | 86.67% | 4.80 | 0.561 | 0.117 |
| | d7 严格遵守工程师职业规范、专业技术标准和行业政策法规 | 5 | 80.00% | 4.80 | 0.414 | 0.086 |
| | d8 家国情怀、全球视野和社会责任感 | 5 | 73.33% | 4.73 | 0.458 | 0.097 |
| e 评价与改良 | e1 查找设计方案和问题解决过程中的不足之处 | 4 | 33.33% | 4.07 | 0.799 | 0.196 |
| | e2 判断问题解决方案的目标达成度 | 4 | 26.67% | 4.00 | 0.756 | 0.189 |
| | e3 多维度评价工程创造物的价值 | 5 | 80.00% | 4.73 | 0.594 | 0.126 |
| | e4 及时修正或改进方案 | 5 | 93.33% | 4.93 | 0.258 | 0.052 |
| | e5 坚持持续质量改进的工程管理理念 | 4 | 26.67% | 4.00 | 0.756 | 0.189 |

### 4.3 指标赋权

考虑到解决复杂工程问题的能力具有分层交错的特点且难以定量描述，本研究选用层次分析法进行指标赋权。层次分析法是美国匹兹堡大学教授萨蒂于20世纪70年代提出的多目标决策分析法，适用于解析多因素构成的复杂系统。层次分析法通常包含建立层次结构模型、构造判断矩阵、层次单排序及其一致性检验、层次总排序及其一致性检验四个步骤。

**1. 建立层次结构模型**

以“解决复杂工程问题的能力”为决策目标（目标层），将表8中一级指标的5个要素确定为准则层，将二级指标的33个要素确定为因子层，以此构建三个层次的结构模型。

**2. 构造判断矩阵**

采用1~9比率标度法，请德尔菲法专家组的15名专家对准则层和因子层各要素的重要性进行两两比较，共得到90个判断矩阵。然后，根据专家调查结果，通过几何平均值汇总计算指标得分，最终形成6个综合判断矩阵（见表9~表14）。

**3. 层次单排序及一致性检验**

采用和积法计算判断矩阵的最大特征根 $\lambda_{max}$ 及其对应特征向量，该特征向量即为同层指标对上层指标相对重要性的排序权值，具体数值见表15的权重和同级权重。同时，对判断矩阵进行一致性检验，计算公式为 CR=CI/RI，其中 $CI=(\lambda_{max}-n)/(n-1)$，$n$ 为判断矩阵的阶数，RI为平均随机一致性指标（RI取值查表可得[39]）。CR<0.1时，则认为层次单排序的结果具有较好一致性[39]。经计算，一级指标和二级指标的判断矩阵均通过一致性检验，结果见表9~表14。

**表9　一级指标综合判断矩阵与一致性检验**

| | a | b | c | d | e |
|---|---|---|---|---|---|
| a | 1 | 2.266 7 | 0.355 6 | 0.511 1 | 1.366 7 |
| b | 0.483 3 | 1 | 0.352 2 | 0.494 4 | 1.266 7 |
| c | 2.933 3 | 3.066 7 | 1 | 1.333 3 | 3.866 7 |
| d | 2.066 7 | 2.333 3 | 0.833 3 | 1 | 2.733 3 |
| e | 1.011 1 | 0.866 7 | 0.267 8 | 0.383 3 | 1 |
| 一致性检验 | $\lambda_{max}$=5.289 3；CI=0.072 3；RI=1.12；CR=0.064 6<0.1 | | | | |

**表10　“发现问题”下属二级指标综合判断矩阵与一致性检验**

| | a1 | a2 | a3 | a4 | a5 |
|---|---|---|---|---|---|
| a1 | 1 | 2.533 3 | 2.066 7 | 1.666 7 | 3.066 7 |
| a2 | 0.416 7 | 1 | 0.933 3 | 0.383 3 | 1.188 9 |
| a3 | 0.511 1 | 1.233 3 | 1 | 0.444 4 | 1.622 2 |

续表

| | a1 | a2 | a3 | a4 | a5 |
|---|---|---|---|---|---|
| a4 | 0.666 7 | 2.866 7 | 2.333 3 | 1 | 2.666 7 |
| a5 | 0.338 9 | 1.066 7 | 0.822 2 | 0.388 9 | 1 |
| 一致性检验 | $\lambda_{max}$=5.264 3;CI=0.066 08;RI=1.12;CR=0.059<0.1 | | | | |

**表 11 “表征问题”下属二级指标综合判断矩阵与一致性检验**

| | b1 | b2 | b3 | b4 | b5 | b6 |
|---|---|---|---|---|---|---|
| b1 | 1 | 2.533 3 | 2.066 7 | 1.666 7 | 3.066 7 | 2.133 3 |
| b2 | 0.416 7 | 1 | 0.933 3 | 0.383 3 | 1.188 9 | 2.266 7 |
| b3 | 0.511 1 | 1.233 3 | 1 | 0.444 4 | 1.622 2 | 2.533 3 |
| b4 | 0.666 7 | 2.866 7 | 2.333 3 | 1 | 2.666 7 | 1.466 7 |
| b5 | 0.338 9 | 1.066 7 | 0.822 2 | 0.388 9 | 1 | 0.455 6 |
| b6 | 0.522 2 | 0.455 6 | 0.422 2 | 0.866 7 | 2.266 7 | 1 |
| 一致性检验 | $\lambda_{max}$=6.410 5;CI=0.082 1;RI=1.26;CR=0.065 2<0.1 | | | | | |

**表 12 “设计方案”下属二级指标综合判断矩阵与一致性检验**

| | c1 | c2 | c3 | c4 | c5 | c6 | c7 | c8 | c9 |
|---|---|---|---|---|---|---|---|---|---|
| c1 | 1 | 3.333 3 | 2.066 7 | 2.866 7 | 2.266 7 | 3.866 7 | 2.333 3 | 2.133 3 | 2.733 3 |
| c2 | 0.307 8 | 1 | 0.327 8 | 0.455 6 | 0.361 1 | 2.066 7 | 0.388 9 | 0.327 8 | 0.422 2 |
| c3 | 0.511 1 | 3.066 7 | 1 | 2.666 7 | 2.133 3 | 3.533 3 | 2.333 3 | 2.066 7 | 2.533 3 |
| c4 | 0.361 1 | 2.266 7 | 0.394 4 | 1 | 0.577 8 | 2.666 7 | 0.433 3 | 0.411 1 | 0.555 6 |
| c5 | 0.477 8 | 2.866 7 | 0.522 2 | 1.933 3 | 1 | 3.466 7 | 0.588 9 | 0.477 8 | 0.533 3 |
| c6 | 0.271 1 | 0.555 6 | 0.288 9 | 0.394 4 | 0.296 7 | 1 | 0.316 7 | 0.311 1 | 0.361 1 |
| c7 | 0.444 4 | 2.666 7 | 0.444 4 | 2.466 7 | 1.866 7 | 3.266 7 | 1 | 0.477 8 | 2.066 7 |
| c8 | 0.522 2 | 3.066 7 | 0.511 1 | 2.533 3 | 2.266 7 | 3.266 7 | 2.266 7 | 1 | 2.666 7 |
| c9 | 0.383 3 | 2.466 7 | 0.416 7 | 1.933 3 | 2.066 7 | 2.933 3 | 0.555 6 | 0.394 4 | 1 |
| 一致性检验 | $\lambda_{max}$=9.685 8;CI=0.085 7;RI=1.46;CR=0.058 7<0.1 | | | | | | | | |

**表 13 “实施方案”下属二级指标综合判断矩阵与一致性检验**

| | d1 | d2 | d3 | d4 | d5 | d6 | d7 | d8 |
|---|---|---|---|---|---|---|---|---|
| d1 | 1 | 2.266 7 | 2.066 7 | 0.488 9 | 2.666 7 | 3.133 3 | 1.933 3 | 3.866 7 |
| d2 | 0.455 6 | 1 | 0.488 9 | 0.422 2 | 1.933 3 | 2.266 7 | 0.455 6 | 3.133 3 |
| d3 | 0.488 9 | 2.066 7 | 1 | 0.488 9 | 2.133 3 | 2.666 7 | 0.477 8 | 3.466 7 |
| d4 | 2.066 7 | 2.466 7 | 2.066 7 | 1 | 2.933 3 | 3.533 3 | 2.066 7 | 4.333 3 |
| d5 | 0.394 4 | 0.533 3 | 0.477 8 | 0.361 1 | 1 | 1.966 7 | 0.422 2 | 2.866 7 |
| d6 | 0.341 1 | 0.455 6 | 0.388 9 | 0.301 1 | 0.588 9 | 1 | 0.338 9 | 2.266 7 |

续表

| | d1 | d2 | d3 | d4 | d5 | d6 | d7 | d8 |
|---|---|---|---|---|---|---|---|---|
| d7 | 0.533 3 | 2.266 7 | 2.133 3 | 0.488 9 | 2.466 7 | 3.066 7 | 1 | 3.666 7 |
| d8 | 0.273 3 | 0.327 8 | 0.294 4 | 0.243 3 | 0.355 6 | 0.455 6 | 0.287 8 | 1 |
| 一致性检验 | $\lambda_{max}$=8.433 5；CI=0.061 9；RI=1.41；CR= 0.043 9<0.1 | | | | | | | |

**表 14 "评价与改良"下属二级指标综合判断矩阵与一致性检验**

| | e1 | e2 | e3 | e4 | e5 |
|---|---|---|---|---|---|
| e1 | 1 | 2.533 3 | 2.066 7 | 1.666 7 | 3.066 7 |
| e2 | 0.416 7 | 1 | 0.933 3 | 0.383 3 | 1.188 9 |
| e3 | 0.511 1 | 1.233 3 | 1 | 0.444 4 | 1.622 2 |
| e4 | 0.666 7 | 2.866 7 | 2.333 3 | 1 | 2.666 7 |
| e5 | 0.338 9 | 1.066 7 | 0.822 2 | 0.388 9 | 1 |
| 一致性检验 | $\lambda_{max}$=5.205 2；CI=0.051 3；RI=1.12；CR= 0.045 8<0.1 | | | | |

### 4. 层次总排序及一致性检验

计算层次单排序权值后，用准则层的权值进行加权综合，可得到因子层总排序权值，即因子层所有指标对目标层的相对重要性权重，结果见表 15。层次总排序的一致性检验公式为 $CR=\sum_{i=1}^{n}a_i CI_i \Big/ \sum_{i=1}^{n}a_i RI_i$，$a_i$ 为准则层的权重，$CI_i$ 为与 $a_i$ 对应的因子层判断矩阵的一致性指标，$RI_i$ 为与 $a_i$ 对应的因子层判断矩阵的随机一致性指标。可得 CR=0.054 1<0.1，达到一致性检验要求。

**表 15 复杂工程问题解决能力评价指标体系权重汇总**

| 一级指标（准则层） | 权重 | 二级指标（因子层） | 同级权重 | 全局权重 | 排序 |
|---|---|---|---|---|---|
| a | 0.154 | a1 | 0.334 | 0.051 | 6 |
| | | a2 | 0.122 | 0.019 | 21 |
| | | a3 | 0.148 | 0.023 | 19 |
| | | a4 | 0.284 | 0.044 | 8 |
| | | a5 | 0.112 | 0.017 | 24 |
| b | 0.110 | b1 | 0.165 | 0.018 | 23 |
| | | b2 | 0.271 | 0.030 | 14 |
| | | b3 | 0.266 | 0.029 | 15 |
| | | b4 | 0.116 | 0.013 | 29 |
| | | b5 | 0.072 | 0.008 | 33 |
| | | b6 | 0.109 | 0.012 | 30 |

续表

| 一级指标（准则层） | 权重 | 二级指标（因子层） | 同级权重 | 全局权重 | 排序 |
|---|---|---|---|---|---|
| c | 0.361 | c1 | 0.218 | 0.079 | 1 |
| | | c2 | 0.047 | 0.017 | 25 |
| | | c3 | 0.177 | 0.064 | 3 |
| | | c4 | 0.067 | 0.024 | 18 |
| | | c5 | 0.092 | 0.033 | 13 |
| | | c6 | 0.036 | 0.013 | 27 |
| | | c7 | 0.116 | 0.042 | 9 |
| | | c8 | 0.152 | 0.055 | 4 |
| | | c9 | 0.095 | 0.034 | 12 |
| d | 0.271 | d1 | 0.192 | 0.052 | 5 |
| | | d2 | 0.099 | 0.027 | 17 |
| | | d3 | 0.127 | 0.034 | 11 |
| | | d4 | 0.245 | 0.066 | 2 |
| | | d5 | 0.078 | 0.021 | 20 |
| | | d6 | 0.058 | 0.016 | 26 |
| | | d7 | 0.163 | 0.044 | 7 |
| | | d8 | 0.038 | 0.010 | 31 |
| e | 0.104 | e1 | 0.123 | 0.013 | 28 |
| | | e2 | 0.179 | 0.019 | 22 |
| | | e3 | 0.076 | 0.008 | 32 |
| | | e4 | 0.281 | 0.029 | 16 |
| | | e5 | 0.341 | 0.036 | 10 |

### 5. 指标权重解读

一级指标项中，“设计方案”权重最高，表明工程设计是工程建造的起始性和定向性环节[40]，对解决复杂工程问题具有特殊重要性。近年来，国际工程教育专业认证组织和工程教育领域具有国际影响力的学校不断对学生创新设计能力提出要求[41]，工程设计能力培养成为工程教育的重要关注点。权重位列第二的是“实施方案”，这是因为工程活动是一种切实的造物实践[42]，因此将设计理念付诸实践就至关重要。随着工程教育从科学范式转向工程范式，亟须加快构建工程实践育人体系，着力提高学生的工程实践能力。值得一提的是，“发现问题”在五项指标中亦具较高权重，表明工程人才的开拓精神、批判意识、集成创新能力、市场调研能力、学科洞察力等日渐获得关注。

二级指标项中，从同级权重看，就“发现问题”而言，“好奇心、探索欲和批判精神”权重最高，强调探索问题的内驱力是发现优质工程问题的第一步；就“表征问题”而言，权重最高的是"灵活运用多学科和交叉学科知识",说明数学和自然科学知识、工程基础知识、工程专业知识、学科前沿知识、交叉学科知识、人文社科知识及必要的工具性知识,是本质上洞察与解析复杂工程问题的关键;就"设计方案"和"实施方案"而言,权重最高的分别为"运用工程中的系统化原则进行方案设计"和"运用系统方法进行项目实施和管理",二者均提及工程的系统性,突显综合集成的系统思想在问题解决不同环节的重要作用;就"评价与改良"而言,"坚持持续质量改进的工程管理理念"权重最高,强调工程人才精益求精、追求卓越和吃苦耐劳的科学精神。

从全局权重看,权重位列前十位的除上述提及的 a1、c1、d4、e5 四项指标,还包括识别或预测问题(a4)、提出与选择设计方案(c3)、制定方案实施计划(c7)、设计实验(c8)、开展实验(d1)、遵守职业规范(d7)六项指标,一方面进一步说明了工程设计与工程实践是解决复杂工程问题的核心要素,另一方面突出了工程师职业规范、专业技术标准和行业政策法规在工程活动中的重要性。

### 4.4 评价等级确立

参照量规设计方法,以二维表的形式构建解决复杂工程问题的能力评价量规,量规开发遵循自上而下的原则,即从工科本科生解决复杂工程问题的能力评价指标体系出发进行研制。量规有三个组成要素:评价维度、评价等级和描述符。评价维度是反映学生表现的重要观测点,本研究以评价指标体系的二级指标项为评价维度。评价等级是描述学生表现好坏的等级序列,本研究从优秀、良好、中等、差四个维度确定指标项的评价等级。描述符指达到某一等级或水平的具体表现。以"设计方案"为例,表 16 呈现了其下属二级指标的评价量规。

表 16 "设计方案"下属二级指标评价量规

| 评价维度 | 差 | 中等 | 良好 | 优秀 |
|---|---|---|---|---|
| c1 | 对系统理论和系统分析方法比较陌生,不具有系统集成思维 | 能够在老师指导下应用部分系统理论和系统分析方法进行方案设计 | 能够独立应用部分系统理论和系统分析方法进行方案设计 | 具有系统集成思维,能够熟练应用系统理论和系统分析方法进行方案设计 |
| c2 | 未明确利益相关者需求,且未考虑使用新兴技术 | 具有了解利益相关者需求的意识,但缺乏相关调研技能,未考虑使用新兴技术 | 能够识别一定利益群体需求,具有追求卓越的精神,敢于尝试应用新兴技术 | 能够识别并权衡多元利益群体需求,具有追求卓越的精神,善于应用新兴技术 |
| c3 | 无法提出备选方案,缺乏方案比较意识 | 能够提出 1~2 个备选方案,但难以对比产生最优方案 | 能够提出多个备选方案并建立相应模型,通过一定分析技术进行方案比较,选出最优方案 | 能够提出多个备选方案并建立相应模型,通过预测、优化、仿真、评价等多元技术对方案进行定性与定量分析,选出最优方案并证明其合理性 |
| c4 | 不能识别、评估和预防风险 | 能够查找工程项目可能面临的风险,但无法确定风险类型,且不能进行风险评估和确定防范措施 | 能够查找工程项目可能面临的风险,找到风险源、主要风险因素和次要风险因素,但难以评估和预防风险 | 能够查找工程项目可能面临的风险,找到风险源、主要风险因素和次要风险因素,评估风险发生的可能性和危害程度,并事先确定防范措施 |

续表

| 评价维度 | 差 | 中等 | 良好 | 优秀 |
|---|---|---|---|---|
| c5 | 对工程准则、实践规范和行业政策法规基本不了解 | 对工程准则、实践规范和行业政策法规有一定了解，但在方案设计时未严格遵守相关准则 | 熟悉工程准则、实践规范和行业政策法规，方案设计基本遵守相关准则 | 熟练掌握工程准则、实践规范和行业政策法规，方案设计严格遵守相关准则 |
| c6 | 没有对方案整体实施效果做出预设，并且未制定工程验收标准 | 对方案整体实施效果做出预设，但未制定工程验收标准 | 对方案整体实施效果做出预设，并制定工程验收标准，但标准可适性不强 | 对方案整体实施效果做出预设，并从产品、工艺、系统和服务等多方面制定工程验收标准，标准灵活适用 |
| c7 | 未制订方案实施计划 | 方案实施计划较笼统，可操作性差 | 方案实施计划内容较丰富，条理较清楚，具有一定可操作性 | 方案实施计划内容翔实、思路清晰，可操作性强 |
| c8 | 不能正确选用技术、资源和工具设计实验，对实验室规章制度和相关伦理准则不了解 | 能够正确选用一定的技术、资源和工具设计实验，但建模、搭建实验装置、控制变量等能力较薄弱，对实验室规章制度和相关伦理准则不了解 | 能够正确开发、选用一定的技术、资源和工具搭建实验装置、确定所用模型、考虑变量和限制条件，基本遵守实验室规章制度和相关伦理准则 | 能够有效开发、选用恰当的技术、资源和工具搭建实验装置、确定所用模型、考虑变量和限制条件，并严格遵守实验室规章制度和相关伦理准则 |
| c9 | 不能设计满足特定需求的系统、部件或工艺流程 | 能够设计满足特定需求的系统、部件或工艺流程，但操作不熟练，并且未考虑限制性因素的影响 | 能够设计满足特定需求的系统、部件或工艺流程，但对限制性因素的考虑不足 | 能够在权衡可制造性、成本、美观性、可持续性、可维护性等限制因素的基础上，设计满足特定需求的系统、部件或工艺流程 |

### 4.5 评价指标应用

选取 L 高校作为评价指标体系试点，该校是以工科为主的教学研究型地方高校，与地方经济发展联系紧密，能在一定程度上反映地方高校工科本科生发展水平。以该校机械、电气、电子信息、自动化 4 个本科专业的 128 名毕业生为评价对象，被评者既包括机械设计制造及其自动化、电气工程及其自动化等传统工科专业学生，又包括光电信息科学与工程、机器人工程等新工科专业学生，样本有一定代表性。通过发放线上问卷，要求毕业生根据评价指标体系及其量规表，以自评形式对个人解决复杂工程问题的能力做出评价。收回评价数据后，运用模糊综合评价法进行统计分析。模糊综合评价法指应用模糊数学隶属度理论将定性评价转化为定量评价，借助模糊关系合成原理，将模糊不清、不易量化的因素定量化，根据多种因素对被评事物隶属等级状况进行综合评价的方法[43]。本研究进行模糊综合评价的步骤和结果如下。

#### 1. 建立评价因素集与评语集

以解决复杂工程问题能力评价指标体系的 33 个二级指标构建评价因素集，$\boldsymbol{U}=\{U_1, U_2, \cdots, U_n\}$（$n=33$）。将评语集分为四个等级，$\boldsymbol{V}=$\{优秀，良好，中等，差\}。为进一步量化处理评价结果，对评价等级分别赋值 100、75、50、25，按百分制量化等级，组成量化评语集

$V=\{100, 75, 50, 25\}$，规定 80~100 为优秀，70~80 为良好，60~70 为中等，0~60 为差。

**2. 评价因素权重分配**

已通过层次分析法求得各项指标的权重，由此可得一级指标的权重向量为 $\boldsymbol{W}=(0.154, 0.110, 0.361, 0.271, 0.104)$，各二级指标的权重向量分别为 $\boldsymbol{W}_a=(0.334, 0.122, 0.148, 0.284, 0.112)$，$\boldsymbol{W}_b=(0.165, 0.271, 0.266, 0.116, 0.072, 0.109)$，$\boldsymbol{W}_c=(0.218, 0.047, 0.177, 0.067, 0.092, 0.036, 0.116, 0.152, 0.095)$，$\boldsymbol{W}_d=(0.192, 0.099, 0.127, 0.245, 0.078, 0.058, 0.163, 0.038)$，$\boldsymbol{W}_e=(0.123, 0.179, 0.076, 0.281, 0.341)$。

**3. 单因素模糊评判**

通过向毕业生发放调查问卷，要求以评价指标体系和量规表为依据，对其解决复杂工程问题的能力做出评价，调查收回有效问卷 120 份，有效回收率为 93.75%。根据评价结果构建隶属度矩阵，以指标项 a1 为例，若 24 人选择优秀，21 人选择良好，68 人选择中等，7 人选择差，则优秀的隶属度为 24/120 = 0.20，同理求得良好、中等和差的隶属度分别为 0.18、0.57、0.06。33 项二级指标的隶属度见表 17。

**表 17　复杂工程问题解决能力评价指标隶属度统计表**

| 二级指标（因子层） | 评价结果 | | | | 二级指标（因子层） | 评价结果 | | | |
|---|---|---|---|---|---|---|---|---|---|
| | 优秀 | 良好 | 中等 | 差 | | 优秀 | 良好 | 中等 | 差 |
| a1 | 0.20 | 0.18 | 0.57 | 0.06 | c7 | 0.40 | 0.36 | 0.22 | 0.03 |
| a2 | 0.13 | 0.35 | 0.46 | 0.07 | c8 | 0.43 | 0.38 | 0.17 | 0.02 |
| a3 | 0.13 | 0.29 | 0.50 | 0.08 | c9 | 0.26 | 0.38 | 0.37 | 0 |
| a4 | 0.18 | 0.27 | 0.49 | 0.07 | d1 | 0.18 | 0.36 | 0.43 | 0.03 |
| a5 | 0.21 | 0.38 | 0.33 | 0.08 | d2 | 0.28 | 0.21 | 0.43 | 0.08 |
| b1 | 0.42 | 0.41 | 0.14 | 0.03 | d3 | 0.24 | 0.38 | 0.32 | 0.06 |
| b2 | 0.23 | 0.32 | 0.42 | 0.03 | d4 | 0.20 | 0.20 | 0.49 | 0.11 |
| b3 | 0.21 | 0.37 | 0.38 | 0.05 | d5 | 0.23 | 0.28 | 0.41 | 0.08 |
| b4 | 0.38 | 0.33 | 0.28 | 0.02 | d6 | 0.21 | 0.24 | 0.46 | 0.09 |
| b5 | 0.17 | 0.39 | 0.40 | 0.04 | d7 | 0.17 | 0.25 | 0.54 | 0.04 |
| b6 | 0.20 | 0.40 | 0.37 | 0.03 | d8 | 0.14 | 0.31 | 0.46 | 0.09 |
| c1 | 0.19 | 0.33 | 0.43 | 0.06 | e1 | 0.35 | 0.33 | 0.32 | 0.01 |
| c2 | 0.27 | 0.37 | 0.32 | 0.05 | e2 | 0.23 | 0.36 | 0.41 | 0 |
| c3 | 0.25 | 0.41 | 0.32 | 0.03 | e3 | 0.21 | 0.30 | 0.48 | 0.02 |
| c4 | 0.22 | 0.46 | 0.30 | 0.07 | e4 | 0.40 | 0.39 | 0.18 | 0.03 |
| c5 | 0.18 | 0.40 | 0.36 | 0.07 | e5 | 0.17 | 0.19 | 0.60 | 0.04 |
| c6 | 0.26 | 0.35 | 0.32 | 0.08 | — | — | — | — | — |

根据隶属度统计结果建立评价矩阵 $\boldsymbol{R}$。分别用 $\boldsymbol{R}_a$、$\boldsymbol{R}_b$、$\boldsymbol{R}_c$、$\boldsymbol{R}_d$、$\boldsymbol{R}_e$ 表示发现问题、表征问题、设计方案、实施方案、评价与改良下属二级指标的隶属度集合：

$$\boldsymbol{R}_a=\begin{bmatrix}0.20 & 0.18 & 0.57 & 0.06\\ 0.13 & 0.35 & 0.46 & 0.07\\ 0.13 & 0.29 & 0.50 & 0.08\\ 0.18 & 0.27 & 0.49 & 0.07\\ 0.21 & 0.38 & 0.33 & 0.08\end{bmatrix}$$

$$\boldsymbol{R}_b=\begin{bmatrix}0.42 & 0.41 & 0.14 & 0.03\\ 0.23 & 0.32 & 0.42 & 0.03\\ 0.21 & 0.37 & 0.38 & 0.05\\ 0.38 & 0.33 & 0.28 & 0.02\\ 0.17 & 0.39 & 0.40 & 0.04\\ 0.20 & 0.40 & 0.37 & 0.03\end{bmatrix}$$

$$\boldsymbol{R}_c=\begin{bmatrix}0.19 & 0.33 & 0.43 & 0.06\\ 0.27 & 0.37 & 0.32 & 0.05\\ 0.25 & 0.41 & 0.32 & 0.03\\ 0.22 & 0.46 & 0.30 & 0.03\\ 0.18 & 0.40 & 0.36 & 0.07\\ 0.26 & 0.35 & 0.32 & 0.08\\ 0.40 & 0.36 & 0.22 & 0.03\\ 0.43 & 0.38 & 0.17 & 0.02\\ 0.26 & 0.38 & 0.37 & 0\end{bmatrix}$$

$$\boldsymbol{R}_d=\begin{bmatrix}0.18 & 0.36 & 0.43 & 0.03\\ 0.28 & 0.21 & 0.43 & 0.08\\ 0.24 & 0.38 & 0.32 & 0.06\\ 0.20 & 0.20 & 0.49 & 0.11\\ 0.23 & 0.28 & 0.41 & 0.08\\ 0.21 & 0.24 & 0.46 & 0.09\\ 0.17 & 0.25 & 0.54 & 0.04\\ 0.14 & 0.31 & 0.46 & 0.09\end{bmatrix}$$

$$\boldsymbol{R}_e=\begin{bmatrix}0.35 & 0.33 & 0.32 & 0.01\\ 0.23 & 0.36 & 0.41 & 0\\ 0.21 & 0.30 & 0.48 & 0.02\\ 0.40 & 0.39 & 0.18 & 0.03\\ 0.17 & 0.19 & 0.60 & 0.04\end{bmatrix}$$

**4. 模糊综合评判**

选用 $M(\cdot,\oplus)$加权平均型算子合成权重向量与评价矩阵，求取模糊综合评价向量。以

“发现问题”为例,其权重向量为 $W_a=(0.334,0.122,0.148,0.284,0,112)$,评价矩阵为

$$R_a=\begin{bmatrix}0.20 & 0.18 & 0.57 & 0.06\\0.13 & 0.35 & 0.46 & 0.07\\0.13 & 0.29 & 0.50 & 0.08\\0.18 & 0.27 & 0.49 & 0.07\\0.21 & 0.38 & 0.33 & 0.08\end{bmatrix}$$

合成 $R_a$ 和 $W_a$ 后,可得综合评价向量 $P_a$ 为

$$P_a=W_a\circ R_a$$

$$=(0.334,0.122,0.148,0.284,0.112)\circ\begin{bmatrix}0.2 & 0.18 & 0.57 & 0.06\\0.13 & 0.35 & 0.46 & 0.07\\0.13 & 0.29 & 0.5 & 0.08\\0.18 & 0.27 & 0.49 & 0.7\\0.21 & 0.38 & 0.33 & 0.08\end{bmatrix}$$

$$=(0.175\ 2,0.263,0.493,0.068\ 8)$$

同理求得 $P_b$、$P_c$、$P_d$、$P_e$ 的综合评价向量:

$$P_b=W_b\circ R_b$$
$$=(0.264\ 9,0.361\ 7,0.338\ 7,0.034\ 8)$$
$$P_c=W_c\circ R_c$$
$$=(0.273\ 2,0.374\ 6,0.314,0.038\ 3)$$
$$P_d=W_d\circ R_d$$
$$=(0.204\ 9,0.275\ 5,0.45,0.069\ 7)$$
$$P_e=W_e\circ R_e$$
$$=(0.27,0.301\ 6,0.403\ 6,0.024\ 8)$$

基于上述结果构建目标层(工科本科生解决复杂工程问题的能力,记作 H)的模糊综合评价矩阵:

$$R_H=\begin{bmatrix}0.175\ 2 & 0.263 & 0.493 & 0.068\ 8\\0.264\ 9 & 0.361\ 7 & 0.338\ 7 & 0.034\ 8\\0.273\ 2 & 0.374\ 6 & 0.314 & 0.038\ 3\\0.204\ 9 & 0.275\ 5 & 0.45 & 0.069\ 7\\0.27 & 0.301\ 6 & 0.403\ 6 & 0.024\ 8\end{bmatrix}$$

最后求出目标层的模糊综合评价向量:

$$P_H=W\circ R_H$$

$$=(0.154,0.110,0.361,0.271,0.104)\circ\begin{bmatrix}0.175\ 2 & 0.263 & 0.493 & 0.068\ 8\\0.264\ 9 & 0.361\ 7 & 0.338\ 7 & 0.034\ 8\\0.273\ 2 & 0.374\ 6 & 0.314 & 0.038\ 3\\0.204\ 9 & 0.275\ 5 & 0.45 & 0.069\ 7\\0.27 & 0.301\ 6 & 0.403\ 6 & 0.024\ 8\end{bmatrix}$$

$$=(0.238\ 3,0.321\ 5,0.390\ 4,0.049\ 7)$$

比较可得，综合评价向量 $\boldsymbol{P}_{H}$ 的最大隶属度为 0.390 4，对应的评价等级为中等，按最大隶属度原则辅以加权平均原则，判定该毕业生群体解决复杂工程问题的能力处于中等水平。通过评级对各项指标进行赋值处理，得到该校工科本科生解决复杂工程问题的能力评分汇总表（见表 18）。

**表 18　解决复杂工程问题能力评分汇总**

| 目标层 | 评价值 | 准则层（一级指标） | 评价值 | 因子层（二级指标） | 评价值 |
|---|---|---|---|---|---|
| 解决复杂工程问题的能力 | 68.71 | 发现问题 | 63.62 | a1 | 70.35 |
| | | | | a2 | 69.95 |
| | | | | a3 | 68.35 |
| | | | | a4 | 70.40 |
| | | | | a5 | 71.25 |
| | | 表征问题 | 71.42 | b1 | 78.55 |
| | | | | b2 | 72.90 |
| | | | | b3 | 72.85 |
| | | | | b4 | 77.75 |
| | | | | b5 | 71.75 |
| | | | | b6 | 72.95 |
| | | 设计方案 | 72.07 | c1 | 71.60 |
| | | | | c2 | 74.35 |
| | | | | c3 | 74.95 |
| | | | | c4 | 74.70 |
| | | | | c5 | 71.70 |
| | | | | c6 | 72.85 |
| | | | | c7 | 78.20 |
| | | | | c8 | 78.85 |
| | | | | c9 | 75.95 |
| | | 实施方案 | 65.4 | d1 | 72.05 |
| | | | | d2 | 71.30 |
| | | | | d3 | 72.70 |
| | | | | d4 | 68.15 |
| | | | | d5 | 70.75 |
| | | | | d6 | 69.50 |
| | | | | d7 | 70.35 |
| | | | | d8 | 68.45 |

续表

| 目标层 | 评价值 | 准则层（一级指标） | 评价值 | 因子层（二级指标） | 评价值 |
|---|---|---|---|---|---|
| 解决复杂工程问题的能力 | 68.71 | 评价与改良 | 70.42 | e1 | 77.35 |
| | | | | e2 | 74.35 |
| | | | | e3 | 73.20 |
| | | | | e4 | 77.85 |
| | | | | e5 | 69.75 |

**5. 结果分析**

表 18 显示，各一级指标的评价值差值略大，“设计方案”得分最高，“发现问题”和“实施方案”得分较低，说明样本高校毕业生工程设计能力整体良好，据了解，该校借鉴麻省理工学院课程建设经验，注重开设产品、项目等设计开发类课程，大一开始分层次、系统性培养学生的工程设计能力，为学生解决复杂工程问题营造了良好环境。然而，该校相关教师指出，学生习惯于接受已设计好的工程问题，不善于探索和解决实际存在的复杂工程问题，发现问题的能力偏弱。从“发现问题”下属的因子层来看，与市场需求、社会需要、学科前沿相关的两项指标（a2、a3）得分低，说明学生提出问题前对问题价值和意义的考查存在欠缺。同时，学生的工程实践能力不容乐观，工程设计与工程实践密切相关，虽然工程设计能力整体良好，但工程实践能力并未呈向好趋势。为进一步分析原因，笔者对专业人才培养方案予以解读，并咨询相关专业任课教师，最终发现学生工程实践能力较低极大程度是由于考评机制不完善，部分设计类课程仍采用传统卷面考试评价，虽有教师尝试运用研究性报告、设计类作品等新型评价方式，但缺乏系统有效的评价标准，难以参照标准甄别课程教学、学生能力水平等方面存在的问题。从因子层指标得分的全局分布看，技术能力得分整体高于非技术能力，得分较低项涉及需求分析（a2、a3）、工程思维（b5）、职业道德修养（c5）、系统思维（d4）、交际技能（d6）、社会责任感（d8）、持续改进理念（e5）等要素，说明学生的大工程素质有待提高。

## 5　结论与建议

### 5.1　研究结论

解决复杂工程问题能力是包含多项子能力的高层次认知操作序列，由发现问题、表征问题、设计方案、实施方案、评价与改良五种能力构成。其中，发现问题是前提，强调根据现实需求确定工程实践的着力点和突破口；表征问题是基础，强调运用分析技术、多学科原理和信息资源，对工程问题形成全面认知；设计方案是关键，强调基于系统化原则，通过构思、比较与优化，创造性地提出问题解决新方案；实施方案是根本，强调综合应用科学知识、技术手段和工具资源，通过团队合作将工程蓝图转化为科技成果；评价与改良是保障，强调全方位审查问题，多维度评价效果，及时修正或改进方案。

工科本科生解决复杂工程问题的能力评价指标体系中，各项指标相对重要性权值有所差异。就一级指标而言，"设计方案"与"实施方案"权重最高，工程设计能力与工程实践能力是评价学生解决复杂工程问题能力的关键指标，而"发现问题"亦具有较高权值，问题探究能力逐渐成为评价关注点。就二级指标而言，权重排名前十的指标涵盖探索精神、多学科和交叉学科知识应用、系统思维、方案比较与优化意识、持续改进理念、职业道德修养、实验技能等内容，这些能力对解决复杂工程问题具有特殊意义，成为相对重要的评价考查点。

从样本高校调查结果看，工科本科生解决复杂工程问题的能力总体处于中等水平。由于该校采用多层次、立体化人才培养模式，学生工程设计能力良好，但发现问题和实施方案的能力偏弱。一方面是由于好奇心、探索欲、批判精神等内部动机不足，问题探究机会和情境缺失；另一方面是由于考评机制不完善，学习评价方式单一，缺乏系统有效的评价标准。与分析问题、运用工具、设计实验等技术能力相比，学生的学科敏锐度、市场调研能力、工程意识、系统思维、职业道德感、交际技能等非技术能力亟待提高。

### 5.2 对策建议

基于研究结论，建议从四个方面加强工科本科生解决复杂工程问题能力的培养。

#### 1. 关注工程人才素质的全面性与完整性

从逻辑上讲，素质与知识、能力并不处于同一逻辑平台[44]，素质是包含知识、能力、品德、意识、思维等要素的内涵丰富的概念。随着大工程时代的到来，工程日渐演化为涵盖政治、经济、文化、伦理、环境等领域的综合集成系统，工程师的职能范围不仅局限于解决专业技术问题，还要考虑环境保护、文化创新、人文关怀等问题。这要求工程教育以"大工程观"为指导，培养学生的"大工程素质"。"大工程观"是以系统、整合、应变、再循环视角分析和解决复杂工程问题的现代工程理念，主张回归工程本真，注重技术要素与非技术要素的交叉融合。"大工程观"对工程教育改革具有重要指引作用，大工程背景下的工程教育强调学科交叉、知识综合、能力多维立体、思维系统活跃、专业意识强烈和道德品质健全。因此，工程教育不仅要注重多学科知识学习与技能培养，更要加强人文教育、哲学教育和工程伦理教育。

#### 2. 注重创新、设计与实践能力提升

创新、设计与实践能力培养不应独立进行，而应作为整体融入人才培养全过程，多方面、分层次、分阶段、分模块构建工程实践教育体系和创新实践平台。具体而言，首先要明确不同年级学生创新、设计与实践能力培养的重点。对于大一学生，可通过实验、上机实习、生产劳动和课程内项目等实践形式，激发其动手兴趣，培养基本操作技能；大二起，逐渐接触设计类项目，合作解决简单工程问题，同时加强专业实习、生产实习、实验设计等训练；大三起，引入有一定难度的复杂工程项目，让学生熟悉工程设计的基本流程，掌握常用的工程实践技能；进入大四，通过毕业设计、学科竞赛、大型工程或科研项目、创业实践等培养学生合作解决复杂工程问题的能力。其次，要加强课程体系的模块化设置，课程模块化的目的在于分类细化工程实践教育的操作要点。根据已有研究，可将实践类课程分为实习实践、实验实践、设计实践、军训和社会实践、创新创业实践，然后分模块明确教学重点[45]。最后，通过多学科

交叉融合、产教和校企合作为创新、设计与实践能力培养营造良好环境。一方面,加强校内工程训练中心建设,提高工科教师实践能力与工程素养,注重学科专业之间的协作与共享;另一方面,积极探索产学研合作有效机制,通过成果转化、技术服务和产品研发与企业、科研单位等进行合作,共建校外实践教学基地。

**3. 强化工程意识与工程思维培养**

工程思维和工程意识培养可从四个方面着手:一要注重科学原理(尤其是科学第一性原理)的学习与探索,引导学生将复杂工程问题与科学原理相联系,分析事物发展变化的规律,抓住问题本质,寻求最基本的命题假设和最合理的解决方案;二要培养学生对工程的系统性认知,让学生理解复杂工程问题根本上是一个系统问题,解决复杂工程问题应善于运用系统理论和系统分析方法,着眼于整体,综合考虑多种影响因素,处理好整体与部分、部分与部分之间的关系;三要训练学生辩证分析和处理问题的能力,日常教学中,建议设置包含多重矛盾冲突的工程问题,如工程建造与环境保护、经济效益与安全质量、已有技术的引进与新技术的自主研发、个人竞争与团队协作等矛盾,使学生在处理矛盾冲突的过程中学会通过权衡和协调找到最佳平衡点;四要培养学生的优化意识,建议多向学生提供开放性工程问题,鼓励学生从不同视角探索解决问题的方法、路径和手段,通过反复修正与完善,找到解决问题的最优方案。

**4. 构建多维立体学习评价体系**

评价学生解决复杂工程问题的能力是一项多主体参与,运用多种评价方法,融技术能力、非技术能力、专业素养等多元评价要素为一体的综合性活动。为增强评价的科学性、有效性与可行性,课程实施者应结合人才培养目标、毕业要求和课程目标,明确解决复杂工程问题的能力在课程层面的具体表现,构建相应的评价标准,根据标准的能力指标点选择恰当的评价方法。在此过程中,要注意评价方式多元化,不能单纯采用卷面考试,更不能仅通过学期末的一次考核判定能力强弱,而要综合运用系统设计方案、项目作品展示、研究性报告、专题研讨会等多种评价方式,平衡好形成性评价与终结性评价、传统学生评价与发展性学生评价之间的关系。同时,构建学生、行业企业代表、一线教师和工程教育专家等组成的评价共同体,从不同视角监测教学质量和学生能力发展状况。评价技术选择上,要充分利用现代信息技术和大数据构建智慧教学系统,创设真实或模拟真实工程问题情境,记录学生解决复杂工程问题过程中的行为表现,创建学生成长档案,为教学和学习评价提供依据。

**参考文献**

[1] World Economic Forum. The Future of Jobs: Employment, Skills and Work Force Strategy for The Fourth Industrial Revolution [EB/OL]. (2020-02-12) [2022-11-23]. https://www3.weforum.org/ docs/WEF_Future_of_Jobs.pdf.

[2] World Economic Forum. The Future of Jobs Report 2020[EB/ OL]. (2020-09-12) [2022-11-23]. https://www3.weforum.org/docs/WEF_Future_of_Jobs_2020.pdf.

[3] 孔寒冰. 工程链:工程教育的新挑战[J]. 高等工程教育研究,2009(2):23-26,70.

[4] International Engineering Alliance. Graduate Attributes and Professional Competencies [EB/OL].(2021-09-01)[2023-02-05]. https://www.ieagreements.org/assets/Uploads/Documents/IEA-Graduate-Attributes-and-Professional-Competencies-2021.1-Sept-2021.pdf

[5] 林健. 面向未来的新工科建设[M]. 北京:高等教育出版社,2021.

[6] BAILEY R, SZABO Z. Assessing engineering design process knowledge[J]. International journal of engineering education,2006(3):508-518.

[7] JINS H, SONG K, SHIN D H, et al. A performance-based evaluation rubric for assessing and enhancing engineering design skills in introductory engineering design courses[J]. International journal of engineering education,2015(4):1007-1020.

[8] LIEW C P, PUTEH M, HAMZAH S H. Comparative study of engineering design project assessment rubrics to address the Washington Accord's Complexity attributes[J]. ASEAN journal of engineering education,2020(1):71-94.

[9] 林健. 如何理解和解决复杂工程问题[J]. 高等工程教育研究,2016(5):17-26,38.

[10] 王章豹,张宝. 培养新工科人才解决复杂工程问题能力的探讨[J]. 高教发展与评估,2019,35(6):74-85,111.

[11] 杨毅刚,孟斌,王伟楠. 如何破解工程教育中有关"复杂工程问题"的难点[J]. 高等工程教育研究,2017(2):72-78.

[12] 蒋宗礼. 本科工程教育:聚焦学生解决复杂工程问题能力的培养[J]. 中国大学教学,2016(11):27-30,84.

[13] JONASSEN D H. Toward a design theory of problem solving[J]. Educational technology research and development, 2000(4):63-85.

[14] 王小明. 学习心理学 [M]. 北京:中国轻工业出版社,2009:231-232.

[15] JONASSEN D H. Instructional design models for well-structured and Ill-structured problem-solving learning outcomes[J]. Educational technology research and development, 1997(1):65-94.

[16] JONASSEN D, STROBEL J, LEE C B. Everyday problem solving in engineering: lessons for engineering educators[J]. Journal of engineering education,2006(2): 139-151.

[17] PHANG F A, ANUAR A N, AZIZ A A, et al. Perception of complex engineering problem solving among engineering educators[C]// Engineering Education for A Smart Society World Engineering Education Forum & Global Engineering Deans Council. Cham: Springer, 2018:215-224.

[18] 杜威. 我们怎样思维[M]. 姜文闵,译. 北京:人民教育出版社,1991.

[19] WALLAS G. The art of thought[M]. New York: Harcourt Brace,1926.

[20] 陈琦. 教育心理学:原理与应用[M]. 合肥:安徽教育出版社,2004.

[21] 袁维新,吴庆麟. 问题解决:涵义、过程与教学模式[J]. 心理科学,2010(1):151-154.

[22] SIMON H A, NEWELL A. Human problem solving: the state of the theory in 1970[J]. American psychologist, 1971(2):145-159.

[23] GICK M L. Problem-solving strategies[J]. Educational psychologist,1986(1-2):99-120.

[24] BRANSFORD J D, STEIN B S. The ideal problem solver [M]. New York: W. H. Freeman, 1983:12.
[25] 李一茗,黎坚. 复杂问题解决能力的概念、影响因素及培养策略[J]. 北京师范大学学报(社会科学版),2020(5):36-48.
[26] WOODS D R. An evidence-based strategy for problem solving[J]. Journal of engineering education, 2000(4):443-459.
[27] Organization for Economic Cooperation and Development. PISA 2012 Results: Creative Problem Solving Students' Skills in Tackling Real-Life Problems (Volume V) [EB/OL]. (2014-02-12) [2022-11-27]. https://www.oecd.org/pisa/keyfindings/PISA-2012-results-volume-V.pdf.
[28] 张俊娟. 问题解决能力培训全案[M]. 北京:人民邮电出版社,2014.
[29] FISCHER A, NEUBERTJC. The multiple faces of complex problems: a model of problem solving competency and its implications for training and assessment[J]. Journal of dynamic decision making, 2015(1):1-14.
[30] FUNKE J. Complex problem solving: a case for complex cognition[J]. Cognitive processing,2010(11):133-142.
[31] 袁勤俭,宗乾进,沈洪洲. 德尔菲法在我国的发展及应用研究[J]. 现代情报,2011(5):3-7.
[32] LIKERT R. A technique for the measurement of attitudes[J]. Archives of psychology, 1932(140):1-55.
[33] 艾尔·巴比. 社会研究方法[M]. 邱泽奇,译. 北京:华夏出版社,2000.
[34] 王志强,张浩然. 基于巡回指导教师视角的巡回指导能力指标体系建构研究[J]. 中国特殊教育,2022(7):71-81.
[35] 龚雪. 糖尿病专科护士首次认证评价指标体系的构建[D]. 广州:暨南大学,2014.
[36] 侯雨欣,王冲. 基于德尔菲法与因子分析的大学生信用评价指标筛选研究[J]. 四川师范大学学报(社会科学版),2016(5):34-41.
[37] VON DER GRACHT H A. Consensus measurement in delphi studies: review and implications for future quality assurance[J]. Technological forecasting and social change, 2012(8):1525-1536.
[38] 王春枝,斯琴. 德尔菲法中的数据统计处理方法及其应用研究[J]. 内蒙古财经学院学报(综合版),2011(4):92-96.
[39] 许树柏. 层次分析法原理[M]. 天津:天津大学出版社,1988.
[40] 雷庆,王敏. 从课程视角看工程设计能力培养[J]. 高等工程教育研究,2011(5):152-156.
[41] 李宏伟,朱爱斌,陈天宁,等. 基于设计思维的工程设计能力培养教学实践研究[J]. 高等工程教育研究,2022(3):85-90.
[42] 王章豹. 工程哲学与工程教育[M]. 上海:上海科学技术出版社,2018.
[43] 杜栋,庞庆华,吴炎. 现代综合评价方法与案例精选[M]. 北京:清华大学出版社,2008.
[44] 朱高峰. 工程教育中的几个理念问题[J]. 高等工程教育研究,2011(1):1-5.
[45] 王章豹. 大工程时代的卓越工程师培养[M]. 上海:上海科技教育出版社,2017.

# 面向卓越工程师培养的现代产业学院高质量发展：目标、策略与路径①

胡德鑫　逄丹丹　顾佩华

**摘要：**现代产业学院是深化产教融合和夯筑卓越工程师人才培养的新型组织。基于我国首批50家现代产业学院的范例，解析当前现代产业学院建设的兴起动因与建设目标、建构逻辑与融合策略、未来行动路径。研究显示，布局战略性新兴产业，服务国家重点领域；赋能产教深度融合，引领区域经济社会发展；创新工程教育组织形式，深化新工科建设；变革人才培养模式，造就新时代卓越工程师，共同形塑现代产业学院的兴起动因与建设目标。进一步，当前现代产业学院的建构逻辑与融合策略集中在构建多元利益主体协同参与的混合式组织架构；注重基于OBE理念的人才培养方案反向设计；创建浸润真实工程环境的项目式教学范式。最后，指出未来推进现代产业学院高质量发展的行动路径。

**关键词：**现代产业学院；产教融合；工程教育；卓越工程师；人才培养

## High-Quality Development of Modern Industrial Colleges for Cultivating Excellent Engineers:Objectives, Strategies and Paths

*Hu Dexin, Pang Dandan, Gu Peihua*

**Abstract:** Modern industrial college is a new organization to deepen the integration of production and education and cultivate excellent engineers. Based on the first batch of 50 modern industrial colleges in China, this paper analyzes the rise motivation and construction goal, construction logic and integration strategy, and future action path of the construction of modern industrial colleges. Our research shows that the rise motivation and construction goal of modern industrial colleges are jointly shaped by: the layout of strategic emerging industries to serve the national key areas; empowering the deep integration of industry and education for regional economic and social development; innovating the organizational form of engineering education and deepening the construction of new engineering disciplines; changing the talent training mode and cultivating excellent engineers in the new era. Further, the current construction logic and integration strategy of modern industrial colleges focuses on the construction of a hybrid organizational structure with multi-stakeholder collaborative participation; it emphasizes the reverse design of talent training programs based on the OBE concept; it creates a project-based teaching paradigm that infiltrates the real engineering environment. Finally, this paper points out an action path to promote the high-quality development of modern industrial colleges in the future.

① 本文刊登于《中国高教研究》2023年第12期第16~23、78页。

**Keywords:** modern industrial college; the integration of production and education; engineering education; excellent engineer; talent training

## 1 问题提出

作为高校与地方政府、行业企业等多主体共建共管共享的新型组织形态，现代产业学院对解决产教脱节问题、培养卓越工程师和服务战略性新兴产业发展具有重要意义[1]。2020年8月，《现代产业学院建设指南（试行）》（以下简称《指南》）正式出台。《指南》指出，要培养适应和引领现代产业发展的高素质应用型、复合型、创新型人才，并为现代产业学院的建设目标、原则、任务与重点指明未来发展方向。2021年12月，教育部公布首批现代产业学院名单，覆盖以天津中医药大学、沈阳化工大学等应用型高校为主体的49所高校的50家现代产业学院，标志着现代产业学院建设逐步由政策设计走向实践落地。2023年3月，《关于开展第二批现代产业学院建设工作的通知》正式发布，这在相当程度上表明现代产业学院建设在持续走深、走实。总的来看，作为工程教育组织领域改革的新形态，现代产业学院在实践过程中必然面临制度重构、组织创新、多方协同、保障机制等领域诸多的问题与挑战，亟须学术界进行较深的分析与总结。

随着《指南》的印发，如何科学推进现代产业学院建设已初步引起学术界的关注与探讨。从当前已有研究来看，聚焦现代产业学院的学术研究主要集中在以下两个方向。一是从理论层面剖析现代产业学院的概念内涵、属性特征等问题。如李名梁和史静妍[2]对现代产业学院的内涵逻辑进行了充分诠释，旨在通过明确目标定位，指导现代产业学院高质量建设；周继良和匡永杨[3]通过比较现代产业学院与企业大学的组织属性，明晰其共同点与异质性，以期找到两者未来的合作空间进而拓展产教合作形式；曹雨平等[4]基于组织生态理论考查现代产业学院特有的可持续发展机制设计，归纳总结现代产业学院功能有效实施的关键节点。二是从实践层面探讨现代产业学院的发展现状、现实挑战或经验成就，进而提出未来优化对策，主要采用理论思辨分析与实践案例分析两种思路。前者如蒋惠凤等[5]与张元宝等[6]指出当前现代产业学院建设的现实困境，并分别运用组织生态学理论和共生理论提出应对策略与改革路径，以期推动现代产业学院有序发展。后者则注重采用案例分析法，以单个或多个现代产业学院为研究对象展开研究。如柯婷和王亚煦[7]与陈雄寅等[8]分别考查粤港澳大湾区和苏粤浙闽沿海四省首批现代产业学院的建设成效，在总结分析其实践经验的基础上，切实有效地提出未来现代产业学院的建设路径。

总体而言，当前研究尚存在两个突出问题。一是从研究内容来看，现代产业学院相关理论研究仍处于起步阶段。这使得系统性的研究成果数量相对较少，研究内容呈现广而不精、散而不深的特点，最终导致研究结论的实用性和普适性不强。二是从研究设计来看，现有的文献多侧重以单案例或几个案例为基础的实践应用总结，缺乏对现代产业学院整体建设情况的深度分析，难以支撑大规模的应用实践。鉴于此，本研究运用案例研究法和文本分析法相结合的方式，通过对我国首批50家国家级现代产业学院兴起动因与建设目标、建构逻辑与融合策略、未来推进高质量发展的行动路径进行深度解析，以期为未来现代产业学院的可持续高质量发展提供科学参考。

## 2 研究设计

### 2.1 案例选取

本研究选取我国首批50家国家级现代产业学院作为案例研究对象。这些学院经过层层筛选，在办学定位、服务产业、前期基础、建设成效、育人模式、政产学研协同、支撑保障和建设投入等方面均满足申报条件，因此有足够的禀赋在组织创新和模式探索的过程中开发出更多可复制、可推广的新路径，能够充分满足典型性这一案例选择首要标准。此外，作为贯彻"分区论证、试点先行、分批启动"原则，严格遵照《指南》培育建设的第一批试点，50家国家级现代产业学院全面覆盖新工科、新医科、新农科、新文科"四新"领域，广泛分布于全国东、中、西部的24个省（区、市），其主办高校更是涵盖"双一流"建设高校、省属普通高校等多种类型，在资料丰富性上能够为开展探索性多案例研究提供有效支撑。

### 2.2 分析框架

现代产业学院是深化产教融合和夯筑卓越工程师人才培养的新型组织，为厘清现代产业学院与传统产业学院的区别，更好地发挥其组织效能，需要从价值论、认识论和方法论三个维度展开研究。探析现代产业学院的建设动因与目标，现代产业学院在实践中通过何种策略响应建设目标，未来又有哪些行动路径能够推动现代产业学院资源效率提升。因此，本研究构建起"目标—策略—路径"的分析框架，（图1）并使用该框架考查首批50家国家级现代产业学院，以期通过次第回答现代产业学院建设的"为何"（兴起动因与建设目标）、"何以"（建构逻辑与融合策略）以及"何为"（未来推进高质量发展的行动路径）问题，剖析其高质量发展的内在机理与实施路径，进一步为未来现代产业学院的高水平建设与持续革新指明方向。

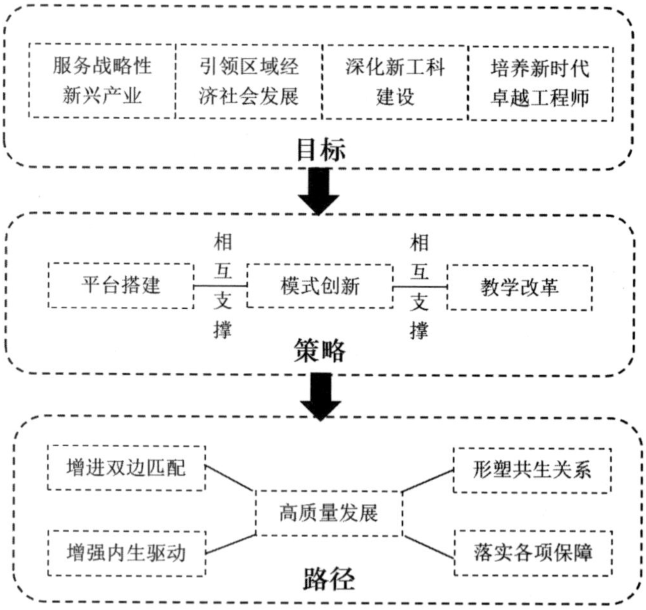


图1 现代产业学院分析框架

## 3　现代产业学院的兴起动因与建设目标标准的实施程序

### 3.1　布局战略性新兴产业，服务国家重点领域

21 世纪以来，新一轮科技革命和产业变革不断向纵深发展。在此背景下，战略性新兴产业以其高技术、低能耗、高增长、强引领的特点，被视为世界主要经济体的竞争高地，深刻影响着世界经济格局的演变。特别是新冠疫情后，战略性新兴产业作为新一轮世界经济复苏的重要支撑点和着力点已成为国际社会的普遍共识。当前，我国战略性新兴产业发展势头强劲，规模持续壮大，但仍面临价值链“低端锁定”、核心技术“卡脖子”等风险与挑战。科技创新是战略性新兴产业紧跟世界前沿的重要法宝，更是战略性新兴产业高质量发展的不竭动力源泉与必然选择，而科技创新的一个重要来源便是高校。现代产业学院是高校在新的起点上发挥自身主动性，超前谋划布局，开展科技创新与孵化新兴产业的重大探索。首批 50 家国家级现代产业学院急国家之所急，研国家之所需，瞄准人工智能、轨道交通装备、智能制造装备、生物医药工程等前沿领域，实现九大战略性新兴产业服务的全覆盖（表 1）。

**表 1　首批现代产业学院对接产业情况**

| 战略性新兴产业 | 主要产业服务面向对象 | 代表性现代产业学院 | 计数 |
|---|---|---|---|
| 新一代信息技术产业 | 人工智能、互联网与云计算、大数据服务等 | 广州大学智能软件学院 | 19 |
| 高端装备制造业 | 轨道交通装备产业、智能制造装备产业等 | 中南大学轨道交通现代产业学院 | 13 |
| 新材料产业 | 新型建筑材料制造、先进石化化工新材料等 | 东华大学新材料现代产业学院 | 5 |
| 生物产业 | 生物医药产业、生物农业及相关产业等 | 广州医科大学金域检验学院 | 6 |
| 新能源汽车产业 | 新能源汽车整车制造、新能源汽车装置等 | 河北工业大学智能汽车产业学院 | 5 |
| 新能源产业 | 太阳能产业、风能产业和智能电网产业等 | 南京师范大学南瑞电气与自动化学院 | 3 |
| 节能环保产业 | 高效节能产业、资源循环利用产业等 | 西南石油大学天然气现代产业学院 | 4 |
| 数字创意产业 | 设计服务等 | 吉林建筑大学亚泰数字建造产业学院 | 1 |
| 相关服务业 | 通用航空生产服务等 | 内蒙古师范大学旅游学院 | 1 |

注：根据《战略性新兴产业分类与国际专利分类参照关系表（2021）》整理。

现代产业学院作为一种新型的高校二级教学科研单位，在科技创新上具有较强的平台优势：一是资源优势，高校作为围绕知识而活动的场域，能够产生多源知识，缩短知识流动距离，使知识在跨界交换和整合中实现迭代更新；二是组织优势，现代产业学院虽然是多元主体共建，但不影响其公共属性[3]，相比于企业大学等市场组织，能够规避掉逐利动机驱动下的排他性与竞争性，推动科学技术在更加开放共享的氛围中实现创新；三是机制优势，现代产业学院赋能校企深度合作，通过横向课题开发和团队技术攻关孵化科技创新成果，最新的科研成果反过来又被利用到科研资源建设和学科发展当中，高质量大学教育和高水平科技创新联动发展，在正反馈循环中形成科技创新的“乘数效应”[9]。对于以科学技术作为强支

撑的战略性新兴产业来说，现代产业学院的意义在于依托自身优势建设科技创新策源地，破解创新内生动力不足难题，并进一步完善技术推动与需求拉动互补的产业发展激励机制，最大程度发挥科技创新赋能战略性新兴产业高质量发展的作用。

### 3.2 赋能产教深度融合，引领区域经济社会发展

产教融合是教育链、人才链与产业链、创新链有机衔接的重要保障，我国高度重视产教融合工作的推动与发展。2017 年，我国颁布了第一份以“产教融合”为主题的文件《关于深化产教融合的若干意见》。此后，高等教育产教融合的政策密集出台，产教融合新型平台建设的多样化探索相继展开，相关概念的界定也在不断丰富。《指南》在已有文件的基础上，创造性地提出搭建“多主体共建共管共享的现代产业学院”，特别是“共享”概念的提出，赋予产教融合新的内涵。“共享”是一种新兴的经济形态，在共享经济模式下，商品和服务的生产者与消费者边界淡化，产消者这一新的社会角色应运而生。产消者是指那些兼具生产功能的消费者，既能通过参与生产服务活动来创造价值，又能通过消费活动来享用价值[10]。现代产业学院特有的共享属性决定着高校、地方政府、行业企业各主体以产消者的身份参与人才培养与科技转化的全过程。以企业为例，在供给侧，企业深度参与高等教育教学改革；在需求侧，企业共享高校人才培养成果。同样，四链闭环上的其他主体均能实时对接供给侧与需求侧两端的信息与资源。产消者机制有助于实现供需两端精准匹配，有助于缩短供需相互反馈的响应时间，有助于破解人才培养与产业发展“两张皮”问题，是现代产业学院相较于传统产业学院彰显出强劲韧性与活力的关键[2]。总的来看，现代产业学院以应用型高校为主阵地，通过校企融通参与区域产业生态体系建构；反过来，地方产业发挥资源禀赋优势，推进当地应用型高校深化办学定位，实现特色发展。当应用型高校与地方产业以现代产业学院为联结点，战略互嵌、同频共振、联动发展时，将最大程度提升两者间的相互支撑作用，将最大范围发挥两者协同的递归效应，将最强有力地推动区域经济社会长效发展。

### 3.3 创新工程教育组织形式，深化新工科建设

“现代产业学院”的表述最早出现在 2018 年 2 月印发的《教育部 2018 年工作要点》中，作为“提升高等学校科学研究和社会服务水平”工作要点中的一项举措被提出。同年 3 月，《教育部办公厅关于公布首批“新工科”研究与实践项目的通知》中正式提出“面向当前产业急需建立现代产业学院”。同年 10 月颁发的《教育部 工业和信息化部 中国工程院关于加快建设发展新工科实施卓越工程师教育培养计划 2.0 的意见》，又将其作为改革任务和重点举措之一再次强调[11]。2020 年 7 月，《指南》颁布，明确提出以“扎实推进新工科建设再深化、再拓展、再突破、再出发”为目标导向。在《指南》的指导下，2021 年 12 月，首批现代产业学院名单公布，建设工作走向实际落地。从提出构想到走向落实，溯源现代产业学院的生成逻辑，其目标定位始终紧紧围绕于服务新工科建设这一核心点。从工程教育范式的变革趋势来看，在由技术范式向科学范式再向工程范式的转变过程中，强化知识跨界整合和回归工程实践是一批传统工科改造和升级的必由之路，然而传统的二级学院难以突破知识割据和资源不流通的障碍，因此迫切需要建立能够汇集多学科信息、共享多部门资源的新型协同

创新平台。现代产业学院积极探索学科交叉建设和产业跨界融合经验，譬如，在已公布的首批现代产业学院名单中，河北工业大学智能汽车产业学院依托车辆工程、电子科学与技术、物联网工程等相关优势专业，联合长城汽车、中汽研（天津）等区域内龙头汽车企业，以工程项目为牵引，以服务产业发展为导向，打破学科专业和体制机制壁垒，有效发挥产教协同和工工交叉“1+1>2”效应。现代产业学院这一协同平台的建立，不仅突破工程教育内部纵向改革的边界，不断拓展横向交叉的学科外延，还真正实现从“学科导向”到“产业需求导向”的理念转变。从该层面来说，现代产业学院是新工科内涵与外延的再丰富，是新工科建设机制与手段的再出发。

### 3.4 变革人才培养模式，造就新时代卓越工程师

作为一项多主体参与的新工科人才培养教育改革创新实践[7]，现代产业学院的根本任务在于育人，在于培养一批面向现代产业发展，具备突出工程项目实践能力、工程问题解决能力、工程技术创新能力的高素质应用型、复合型、创新型卓越工程师。在专业建设上，现代产业学院以适配产业发展为导向，打破传统学科制度壁垒，整合高校其他二级学院的优质教学资源。依托组织创新优势，推动多学科交叉融合，聚焦行业高水平复合型技术技能人才培养，不断增强人才对区域产业和经济社会高质量发展的适应性[12]。在教师队伍配备上，现代产业学院对接校企两端，设置互聘互认机制，教师进企业，工程师进课堂，校企人才双向流动，校内校外师资形成优势互补。在高水平“双师双能型”教学创新团队的共同授课、联合指导下，学生能够接收到更多新知识、新理论、新观念，进而不断提高自身的综合素质。在课程内容改革上，现代产业学院的多主体共建模式决定了行业企业将深度参与课程建设与教材开发，最新的行业标准、企业技术、工艺流程和管理经验将成为课程教学内容迭代更新的重要参考依据[12]。课程体系得以重构，课程结构持续优化，课程内容实现与产业需求的充分对接，学生对产业的认知程度全面提高。在教学方法创新上，现代产业学院依托行业企业技术革新项目，利用真实生产线环境，开展浸润式实景、实操、实地教学，在真实的社会问题情景中强化理论与实践的结合，促成学生学做贯通，着力提高学生的动手实践能力和解决复杂问题的能力。在教学评价设计上，现代产业学院天然的多主体属性驱动教学评价由传统的单一标准向多元向度转变，企业导师、校内导师、行业代表等多个主体均被吸纳到教学评价环节中，学生的综合能力得以全面考查。总的来说，现代产业学院以全方位变革培养要素有力地托举新时代卓越工程师成长。

## 4 现代产业学院的建构逻辑与融合策略

### 4.1 平台搭建：构建多元利益主体协同参与的混合式组织架构

作为高校、政府、企业、研究院、行业协会中至少两个主体参与共同建设的新型产教融合载体（表 2），现代产业学院的组织形态明显区别于传统的高校二级学院，是一种典型的混合型组织。混合型组织是伴随着公共部门、私营部门、第三部门间边界模糊，不同部门间相互

渗透,应运而生的一种杂糅两种及两种以上组织核心要素的组织模式,已逐渐成为解决复杂社会问题的有力工具。混合型组织的出现改变原有校企双方科层体系下两条平行线无法相交的状态[13],为高校与社会相关领域建立合作提供良好的契机。高校内部的校院两级隶属关系,以及企业内部的层级制管理关系,都属于单维组织模式。这种模式存在信息来源单一、对外界变化反应不灵敏、缺乏创造性等瓶颈,难以突破。相比之下,混合型组织的优势在于能够整合各方优势资源和稀缺资源,实现社会整体效益的最大化;能够打破以往高校成果单向输出模式,建立起高校与外界环境的动态联系;能够促进异质性知识的交流碰撞,激发组织的学习力、创造力以实现自身高质量发展。

**表 2　首批现代产业学院多元主体共建模式分布情况**

| 共建模式 | 代表性现代产业学院 | 数量 | 占比 |
| --- | --- | --- | --- |
| 校-企 | 天津中医药大学中药制药现代产业学院 | 31 | 62% |
| 政-校-企 | 吉林农业大学参茸道地药材现代产业学院 | 10 | 20% |
| 校-企-研 | 南京师范大学南瑞电气与自动化学院 | 3 | 6% |
| 政-校 | 重庆邮电大学工业互联网学院 | 2 | 4% |
| 政-校-研 | 盐城工学院新能源学院 | 1 | 2% |
| 政-校-企-行 | 佛山科学技术学院半导体光学工程产业学院 | 1 | 2% |
| 校-企-行 | 福建工程学院智能制造产业学院 | 1 | 2% |
| 校-企-研-行 | 广西科技大学智能车辆(制造)与新能源汽车产业学院 | 1 | 2% |

混合型组织的使命在于,通过合理安排多维制度逻辑、加强多重利益相关主体互动,实现对多重需求、多维期望的响应。最终,达成各利益相关主体多维价值的共创共享[14]。现代产业学院的基因中蕴含着成为混合型组织的先天条件,但还需要建立起科学合理的组织架构与运行制度才能充分发挥出混合型组织的突出优势、担负起实现整体效益最大化的使命。虽然当前尚未形成相对成熟的现代产业学院组织架构,但首批 50 家现代产业学院普遍正在着力探索多主体协同下理事会领导的院长负责制这种三级组织架构的搭建(图 2),并相继制定出一系列规章制度配合三级组织架构平稳有序运行。在这一组织架构设计中,第一层级的高校、企业、科研院所等多个利益相关主体代表组成理事会,作为学院的最高决策层对资源投入、发展方向等重大事项进行协商和表决;第二层级的院长对接理事会,对理事会的重大决策进行落实,并负责学院发展、运行等相关管理事宜;第三层级的各业务部门承接院长下放的行政、教学、对接产业等管理权限与责任,履行学院的各项基本职能。相比于传统的二级学院组织架构,现代产业学院典型的三级组织架构在决策层增设理事会这一机制,在赋予学院更大独立自主权的同时,为多方相关利益主体提供更多沟通交流机会,为畅通多方资源有效融合渠道奠定良好基础;在管理层明确院长作为学院运营管理的第一责任人,有效规避在办学过程中各方权责边界划分不清现象的发生,极大提升现代产业学院作为多主体参与共建组织的运行效率;在运行层增设产业服务部门,将其作为沟通校企、整合资源的窗口,开展产业技术研究和改造、科研成果转化与应用等工作,将服务产业工作提升到与人才

培养、行政管理事务一致的高度，高度重视产教融合对产业转型升级的促进作用。总体而言，理事会领导下院长负责的三级组织架构从顶层设计层面打破“引企入教”的制度性障碍，保障现代产业学院科学有效地发挥混合型组织优势，为集聚创新要素、深化产教融合和激发产业发展活力提供源源不竭的新动能。

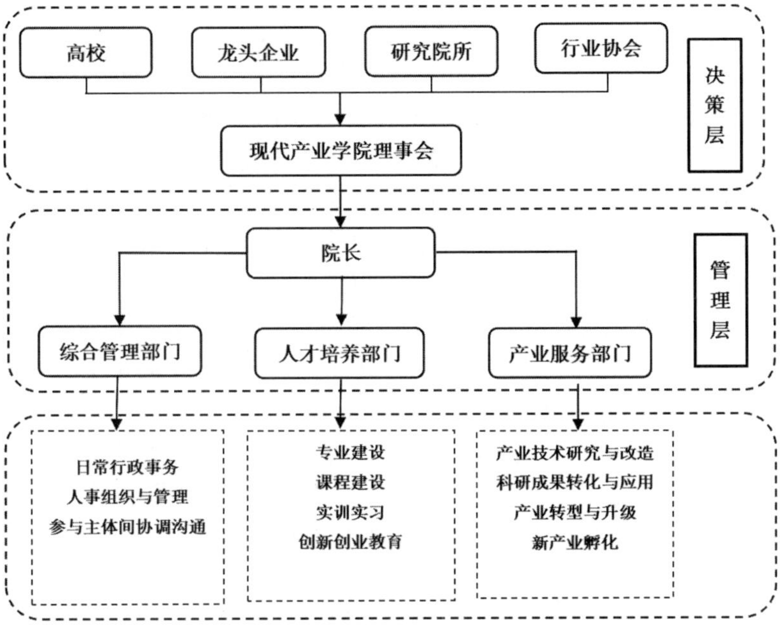


**图 2 现代产业学院的典型组织架构设计**

### 4.2 模式创新：基于 OBE 理念的人才培养方案反向设计

成果导向教育（outcome based education，OBE）是一种以学习成果为中心的教育理念，其核心要义是“学生中心、成果导向、持续改进”。相较于传统教育理念下过分强调学生有限知识习得，OBE 理念主张要以提升学生综合能力为中心，以促进其全面发展为要旨；相较于传统教育流程下高校提前单线程安排好学生的学习内容，OBE 理念强调要遵循“反向设计”原则，依据相关利益主体对学生的要求与预期成果反向设计学生的学习任务；相较于传统教育模式下人才培养方式惯性沿袭原有路径，OBE 理念强调要在外界环境的动态变化中持续改进人才培养方式方法以增进育人模式的先进性。OBE 理念与现代产业学院增强学生社会适应性、提高学生自主创新能力等人才培育目标存在诸多联结点。此外，OBE 理念已被充分纳入工程教育认证领域并发挥成效，美国工程与技术认证委员会（Accreditation Board for Engineering and Technology，ABET）将 OBE 理念贯彻到工程教育专业认证标准中，我国新工科建设指南（亦称“北京指南”）中也明确指出要全面落实“学生中心、成果导向、持续改进”的国际工程教育专业认证理念。因此，对于以“培养新时代卓越工程师”为己任的现代产业学院来说，在人才培养各环节中积极贯彻 OBE 理念是提升其育人成效的必然选择。

在 OBE 理念的指导下，首批现代产业学院积极开发出一系列人才培养新举措。譬如，天津中医药大学中药制药现代产业学院基于中药制药行业岗位需求和区域发展人才需要，规划产、教、研三位一体的学生学业发展模式，制定兼顾三方利益的人才培养方案；常州大学阿里云大数据学院基于行业需求、能力标准反向设计课程体系，构建符合人才培养定位的新课程体系，并利用阿里云、中软等行业主流领先技术不断迭代课程内容，形成基于产业技术前沿的课程资源；江西理工大学先进铜产业学院与江铜集团签订定向合作协议，培养符合企业需要的专业人才；吉林农业大学参茸道地药材现代产业学院协同6家参茸产业龙头企业开设道地药材参茸产业定制班，打造行业紧缺人才。除上述典例中更新人才培养方案、迭代课程内容、签订定向合作协议和校企共同开设定制班等路径外，首批50家现代产业学院还展开各式各样基于OBE理念的实践探索，并逐步摸索出一种以OBE理念为导向的人才培养新模式（图3）。与传统基于OBE理念的人才培养方式相比，这一培养模式有显著优势。它以当前行业发展趋势为逻辑起点，强化行业企业的参与。密切掌握行业发展动态的龙头企业，利用现代产业学院这一合作平台，将用人单位需求传递给高校，有效避免人才培养方案老化、人才培养标准与现实需要脱节等问题；以启用校外导师和吸纳前沿技术作为课程资源等直接或间接的方式强化企业在各项人才培养环节中的参与，丰富人才培养内容，深刻转变以往课堂讲授比重过大，实践教学环节不受重视的倾向；通过企业参与教学，增进了育人环节与人才的直接接触，大幅缩短人才资源供需双方相互反馈的时间与距离，在企业先后对接育人环节与用人环节的基础上促成人才培养机制自我改进能力的生成。总的来说，这一模式充分响应OBE理念的"学生中心、成果导向、持续改进"核心要义，通过重构人才培养流程将产业链与教育链有机衔接起来，极大提高人才培养与产业发展的契合度，是现代产业学院培育新时代卓越工程师的重要抓手。

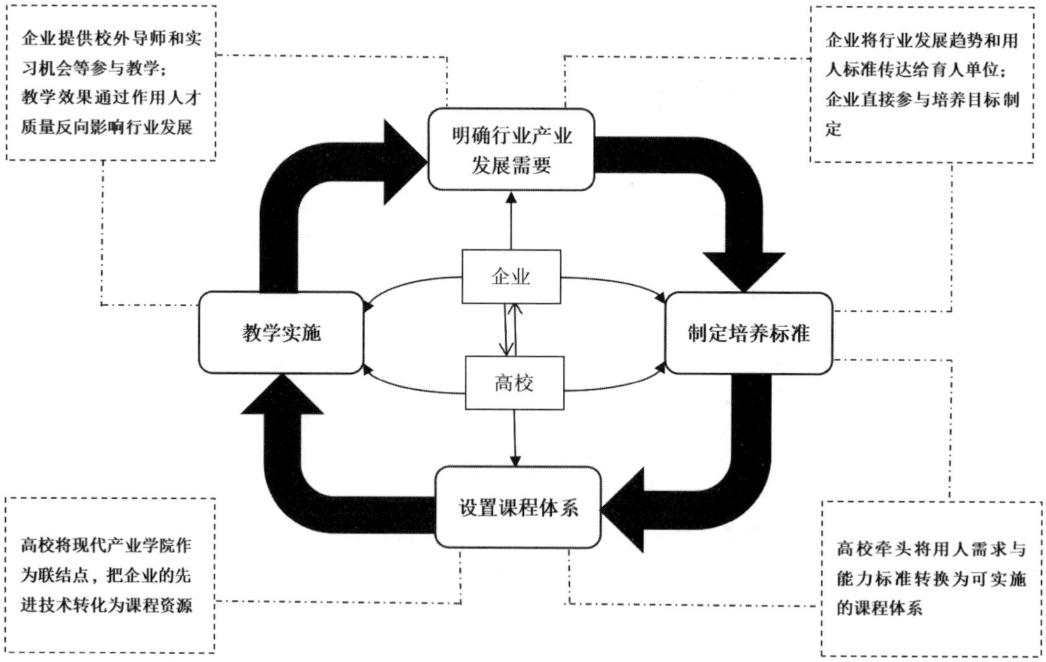


**图3　以OBE理念为导向的人才培养关键环节流程**

### 4.3 教学改革：创建浸润真实工程环境的项目式教学范式

课程教学是人才培养的实际落脚点，是人才培养目标最终得以实现的重要依托。传统的理论式课堂教学模式以教师讲授为主，存在重理论、轻实践的问题。这一模式已然无法满足学生的发展需要，也不能适应当前日新月异的人才需求。特别是对于面向学生创新与实践能力培养的工程教育来说，传统课堂教学与工程实践训练相分离的教学范式致使学生在相对孤立的知识点与技能训练下无法打通知识与能力之间的界面障碍，难以实现知识向能力的有效转变[15]，因此迫切需要探索新的改革方向。项目式教学并非新概念，它源自杜威的“做中学”理念，由克伯屈的设计教学法发展而来，早在 20 世纪 70 年代就已经引发欧美教育界的广泛讨论和实践探索。项目式教学的核心思想是问题导向、项目驱动，强调在解决问题的真实情境中展开教学活动，并通过教学项目的实施将理论与实践有机结合起来，使学生获得运用新知识和新技能解决实际问题的能力。伴随着建设现代产业学院等卓越工程师产教联合培养工作的深入推进，工程教育领域的项目式教学也因企业这一主体的参与焕发出新的活力，因产业中真实工程项目的引入迎来更为广阔的应用空间。经调研发现，首批现代产业学院中的半数以上均不约而同地在各自官网、相关媒体报道中提及项目式教学或项目式课程这一概念，其中更是有 16 家在文件中明确强调要依托项目开展教学内容与教学方式的改革。

现代产业学院具备独特的平台优势和资源禀赋，这些特质与项目式教学功能设计之间存在很强的适配性。作为产教进一步深度融合的载体，现代产业学院利用合作企业的资源优势，以项目为载体，让师生直接参与企业技术研发和技术服务，科研项目直接作为毕业选题。在真实工程案例、真实企业氛围、真实项目经历、真实工作压力“4R”环境下进行项目式教学（图 4），能够最大程度激发项目式教学范式的效能，有效推动组织目标达成。

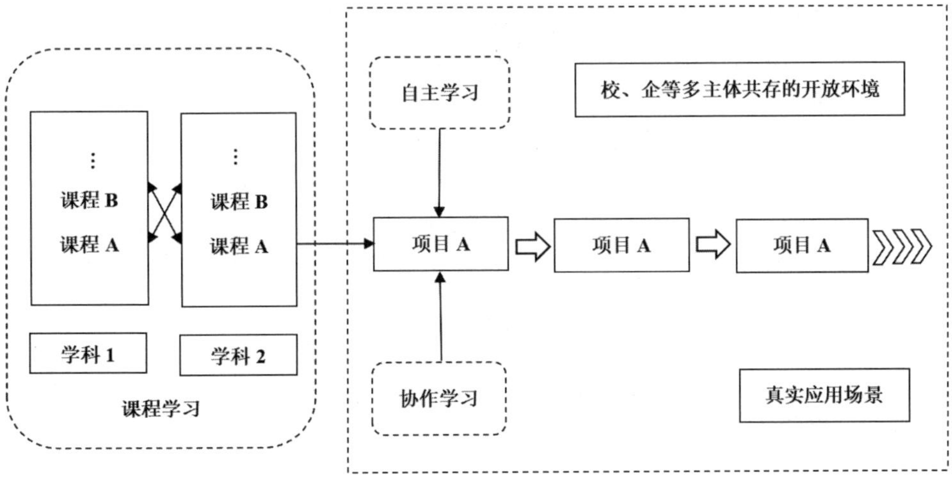


**图 4 现代产业学院中的项目式教学范式**

在现代产业学院中推进项目式教学优势主要表现在四个方面。一是项目作为载体助推学科交叉建设落地。被解构的单一学科知识无法支撑项目经历一个完整的生命周期，为推动项目实施，现代产业学院必须主动打破学科壁垒，并利用此契机重构课程体系，强化课程间的跨模态知识迁移与学科间的交叉融合。二是项目式教学驱动学习方式变革。学生通过课程学习获取的显性知识仅占其知识体量的一小部分，为顺利完成项目，学生还需要在真实的应用场景中转变学习方式，从接受学习转向发现学习，对缄默知识进行自主学习，还需要在多主体共存的开放环境中学会与团队成员协作学习。三是通过开发真实工程环境的教学资源和重组实践教学体系强化工程深度学习。学生在深度参与一个个工程项目中加强对知识的理解，增强理论联系实际与解决复杂问题的能力，实现新工科知识增长、新产业能力培养和新时代素质提升。四是项目作为多主体开展深度合作的方式之一，赋能科教与产教双融合，将学习过程转变为解决企业实际问题的过程，在解决真实问题的过程中实现产学并举，研创结合。总的来说，浸润真实工程环境的项目式教学范式在发挥新时代卓越工程师能力培养这一突出优势的基础上，还能积极应对现代产业学院交叉学科建设、产教深度融合等发展需要，是现代产业学院高质量发展不可或缺的一部分。

## 5 未来推进现代产业学院高质量发展的行动路径

### 5.1 强化政府引导，增进多边匹配

校企匹配是最大程度发挥现代产业学院中各方主体资源优势和融合效应的前提基础。当前我国各级政府部门管理着大部分信息数据资源，表明其具备掌握区域内各所高校与各家企业基本特征的资质禀赋，说明地方政府有把握区域内各所高校与各家企业基本特征的资质禀赋，因此要充分发挥地方政府在现代产业学院筹备初期的引导作用，驱动适配企业与高校进行精准对接。

（1）探索建立资源匹配机制。地方政府应深度分析区域产业优势和人才需求，结合地方未来发展规划，优选适合建设现代产业学院的各方主体。通过坚持优中选优原则，推动现代产业学院创新突破。

（2）在明确产业发展需要和高校办学定位的基础上，为适配的高校、企业等主体提供平等对话交流的机会，引导双方建立起良好的合作关系，共同服务区域经济社会高质量发展。

（3）予以适当的政策倾斜和财政资金支持。通过出台配套政策与设立专项基金等方式发挥政府的能动作用，充分激发各主体参与现代产业学院建设的积极主动性，为双边或多边合作共建现代产业学院提供有效支撑引领。

（4）持续把控现代产业学院建设方向，以避免高校、企业等单一主体在信息未完全对称的匹配初期受到干扰走偏走样，要充分调动政府的治理优势弥合信息差，促进适配的多主体朝着正确方向共同发力。

### 5.2 理顺利益关切，形塑共生关系

驱使高校、行业企业等多个异质性组织参与现代产业学院共建的引擎是促进自身价值增值，参与主体间的关系实质是正和博弈关系。由于各方组织在规章制度、价值观念等方面

存在一定差异，正和博弈关系并不稳固，因此，亟须建立多方利益相关主体间的相互信任，推动这种关系向共生关系演进，进而形成主体合力。

（1）强化主体间的战略共识，通过聚焦利益结合点，在现代产业学院战略层面创设满足多方利益诉求的共同使命与愿景，推动共建主体加快形成利益耦合、战略互嵌、同频共振的发展格局，以促进现代产业学院有效发挥产教融合成效。

（2）健全利益分配机制，借此规避共建过程中的利益矛盾与冲突，维护主体关系稳定。此外，由于在现代产业学院的人才培养、产品研发等主要环节中发生的知识转移具有复杂性和难以界定性，提前签订的契约难以兼顾实践中的各种细节，因此还要探索建立具有弹性的事后利益补偿机制，真正构建起公平合理的校企共生利益链条，实现风险共担，利益共享[16]。

（3）加强现代产业学院中的文化建设。参与共建的各个组织可能会呈现出截然不同甚至是抵牾的价值取向，严重威胁其和谐共生关系，因此要以多方主体价值认同的“最大公约数”为抓手，加快建立新的组织文化，通过营造和谐共生的深层文化氛围，促进各主体同呼吸、共命运。

### 5.3 完善激励机制，增强内生驱动

现代产业学院建设和发展是一个长期的过程，其人才培养、科技成果孵化等功效的发挥往往需要较长的周期，因此在短期内实现快速获利的可能性不大[17]。这就需要在机制设计层面，开发出能够与长期能力建设性工具紧密配合的短期激励性工具[18]。通过这种方式，推动现代产业学院完成阶段性任务与长期规划，获取源源不断的发展动力。

（1）为发挥市场竞争的激励作用，应尽快确立现代产业学院的独立法人地位。法人实体是参与市场经济活动的重要资格凭证，只有参与市场经济活动才能实现资源增值，才能利用激烈的市场竞争充分激发现代产业学院建设的紧迫感与危机感，进而推动现代产业学院向上向好发展。

（2）探索建立包含成果奖励制度、绩效分配制度和个人荣誉制度等在内一系列的现代产业学院内部激励制度体系[19]，以创新内部激励制度，调动各参与主体的工作积极性，通过提升现代产业学院各个环节的运行效率，促进其内生动力累积增长。

（3）开展建设成效评价。评价具有重要的导向作用，有助于审视和检查建设过程中的问题并为后续改进提供依据，能从外部推动现代产业学院高质量建设，因此要定期吸纳多方利益相关主体展开对现代产业学院建设成效的全方位评价，在常规性的质量检查评价中驱动外部推动力向内部自驱力转化。

### 5.4 优化顶层设计，落实各项保障

由于第一批国家级现代产业学院名单公布至今还不到两年的时间，第二批国家级现代产业学院申报工作目前还未结束，现代产业学院仍属于处在探索建设初期的新生组织，其发展模式尚不成熟，在实践过程中可能会面临诸多不确定因素和挑战，因此亟须从顶层设计层面提前安排好各项保障工作，为现代产业学院的可持续高质量发展保驾护航。

（1）完善知识产权保护机制，保障现代产业学院作为智力成果完成人享有正当权利的

合法性，从而充分调动其在新产品生产和新技术孵化等工作中的积极性与创造性，有效发挥其在科技创新领域的突出优势。

（2）探索建立相应的资格认证制度。一方面，要通过形成规范性的协议章程完善资本的准入准出规则，方便对参与主体进行管理的同时也确保其享有不可剥夺的受益权；另一方面，要充分保障参与共建主体的招聘人才优先权[20]，防止"人才盗猎"现象发生后严重损害行业企业合作意愿。

（3）建立稳定的资源保障制度。现代产业学院服务于高技术和高资本密集的战略性新兴产业，对资源投入依赖性很强。因此，需做好物力、财力等资源保障。对内，确保各方主体对现代产业学院建设的稳定投入；对外，积极探索多元经费筹措渠道，如与市场中的上下游企业开展合作等，汇聚多方资源，推动现代产业学院的建设持续深入。

**参考文献**


[1] 林健，耿乐乐. 现代产业学院建设：培养新时代卓越工程师和促进产业发展的新途径[J]. 高等工程教育研究，2023（1）：6-13.

[2] 李名梁，史静妍. 我国现代产业学院：内涵诠释、逻辑进路及研究转向[J]. 教育与职业，2023（10）：13-20.

[3] 周继良，匡永杨. 现代产业学院与企业大学的组织属性、特征与合作空间[J]. 黑龙江高教研究，2023，41（7）：42-49.

[4] 曹雨平，张兵，邹一琴. 现代产业学院可持续发展机制设计——基于组织生态学理论[J]. 高等工程教育研究，2023（1）：111-115，156.

[5] 蒋惠凤，张兵，刘益平. 组织生态学视角下现代产业学院高质量发展：内涵、困境与路径[J]. 中国高教研究，2022（12）：88-93.

[6] 张元宝，杨国兴，毛防华. 应用型高校现代产业学院高质量发展：内涵、困境与路径——基于共生理论的视角[J]. 江苏高教，2023（7）：52-59.

[7] 柯婷，王亚煦. 现代产业学院人才培养体系建设——以粤港澳大湾区首批全国现代产业学院为例[J]. 科技管理研究，2022，42（18）：80-86.

[8] 陈雄寅，周跃良，贾铁刚. 苏粤浙闽等沿海四省现代产业学院建设现状及启示[J]. 中国职业技术教育，2022（24）：46-53.

[9] 严纯华. 推动大学教育和科技创新联动发展[N/OL].（2021-08-16）[2023-07-21]. http://t-heory.people.com.cn/n1/2021/0816/c40531-32193931.html.

[10] 项典典，包莹，焦冠哲. 数字经济视域下的产消者：研究述评与展望[J]. 外国经济与管理，2022，44（3）：36-52.

[11] 教育部 工业和信息化部 中国工程院关于加快建设发展新工科实施卓越工程师教育培养计划 2.0 的意见[EB/OL].（2018-10-08）[2023-07-21]. http://www.moe.gov.cn/src-site/A08/moe_742/s3860/201810/t20181017_351890.html.

[12] 邓小华，王晞. 现代产业学院的基本职能与运行机制[J]. 职教论坛，2022，38（7）：37-44.

[13] 吴金栋. 高校合作型组织创新的研究[J]. 中国软科学，2022（S1）：98-101.

[14] 肖红军，阳镇. 混合型组织的可持续成长：多重紧张的战略响应[J]. 经济与管理研究，

2022,43(3):114-129.

[15] 孙康宁,于化东,梁延德.基于新工科的知识力、实践、创新一体化培养教学模式探讨[J].中国大学教学,2019(3):93-96.

[16] 黄红武,李宁,刘国买,等.现代产业学院组织模式的创新构想与实现路径[J].中国高等教育,2022(20):36-38.

[17] 陈小中.高职现代产业学院的内涵逻辑、运行掣肘与发展路径[J].教育与职业，2022(12):28-35.

[18] 肖纲领,李威,林荣日.地方本科院校产教融合制度建设困境的审视与纾解——组织社会学新制度主义的视角[J].高教探索,2023(3):12-18,70.

[19] 邓小华,付传.现代产业学院运行的知识逻辑及治理路径——知识基础理论视角[J].高等工程教育研究,2023(3):120-124,144.

[20] 苏新留,曹留成.政校企协同建设现代产业学院的逻辑、问题与策略[J].教育与职业，2023(12):50-57.

# 新工科研究与实践的发展现状、成效评价与未来趋势①

林佳妮　胡德鑫　夏淑倩　顾佩华

**摘要：**新工科研究与实践项目是推动工程教育持续革新、赋能新工科高质量发展的重要载体。基于第二批845个全国新工科研究与实践项目的申报与建设材料，系统分析我国新工科研究与实践的发展现状、成效评价与未来趋势。在对我国新工科研究与实践发展现状进行简要分析的基础上，系统评价其在专业优化调整、教材体系建设、一流核心课建设、工科教师成长共同体培育、教学技术新突破等方面取得的发展成效。进一步，对新工科研究与实践中理念深化、师资建设、产教融合和卓越工程师培养等方面的问题与挑战进行研判，进而指出未来新工科研究与实践的治理路径。

**关键词：**新工科；新工科研究与实践项目；工程教育；卓越工程师

## Development Status, Effectiveness Evaluation,and Future Trends Analysis of Emerging Engineering Education Research and Practice

*Lin Jiani, Hu Dexin, Xia Shuqian, Gu Peihua*

**Abstract:** The Emerging Engineering Education Research and Practice Projects is an vital vehicle for driving continuous innovation of emerging engineering education and empowering the high-quality development of engineering education. Based on the application and implementation data of the second batch of 845 projects, this paper analyzes systematically the current development status, effectiveness evaluation, and future trend of emerging engineering education research and practice in China. Based on a brief analysis of the current development status, this paper systematically evaluates the development achievements made in professional optimization and adjustment, textbook system construction, first-class core course construction, engineering teacher growth community, and new breakthroughs in teaching technology. Furthermore, we analyze and assess the issues and challenges in the deepening of concepts, teacher development, integration of industry and education, and the cultivation of outstanding engineers in the research and practice of emerging engineering education, and further point out the governance path for future.

**Keywords:** emerging engineering education; the Emerging Engineering Education Research and Practice Project; engineering education; outstanding engineer

① 本文刊登于《高等工程教育研究》2024年第2期第38~43页。

## 引言

全面深化新工科建设，具体落实到组织模式创新、培养机制创新、内容方法创新和理论实践创新等方面，其中新工科研究与实践项目成为推动从理论深化到实践创新的重要举措。2017 年 6 月，教育部开展首批全国新工科研究与实践项目研究，积极探索新工科建设的新模式、新结构、新质量、新理念、新体系，聚焦于新工科建设的整体制度设计和理论范式建构[1]。在首批项目取得成效的基础上，教育部提出开展第二批全国新工科研究与实践项目，旨在推动新工科建设从理念向实践行动的真正落地。2020 年 3 月，教育部发布《第二批新工科研究与实践项目指南》（简称《指南》）。《指南》围绕理念深化、结构优化、模式创新等八个方面 34 个选题方向展开。10 月，《教育部办公厅关于公布第二批新工科研究与实践项目的通知》中认定 845 个项目。基于此，本研究根据第二批新工科研究与实践项目的相关材料，采用文本分析法、多案例研讨法、词频分析法等方法与工具，着重探讨我国新工科研究与实践的发展现状、成效评价与未来态势。

## 1　研究设计

### 1.1　资料来源

全国新工科研究与实践项目包括 273 个新工科综合改革类项目和 572 个新工科专业改革类项目，项目分为理念深化、结构优化、模式创新、师资建设、创新创业教育、协同育人、共同体构建和质量提升八类选题方向，涵盖新工科理念研究类项目群、专业结构改革项目群、高层次人才培养项目群等诸多项目群。本研究资料来自第二批全国新工科研究与实践项目立项的 845 个项目申报与结项材料，并结合项目实施过程中的新闻报道、学术论文资料、学术会议、结项专家评议意见进行综合分析。

### 1.2　研究方法

本文主要采用文本分析法、多案例研讨法、词频分析法等方法与工具。文本分析法强调对文字性内容进行量化，从而发现定性资料中所隐藏的规律性问题。文本分析法作为本研究的核心方法，通过对第二批新工科研究与实践项目文字性内容的深度挖掘，旨在探讨新工科研究与实践的发展现状和取得的成效，以及研判其存在的问题。多案例研讨法基于理论抽样原则，对两个以上案例进行比较分析，以识别案例单元的相似性和异质性。本研究通过理论抽样选取成效显著的典型项目进行多案例分析，以总结新工科研究与实践取得的实际成效。词频分析法是文本挖掘的一种重要工具，用于计算和分析文档文本中核心关键词的出现次数，其原理是通过词汇出现频率的变化来确定热点及其变化趋势。本研究借助词频分析法，以 845 个立项项目的名称为基础，利用 Python 软件绘制词云图，确定新工科研究重点领域。

## 2 新工科研究与实践的发展现状

### 2.1 项目选题的覆盖度分析

与《指南》中的选题方向进行对比,“结构优化”“协同育人”选题方向的项目数最多,分别为306项和201项,“理念深化选题”项目数最少,仅有17个项目。通过与《指南》中的34个选题方向进行对比,考查所有立项项目在课题方向上的达成度与覆盖度(表1)。845个立项项目实现对《指南》中34个课题的全覆盖,初步实现《指南》规划的预期目标。不同选题方向的立项数量在一定程度上反映了《指南》的达成度。在数量上,“传统工科专业改造升级探索与实践”“新工科人才培养实践创新平台建设探索与实践”“新工科产教融合、校企合作机制模式探索与实践”三个选题方向达成度较高,占比均超过总项目数的10%。总的来看,第二批新工科研究与实践项目的聚焦性较强,对专业结构优化、人才培养实践、产教融合育人等主题能够深入开展研究,但部分选题(如理念深化、质量提升等)的立项数量较少,可能影响研究的多元性与深入性。

**表1 845个立项项目对《指南》34个选题方向的覆盖情况**

| 选题方向 | 课题编号 | 研究课题名称 | 立项项目数 |
|---|---|---|---|
| 理念深化(17项) | 1 | 新工科人才培养若干基本理论问题研究 | 9 |
| | 2 | 新工科教育科学研究的理论特征分析与发展研判 | 1 |
| | 3 | 新工科人才的工程伦理意识与职业道德和规范研究 | 3 |
| | 4 | 新工科建设再深化、再拓展、再突破、再出发关键问题研究 | 4 |
| 结构优化(306项) | 5 | 未来战略必争领域紧缺人才培养机制探索与实践 | 69 |
| | 6 | 新工科专业结构调整优化机制探索与实践 | 21 |
| | 7 | 传统工科专业改造升级探索与实践 | 169 |
| | 8 | 新工科通专融合课程及教材体系建设 | 47 |
| 模式创新(135项) | 9 | 跨学科、多学科交叉的创新型工程教育组织模式研究与实践 | 78 |
| | 10 | 聚焦科技创新领军人才培养的未来技术学院建设探索与实践 | 6 |
| | 11 | 面向区域产业急需的现代产业学院建设探索与实践 | 40 |
| | 12 | 以软件高端人才培养为导向的特色化示范性软件学院建设探索与实践 | 11 |
| 师资建设(39项) | 13 | 新工科师资能力标准体系探索与构建 | 3 |
| | 14 | 工学院院长教学领导力提升探索与实践 | 2 |
| | 15 | 多层次教师培训体系探索与实践 | 7 |
| | 16 | 高校教师与行业人才双向交流机制探索与实践 | 3 |
| | 17 | 新兴技术范式下的教师教学方法创新与实践 | 24 |

续表

| 选题方向 | 课题编号 | 研究课题名称 | 立项项目数 |
|---|---|---|---|
| 创新创业教育（78项） | 18 | 新工科人才创意创新创业能力培养探索与实践 | 59 |
| | 19 | 新工科建设创新创业教育类课程体系建设 | 4 |
| | 20 | 新工科人才创新创业教育实践平台开发与保障 | 15 |
| 协同育人（201项） | 21 | 新工科产教融合、校企合作机制模式探索与实践 | 87 |
| | 22 | 新工科人才培养实践创新平台建设探索与实践 | 98 |
| | 23 | 结果导向的实习实训保障制度体系建设探索与实践 | 4 |
| | 24 | 新形态复合型教育教学资源体系构建 | 12 |
| 共同体构建（38项） | 25 | 新工科建设国际化人才培养模式和机制研究 | 21 |
| | 26 | 区域新工科教育共同体建设及实践 | 5 |
| | 27 | “一带一路”新工科教育共同体建设 | 11 |
| | 28 | 国际工程教育的中国标准和中国方案研究 | 1 |
| 质量提升（31项） | 29 | 新工科人才学习质量提升路径的探索与实践 | 17 |
| | 30 | 新工科建设全链条标准体系构建与研制 | 4 |
| | 31 | 新工科理念下的专业认证制度体系构建 | 1 |
| | 32 | 新工科背景下的工程教育三级认证标准构建 | 5 |
| | 33 | 新工科建设专业认证制度与工程师注册制度的有效衔接机制探索 | 3 |
| | 34 | 新工科建设视域下的工程教育文化建设与评价机制 | 1 |

### 2.2 高校组别的选题覆盖度分析

第二批项目第一申报单位共计367个，第二参与单位有35个。按第一单位统计，工科优势高校组立项326项，占立项总数的38.58%；综合性高校组立项156项，占立项总数的18.46%；地方高校组立项363项，占立项总数的42.96%。通过计算各组别在八大选题中的占比（表2），可分析各组别对相关选题的关注程度，该占比在一定程度上反映了该组别在相关选题上的达成度。一方面，所有组别对“结构优化”“协同育人”“模式创新”等选题的关注度较高。另一方面，不同组别对选题的关注度也存在差异，工科优势高校组“结构优化”“共同体构建”“质量提升”选题的占比高于另外两个组别，说明工科优势高校在已有基础上，对传统专业升级改造和新专业设置有更大的建设需求，对形成工科研究共同体具有引领作用，对工科教学质量提升有一定理论或实践基础。综合性高校组“模式创新”“师资建设”“理念深化”选题的占比高于另外两个组别，说明综合性高校对组织模式创新、工科教师能力提升、学科交叉融合等研究有较大需求，并且表现出有较好的集合本单位资源开展研究的能力。地方高校组“创新创业教育”“协同育人”选题的占比高于另外两个组别，这体现了地方高校服务区域建设发展，在产教协同育人、建设产业学院方面的研究需求更大，并且具有结合区域优势、调动企业等资源、开展项目研究的优势。

**表 2　各组别八大选题占比**

| 选题类别 | 工科优势高校组 | 综合性高校组 | 地方高校组 |
|---|---|---|---|
| 理念深化 | 2.76% | 3.21% | 0.83% |
| 质量提升 | 3.99% | 3.21% | 3.58% |
| 师资建设 | 4.60% | 8.97% | 2.75% |
| 共同体构建 | 6.44% | 2.56% | 3.58% |
| 创新创业教育 | 7.98% | 9.62% | 10.19% |
| 模式创新 | 11.04% | 19.87% | 18.73% |
| 协同育人 | 19.63% | 17.95% | 30.03% |
| 结构优化 | 43.56% | 34.62% | 30.30% |

注:由于四舍五入,总计不等于 100%。

## 2.3　项目研究的重点领域分析

根据 845 个立项项目名称中关键词出现的频次,本研究在剔除“工科”“建设”“研究”“探索”“工程”等重复或非主题性词语后,运用 NVivo 软件绘制了词云图(图 1),字号越大,说明该词语在 845 个立项项目名称中出现的频次越高,这一结果对确定《指南》达成度的重点领域具有重要参考价值。结果显示,“实践”“专业”“人才”“培养”“创新”等词语的字号较大,说明这些词语在项目名称中出现的频次较高。

**图 1　第二批项目达成度的重点领域词云图**

根据上述结果判断,工程实践、专业建设、人才培养、融合创新是《指南》达成度的重点领域。此外,通过对 200 余项立项项目标题中含有“跨学科”“多学科”“交叉”“融合”等关键词的项目进行分析,发现立项项目对“工工交叉”“工医交叉”“理工融合”“工文融合”“工农融合”等方向均有覆盖,通过学科交叉推进新工科的趋势明显。

### 2.4 优秀项目的聚合性分析

项目结题验收中共有 120 个被评选为优秀项目,优秀项目的聚类分析可以反映不同选题方向研究成果的数量差异(图 2)。“传统工科专业改造升级探索与实践”方向的优秀项目最多,占总优秀项目数量的 19.17%;其次是“新工科人才培养实践创新平台建设探索与实践”方向,占比为 10.83%;再次是“未来战略必争领域紧缺人才培养机制探索与实践”方向,占比为 10%。其余选题的优秀项目占总优秀项目的比例均在 10%以下。优秀项目占某一选题立项项目数量的比重可以反映该选题的建设情况。尽管部分选题方向优秀项目数量较少,但其占该选题项目总数的比重较高,如“新工科通专融合课程及教材体系建设”方向有 9 个项目获评优秀项目,在 47 个立项项目中的占比为 19.15%。从项目实施的关键领域来看,“土木、建筑、水利、海洋类”“计算机和软件工程类”“人工智能类”“材料类”“航空航天、交通运输类”“能源电子、核工程类”等领域的立项数量及优秀项目数量均较多,说明这些领域的研究内容较为丰富。

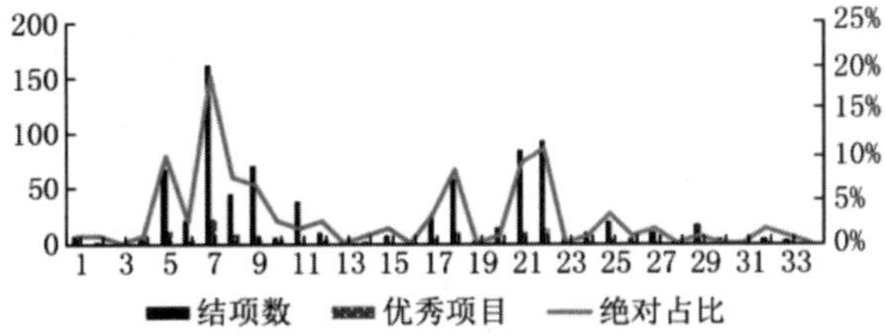


**图 2 120 个优秀项目在《指南》34 个选题方向的聚合程度**

## 3 新工科研究与实践的成效评价

### 3.1 推动专业优化调整

专业是人才培养的基本单元,“新工科专业建设需聚焦新专业设置、传统专业升级、交叉融合出新”已成为重要共识,既是教与学的交汇点,又是第二批项目研究最集中的选题。项目面向新经济发展需要、制造强国战略目标、制造业战略性结构调整需求,聚焦于“传统工科项目的升级改造”与“新工科专业结构调整优化机制”。一是在战略层面明确人才培养定位。项目组根据国家发展战略、行业重大需求和学科前沿的变化对专业人才培养提出的新要求,结合区域发展和学校规划调整优化专业设置,创新人才培养理念,重塑人才培养目标,培养未来发展所需人才。二是在组织层面构建跨学科、多学科交叉平台。“工科优势高校新工科建设再深化、再拓展、再突破、再出发关键问题研究(E-LNYJ20200109)”等项目根据新技术和新产业发展趋势,推动学科交叉融合,突破制约传统工科专业创新人才培养的内部机制障碍,打破学院间体制壁垒,积极成立跨学院、跨学科的新专业。三是在实践层面深化校企协同机制,关注学生创新能力培养。“面向产业前沿的跨学科创意创新创业能力训练体系(E-CXCYYR20200901)”等项目持续深化产教融合,打造有组织的联合科研合作和人才培养平台,将产业最新技术和应用平台引入课堂教学与专业实践。

### 3.2 推动教材体系建设

教材是开展人才培养的有效载体，教学改革的关键落实点在于教材。第二批新工科项目以产业需求为导向，坚持“建用并进、持续改进、共建共享、智能教学”的理念，建设了一批针对新技术、新模式、新业态的新工科教材，构建适应新工科人才培养的教材体系。一是完善新兴领域教材体系建设。教材编写凸显前沿性、交叉性与综合性，引入产业元素，突出教材内容与工程实践、产业应用紧密结合的特点。“人工智能通专融合课程及教材体系建设（E-RGZN20201024）”等项目持续推进系列教材建设，支撑面向人工智能人才培养的核心知识体系和课程体系。二是开发新形态教学资源。改变教材传统的呈现形式，采用全新数字化融媒体形式，将过去平面二维、静态、抽象的专业知识以三维、动态、立体形式呈现，拓展教材内容的立体互动表现方式。“智能制造模块化新形态教材建设（E-ZNZZ20201201）”等项目采用主干教材+模块教材的方式策划、出版了系列智能制造模块化新形态教材，既能满足智能制造工程专业人才培养的需求，又能满足机械工程、自动化等专业学生选修课程的需求。三是创建教材教学资源新平台。建设支撑模块化课程体系的新工科教材资源平台，“智能时代面向新工科的自动化专业模块化课程体系建设与实践（E-ZDH20201611）”项目集合 20 余所高校围绕学科基础类、智能检测与建模类、智能控制类、智能分析与决策类等课程模块，出版一系列新工科立体化教材。

### 3.3 推动一流核心课建设

课程是一流本科教育建设的关键要素，教育教学改革向深处推进的关键是课程建设。第二批项目在课程上聚焦于“新工科通专融合课程”“新工科创新创业类课程”，形成以下特色。一是重构体系，打造横纵交叉通专融合课程群组。新工科建设的发展改革理念和教育教学理念在实际课程中得到落实，“主辅双修”“专通融合”“交叉融合”“本研贯通”的课程体系成效显著。课程群成为培养具有创新能力和综合素质的高水平人才的重要载体，“多学科交叉融合的人工智能新兴工科专业建设探索与实践（E-RGZN20201023）”项目横向上人工智能、大数据等新兴技术与传统学科的跨专业交叉融合，形成覆盖多个领域，涵盖基础课程、专业课程、通识课程的多学科交叉的课程群。二是“跨界”培养，聚焦产学研协同实践育人新模式。以课程建设为中心，深化校企合作，突出人才输出导向，鼓励企业参与新工科课程改革，将企业先进技术融入相关专业课程中。“面向未来技术的学科交叉平台建设，赋能创新型工程人才培养（EDXKJC20200515）”项目组以社会需求为牵引，引入校企资源共建共享，深入推进实践育人模式实施，同国内外知名企业共建校企联合实验室、联合培养基地等平台及实习实训基地，提升学生探索能力和应用能力。三是示范引领，争创“一流课程”提升课程整体质量。课程质量决定人才培养质量，全面打造“金课”势在必行。“智慧化工与创新驱动背景下的化工类专业改造、升级研究与实践（EHGZY20202004）”项目充分利用线上条件和平台改革专业核心课程，开发一批更具时代性、数字化、智能化的新形态课程。

### 3.4 构建工科教师成长共同体

师资队伍质量是高校教育教学质量的根本保证，师资队伍的建设是学生培养质量的决定性因素。第二批项目聚焦“新工科师资能力培养”“多层次教师培训体系”“教师教学方法创新”等方向，对师资建设进行了实践与研究。一是打造高素质“双师双能”教师队伍。组建“双师”培训专家库和团队，以“先进教育理念”“教学技能提升”“实践技能提升”“伴随式指导”等为重点内容开展培训，提升教育教学能力。“新工科背景下 IT 类专业多层次教师培训体系探索与实践（EJSJRJ20201304）”项目深化校企融合，与企业针对性制订全国高校人工智能开发技术师资培训计划，构建“双师双能”教师能力培训体系，鼓励教师到企业锻炼和行业企业专家、技术骨干到大学兼职，促进校企双向交流。二是以新技术新媒体赋能师资培训。“基于新技术和新媒体的新工科师资培训体系建设（E-SZNL20200701）”项目围绕信息技术学科前沿领域和产业交叉技术，组织高校教育专家和企业研发工程师，为高校教师搭建学习和实践产业前沿技术的培训平台，提升教师的工程实践能力和教育教学水平。三是创新教师考评机制，强化激励机制。“‘双师双能型’航海类教师培养培训体系建设研究（ESZNL20200706）”项目科学设置评价标准，修订教师职称评价标准，增加行业影响及社会服务业绩成果的考核权重。

### 3.5 促进教学技术新突破

技术是实现从学习革命、质量革命到高质量发展的突破性切口和创新性路径，是中国高等教育实现从全面并跑到战略领跑的重大突破。第二批项目聚焦“新兴技术范式下的教师教学方法创新与实践”等方向，对技术发展进行研究与 实践。一是构建数字化教学环境。面向工业 4.0 时代产业需求，以人工智能等新兴技术为驱动，构建数字化、网络化虚拟仿真实践空间，培养相关技术运用能力。“面向新工科的智慧环境下‘智能+’专业课堂教学模式改革探索与实践（ESZNL20200705）”项目利用智慧教室等信息技术优势，促进现代信息技术与教育教学深度融合，重塑教育教学形态。二是丰富教学实践手段。“京津冀区域材料新工科人才教育共同体构建与运行机制研究（E-CL20201902）”项目利用新技术带来的新机遇，将教学组织方式重组再造，实现教学模式实时切换、线上线下“双空间”互动教学。探索专业课程数字化改造的新途径，颠覆传统教学方式，利用增强现实（AR）、虚拟现实（VR）等技术，结合国家一流虚拟仿真课程，创新人才培养模式和教学方式。三是探索建设新型基层教学组织。建设虚拟教研室，促进人才培养各方合作互通，探索教学研究新形态，构建校企结合、专兼结合、虚实结合的高水平、多元化教学发展共同体，以新技术新工具推动新型教育模式推广。

## 4 新工科研究与实践未来治理路径

### 4.1 新工科研究与实践的问题研判

第一，理念深化层面的研究有待丰富。新工科研究与实践的发展现状、成效评价与未来趋势研究需强调将理论知识运用到实际中去，通过不断实践，逐渐形成工程教育新的教育理念和方法，从而实现持续迭代与创新。根据所有立项项目在《指南》八大选题的达成度分析结果,“理念深化”选题达成度最低,仅立项17项,占总项目数的2%。此外,在其他选题实施过程中,项目普遍关注实践,缺少理论支撑。

第二,师资建设层面的研究有待强化。第二批项目围绕“师资建设”方面的立项项目较少,占比不足5%,主要包括新工科师资能力标准、工学院院长教学领导力、高校教师与行业人才双向交流机制等主题。研究显示,教学队伍工程经验普遍不足,部分教师从大学校门出来就开始任教,并没有实际工程经验;教师队伍是推动工作做实做细做深的核心,直接相关的就是教师评价和激励机制的建立。

第三,产教融合层面的联动有待加强。第二批项目普遍关注到产教融合和校企联动,但在具体实践中仍存在突出问题。例如,工业制造一线和实体经济主流领域的拔尖创新人才缺乏,学校教育与企业培训之间存在衔接空白,人才的知识理论与实践应用的结合上出现脱节、错位[2]。有专家指出,当前教学内容更新严重滞后,产业端核心技术和工艺最新的变化如何敏捷快速地对接到专业教学、课程建设、教材建设,也是需要进一步下功夫的地方。

第四,自主培养卓越工程师能力仍需提升。从国内外发展态势来看,目前存在多样的工科学生类型[3],与其他学科相比,工科博士去往学术界的比例呈现持续下降的态势[4],但大部分高校的现行培养目标与模式相对单一。新工科已经历多年实践,我国高校如何进一步向世界一流大学迈进,自主培养多样化的高精尖人才,值得进一步探讨。

### 4.2 新工科研究与实践的未来治理路径

一是持续加强高水平的新工科理论与实践供给。总结长期以来工程教育改革探索与实践的经验,以推进工程教育范式转变赋能新工科的本质性变革[5]。新工科研究与实践项目已成为高校工程教育改革理论研究与实践探索的重要载体。要以新工科研究与实践项目为载体,持续推动工程教育在理念深化、结构优化、模式创新、师资建设、创新创业教育、协同育人、共同体构建和质量提升等领域的研究持续革新,促进理论研究成果有效融入实践改革创新中,推动新工科教育范式的形成与持续迭代,进而构建起新工科教育的“中国范式”“中国理论”和“中国主张”。

二是推进构建科学的工科教师评聘与激励机制。研究显示,当前大部分工科教师缺乏工程实践经历,忽视解决实际问题的工程能力的培养[6]。要建立跨学院联聘制度,鼓励在新工科校级平台组建跨学科、跨学院教学团队,开展多学科交叉专业的培养方案制订、课程设计(特别是项目式课程设计),通过共建和共享课程带动全校课程水平和育人水平的整体提升。要深化高校教师岗位分类改革研究,探索建立有别于学术型工科教师的“工程实践型”教师评聘体系。要拓宽工程教师来源渠道,加强与企业的深度合作,积极吸纳工业界的技术人员到高校担任工程实践指导教师。要完善工科教师工程职称晋升评价制度,将培养学生的工程实践能力纳入职称考评体系,逐步推动论文导向转为解决实际问题导向。

三是推动以产教融合为核心的工程教育治理共同体建设。当前,政府、企业、行业协会等多个利益主体尚未充分发挥协同作用。应加强顶层设计,构建多元利益主体深度参与的产教融合协同治理框架,涵盖产教融合基本要素、相关主体和整体过程,并通过健全制度设计、整合优势资源、高效组织运行、培育高水平师资等,提供有效支撑[7]。在持续推进未来技术学院、现代产业学院、国家卓越工程师学院建设的同时,要将传统行业头部企业和创新型企业引入高校，参与人才培养方案制定、课程设计与教学、实习实践等全过程，着力推进科教融合、产教融合，实现人才培养供给与行业产业需求的高度耦合[8]。

四是聚焦卓越工程师人才自主培养改革。要聚焦卓越工程师核心素养标准研究，该标准强调工科学生在专业领域需要具备的综合理论知识与实践能力，这包括但不限于专业知识、学科精神、创新能力、团队协作、跨学科能力和社会责任感等[9]。要推进多元化项目式课程教学，鼓励开展以问题为导向的教学，使学生将课程核心知识与实际应用相结合，切实提升其复杂工程问题解决能力。在现有认证标准基础上，针对新工科人才培养目标、课程与教学、毕业要求、师资队伍等核心要素，构建全过程、全周期和全角度的卓越工程师人才质量评价与反馈机制。推动与工程教育相衔接的注册工程师制度[10]，制定卓越工程师能力评价标准，切实提升卓越工程师人才自主培养能力。

## 参考文献

[1] 刘坤，代玉，张志金，等. 首批新工科研究与实践项目指南达成度评价及未来发展研判[J]. 高等工程教育研究，2021(1)：31-38.

[2] 刘志军，夏远景，朱泓. 以卓越计划 2.0 版为契机推进高等工程教育改革[J]. 西北工业大学学报(社会科学版)，2018(1)：35-39.

[3] 罗英姿，韩霜，李雪辉. 学生需求视角下工程类专业学位博士教育质量评价研究[J]. 西北工业大学学报(社会科学版)，2023(1)：42-52.

[4] 胡德鑫，王君. 美国博士学位获得者职业选择的结构特征与演进趋势解析[J]. 西北工业大学学报(社会科学版)，2023(4)：69-78.

[5] 顾佩华. 新工科与新范式：概念、框架和实施路径[J]. 高等工程教育研究，2017(6)：1-13.

[6] 王迪，王秀秀. 工科教师专业发展现状及对策研究[J]. 高等工程教育研究，2023(3)：89-95.

[7] 胡德鑫. 学科演进视域下新工科建设制度困境与行动路径[J]. 高等工程教育研究，2020(3)：49-54.

[8] 胡德鑫，逄丹丹. 中国高等工程教育百年发展史回眸：历史演进、变革逻辑与未来趋向[J]. 高校教育管理，2023，17(6)：100-113.

[9] 刘怡，张炜. 一流大学卓越工程师核心素养构成及发展状况调查[J]. 高等工程教育研究，2023(6)：59-65.

[10] 胡德鑫，徐文君，常乔丽，等. 国际注册工程师资质认证制度的建构逻辑与改革趋向[J]. 高等工程教育研究，2023(2)：87-95.

# 基于产出导向工程教育理念的毕业要求达成评价(上)①

朱　露　胡德鑫　王凯峰　顾佩华

**摘要:**工程教育专业认证中的毕业要求达成评价是专业自我评价与认证组织考查评价的重点和难点。本文以国际典型大学和认证组织为研究对象,分别解析学校评价实践和认证组织评价制度体系的案例。研究表明:学校毕业要求达成评价聚焦课程质量评价,主要在对毕业要求具有强支撑作用的专业必修课和实践性教学环节中进行,采用直接辅以间接、定量结合定性、过程对照结果的综合评价模式获取数据,通过对不同类型数据构建完整证据链以三角验证评价结果,综合应用定量分析评判法与定性分析描述法判断达标程度,评价过程重视多元主体协同参与,其本质是以持续改进为导向的周期性循环评价;认证组织基于工程师职业能力标准构建毕业要求框架,统筹设计毕业要求达成评价机制,通过分专业大类细化毕业要求、提供指标点分解样例、明确考查重点与实施细则、制定评价指导方针与评估量规,建立系统化、科学化、规范化的评价指导体系。

**关键词:**OBE;工程教育专业认证;毕业要求达成评价;专业自评;认证组织考评

## On the Evaluation of the Achievement of Graduate Outcomes based on Outcome-based Engineering Education Principles (Part 1)

*Zhu Lu, Hu Dexin, Wang Kaifeng, Gu Peihua*

**Abstract:** The evaluation of the achievement of graduate outcomes in engineering education accreditation is a difficult and challenging task of the program's self-evaluation and accreditation organization's review of engineering education. Taking several typical universities and accreditation organizations as the study objects, this paper carries out case analyses of schools' self-evaluation practices and accreditation organizations' evaluation systems. The results show that the school-level evaluation of the achievement of graduate outcomes focuses on the evaluation of course quality. This is mainly carried out in the professional compulsory courses and practical training that strongly support graduate outcomes, through a comprehensive evaluation model in which direct assessment is supplemented by indirect assessment, quantitative assessment is combined with qualitative assessment, formative assessment is compared with summative assessment. During the evaluation, a complete evidence chain is constructed based on multiple types of data to triangulate the evaluation results, and quantitative analysis evaluation methods combined with qualitative analysis description methods are comprehen-

① 本文刊登于《高等工程教育研究》2024 年第 3 期第 42~57 页。

sively applied to determine the degree of achievement. The importance was attached to the collaborative participation of multiple stakeholders and the essence of the evaluation is a periodic cyclic evaluation oriented towards continuous improvement. Accreditation organizations build a framework of graduate outcomes based on professional competency standards for engineers, design procedures and associated processes for evaluating the achievement of graduate outcomes in a coordinated manner, and establish a systematic, scientific and standardized evaluation guidance system by refining graduate outcomes by program categories, providing examples of indicators, clarifying elements and implementation details of evaluation and formulating the assessment guidelines.

**Keywords:** OBE; accreditation for engineering programs; evaluation of the achievement of graduate outcomes; program's self-evaluation; accreditation organization's review

## 1 问题提出

根据产出导向教育（OBE）理念，《华盛顿协议》各成员组织制定了具有国际实质等效性的工程教育专业认证标准。其中，反映学生培养质量和水平的毕业要求，是《华盛顿协议》判断其成员组织认证体系实质等效性的重点关注项，也是专业人才培养自我评价与认证组织考查评价的重要内容。通过毕业要求达成评价，专业建设者对教育教学活动进行全过程、全要素、全方位监测，根据评价结果有针对性地采取改进措施，将教育改革落实到具体教学环节，持续推进人才培养质量提高与专业高水平发展。作为工程教育专业认证的重要环节，毕业要求达成评价对学校建立产出导向课程体系与考核要求、贯彻落实持续改进机制具有引导和促进作用。因此，亟须从学校和认证组织两个视角，进一步明确毕业要求达成评价的内容要素与实施策略，构建产出导向的毕业要求达成评价参考方案。

### 1.1 评什么：学生毕业时的知识、能力和素养是否达标

毕业要求是学生毕业时在知识、能力、素养方面应达到的基本水平[1-3]。工程教育领域的毕业要求涉及三个方面：国际工程教育互认体系的毕业要求，如《华盛顿协议》的毕业生素质（graduate attributes）[4]、欧洲工程教育专业认证体系的专业产出标准（program outcomes）[5]；各国/地区工程教育专业认证标准中的毕业要求，简称标准毕业要求；学校具体专业制定的毕业要求，简称专业毕业要求。毕业要求达成评价以毕业生的能力要素和能力水平为评价内容，科学制定毕业要求并明确其内容构成是有效开展毕业要求达成评价的第一步。从认证组织视角看，我国工程教育专业认证协会制定了统一的毕业要求框架，但未分专业领域制定指导性的毕业要求，且由于还没有实施注册工程师制度，尚未实现毕业要求与工程师职业能力标准相衔接。从学校视角看，参与认证的高校虽然根据各自办学特色制定专业毕业要求、设置毕业要求指标点，但一些专业毕业要求的可衡量性及其对标准毕业要求的覆盖性不足[6]。如何制定清晰明确、可落实且可评价，既符合认证标准，又具有培养特色的专业毕业要求成为学校面临的一个挑战。

### 1.2 怎么评：学校和认证组织如何科学证明毕业要求达成

毕业要求达成评价包括专业自我评价和认证组织考查评价两个关键环节。专业自我评

价是学校通过直接和间接方式，系统收集最具代表性且能反映毕业生学习结果（产出）的评价数据，定量统计和定性分析评价结果后，对毕业生是否达成、如何达成以及何种程度上达成专业毕业要求做出的评价。认证组织考查评价由认证专家通过审阅自评报告、开展现场考查，判断参与认证的专业是否符合标准毕业要求的达成情况。目前，学校毕业要求达成评价存在评价方法单一（主要以课程考试算分法为主）、评价未聚焦课程目标达成、外部利益相关者参与评价的体制机制不健全、基于评价结果的改进措施不系统和不严谨等问题[7]。认证组织毕业要求达成评价面临考评要素和评价实施细则不明确，专家考查以质性判断为主，缺乏客观评估量规，评价指导材料不完善等问题。学校如何客观真实验证毕业生质量达到预期并实现专业持续改进，认证组织如何科学合理评判专业人才培养质量达标，是卓越工程师培养与工程教育专业认证的重点与难点之一。

## 2 研究设计

### 2.1 研究思路

采用探索性多案例研究策略，分别从学校和认证组织双维视角剖析毕业要求达成评价的国际案例做法，通过分项比较与系统整合，探寻学校之间、认证组织之间毕业要求达成评价的异同。学校方面的案例分析侧重从评价周期、评价过程、评价方法、用于评价的课程、评价结果、持续改进等方面展开，认证组织方面的案例分析聚焦考查要素、评价指导、评价体制机制等内容。根据学校自评和认证组织考评的国际成熟经验，结合 OBE 理念，凝练毕业要求达成评价的核心要素，探索可供参考的评价体系和策略，立足学校和认证组织两个不同评价主体，分类构建毕业要求达成评价参考方案。同时，以机械工程专业为例，对学校如何有效开展毕业要求达成评价进行举例说明。

### 2.2 案例选择

所选案例包括代表性学校的专业自评实践和典型认证组织的毕业要求达成评价制度体系。首先，以较早建立工程教育专业认证制度的美国为切入点，查找美国高校参与美国工程与技术认证委员会（Accreditation Board for Engineering and Technology，ABET）专业认证的自评报告，根据评价实践是否系统科学、评价方法是否适切多样、评价结果是否得到有效应用，以圣路易斯大学、华盛顿大学、佛罗里达大学三所高校的计算机工程专业为样例，对学校毕业要求达成评价进行深度案例解析。其次，从《华盛顿协议》成员中选取美国、加拿大、英国和澳大利亚的认证组织作为毕业要求达成评价的案例分析对象，其典型性体现在两方面：一是其认证组织的工程教育专业认证历史悠久且最早加入国际互认组织；二是构建了相对完备的毕业要求达成评价指导体系。

# 3　案例分析

## 3.1　学校方面毕业要求达成评价的比较分析

### 3.1.1　圣路易斯大学的实践经验

**1. 案例描述**

圣路易斯大学计算机工程专业在2018—2019年认证期内通过ABET认证,全面采纳ABET 11条毕业要求(a~k)并设置指标点(indicators)。该校毕业要求达成评价按照三年轮动时间表进行,每年参与评价的指标有所不同,通常控制在4个以内,三年时间内完成对11条毕业要求的评价,在ABET六年认证有效期内可系统收集两轮评价数据。

从评价过程上看,如图1所示,圣路易斯大学毕业要求达成评价形成以课程质量评价为核心的持续改进机制。评价过程的第一步是将毕业要求分解为指标点。指标点作为对毕业要求的具体解释,可通过课程相关材料进行有效测量。然后,选择支撑毕业要求达成评价的课程,并将指标点与不同类型的课程相联系,大多数情况下,还需确定用于指标点达成评价的考核任务。对于顶点课程(capstone course)或设计类项目,一般通过学习材料集(包括项目记录、技术报告、技术演示等)获取评价数据。最后,设计每门参评课程的指标点评估量规,通过评估量规对分层抽样得到的学生作业进行评价,汇总计算指标点得分后即可获得毕业要求达成评分。根据评价结果,专业通常会采取两类改进措施[8]:一是改进课程,包括调整课程设置、完善课程材料、修订课程目标等;二是改进评估程序,包括优化指标点设计、重新选择用于评价的课程等。

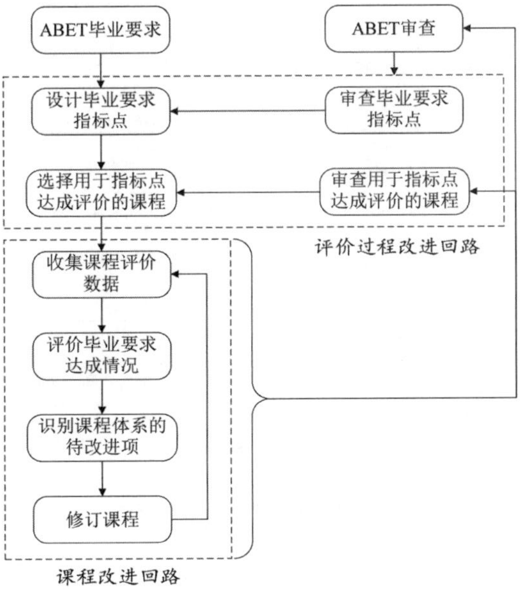


图1　圣路易斯大学计算机工程专业毕业要求达成评价与持续改进机制[8]

从评价方法上看，圣路易斯大学毕业要求达成评价采用直接评价与间接评价、定量评价与定性评价相结合的方式。直接定量评价通过核心课程量规法实施。在三年评价周期内，圣路易斯大学从22门专业核心课中选取9门课程（5门课程开设于大三，2门课程开设于大二，大一和大四的课程分别仅有1门）用于毕业要求达成评价，各年份的参评指标存在差异，每年支撑评价的课程选择也因此不同。参评课程中既包括用于评价学生低阶认知水平（知识和理解层次）的“半导体”“电气与计算机工程简介1”等专业基础课，又包括用于评价学生高阶认知水平（应用、分析、综合、评价层次）的“数字实验”“线性系统实验”“微处理器实验”“高级设计”等专业课和综合性项目实践课，还包括先修课与强化课的组合（如“初级设计”和“高级设计”），从而保证处于不同认知目标层次的毕业要求有足够的课程评价数据支撑达成。实施课程评价时，首先，将各项毕业要求分为若干指标点（见表1）；然后，在指标点与9门专业核心课及其课程目标之间建立联系；最后，通过制定三级量规表（见表2），建立用以判断课程目标达成情况的评分准则，在计算指标点得分的基础上，对各项毕业要求达标程度进行定量评价。判断课程目标达成时，无须评价课程的全部学生作业，而是基于课程量规表对随机抽取的6份作业进行打分并对分数进行排序，计算最高分、最低分和中间分的平均值，最终得分即为对应指标点的达成评分。间接定性评价包括毕业生调查、学习档案袋、校友调查、工业咨询委员会反馈等形式，旨在从不同维度和视角获取多元主体对毕业要求达成情况的态度和看法。直接定量评价辅以间接定性评价有利于克服单一评价模式的弊端，但可以看出，基于课程的直接考核是毕业要求达成评价的重点，以定性调查为代表的间接评价只是辅助评价手段，可作为三角检验的数据来源。

**表1　圣路易斯大学计算机工程专业毕业要求指标点及对应课程目标（以毕业要求a为例）**

| 指标点 | 支撑课程 | 课程目标 |
|---|---|---|
| 1. 能够应用科学原理对系统进行数学描述 | ECE2103 | 查找RLC电路的频率响应 |
| | ECE3130 | 绘制半导体的能带图并计算载流子浓度 |
| | ECE3151 | 开发一个从自相关函数估计回波增益的映射函数 |
| | ECE4800/ECE4810 | 通过项目笔记本、技术报告或技术演示展示技术成果 |
| 2. 能够开发和分析系统的数学模型 | ECE2103 | 查找电路的戴维南等效项 |
| | ECE3130 | 为半导体器件（如二极管或晶体管）建立数学模型 |
| | ECE3151 | 开发滤波器的脉冲响应，以消除声学信号中的回波 |
| | ECE4800/ECE4810 | 通过项目笔记本、技术报告或技术演示展示技术成果 |
| 3. 能够应用数学和工程知识综合组件或系统 | ECE2103 | 设计具有所需频率响应的RLC电路 |
| | ECE3151 | 开发一种软件模块，用于消除声音信号中的回声 |
| | ECE4800/ECE4810 | 通过项目笔记本、技术报告或技术演示展示技术成果 |

注：毕业要求a为数学、科学和工程知识的应用能力。

资料来源：根据https://www.slu.edu/provost/educational-pro-gram-development-review/assessment-student-learning/program-level/pks/computer-engineering _bs_report_2018.pdf的部分内容翻译整理而成。

**表 2　圣路易斯大学计算机工程专业课程目标达成情况的评估量规（范例）**

| 指标点 | 评价等级 | | |
|---|---|---|---|
| | 1=不符合预期 | 2=符合预期 | 3=超出预期 |
| ECE2103 电路实验 | | | |
| 1 | 频率响应函数不正确，或滤波器类型说明不正确 | 频率响应函数正确，滤波器类型说明正确，但缺少详细计算信息或信息不充分 | 频率响应函数正确，计算详细，滤波器类型说明正确 |
| 2 | 戴维南模型不正确或模型正确但组件值不正确 | 戴维南模型正确，组件值也正确，但缺少详细计算信息或信息不充分 | 戴维南模型正确，组件值也正确，并展示计算细节 |
| 3 | RLC 电路值不正确，无法实现具有所需频率响应的滤波器 | RLC 电路值正确，可实现具有所需频率响应的滤波器，但计算缺失或不充分 | RLC 电路值正确，实现具有所需频率响应的滤波器，所有计算准确无误 |

资料来源：根据 https://www.slu.edu/provost/educational program development review/assessment-student learning/programlevel/pks/computerengineering_bs_report_2018.pdf 的部分内容翻译整理而成。

从评价结果及其应用上看，圣路易斯大学毕业要求达成评价的明显特征是通过制定量规表，对指标达成情况进行赋值处理，并设定需要采取改进措施的阈值。就直接评价而言，教师根据表 2 所示的三级量规，对 9 门专业核心课的课程目标达成情况进行赋分，求取平均值后得到每条毕业要求的达成评分（见表 3）。就间接评价而言，各种定性调查同样以赋值的方式量化处理调查结果，以毕业生调查为例，该项调查邀请毕业生对何种程度上达成各项毕业要求进行自我判断，答案选项包括完全赞同、赞同、一般赞同、不赞同、完全不赞同，分别赋值 3、2.5、2、1.5、1，汇总计算后的得分即可反映毕业要求达成情况。为增强评价结果与持续改进之间的关联性与协调性，圣路易斯大学还制定了根据评分有针对性地采取改进措施的基本原则。如果毕业要求达成得分介于 2.5~3，则无须做出改进；得分介于 2~2.5，可考虑做出一定改进；得分< 2，则必须做出改进。专业改进重在优化课程体系以及与课程相关的评价手段，通常表现为删除不必要课程，根据内外部需求增设新课程，对现有课程不合适的部分进行调整，同时涉及指标点、课程目标等配套制度改革。

**表 3　圣路易斯大学计算机工程专业 2016—2018 年毕业要求 a 达成评价结果[8]**

| 参评课程 | 开设学期 | 支撑指标点 | 达成评分 |
|---|---|---|---|
| ECE2103 | 18 年春季学期 | a-1 | 2 |
| ECE3130 | 17 年春季学期 | a-1 | 2 |
| ECE3151 | 16 年秋季学期 | a-1 | 3 |
| ECE4800/4810 | 16 年秋季至 17 年春季学期 | a-1 | 2.33 |
| 平均分：2.33 | | | |
| ECE2103 | 18 年春季学期 | a-2 | N/A |
| ECE3130 | 17 年春季学期 | a-2 | 2 |
| ECE3151 | 16 年秋季学期 | a-2 | 2 |
| ECE4800/4810 | 16 年秋季至 17 年春季学期 | a-2 | 3 |

续表

| 参评课程 | 开设学期 | 支撑指标点 | 达成评分 |
|---|---|---|---|
| 平均分:2.33 | | | |
| ECE2103 | 18 年春季学期 | a-3 | 2 |
| ECE3151 | 16 年秋季学期 | a-3 | 3 |
| ECE4800/4810 | 16 年秋季至 17 年春季学期 | a-3 | 2 |
| 平均分:2.33 | | | |
| 综合评分:2.33 | | | |

注:毕业要求 a 为数学、科学和工程知识的应用能力;N/A 表示评价数据收集不充分,评价结果为 N/A 的课程不参与计分。

#### 2. 案例评析

圣路易斯大学将毕业要求分解为指标点,基于指标点制定课程目标,在毕业要求、指标点与课程目标之间建立对应关系,使概括程度较高的毕业要求由科学合理、可衡量、可评价的课程目标进行落实,增强了毕业要求达成评价的可靠性与可操作性。值得注意的是,同一项毕业要求的不同指标点对应支撑的课程群大多保持一致(如表 1 所示,毕业要求 a 的 3 个指标点基本均由 ECE2103、ECE3130、ECE3151、ECE4800/ECE4810 4 门课程支撑),说明指标点并不是对毕业要求内容的简单分解,指标点之间具有内在逻辑关联,可按照一定逻辑关系组合形成有机整体,从而有效保证了能力培养与评价的系统性和完整性。此外,圣路易斯大学借助评估量规为课程目标评价提供统一判断依据,并根据量规表的评估等级量化处理评价结果,一定程度上避免了评价的主观臆断,也有利于根据定量目标值直观判断毕业要求达成情况。

### 3.1.2　华盛顿大学的实践经验

#### 1. 案例描述

2019—2020 年认证期内,华盛顿大学计算机工程专业直接采用 ABET 7 条能力指标作为毕业要求,未设置专业层面上的毕业要求指标点,但在课程层面将毕业要求分解为若干绩效指标(performance indicators,又称课程目标)。华盛顿大学毕业要求达成评价未覆盖所有专业核心课,而是在部分顶点课程中进行,每三年系统收集一轮毕业要求达成评价数据。

顶点课程是开设于大四的综合性专业限选课(selective elective course),在顶点课程中,学生以团队形式合作完成包括方案设计、建造实施、效果评估、成果展示等任务的大型实质性项目,共同解决复杂工程问题。华盛顿大学的顶点课程按主题设置,涵盖嵌入式系统、虚拟现实、操作系统、声音和媒体、动画、机器人、安全、计算生物学、人机交互、可访问性、自然语言处理和资源受限环境技术等领域;各领域分别开设相应的顶点课程供学生选择,每名学生至少选修一门顶点课程才能达到毕业要求。实施评价时从近三年的顶点课程中选择一定数量的课程开展评价,每年通过个别顶点课程(分别开设于上下两个学期)获取评价数据,按照三年轮换时间表循环评估参评课程。由于顶点课程对达成各项毕业要求具有强支撑作用,能系统反映各项毕业要求的达成情况,从而实现每年对所有毕业要求进行评价,各项毕业要求在一年内经历两轮评估,三年收集的顶点课程评价数据即作为毕业要求达成评价数据之一。

从评价过程上看,如图2所示,华盛顿大学毕业要求达成评价与持续改进机制中有两个反馈回路(feedback loop)[9]。大反馈回路从整体视角对何种程度上达成毕业要求和培养目标进行评价,评价数据源于对毕业生、在校生、工业界代表的调查,外部咨询委员会评估,学生咨询委员会反馈,教师与专业负责人、教学协调人员等之间的会谈等。小反馈回路用于评价不同课程对达成毕业要求的贡献度,评价数据主要通过教师对课程目标达成情况的判断、学生评教和课程学习反馈、师生交谈等方式获得。大小反馈回路体现了宏观与微观相结合的评价思路,可从不同渠道获取多元利益主体的评价反馈,实现毕业生能力的三角测评,从而全面诊断培养方案和教学实践中存在的问题,有的放矢地对课程设置、教学大纲、毕业要求、培养目标等加以改进。

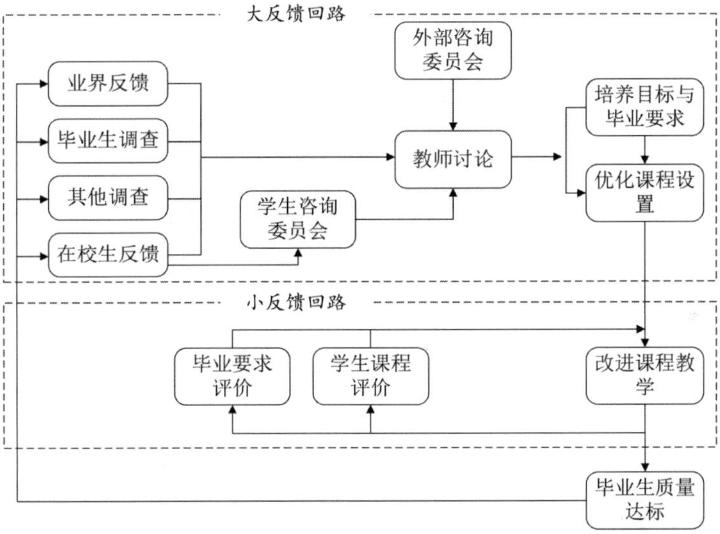


**图2 华盛顿大学计算机工程专业毕业要求达成评价与持续改进机制[9]**

从评价方法上看,根据评价内容性质与方法应用模式的不同,华盛顿大学毕业要求达成评价方法分为直接评价和间接评价(见表4)。直接评价基于可衡量的学习产出直接考查或观察学生知道什么或能够做什么,具体包括顶点课程任务、常规课程作业和针对性课程作业。其中,顶点课程是华盛顿大学毕业要求达成评价的主要对象,该类课程面向培养毕业要求中的多种能力,能综合全面反映毕业要求达成程度。华盛顿大学未将毕业要求分解为指标点,但教师设置了课程层面的绩效指标,并根据绩效指标评价学生表现。评价结果分为高、中、低三等,教师在三个等级的学生作业中进行分层抽样,通过所选样本的评价结果反映课程目标达成情况,最后根据课程目标达成情况综合判断毕业要求达成情况。学校规定各项毕业要求中等和高等水平人数至少占总人数的80%才能视为合格。间接评价用以从各种角度评价学生的非智力品质(如情感、态度和价值观),具体包括来自学生和用人单位的实习反馈、校友调查、毕业生调查、学习氛围调研、每门课程的教师交接文件、教师反思等。毕业要求达成评价以直接评价为主，间接评价为辅。常规课程作业、针对性课程作业以及顶点课程任务等直接评价的频率较高，校友调查、毕业生调查、学习氛围调研等间接评价通常每年一次，来自学生和用人单位的实习反馈在每轮实习期获得。

**表 4　华盛顿大学计算机工程专业毕业要求及其评价方法的对应关系[9]**

| 毕业要求 | 主要评价方法 | 辅助评价方法 |
| --- | --- | --- |
| SO1 | 常规课程作业；针对性课程作业；顶点课程任务 | 毕业生调查；用人单位反馈；每门课程的教师交接文件 |
| SO2 | 针对性课程作业；顶点课程任务 | 用人单位反馈；教师反思 |
| SO3 | 针对性课程作业；顶点课程任务 | 用人单位反馈；校友调查 |
| SO4 | 针对性课程作业；顶点课程任务 | 用人单位反馈；毕业生调查 |
| SO5 | 针对性课程作业；顶点课程任务 | 用人单位反馈；学习氛围调研 |
| SO6 | 针对性课程作业；顶点课程任务 | 校友调查 |
| SO7 | 针对性课程作业；顶点课程任务 | 用人单位反馈；校友调查 |

从评价结果及其应用上看，华盛顿大学毕业要求达成评价结果以质性数据为主，一是教师根据顶点课程目标对学生表现的等级划分，二是通过在校生、毕业生、用人单位等获得的能力反馈。对于以课程考核为代表的直接评价结果，华盛顿大学对照毕业要求逐条说明在各项能力培养上采取的改进措施，主要表现为课程体系优化和教学模式创新。对于以定性调查为代表的间接评价结果（见表 5），学校将其作为修订毕业要求和培养目标、调整课程设置、改进教学方法、健全评价机制以及优化资源配置的补充性依据。整体而言，华盛顿大学毕业要求达成评价的核心是以学习产出为导向的课程质量评价，根据评价结果优化课程设置是持续改进的一大重点。

**表 5　华盛顿大学计算机工程专业基于间接评价结果做出的改进（范例）[9]**

| 评价时间 | 待关注项 | 评价方法 | 改进措施 |
| --- | --- | --- | --- |
| 2014—2015 年 | 学生、教师和行业要求提供更多学习数据科学的机会 | 调查 | 在计算机科学本科专业中增设数据科学方向，计算机工程专业的学生可选修这个方向的课程 |
| 2014—2015 年 | 学生希望获得更多类似于毕业设计的体验 | 调查 | 增设 CSE495 项目实践课，为学生提供除顶点课程以外的其他实践类课程 |
| 2014—2015 年 | 学生对机器学习（ML）、自然语言处理（NLP）和可视化的兴趣高涨 | 调查与用人单位反馈 | 创建了四门新的 400 级课程：自然语言处理、机器学习、机器人学和数据可视化 |
| 2016—2017 年 | 学生希望获得更多互动体验 | 调查和学生反馈 | 成立学生顾问委员会和学生交流小组 |

**2. 案例评析**

华盛顿大学毕业要求达成评价注重多主体协同参与和多种方法配合使用，遵循宏观定性调查与微观课程质量评价相结合的评价思路，一方面有利于从不同主体视角综合判断毕业要求达成情况,另一方面有利于通过不同类型数据评价三角验证结果。该校虽然未在专业层面将毕业要求分解为指标点,但在课程层面对毕业要求进行要素分解,即直接将毕业要求细化落实至具体课程目标。这一做法的优点是容易得到相对规范的课程目标集,评价方法简洁,但没有统一的毕业要求指标点进行指导,教师可能难以准确把握毕业要求的内容要素,容易对毕业要求产生片面而模糊的理解,不利于制定明确具体、易于衡量的课程目标。此外,华盛顿大学选择顶点课程进行毕业要求达成评价,该类课程综合实践性较强,有助于系统评价学生解决复杂工程问题的能力,但由于未将专业领域内的先修课纳入评价,导致无法获取形成性评价数据,不利于通过对比过程数据和结果数据全面反映毕业要求达成情况。

### 3.1.3 佛罗里达大学的实践经验

#### 1. 案例描述

2012—2013年认证期内,佛罗里达大学计算机工程专业的毕业要求与ABET 11条能力指标(a~k)保持一致,没有独立设置毕业要求指标点。毕业要求达成评价周期为四年,直接评价数据按学期收集,间接评价数据按年度获取,根据四年学制内获得的直接与间接评价数据系统反映毕业要求达成情况,数据整理、分析和验证工作由学院课程委员会(course committee)和协调组(coordinator)共同负责。

从评价过程上看,佛罗里达大学聚焦课程与教学质量监控,形成课程群量化评价—独立课程质性评价—学生自主评价—协调组综合评判—全方位持续改进的贯通式、一体化评价机制。课程群量化评价的第一步是从课程体系中选择支撑毕业要求达成评价的课程群(见表6),涵盖17门专业必修课(总共34门课)。参评课程选自不同年级,多集中于高年级,其中既包括专业必修课,也包括少量专业限选课,课程之间形成先修课与强化课的对应衔接关系,如"数字逻辑与计算机系统"的强化课是"微处理器应用","计算机组织概论"的强化课是"操作系统"和"软件工程概论"。各门课程的评价工具由教师自行设计,包括内置于课程作业中的典型问题、期末考试、平时测验等,评价结果采用李克特五级量表进行赋分。专业负责人会同教师确定各项毕业要求的达标阈值,毕业要求指标项的达成评分即为对应支撑课程的得分平均值。独立课程质性评价用于判断单门课程对实现各项毕业要求的贡献度,责任机构是课程委员会。每门课程均设立有相应的课程委员会,负责对课程群定量评价结果进行定性分析,为改进课程教学、增强课程间的关联性与协调性、优化评价程序与标准等提供咨询建议。学生自主评价通过学生焦点小组(student focus groups)和学生焦点退出调查(student focus exit surveys)进行,前者根据学生在设计类课程中的表现与自我评价结果判断毕业要求达成情况,并了解学生对计划改进措施的看法,后者以访谈方式对毕业生就业计划、课程体系优化建议、学习满意度等进行全面调查。协调组负责整合比较、系统分析上述各来源的评价数据,必要时还可参考国家教育质量标准、工业咨询委员会建议等补充性依据辅助判断毕业要求达成情况,根据判断结果查找问题项和待改进项,从而对课程体系、教学设施、评价过程等进行全面优化。

从评价方法上看,佛罗里达大学构建直接评价辅以间接评价、定量评价结合定性评价、形成性评价与总结性评价并重的综合评价体系。该校毕业要求达成评价以课程质量的直接定量评价为主，收集数据的过程中，既通过课程作业、平时测验实施形成性考核，又通过期末考试、项目设计等实施终极考核，注重教学评价的连续反馈，加之运用李克特量表量化处理评价结果，从而有效保证了评价的客观性、及时性和有效性。就所选课程对毕业要求的支撑强度而言，一门课程通常支撑 2~4 条毕业要求， 1 条毕业要求最少由 3 门课程支撑，设计类课程可强支撑所有毕业要求，建立了相对科学的评价支撑关系。然而，单纯采用量化评价可能导致统计数据的机械堆砌，有时虽然能计算出具有一定统计意义的评价结果，但并未得到具有教学改进作用的实质性结论。为此，该校又通过课程委员会对毕业要求达成情况进行质性判断，将其作为课程定量评价数据的补充。在间接评价方面，数据获取途径包括学生焦点小组、毕业生调查和工业咨询委员会反馈，间接评价数据一般是以提问方式获得的态度、观点和建议，主要用于验证和补充直接评价结果。

**表 6　佛罗里达大学计算机工程专业用于毕业要求达成评价的课程与毕业要求的对应关系[10]**

| 参评课程 | 毕业要求 | | | | | | | | | | |
|---|---|---|---|---|---|---|---|---|---|---|---|
| | a | b | c | d | e | f | g | h | i | j | k |
| CIS 导论 | | | X | | X | | | | | | X |
| 离散结构及应用 | X | | | | | | | | | | X |
| 数据结构与算法 | X | | | | X | | | | | | X |
| 计算机组织概论 | X | | X | | X | | | | | | |
| 软件工程概论 | | | | X | | | X | | | | |
| 操作系统 | | | X | | | | | | | | X |
| 数值分析 | X | X | | | X | | | | | | |
| 公司互联网基金 | | X | | | | | | | | | X |
| 计算机相关的法律和社会问题 | | | | | | X | | X | X | X | |
| 高级设计（CIS/CEN-4914） | X | X | X | X | X | X | X | X | X | X | X |
| 电路 1 | X | | | | | | | | | | X |
| 离散时间信号与系统 | X | | | | | | | | | | X |
| 电子电路 1 | | X | X | | | | | | X | | |
| 数字逻辑与计算机系统 | | | X | | | | | | | | X |
| 数字化设计 | X | | X | | X | | | | | | X |
| 微处理器应用 | X | | X | | X | | X | | | | X |
| 高级设计（EEL-4914C） | | X | X | X | X | X | X | X | X | X | X |

从评价结果及其应用上看，佛罗里达大学毕业要求达成评价结果以量化数据为主，质性数据作为补充，持续改进在不同类型数据相互佐证的基础上进行。量化数据按照李克特量表进行标准化处理，规定 80%及以上的学生在该指标项上满足能力要求且达成评分≥3 视为该项毕业要求达成[10]。根据量化评价结果（见表 7），能直观看到各门课程在各项毕业要求上的达成评分，对比不同毕业要求指标项的得分差异，从而判断单项毕业要求达成情况、

毕业要求整体达成情况以及课程体系存在的问题,问题改进措施一般包括优化课程结构(如增删课程或改变课程性质和学时)、调整课程内容(如删除陈旧知识、补充新知识)、改进教学方法和学习形式(如引入团队合作)等。质性评价数据以提取核心观点和重要建议的方式呈现,主要反映学生学习需求、教师教学期望和行业企业用人标准,为改进课程教学及其相关要素(如教学设施)提供参考。

**表 7　佛罗里达大学计算机工程专业毕业要求达成评分(以毕业要求 a 为例)[10]**

| 2007—2011 年度参评课程 | 达成毕业要求的学生比例 | 平均李克特值 |
|---|---|---|
| 离散结构及应用 | 76.5% | 3.4 |
| 数据结构与算法 | 73.5% | 3.3 |
| 计算机组织概论 | 79.3% | 3.8 |
| 数值分析 | 83.9% | 3.5 |
| 高级设计(CIS/CEN-4914) | 94.2% | 4.5 |
| 高级设计(EEL-4914C) | 96.0% | 4.4 |
| 电路 1 | 72.5% | 3.8 |
| 离散时间信号与系统 | 74.2% | 3.6 |
| 微处理器应用 | 90.5% | 3.6 |
| 平均值 | 82.29% | 3.77 |

注:毕业要求 a 为数学、科学和工程知识的应用能力。

**2. 案例评析**

佛罗里达大学设立课程委员会和协调组,评价数据的整理、分析与验证工作由独立性和专业性较强的组织机构负责,从而实现数据常态监测和规范管理。评价时采用直接辅以间接、定量结合定性、过程对照结果的综合评价模式获取数据,融合不同类型数据构建完整证据链,并在此基础上交叉比较、综合分析评价结果,有效保证了数据来源的多样性与评价结论的稳定性和可靠性。分析处理评价结果主要采用定量分析评判法,既设定定量目标值,又划定目标率,有利于根据量化数据直观反映毕业要求达成情况,但未使用量规表等定性分析描述法为课程评价、毕业生调查等提供统一判分依据,评价者可能因认知偏差导致判断不准确。此外,佛罗里达大学未对毕业要求进行要素分解,虽然将毕业要求矩阵式映射至用于评价的课程,但没有明晰毕业要求与课程教学目标之间的对应关系,一定程度上不利于准确判断专业是否全面达成毕业要求中的各项指标。

### 3.1.4　三所大学毕业要求达成评价的异同比较

同为经 ABET 认证的高校,三所大学计算机工程专业毕业要求达成评价的理念和实施逻辑基本保持一致,都以产出为导向,注重专业持续改进。但由于专业认证是以标准为参照的合格评估,为学校自主创新与特色化发展预留空间,专业享有评价自主权,三所高校因此表现出各自不同的评价特点,具体可从评价周期、评价过程、评价方法、用于评价的课程、评价结果、评价结果应用六个方面比较其异同（见表 8）。

**表 8　三所大学计算机工程专业毕业要求达成评价的异同**

| 比较维度 | | 圣路易斯大学 | 华盛顿大学 | 佛罗里达大学 |
|---|---|---|---|---|
| 评价周期 | 同 | 以一定年限为循环周期的持续改进性评价 | | |
| | 异 | 三年一周期，每年对个别毕业要求进行评价 | 三年一周期，每年对所有毕业要求进行评价 | 四年一周期，每年对个别毕业要求进行评价 |
| 评价过程 | 同 | 面向产出的评价机制与持续改进机制，多元主体协同参与机制 | | |
| | 异 | 通过课程质量评价和定性调查获取数据 | 注重数据、人员、方法的三角检验 | 通过课程质量评价和定性调查获取数据 |
| 评价方法 | 同 | 直接评价与间接评价相结合的综合评价模式 | | |
| | 异 | 以核心课程量规评价为主 | 以顶点课程绩效指标评价为主 | 以课程群定量评价为主 |
| 用于评价的课程 | 同 | 通过对毕业要求具有强支撑作用的课程进行评价 | | |
| | 异 | 专业核心课 | 顶点课程 | 专业核心课 |
| 评价结果 | 同 | 注重评价结果的可视化呈现 | | |
| | 异 | 量化数据辅以质性数据 | 以质性数据为主 | 量化数据融合质性数据 |
| 评价结果应用 | 同 | 基于评价结果促进专业持续改进 | | |
| | 异 | 聚焦课程和评价程序改进 | 强调人才培养全方位改进 | 重点关注课程改进，兼顾其他相关要素优化 |

## 3.2　认证组织方面毕业要求达成评价的比较分析

### 3.2.1　美国工程与技术认证委员会：注重毕业要求达成评价的全流程指导

自美国 ABET 工程教育专业认证标准《工程标准 2000》（Engineering Criteria 2000）颁布以来，ABET 认证实现从输入导向到产出导向、从重数量达成到重质量提升的转变，反映学生学习水平和质量的毕业要求成为专业认证的重点关注项和考查项。为引导学校贯彻落实产出导向教育理念，形成教育质量持续改进的长效机制，ABET 注重毕业要求达成评价指导，通过定期召开专题研讨会、补充完善认证辅助性参考文件，对评价计划、过程、策略、方法、周期、达标判断等方面予以指导。评价指导相关内容覆盖评价全过程，涉及评价准备、评价实施和持续改进三个阶段。

正式评价前，ABET 倡导构建毕业要求达成评价与持续改进机制并对其科学性、合理性与有效性进行自我评估，自我评估通过量规表（见表 9）进行，重在审查利益相关者参与机制，培养目标与毕业要求的公开性、可衡量性和适切性，教学环节对毕业要求的支撑度，评价方法综合使用情况，基于评价结果的改进措施等内容。同时，建议针对每项毕业要求制定详细评价计划（见表 10），明确毕业要求指标点、用于评价的课程与实践性教学环节、形成性和总结性评价数据来源、评价方法、评价时间、达标阈值等要素，并确定各类评价活动的责任人。关于评价时间，ABET 提倡以两年或三年为一个周期推进循环评价与持续改进，每年选择一定数量的毕业要求进行评价，不同年份重点关注的评价活动可有所侧重。ABET 指出，制定评价时间表只是为了系统规划评价活动，专业应根据评价结果适时调整评价计划，例如，收集多轮数据后发现某些指标的达成度始终较高，而某些指标一直较难达标，新一轮评价周期则应增加未达标项的被评次数[11]。

**表 9　ABET 毕业要求达成评价与持续改进机制的自我评估量规[12]**

| 利益相关者参与机制 | 得分 | 培养目标 | 得分 | 毕业要求 | 得分 | 毕业要求与教学实践的关联度 | 得分 | 评价过程 | 得分 | 评价结果分析与应用 | 得分 |
|---|---|---|---|---|---|---|---|---|---|---|---|
| 明确利益相关者 | | 制定明确的专业培养目标 | | 制定明确的毕业要求，毕业要求涵盖学生毕业时应具备的知识、能力和素养 | | 有相应的课程或教学环节支撑毕业要求达成 | | 毕业要求达成评价具有持续性和系统性 | | 系统分析评价数据 | |
| 主要利益相关者参与制定专业培养目标 | | 专业培养目标具有公开性 | | 毕业要求具有可衡量性 | | 通过毕业要求评价数据系统评价教学实践 | | 每条毕业要求采用不同方法评价 | | 评价结果由决定专业改进工作的负责人进行分析 | |
| 主要利益相关者参与定期评价专业培养目标 | | 专业培养目标具有可衡量性 | | 毕业要求具有公开性 | | 必要时根据评价结果改进课程体系和教学实践 | | 配合使用直接评价法和间接评价法 | | 通过评价结果诊断课程体系和教学实践中存在的问题 | |
| 与利益相关者建立持续稳定的合作伙伴关系 | | 专业培养目标符合学校使命 | | 毕业要求支撑培养目标达成 | | — | — | 审查评价过程的可持续性和有效性 | | 将评价结果用于专业持续改进 | |
| — | — | 定期评价专业培养目标以使其符合外部利益相关者的需求 | | 毕业要求被分解为若干绩效指标 | | — | — | 必要时根据评价流程调整评价方法 | | — | — |

注：评分包括 6 个等级，1=尚未建立评价机制，2=评价机制开发中，3=评价机制已建立但刚开始实施评价，4=评价机制已建立且实施过评价，5=已实施评价且评价效果良好，6=已实施评价且至少进行一轮改进工作。

**表 10　ABET 毕业要求各指标项的评价计划表（示例）**

| 指标点 | 支撑评价的课程或教学环节 | 评价方法 | 总结性评价数据 | 形成性评价数据 | 评价周期 | 数据收集时间 | 达标阈值 |
|---|---|---|---|---|---|---|---|
| 参与制定团队合作目标和工作计划 | CSCI：2210；2720；4230；4911 | 同伴评价 | 4911 | 2210（评价周期的第一年） | 2 年 | 2014 年、2016 年、2018 年 | 80% |
| | | 教师评价 | 4911 | | | | |
| | | 高级调查 | 线上调查 | | | | |

续表

| 指标点 | 支撑评价的课程或教学环节 | 评价方法 | 总结性评价数据 | 形成性评价数据 | 评价周期 | 数据收集时间 | 达标阈值 |
|---|---|---|---|---|---|---|---|
| 致力于营造团队协作环境 | CSCI;2210;2720;4230;4911 | 同伴评价 | 4911 | 2210(评价周期的第一年) | 2年 | 2014年、2016年、2018年 | 80% |
| | | 教师评价 | 4911 | | | | |
| | | 高级调查 | 线上调查 | | | | |
| 鼓励包容性的团队合作氛围 | CSCI;2210;2720;4230;4911 | 同伴评价 | 4911 | 2210(评价周期的第一年) | 2年 | 2014年、2016年、2018年 | 80% |
| | | 教师评价 | 4911 | | | | |
| | | 高级调查 | 线上调查 | | | | |
| 在实现团队目标的过程中表现出可靠性 | CSCI;2210;2720;4230;4911 | 同伴评价 | 4911 | 2210(评价周期的第一年) | 2年 | 2014年、2016年、2018年 | 80% |
| | | 教师评价 | 4911 | | | | |
| | | 高级调查 | 线上调查 | | | | |

毕业要求:学生能够有效地进行团队合作。

资料来源:根据 ABET 官网上毕业要求达成评价的相关文件和视频资料翻译整理而成。

评价过程中,ABET 提出将毕业要求分解为绩效指标,建立支撑毕业要求达成的课程图,选择恰当的评价工具或方法系统收集数据,根据达标阈值判断毕业要求达成情况并查找人才培养的弱项和问题项,最后将评价结果用于专业持续改进。选择用于评价的课程时,应重视发挥最终设计类问题(ultimate design problem)对毕业要求达成评价的强支撑作用,该类问题没有明确的解决方案,要求学生了解用户需求,考虑多种条件限制和约束,通过不断迭代优化,以系统集成的方法合作解决问题[13]。在数据收集上,ABET 关注两类数据来源,一是形成性评价数据,二是总结性评价数据,对比两类数据可判断学生进步幅度。形成性评价与总结性评价数据一般通过直接辅以间接的综合评价模式获得,直接评价包括行为观察、课程考试或平时作业、学习档案袋、标准化测验等方法,间接评价通过焦点小组、访谈、问卷等方式进行。一方面,ABET 建议将直接评价数据作为持续改进的主要依据。ABET 指出,直接评价的置信度和有效度取决于是否使用一系列明确而可衡量的绩效指标来界定毕业要求,如果毕业要求未被明确界定,则容易导致直接评价因缺乏客观评价依据而变成无根据的主观臆断[14]。对于直接评价中的考试成绩分析法,ABET 认为,考试成绩虽然能整体反映学生的学习水平,但由于成绩受教师评分标准、考试内容等多种因素影响,其本身是一个衡量标准,难以根据成绩推断学生具体知道什么或能够做什么,因此,考试成绩与量规表配合使用能使分数更具解释力,课程考试关注的重点不应是分数,而是分数代表的学生知识、能力和素养水平[15]。另一方面,对于难以直接测量的态度、观点、价值观等隐含品质,ABET 主张通过访谈、问卷等间接评价方式进行测评,间接评价数据主要作为直接评价数据的补充和验证。而有效的间接评价取决于调查工具的质量,ABET 强调,设计访谈提纲或编制调查问卷时要注意问题和测试题项准确反映评价内容,通过恰当的抽样方式获得具有代表性和典型性的调查样本,保证问卷填答率,并对调查结果进行科学分析与合理解释[16]。

获得评价数据后,ABET 建议对评价参与者、评价内容、数据收集过程、评价周期、达标阈值、各项毕业要求达成情况、人才培养中的弱项和问题项、改进措施、优化趋势等进行归档整理,从而发现评价过程本身以及教育教学体系中存在的问题,系统分析产出导向教育理念和持续改进机制落实情况,在此基础上进行进一步改进。那么,多少数据足以证明毕业要求达成?如何避免收集无效数据?ABET 指出,一是要确保评价方法或工具与所要评价的学习产出相匹配,换言之,只有对毕业要求的内容有清晰认识(一般通过细化设置指标点明确毕业要求的内容构成),才能找到与之相匹配的评价方法;二是要科学设定评价周期,根据教学需要确定每年参与评价的指标,明确评价各项指标的意图以及相关评价数据的用途[17]。

### 3.2.2 加拿大工程师协会:明确毕业要求达成评价的考查要素与实施细则

加拿大工程师协会(Engineers Canada,EC)下属加拿大工程认证委员会(Canadian Engineering Accreditation Board,CEAB)通过颁布系列文件,制定毕业要求达成评价实施细则,为专业自评和专家考评提供详尽指导。

一是在工程教育专业认证标准中细化毕业要求达成评价的五个要素,具体包括:组织结构和参与机制(organization and engagement),要求成立专门机构负责毕业要求达成评价与专业可持续发展,这一过程有教职员工和工业界代表参与;课程图(curriculum maps),要求构建以展示毕业要求、课程体系(或教学环节)、学期学时之间关系的书面化课程图;指标点(indicators),要求为每条毕业要求建立一套可衡量且有文档记录的指标点,描述学生达到何种能力水平才可视为达成毕业要求;评价工具(assessment tools),要求对毕业要求达成评价工具进行明确规定,并将其作为获得学生在六年或更短时间内关于 12 条毕业要求学习数据的基础;评价结果(assessment results),要求在 6 年一周期或更短时间内,至少获得完整一轮毕业要求达成评价数据,评价结果要足以证明学生达成 12 条能力指标。同时,EC 还通过制定《毕业要求与持续改进评估量规》(The Graduate Attributes and Continual Improvement Rubrics),对五个考查要素的达成项与未达成项给予内涵说明。以指标点这一考查项为例,达成项的具体描述是指标点可衡量且全面覆盖毕业要求的内容要素,指标点与毕业要求预期达成的学习水平一致,指标点数量与毕业要求的可持续数据收集计划相符;未达成项表述为指标点不能充分描述并涵盖毕业要求的核心内容,指标点与毕业要求预期达成的学习水平不相符,指标点数量与毕业要求的可持续数据收集计划不相符[18]。评估量规为认证专家进行毕业要求达成评价提供统一评判标准,一定程度上可避免评价的主观臆断性。

二是发布《产出导向标准指南》(A Guide to Outcomes-Based Criteria),该指南作为专家考评的指导性文件,对上述五个考查要素的评价实施细则进行进一步说明,为认证专家全方位考查专业毕业要求达成、多渠道收集毕业要求达标证据制定行动方针。不同考查要素的指导内容主要由考查要求、参考问题以及评价策略三部分构成(示例见表 11)。其中,考查要求是对考查要素的内容说明,参考问题细化了对应考查要素涵盖的考查点,评价策略针对每个问题分析出可能存在的未达标情况。为有效判断毕业要求是否达成,指南还分项制定了 12 条毕业要求的评价指导方针,要求专业通过审查评价工具、评价结果以及评价结果应用情况反映毕业要求达成情况。各项毕业要求的评价指导方针具有相似性,大致包含以下三大内容[19]:其一,有多少课程教学活动支撑该项毕业要求,针对这一问题,要求列出完整课程体系和相关教学环节;其二,是否选择特定课程或教学环节用于毕业要求达成评价,毕业要求指标点是否与毕业要求相关联,该类问题旨在审查指标点与用以评价的课程、毕业要求之间的关联性；其三，指标点与毕业要求规定达到的能力水平之间是否存在差距，这一问题重在考查指标点与毕业要求所涵盖的能力要素是否相符。由此可见，CEAB 将指标点作为毕业要求达成评价的考查重点，并为认证专家审查指标点分解情况予以指导。

**表 11　加拿大工程师协会《产出导向标准指南》的部分考查要求及评价指导[19]**

| 考查要素 | 考查要素 | 参考问题 | 评价策略 |
|---|---|---|---|
| 毕业要求指标点 | 列出每条毕业要求包含的指标点以及用于评价指标点达成的课程 | 填写表格时是否遵照相关说明？ | ①查找未提供完整指标点的毕业要求。<br>②判断用于评价毕业要求达成的课程和用于评价毕业要求指标点达成的课程是否不一致 |
| | | 指标点是否与毕业要求相符（或与毕业要求直接相关）？ | ①查找与毕业要求或毕业要求各组成部分不相符或不相关的指标点。<br>②查找涵盖单项毕业要求多个方面的指标点（即不具体的指标点） |
| | | 每项毕业要求是否有足够的指标点？ | 查找指标点未涉及的毕业要求内容（即指标点的内容覆盖面与毕业要求内容覆盖面之间的差距） |
| | | 是否有哪项毕业要求的指标点过多？ | ①判断指标点是否交叉重复（重叠部分是冗余还是有价值的交叉）。<br>②对专业或学校评估计划的可持续性进行评论 |
| | | 指标点是否可衡量？ | ①找出评价难度较大的指标点。<br>②提供判定该指标点可衡量性差的理由 |
| | | 是否恰当选择用于评价指标点达成的课程？ | ①找出可能不适合特定教学水平的指标点。<br>②找出不必要或冗余的用于评价指标点达成的课程 |

资料来源：根据 https://engineerscanada.ca/sites/default/files/ draft_program_visitor_guide_v1.25.pdf 的部分内容翻译整理而成。

### 3.2.3　英国工程委员会：构建统筹规划，分专业落实的评价机制

作为经英国皇家特许的工程师职业管理机构，英国工程委员会（Engineering Council United Kingdom，ECUK）不直接参与工程教育专业认证工作，而是通过授权的方式，让符合条件的工程专业学会成为被许可方，将具体认证事项交由各专业学会负责。目前，具有 ECUK 授权资格的专业学会共 39 个[20]，39 个专业学会在遵循 ECUK 统一性认证规定的基础上，构建各自特有的认证标准和程序。统一性规定是指由 ECUK 制定的高等教育专业认证标准（Accreditation of Higher Education Programs，AHEP），其中包含所有专业学会必须遵循的学习产出标准（简称 AHEP 毕业要求）。AHEP 毕业要求衍生于英国工程职业能力与责任标准（The UK Standard for Professional Engineering Competence and Commitment，UK-SPEC），从自然科学与数学、工程分析、设计与创新、工程师与社会、工程实践五个维度设定毕业生应达到的知识、能力和素养水平[2]，成为被授权学会制定具体毕业要求的参考框架。解读 AHEP 毕业要求需要以 UK-SPEC 为背景，UK-SPEC 规定了成为注册工程师（特许工程师、工程技师和工程技术员）应具备的能力，涵盖知识与理解，设计、开发与解决工程问题，责任、管理与领导力，沟通与人际交往能力，个人与专业承诺五个方面，AHEP 毕业要求则基于上述 UK-SPEC 制定而成[21]。除此之外，AHEP 还以细化毕业要求达成评价要点（见图 3）的方式对被授权学会审查专业毕业要求达成情况予以指导。可以看出，ECUK 通过统

筹规划工程师职业能力标准、AHEP 毕业要求框架及其考查点,构建毕业要求达成评价总方针,为专业学会和学校制定毕业要求、开展毕业要求达成评价指明方向。

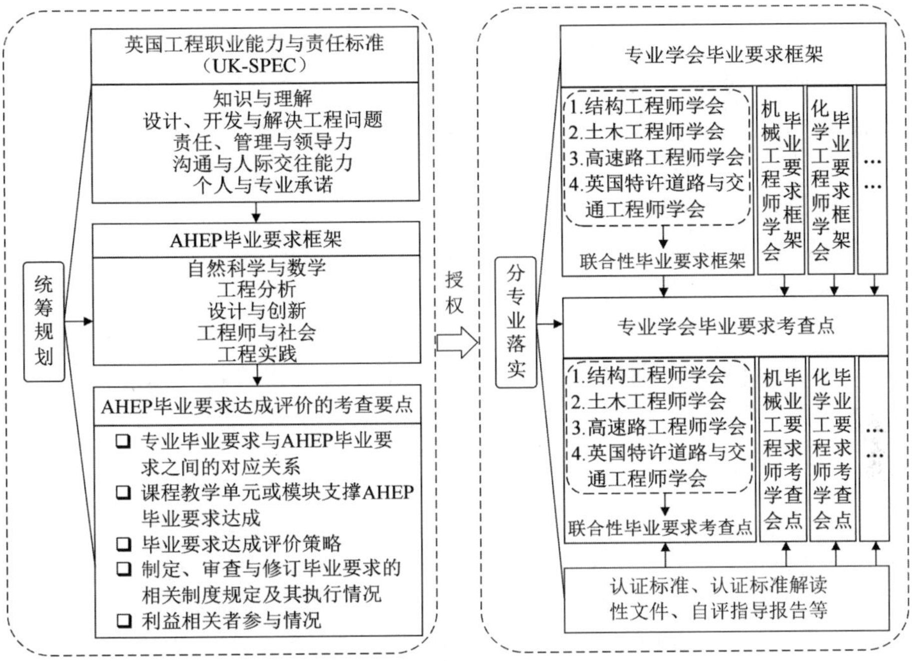


**图 3 英国工程委员会毕业要求达成评价机制**

同时,专业学会在遵循 ECUK 认证总要求的基础上,又对个别专业的毕业要求框架和毕业要求达成评价的考查要点进行进一步细化和落实。例如,土木工程师学会、结构工程师学会、高速路工程师学会、英国特许道路与交通工程师学会共同组建联合评审委员会,对建筑工程领域内的土木、结构、运输等相关工程专业实施认证。联合评审委员会聚焦工程设计、可持续性、健康与风险管理、专业素养、伦理、多样性与包容性等维度,从知识和理解能力、智力能力、实践技能、通用性可迁移能力四方面,制定适用于建筑工程相关专业的毕业要求,并给出具体评价各维度能力要素的方法[22]。再如,化学工程师学会的毕业要求由通用性毕业要求和特殊性毕业要求两部分组成,通用性毕业要求即 AHEP 毕业要求,特殊性毕业要求针对以化学工程专业为背景的毕业要求,强调数学、自然科学和相关工程基础、化学工程原理、化学工程实践、化学工程设计和嵌入式学习[23]。除了制定专业领域的毕业要求框架,专业学会还在认证标准、认证标准解读性文件以及专业自评报告中明确毕业要求达成评价的考查要点,从专业层面落实毕业要求达成评价的实施细则。

### 3.2.4 澳大利亚工程师协会:基于职业能力标准设计毕业要求及其指标点

澳大利亚工程师协会(Engineers Australia, EA)是澳大利亚工程教育专业认证和工程师职业资格认证的统筹管理机构,也是国家统一的工程实践能力评估机构,具有制定工程师职业能力标准、构建工程教育专业认证和工程师资质认证体系、促进工程师终身职业发展等职能。EA 工程师职业能力标准包括一阶能力标准和二阶能力标准。一阶能力标准将工程技术人才划分为专业工程师、工程技师和工程技术员三类，针对每一职业类型，从知识与技能基础、工程应用能力、专业与个人素养三方面制定毕业生从事工程实践应具备的基本能力[24]。二阶能力标准设定授予上述三类工程技术人才特许资质应满足的能力要求，涉及专业承诺、对社区的义务、工作场所中发挥的价值和技术熟练程度四方面[25]，获得特许资质的从业人员可得到世界各地政府、企业和公众的广泛认可，是工程技术人才能独立从事工程实践的重要标志。EA 基于工程师职业能力标准设计教育产出框架，其工程教育专业认证的毕业要求源于一阶能力标准中专业工程师的相关能力描述，这也充分体现澳大利亚工程教育专业认证与工程师职业资格认证相衔接，EA 毕业要求由三大能力（知识与技能基础、工程应用能力、专业与个人素养）和 16 个能力要素构成。为深化学校对能力标准的理解并加强课程教学和专业自评指导，EA 还专门设置指标点供学校参考（见表 12），从而增强毕业要求达成评价的可操作性。需要强调的是，概念内涵丰富的毕业要求一般被分解成多个指标点，而对于内容要素相对简单的毕业要求，则仅通过单一指标点对毕业要求进行具体解释。此外，指标点不是对上位概念的简单分解，指标点之间具有较强的逻辑关联，能力评价和能力培养都要以系统、整体的方式进行[26]。

**表 12　澳大利亚工程师协会一阶能力标准（以“知识与技能基础”维度为例）**

| 评价维度 | 能力要素 | 指标点 |
|---|---|---|
| 知识与技能基础 | 对自然科学以及工程科学相关理论有全面理解 | 从现象学层面学习工程专业，应用自然科学和工程原理进行系统的调查、解释、分析、设计等工程实践活动 |
| | 对作为工程学科基础的数学、数值分析、统计学、信息与计算科学有概念性理解 | 开发并熟练应用工程学科领域内与调查、解释、评价、表征、预测、评估、建模、决策、测量、知识管理、沟通等相关的技术和工具 |
| | 深入了解工程学科的专业知识体系 | 在工程学科的至少一个专业实践领域内熟练掌握先进技术知识和技能 |
| | 对工程学科内的知识发展和研究方向有敏锐洞察力 | a. 在工程学科的至少一个专业实践领域内，确定并批判性地评估当前的技术发展、新兴问题及其跨学科联系 |
| | | b. 通过选定的研究文献，为工程学科至少一个专业领域内的工程实践提供信息 |
| | 了解工程设计相关知识和影响工程学科的背景因素 | a. 确定并应用与工程学科相关的系统设计原则 |
| | | b. 识别并理解工程系统与人在社会、文化、环境、商业、法律和政治背景中的互动，包括工程学在可持续发展中的积极作用以及工程活动的潜在负面影响 |
| | | c. 了解与国际工程实践和全球运营环境相关的问题 |
| | | d. 了解与工程学科相关的人文因素 |
| | | e. 了解商业和企业管理的基本原理 |
| | | f. 确定工程师队伍的结构、作用和能力 |

续表

| 评价维度 | 能力要素 | 指标点 |
|---|---|---|
| 知识与技能基础 | 理解特定专业可持续工程实践的范围、原则、规范、责任和界限 | a. 理解工程实践标准和规范,以及适用于工程学科的法律法规要求 |
| | | b. 理解安全工程准则、风险管理和专业工程师的健康与安全责任,包括适用于工程学科的立法要求 |
| | | c. 理解可持续工程实践的社会、环境和经济原则 |
| | | d. 理解工程项目管理的基本原则,将其作为计划、组织和管理资源的基础 |
| | | e. 理解系统工程的正式结构和方法,将其作为管理复杂性和可持续性的基础 |

资料来源:根据 https://www.engineersaustralia.org.au/sites/default/files/2022-07/stage-1-competency-standard-professional-engineer.pdf 的部分内容翻译整理而成。

为深化学校对工程教育专业认证标准的理解并增强专业自评的可操作性, EA 颁布自评报告模板、认证标准用户指南,在细化标准考查要素、提供标准达成范例的基础上明确了毕业要求达成评价策略。概括总结毕业要求相关规定后发现,EA 从毕业要求的制定、实现、合理性审查、达成评价以及持续改进等多方面对专业提出要求,具体包括:专业毕业要求覆盖标准毕业要求,毕业要求支撑培养目标达成,课程体系支撑毕业要求达成,毕业要求被分解为若干指标点,规范化制定、审查与修订毕业要求的制度体系,多元化评价方法,系统健全的评价程序与真实可靠的评价结果,根据评价结果推动专业持续改进,有专门的组织机构或体制机制保障外部利益相关者参与制定、评价、审查与修订毕业要求。值得一提的是,EA 重视发挥指标点的评价功能,明确规定毕业要求应包含可衡量的绩效指标(performance indicator),基于多维绩效指标的评价要结合定量和定性评价措施,充分吸纳多元利益相关者反馈。不仅如此,EA 还将行业、企业参与毕业要求达成评价作为考查重点,建议以咨询委员会的形式(如工业咨询委员会)吸引行业、企业参与毕业生质量评价。

### 3.2.5 四个组织毕业要求达成评价的异同比较

作为工程教育专业认证的核心参与主体之一,认证组织扮演着制度管理者、监督检查者和变革领导者的角色,在毕业要求达成评价中,具有诊断、监控、鉴定、激励、导向等功能。ABET、EC、ECUK 和 EA 均通过明确毕业要求达成评价要素,通过顶层设计、统筹规划专业自评和专家考评制度,构建系统化、科学化、规范化的毕业要求达成评价指导体系。虽然同为《华盛顿协议》正式成员,但各组织保持认证体系实质等效性的同时又各具本土特色,具体可从考查要素、评价指导、评价体制机制三个方面比较其异同(见表 13)。

**表 13　四个组织毕业要求达成评价的异同比较**

| 比较维度 | | 美国工程与技术认证委员会（ABET） | 加拿大工程师协会（EC） | 英国工程委员会（ECUK） | 澳大利亚工程师协会（EA） |
|---|---|---|---|---|---|
| 考查要素 | 同 | 明确毕业要求达成的考评点 | | | |
| | 异 | 分阶段明确毕业要求达成评价的考查重点 | 凝练毕业要求达成评价的五项要求 | 分专业细化毕业要求达成评价点 | 通过设置指标点对毕业要求进行要素分解 |
| 评价指导 | 同 | 形成健全的毕业要求达成评价指导体系 | | | |
| | 异 | 定期举办专题研讨会，实时更新认证辅助性参考文件 | 制定专业自评和专家考评指南 | 分专业制定毕业要求达成评价的实施细则 | 颁布自评报告模板、毕业要求解读性文件等指导材料 |
| 评价体制机制 | 同 | 注重毕业要求达成评价的顶层设计与统筹规划 | | | |
| | 异 | 注重评价全流程指导的同时鼓励专业构建特色化评价机制 | 统一制定毕业要求达成评价相关规定 | 根据工程师职业能力标准统筹设计毕业要求 | 统一将工程师职业能力标准及其指标点作为毕业要求框架 |

# 4　结论与启示

## 4.1　研究结论

毕业要求达成评价包括专业自我评价和认证组织考查评价两个关键环节，通过综合专业自评结果与专家考评结果，得出最终评价结论。

学校方面的毕业要求达成评价是专业教师及管理人员，联合在校生、毕业生、行业、企业代表，综合运用不同评价方法全面采集数据，在确定达标依据的前提下系统分析评价结果，进而根据数据和证据找差距、查问题并促进整改的过程。①从评价周期上看，毕业要求达成评价是以一定年限为循环周期的持续改进性评价，每年可选择个别指标进行评价，一个周期内评完所有指标。②从评价数据上看，毕业要求达成评价数据包括课程评价数据和主观判断数据，课程评价数据源于对强支撑毕业要求达成的专业必修课和实践性教学环节开展的评价，主观判断数据源于对毕业生、用人单位等实施的问卷调查或访谈。③从评价方法上看，采用直接评价辅以间接评价、定量评价结合定性评价、形成性评价对比总结性评价的综合评价模式，通过不同类型数据交叉比较、综合分析、相互佐证评价结果。④从评价过程上看，实施评价时以课程质量评价为主，定性调查为辅，注重教师、学生、行业、企业等多元主体协同参与。⑤从评价结果及其应用上看，结合定量目标值和定性等级描述综合判断毕业要求达成情况，根据评价结果诊断人才培养体系、评价过程中的问题和不足，从而对培养目标、毕业要求、课程体系、教学过程等进行全方位改进。

认证组织方面的毕业要求达成评价是认证专家基于自评报告审阅结果和现场考查情况，对专业毕业要求是否符合认证标准中的毕业要求、专业在何种程度上达成其设定的毕业要求进行的综合评判，评价结果将作为认证通过与否的重要依据。为保证评价的科学性与可行性，认证组织统筹设计毕业要求达成评价机制，形成规范统一的评价指导体系。其一，基于工程师职业能力标准构建毕业要求框架,实现工程教育质量要求与工程师职业胜任力要求相衔接。其二,分专业大类细化标准毕业要求,提出不同专业工科生解决复杂工程问题应满足的知识、能力和素养要求。其三,通过在认证标准中提供毕业要求指标点分解样例,为学校制定专业毕业要求和课程目标给予指导。其四,提炼毕业要求达成评价的考查重点,并在此基础上制定评估量规和专家考评实施细则建议,为专家考评建立工作方针。其五,注重毕业要求达成评价的全流程指导,分别从评价准备、评价实施、持续改进三个阶段明确操作要点,为专业自评确立行动指南。

### 4.2 经验启示

#### 1. 基于三所大学计算机工程专业毕业要求达成评价实践经验的启示

汲取三所大学计算机工程专业毕业要求达成评价的成熟经验,从评价机构与队伍、评价周期与计划、评价过程与方法、数据处理与判断、评价结果与应用等方面总结对我国高校开展毕业要求达成评价的启示。

(1)通过设立专业性组织或部门实现毕业要求达成评价的管办评分离。

毕业要求达成评价应由专门的组织或部门承担,确立评价责任机构可参照佛罗里达大学的做法,实行统一管理、分工合作制度。首先建立学校或院系层面的评价领导机构来统筹规划、协调和监督评价工作,然后以课程或教学环节为单位成立工作委员会或质量审查组来组织开展评价,评价时保证教师、学生、行业、企业代表等多元利益相关方协同参与,可通过设立工业咨询委员会和建设毕业生跟踪评价系统推动行业、企业和毕业生参与评价。

(2)通过科学设定评价周期与评价实施计划促进专业持续改进。

毕业要求达成评价以一定年限为循环周期,以持续改进为最终目的。虽然华盛顿大学要求所有指标做到一年一评,但本文认为,为保证有充足的时间落实改进措施,圣路易斯大学和佛罗里达大学每年选择一定数量的指标进行评价的做法更可取。因此,建议以2~4年为循环周期推进专业持续改进,通过制定评价时间表明确规定年度参评指标和评价活动,并在此基础上制订详细的评价计划。

(3)通过综合运用多种评价方法系统收集评价数据和达标证据。

毕业要求达成评价聚焦两大内容:一是教学质量内部评价,重点关注是否建立完善的教学过程质量监控机制和课程目标达成情况评价机制,主要选择对毕业要求具有强支撑作用的专业必修课和实践性教学环节进行评价,评价时应充分发挥顶点课程和设计类项目对评价的显性支撑作用;二是教学质量外部评价,主要以调查的方式了解用人单位、校友等外部利益相关者对毕业要求达成情况的判断。收集内外部评价数据可综合三所大学用到的方法,采用以直接评价为主、辅以间接评价,定量评价结合定性评价,形成性评价对比总结性评价的模式。

(4)通过定量分析评判法与定性分析描述法全面判断毕业要求达成情况。

根据三所大学处理评价数据的方法,既可将定量目标值作为达成标准,亦可将量规表或其他定性等级描述作为达成依据。判断毕业要求达成情况时,可参照佛罗里达大学的做法,将直接、定量数据作为判定毕业要求达成情况的主要依据,将间接、定性数据作为佐证评价结果的补充依据，同时通过形成性评价和总结性评价数据对比验证评价结果。此外，应选用恰当的数据合成方法处理评价结果，如采用加权平均法合成量化数据，采用模糊综合评价法将模糊数据转化为普通数据，并运用现代信息技术辅助分析评价数据。

（5）根据评价结果查找薄弱环节和存在的问题并对人才培养体系进行全方位改进。

毕业要求达成评价的根本目标是根据评价结果查找人才培养中的薄弱环节和存在的问题并促进整改。可首先参照圣路易斯大学和佛罗里达大学的做法，结合质性和量化评价数据找差距、查问题，然后借鉴华盛顿大学的经验，对培养目标、毕业要求、课程设置、教学方法、评价程序等进行全面改进。为保证改进措施得以有效落实，还需建立完善的评价结果反馈机制和改进效果监测机制：一方面，通过正式渠道及时将评价结果反馈给教师和教学管理人员；另一方面，通过周期性审核评估制度与适当的奖惩机制促进改进措施落地生效。

**2. 基于四个认证组织毕业要求达成评价制度体系建构经验的启示**

综合四个认证组织毕业要求达成评价制度体系的建构经验，从标准毕业要求的优化与细化、专家考评与专业自评的配套指导资源建设等方面，总结对我国工程教育专业认证协会开展毕业要求达成评价的启示。

（1）优化认证标准中毕业要求的框架体系与内容要素。

可借鉴英国工程委员会和澳大利亚工程师协会的经验，在综合考虑未来行业和产业发展需求，以及国内和国际人才培养质量要求的基础上，制定认证标准中的毕业要求，使标准毕业要求与国际工程教育质量标准实质等效、与我国本科教学质量标准相符、与工程师职业能力标准相衔接。同时，通过分专业大类细化毕业要求、设置毕业要求指标点（或观测点）样例，为学校深刻理解认证标准中的毕业要求、有效制定本专业领域的毕业要求提供参考。

（2）健全辅助性参考文件以加强专家考评指导。

健全专家考评指导的辅助性参考文件可参照加拿大工程师协会的做法。一是要明确毕业要求达成评价的考查重点，例如将组织基础和多元利益相关者参与机制、参评课程与毕业要求之间的对应支撑关系、指标点分解情况、评价方法的多样性与适切性、评价结果及持续改进效果五个维度作为毕业要求达成评价的核心考查要素。二是要针对不同考查重点制定达成情况评估量规，确定各考查维度的评价等级以及有关各等级的具体描述，从而为认证专家判断达标程度提供统一依据。三是要根据评价考查重点制定评价实施细则，研制各考查重点的细化要求，为认证专家提供可供参考的评价策略。

（3）完善毕业要求达成评价的专业自评指导体系。

完善专业自评指导体系可参照 ABET 的做法，分阶段——评价准备、评价实施和持续改进——提供评价指导建议，加强配套指导资源建设。具体而言，一是要健全学校毕业要求达成评价相关的工作办法和操作指南，明确评价实施流程、方法策略与注意事项。二是要加强学校毕业要求达成评价培训，可在认证协会现行培训体系中专门设置毕业要求达成评价培训的内容，培训工作由经验丰富的认证专家或优秀案例学校的专业认证负责人承担。三是要畅通高等教育利益相关者之间的沟通交流渠道，加强产出导向教育理念与实践的探讨，通过定期举办论坛，为经验共享、需求反馈和答疑解惑搭建平台。

## 5 结语

毕业要求达成评价是工程教育人才培养质量的重要环节，以认证组织层面、专业层面和课程层面的学习产出标准为质量准则，以认证专家、学校管理者、教师、在校生、毕业生、用人单位等多元利益相关者为参与主体，通过全面收集最具代表性且能反映教学与学习产出达成的反馈信息，为学校提高专业人才培养质量提供有力证据，为认证组织判断专业达标与否提供重要支撑，从本质上看，其实质是以持续改进为目的的周期性循环评价。通过对美国三所高校计算机工程专业的毕业要求达成评价实践和《华盛顿协议》四个成员组织的毕业要求达成评价制度体系进行比较研究后发现，毕业要求达成评价包括专业自我评价和认证组织考查评价两个核心环节，最终评价结果由专业相关人员和认证专家共同决定，专业自评和专家考评的内容重点和实施策略存在差异，因此，如何立足学校和认证组织两个不同主体，分类构建具有实际应用价值的毕业要求达成评价参考方案，仍有待深入研究。上述案例为我国构建毕业要求达成评价方案提供了重要参考，但在借鉴国际案例成熟经验的基础上，还需结合我国工程教育特色和专业认证制度，从学校实施框架和认证组织考查框架两个方面，进一步探索兼具国际等效性与国内适应性的毕业要求达成评价参考方案。

### 参考文献

[1] Accreditation Board for Engineering and Technology. Criteria for accrediting engineering programs，2023-2024[EB/OL]. [2023-05-24]. https://www.abet.org/wp-content/uploads/2023/03/23-24-EAC-Criteria_FINAL2.pdf.

[2] Engineering Council United Kingdom. The accreditation of higher education programmes（AHEP）[EB/OL]. [2023-05-24]. https://www.engc.org.uk/media/3464/ahep-fourthedition.pdf.

[3] Engineers Ireland. Accreditation criteria[EB/OL]. [2023-05-24]. https：//www.engineersireland.ie/Professionals/Membership/Become-a-member/Accredited-third-level-courses/Accreditation-criteria-procedure-and-training.

[4] International Engineering Alliance. Graduate attributes & professional competencies[EB/OL]. [2023-05-24]. https://www.ieagreements.org/assets/Uploads/Documents/IEAGraduate-Attributes-and-Professional-Competencies-2021.1Sept-2021.pdf.

[5] ENAEE. EUR-ACE® framework standards and guidelines（EAFSG）[EB/OL]. [2023-05-24]. https://www.enaee.eu/wp-content/uploads/2021/05/eafsg_brochure_2017_online.pdf.

[6] 李志义. 对毕业要求及其制定的再认识[J]. 高等工程教育研究，2020（5）：1-10.

[7] 中国工程教育专业认证协会. 工程教育认证通用标准解读及使用指南（2022 版）[EB/OL]. [2023-08-26]. https://www.ceeaa.org.cn/gcjyzyrzxh/rzcxjbz/gjwj/gzzn/index.html.

[8] Saint Louis University. ABET self-study report for the computer engineering program at Parks College of Engineering，Aviation and Technology Saint Louis University[EB/OL]. [2023-08-07]. https://www.slu.edu/provost/educationalprogram-development-review/assessment-

student-learning/program-level/pks/computer-engineering_bs_report_2018.pdf.
[9] University of Florida. ABET self-study report for computer engineering[EB/OL]. [2023-09-11]. https://cpe.eng.ufl.edu/wp-content/uploads/2019/06/ABET-2012CpE-SelfStudy.pdf.
[10] Accreditation Board for Engineering and Technology. Establishing time lines and responsibilities[EB/OL]. [2023-09-20]. https://assessment.abet.org/wp-content/uploads/2022/09/Establishing-Timelines-and-Responsibilities-09.09.20.pdf.
[11] Accreditation Board for Engineering and Technology. Selfassessment：continuous improvement of program-level assessment of student learning[EB/OL]. [2023-09-20]. https://assessment.abet.org/wp-content/uploads/2022/09/Self-Assessment_with-instructions.pdf.
[12] Accreditation Board for Engineering and Technology. Program assessment：the ultimate design problem[EB/OL]. [2023-09-20]. https://assessment.abet.org/wp-content/uploads/2022/09/Program-Assessment_The-Ultimate-Design-Problem-09.09.20.pdf.
[13] Accreditation Board for Engineering and Technology. The importance of direct measures[EB/OL]. [2023-09-20]. https://assessment.abet.org/wp-content/uploads/2022/09/Importance-of-Direct-Measures-09.09.20.pdf.
[14] Accreditation Board for Engineering and Technology. Using course or testgrades for program assessment[EB/OL]. [2023-09-20]. https://assessment.abet.org/wp-content/uploads/2022/09/Using-Course-or-Test-Grades-for-Program-Assessment-09.09.20.pdf.
[15] Accreditation Board for Engineering and Technology. Surveys and questionnaires：Do they measure up[EB/OL]. [2023-09-20]. https://assessment.abet.org/wp-content/uploads/2022/09/Surveys-and-Questionnaires-09.09.20.pdf.
[16] Accreditation Board for Engineering and Technology. How many data are too many[EB/OL]. [2023-09-20]. https://assessment.abet.org/wp-content/uploads/2022/09/HowMany-Data-Are-Too-Many-09.09.20.pdf.
[17] Engineers Canada. Graduate attributes and continual improvement rubrics[EB/OL]. [2023-05-16]. https://engineerscanada.ca/sites/default/files/2021-11/gaci-rubrics-en.pdf.
[18] Engineers Canada. A guide to outcomes-based criteria( draft )[EB/OL]. [2023-05-16]. https://engineerscanada.ca/sites/default/files/draft_program_visitor_guide_v1.25.pdf.
[19] Engineering Council United Kingdom. Professional engineering institutions[EB/OL]. [2022-05-17]. https://www.engc.org.uk/licensees.
[20] Engineering Council United Kingdom. The UK standard or professional engineering competence and commitment( UKSPEC )( Fourth edition )[EB/OL]. [2023-05-17]. https://www.engc.org.uk/media/3877/uk-spec-v12-web.pdf.
[21] Joint Board of Moderators. Guidelines for developing degree programmes( AHEP4 )[EB/OL]. [2023-05-17]. https://www.jbm.org.uk/media/hdojdcyf/guidelines-for-developing-degree-programmes_ahep4.pdf.
[22] Institution of Chemical Engineers. Accreditation of chemical engineering programes[EB/OL]. [2023-05-17]. https://www.icheme.org/media/17198/accreditation-guidance-october-

2021.pdf.

[23] Engineers Australia. Stage 1 competency standard for professional engineer [EB/OL]. [2023-08-31]. https://www.engineersaustralia.org.au/sites/default/files/2022-07/stage-1-competency-standard-professional-engineer.pdf.

# 基于产出导向工程教育理念的毕业要求达成评价(下)①

朱 露 胡德鑫 王凯峰 顾佩华

**摘要:**借鉴工程教育专业认证中毕业要求达成评价的国际案例经验,基于OBE(成果导向教育)理念,立足学校和认证组织双维度视角,提出未来工程教育专业认证的毕业要求达成评价参考方案。该参考方案由学校方面毕业要求达成评价的参考性实施框架和认证组织方面毕业要求达成评价的参考性考查框架两部分组成。学校方面毕业要求达成评价的参考性实施框架分为评价准备、评价实施和持续改进3个阶段,涵盖11个环节。认证组织方面毕业要求达成评价的参考性考查框架包括毕业要求参考性内容和毕业要求达成参考性评价方法,前者为学校制定专业毕业要求建立基准,后者旨在从认证组织方(认证机构)为专家考评与专业自评提供参考。为协助学校理解和应用参考方案和方法开展毕业要求达成评价,通过一个机械工程专业的虚拟案例,对专业毕业要求达成评价的参考性实施框架进行演示操作流程。需要强调的是,本文是一个探索性成果,希望能够起到抛砖引玉的作用,在根据《华盛顿协议》新版毕业要求(GAPC21)修订中国工程教育专业认证毕业要求的关键时期,推动开展更广泛且深入的工程教育专业认证相关理论与实践研究,持续提高工程教育质量与水平。

**关键词:**OBE;工程教育认证;毕业要求达成评价;专业自评;认证组织考评

## On the Evaluation of the Achievement of Graduate Outcomes based on Outcome-based Engineering Education Principles (Part 2)

*Zhu Lu, Hu Dexin, Wang Kaifeng, Gu Peihua*

**Abstract:** Drawing on the international cases' experience in the evaluation of the achievement of graduate outcomes and based on OBE (outcome-based education) education principles, this study constructs a future referenced scheme for the evaluation of the achievement of graduate outcomes of engineering education from the dual perspectives of schools and accreditation organizations. The referenced scheme comprises two components: the school's referenced implementation scheme and the accreditation organization's referenced review scheme. The school's referenced implementation scheme is generally divided into three stages—evaluation preparation, evaluation implementation and continuous improvement with 11 steps.The accreditation organization's referenced review scheme includes the referenced content of graduate outcomes and the referenced evaluation methods. The former provide reference for schools to formulate program's graduate outcomes, the latter aims to provide ref-

① 本文刊登于《高等工程教育研究》2024年第4期第37~53页。

erence for expert evaluation and program self-evaluation from the perspective of the accreditation organization. In order to further explain how schools understand and utilize the referenced scheme, an evaluation of graduate outcomes of a mechanical engineering program as a virtual example was included to illustrate the school's referenced scheme. It should be emphasized that this is an exploratory study. It is authors' hope that this study would inspire more theoretical and implementation research explorations and continuously improve the quality and level of engineering education during the critical period of revising the graduate outcomes of China Engineering Education Accreditation Criteria based on GAPC21 of Washington Accord.

**Keywords:** OBE; accreditation for engineering programs; evaluation of the achievement of graduate outcomes; program's self-evaluation; accreditation organization's review

## 引言

《基于产出导向工程教育理念的毕业要求达成评价(上)》对美国三所大学计算机工程专业的毕业要求达成评价实践和《华盛顿协议》四个成员组织的毕业要求达成评价制度体系开展了国际比较,总结出对高校和工程教育专业认证组织开展毕业要求达成评价的启示。本文在借鉴毕业要求达成评价国际案例经验和产出导向教育(OBE)理念的基础上,结合我国工程教育特色与专业认证制度,提出未来工程教育专业认证的毕业要求达成评价参考方案(本研究为探索性研究)。选取机械工程专业毕业要求评价的虚拟案例,对学校如何开展毕业要求达成评价进行演示操作。需要强调的是,工程教育专业认证标准达成评价涉及学生、培养目标、毕业要求、持续改进、课程体系、师资队伍、支持条件等7个方面,在认证评价中,需整体把握、系统评价7项标准的达成情况。本研究聚焦毕业要求达成评价,通过研制产出导向的毕业要求达成评价参考方案,探索工程教育转型新时期专业认证工作的重要性,旨在激发更广泛且深入的工程教育专业认证相关理论与实践研究。

## 1 未来工程教育专业认证的毕业要求达成评价参考方案的思考

工程教育专业认证的毕业要求达成评价参考方案包括两部分:一是学校方面毕业要求达成评价的参考性实施框架;二是认证组织方面毕业要求达成评价的参考性考查框架。

### 1.1 学校方面毕业要求达成评价的参考性实施框架

从学校方面看,学校开展毕业要求达成评价前,需首先明确专业毕业要求的内容构成,继而构建产出导向评价方法体系和持续改进机制,并将其付诸实践。学校层面的毕业要求达成评价参考性实施框架借鉴了美国工程与技术认证委员会(ABET)的评价指导建议,从评价准备、评价实施和持续改进三个阶段明确了毕业要求达成评价的操作要点,共包含11个实施环节(见图1)。

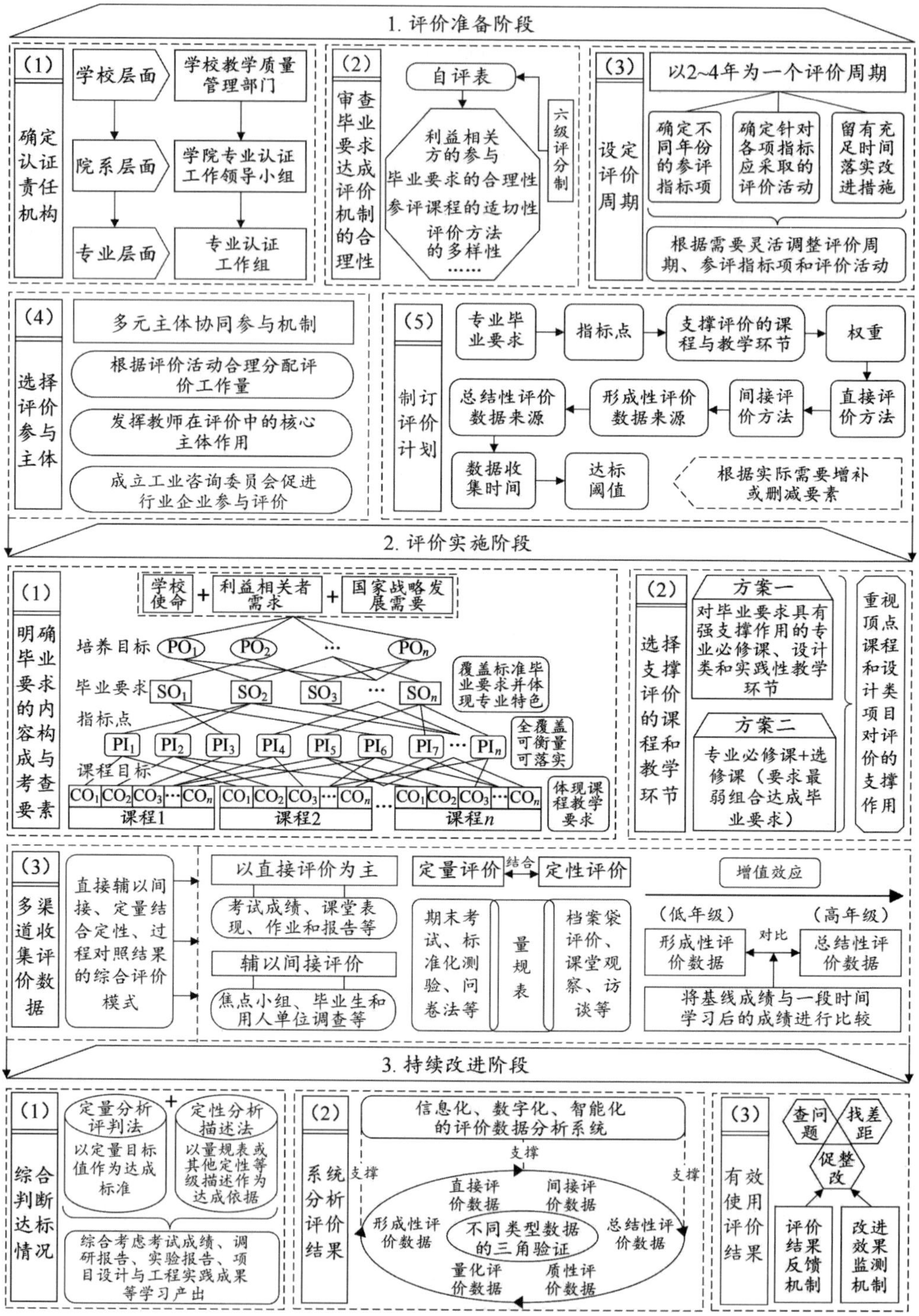


**图 1　学校方面毕业要求达成评价的参考性实施框架**

[PO、SO、PI、CO 分别为培养目标( program outcome )、毕业要求( student outcome )、指标点( performance indicator )、课程目标( course outcome )]

**1. 评价准备阶段**

（1）确定认证责任机构。

确定认证责任机构可借鉴佛罗里达大学“统筹协调、分散管理”的组织建设经验。首先，成立学校专业认证领导机构（如学校教学质量管理部门），负责学校层面认证工作的领导和统筹组织。其次，对于参与认证专业的学院，成立院级专业认证领导机构（如学院专业认证工作领导小组）来领导学院层面专业认证的具体工作，其中包括领导和组织开展毕业要求达成评价工作。院级专业认证领导机构可由学院主管教学负责人、教育委员会成员、参加认证的专业负责人、工程实践领域专家、教师代表等组成，学校教学质量管理部门可委派代表参与院级认证组织工作。最后，对于每个参加认证的专业，成立以系或专业负责人牵头的专业认证工作组，负责组织开展认证准备和评价工作，其中涉及开展毕业要求达成评价、反馈评价信息、为改进教育教学与评估程序提供建议等工作。需要说明的是，毕业要求达成评价仅是学校、院系、专业三级认证责任机构的职能之一，在真实的认证评价中，各级认证机构需领导和组织开展包括毕业要求在内的认证标准整体达成情况的评价工作。

（2）审查毕业要求达成评价机制的合理性。

专业开展毕业要求达成评价之前，需通过自评表对毕业要求达成评价与持续改进机制的合理性进行自我评价，评价标准包括：有多元利益相关者参与培养目标与毕业要求的制定、修订与评价；毕业要求需支撑培养目标达成，全面覆盖国家认证标准中的毕业要求；用于毕业要求达成评价的课程和教学环节能够系统性反映学生学习产出；采用直接辅以间接、定量结合定性、过程对照结果的综合评价模式采集数据；根据评价标准判断达标情况，识别人才培养中的薄弱环节和问题项并持续改进，同时构建信息反馈机制与改进效果监测机制，保障评价结果的有效使用。计分可参考 ABET 六级评分制（见《基于产出导向工程教育理念的毕业要求达成评价（上）》中的表 9），也可根据专业特点，制定合理的评分办法，对现有评价体系、评价执行情况和持续改进情况进行自我评价，若有得分较低的项目，应对其做出改进后再开展毕业要求达成评价。

（3）设定评价周期。

毕业要求达成评价是以持续改进为导向的周期性评价。参考美国三所大学设定评价周期的实践经验并结合 ABET 的评价指导建议，完整一轮毕业要求达成评价的周期一般为 2~4 年，如果以 2 年或 3 年为一个评价周期，在 6 年认证有效期内可进行 3 轮或 2 轮评价；如果以 4 年为一个评价周期，则在本科四年学制内系统收集一轮评价数据。设定评价周期时，应考虑持续改进各阶段的作用，明确不同年份的参评指标及对应的具体评价活动，确保每项毕业要求和每届学生在一个周期内接受至少一次评价，但无须每年对所有毕业要求和学生开展评价，需留有足够时间落实改进措施。以 2 年周期表为例，表 1 中共有 11 条毕业要求，每年参与评价的指标在 6 个以内，每条毕业要求在 6 年认证有效期内可经历 3 轮评价。除了确定年度参评指标，还需在各年份有针对性地开展评价活动。如表 2 所示，可将评价活动及相关工作分为 8 个步骤。各年份进行的评价活动可有所差异，但需要注意的是，每个周期都要有完整的数据分析过程，形成评价报告并归档，如实反馈评价结果，并在评价周期结束后的第二学年及时做出改进。专业可根据评价结果动态调整评价周期、参评指标及评价活动，若某些指标达标率较高，而另一些指标始终较难达标，则应增加未达标项的被评次数。

**表 1　以两年为一个周期的评价时间表示例**

| 毕业要求 | 第 1 周期 | | 第 2 周期 | | 第 3 周期 | |
|---|---|---|---|---|---|---|
| | 第 1 年 | 第 2 年 | 第 3 年 | 第 4 年 | 第 5 年 | 第 6 年 |
| A | ● | | ● | | ● | |
| B | | ● | | ● | | ● |
| C | ● | | ● | | ● | |
| D | ● | | ● | | ● | |
| E | | ● | | ● | | ● |
| F | ● | | ● | | ● | |
| G | | ● | | ● | | ● |
| H | ● | | ● | | ● | |
| I | | ● | | ● | | ● |
| J | ● | | ● | | ● | |
| K | | ● | | ● | | ● |

**表 2　负责人、评价活动与评价时间之间的关系[1]**

| 负责人 | 评价活动 | 第 1 周期 | | 第 2 周期 | | 第 3 周期 | |
|---|---|---|---|---|---|---|---|
| | | 第 1 年 | 第 2 年 | 第 3 年 | 第 4 年 | 第 5 年 | 第 6 年 |
| 认证责任机构 | 1. 审查指标点设置的合理性 | ● | | | ● | | ● |
| 全体教师、认证责任机构 | 2. 建立课程（或教学环节）与指标点之间的对应关系矩阵 | ● | | | | ● | |
| 专业教师、认证责任机构 | 3. 根据对应支撑关系选择用于毕业要求达成评价的课程和教学环节 | ● | | | | ● | |
| 认证责任机构、专业教师 | 4. 开发和选择评价方法 | ● | | | ● | | ● |
| 专业教师、认证责任机构 | 5. 收集数据 | | ● | ● | | ● | |
| 认证责任机构 | 6. 分析数据并对评价过程的合理性进行评价 | | ● | | ● | | ● |
| 认证责任机构 | 7. 报告评价结果 | | ● | | ● | | ● |
| 专业教师 | 8. 采取改进措施 | | | ● | | ● | |

（4）选择评价参与主体。

毕业要求达成评价需要多元主体协同参与，包括教师、在校生、校友、用人单位、行业或企业等利益相关者，专业应根据评价活动有针对性地选择评价主体，合理分配评价工作量。教师作为核心参与主体，既是评价数据的收集者，也是持续改进的践行者，要充分发挥教师在评价和改进工作中的主要作用，使其恰当选择支撑评价的课程，运用多种评价方法查找教学中存在的问题，并将改进工作落实至具体教学环节。此外，还要重视行业、企业对人才培养和毕业要求达成情况的评价与反馈，为保障行业、企业参与评价，建议成立由企业代表、校友、骨干教师和相关领域专家组成的工业咨询委员会（Industrial Advisory Board），协助专业了解产业发展趋势以及企业对工程技术人才的最新需求。工业咨询委员会的职能不限于工程教育专业认证工作，更不限于毕业要求达成评价。

（5）制订评价计划。

制订评价计划的目的是对各项毕业要求的评价实施流程进行规划，其基本构成要素如表3所示。需要说明的是，专业可自主决定是否将毕业要求分解为指标点，若不分解，则直接建立评价课程与毕业要求的对应关系，但需保证课程目标明确、课程内容充分、考核方法适当。由于毕业要求达成评价需关联不同类型数据以构建完整证据链，因此，除依据直接评价与间接评价、定量评价与定性评价得到的数据判断达标程度，还需通过形成性评价数据和总结性评价数据纵向比较学生在一段学习时间内不同时间点上的发展与变化，根据学习进步幅度判断毕业要求达成情况，进而验证其他方法的评价结果。形成性评价数据一般源于低年级课程，而总结性评价数据通常来自高年级课程。表3仅为一个示例，其科学性与合理性尚待在教学实践中进一步检验。

**表3　毕业要求各指标项评价计划表示例**

<table>
<tr><th>专业毕业要求</th><th>指标点</th><th>用于评价的课程、设计类和实践性教学环节</th><th>权重</th><th>评价方法</th><th>形成性评价数据来源</th><th>总结性评价数据来源</th><th>数据收集时间</th><th>达标阈值</th></tr>
<tr><td rowspan="8">毕业要求1：描述…</td><td rowspan="4">1.1 描述…</td><td>课程A</td><td>0.3</td><td rowspan="8">评价方法具有多样性，注意做到直接评价辅以间接评价，定量评价结合定性评价</td><td rowspan="8">课程A（通常开设于第一或第二学年）</td><td rowspan="8">课程B（通常开设于第三或第四学年）</td><td rowspan="8">2016年、2018年、2020年</td><td rowspan="8">既可以是定量目标值，也可以是定性等级描述</td></tr>
<tr><td>课程B</td><td>0.2</td></tr>
<tr><td>课程C</td><td>0.5</td></tr>
<tr><td>……</td><td>…</td></tr>
<tr><td rowspan="4">1.2 描述…</td><td>课程A</td><td>0.2</td></tr>
<tr><td>课程B</td><td>0.2</td></tr>
<tr><td>课程C</td><td>0.6</td></tr>
<tr><td>……</td><td>…</td></tr>
</table>

注：此表参考ABET毕业要求各指标项的评价计划表（见《基于产出导向工程教育理念的毕业要求达成评价（上）》中的表10）研制而成，表中的权重数值、数据收集时间均为虚拟数据。

**2. 评价实施阶段**

（1）明确毕业要求的内容构成与考查要素。

中国工程教育专业认证协会通用标准中的毕业要求为学校制定专业毕业要求建立基准，但并不要求专业毕业要求与标准毕业要求完全相同，学校可根据自身办学理念与发展特色，结合社会经济发展需求，制定符合专业定位和培养目标的毕业要求。专业毕业要求应全面覆盖标准毕业要求，反映学生毕业时的培养要求，按照教育和人才培养规律，还应体现学生认知发展过程中各阶段的培养要求，落实于不同学习阶段的课程目标和培养内容之中，为优化课程体系提供依据和指导。确定毕业要求框架之后，需进一步细化和明确毕业要求的内容要素，可参考圣路易斯大学将毕业要求分解为指标点（indicators）的做法。指标点是通过分解毕业要求而得到的关于学生学习表现的具体陈述。设置毕业要求指标点应遵循全覆盖、可衡量和可落实的原则。“全覆盖”指有足够数量的指标点反映每条毕业要求包含的全部能力要素。指标点设置应该科学合理，不宜过分复杂，指标点数量过多容易增加教学系统的复杂性，数量过少则难以详细说明能力所包含的具体行为表现。“可衡量”指运用恰当的认知行为动词具体化呈现学习产出，选择认知行为动词时要避免使用不可测量的抽象概括的词汇，可根据布鲁姆教育目标分类学确定认知层次，从对应认知层次中选择能准确反映学习表现的动词，并以“认知行为动词+学习产出内容”的结构描述指标点。“可落实”意味着指标点有具体课程或教学环节支撑，指标点达成情况可采用适当考核方式进行评价，指标点内容体现专业特色。值得一提的是，虽然我国2022版《工程教育认证自评报告指导书》没有要求专业设置毕业要求指标点[2]（给大学和专业留有实施的余地），《基于产出导向工程教育理念的毕业要求达成评价（上）》介绍的美国三所大学中也有未设置指标点的案例，并且有学者从控制论视角指出指标点的弊端[3]，但从我国目前工程教育专业认证的情况看，还有很多高校没有进行专业认证，缺乏认证经验的专业直接将标准毕业要求作为专业毕业要求，承担课程教学的教师可能较难把握毕业要求的内容要素以及毕业要求与课程内容之间的关系[4]。因此，将毕业要求分解为指标点并根据指标点制定课程目标、教学内容和考核方法，更有助于教师将毕业要求落实到教学过程中，也有利于得到更准确的评价结果。

（2）选择支撑评价的课程和教学环节。

根据美国三所大学选择参评课程的经验，毕业要求达成评价以面向产出的课程质量评价为核心，主要在对毕业要求具有强支撑作用的专业核心课、设计类和实践性教学环节中进行。专业核心课包括工程基础课、专业基础课、专业课和工程实践课（含项目制课程），一般应为专业必修课；设计类和实践性教学环节主要指毕业设计、生产实习、科技创新和各种实施工程项目的活动，即课堂教学以外的其他培养环节。如果专业必修课和选修课一同考查，要从设定的必修课和选修课组合中找到最弱组合，只有最弱组合满足认证标准中的各项要求，才能通过专业认证的要求，这一点务必注意。对基于课程数据的评价，专业应重点关注用于毕业要求达成评价的课程和教学环节是否选择恰当，专业核心课和项目实践类课程能否充分体现对评价的主要支撑作用。此外，还应考虑毕业要求（或指标点）所处目标层次，含有高层次认知行为的毕业要求或指标点应由多门课程及对应的考核办法或综合性设计项目支撑，但要注意课程之间的内在逻辑，可同时选择支撑毕业要求的先修课和强化课进行评价以增强能力评价的关联性与系统性。评价过程中，要重视对顶点课程和设计类项目的考查，不仅应通过直接评价法考查技术能力指标达成情况，还应通过间接评价法考查非技术能力指标达成情况，换言之，对于支撑毕业要求指标项数量较多的课程或教学环节，其评价方法应更具考查学生解决复杂工程问题能力的综合集成性。

（3）采用综合方法收集数据并进行评价。

收集数据的过程中,要注意评价方法的适切性与多元化,根据教学目标选择恰当的评价方法,运用不同方法系统获取佐证材料。我国工程教育毕业要求达成评价的常用方法有课程考核成绩分析法、评分表分析法(也叫量规表法)、问卷调查、学生访谈、标准化测验和模拟测验[5]。整体而言,专业较多选用课程考试平均算分法,对量规表法、问卷调查、访谈等其他评价方法运用不多。为增强专业自证的全面性、可信性与去主观性,应根据毕业要求所处目标层次的不同,选择合适的评价方法。可综合美国三所大学毕业要求达成评价所用方法,采用以直接评价为主,辅以间接评价,定量评价与定性评价相结合的模式。一般而言,可通过课程考核成绩、标准化测验等直接或定量评价法收集技术性指标评价数据,通过焦点小组、访谈等间接或定性评价法收集非技术性指标评价数据,但不论哪种方法,都应通过量规表为其制定统一评分准则,促使教师、学生、工业界代表等协作开发量规表并参与量规评价。此外,目前课程评价多以最终考核成绩的均值作为评价结果,其实质是总结性评价,这种评价模式容易忽视学生的主观努力程度和实际进步幅度,不利于真实反映学习效果。因此,建议将增值评价(value-added assessment)纳入课程评价体系,在考虑不受教师或学校控制的影响因素(如学生已有知识水平)的前提下,通过收集形成性评价数据和总结性评价数据,将学生起点水平与实际学习结果进行比较,以其进步幅度为评价标准,观察学生的成长变化过程,考查学校和教师对学生学习产出影响的净效应,以此判断毕业要求达成情况。评价过程中可采用科学的抽样方法,根据学生数量,从好、中、差的或适当增加评价等级的学生作业或试卷中等比例抽取具有统计意义的样本,从而避免无效或重复收集数据。

**3. 持续改进阶段**

(1)综合判断达标程度。

由于毕业要求达成评价聚焦课程总体质量评价,因此课程评价数据也就成为判断毕业要求达成情况的主要证据。实施课程评价时要恰当选择用于评价的课程,以赋权方式确定各门课程对毕业要求的支撑强度并制定评价标准,根据美国三所大学判断达标程度的做法,建议综合运用定量分析评判法和定性分析描述法判断毕业要求达成情况。为保证评价的客观性与准确性,不能单纯根据考试成绩计算毕业要求达成评分,而要同时考查调研报告、实验报告、项目设计与工程实践成果等学习产出,确定不同考核评价方式与毕业要求、课程目标之间的对应关系及其占总评成绩的比例,以量规表的形式制定评价依据并对评价结果进行赋值处理,计分一般采用百分制或五级评分制,评价值可通过加权计算求得,达到某个定量目标值则视为达成。除了课程评价数据,还需通过问卷调查、访谈、焦点小组等间接评价法了解毕业生、用人单位等利益相关者对毕业要求达成情况的看法,由于间接评价法可能受个体主观因素影响,因此除了保证问卷题目、访谈问题等与评价目标相匹配,还应通过量规表或其他定性等级描述为被调查者回答问题提供答案依据。问卷调查结果可使用李克特五级评分制计算评价值并设定目标值,而访谈、焦点小组的调查结果则主要通过不断抽象概括得到实质性结论。对于增值评价,判断毕业要求达成情况最简单的思路就是计算两个不同时间点学习成效的绝对变化,将某个成绩增值作为达成毕业要求的目标值。目前可用的增值评价方法有描述统计法、统计回归法、机器学习算法等[6]。但增值评价不能只关注分数,还应全面评价学生德智体美劳多个维度的增值,因此,如何融合多种评价方法(定量与定性、自评和他评）以准确测量变化幅度，以及如何建立统一的增值评价标准，成为开展增值评价面临的两个挑战。对上述不同来源的数据进行归一化处理后，即可得到毕业要求达成情况的总评结果。

（2）系统分析评价结果。

分析通过多种方法得到的评价数据，要做到交叉比较、系统归纳和相互佐证，建议采用三角检验法验证评价结果。所谓三角检验，是指由不同调查者运用不同数据、方法和证据来证明同一命题或结论的方法，其基本原理是求证多个独立检测结果与研究发现的一致性，包括数据三角检验、人员三角检验、方法三角检验和理论三角检验[7]。由于理论三角检验尚存争议[8]，本研究仅对前三种三角检验法在毕业要求达成评价中的运用进行探讨。数据三角检验是指根据不同来源的数据检验评价结果。例如，首先通过直接评价和定量评价数据初步判定评价结果；然后通过间接评价和定性评价数据辅助佐证评价结果；最后，通过对比形成性评价数据和总结性评价数据进一步验证评价结果。人员三角检验是指根据不同评价主体收集的数据检验评价结果。例如，判断通过教师评价、用人单位反馈以及学生自评得到的数据是否一致。方法三角检验是指根据不同评价方法得到的数据检验评价结果。例如，顶点课程评价可通过量规表、课程日志、调查问卷三角检验解决复杂工程问题的能力的评价结果[9]。三角检验过程中要注意把握不同类型数据之间的关联性和相互佐证性，如果不同方法得出的评价结果存在较大差距，应认真反思评价方法的适切性以及数据的真实可靠性，必要时对评价方案进行调整，通过其他评价方法进行二次检验。在此过程中，要选择适当的数据合成方法对数据进行汇总整理，对于普通量化数据，可通过加权平均法，逐级向上使用同一算法进行处理，直至将全部数据在一级指标上归并为一个合成值；对于质性评价数据（如关于优、良、中、差的等级评定结果），可通过模糊综合评判法将模糊数据转化为普通量化数据。

此外，要善用 SPSS、SAS 等评价信息处理工具，有条件的学校还可应用现代信息技术构建信息化、数字化、智能化的评价数据分析系统，以高效管理和分析评价结果。

（3）有效使用评价结果。

得到评价结果后，更为重要的是基于数据和证据诊断人才培养中存在的短板和不足，全面优化包括培养目标、毕业要求、课程、教学过程、师资配置、支持条件等在内的人才培养体系，必要时还应调整评价实施程序。在合成分项评定结果的基础上，对整体评价结果进行综合描述与判断，总结得出客观合理且具有正确导向性的评价结论，据此发现问题、找到差距、确定改进方向并落实改进工作。为确保改进措施有效落实，一是要建立稳定的信息反馈机制，由专业管理人员将评价过程数据、评价结果和发现的问题及时反馈给有关各方，为相关部门进行教育决策提供参考，为改进课程教学提供依据，尤其要明确课程教师应承担的改进职责，调动教师改进教学方法、优化考核评价方式的积极性；二是要建立常态化的改进效果监测机制，由持续改进的责任人协同利益相关主体，定期对课程体系修订情况和教学质量提升情况进行审查并形成相应的文档记录。

### 1.2 认证组织方面毕业要求达成评价的参考性考查框架

从认证组织方面看，认证组织应做好毕业要求以及毕业要求达成评价的顶层设计和指导工作，出台并落实毕业要求达成评价实施细则与指导文件。如图 2 所示的认证组织方面毕业要求达成评价的参考性考查框架，由毕业要求参考性内容和毕业要求达成参考性评价方法两部分组成。强调参考性，说明这个框架没有经过严格的科学检验和实践论证，其功能仅用于辅助说明评价方法。毕业要求参考性内容为学校制定专业毕业要求提供基准，毕业要求达成参考性评价方法旨在从认证组织层面为专家考评与专业自评提供参考。

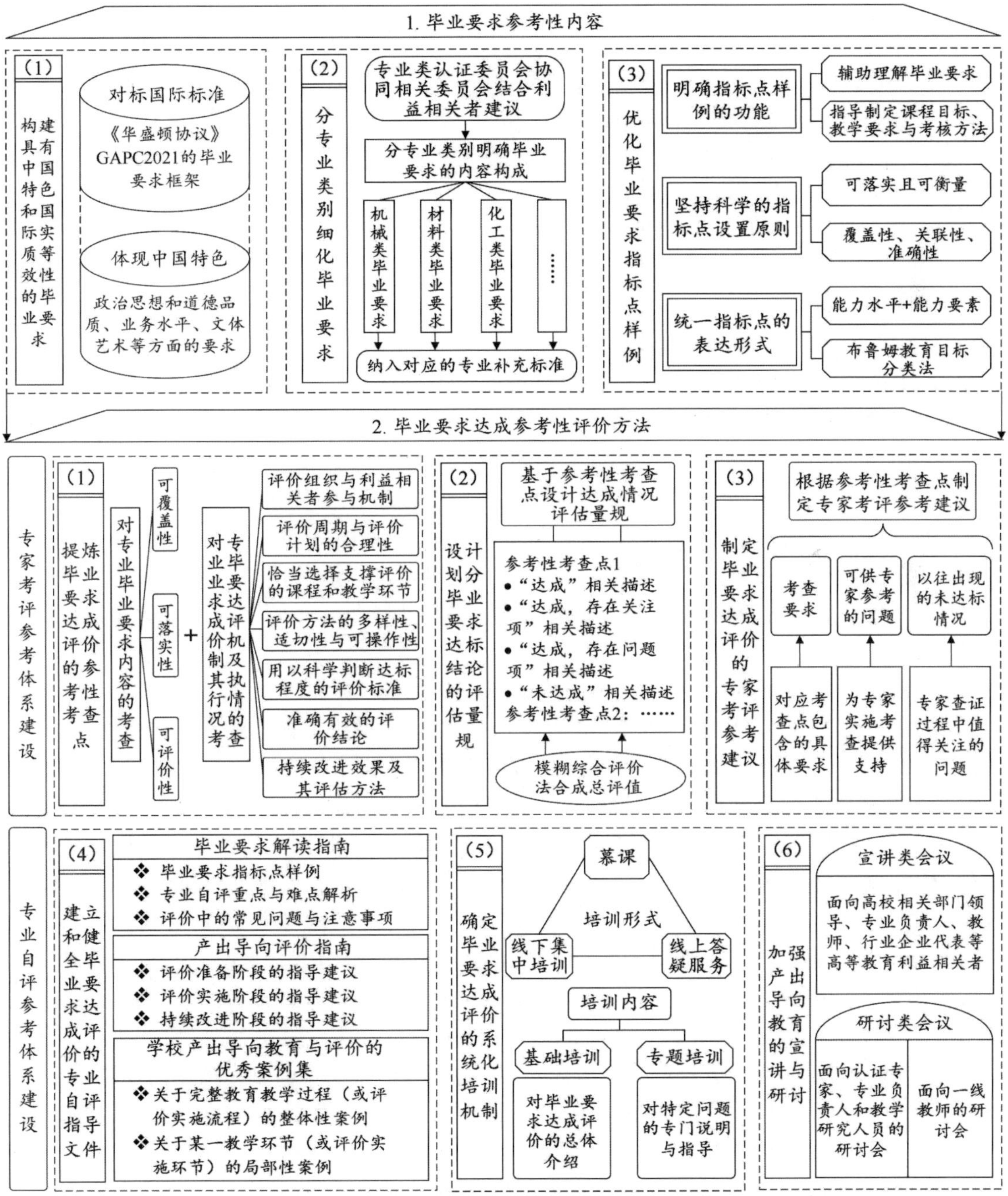


**图 2　认证组织方面毕业要求达成评价的参考性考查框架**

**1. 毕业要求参考性内容**

（1）构建具有中国特色和国际实质等效性的毕业要求。

我国工程教育专业认证通用标准中的毕业要求（简称标准毕业要求）是学校制定专业毕业要求的基础，为面向未来行业和产业发展需求、国家战略发展需要以及国际工程技术人才质量要求培养未来工程师，通用标准中的毕业要求应该与国际标准实质等效，同时体现中国特色，指导学校培养具有国际竞争力、服务国家和社会发展的工程技术人才。首先，标准毕业要求要符合（或高于）已有国际工程教育质量标准，如《华盛顿协议》颁布的第四版《毕业要求和职业胜任力-2021》（GAPC21）；其次，标准毕业要求还要体现我国工程技术人才培养的特色和特殊要求，包括政治思想和道德品质、业务水平、文体艺术等方面的要求；最后，应根据国家、产业、社会以及国际认证组织对工程技术人才需求的最新变化，定期修订标准毕业要求，增强标准毕业要求的动态适应性。

（2）分专业类别细化毕业要求。

目前，我国现行工程教育专业认证标准中的毕业要求是面向所有工科专业的普适性要求，由于解决不同专业领域复杂工程问题应具备的知识、能力和素养存在差异，以及快速发展的科技对专业的影响不同，建议借鉴英国工程委员会的经验，分专业大类（如机械工程类专业、电子工程类专业等）深入研究毕业要求的内容构成。可由中国工程教育专业认证协会的各专业类认证委员会协同相关委员会，结合利益相关方的意见与建议，通过充分了解、科学研判国家、产业和社会对不同领域工程技术人才的能力需求，从大类专业视角制定工程人才培养的补充性要求，以此最终形成专业大类毕业要求并将其纳入专业补充标准。这里需要说明的是，认证标准中的专业类毕业要求不作为学校制定专业毕业要求的统一模板，仅为学校提供参考框架，鼓励学校结合办学定位、专业特点、行业和区域特色以及学生发展需求，增加或强化某些方面的知识、能力和素养要求，促进专业人才培养的本土化与特色化创新发展。

（3）优化毕业要求指标点（或称为内涵观测点）样例。

由于毕业要求是概括程度较高的概括性能力描述，为准确把握毕业要求的内容和内涵，认证组织需进一步分解和细化毕业要求，建议参考澳大利亚工程师协会的做法，通过在标准毕业要求中提供指标点样例，为学校制定专业毕业要求提供参考。目前，中国工程教育专业认证协会在《工程教育认证通用标准解读及使用指南》中给出各项毕业要求的内涵观测点（又称指标点），随着认证协会按照《华盛顿协议》GAPC21 相关要求修订标准毕业要求，建议继续明确指标点设置原则，在认知程度表达、指标点形式结构等方面给出具体建议，以便于新参加认证专业把握与实施。首先，建议明确指标点样例的用途和功能，在标准毕业要求中提供指标点样例主要是为了帮助专业较深入地理解和把握毕业要求包含的能力要素，在此基础上制定课程目标和课程教学具体要求并确定考核方法。其次，建议设计指标点从两方面考虑：其一，指标点应该可落实且可衡量，指标点是对毕业要求更为细化的描述，可采用适当的评价方法判断指标点达成情况；其二，指标点应该具有覆盖性、关联性和准确性，覆盖性是指所有指标点组成的集合不可遗漏毕业要求包含的能力要素，关联性意味着同一项毕业要求分解出的指标点可按照一定逻辑关系组合形成系统整体，准确性要求指标点符合毕业要求规定应达到的认知水平。此外,建议指标点达成要有统一的表达形式。考虑采用"认知水平+能力要素"的形式,按毕业时的目标要求分解出能力要素,并根据布鲁姆教育目标分类法,恰当选择对应认知层次。

**2. 毕业要求达成参考性评价方法**

(1)提炼毕业要求达成评价的参考性考查点。

为帮助认证专家把握毕业要求达成评价的基本要求,使认证工作评价更加科学可行,建议借鉴加拿大工程认证委员会提炼毕业要求达成评价要点的做法,在认证辅助性参考文件中进一步明确毕业要求达成评价的参考性考查点。本研究将毕业要求达成评价的参考性考查点总体归为两类:对毕业要求内容的考查,对毕业要求达成评价机制及其执行情况的考查。对专业毕业要求内容的考查有三个考查点:专业毕业要求的可覆盖性、可落实性与可评价性。"可覆盖性"关注专业毕业要求是否在能力要素和能力水平上全面覆盖认证标准中的毕业要求,"可落实性"关注毕业要求能否与课程目标、课程教学和课程评价形成合理的对应支撑关系,"可评价性"关注每项毕业要求能否通过不同考核方式进行有针对性的评价。对毕业要求达成评价机制及其执行情况的考查包括七个重点。一是评价组织与利益相关者参与机制,要求明确认证责任机构并促进利益相关方共同参与评价,尤其是要有健全的机制保障行业和企业的参与。二是评价周期与评价计划的合理性,要求以一定年限为循环周期推进专业持续改进,合理规划评价周期、年度参评指标和评价工作。三是恰当选择支撑评价的课程和教学环节,要求选择最具代表性且能证明毕业要求达成的专业必修课、设计类和实践性教学环节进行评价,如果将选修课用于评价,应提供客观评价标准和有效达标证据,并且要证明选修课与必修课的最弱组合达成毕业要求。四是评价方法的多样性、适切性与可操作性,要求综合多种评价方法开展评价,对基于课程数据的评价,需根据不同课程的教学目标恰当选择评价方法;对基于主观判断的评价,需有针对性地选择调查群体与合适的调查工具。五是科学判断达标程度的评价标准,要求不论使用哪种评价方法,都要为其制定明确的评价依据,既可是定量目标值,也可是定性等级描述。六是准确有效的评价结论,要求主要根据直接、定量评价数据判断达标情况,结合间接、定性评价数据补充验证评价结果,通过形成性评价与总结性评价数据对比验证评价结果,并能够基于评价结果识别弱项和问题项。七是持续改进效果及其评估方法,要求通过建立评价信息反馈机制和改进效果监测机制,保证改进措施落地见效。

(2)设计划分毕业要求达标结论的评估量规。

在明确参考性考查点的基础上,为判断各考查点的达标情况,建议参考加拿大工程认证委员会设计毕业要求与持续改进评估量规(rubrics)的做法,通过制定毕业要求达成情况评估量规,为划分达标结论提供统一评判依据。目前,认证专家判断认证标准达成情况的结论有四类:达成;达成,存在关注项;达成,存在问题项;未达成。毕业要求达成情况评估量规的评价等级可按照以上四种结论划分,评价内容可参考上文提到的参考性考查点,各考查点不同等级的达标描述应具有区分度。"达成"意味着专业完全满足或高于考查要求,没有弱项和问题项;"达成,存在关注项"意味着专业满足考查要求,但存在需要关注的方面,这些方面可能对保持达标状态产生潜在影响;"达成,存在问题项"意味着专业满足考查要求,但存在需要改进的问题，需在认证有效期内予以改进；“未达成”意味着专业存在不达标的指标项，无法满足考查要求。以“评价方法的多样性、适切性与可操作性”为例（见表4），其评估量规由参考性考查点、细化要求、指标权重和评价等级四个要素构成，各评价等级分别赋分100、75、50、25，建议在认证专家完成单项指标评价（评分）后，通过模糊综合评价法求得该考查点的综合评分，评分介于80~100为“达成”，70~80为“达成，存在关注项”，60~70为“达成，存在问题项”，60以下为“未达成”。需要说明的是，表4中的权重均未给出具体数值，仅用A、B、C、D表示，参考性考查点及其细化要求的权重值需通过层次分析法或熵权法等赋权方法进一步研究。此外，设计划分毕业要求达标结论的评估量规只是一种学术性探索，具体评价方法需要由有认证经验的专家和相关委员会确定。

**表4 毕业要求达成情况评估量规示例**

| 参考性考查点 | 全局权重 | 细化要求 | 细化权重 | 达成（100） | 达成，存在关注项（75） | 达成，存在问题项（50） | 未达成（25） |
|---|---|---|---|---|---|---|---|
| 评价方法的多样性、适切性与可操作性 | 权重A | 评价方法的多样性 | 权重B | 综合多种方法开展评价，做到以直接评价为主，辅以间接评价，定量评价结合定性评价，形成性评价对比总结性评价 | 综合多种方法开展评价，以直接评价和定量评价为主，以间接评价和定性评价作为补充，但没有通过形成性评价数据和总结性评价数据对比验证评价结果 | 综合直接评价法和间接评价法开展评价，但未将直接评价作为主要评价方法，直接评价数据和间接评价数据占比不合理 | 评价方法单一，主要采用课程考核成绩平均算分法，没有通过间接评价数据和定性评价数据补充验证评价结果 |
| | | 评价方法的适切性 | 权重C | 对基于课程数据的评价，根据课程教学目标恰当选择评价方法；对基于主观判断的评价，选用与评价目标相匹配的评价方法，能证明评价过程和评价工具的科学性与合理性 | 对基于课程数据的评价，根据课程教学目标恰当选择评价方法；对基于主观判断的评价，做到评价方法与评价目标相匹配，但无法证明评价对象是否选择恰当，评价观测点是否明确合理，评价标准是否客观科学 | 对基于课程数据的评价，能根据课程教学目标选择评价方法，但无法通过评价方法观测到充分反映教学目标达成的学习行为，即评价方法的适切性不足；对基于主观判断的评价，采用访谈、调查等方法进行了评价，但评价目标不明确，没有科学且详细的评价标准 | 对基于课程数据的评价，所用评价方法与课程性质和教学目标不匹配，没有基于主观判断的评价 |
| | | 评价方法的可操作性 | 权重D | 每种评价方法都有客观且详细的评价标准，充分发挥量规表在不同评价方法中的作用 | 评价方法有统一评价标准，发挥了量规表在间接评价和定性评价中的作用，但没有通过量规表为课程考试成绩提供统一评分依据 | 评价方法有统一评价标准，但未使用量规表为不同评价方法提供详细的评价依据 | 评价方法没有统一的评价标准 |

（3）制定毕业要求达成评价的专家考评参考建议。

参考加拿大工程认证委员会制定专家考评实施细则的做法，通过制定专家考评参考建议,对毕业要求达成评价的参考性考查点进行进一步细化,从认证专家视角明确毕业要求达成评价的考查要素、实施策略与评估准则,以方便专家进行考评工作。专家考评参考建议由认证协会相关委员会以及熟悉认证工作的专家、企业和行业代表共同制定,随着科技发展、工程教育进步以及认证实践中发现的新问题,不断修订。以“评价方法的多样性、适切性与可操作性”为例(见表5),其专家考评参考建议可考虑由四部分组成:参考性考查点、考查要求、可供专家参考的问题、以往出现的未达标情况。“参考性考查点”包括上文提出的毕业要求达成评价的10个参考性考查点,但不限于这些考查建议;“考查要求”是对应考查点涉及的具体要求,需覆盖参考性考查点包含的全部内容要素,对学校提出具有可操作性的评价要求;“可供专家参考的问题”为专家有效开展评价提供支持,应简练、明确、具体,不需要一个问题考查多个方面;“以往出现的未达标情况”是以往专业认证中发现的真实和常见的未达标问题,用于提醒专家在考查过程中值得关注的参考和潜在问题。

**表5 毕业要求达成评价的专家考评参考建议演示说明(非实际例子)**

| 参考性考查点 | 考查要求 | 可供专家参考的问题 | 以往出现的未达标情况 |
| --- | --- | --- | --- |
| 评价方法的多样性、适切性与可操作性 | 对基于课程数据的评价,要求列出参评课程和教学环节所用到的评价方法,提供试卷、作业题目、综合设计作品、论文、报告等考核资料;对基于主观判断的评价,要求列出用以间接评价毕业要求达成的调查方法并展示调查工具(如访谈提纲、问卷等);同时要求提供每种评价方法的评价标准以及评价方法的合理性审核记录 | 是否通过不同评价方法收集数据? | ①仅通过课程考核成绩算分法获取评价数据 |
| | | | ②仅有总结性评价数据,没有形成性评价数据 |
| | | | ③仅有定量评价数据,没有定性评价数据 |
| | | 是否综合运用多种评价方法交叉比较、相互佐证评价结果? | ①分析数据时未做到以直接、定量评价数据为主,以间接、定性评价数据为辅 |
| | | | ②未合理选择形成性评价数据和总结性评价数据来对比验证评价结果 |
| | | 是否根据课程或其他培养环节的教学目标恰当选择评价方法? | ①无法通过所选评价方法观测到充分反映教学目标达成的学习行为 |
| | | | ②运用考核低阶认知目标的评价方法考核高阶认知目标 |
| | | 以调查为主的评价方法是否有明确的评价目标、合适的评价对象和科学的评价工具? | ①问卷调查、访谈等的评价观测点不明确,所得调查结果解释力不足 |
| | | | ②访谈提纲和问卷题项设置不合理,难以获得可靠稳定的评价结果 |
| | | | ③抽样方式不恰当,未选取具有典型性和代表性的调查对象 |
| | | 各种评价方法是否有客观合理的评价标准? | ①评价标准模糊笼统,不能为判定评价结果提供详细依据 |
| | | | ②评价标准与评价内容的关联性不强,遗漏或超出评价内容所包含的要素 |
| | | 是否清晰记录每种评价方法的实施过程与合理性审查过程? | ①没有对评价方法所涉及的评价时间、评价对象、评价标准、评价结果等信息进行归档整理 |
| | | | ②没有定期审查评价方法的合理性并形成相关记录档案 |

注:表中内容可能有不恰当之处,专家考评参考建议需要由认证经验丰富的专家和相关委员会制定。

(4)建立和健全毕业要求达成评价的专业自评指导文件。

目前,我国工程教育专业认证协会出台了《工程教育认证毕业要求达成评价指导手册

(试行)》,对毕业要求达成评价时间与周期、机构与人员、过程与方法等问题予以阐释,成为健全毕业要求达成评价指导文件体系的基础。鉴于我国工科专业数量大、涉及领域广、新增专业多、学校的办学层次不同等情况,为充分发挥专业认证在工程教育质量保障中的关键作用,需不断提高学校方面毕业要求达成评价的可操作性,不断增加和修订相关辅助性参考文件,通过制定毕业要求解读指南、产出导向评价指南、学校产出导向教育与评价的优秀案例集等工作文件,对毕业要求在教学过程中的实施情况、毕业要求的内涵观测点、评价实施流程、评价方法和策略、评价注意事项等进行进一步说明,协助新参加认证的学校和专业建立产出导向课程体系、持续提高教育教学质量和顺利完成认证准备工作。具体建议如下。①关于毕业要求解读指南,可给出对每条毕业要求的参考性解释说明,其中包括指标点样例、专业自评重点与难点解析以及评价中的常见问题与注意事项,指南仅作为辅助专业理解毕业要求的参考文件,主要是为了帮助专业查证专业毕业要求是否全面覆盖认证标准中的毕业要求,引导专业将毕业要求真正落实到制定课程目标、设计教学内容和确定考核方法中。②关于产出导向评价指南,以认证协会现有指导手册为基础,考虑从评价准备、评价实施和持续改进三个阶段不断补充、细化和优化毕业要求达成评价的操作流程。评价准备阶段的指导可以包括确立认证责任机构的基本思路、审查评价机制合理性的办法、设定评价时间与周期的基本原则、保障利益相关者参与评价的方法、评价计划参考范例等内容,评价实施阶段的指导可以包括设置毕业要求指标点的基本原则、选择参评课程(支撑毕业要求的达成)的基本思路、可供参考的评价方法及相关介绍,持续改进阶段的指导可以包括判断达标程度的方法、处理不同类型评价数据的方法、让持续改进措施落地见效的方法等内容。③学校产出导向教育与评价的优秀案例集,建议认证专家在实施考查过程中有意识地收集值得借鉴的学校优秀案例,认证协会根据专家推荐和评估,选择具有典型性和参考性的优秀案例汇编成案例集供学校学习,案例既可以是关于完整教育教学过程(或评价实施流程)的整体性案例,也可以是关于某一教学环节(或评价实施环节)的局部性案例(某方面的案例),随着时间推移,考虑阶段性更新案例集,保证案例的参考价值。

(5)确定毕业要求达成评价的系统化培训机制。

中国工程教育专业认证协会已面向学校开展毕业要求达成评价相关培训,为参评专业提供了有效帮助和指导。随着认证工作的深入开展,建议进一步健全培训体系,特别是帮助准备参加认证的专业学习掌握产出导向评价的基本理念、要求、内容、流程与方法,让学校在深刻理解标准毕业要求的基础上科学制定专业毕业要求,有效开展毕业要求达成评价。由于我国专业点较多,培训可通过制作慕课课程资源、组织线下集中培训、提供线上答疑服务等方式进行。设置培训内容应结合专家建议和学校需求,可包括基础培训和专题培训两部分。基础培训是对毕业要求达成评价的总体介绍,涉及标准毕业要求的内容解读、认证考查的基本要求、评价重点与难点、评价实施流程等方面,一般通过录制慕课供学校学习。专题培训旨在为某一评价环节或特定问题提供专门说明与指导,如产出评价方法专题培训、指标点专题培训、量规表专题培训等,主要以线下集中培训的方式进行。为增强学校与认证专家间的实时互动,还可于官网上定期征集学校在评价中遇到的问题与困难,针对典型或共性问题,组织专家召开线上答疑会,解答学校方面的问题。

（6）加强产出导向教育的宣讲与研讨。

为加强毕业要求达成评价的常态化指导，除了为学校提供专门培训，还建议通过定期举办宣讲会和专题研讨会，向社会和高校宣讲产出导向教育理念，推广产出导向评价的成熟经验与做法，并就毕业要求达成评价的重难点环节和重难点问题进行专门研讨。宣讲会与研讨会可同期举办，以提高会议效率并形成规模效应。宣讲会主要面向高校相关部门领导、专业负责人、教师、行业和企业代表等高等工程教育的利益相关者，旨在帮助多元主体深刻理解产出导向教育理念并以其为指导进行专业建设和人才培养质量评价，宣讲内容可包括工程教育专业认证标准、产出导向教育的核心理念、面向产出的教育质量评价与持续改进机制建设、以毕业要求为导向的课程体系建设、毕业要求达成评价等认证工作的基本流程与要求等。研讨会面向认证专家、院系专业负责人、教学研究人员及一线教师，旨在选择特定主题对产出导向教育相关问题进行深入研讨，提高专业对产出导向教育理念的认识，引导专业将产出导向教育理念落实于教学实践。专题研讨会可分对象进行，面向认证专家、专业负责人及教学研究人员的研讨会应重点关注毕业要求的制定与修订、课程体系的设计与优化、教学运行机制的持续改进等内容，面向一线教师的研讨会应重点关注教学法、教学评价法、课程建设等内容。

## 2 学校毕业要求达成评价示例

以机械工程专业为虚拟案例，对学校毕业要求达成评价的参考性实施框架进行演示性举例说明。需要强调的是，下文中的示例是一个虚拟案例，仅用于辅助说明如何使用本文提出的评价方法，案例中涉及的组织机构、工作方式及各类数据均为虚拟数据，所以相关结论也是虚拟性的，不具实质性指导意义。

为了辅助说明这个虚拟案例，首先根据标准毕业要求、《华盛顿协议》GAPC21 的毕业要求草拟机械工程专业的毕业要求（见表 6），再次强调，这个样例的机械工程专业毕业要求没有实质性参考价值。

**表 6 《华盛顿协议》GAPC21 的毕业要求与虚拟性机械工程专业毕业要求的比较**

| 《华盛顿协议》GAPC21 的毕业要求 | 机械工程专业毕业要求（虚拟性） |
|---|---|
| A. 工程知识。运用数学、自然科学、计算与工程基础知识以及 WK1~WK4 规定的工程专门知识，开发复杂工程问题的解决方案 | A. 工程知识。能够将数学、自然科学、计算机技术、工程基础和专业知识，包括工程图学、设计、计算、检测、控制、自动化等基本理论知识应用于解决机械领域装备和系统设计与制造等复杂工程问题 |
| B. 问题分析。基于可持续发展的整体考虑，运用数学、自然科学和工程科学的第一性原理，识别、描述并通过研究文献分析复杂工程问题，得出经证实的结论（WK1~WK4） | B. 问题分析。能够应用数学、自然科学、工程科学的第一性原理，识别、表达并通过文献研究分析机械工程领域的复杂工程问题，综合考虑可持续性发展的要求，以获得有效结论 |
| C. 设计/开发解决方案。为复杂工程问题设计创造性的解决方案，设计系统、部件或流程以满足特定需求，适当考虑公共健康与安全、全寿命周期成本、净零碳以及按照要求考虑资源、文化、社会和环境等（WK5） | C. 设计/开发解决方案。能够针对机械工程领域的复杂工程问题，开发和设计创新性解决方案，方案包括设计满足要求的系统、部件、零件和相关工艺流程，并从公共健康与安全、全生命周期成本与净零碳要求、法律与伦理、社会责任、文化等角度分析方案的可行性 |

续表

| 《华盛顿协议》GAPC21 的毕业要求 | 机械工程专业毕业要求（虚拟性） |
|---|---|
| D. 调查研究。使用包括基于研究的知识、实验设计、数据分析和解释以及信息综合等在内的研究方法，对复杂工程问题进行调查研究，以提供可靠的结论（WK8） | D. 研究。能够基于科学原理、采用科学方法和技术手段对机械工程领域的复杂工程问题进行分析与研究，包括设计实验、完成实验、分析与解释实验数据并通过信息综合得到合理有效的结论 |
| E. 现代工具的使用。创造、选择和应用适当的技术、资源以及现代工程和信息技术工具，包括预测和建模，以解决复杂工程问题（WK2 和 WK6），并认识到其中的局限性 | E. 现代工具的使用。能够针对机械工程领域的复杂工程问题，开发、选择与使用适当的技术、资源、现代工程和信息技术工具，包括对复杂工程问题的建模、模拟与预测，以提出复杂机械工程问题解决方案，并认识到方案的局限性 |
| F. 工程师与社会。在解决复杂工程问题时，分析和评估可持续发展对以下方面的影响：社会、经济、可持续性、健康和安全、法律框架和环境（WK1、WK5 和 WK7） | F. 工程与可持续发展。在解决复杂机械工程问题时，能够基于机械工程和相关学科知识，分析和评价工程实践对健康、安全、环境、法律以及经济和社会可持续发展的影响，并清楚工程师应承担的责任 |
| G. 伦理。运用伦理原则，遵循工程实践的职业伦理和规范，遵守相关的国家和国际法律，表现出对多样性和包容性需求的理解（WK9） | G. 伦理和职业规范。具有工程报国、工程为民的自觉与意识，具有人文社会科学素养和社会责任感，理解和应用工程伦理，在工程实践中遵守工程职业道德、规范和相关法律，履行工程师职业责任 |
| H. 个人和团队工作。在多样性和包容性的团队中，以及在多学科、面对面、远程和分布式的环境中，作为个人、成员或领导者有效地发挥作用（WK9） | H. 个人和团队工作。能够在多样性、多学科背景下的团队中，承担个人、团队成员以及团队负责人的角色，并能有效发挥积极作用 |
| I. 沟通。就复杂工程活动与工程界和整个社会有效且包容性地进行沟通，例如能够理解和撰写实际的报告和设计文件，进行有效展示，同时考虑到文化、语言和学习的差异 | I. 沟通交流。能够就复杂机械工程问题与业界同行及社会公众进行有效沟通和交流，撰写工程报告、设计文件、陈述和发言，清晰表达和回应相关指令；能够在跨文化背景下进行有效沟通和交流，理解和尊重语言和文化差异 |
| J. 项目管理和财务。作为团队的成员和领导者，将对工程管理原则和经济决策知识的理解，运用于自己的工作中，并在多学科环境下进行项目管理 | J. 项目管理和财务。理解并掌握工程项目相关的管理知识、原理与经济决策方法，并能够有效用于多学科环境下的项目管理实践中 |
| K. 终身学习。认识到以下需求，为其做好准备并具有相应能力：①独立学习、终身学习；②适应新型技术和新兴技术；③在最广泛的技术变革背景下进行批判性思考（WK8） | K. 终身学习。具有自主和自觉学习及终身学习的意识和能力，以批评性思维分析和理解快速发展的新技术与变革对工程和社会的影响，主动适应新技术变革 |

注：在中国工程教育专业认证协会和机械工程分委员会没有颁布官方专业类毕业要求标准的情况下，为了说明本文的毕业要求达成评价参考方案，上述毕业要求是作者参考《华盛顿协议》GAPC21 提出的虚拟性毕业要求，真实的机械工程毕业要求应根据中国工程教育专业认证协会颁布的国家标准，由机械工程学会相关委员会制定专业补充标准。

## 2.1 评价准备阶段

### 1. 成立学校、院系、专业层面的认证责任机构

学校一般都有教学质量评估中心或教学质量管理中心，如果学校没有这样的机构，可以设立一个机构或由教务管理部门负责学校层面的教学数据监测、专业认证、专项评估等教学质量管理工作。在专业认证中，学校教学质量管理机构主要负责推进认证评估规范性建设以及监督教学质量持续改进效果。由于专业认证是一项长期工作，建议由学院教学委员会作为学院专业认证工作领导小组，负责学院参加认证的各专业的领导和组织工作，其中包括

指导各专业进行认证标准达成评价，毕业要求达成评价只是专业自评工作之一。在各个专业的毕业要求达成评价中，学院专业认证工作领导小组和专业认证工作组共同负责明确毕业要求达成评价实施流程、制订评价计划、落实评价分工、汇总分析毕业要求达成评价结果、提供人才培养改进建议、建立教学质量责任追究制度等工作。

**2. 根据自评表审查毕业要求达成评价机制的合理性**

为保证认证工作的有序进行，在学校教学质量评估中心领导下，学院专业认证工作领导小组，协同各参评专业的认证工作组，应出台相关制度文件明确专业认证标准的达成要求，其中涉及毕业要求达成评价相关要求。需要强调的是，这个虚拟示例主要集中在毕业要求达成评价方面，在真实案例中，需针对每项认证标准（毕业要求只是其中一项）进行准备工作。对于毕业要求达成评价，建议专业开展评价之前使用自评表（见表 7）审查评价机制的合理性，自评表可在示例表格的基础上进行适当补充与改进。评价机制的自我审查工作可分要素进行，例如，多元利益相关者参与机制、培养目标和毕业要求的合理性由院系管理者和专业负责人进行审查，参评课程和教学环节的适切性、评价过程的合理性由专业负责人协同课程教师进行审查，评价结果的使用情况由专业负责人或专业认证专家进行审查。

**表 7　毕业要求达成评价与持续改进机制的自评表示例**

| 多元利益相关者的参与 | 得分 | 培养目标 | 得分 | 毕业要求 | 得分 | 支撑评价的课程和教学环节 | 得分 | 评价过程 | 得分 | 评价结果及其使用 | 得分 |
|---|---|---|---|---|---|---|---|---|---|---|---|
| 明确毕业要求达成评价的利益相关者 | | 制定符合学校使命、专业人才培养特色、国家战略发展需要的培养目标 | | 专业毕业要求全面覆盖认证标准中的毕业要求 | | 主要选择对毕业要求具有强支撑作用的专业必修课和实践性教学环节进行评价（如果选修课与必修课一同考查，要求最弱组合达成毕业要求） | | 采用直接评价辅以间接评价，定量评价结合定性评价，形成性评价对比总结性评价的方式获取数据 | | 根据定量目标值和定性等级描述综合判断毕业要求达成情况 | |
| 主要的利益相关者参与制定、修订培养目标和毕业要求 | | 培养目标明确、公开、可衡量 | | 专业毕业要求支撑培养目标达成 | | 支撑评价的课程中有顶点课程或设计类项目 | | 根据教学目标选择恰当的评价方法 | | 通过不同类型数据相互佐证评价结果 | |
| 主要的利益相关者参与毕业要求达成评价 | | 定期评价培养目标达成情况 | | 专业毕业要求明确、公开、可衡量 | | 根据评价结果适时调整用于评价的课程或教学环节 | | 每种评价方法有客观合理的评价标准 | | 根据评价结果查找课程体系、教学实践中的弱项和问题项并予以改进 | |
| 有稳定健全的利益相关者参与机制 | | 定期根据工程教育的内外部需求修订培养目标 | | 定期评价专业毕业要求达成情况 | | 支撑评价的课程之间具有一定的逻辑关联，有先修课，也有强化课 | | 每条毕业要求采用不同方法进行评价 | | 有稳定的评价结果反馈机制 | |

续表

| 多元利益相关者的参与 | 得分 | 培养目标 | 得分 | 毕业要求 | 得分 | 支撑评价的课程和教学环节 | 得分 | 评价过程 | 得分 | 评价结果及其使用 | 得分 |
|---|---|---|---|---|---|---|---|---|---|---|---|
| — | — | — | — | 定期对专业毕业要求进行合理性审查并予以修订 | — | — | — | 定期审查评价过程的合理性 | — | 有健全的持续改进效果监测机制 | — |

注：评分包括6个等级（只是建议和为了辅助说明样例），1=尚未建立评价机制，2=评价机制开发中，3=评价机制已建立但刚开始实施评价，4=评价机制已建立且实施过评价，5=已实施评价且评价效果良好，6=已实施评价且至少进行一轮改进工作。需要说明的是，这是一个虚拟示例，真实的认证专业可根据各自的情况确定是否需要评分、怎么评分等。

**3. 以3年为一个循环周期制定评价时间表**

以机械工程专业为例，假设其毕业要求由A~K 11条能力指标（均为虚拟指标）构成，毕业要求达成评价按3年周期表循环进行，在我国工程教育专业认证的6年认证有效期内，可完整收集2轮评价数据。如果认证结论是“通过认证，有效期6年（有条件）”，需要在第3年提交中期报告。如表8所示，该专业共有11条毕业要求，每年参与评价的毕业要求为3条或4条，每条毕业要求在6年认证有效期内可经历2轮评价，每个周期评完所有指标。由于年度参评指标不同，选择支撑指标评价的课程和教学环节也就不同。用于评价的课程来自大一至大四不同年级（通常多集中于大三，大一、大二和大四阶段的课程较少），从而保证每届学生在一个周期内接受过评价。

**表8　机械工程专业毕业要求达成评价周期表示例**

| 专业毕业要求 | 第一个周期 | | | 第二个周期 | | |
|---|---|---|---|---|---|---|
| | 第1年 | 第2年 | 第3年 | 第4年 | 第5年 | 第6年 |
| A. 工程知识 | ● | | | ● | | |
| B. 问题分析 | | ● | | | ● | |
| C. 设计/开发解决方案 | | | ● | | | ● |
| D. 研究 | ● | | | ● | | |
| E. 现代工具的使用 | | ● | | | ● | |
| F. 工程与可持续发展 | | | ● | | | ● |
| G. 伦理和职业规范 | ● | | | ● | | |
| H. 个人和团队工作 | | ● | | | ● | |
| I. 沟通交流 | | | ● | | | ● |
| J. 项目管理和财务 | ● | | | ● | | |
| K. 终身学习 | | ● | | | ● | |

确定评价周期和年度参评指标之后，还需确定不同年份应开展的评价工作以及各项工作的负责人。此外，应根据评价结果适时修订评价周期、参评指标和评价计划。例如，经一

轮评价，学生的工程伦理素养未达标，采取教学改进措施后，可在第二个周期连续三年对该指标进行评价。

**4. 制订各项毕业要求的评价实施计划**

制订评价计划需明晰每条毕业要求的评价实施策略。以“问题分析”为例（见表9），该项毕业要求由6门课程提供评价支撑，各门课程的支撑强度有所不同，课程权重值之和为1。该项毕业要求达成评价以课程测验及其他考试、实验、项目设计与实施为主，问卷调查和访谈为辅，每3年系统收集一轮评价数据。其中，课程测验及其他考试、实验、项目设计与实施根据课程考核成绩分析法计算评价值，以量规表为评价依据，评价结果达到某个定量目标值则视为达成。建议问卷调查和访谈不基于单门课程进行，而是从毕业生和用人单位视角总体判断毕业要求达成情况，采用李克特五级量表设计答案选项，评价结果达到“一般认同”及以上等级则视为达成。为进一步验证评价结果，还可通过对比形成性评价数据和总结性评价数据判断学生进步幅度，增值达到某个定量目标值则视为达成。目前，计算学习成绩（成效）的增值有不同算法与模型，如OLS线性回归模型、学生成长百分位模型、残差模型、交叉分类模型等[10]，任课教师应结合教学目标与评价目标选择合适的增值评价模型，协同专业负责人或课程组负责人确定判断毕业要求达成的目标增值。

**表9　机械工程专业毕业要求达成评价计划表示例（以“问题分析”为例）**

| 专业毕业要求 | 参评课程与教学环节 | 权重 | 直接评价法 | 间接评价法 | 形成性评价数据来源 | 总结性评价数据来源 | 数据收集时间 | 达标阈值 |
|---|---|---|---|---|---|---|---|---|
| B问题分析 | 机器人技术 | 0.15 | 课程测验及其他考试、实验、项目设计与实施 | 对毕业生及用人单位的问卷调查和访谈 | 设计与制造基础Ⅰ（开设于大一） | 设计与制造基础Ⅲ（开设于大三） | 2017年、2020年、2023年 | 1. 在课程考核中，毕业要求评价值≥某个定量目标值；2. 在问卷调查和访谈中，评价结果处于“一般认同”及以上等级；3. 在增值评价中，增值≥某个定量目标值 |
| | 设计与制造基础Ⅰ | 0.16 | | | | | | |
| | 流体力学与液压传动 | 0.15 | | | | | | |
| | 机电控制系统 | 0.15 | | | | | | |
| | 设计与制造基础Ⅲ（数字化设计与制造） | 0.16 | | | | | | |
| | 包含设计、建造与运行的综合性项目实践 | 0.23 | | | | | | |

注：表中的课程、权重数值、达标阈值、数据收集时间均为虚拟数据。

## 2.2　评价实施阶段

**1. 明确专业毕业要求的内容构成**

《华盛顿协议》第四版《毕业要求和职业胜任力-2021》（GAPC21）的颁布，为成员组织制定认证标准中的毕业要求提供新的参考框架。与2013版相比，2021版毕业要求从12条精简为 11 条，新增第一性原理、数字素养、批判性思维等元素，同时进一步强调可持续发展、工程伦理、终身职业发展等的重要性。目前，中国工程教育专业认证协会已展开标准毕业要求的修订工作，修订后的毕业要求在基本框架上将与 GAPC21 毕业要求实质等效。因此，本研究以 GAPC21 的 11 条毕业要求为基准，结合机械工程领域的特征，制定虚拟性机械工程专业的毕业要求（见表 6），主要用于辅助说明本研究提出的评价方法。需要强调的是，制定专业毕业要求不仅要全面覆盖标准毕业要求，而且要有反映本校和本专业特点的补充性要求，重视毕业要求的前瞻性与导向性，根据国家、产业、社会对工程技术人才的最新需求适时修订毕业要求，使之引导工程教育持续改进。

**2. 选择对毕业要求具有强支撑作用的专业必修课、设计类和实践性教学环节进行评价**

专业开设的课程和教学环节对达成毕业要求的支撑强度有所不同，通常表现为强支撑、中等支撑、弱支撑或无支撑形式，一般选取强支撑毕业要求达成的课程和教学环节进行毕业要求达成评价。综合国内机械工程专业的课程体系，从中选取 12 门对毕业要求具有强支撑作用的课程、设计类和实践性教学环节进行评价（见表 10），其中包括 7 门专业必修课（设计与制造基础Ⅰ、机械工程导论、机器人技术、流体力学与液压传动、机电控制系统、设计与制造基础Ⅲ、机械制造装备设计）、5 个教学环节（制造技术基础训练，机械装备拆装实习，包含设计、建造与运行的综合性项目实践，生产实习，毕业设计）。参评课程源于大一至大四不同学年，本样例中课程多集中于大三学年，其中包括先修课（如设计与制造基础Ⅰ）与强化课（设计与制造基础Ⅲ）的组合。一条毕业要求通常由三门及以上课程支撑，一门课程最少支撑两条毕业要求，包含设计、建造与运行的综合性项目实践强支撑所有毕业要求。一般而言，支撑技术性指标的课程相对较多，支撑非技术性指标的课程相对较少，这是因为沟通交流、终身学习等非技术能力难以单纯通过课堂教学获得，也无法仅通过以知识和技能传授为目的的课程进行考查，只有顶点课程或设计与实践类项目才能有效支撑非技术能力指标达成评价。需要说明的是，课程及课程选择均为虚拟设计，在真实的专业认证工作中，选择支撑毕业要求达成的课程内容、课程数量等都需要系统思考。

**表 10　机械工程专业支撑毕业要求达成评价的课程示例**

| 参评课程 | 修读学期 | 毕业要求 | | | | | | | | | | |
|---|---|---|---|---|---|---|---|---|---|---|---|---|
| | | A | B | C | D | E | F | G | H | I | J | K |
| 设计与制造基础Ⅰ | 大一上 | H | H | | | | | | | | | |
| 机械工程导论 | 大一下 | H | | | | | H | H | | | | |
| 机器人技术 | 大二下 | H | H | | | H | | | | | | |
| 流体力学与液压传动 | 大三上 | H | H | | | | | | | | | |
| 制造技术基础训练 | 大三上 | | | | | H | | H | | | | |
| 机电控制系统 | 大三下 | H | H | H | | | | | | | | |
| 设计与制造基础Ⅲ（数字化设计与制造） | 大三下 | | H | H | H | H | | | | | | |
| 机械制造装备设计 | 大三下 | | | H | H | H | | | | | | |

续表

| 参评课程 | 修读学期 | 毕业要求 | | | | | | | | | | |
|---|---|---|---|---|---|---|---|---|---|---|---|---|
| | | A | B | C | D | E | F | G | H | I | J | K |
| 机械装备拆装实习 | 大三下 | | | H | H | H | | | H | | | |
| 包含设计、建造与运行的综合性项目实践 | 大三下 | H | H | H | H | H | H | H | H | H | H | H |
| 生产实习 | 大四上 | | | | | H | H | H | H | H | H | H |
| 毕业设计 | 大四下 | | | H | H | | H | H | | H | H | H |

注：表中 H（High）表示课程强支撑毕业要求达成，中等支撑可用 M（Medium）表示，弱支撑或无支撑可用 X 表示。这个样例只标示了强支撑毕业要求达成的课程，在没有明确课程内容的情况下，此表仅用于演示性说明。

### 3. 运用多元评价方法分类采集评价数据

毕业要求达成评价数据包括两类：课程评价数据和基于调查的主观判断数据。课程评价数据源于支撑评价的课程和教学环节，是毕业要求达成评价的主要数据来源；主观判断数据源于对毕业生、用人单位等利益相关者的调查，是毕业要求达成评价的补充性证据。

对基于课程的评价，主要根据课程目标达成评分对毕业要求达成情况进行综合判断，大致包含以下步骤。一是建立毕业要求与支撑评价课程之间的对应关系，通过赋权确定每门课程对毕业要求的支撑强度。二是由专业认证工作组指定专人对课程评价材料（如试卷、实验报告、项目设计与实践成果等）、评价标准（主要以量规表的形式制定评价标准）的科学性与合理性进行确认。三是通过分层抽样选取具有代表意义的样本计算课程目标达成评分，保证样本好、中、差三个等级的占比基本均等。以“机电控制系统”为例（见表 11），该门课程支撑工程知识、问题分析、设计/开发解决方案 3 条毕业要求，选取课程测验及其他考试、实验、项目设计与实施三种评价方法判断课程目标达成情况。工程知识属于布鲁姆教育目标分类中的“记忆”和“理解”层次，通过课程测验及其他考试进行评价；问题分析属于布鲁姆教育目标分类中的“应用”和“分析”层次，通过实验和项目报告进行评价；设计/开发解决方案属于布鲁姆教育目标分类中的“评价”和“创造”层次，通过综合性项目设计与实施进行评价。已知课程成绩总分为 100 分，课程测验及其他考试占 50 分，实验和项目报告占 20 分，项目设计与实施占 30 分（真实的占分比例要根据具体课程内容和要求合理分配），课程对各项毕业要求的支撑权重为 0.2、0.15、0.2，每种评价方法有明确的评价标准。实施评价时，抽取一个教学班的考核成绩作为样本，分别计算样本中所有学生课程测验及其他考试、实验和项目报告、项目设计与实施的平均分，并根据平均分、目标分和权重计算课程目标达成度评价值以及基于该门课程得到的毕业要求评价值，课程目标评价值=平均分/目标分，毕业要求评价值=权重×（平均分/目标分）。同理求得其他课程对应支撑的毕业要求的达成度评分，进而汇总计算各项毕业要求的达成情况评价值（如表 12 所示），一般取各项毕业要求最终评价结果中的最小值作为毕业要求达成情况的总评结果，根据设定的定量目标值（如评价值≥0.75）判断毕业要求是否达成。

**表 11　课程目标达成情况评价信息(以“机电控制系统”课程为例)**

| 课程目标 | 支撑毕业要求 | 支撑权重 | 评价方法 | 目标分(满分) | 学生平均得分 | 课程目标评价值 | 毕业要求评价值 |
|---|---|---|---|---|---|---|---|
| 课程目标 1 | A | 0.2 | 课程测验及其他考试 | 50 | 35 | 0.7 | 0.14 |
| 课程目标 2 | B | 0.15 | 实验和项目报告 | 20 | 16 | 0.8 | 0.12 |
| 课程目标 3 | C | 0.2 | 项目设计与实施 | 30 | 24 | 0.8 | 0.16 |

注:表中的数据包括权重均为虚拟数据。

**表 12　基于课程考核成绩的毕业要求达成评价结果示例**

| 参评课程 | 毕业要求 A | 毕业要求 B | 毕业要求 C | …… | |
|---|---|---|---|---|---|
| C1 | 0.12 | 0.16 | | …… | 毕业要求达成情况的总评结果(取各项毕业要求最终评价结果中的最小值) |
| C2 | 0.15 | | | …… | |
| C3 | 0.14 | 0.12 | 0.16 | …… | |
| C4 | 0.17 | 0.14 | | …… | |
| C5 | 0.13 | 0.16 | 0.12 | …… | |
| C6 | | | | …… | |
| C7 | 0.11 | 0.10 | | …… | |
| C8 | | 0.15 | 0.12 | …… | |
| C9 | | | 0.15 | …… | |
| C10 | | | 0.17 | …… | |
| C11 | | | | …… | |
| C12 | | | 0.16 | …… | |
| 评价结果 | 0.82 | 0.83 | 0.88 | …… | 0.82 |

注:表中的数据均为虚拟数据。

由于上述课程评价方法是以最终学习产出为判断依据的总结性评价,较难反映学生在学习过程中的实际进步幅度,因此,可通过对比先修课(如设计与制造基础Ⅰ)和强化课(如设计与制造基础Ⅲ)的学习效果进一步验证毕业要求是否达成(也是虚拟性说明)。首先,由专业认证工作组或专业教学委员会协同教师开发专门用于评价某项毕业要求达成情况的量表或试卷;然后,运用量表或试卷,在支撑评价的先修课结课时进行能力前测,在支撑评价的强化课结课时进行能力后测;最后,选用适当的增值评价模型计算前后两次测试的成绩增值,增值达到某个定量目标值则视为对应支撑的毕业要求达成。例如,如果运用量表对同一个教学班进行前后对比测试,计算前后两次得分的标准化差值即可得到能力增值;如果通过考试分数反映进步幅度,则可通过百分等级成长模型、残差模型等更高阶的方法计算增值和确定达成值。

基于调查的主观判断性评价，通过问卷调查和访谈收集毕业生、用人单位对毕业要求达成程度的反馈。问卷题目和访谈问题可直接采用11条毕业要求，答案选项可参考李克特五级量表分为完全认同、基本认同、一般认同、基本不认同、完全不认同五个等级。为便于汇总计算问卷调查结果，由学院专业认证工作领导小组协同专业认证工作组对毕业要求进行赋权，并通过模糊综合评价法合成最终评价值，访谈结果主要由访谈人员对访谈文本进行逐级编码后得出最终评价结论，问卷调查与访谈的评价结果在"一般认同"及以上等级视为毕业要求达成。

### 2.3 持续改进阶段

#### 1. 根据定量目标值和定性等级描述综合判断达标程度

由于采用的评价方法不同，针对每种方法设定的达标阈值也就不同，判断达标程度主要以定量目标值和定性等级描述为依据。对基于课程考核成绩分析法的评价，其达成值多为定量目标值，定量目标值包括课程目标达成值和毕业要求达成值。通过衡量实际所得评价值与达成值之间的差距，即可判断目标达成情况。以机电控制系统课程为例，根据表11，课程目标1的评价值为35/50 = 0.7，假设课程目标达成值为0.6，则说明课程目标1达成；通过该课程评价毕业要求A达成情况的结果为0.2 ×（35/50）= 0.14，假设目标值为0.15，则说明该课程对达成毕业要求A的贡献度不足。除了根据单一课程判断达标程度，还需汇总多门课程评价结果，整体判断毕业要求达成情况，毕业要求总评值为支撑毕业要求达成的各门课程评价值之和。以机械工程专业为例，假设毕业要求A由设计与制造基础Ⅰ，机械工程导论，机器人技术，流体力学与液压传动，机电控制系统，包含设计、建造与运行的综合性项目实践6门课程支撑评价，各门课程支撑该项毕业要求达成的评价结果分别为0.12、0.15、0.14、0.17、0.13、0.11，毕业要求A的总评值为0.12 + 0.15 + 0.14 + 0.17 + 0.13 + 0.11 = 0.82，假设目标值为0.75，则说明毕业要求A达成。如果通过增值评价辅助验证评价结果，其达成值一般也为定量目标值。例如，选择设计与制造基础Ⅰ、设计与制造基础Ⅲ2门课程辅助验证"问题分析"这条毕业要求的达成情况，可以运用同一份成熟量表分别在2门课程学习结束后对学生实施问卷调查，量表包含对问题分析能力的测试题，采用李克特五级评分制计分，两次调查后求取总评结果的增值，增值达到某个定量目标值则视为该项毕业要求达成。如果通过毕业生调查、用人单位调查等方式进一步证实毕业要求达成情况，其达成值通常为定性等级描述，划分为完全认同、基本认同、一般认同、基本不认同、完全不认同五个等级，由专业的调查人员对问卷数据或访谈文本进行分析，并对各项毕业要求的达成情况进行等级划分。访谈文本分析一般采用逐级编码、不断抽象比较的方式，由经验丰富的编码人员从访谈文本提炼能系统反映达标程度的概括性结论。问卷数据一般采用模糊综合评价法合成毕业要求总评结果。问卷和访谈结果为"一般认同"及以上等级则视为达成。

需要说明的是，如果所选课程不满足对某一条毕业要求的支撑，有两种办法解决这个问题：①修改课程目标和课程内容，增加支撑不足方面的课程内容，在课程迭代中达到支撑目标；②增加支撑课程，聚焦不达标的毕业要求的具体内容，在专业课程体系中选择对缺失方面有支撑的必修课程参与毕业要求达成评价。具体选择哪种或两种办法都选，由专业认证工作组决定，再由相应教学委员会批准。

**2. 基于不同类型数据相互佐证评价结果**

以机械工程专业为例，假设该专业毕业要求达成评价通过课程考核成绩分析法（具体考核方法结合课程内容与布鲁姆教育目标分类法确定）、增值评价（此处以量表为评价工具）、问卷调查和访谈四种方式进行。总体判断毕业要求达成情况时，将课程考核成绩作为主要依据，将增值评价结果作为补充依据，并通过问卷调查和访谈数据进一步验证达标结论，最终评价结果在对不同类型数据进行交叉检验后得出。如表 13 所示，不同评价方法得到的达标结论可能存在差异，根据差异性评价结果判断达标情况一般有以下三种情况。当多数评价方法所得结论为“达成”，少数为“未达成”时，最终视为达成，如毕业要求 C 和 I。当多数评价结果为“未达成”，少数为“达成”时，最终视为未达成，如毕业要求 F 和 G。当“达成”与“未达成”数量均等时，需通过其他评价方法或重复之前的评价方法重新检验评价结果，如毕业要求 K。

**表 13　毕业要求达成评价结果汇总示例**

| 毕业要求 | 评价方法 | | | | | | | |
|---|---|---|---|---|---|---|---|---|
| | 课程考核成绩分析法 | | 增值评价 | | 问卷调查（针对毕业生） | | 访谈（针对用人单位） | |
| | 评价值（假设目标值为 0.75） | 达标情况判断 | 评价值（假设目标值为 0.009） | 达标情况判断 | 评价结果（假设目标等级为“一般认同”） | 达标情况判断 | 评价结果（假设目标等级为“一般认同”） | 达标情况判断 |
| A | 0.872 | 达成 | 0.0120 | 达成 | 完全认同 | 达成 | 基本认同 | 达成 |
| B | 0.780 | 达成 | 0.0150 | 达成 | 基本认同 | 达成 | 基本认同 | 达成 |
| C | 0.834 | 达成 | 0.0087 | 未达成 | 基本认同 | 达成 | 一般认同 | 达成 |
| D | 0.821 | 达成 | 0.0170 | 达成 | 基本认同 | 达成 | 基本认同 | 达成 |
| E | 0.856 | 达成 | 0.0180 | 达成 | 基本认同 | 达成 | 基本认同 | 达成 |
| F | 0.748 | 未达成 | 0.0083 | 未达成 | 一般认同 | 达成 | 基本不认同 | 未达成 |
| G | 0.736 | 未达成 | 0.0091 | 达成 | 基本不认同 | 未达成 | 基本不认同 | 未达成 |
| H | 0.762 | 达成 | 0.0095 | 达成 | 一般认同 | 达成 | 一般认同 | 达成 |
| I | 0.747 | 未达成 | 0.0094 | 达成 | 一般认同 | 达成 | 一般认同 | 达成 |
| J | 0.754 | 达成 | 0.0099 | 达成 | 基本认同 | 达成 | 基本认同 | 达成 |
| K | 0.755 | 达成 | 0.0093 | 达成 | 基本不认同 | 未达成 | 基本不认同 | 未达成 |

注：表中的数值均为虚拟数据。

**3. 切实保障改进措施落地见效**

基于评价结果促进专业持续改进需凝聚多方力量，强化协调配合。首先，由学院专业认证工作领导小组协同专业认证工作组做好评价数据的统计、分析和整理工作，形成毕业要求达成评价结果分析报告并及时反馈给专业负责人、教学研究人员和教师。然后，由专业认证工作组与专业相关人员根据评价报告诊断人才培养中存在的问题。一方面,专业骨干教师组应基于毕业要求评价值,分析毕业生能力的薄弱环节,进而优化课程体系、健全师资队伍和改善教学条件。另一方面,教师和教研人员应根据毕业要求及课程目标评价值,查找未达标项和达成值偏低项,进而改进教学方法、调整教学内容和优化评价方式。最后,学院专业认证工作领导小组协同专业认证工作组要定期监测持续改进效果,包括对各专业培养目标与毕业要求达成情况、课程体系、教学模式、评价方法、师资队伍、资源配置等改进情况的全方位监测。

## 3 研究结论与展望

工程教育专业认证中的毕业要求达成评价是实现专业培养目标与加强专业建设的重要抓手,是专业自评与专家考评的重点和难点。借鉴国际上三所大学和四个认证组织毕业要求达成评价的经验,结合我国工程教育特色和专业认证制度,从学校和认证组织两个评价主体出发,提出产出导向的毕业要求达成评价参考性虚拟方案。该方案由学校方面毕业要求达成评价的参考性实施框架和认证组织方面毕业要求达成评价的参考性考查框架两部分组成。学校实施框架包括评价准备、评价实施、持续改进三个阶段,细分为 11 个环节。认证组织考查框架涵盖毕业要求参考性内容和毕业要求达成参考性评价方法,前者为学校制定专业毕业要求建立基准,后者为认证专家和学校开展毕业要求达成评价提供参考。

需要说明的是,该方案只是一个研究探索,对中国工程教育专业认证协会和参加认证的学校和专业的指导意义有限,甚至参考价值有限。此方案的研究目的是抛砖引玉,由于工程教育专业认证在提高工程教育质量方面具有不可替代的作用,希望开展更加广泛的研究与讨论,持续提高工程教育专业认证水平和工程教育人才培养质量,力求在经验借鉴的基础上实现卓越工程人才培养与评价的再创新。当前,中国工程教育专业认证协会正在根据 GAPC21 修订我国的认证标准,本文中任何理念、方法、观点与即将出台的中国工程教育专业认证修订标准有矛盾和不一致之处,最终以中国工程教育专业认证协会的标准及相关文件为准。此外,笔者受专业背景和学习经历的限制,对毕业要求达成评价的理解可能有不深入、不全面甚至不恰当的地方,愿与工业界、教育界同行就毕业要求达成评价方案的优化展开交流。

### 参考文献

[1] Accreditation Board for Engineering and Technology. Establishing timelines and responsibilities[EB/OL].(2022-09-09)[2023-09-20]. https://assessment.abet.org/wp-content/uploads/2022/09/Establishing-Timelines-and-Responsibilities-09.09.20.pdf.

[2] 中国工程教育专业认证协会. 工程教育认证自评报告指导书[EB/OL].(2022-05-12)[2023-10-03]. https://www.ceeaa.org.cn/gcjyzyrzxh/rzcxjbz/gjwj/gzyb/xxgzyb/index.html.

[3] 戴先中. 工程教育专业认证中毕业要求分解指标点的利弊[J]. 高等工程教育研究,2022(3):60-66.

[4] 蒋宗礼. 提高课程教学站位[J]. 中国大学教学,2021(Z1):35- 41.

[5] 中国工程教育专业认证协会. 工程教育认证毕业要求达成评价指导手册[Z]. 2015:8-11.
[6] 王霞,毛秀珍,张丽. 教育增值评价:模型、应用及研究展望[J]. 教育学报, 2023(4): 109-122.
[7] MATHISON S.Why triangulate[J].Educational researcher,1988(2):13-17.
[8] MILLERS S I. Some comments on the logic of triangulation[J].International journal of experimental research in education,1983(2):200-212.
[9] FERDIAN R. 2020 12th International Conference on Information Technology and Electrical Engineering [C]. New York:IEEE,2020.
[10] 朱珂,张晨雨,刘玉莹,等. 国际视阈下教育发展增值评价模型的比较研究[J]. 远程教育杂志,2023(1):60-71.

# 国际视野下我国工程教育转型的发展路径与思考
## ——天津大学新工科教育中心主任顾佩华教授访谈录

顾佩华

顾佩华教授系加拿大工程院院士、教育部长江学者讲座教授、国际生产工程科学院( the International Academy for Production Engineering, CIRP )会士、加拿大自然科学与工程研究会( the Natural Sciences and Engineering Research Council of Canada, NSERC )全生命周期工程设计讲席教授( Chair in Life Cycle Design Engineering )。现任天津大学新工科教育中心主任、天津大学浙江国际创新设计与智造研究院院长、机械工程学院教授。曾担任汕头大学执行校长、加拿大卡尔加里大学( University of Calgary )机械与制造工程系主任、工学院副院长,教育部"CDIO 工程教育模式研究与实践课题组"组长,中国 CDIO 工程教育联盟主席。曾任 CIRP 设计科学与技术委员会主席,机械工程设计委员会副主任委员,担任多个学术杂志的编委或副主编。

自教育部于 2017 年正式启动新工科建设后,先后形成了"复旦共识""天大行动""北京指南"等指导性文件,推动了工科优势高校和大批普通高校参与践行新工科建设。在一系列的新工科改革行动中,许多高校都涌现了面向新业态的工科专业设置、工科人才培养方案和产教融合模式,为我国工程教育转型发展提供了新模板。新工科建设迄今已实施 8 年,顾佩华教授全程参与新工科建设工作,负责新工科建设"天大方案"设计和多学院、多学科培养平台的试点实施工作,并多次在研讨会上对新工科建设提出独到见解,所著《新工科与新范式:概念、框架和实施路径》《新工科建设发展与深化的思考》《新工科与新范式:实践探索和思考》等成为工程教育领域关于新工科主题研讨的重要文献。本文围绕当前世界范围内工程教育转型发展与我国工程教育近年来的探索实践及路径,结合对新工科建设的思考与未来发展等问题,对顾佩华教授进行专题访谈。

### 一、国际范围内工程教育的转型发展

**问:请从国际范围内工程教育的转型发展、工程师的全链条培养等方面谈一谈工程教育面临的挑战,以及我国的工程教育转型( 以新工科为例 )中需要关注的问题?**

我从 1985 年开始到加拿大麦克马斯特大学( McMaster University )攻读博士学位,当时我们国家与北美的工程教育在硬件条件和培养体系方面有较明显的差距。1999 年我担任

加拿大卡尔加里大学机械与制造工程系主任，面对企业很难找到满足需要的工程师和工科毕业生就业难的问题，参与发起成立加拿大设计工程网络（Canadian Design Engineering Network，CDEN），推动加拿大工程教育改革，改革旨在提高工科毕业生的设计与工程创新能力。2005 年我回国在汕头大学推动 CDIO 工程教育改革，与 2004 年美国麻省理工学院（MIT）领导的国际 CDIO 工程教育改革几乎同步。从近十多年全球高等教育的发展来看，2010 年教育部启动卓越工程师教育培养计划，改革人才培养体制机制，推动校企合作，显示了与世界赛跑的决心。2013 年美国“斯坦福 2025 计划”启动，全面改变大学的办学模式，是一个具有颠覆性的创新尝试。美国 2017 年开始的 MIT 新工科教育转型计划（New Engineering Education Transformation，NEET）的目的是重构本科教育。同一时期，2016 年中国成为《华盛顿协议》正式成员，在 2016—2017 年提出开展新工科建设，开启了我国高校面向未来、面向产业的工程教育变革与创新。通过与国际上多所大学的工程教育创新计划对比分析可见，与我们的卓越工程师教育培养计划目的相似，近年来全球范围内的工程教育变革方案都是要培养新工业革命时代产业需要的工程技术人才。

从工程教育的挑战来看，2018 年 3 月 MIT 委托的《全球一流工程教育发展现状》（The Global State of the Art in Engineering Education）报告指出，美国工程教育存在以下几方面问题：基于学科、院系的工程教育妨碍教学创新，是实现卓越工程师教育的障碍；教师评价和考核系统对教学贡献激励不够，导致教师对学生工程能力培养投入不足，对本科教育改革参与和投入的精力有限；公立大学经费有限，政府对大学教育质量和招生数量的期待却越来越高；专业认证（特别是 EC 2000 产出导向的认证标准）的实施，对提高美国工程教育质量起到了重要作用。就我个人观察，国内的问题可能包括以下几个方面：现行大学管理体制很难实现跨学科培养，跨学院自由选课也很难实现；现在的培养体系导致学生知识面窄，很多学校给学生提供工程动手实践的机会还偏少，学生过度关注分数和保研等；指标导向的教师考核使得教师缺乏参与教育改革的动力，影响了教师育人的积极性；产学合作缺少制度保障；如何将国家和学校关注的先进理念转化为教师的日常教学活动的机制值得进一步探索。由此可知，中国和国际工程教育发展面临相似的挑战：全球科技和产业快速发展，在很多技术领域，企业走在了大学前面，教师知识的更新和工程创新能力的提高需要体制机制的保障，产业需要掌握新技术和新知识的工程创新人才，以适应未来科技产业发展；世界各国大学传统培养模式、课程体系、课程内容、教学方法等的更新和修订周期，与快速发展的科学技术和新知识不适应、不协调，高等工程教育需要进行深刻变革和全面创新，培养产业发展需要的工程创新人才。从世界工程教育新发展和面临挑战这两个维度进行分析，可以大体上判断出：我国与世界先进工程教育基本处在同一新发展起点上，当前是我国建设工程教育强国的历史契机。

欧洲在工程创新方面的成绩突出，工程教育起源于欧洲，最早是在法国、德国、英国，后来才是美国，但美国工程教育无论从体量还是水平上来看都值得我们重视，美国工程教育是我国建设工程教育强国的重要参考。比较中美两国，很多方面我们都有优势，但仍有一些方面需要努力。20 世纪 60 年代美国工程教育的工程实践与工程科学达到较好的平衡，随着工程实践教师的退休，原先的教师逐渐被工程科学的教师所代替，美国工程教育形成了工程科学导向的课程体系和教师队伍，也出现了工科不“工”现象。从 20 世纪 80 年代到 90 年代，工业界对美国大学缺乏工程师能力培养表现了极大的关切和担心，开始积极推动员工教育，对工程师的培养进行改革和创新。波音公司提出了 10 条理想工程师的特征，这些特征到今天仍然是衡量工程师质量的重要指标。美国政府通过行政任命和政府部门的工作，设立国家自然科学基金专项项目，推动工程教育专业认证，美国工程院、具有引领意识的大学或院领导都积极推动工程教育改革与创新。1984 年里根任命 MIT 机械系徐南构（Nam P. Suh）教授负责建设美国国家科学基金委员会（National Science Foundation，NSF）的工程部，要求 NSF 工程部保障美国进入 21 世纪后仍能长期占据全球工程领导地位。美国工程研究中心（Engineering Research Center，ERC）设有本科教育计划，职业生涯奖的申请要求有研究计划和教学计划，这些措施保证优秀工科教师培养更多优秀的工科毕业生。与美国相比，中国具有明显的体制机制优势，可以大范围推动工程教育深刻改革和全面创新，中美工程教育竞争内容与特点的比较如表 1 所示。

**表 1　中美工程教育竞争内容与特点的比较**

| 竞争内容 | 中国 | 美国 | 比较分析 |
|---|---|---|---|
| 特征 | 工程技术教育：注重专业教育，专业课多，需要加强自然科学和工程基础课程 | 工程科学教育：注重工程基础，企业不再提供以往的培训，开始提高设计与解决复杂问题的能力 | 美国大学教师中具有工程经验的少；中国大学教师队伍中，在企业中工作过的也较少 |
| 体制机制 | 全面推动力：具有全面推进工程教育改革与创新的体制机制优势，需要政府下决心推进，学校认真实施 | 全面推动力：缺乏体制机制条件和能力实现全面推动 | 美国缺少全面推进的体制机制；中国具有体制优势，需要真干实做，不炒作 |
| | 外部驱动力：来自政府、校友、用人单位、招生和教育成果奖，以及大学评估和排名 | 外部驱动力：来自产业、校友、用人单位、招生和提高学校的名声 | |
| | 执行力：来自教育主管部门、大学评估等，学校“一把手”下决心改革教师评价体系，就能实现一流教育 | 执行力：方案需要多次从下到上、从上到下反复辩论，耗时会很长 | |
| | 创新力：学校领导会主动提出新教育理念或模式，但在实施上不够深入 | 创新力：新领导会提出学术规划，其中包括教育理念和模式，会持续推进 | 美国大学师生普遍期待新校长的新学术战略规划 |
| 教育教学 | 跨学科培养：虽然难，校领导可以推动，而且必须推动，这是卓越工程师教育培养的重要方面，希望不久的将来可以实现 | 跨学科培养：难，校领导很难推动，院长可以推动（与我国工程专业不同，美国一个专业由多个学科的课程组成） | 中国是一个学科办专业，领域太窄；美国是一个系内多个一级学科办专业 |
| | 课程体系和要求：课程体系有多年传承，课程多，课程难度不高，考核单一 | 课程体系和要求：通过多年认证和改进迭代，课程体系内容和难度稳定。学术体系规范化，大改动不容易 | 美国学术管理规范，中国正在逐步规范化 |
| | 质量保证：正在通过专业认证建立 | 质量保证：除新专业外，已通过专业认证系统建立了质量保证 | 美国于 1932 年认证，中国于 2006 年试点 |
| 教师 | 能力：学校之间差距较大；<br>评价：教师考核指标化，教师集中精力完成指标要求 | 能力：学校之间有差距，但差距不大；<br>评价：教师考核比较客观，总体考核非指标化 | 美国工程专业认证成熟，教师队伍教学能力比较平均；教师工作和行为是考核要求的反映 |

续表

| 竞争内容 | 中国 | 美国 | 比较分析 |
|---|---|---|---|
| 学生 | 课程多、学习努力、过度关注课程分数 | 贷款上学，关注教学质量，要学到真本领，对知识和技能有要求 | 中国学生关注成绩和升学，课程多；美国学生希望自己学到知识、技能和真本领 |
| 产业参与 | 产业/职业协会参与认证工作和接受实习，对大学教育质量不太关注 | 推动工程教育进步的重要力量。企业从用人单位和职业协会角度关注大学教育质量和人才培养 | 美国企业和职业协会比较积极地关注工程教育改革发展 |
| 克服挑战 | 提高本科教育质量和水平，学校要真正下决心，把口号变成教职工的实际行动 | 缺少实质性的动力和能力 | 大学核心价值观和教师立德树人榜样力量非常关键 |

**问：关于工程教育模式创新方面有哪些值得推荐的先进案例，请您具体谈一谈。**

欧林工学院（Olin College of Engineering）的建设背景是20世纪八九十年代，受到日本与德国先进制造业水平的影响，当时美国社会有悲观情绪，认为先进和高质量产品和技术被日本和德国主导，而中低端产品市场由中国产品占领，美国的制造业没有国际竞争力，工程教育人才培养不能满足企业的需求。工程科学主导的工程教育需要回归工程，呼吁进行深刻变革，欧林基金会希望将仅有的5亿美元捐给一所美国高校，推动工程教育改革。由于已有的美国大学学术和教育体系很难做出重大改变，最后欧林基金会决定建立欧林工学院，使之成为探索工程教育改革的试验田[1-2]。就是这样一所只有40名左右教师、350多名本科生的学院，全面改革和创新了工程教育，建校20年，先后接待了3000多名到访者[3-5]，对推动美国和世界工程教育进步做出了重要贡献。

除了欧林工学院外，美国MIT、斯坦福大学等国际高校，以及我国多所高水平大学的工程教育实践均值得广泛交流和互相借鉴，有助于切实提高人才培养水平和质量，支持产业创新发展。

## 二、工程教育转型中的大学管理与高等教育内涵建设

**问：工程教育转型涉及大学管理和人才培养理念等很多问题，这与高等教育内涵式发展有着密切关系，请您谈一谈其中的问题与挑战。**

通过新办大学、扩招、大学合并等举措，中国不仅成为世界高等教育规模最大的国家，其高等教育也从大众化向普及化发展。“985工程”“211工程”“双一流”建设持续投入，科研经费大幅度增长，中国研究型大学特别是“985工程”大学的科研能力和水平、SCI（科学引文索引）论文数量、ESI（基本科学指标数据库）排名、大学排名等快速进步。与办学规模的快速发展相比，教育质量也大幅度提升。但是企业特别是高科技企业存在用工荒，同时有些领域的毕业生就业质量仍然有待提升。SCI/ESI论文数量和质量、高校的科研能力迅速提高，但是科技创新驱动的工业创新发展仍需更多努力。发挥体制优势，高等教育发展取得了有目共睹的成就，如何继续发挥体制优势，提高教育质量和人才培养水平，实现内涵式发展，是新时代重要的命题。党的十八大提出推动高等教育内涵式发展，党的十九大提出实现高

等教育内涵式发展，因此当前的“双一流”建设和地方政府提出的高水平大学建设计划，应该理解为大力推进和实施高等教育的内涵式发展。高等教育内涵式发展是相对于外延式发展提出的，是以“质量提升、结构优化、效益提高”等为主要特征的发展方式。对一所大学而言，内涵式发展可以理解为，在发展过程中注重优秀大学文化建设，通过塑造核心价值观、建立先进办学理念、凝练办学特色、优化内部结构、建立制度体系、持续提高办学质量、培育优秀文化等，激活学校内在动力，实现提高教育质量、科技创新水平、办学效益等办学目标。

在高等教育内涵式发展的过程中，我们也要思考关于新工科教育的内涵，自教育部提出新工科建设以来，讨论不断深化，新工科教育的内涵是面向未来科技和产业变革的新工程教育创新与重构；探索建立新时代工程教育的新模式和新范式；以新理念、新模式、新课程体系、新的教与学方法、质量标准和新要求等建设新工科专业，升级现有工科专业，持续改进和持续创新工程教育；深化改革学校工程教育学术体制机制，确保人才培养持续满足企业发展需要；面向未来、面向产业、面向人类可持续发展，培养社会和产业需要的未来创新型卓越工程师、项目和产业产品经理人、工程管理专家、企业家、工程科学家和领军者；等等。新工科要有变革和创新，就是要用新的模式、新的要求来培养新时代需要的人才。面向人工智能特别是生成式人工智能技术（generative artificial intelligence，GAI）、大语言模型（large language model，LLM）和未来人工通用智能（artificial general intelligence，AGI）以及其他科技发展与应用，企业发展模式与工科人才需求都会持续产生变化，面对这样的不确定性，未来卓越工程创新人才培养目标，除满足工程教育认证毕业要求的知识、能力、素质外，还应具备更多元的素养和卓越工程能力，毕业生要具有主动适应未来科技发展和个人职业生涯变化的能力和自觉性（图 1）。

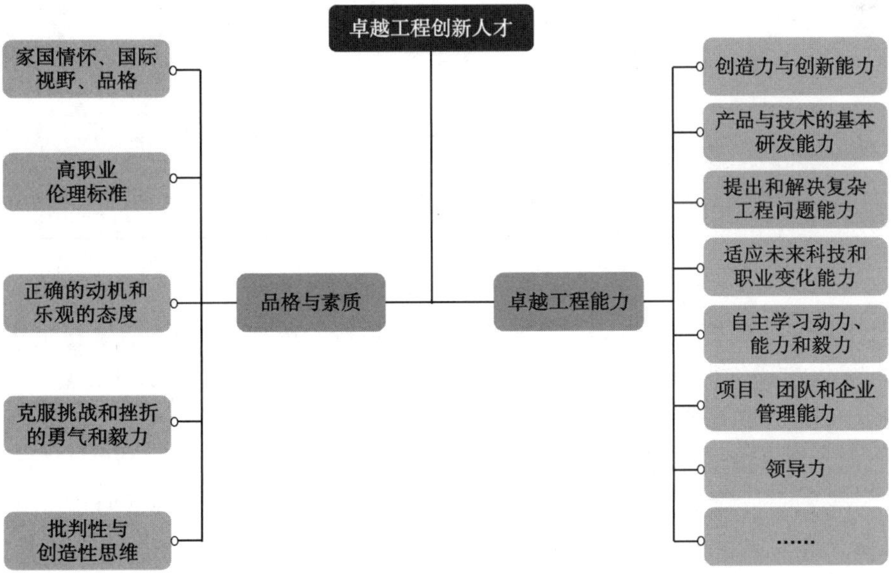


**图 1　卓越工程创新人才培养目标**

**问：新工科概念发轫至今，在工程教育转型的理念、改革举措等方面有哪些值得借鉴的经验和实践启示？**

新工科的建设，要走高校内涵建设的路径，至少涉及以下方面。一是服务国家发展、以人为本、追求卓越、面向未来、面向世界的办学理念。坚持服务国家和地方的发展，面向世界、面向未来、集全校和各方智慧，确定学校的使命、愿景、办学目标、阶段性战略发展规划等；坚持以学生为中心，以教师为本，追求卓越，凝聚全校的共识，形成合力，实现办学目标。二是建设高水平教师队伍，建立人才培养体系，持续提高科研和学术水平。建设高水平教师队伍，提高教师的工程能力和教学能力，建立先进人才培养体系，创新教育理念，持续提高教育教学质量；提高教师科研和创新能力，提高办学水平和效益。三是注重学校文化建设。大学精神文化建设是学校内涵建设的核心内容之一；优秀大学文化体现在师生的理想和追求、道德规范、校园氛围、校风、教风、学风等方面；只有大学坚持和追求真理，才能使社会相信真理。四是提高大学管理水平，激发内部原动力。学校发展要依靠内生动力、内部潜力、内部创造力等的组织和优化；提高教育资源整合力、组织执行力、教学能力、科研能力，提高办学质量和效益。

然而，学生如何发现内涵建设的好学校？通过各种大学排名？我们对比分析了 U.S. News 世界大学排名与美国国内大学排名，发现两者的区别如表 2 所示，这些大学都是私立大学，事实上还有很多优秀的、有特色的大学在这两项排名上没能得到一致的结果。这些优秀大学大多经过较长时间建设而成，学校的核心价值观、大学文化、办学水平，都经历了相当长的历史积淀，而不是刻意按照排名指标打造而成的。

**表 2　大学排名指标分析与教育质量和办学水平的关系——以美国为例**

| 比较方面 | U.S. News 世界大学排名指标分析 | U.S. News 美国大学排名指标分析 |
|---|---|---|
| 关注重点 | 主要与研究相关，如科研水平、声誉、竞争力 | 主要与人才培养有关，可以为学生选择学校作参考 |
| 均进入前 10 名的高校 | 哈佛大学、普林斯顿大学、耶鲁大学、哥伦比亚大学、麻省理工学院、斯坦福大学、加州理工学院、约翰斯·霍普金斯大学 | |
| 均进入前 15 名的高校 | 增加芝加哥大学 | |

资料来源：U.S. News 2015—2017 年的排名数据。

因此，指标导向的管理与着眼于高等教育内涵建设的精神不相符（表 3），尤其在科研学术方面，指标化的评价很难体现学科之间的差别，一定要尊重研究领域的特点，主要评价科研成果的影响和贡献；重要的技术发明和创新也不一定有英文文章的发表，如德国和日本是制造强国，虽然他们的教授发表 SCI/ESI 的文章数量有限，但是工程实践和科技创新水平高。尽管实践表明行政主导的指标导向的管理效率高、发展快、见效快，但指标导向的管理的短期效益是否与大学以人为本的公平、公正和追求真理等价值观相符合？是否与教育和科研的质量、发展规律及追求卓越的学术精神相一致？是否与优秀大学文化建设和耐心沉淀相协调？是否与建设真正意义上的一流大学相符合？这些问题仍值得进一步思考。

**表 3　指标导向的管理与内涵建设分析**

| | 指标导向的管理 | 内涵建设 |
|---|---|---|
| 本质区别 | 行政主导分配指标到学校单位完成，以达到指标为办学目标 | 以指标数据为参考和支撑，制定学校计划和政策提高办学质量、水平和效益 |
| 典型例证/判定依据 | 学校将科研经费、人才引进、SCI/ESI/核心期刊等论文、各种奖项等指标分配给学院/系完成，并作为院系考核指标；<br>将人才计划评选、教师聘用和晋升、年度考核等指标化和数字化；<br>科研通过 SCI/ESI 等论文数量、影响因子、项目、经费、各种奖项等确定教师的薪酬和奖励金额；<br>教学通过名师、精品课、教学成果奖、教学工作量等确定岗位津贴；<br>…… | **学校内部：**<br>学校定位、办学特色、愿景和使命；<br>为实现愿景和使命，制定阶段性战略目标和学术规划；<br>学校的校风、教风、学风，通过制度建设，营造公平、公正、民主、平等和包容的学校文化等；<br>教师和学生在学校的地位，学校制度对教职工的尊重，行政系统对服务于学生、教师、教学、科研的认识与自觉性；<br>对本科教育和人才培养的重视；<br>……<br>**学校外部：**<br>学校在社会、业界和同行中的声誉和影响；<br>知名校友和广大校友的成就；<br>学生报考情况；<br>教师在其领域的影响；<br>网站的宣传和介绍可以体现学校的主体和主人（观察和分析哈佛大学、斯坦福大学、MIT 等著名大学网站内容）；<br>…… |

一流大学建设要以实际行动提升工程教育人才培养质量与水平，真正实现以学生发展和培养为中心，需要从体制机制上鼓励校内学院、学科、专业通力合作与协同发展。在工程教育转型的过程中，改革教师评价标准的目的是要求教师群体肩负起育人的责任，而完成这些任务则需要学校和学院的主要管理者来改变大学指标导向的管理方式。不可否认，指标导向的管理对大学和学科排名起到了促进作用，学校将指标分到学院，学院再分给系/学科，学科再分到研究所或教师个人。教师关注各自指标的完成，对大学优秀文化建设、核心价值观塑造、院系发展、人才发展，特别是学生工程能力培养等关心不够。完成了指标，学校可能也达不到一流大学建设目标。真正的一流大学不是按照指标建设的，但是一流大学的各类指标水平都很好，这是真正的一流大学应有的特质。建立工程教育新体制机制，特别需要改革教师聘任、考核、晋升的评价体系，弱化评价指标，实施教学、科研、服务综合贡献评价。鼓励教师参加国家和地方工程科技攻关，积极参与校企合作，培养学生解决高难度复杂工程问题能力的同时，提高教师自身的工程能力。

新工科教育不是指要办新专业。从工程教育发展的历史看，最早只有工程专业，后来出现土木工程、机械工程，到现在光电子工程、生物医学工程等，我们一直在根据产业发展需求办新专业。一百年前的机械工程，现在仍叫机械工程，内容却已改变，因为企业和产业的基础已经发生变化，今天数字化技术对人类的影响要超过 100 多年前的电气化。新工科应对新的变革，要培养学生面向世界，面向产业，面向未来。学生要有专业能力，人品也很重要，因为在技术可以做很多事的时候，更体现出伦理标准的重要性。学生的适应能力也很重要，在智能化时代，随着产业快速发展与变革，企业对人才的需求也会持续变化，未来工程技术人员的工作环境也要变化，需要更强的适应能力。此外终身学习的能力、毅力和主动性也很重要，学生需具备自主学习的能力、动力和毅力，自觉开展学习。新工科的改革从课程改革开始，要求学生有很好的知识基础，要用新的理念，创造新的模式、新的培养体系、新的教学内容、新的学习和教育方法，要有新的标准、新的质量要求。

简而言之，我们要持续创新人才培养体系来应对产业、企业将来的变化。科技发展会催生新产业和新企业，也会颠覆没有与时俱进的传统企业，华为、比亚迪、腾讯、百度等企业就是科技推动快速发展起来的。传统产业也采用新技术，沃尔玛在准备进入自己的元宇宙时代。1997 年，在韩国的一次学术会议上，时任韩国副总理兼教育部部长提出科技发展越来越快，颠覆了很多传统的产业、企业，也催生了很多新的企业，这迫使大学要贴近企业，培养企业需要的人，要进行教育范式的转变，这也离不开高校内涵建设的支撑与助力。韩国是世界上最具有创新力的国家之一，这与其重视人才培养有关。

## 三、新工科“天大方案”的实施与反思

**问：您参与了新工科“天大方案”的设计和实施，有哪些经验可以分享给其他院校的同行？**

2010 年 6 月 23 日，教育部在天津大学召开卓越工程师教育培养计划启动会，我们认为这是“天大方案”1.0；2019 年 4 月 29 日，教育部“六卓越一拔尖[①]”计划 2.0 启动大会在天津大学召开。天津大学最早发布新工科建设方案，提出以新工科教育实现本科卓越工程师培养，推动世界一流工程教育发展，以实际行动实现对中国工程教育的引领，为建设工程教育强国做出贡献。根据卓越工程师教育本科培养标准构建卓越工程师教育，包括核心理念、多学科跨学科的培养平台、课程和培养体系建设路径、整体融合和结果导向的课程建设、全面质量保障体系、书院-导师制全人教育和全面培养等。其核心内涵包括：品格塑造，即以立德树人统领人才培养全过程，通过课程、项目、课外活动和社会服务等方式培养学生家国情怀、伦理道德和核心价值观；新文理教育，即由中国特色的新文理教育培养学生的终身能力，如想象力、科学精神、科学态度、思维和思辨、分析和判断、伦理推断、沟通、写作、团队合作、创业、管理、领导和终身学习等方面的能力，以适应未来职业发展和要求；多学科工程教育，即培养学生宽厚的自然科学、数学和工程科学基础，严谨的工程态度，多学科和跨学科分析与决策能力、设计和建造能力、提出和解决复杂工程问题的能力、工程创造和创新能力；个性化专业培养，即以卓越目标和学生职业目标发展为导向提供最新专业知识、能力、职业素养，鼓励毕业生团队自主研发技术或产品，开展技术创业[6]。

“天大方案”设计的课程体系是一个整体，是以课程项目、课程群项目、本科研究项目、多学科大团队科技挑战项目、毕业项目 5 种项目为节点，建设柔性连接的模块化课程体系，优化学生四年的培养和成长路径。在多学科和跨学科培养平台上，实现教-研-学融合、校企融合协同育人、多学科交叉融合、国内-国际合作，全校的创客空间、重点实验室、工程中心、科研和教学平台等有组织和有计划地对本科生开放，将 5 种项目有机结合，支持学生团队在毕业时产出技术或产品，鼓励研究型大学毕业生技术创业。为支持毕业生创业，建设校内和

① “六卓越一拔尖”计划，是指卓越工程师教育培养计划、卓越医生教育培养计划、卓越农林人才教育培养计划、卓越教师培养计划、卓越法治人才教育培养计划、卓越新闻传播人才教育培养计划、基础学科拔尖学生培养计划。

协助建设校外科技孵化器和加速器。

同时参考了斯坦福大学、MIT、以色列理工学院的创新创业实践，鼓励和协助毕业生科技创业，希望未来能够在天津大学周围建成科技创新公司群。例如，“天大方案”中关于未来智能机器与系统平台的建设，对标于MIT的“新机器”主题。通过整合机械、精密仪器、自动化、微电子、计算机等学院的十几个专业课程体系，设置多学科培养平台必修课、专业必修课、平台选修课，支持学生跨学院、跨专业选课，实现学生的个性化培养。2021年开始实施的毕业项目，旨在支持学生团队在毕业时能够实现技术创业，这是研究型大学支持地方创新经济发展的重要贡献。

关于新工科改革的反思，我们认为，任何教育改革都应该使每个相关学生受益。未来智能机器与系统平台在2019级新生中试点实施后，本应让相关专业二年级、三年级和四年级学生参与和受益。但由于种种原因，受益面没能扩大到更多的学生。校领导要求实体化建设天津大学新工科教育中心，新工科教育不能只局限在试点班，要逐步实现全校学生培养的全覆盖，天津大学新工科教育中心正在推进落实校领导的要求。

**问：您曾经判断“后疫情时代我国的新基建、新产业、新科技、新经济发展需要大量创新工程科技人才，势必对工程教育和人才培养提出新的要求，为新工科再深化、再拓展指明新方向，也是新工科再突破和再出发的新起点”，请您谈一谈当前“智能涌现”背景下，对于我国新工科建设发展的新思考。**

李培根院士于2023年6月发文指出，人类社会发展正面临拐点，他呼吁“科学家、工程师、政治家、教育工作者乃至全社会的共同努力。由于真正面对拐点的是未来的精英们，如何培养应对拐点到来的人才，这就需要教育率先做好转型变革的准备”[7]。李院士分析了多年前“VUCA①”概念在新时期的意义，特别是科技带来的各种不确定性，专业和学科边界等方面的模糊性，希望各个专业的教师“透视VUCA，全面审视当前专业教育中存在的、严重滞后于科学与技术发展现状与趋势问题”[7]，在数字空间改造工程专业。

以ChatGPT为代表的人工智能工具，展示了GAI技术的潜力，虽然还不能比较准确地预测GAI对人类社会的影响，但可以想象影响将是广泛和深刻的，人类需要尽快做好准备。就工程教育而言，GAI发展包括细分领域GPT的不断出现，将会改变未来的企业及其用人要求，也会改变教师的工作和学生的学习，将对工程教育产生重要影响。智能机器与系统如智能制造技术逐渐取代重复性简单技能型工作，主要是蓝领工作。研究表明，具有一定技术含量和需要高等教育才能适应的工作，如软件编程、区块链工程、数据分析、量化金融分析、会计和纳税工作、以写作为主的助手性工作、公共关系等工作，都会不同程度地受到GAI工具的影响。智能时代社会和产业的发展，导致对人才需求的改变，高等工程教育必须为这些改变的到来做好准备。

OpenAI与宾夕法尼亚大学组成的研究团队研究了OpenAI最新一代语言处理模型GPT-4对美国劳动力的影响。他们发现，GPT-4可能对技术工作和接受过高等教育、年薪达到8万美元的白领阶层产生影响，而对简单重复性的蓝领工作的影响相对小。

对教育本身的影响最直接的是对学生考核的影响，比尔·盖茨亲身体验ChatGPT，让其回答AP Biology的考试题目（60个选择题和6个开放题目），60个选择题答对了59个，6

① “VUCA”是volatility（易变性）、uncertainty（不确定性）、complexity（复杂性）、ambiguity（模糊性）的缩写。

个开放式（open-ended）题目回答得很好，成绩达到 A 或 A+[8]，说明 GAI 能够通过考试。澳大利亚 7 所大学的多学科联合研究表明，ChatGPT 的应用给验证考核真实性和检测剽窃带来一定挑战。跨学校和学科研究通过运用 ChatGPT 对 10 个课程的考核进行分析后发现，目前的考核对 ChatGPT 不构成挑战，需要更改规则。因为只需对输入提示进行很少的修改，ChatGPT 就可以通过考核。随着未来版本基于更大规模的数据集进行训练，ChatGPT 的回答质量将进一步提升。因此，世界工程教育将迎来新一轮的变革与转型，中国工程教育应该在这轮变革和转型过程中实现工程教育强国建设。

**问：面向未来，在工程师自主培养方面如何进一步发挥我国工科优势高校的作用？应该如何探索我国工程教育创新模式，以应对国际工程教育改革趋势，实现科技强国目标？**

如何深化新工科教育，迎接新一轮工程教育转型和变革，适应智能时代对工程教育的新要求，需要世界各国工程教育的探索和实践，这也是我国工程教育发展的新机遇和新挑战。

党的二十大报告强调教育、科技、人才协同发展。教育是培养人才的核心，科技是社会进步的动力。在高校层面，人才培养既包括学生的成长，也涉及教师队伍的建设，二者共同构成大学的核心竞争力。教育是人才培养，而人才培养也包括教师的培养，教师也是人才，负责教育和科研。应以国家重大需求项目为聚焦点，组织好多学科教师和学生团队，持续攻关合作，完成重要的科技计划和项目，解决国家科技发展的问题。严格的教师考核系统需要有很好的支持体系，这样才能使得教师这一人才群体得到很好的发展。让每位教师都能得到发展，是建设教育强国的关键支撑。

人才自主培养还涉及教材，教材内容通常是相对稳定的基础理论和专业基础知识，对于专业课，如果过分强调教材，就难以及时反映最新的科研成果，这使得研究与课堂教学间存在脱节，而作为辅助教材的学术文章、报告、课件、讲义等能够把新东西及时带到课堂上，授课的材料应该是多种多样的。对于普通学校来说，为了保障教学质量，教材很重要；一流大学培养拔尖创新人才的基础课程也可以依照教材，但专业课程一定要吸收最新的成果，让学生学习到最新的内容。

我国要自主培养优秀的工程师，就要发挥工科优势高校的作用，提高整体工程教育的水平。工科优势高校一定要依靠多年以来社会和国家的支持、学校自身的努力，承担起带头的责任，带动整个工程教育发展。工科优势高校要在人才培养、教材编写、教师的培育上依托国家层面在体制机制上的作用。

社会、产业、工业在变化，要紧密结合产业的发展。让大量有工程实践经验的人才进入大学，改变工科教师队伍的组成，改变教学生态体系，提高工程能力的培养水平。当今时代的工程教育要进行深刻变革，要了解企业需要，本着实事求是的态度进行广泛调研。我们要做出全面改变，培养未来能够支撑中国的企业和工业，参与全世界竞争，只有教育强国才可能成为人才强国、工业强国、科技强国，目标还是要把人才培养好。

## 参考文献

[1] 于海琴，陶正，王连江，等. 欧林：打造工程教育的“实验室”（上）：访欧林工学院校长理查德·米勒[J]. 高等工程教育研究，2018（3）：45-52.

[2] 于海琴，陶正，王连江，等. 欧林：打造工程教育的“实验室”（下）：访欧林工学院校长理

查德·米勒[J]. 高等工程教育研究，2018(4)：40-44，71.

[3] 米勒，王连江，于海琴."新工科"办学的欧林效应：小规模，大影响——理查德·米勒校长与王连江、于海琴的对话[J]. 华东师范大学学报(教育科学版)，2021，39(3)：111-126.

[4] 袁广林. 欧林工学院：工程教育的一种新范式[J]. 高教探索，2022(1)：80-86.

[5] 马廷奇，毛立伟. 美国工程教育产教深度融合的经验与启示：以欧林工学院为例[J]. 现代教育管理，2023(7)：55-65.

[6] 顾佩华. 新工科与新范式：实践探索和思考[J]. 高等工程教育研究，2020(4)：1-19.

[7] 李培根. 迎接拐点：前瞻工程教育的变革[J]. 高等工程教育研究，2023(5)：1.

[8] GATES B. The age of AI has begun[EB/OL].(2023-03-21)[2023-08-31]. http://www.gates-notes.com/The-Age-of-AI-Has-Begun.